Methodological Issues & Strategies in Clinical Research

Second Edition

Edited by
Alan E. Kazdin

American Psychological Association
Washington, DC

Published by
American Psychological Association
750 First Street, NE
Washington, DC 20002

Copies may be ordered from
APA Order Department
P.O. Box 92984
Washington, DC 20090-2984

In the UK and Europe, copies may be ordered from
American Psychological Association
3 Henrietta Street
Covent Garden, London
WC2E 8LU England

Typeset in Goudy by G&S Typesetters, Inc., Austin, TX

Cover designer: Minker Design, Bethesda, MD
Printer: Hamilton Printing Company, Rensselaer, NY
Technical/production editor: Ida Audeh

Library of Congress Cataloging-in-Publication Data

Methodological issues and strategies in clinical research / Alan E. Kazdin, editor.—2nd ed.
    p. cm.
    Rev. ed. of : Methodological issues & strategies in clinical research. 1st ed. © 1992.
    Includes bibliographical references and index.
    ISBN 1-55798-481-6 (hardcover : alk. paper). — ISBN 1-55798-482-4 (pbk. :
alk. paper).
    1. Clinical psychology—Research—Methodology. I. Kazdin, Alan E. II. Title:
Methodological issues & strategies in clinical research.
    [DNLM: 1. Psychology, Clinical—methods. 2. Research Design. WM 105 M5925
1998]
RC467.8.M48   1998
616.89'0072—dc21
DNLM/DLC
for Library of Congress   97–42491
                                                          CIP

British Library Cataloguing-in-Publication Data
A CIP record is available from the British Library

Printed in the United States of America
Second edition, first printing.

CONTENTS

CONTRIBUTORS

Michael E. Addis, Department of Psychology, University of Washington

David H. Barlow, Department of Psychology, Boston University

Alan S. Bellack, Department of Psychiatry, University of Maryland School of Medicine

Daryl J. Bem, Department of Psychology, Cornell University

Peter David Blanck, College of Law, University of Iowa

Stephen J. Ceci, Department of Psychology, Cornell University

Lee Anna Clark, Department of Psychology, University of Iowa

Gregory N. Clarke, Center for Health Research, Portland, Oregon

Jacob Cohen, Department of Psychology, New York University

David A. Cole, Department of Psychology, University of Notre Dame

Michael Cowles, Department of Psychology, York University

Betsy Davis, School of Psychology, University of Oregon

Caroline Davis, Department of Psychology, York University

René V. Dawis, Department of Psychology, University of Minnesota

Mark A. Fine, Department of Psychology, University of Dayton

Robert W. Frick, Department of Psychology, State University of New York at Stony Brook

Roland H. Good III, School of Psychology, University of Oregon

Anthony G. Greenwald, Department of Psychology, University of Washington

Steven C. Hayes, Department of Psychology, University of North Carolina

Grayson N. Holmbeck, Department of Psychology, Loyola University of Chicago

Louis M. Hsu, Department of Psychology, Fairleigh Dickinson University

Neil S. Jacobson, Department of Psychology, University of Washington

Alan E. Kazdin, Department of Psychology, Yale University

Gregory A. Kimble, Department of Psychology, Duke University

Kelly Koerner, Department of Psychology, University of Washington

Gerald P. Koocher, Department of Psychology, Children's Hospital, Boston

Lawrence A. Kurdek, Department of Psychology, Wright State University

Wolfgang Linden, Department of Psychology, University of British Columbia

Brendan A. Maher, Department of Psychology, Harvard University

Alvin R. Mahrer, Department of Psychology, University of Ottawa

Scott E. Maxwell, Department of Psychology, University of Notre Dame

Samuel Messick, Educational Testing Service, Princeton, New Jersey

Mary L. Miers, National Institute of Neurological Disorders and Stroke, Bethesda, Maryland

Dale T. Miller, Department of Psychology, Princeton University

Douglas G. Mook, Department of Psychology, University of Virginia

Karla Moras, Department of Psychiatry, University of Pennsylvania School of Medicine

E. R. Oetting, Department of Psychology, Colorado State University

Sumie Okazaki, Department of Psychology, University of Wisconsin

Deborah A. Prentice, Department of Psychology, Princeton University

Robert Rosenthal, Department of Psychology, Harvard University

Ralph L. Rosnow, Department of Psychology, Temple University

Mary Jane Rotheram-Borus, Division of Social and Community Psychiatry, University of California, Los Angeles Health Sciences Center

Frank L. Schmidt, Department of Management and Organizations, University of Iowa

Nina R. Schooler, Department of Psychiatry, University of Pittsburgh School of Medicine

Lee Sechrest, Department of Psychology, University of Arizona

Joan E. Sieber, Department of Psychology, California State University, Hayward

Bradley Smith, Institute for Addictions Research, State University of New York at Buffalo

Stanley Sue, Department of Psychology, University of California, Los Angeles

Leslie A. Telfer, Veterans Administration Center, Palo Alto, California

Paula Truax, Department of Psychology, University of Washington

Jennifer Waltz, Department of Psychology, University of Washington

Bruce E. Wampold, Division of Counseling Psychology, University of Wisconsin

David Watson, Department of Psychology, University of Iowa

Frances K. Wen, Department of Psychology, University of British Columbia

Allan W. Wicker, Department of Psychology, Claremont Graduate School

Brian T. Yates, Department of Psychology, The American University

PREFACE

This book of readings is designed to improve understanding of methodology and research practices in clinical psychology. Students and professionals who are in training or actively involved in research are the intended audience. Although the primary focus is on clinical psychology, many of the articles address issues that span the field of psychology more generally. The issues and methods raised in the readings are particularly relevant to areas of research within psychology (e.g., clinical, counseling, educational, and school psychology) and to other disciplines (e.g., psychiatry and social work). These areas span theory, research, and application and, hence, share many methodological challenges and opportunities.

The emphasis of this book is on the dominant paradigm that characterizes contemporary scientific research. Among the salient characteristics of this paradigm are the focus on theory, systematic assessment, and quantitative analyses of results. Just as scientific research is not the only way of knowing (e.g., deduction, intuition), the current paradigm is not the only way of studying phenomena empirically (e.g., qualitative research, nonstatistical methods of data evaluation). Nevertheless, it is central that students and professionals master and keep abreast of the dominant paradigm, understand the many methodological options and advances, and be alert to the many obstacles and shoals when designing their studies. The goal of this book is to foster greater understanding of the strengths, limitations, and options of methodology in the context of contemporary research practices.

The book includes articles about experimental design; the principles, procedures, and practices that govern research; assessment; sources of artifact and bias; methods of data analyses and interpretation; ethical issues; and publication and communication of the results of research. The organization of the book conveys features of research that follow in approximate logical and temporal order as they arise in the flow of an investigation. Thus, underpinnings of research, development of the research idea, and procedures within the study obviously precede data analyses and the write-up of the study. The book includes the following sections:

- Background and Underpinnings of Research
- Methods: Principles and Practices
- Assessment
- Data Analysis, Evaluation, and Interpretation
- Special Topics in Clinical Research
- Ethics in Research
- Publication and Communication of Research

The chapter topics follow the flow and sequence of the research process. Underlying this book and the selection of articles is the view that diverse facets of design are integrally related at the outset, that is, they emerge when the study is conceived. For example, in the planning stage of a study, the theory and rationale are (or at least should be) related to the plans for the data analyses and anticipated interpretations of the results. Typically, at this point investigators are not too concerned with analyses of the results or, of course, with the critical issues that will form the basis of the discussion in any report or write-up of the study. Yet, critical thought about how one is likely to analyze the data and the specific conclusions one wishes to draw greatly influence core features of the design, such as the experimental conditions, the plan for their administration between or within subjects, sample size and composition, and the type and range of measures.

Similarly, limitations of a study are usually discussed at the end of the journal article that describes the study. This is clearly the place to discuss them, and many limitations can be identified only when the study is completed. For example, the reader may learn during the study only that 90% of subjects[1] in the control group went on a group vacation and missed the posttest. Yet, many of the questions that are converted later to limitations can be identified and considered before the first subject is tested. If no effects or no differences are obtained, can this investigation be regarded as a strong and careful test of the hypotheses? Do the conditions of the investigation represent a sample of the conditions to which the investigator wishes to generalize? Do the control or comparison groups permit the investigator to comment specifically on what was responsible for group differences? These, of course, are all questions about methodology.

The quality of a study is usually related to the coherence of its conceptualization (hypotheses, predictions), the procedures to test that conceptualization (sample, measures, conditions, data evaluation), and the interpreta-

---

[1] The term *participants* is usually recommended for use in place of the term *subjects*. In the context of research methods, however, there are many participants in research, including persons who design the study (investigators), implement or carry out the procedures to run the study (experimenters), and provide the data (subjects). The term *subjects* is retained to maximize clarity of the reference group.

tions the author makes on the basis of these procedures. Methodology is not just a set of practices, such as random assignment and use of control groups, but more fundamentally pertains to correspondence between what the investigator wishes to say about the findings and what he or she is entitled to say on the basis of how the study was designed and conducted. Although the topics of the present book reflect and are organized according to the flow of research, some of the selected articles transcend and blur boundaries and discrete steps of research; they were selected to convey the interdependence of all phases of research in relation to drawing valid conclusions.

Research design is dynamic and cumulative; methods of design, assessment, and evaluation continually evolve and emerge. Thus, the book can only sample the available articles to address relevant domains to aid the researcher. Articles were selected to address core topics, including generating and testing hypotheses, selecting the sample, developing or selecting measures, designing studies that are statistically powerful, presenting the data, and communicating the results. Several articles from the first edition were retained because they still reflect classic statements on key topics.

In the second edition, articles were added to expand on core concepts, to reflect contemporary issues in research, and to elaborate ethical responsibilities in relation to research participants and to science more generally. Examples include articles on mediators and moderators, methods for studying efficacy and effectiveness of psychotherapy, making research relevant to clinical practice and policy, criteria used by review boards to evaluate scientific and ethical practices in research, and key features of preparing empirical and review papers for publication. Furthermore, since the first edition, the Ethical Principles of Psychologists and Code of Conduct that guide research (and other professional activities) have been revised and expanded (American Psychological Association, 1992).[2] Salient topics central to the design and execution of research are discussed, including ethical issues, oversight of research by committees that review scientific merit and ethical practices, and standards of scientific conduct more generally.

A book of readings on methodology has a great potential for missing the best-seller list. (Moreover, I regret to report that as I prepare this Preface, the movie rights for this book have still not been decided.) Articles in edited volumes are notoriously uneven in quality and level. The topic of methodology adds to the risk by being viewed as dry, technical, and difficult competition against alternatives for Saturday night entertainment. However, I attempted to steer sharply away from the shoals of checkered quality and tedium.

To that end, three considerations guided the selection of articles. First, articles were designed to cover several steps or stages that emerge in planning and executing research. Key stages in the research process include developing

---

[2]References cited in this section and in sections that introduce remaining portions of the book appear in a single reference section at the end of the book.

the research idea; selecting methods, procedures, and assessment devices; analyzing and interpreting the data; and preparing a written report to communicate what was accomplished and why. Second, articles were selected not only to improve our understanding of research methods but also to provide concrete recommendations and practices to guide the design of an investigation. Thus, many of the articles include suggestions that can be readily applied to improve an investigator's research. Finally, an effort was made to identify highly readable articles. Hundreds of articles on methodology and research design within the past several years were identified and evaluated. From these, articles were selected that eschewed technical jargon, extensive formula, and related features that might engender insomnia among the most vigilant. Each of the articles has been published previously. An advantage is they have traversed the review and publication process and hence their merit already has been favorably evaluated in advance of inclusion in this volume. In many cases, the articles are considered to be classics because of the message and clarity of presentation.

The rationale for selecting readable articles extends beyond the obvious. Technical writings and coverage of individual topics are critical to the development of research acumen. At the same time, such writings often require detailed discussion and dialogue to establish the core concepts and to cull their implications. The process of selection in the present book was designed to identify articles whose critical points could be readily gleaned from the articles themselves. Consequently, the book can be used on its own, particularly for graduate and advanced undergraduate courses, or as a supplement to other texts (e.g., Kazdin, 1998; Rosenthal & Rosnow, 1991).

Several persons have contributed to the development of the book. The contributors whose articles are included are gratefully acknowledged not only for their articles but also for the special contribution their work makes to psychology. Gary R. VandenBos, Julia Frank-McNeil, and Ted Baroody of the American Psychological Association provided valuable support. Colleagues (faculty and students) in the Department of Psychology at Yale University provide in an ongoing way a very special environment for deliberating, discussing, and dissecting research issues and hence served as an important impetus for the present book. In addition, many students have commented on the specific articles that are included in the book and thus helped to screen their final selection. While this book was prepared, I received support from a Research Scientist Award (MH00353) from the National Institute of Mental Health and by the John D. and Catherine T. MacArthur Foundation Research Network on Psychopathology and Development. I am extremely grateful for the support and the learning opportunities these grants provided.

Alan E. Kazdin

Methodological Issues & Strategies in Clinical Research

Second Edition

INTRODUCTION

Methodology refers to the diverse principles, procedures, and practices that govern and guide research. Methodology provides ways of filtering, screening, and selecting information. Findings that emerge from methodologically sound research, particularly when replicated, have special status, namely, they can enter the body of scientific knowledge, with all the strengths and limitations that status confers. The principles and practices span all the sciences, and hence scientific research methods constitute a universal language—sort of an epistemological Esperanto. To state that a particular relation or finding emerged from controlled empirical research and has been replicated has meaning that can be grasped among the community of scientists. That meaning includes a level of tentativeness that many nonresearchers (and researchers outside of the context of their laboratories) understandably lament. For example, as we are deciding what to put on our toast (e.g., butter, margarine, jam, nonsweetened jamlike fruit, melted cheddar cheese with a slice of ham and an egg), we are frustrated with the fact that we do not have a clear picture of what to do based on the latest research findings. The findings of what is "good" and "bad" for us are not very clear, and when knowledge does advance, the same breakfast food is likely to be quite good and quite bad for us in different ways. The tentativeness and complexity of such findings occasionally lead the public to be "fed up" with science.

When in our laboratory and poring over our own latest findings, we are not as concerned with the seeming ambiguity. We know and appreciate that a scientific "truth" does not mean that the relation evident in research is certain, true for all time, true for all members of the group (e.g., culture and species) for which it was demonstrated, and true for all circumstances to which it might be applied. Yet much can be said, and we appreciate the findings from research because they signal that particular practices were implemented, controls were used, and special care evidently was taken to rule out, limit, or minimize artifacts and potential sources of bias. The protections of scientific methods are not foolproof by any means, but they represent a leap from ordinary experience in our power to draw inferences and to accumulate knowledge in a systematic way.

Scientific research is essential for understanding natural phenomena and for making advances in knowledge. A number of research methods are available; they have in common careful observation and systematic evaluation of the subject matter under varying conditions. The diverse methods constitute special arrangements and plans of observation that are designed to uncover relations between variables in a relatively unambiguous fashion. The relations may seem apparent in nature when a particular phenomenon is observed casually. Yet, many relations are obscured by the complex interrelations and combinations of many variables as they normally appear. The task of identifying relations is compounded by the characteristics and limits of one's perception. Among complex relations, it is easy and natural for individuals to connect variables perceptually and conceptually and to then integrate these into their belief systems. The relations can be firmly entrenched independently of whether the variables genuinely go together or are related in fact.

In scientific research, one attempts to simplify the complexity of nature and to isolate a particular phenomenon for careful scrutiny. The phenomenon is examined by manipulating or varying values of the variable of interest while controlling extraneous factors that might otherwise influence the results. By controlling or holding constant sources of influence that might vary under ordinary circumstances, the relation between the variables of interest can be examined. The isolation of the phenomenon of interest does not always require the manipulation of conditions. Other ways include fine-grained assessment to permit a more molecular level of analysis of a construct that otherwise would not be possible and statistical or data evaluation techniques to permit separation and control of influences that are normally intertwined. Arranging the conditions of investigation, using special measures, and evaluating the data quantitatively serve as aides to perception. The methods consist of diverse practices, procedures, and decision rules to aid in drawing conclusions and in reaching a consensus about relations observed in research. Among the interesting features of scientific research is that the methods used to reveal nature can contribute significantly to the results. That is, how a study is conducted, the measures that are used, and how the data are analyzed are just a few of the aspects of methodology that influence the specific conclusions the investigator draws. Consequently, the study of methodology and the underpinnings of design and evaluation options is essential.

KEY CHARACTERISTICS OF METHODOLOGY

Although methodology encompasses a number of specific practices and procedures, the significance of the topic derives from several general characteristics. First, methodology is a way of thinking about phenomena of interest. That way of thinking encompasses how we wish to understand, a range of questions about how the world behaves, and a critical approach to the answers we obtain. The way of thinking is quickly revealed in discussions about a particular finding, including questions or comments about whether the way in which the phenomenon was studied could explain the result (e.g., various sources of artifact, bias, or uncontrolled factors), whether the theory or hypotheses that prompted the study are the best account of the findings, and whether the findings are restricted to particular conditions (e.g., sample, methods of manipulating the independent variable or operationalizing the constructs of interest) implemented to study the phenomenon. This way of thinking is not merely critical thinking or skepticism for its own sake; rather, it is a way of generating advances in knowledge that accumulate and elaborate prior findings and that lead to more in-depth understanding.

As an example of the type of thinking involved, consider briefly the reasonably well-established finding that harsh physical (corporal) punishment of children by their parents is often associated with elevated child aggression. (For purposes of the example, I shall gloss over the genuinely critical questions about what defines harsh punishment, what aggression means, and how it is measured.) A statement about the relation, although based on research, conveys the need for additional research based on the questions that immediately emerge. Among the questions, is it really punishment that is the variable that leads to or contributes to aggression or is it something associated with punishment (e.g., lack of parental warmth, single-parent families, poor diet in the homes)? Moreover, can one be sure of the order or sequence, that is, that parental punishment is antecedent to child aggression? It might make sense to propose the opposite order, namely, that aggressive children eventually become so frustrating that parents begin to use corporal punishment after having exhausted alternative discipline strategies. Not all children who are punished harshly are highly aggressive—why, who are they, what influences augment or attenuate the relation between corporal punishment and aggression? If punishment leads to aggression, what are the mechanisms or processes involved (e.g., modeling by the parent, activation of neurological mechanisms that mediate aggressive behavior, genetic influences that contribute both to parent and child aggression)? What characteristics other than aggression are evident among such children? What are parents and families like who engage in harsh practices? Is having two harsh parents worse than one in severity of child aggression? Research is not conducted merely to fill out a periodic table of "facts" or empirical relations among variables. Researchers wish to understand the bases of the relations. The previous questions convey the way of thinking that methodology reflects and prompts. Among the characteristics of the questions are a search for mechanisms, processes, correlates, variations in patterns (e.g., among parents and children with seemingly similar histories or characteristics), and formulation of the questions in ways that they can in principle and practice be answered by further research.

Second, methodology is always evolving and developing. This does not mean that every principle, practice, or procedure changes, but very many do. This makes methodology a very lively topic because many seemingly standard practices in one generation become outdated. New methods are not just a matter of studying old phenomena in new ways. New ways generate new findings and phenomena that have not heretofore been studied. For example, methodology encompasses new ways to measure phenomena of interest and these new methods (e.g., Hubble telescope in astronomy, fast mental resonance imaging [fMRI] in neuroscience) lead to observations of very new phenomena and place previously observed phenomena in a new light.

The advances that methodology provide often are hidden or made explicit only in historical perspective. Perhaps that is fine. However, as a rationale for studying methodology, for improving one's own research, and for making an advance, it is critical that researchers appreciate the nuances and contributions of methodology to substantive advances. Consider a familiar example with a less familiar methodological footnote. The work of Ivan P. Pavlov (1849–1936) may be readily recalled. Indeed, one can ask most college students to recount his work and hear in response the pithy reply, "Wasn't he the classical conditioning guy with the dogs who got a Nobel prize for digestion?" Yes, that was the guy. For present purposes, however, it is useful to note that underlying the important conceptual and empirical advances were critical methodological breakthroughs, particularly in relation to assessment. Pavlov mastered a very difficult surgical technique with his dogs in which a permanent fistula (tube) was implanted in the glands (e.g., salivary) or major organs (e.g., stomach). The fistula permitted secretions—usually drop by drop—to be collected outside of the body so they were not contaminated by other fluids (e.g., gastric fluids in the stomach). The technique, not invented by Pavlov, permitted meticulous quantification (assessment) and fine-grained analyses of responses (conditioned and unconditioned) to various experimental arrangements. It is important that one not only remember and build on the substance of Pavlov's work but also appreciate how advances in assessment more generally facilitated the substantive contribution.

In a related vein, much of graduate training in statistics focuses on, and is restricted to, teaching fairly traditional methods of data analysis such as analyses of variance and multiple regression (Aiken, West, Sechrest, & Reno, 1990). As with assessments, data analyses very much influence conceptualization of phenomena and the findings that are obtained. Less frequently taught analyses (e.g., path analyses, structural equation modeling, individual growth curves, survival analyses) do not merely increase researchers' options for data analyses but also extend what facets of the world are revealed to them.

Even less frequently taught and discussed are the models underlying commonly used statistics. As a general rule, statistics in common use rely on linear models and simple models at that. Among the models is the view that one influence leads to another, as represented by an arrow (Influence A → Outcome B), and that influence tends to be linear. To my knowledge, however, there has been no biblical or other prescription that variables relate to each other in linear ways. It is likely that many relations of interest are nonlinear and nonlinear in diverse ways. Moreover, rather than single arrows, there are multiple arrows and arrows of different lengths (influences that come into play at different times and for different durations). Multiple influences are likely to affect one another as well as the outcome. Statistical models and tests that follow from them make assumptions about how "reality" is constructed and, in the context of individual investigations, what reality can look like.

Third, methodology is characterized by a multiplicity of options, that is, how a particular situation can be arranged or examined so as to reveal nature's secrets. As the area of research includes less experimental control or fewer conditions of the laboratory, greater use of these options is necessary. For example, interpersonal interaction may be studied in a laboratory with college students who are assigned randomly to various experimental conditions. These conditions may be presented by audio or video tape or by highly trained experimenters who deliver prepared scripts. Interaction may also be studied naturalistically in everyday situations in which experimental control, intervention, and potential sources of artifact are pervasive. Inferences can readily be drawn in less well-controlled situations, but to do so requires the investigator to be a bit more innovative and to be aware of, and indeed perhaps to invent, new models and methods to permit inferences to be drawn. In areas where there are field or applied investigations, knowledge of the range of options for design, assessment, and data evaluation is essential. Methodology involves problem solving, where the problem is to draw unambiguous inferences from situations of interest to the investigator. Methodological practices involve potential solutions to the range of specific problems or sources of potential ambiguity.

METHODOLOGY IN CLINICAL PSYCHOLOGY

Although methodology is central to all science in general, there are special reasons to focus on issues related to research in clinical psychology. Clinical psychology embraces standard features of scientific research, such as defining the research idea, generating hypotheses, designing investigations, and collecting and analyzing data. Yet, in clinical psychology and other disciplines in which laboratory, clinical, and applied studies are conducted, the basic steps of research and methodological acumen of the investigator are challenged. The challenges derive from the diversity of topics, samples, and settings in which research is conducted.

The scope of research in clinical psychology is enormous. Among the topics addressed in research are the assessment, diagnosis, clinical course, treatment, and prevention of clinical dysfunction; personality; and cross-cultural differences. The populations studied include children, adolescents, adults, and the elderly and people with special experiences (e.g., homelessness, divorce, imprisonment during prior wars), medical impairment and disease (e.g., cancer, acquired immune deficiency syndrome [AIDS], spinal cord injury, diabetes), or psychological disorder or dysfunction (e.g., depression, anxiety, posttraumatic stress disorder, autism). People in contact with special populations (i.e., those who are exposed to someone with a special condition) themselves are often studied (e.g., children of alcoholic parents, spouses of depressed patients, siblings of physically handicapped children). Research in clinical psychology is conducted in diverse settings (e.g., laboratory, clinics, hospitals, prisons, schools, industry) and in the absence of structured settings (e.g., runaway children, homeless families). Research in clinical psychology is also conducted in conjunction with many other branches of psychology and different disciplines (e.g., criminology, health psychology, neurology, pediatrics, psychiatry, public health).

Understandably, diverse methods of study are required to meet the varied conditions in which clinical psychologists work and the special challenges in drawing valid scientific inferences from these situations. The methodological diversity of clinical research, like the substantive diversity, can be illustrated in many different ways. Studies vary in the extent to which the investigator can exert control over the assignment of cases to conditions or administration of the intervention (e.g., true experiments and quasi-experiments) and the selection of pre-existing groups and how they are followed and evaluated. Moreover, designs (e.g., group and single case), methods of data evaluation (e.g., statistical and clinical), and indeed approaches to the study of clinical phenomena further convey the methodological richness of the field.

The purpose in highlighting the diversity of clinical psychology is to underscore the importance of facility with the methods of research. Special demands or constraints are frequently placed on the clinical researcher. Ideal methodological practices (e.g., random assignment) are not always available, but they are not always necessary. Restrictions also may limit the researcher's options (e.g., a control group might not be feasible, only small sample sizes are available). The task of the scientist is to draw valid inferences from the situation and to use methodology, design, and statistics toward that end. In clinical psychology and related areas of research, the options in methodology, design, and statistics must be greater than those in more basic research areas to permit the investigator to select and identify creative solutions. Clinical research is not in any way soft science; indeed, the processes involved in clinical research reflect science at its best precisely because of the thinking and methodological ingenuity required to force nature to reveal its secrets. Deploying strategies to accomplish this requires an appreciation of the purposes of research and the underpinnings of research strategies.

GOALS AND FOCUS OF THIS BOOK

The goal of this book is to help the reader conduct, recognize, and appreciate high-quality research. *High-quality research* is a broad term that encompasses several distinguishable components. First, of course, is the idea, theory, or prediction that underlies the study and its contribution to knowledge. There is no substitute for a novel conceptualization or an integrative view that permits one to conceive of phenomena in new ways or to recognize entirely new phenomena. Second, how that idea is translated into an investigation is critical. There are many options for evaluating or testing the idea. The quality of the study is determined by the options selected and the extent to which they reveal the phenomenon and rule out various interpretations that might make the results ambiguous. Third, communication of the findings is critically important too. Communication of findings is not merely describing the creative idea and the methods that were used. Rather, communication of findings places the research in the context of what is known and what needs to be known. It is valuable and praiseworthy to be skilled at any one of these three components (just as it is "nice" for a pilot to know how to take off). High-quality research stems from being skilled in each of the components and putting them together in an investigation (it is rather useful for a pilot to know how to land too and to be able to do this after a successful takeoff). This book addresses each of the components of research and is intended to augment skills in their conceptualization and execution. The articles are organized into sections that are designed to reflect the flow of research issues and processes.

The first section, Background and Underpinnings of Research, provides an overview of psychological research in general. Assumptions, goals, and methods of research provide a point of departure for specific sections that follow. In addition, within this initial section are articles that cover the process of developing research ideas. One way to consider the focus of the study is to consider the type of relation the researcher is trying to demonstrate. Evaluation of mediators and moderators is discussed to convey the impact of conceptualization of the independent variables on design and data evaluation issues. Even at this early stage, conceptualization of the study (e.g., hypothesized relations among independent and dependent variables) has implications for how the data might be analyzed.

The second section, Methods: Principles and Practices, includes articles that address procedures, practices, and design options. Articles cover sampling issues related to research subjects, which are familiar, and issues related to the conditions of research, which are less familiar. The methods used to study phenomena, their implications for establishing a relation, and generality of that relation are also presented. This section ends with a discussion of design options and considerations governing their use.

The third section, Assessment, presents scale evaluation and development. Although most research does not involve development of scales, selecting measures is a critical step. The articles on scale evaluation and development convey dimensions that are relevant to the use of measures in research. This section also discusses measurement validity and the relation of characteristics of a measure to the theory about the phenomenon of interest. Ethnic and minority issues are discussed in the context of sampling. The issues, of interest in their own right, raise broader points about sampling, measurement validation, and generality of results.

The fourth section, Data Analysis, Evaluation, and Interpretation, includes several articles that relate data evaluation to other facets of research. Major attention is given to statistical significance testing, including its origins, strengths, and limitations. There is deep concern regarding the uses and misuses of statistical significance and null hypothesis testing. The articles convey the manifold issues involved and options for data presentation and analysis.

In the fifth section, Special Topics in Clinical Research, diverse topics of special interest in areas of clinical work are addressed. Articles discuss evaluation with individual cases in the context of clinical practice and research. Other topics include evaluation of treatment integrity in therapy research, the importance of searching for Treatment × Client interactions in therapy research, and the assessment of clinical significance. Articles also focus on what can be done in the design and evaluation of studies to improve the relevance, disseminability, and generality of research findings and to increase their impact on clinical practice and policy.

In the sixth section, Ethics in Research, multiple ethical issues and practices to guide research and the researcher are presented. The section begins with the American Psychological Association (APA) statement of ethical principles, followed by discussions of the strengths and limitations of the guidelines in relation to research. Also covered in this section is the role of institutional review boards in the oversight of research. Misconduct in science (e.g., fraud, data fabrication, plagiarism), covered in the ethical principles and codes, also is discussed. Finally, an article related to the ethics of authorship (e.g., deciding who is an author, who is first author) is included because of the sensitivity of the issues in collaborative research and particularly in collaborations of students and faculty.

The final section, Publication and Communication of Research, addresses the preparation of manuscripts designed to communicate research. Communication is a logical conclusion to completion of research. From the standpoint of methodology, the rationale for research processes and practices are critically important to convey in the written report of research. The articles in this section are designed to convey the thought processes prompted by methodology that deserves attention in preparing reports on one's own research, reviewing the literature within an area, conducting meta-analyses, and preparing grant applications.

The articles within each section raise points central to the respective aspect or phase of the study. At the same time, many articles connect the research process by spanning different phases of research and hence serve a valuable role in conveying how theory, research design, assessment, and statistical evaluation act in concert. There is a flow to research and a seamless process. A given study is in a sequence and historical tradition in the area of investigation; within the study itself there is a process that does not quite have a clear beginning and end. The write-up of a study ought to point rather clearly to the next studies and hence constitutes a new beginning. The articles in this book have been selected to magnify facets of the research process, to identify components of high-quality research, and to delineate practices that can be adopted to improve investigations.

I

BACKGROUND AND UNDERPINNINGS OF RESEARCH

This book begins at the beginning of the research process, namely, key tenets and underpinnings of research. In this initial set of articles, general issues antecedent to the investigation itself are discussed. The first article discusses assumptions that underlie the research process and different types of research. Articles in this section also discuss the sources and development of ideas necessary for beginning an investigation.

TENETS OF RESEARCH

In the initial article, Gregory A. Kimble discusses the scientific underpinnings, tenets, and approaches of psychological research. Critical issues are examined, including the role of theory, personal experience, and common sense in relation to the development of scientific research. The article provides a useful starting point by making explicit key assumptions about what investigators do in psychological research and how these assumptions relate to the research process and the accumulation of scientific knowledge.

DEVELOPING RESEARCH IDEAS

Research begins with the idea or question for investigation. Identifying and generating an idea for research might be cast aside quickly as creativity, inspiration, and brilliance and hence not usually what is considered to be part of research design. In developing the research idea, creativity is difficult to prescribe. Yet, looking at phenomena in new ways and challenging existing assumptions provide a useful point of departure. In the article by Allan W. Wicker, several strategies are presented to generate novel ideas, including alternative ways of selecting, developing, and playing with ideas; examining the contexts in which phenomena occur; challenging central assumptions; and scrutinizing key concepts. What is particularly novel about this article is the broad range of strategies that are presented and illustrated.

Research usually consists of testing specific hypotheses but also can be used to develop ideas and hypotheses. In the article by Alvin R. Mahrer, two different approaches to research are discussed: hypothesis testing and discovery-oriented research. The article begins by discussing the more familiar hypothesis-testing approach that dominates psychological research in general. In the context of psychotherapy research, hypothesis testing is criticized for its intent, limited yield, and lack of impact on theory or clinical practice. The purpose of discovery-oriented research is to examine the particulars in the area of interest (e.g., client and therapist interaction), to isolate that which is novel and unexpected, and to identify connections and relations. The article sharply contrasts hypothesis-driven versus discovery-oriented research to make the case for the special contribution of the latter. The key point is that exploration, maximum use of the data collected, and creative opportunities for discovery are not fostered in research and in the training of researchers. Indeed, often pejorative terms are used when one explores the data in a seeming unguided fashion ("fishing expedition"). Discovery-oriented evaluation of the data is to be encouraged as a way to generate hypotheses and to extract from a given investigation a range of findings. The study and the way it is analyzed can address hypothesis testing and exploration. Both articles by Wicker and Mahrer are designed to foster more creative approaches to the conceptualization of studies and the data they generate.

CONCEPTUALIZING INDEPENDENT VARIABLES

The idea for a study can derive from considering the ways in which the variables under investigation may relate to one another or another phenomenon (see Haynes, 1992; Kraemer et al., 1997). A key distinction that represents two of the many ways in which variables can relate to the phenomenon of interest is between mediators and moderators (Baron & Kenny, 1986). *Mediators* refer to the reasons, processes, or mechanisms that are responsible for the effect of an intervention or experimental manipulation; *moderators* refer to those variables with which a particular relation interacts (e.g., gender, race). The article by Grayson N. Holmbeck elaborates the nature of this distinction and gives examples of how mediators and moderators are evaluated. The examples not only clarify the distinction but are useful when viewed from a broader perspective. There are different pathways, mechanisms, and relations among variables, and the task for the researcher is to think about these in advance of the study and to ensure that the design, conditions, and data analyses can address these relations. Statistical approaches to evaluate mediators and moderators are also discussed and underscore the importance of considering data-analytic issues early in the research process.

UNDERPINNINGS AND TENETS OF RESEARCH

1

PSYCHOLOGY FROM THE STANDPOINT OF A GENERALIST

GREGORY A. KIMBLE

In recent years the question of whether psychology can be a single, general discipline has been the object of considerable discussion and controversy. Although some scholars have been able to see actual (e.g., Matarazzo, 1987) or potential (e.g., Staats, 1981) unity in the field, a greater number (e.g., Furedy & Furedy, 1982; Kendler, 1981; Koch, 1981) have found disunity and chaos. Discussions of this issue sometimes have taken on the quality of a methodological holy war because the disagreements are partly in the realm of values. Psychology is a house divided. One group of psychologists sees the field in terms of scientific values and accepts the concepts of objectivism, elementism, and nomothetic lawfulness. The group opposed sees psychology in terms of humanistic values and accepts the concepts of intuitionism, holism, and idiographic lawfulness. The positions seem irreconcilable, and the war goes on (Kimble, 1984).

Meanwhile, this epistemic jihad has encouraged the impression in some quarters that our recent family squabbles are a scientific revolution of the

Reprinted from the *American Psychologist, 44,* 491–499. Copyright 1989 by the American Psychological Association.

type that Kuhn (1970) referred to as a "paradigm shift." The time has come, however, to put that myth to rest. There has been no revolution in psychology, just a series of tribal wars that have brought a new look to the battlefield. In particular, the concepts, methods, and subject matter of both cognitive and humanistic psychology, although very different, have gained legitimacy. As a result, the appearance of psychology now is not at all like what it was less than half a century ago. The major assertion of this article, however, is that the altered appearance of psychology is just a change in surface structure. At a deeper level, the structure of psychology is what it always was. The purpose of this article is to describe that structure in the belief that all psychologists may possibly find it acceptable because it will show that intuition, holism, and idiographic lawfulness are now included in the science of psychology and that this science operates within limits set by human values. In this article, I present a series of assertions that define what I take to be the major commitments and styles of thought that characterize scientific psychology. Each of these assertions is followed by explanatory text.

DETERMINISM, EMPIRICISM, AND THE DEFINITION OF PSYCHOLOGY

Two of the basic tenets of traditional science are those of determinism and empiricism. In psychology, those assumptions decide such fundamental issues as the definition of the field.

1. *Behavior is determined by genetic endowment and environmental circumstances. The understanding, prediction, and control of behavior are reasonable scientific ambitions.*

All psychologists accept these statements but in somewhat different ways. For the purely scientific psychologists, the emphasis is on abstract understanding. *Prediction* and *control* are terms that apply to theory and research. For the applied psychologists, the emphasis is on practical understanding. Prediction and control are concepts related to the goal of improving the lives of people. Although there are some psychologists who regard some human actions as otherwise uncaused voluntary expressions of "free will" (Kimble, 1984), I doubt that such a compromise is necessary.

For some time now it has been clear that voluntary acts are amenable to investigation by the methods of science. In an early article, Kimble and Perlmuter (1970) identified five hallmarks of volition. Voluntary behavior is learned, motivated, planned, attended to, and guided to completion by a comparator process. At one level, this analysis solves the problem of volition by reducing it to accepted scientific concepts. At another level, however, the solution creates problems of its own, because terms like *motivation, attention,* and *comparator process* require objective definition. Without it, they violate the second basic tenet of science, the principle of empiricism.

2. The data of science are the publicly confirmable facts of observation. Psychology is the science of behavior.

Although they are an important part of psychology, inner phenomena like thought, emotion, and ambition are not a part of the basic definition because they are not observable. They are concepts, inferences from behavior. They play a key role in the science of psychology, which I will describe after I develop the required foundation, beginning with a correction of some possible misunderstandings of the definition just presented.

Most important, perhaps, the definition does not exclude personal experience, common sense, or intuition from the science of psychology. Although private, they are important sources of hypotheses for the science. The principle of empiricism does not apply to the discovery of ideas but to the establishment of their validity. How one arrives at an idea has no bearing on its truth. It is its acceptance into science that requires objective evidence. Thus, if a man dreams that he was hiking in the mountains, and your intuition tells you that he had the dream because he unconsciously loves his mother, there is nothing in the tenet of empiricism to prevent your thinking that way. No one should take you very seriously, however, until you produce some type of evidence that the hypothesis is not false. If it turns out that such evidence is logically impossible to obtain, as is true of Marxist theory, "scientific" creationism, and some parts of psychoanalytic theory, the hypothesis is not part of science. Falsifiability is the criterion that marks the boundary line between science and nonscience.

Although personal experience plays the same legitimate role as intuition in psychology, it cannot provide the basic data of the science for reasons that become very clear in cases where the experiences of people differ. Suppose that my experience tells me that learning always is sudden and insightful, that men are more intelligent than women, and that people have dependable traits like honesty and sociability that appear in every situation. Suppose, by contrast, that your experience tells you that learning is always gradual, that women are more intelligent than men, and that traits like honesty and sociability are situation specific. Whose experience (if either) shall we accept as valid? You get the point: We cannot decide without a public test. The only alternatives appear to be (a) the creation of an epistemological elitist class whose personal experiences would define the truth for all the rest of us, or (b) the democratic decision that the experiences of everyone have been created equal. Neither of these alternatives is acceptable to science, however, because both of them violate the criterion of falsifiability.

The great problem with a reliance on common sense as evidence of psychological truths is that these truths are so defective (Kohn, 1988). Some of them are wrong ("Genius is closely related to insanity"). Some of them are contradictory ("Every individual human being is unique" versus "People are about the same the whole world over"). Most of the explanations appeal to essences ("People seek the company of others because they are gregarious by nature"). Probably without exception, the truths of common sense are oversimplifications.

COMPLEXITY AND ANALYSIS

Almost nothing important in behavior results from a single gene or from a single environmental influence. Behavior and its determinants are both complex. Multiple causes produce multiple psychological effects. Moreover, causes interact, and the influence of any single variable depends on the values of other variables in the situation. The need to unravel the threads of such complex causality has a fundamental implication.

3. Psychology must be analytic. A nonanalyzing science is an inarticulate science. Even to talk about a subject requires that it be analyzed into elements.

All science analyzes. Lewinian field theory (e.g., Lewin, 1931), which psychology now recognizes as possibly the most constructive holistic theory in its history (Jones, 1985), was very analytic. Lewin's fields contained boundaries, barriers, goals, and paths to goals, along with the individual. The individual was full of separate psychic regions, in various states of tension, separated by more or less permeable boundaries. Acted on by attracting and repelling vectors derived from objects with positive and negative valences, the individual moved with the field, sometimes reorganized it, and sometimes left it for the greener pastures of another level of reality. Lewinian theory was holistic in the sense that it treated behavior as dependent on the totality of many interacting variables, but that feature did not distinguish it from any other well-developed theory, for example that of Hull, one of Lewin's great rivals. The important difference between these theories was a difference in the level of analysis.

The products of analysis are the elements of a science. Because all science is analytic, it is also elementistic at some level. Different levels of analysis, and therefore different elements, are appropriate for different purposes. For example, the psycholinguists have been quite convincing on the point that the communicative functions of language involve overarching plans that control the production of sentences. It is impossible to understand the creation of an utterance in terms of strung-together linguistic units. Mistakes in language are another matter. They are only partly understandable in such holistic terms. I still write longhand, and every sentence that I write is the realization of a linguistic plan. The mistakes I make, however—the slips of the pen—almost always occur when some fragment of a word that should come later sneaks forward and occurs too early. The explanation of such linguistic behavior requires the use of elements that are smaller than a word.

In the history of psychology the elementist–holist argument centered on the question of whether the units of perception are attributes of sensations or organized perceptual patterns. The most important thing that has happened to that question is that it has become a question of fact rather than an item of faith. Research has now produced a blueprint of the answer to the question. The peripheral nervous system is equipped to handle only very elementary inputs: primary qualities, intensities, frequencies, durations, and extents of stimulation. By the time these neural messages reach the brain, however, they have given rise to organizations that endow such patterns of stimulation as those produced by phonemes, psychologically primary colors, visual angles, and the human face with the status of perceptual units. These particular organizing processes appear to be inborn, but experience also contributes to the creation of such units. Anyone who has tried the Stroop test (Stroop, 1935) has had a firsthand demonstration of the fact that words (learned organizations of letters) are extremely powerful perceptual units.

NATURE–NURTURE INTERACTION

Except in the minds of a few radical nativists and empiricists, the nature–nurture issue has long since been settled. The methods of behavioral genetics give quantitative meaning to the now-accepted statement that heredity and environment both contribute to human psychological characteristics but that they contribute to different degrees for different traits. Social attitudes and values are mostly learned (environmental), whereas height and weight are mostly inherited. Intelligence and introversion are somewhere in between. Whatever the proportions, however, the pattern of joint influence always seems to be the same.

4. *For all psychological characteristics, inheritance sets limits on, or creates, a range of potentials for development. Environment determines how near the individual comes to developing the extremes of these potentials.*

Inheritance provides different people with the intellect required to become a chess master, with a vulnerability to schizophrenia, or with the physical gifts required to compete in the Olympic Games. Environment determines whether these potential outcomes are realized. Questions about the relative importance of heredity and environment in the determination of such outcomes are questions for research, some of which is now available. For example, coefficients of heritability have been calculated for intelligence, various traits of personality, and the major forms of psychopathology. These coefficients usually ascribe less than half the variance in psychological traits to inheritance. Such data indicate that, although a biological basis for human diversity exists, the most powerful influences are environmental.

POTENTIAL VERSUS PERFORMANCE

Turning to the short-term dynamics of individual behavior, one encounters a similar pattern. Just as genetic factors put limits on the range of traits a person can develop, these developed traits define the limits of a person's behavior at the moment. Other factors determine whether this behavior reaches the limits of an individual's potential.

5. Individual behavior is the joint product of more or less permanent underlying potentials and more or less temporary internal and external conditions.

The distinction between trait- and state-anxiety shows how this idea works. A person may have a long-lasting potential for becoming anxious, a high level of trait-anxiety. The trait will lie dormant, however, until some threat occurs to throw this person into a state of anxiety. The distinctions in psychological theory between availability and accessibility of memories, linguistic competence and linguistic behavior, and sensitivity and bias provide additional examples. One may possess the memory of a certain person's name, but the memory may escape because of an interfering set. A little boy may know that the correct pronunciation of the word is "fish" although the best that he can do is "fis." Given the same sensory evidence, one subject in an experiment may report the presence of a signal and another may not because of their different criteria for making a positive response.

As in the case of nature and nurture, performance can never exceed the limits set by the underlying potential. Suppose that the anxious person described above has the potential to score 130 on an IQ test. In an anxious state, the person's performance may be much lower than that, but never higher. These statements are inherent in the definition of potential.

MENTALISTIC CONCEPTS

For the radical behaviorists, from Watson (1913) to Skinner (1987), all of this talk about anxiety, criteria, and potentials is offensive because these terms refer to phenomena that are subjective, mentalistic, and unobservable. They are not the raw materials that sciences are made of. In the final analysis, they hold (and I agree) that the only observables available to psychology are the behavior of organisms (responses) and the environmental circumstances (stimuli) in which behavior occurs. Everything else, they say, (but I do not agree) must be excluded if psychology is to be a science. The problem with this radical position is that it sacrifices everything of interest and importance in psychology by its exclusion of mentalistic concepts. Who can possibly care about a psychology that is silent on such topics as thinking, motivation, and volition? What has happened to human experience and the mind in this strangely unpsychological psychology? Do mentalistic concepts have no scientific role at all to play in a behavioristic world of facts? The answers to these questions take us back to a point that came up in connection with the definition of psychology.

6. *Mentalistic concepts enter psychology as inferences from behavior. The observations that define them often suggest causes.*

For as long as there has been a human species, people have noted that members of the species vary. All languages came to include such terms as "intelligence," "introversion," and "industriousness" to describe such variation. In the history of psychology, applications of this descriptive process have been important. They led Pavlov to the concept of the conditioned reflex, Piaget to the idea of developmental stages, and Selye to a recognition of the General Adaptation Syndrome.

In his very first classes in internal medicine as a young medical student, Selye (1976) was impressed with the fact that patients who were supposed to have different diseases shared many of the same symptoms: "They felt and looked ill, had a coated tongue, complained of more or less diffuse aches and pains in the joints, and of intestinal disturbances with loss of appetite" (p. 15). The symptoms that were supposed to help in differential diagnosis, "were absent or, at least, so inconspicuous that I could not distinguish them" (p. 16). This led Selye to the conception of a "general syndrome of disease," which later on became the "General Adaptation Syndrome" and then "stress." Selye hypothesized that the General Adaptation Syndrome was caused by any form of illness or injury to the body and that it was expressed in the symptoms common to all illness.

Selye was thinking in terms that came to be called "intervening variable theorizing." The construct, General Adaptation Syndrome, intervenes conceptually between a determining independent variable (any bodily injury) and a dependent variable (symptoms common to all illness). Figure 1 presents two diagrams of this kind of theorizing. The upper diagram based on the Selye example shows that processes of inference and hypothesis lead to the identification of psychological concepts and the postulation of possible lawful connections. The lower diagram presents the status of these connections as they were seen by Tolman (1938), the most important advocate of intervening variable theorizing. Tolman identified relationships among variables that are of different kinds, depending on whether the system includes intervening variables. Those that he called F-1 laws describe the direct dependence of behavioral phenomena on their determining antecedents. Those that he called F-2 and F-3 laws enter the picture with the introduction of intervening variables. The F-2 laws relate intervening variables to their antecedents. The F-3 laws describe the dependence of psychological phenomena on the intervening constructs.

The great usefulness of the intervening variable approach is that it provides objectivity for unobservable mentalistic concepts. The F-2 and F-3 laws tie them to observable antecedents and behavioral consequences. This permits entry into psychology of the topics that the radical behaviorists

THE GENERAL ADAPTATION SYNDROME

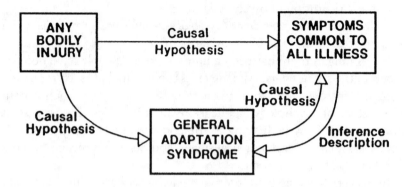

CONCEPTS AND TYPES OF LAWFULNESS

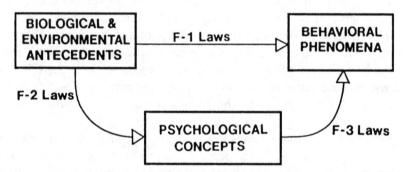

Figure 1. Intervening variable theorizing. *Note:* Psychological concepts are conceived as standing logically between independent variables on the left-hand side of the diagram and dependent variables on the right. The upper panel provides a concrete example and shows how inferences and causal hypotheses figure in the creation of intervening variables. The lower panel presents the more general case and shows how Tolman's (1938) F-1, F-2, and F-3 laws fit into the picture.

would banish. It allows psychology to deal with such conceptions as "attitude," "plan," and "purpose," which most of us take to be important items in the subject matter of the science.

By now, of course, the cat is out of the bag. The approach that I am recommending is the logical-empiricist method that has received strong criticism from the philosophers of science (e.g., Spector, 1966). Public observability as the criterion of scientific truth is harder to pin down than first thoughts might suggest. What is observable to people with one type of physiology or personal history may not be observable to others. This criticism, however, only leads to another important point of understanding. Before abandoning any significant commitment, it is always a good idea to consider the options that would remain in the absence of what one is planning to give up. In this case, the most frequently offered alternatives are to accept personal experience or linguistic practice as the criterion of truth. These are alternatives that science must reject for reasons presented earlier in this article.

At the same time that we recognize the value of intervening variables, we must also recognize and avoid two abuses to which they are commonly subjected. First, concepts are reified too often. They are captured by the mistaken outlook that Stuart Chase (1938) once called "the tyranny of words." According to that misguided view, if there is a word for it in the dictionary, a corresponding item of physical or psychological reality must exist, and the major task of science is to discover the a priori meanings of these linguistic givens. On the current psychological scene, this foolish assumption gives rise to ill-conceived attempts to decide what motives, intelligence, personality, and cognition "really are." It also legitimates unproductive debates over such questions as whether alcoholism is a disease. Those involved in such disputes never seem to recognize that the controversies are always about definitions and not facts. This first misunderstanding is related to the second one.

Concepts are products of definition. They are merely descriptive and explain nothing. If someone says that a man has hallucinations, withdraws from society, lives in his own world, has extremely unusual associations, and reacts without emotion to imaginary catastrophes because he is schizophrenic, it is important to understand that the word *because* has been misused. The symptomatology defines (diagnoses) schizophrenia. The symptoms and the "cause" are identical. The "explanation" is circular and not an explanation at all.

It may be worth the few sentences that it takes to say that circular definitions are not a scientific sin. Definitions must be circular—by definition. They are verbal equations in which the quantity on the left-hand side of the equals sign must be the same as that on the right. The sin is the offering of definitions as though they were explanations, as one can catch the late-night talk show hosts doing almost any evening on the radio. The following are examples of such statements: "Your eight-year-old son is distractable in school and having trouble reading because he has an attention deficit disorder"; and "The stock market crash of October 19, 1987, was caused by widespread economic panic." If I could make just one change in what the general public (and some psychologists) understand about psychology, it would be to give them an immunity to such misuses of definitions.

SCIENTIFIC STRUCTURE OF PSYCHOLOGY

Figure 2 summarizes much of the previous content of this article. The top part of the figure, labeled "Psychology Without Concepts," makes two points: (a) Defined in terms of observable dependent variables, psychology is

PSYCHOLOGY WITHOUT CONCEPTS

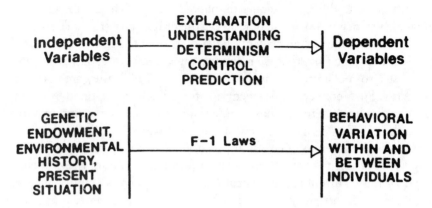

PSYCHOLOGY WITH CONCEPTS

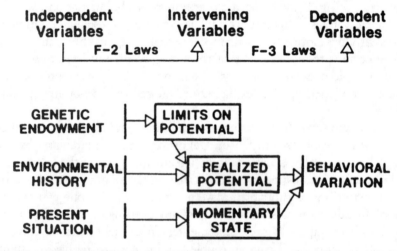

Figure 2. Summary of the argument. *Note:* The upper panel reviews the contributions of the empiricistic and deterministic tenets. The lower panel shows how three major classes of independent variables interact to define intervening variables and how the intervening variables interact in the production of behavior.

the science of behavior; and (b) this science operates on the assumption that behavior is determined. Explanation, prediction, and control are possible. The bottom part of the figure, labeled "Psychology With Concepts," reviews two further points: (a) In the determination of behavior, nature places limits on potentials for development, and environment determines the extent to which these potentials are realized; and (b) the behavior of an individual at any moment is the joint outcome of realized potential interacting with a temporary state.

In its entirety, Figure 2 is a review of the intervening variable approach and the meaning of Tolman's F-1, F-2, and F-3 laws. As an aid to the further development of these ideas, I return now to the concept of stress. Figure 3 presents the current situation of this concept in the general framework shown in Figure 2 and in enough detail to support several interpretative points.

First, the collection of independent and dependent variables has become quite large. Moreover, they *are* variables. Each of them has an infinite number of possible values, and people's positions on these many different dimensions are largely uncorrelated. Such complexity surrounds every important psychological concept. It provides a way for bringing common sense and science together on an important point: Individual uniqueness is no problem for psychology.

7. Every individual is a unique expression of the joint influence of a host of variables. Such uniqueness results from the specific (idiographic) effects on individuals of general (nomothetic) laws.

The contradictory truths of common sense that "every individual is unique" but that "people are the same the whole world over" are really not contradictory. People are the same in that they represent the outcome of the same laws operating on the same variables. They differ in degree and not in kind. People are unique in that the details of those operations differ from person to person.

Second, in Figure 2, the arrows connecting independent variables to concepts give objective meaning to these concepts. They are the operational definitions of the concepts. They are also Tolman's F-2 laws. The arrows connecting concepts to dependent variables are Tolman's F-3 laws. These F-2 and F-3 arrows identify the criteria of useful intervening variables.

8. A concept is acceptable to psychology only if it meets both of two criteria. It must be defined operationally and have a relationship to behavior.

One way in which scientific psychology has become more liberal in recent years is with respect to the requirement for operational definitions of concepts. Although there are still some psychologists who insist on strict and restrictive operational definitions, most of us recognize that our concepts are "open." As knowledge of a concept grows, the number of determining (therefore, defining) variables also increases, as happened with the concept of stress. This state of affairs creates great problems for psychology in the operational realization of its concepts. Such problems do not justify the abandonment of the operational approach, however. "Psychologists must learn to be sophisticated and rigorous in their metathinking about open concepts at the substantive level" (Meehl, 1978, p. 815).

Third, in Figure 3, including "physiology of stress" in the same box as "psychological stress" emphasizes the point that psychological and physiological concepts play identical epistemological roles. The alleged "reality" of

Independent
Variables

Intervening
Variables

Dependent
Variables

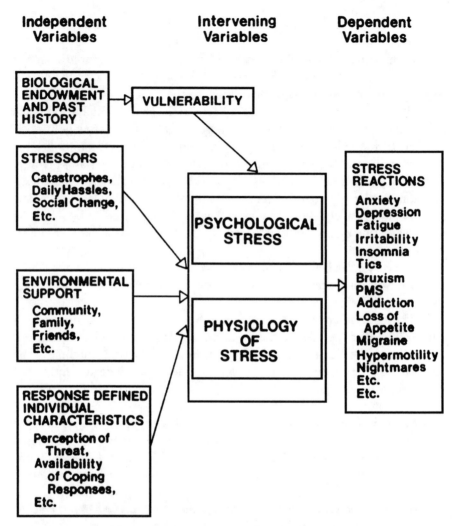

Figure 3. Current status of the concept of stress. *Note:* This figure spells out the details and analyzes the argument of Figure 2. This figure is an explication of concepts in Selye (1976).

physiological concepts may or may not exist. When Mendel proposed the concept of the gene to explain the hereditary transmission of traits, no one had yet observed any corresponding entity. Now we know that genes exist. When Pavlov proposed the concept of cortical irradiation to account for the phenomenon of stimulus generalization, no one had observed a corresponding brain process. So far in the history of psychology, no one has. These examples show that psychological concepts with physiological sounding names differ from other psychological concepts only if the physiological concepts acquire additional meaning through separate operations carried out at the level of physiology. Calling them physiological does not give them physical reality, only surplus meaning. As Donald Hebb (1955) once noted, CNS stands for "conceptual nervous system" until such independent observations have been made.

Finally, the appearance of "response defined individual characteristics" as well as "stressors" on the independent variable side of Figure 3 represents the relevance to the study of stress of both of the two sciences of psychology described by Cronbach (1957). The first science is stimulus–response (S–R) psychology, whose independent variables are situational events. The second science is response–response (R–R) psychology, whose independent variables are the behavior of individuals.

The independent variables of both sciences are independent in the sense that they are the variables from which the scientist makes predictions about behavior. The independent variables of the two sciences differ in that those of stimulus–response psychology can, in principle, be defined without reference to organisms and manipulated directly. Those of response–response psychology lack those properties. Experimental psychology typifies the S–R approach. The effort is to find the laws that relate behavior to environmental variables, for example, amount learned (R) as a function of distribution of practice (S). Psychometric psychology typifies the R–R approach. The effort is to find the laws that relate behavior in one situation to behavior in some other situation, most commonly a test, for example, college grades (R-2) as a function of SAT scores (R-1). The independent variables of R–R psychology sometimes become the dependent variables of S–R psychology. Figure 4 makes this point, using an example based on the concept of intelligence.

PSYCHOLOGICAL THEORY

Networks of the type laid out in Figure 3 represent the present state of theorizing in psychology. They define theoretical concepts, relate these concepts to one another, and identify the laws that connect them to behavior.

9. *A psychological theory puts a collection of concepts and their associated laws into a structure that allows the deduction of behavioral consequences. To show that a fact of behavior is deducible from such a theory is what it means to explain that fact.*

This is the method that Hull (1935) sometimes called the "hypothetico-deductive method." Although that designation has gone out of fashion, it is the method that scientists continue to use whenever they argue that their theories lead to specified predictions. Psychology has made recognizable progress in the sophistication with which it uses the method. Theoretical structures are often expressed in terms of formal logic or mathematics. Many of our concepts have acquired legitimate physiological meaning. The basic method remains unchanged, however.

The only alternative to hypothetico-deductive theorizing that I can think of is the radical empiristic approach, sometimes advocated by the Skinnerians. This alternative would rule out intervening variables, replacing them with an assemblage of F-1 laws like those identified at the top of Figure 2. In this view, theory would arise (if at all) inductively as the individual laws accumulated. Knowledge would provide its own theoretical organization.

One problem with this extreme view is that theory-free investigation is impossible. The choice of empirical questions to study and the selection of dependent and independent variables always entail theoretical assumptions. A second problem is that this approach encourages the delusion that facts somehow give unaided rise to scientific theories. In actuality, theories are creative products of scientific minds. Finally, for many of us the most unattractive aspect of the radical empiricistic view is that it takes the joy out of science. The process of making predictions, testing them, and finding out that they are right is the most exciting part of science. The radical empiricistic approach would rob the scientist of this excitement. In addition, that approach would leave the scientist unable to see the forest through the impenetrable tangle of F-1 trees. For all of those reasons it seems unlikely that theorizing will soon go out of style.

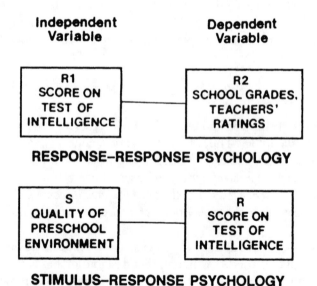

Figure 4. Psychology's two scientific disciplines. *Note:* The psychometric (R–R) and experimental (S–R) sciences of psychology differ in their choice of independent variables. The first uses previous behavior to predict performance, and the second uses stimulus events for that purpose. Depending on their functions, performance measures such as scores on tests can be independent variables (upper panel) or dependent variables (lower panel). Neither of the disciplines is more important than the other (Cronbach, 1957).

Because behavior is so complex and because it is amenable to treatment at so many different levels, an essentially unlimited array of theories is possible. Is there any way to choose among them? Obviously there is. The best theory is the one that survives the fires of logical and empirical testing. An evolutionary metaphor appears to be applicable. Scientific progress will be most rapid when a large pool of theoretical variants exists along with heavy selective pressure in the form of criticism and empirical tests. In the ideal scientific world, psychologists could preach and publish whatever they wanted to, no matter how unpopular, unorthodox, or unlikely to be correct. Physiological, mathematical, behavioristic, and humanistic theories would all participate in the struggle for survival. Freely published criticism would quickly lead to the extinction of the most maladaptive theoretical mutations. Empirical investigations would decide the fate of all the rest. The theories that survived and continued to evolve would be those that were best able to generate and validate behavioral deductions. The great diversity in psychology means that there is a niche for many different theoretical species.

THE QUESTION OF VALUES

I have now done most of what I set out to do in this article showing that the science of psychology is not inimical to the conceptions that characterize the new look in psychology. Intuition and common sense are major sources of ideas for this science. Mental states are concepts without which an acceptable science of behavior cannot exist. The elementism–holism issue disappears because research has shown that what is whole and what is elementary depends on the level of analysis. Human uniqueness is a factual consequence of the complexity of the determination of behavior. Idiographic and nomothetic lawfulness both make their contributions. Every type of theorizing is allowed its day in court. This leaves the question of values. Should scientific or humanistic values control the science of psychology? What should psychology be doing to solve the human problems of our age?

10. *The values that govern the science of psychology are scientific values. Humanistic values govern the behavior of psychological scientists and of psychologists who apply the knowledge gained by science.*

As a science, psychology is dedicated to discovering facts about behavior and creating theories to explain these facts. In this abstract conception, questions of human values do not arise. The scientific value system requires only that psychology discover the most dependable facts and produce the best theories that it can. Reality is more complex than that, however, because the science of psychology deals with living organisms. Research may require deprivation, concealment, deception, threat, punishment, or the invasion of privacy, and such procedures put scientific values into conflict with human values. For every psychological investigation this conflict raises a question: Is it worth it? Do the potential benefits to science and eventually to animal and human lives justify the costs to be extracted here and now? Psychology has wrestled with this issue for years, and guidelines now exist that protect the welfare of animal and human participants in psychological research. In these guidelines, humanistic values take precedence and form the basis for decisions regarding the acceptability of scientific research. In psychology today most research is in conformity with these codes of ethics.

The ethical acceptability of psychological research does not mean that it will answer the great moral questions of our age or decide which social policy is best. Such questions include the right to bear arms versus handgun control, bans on dirty books versus freedom of literary expression, the public's right to know versus the individual's right to privacy, retribution versus rehabilitation as the aim of criminal codes, affirmative action versus traditional indexes of merit, a verdict of "not guilty by reason of insanity" versus one of "guilty but insane," and freedom of choice versus right to life. Much of what scientific psychology knows is relevant to these important questions, but it cannot supply the answers. They must come from decisions that are made beyond the reach of science, in the court of human values.

The distinction that is implied here is one that should be guarded jealously. If psychology is to have a future as a science, it must obey the scientific rules. These rules define the limits of scientific authority. Science gains its strength and credibility by operating within these limits and understanding that, in other realms, it has no special power or status. Already in its short history, psychology has made important scientific contributions. The credibility acquired by reason of those accomplishments must not be mistaken for moral authority, however. It is a misuse of the credibility of psychology to use it as a basis to promote social prejudices or political goals, and the use of our status as psychologists for such purposes is an even worse misuse. The potential cost of these misuses is loss of the very credibility and status that allowed the misuse in the first place (Gould, 1987).

REFERENCES

Chase, S. (1938). *The tyranny of words*. New York: Harcourt, Brace.

Cronbach, L. J. (1957). Two disciplines of scientific psychology. *American Psychologist, 12*, 671–684.

Furedy, J. J., & Furedy, C. (1982). Socratic versus sophistic strains in the teaching of undergraduate psychology: Implicit conflicts made explicit. *Teaching of Psychology, 9*, 14–20.

Gould, S. J. (1987). William Jennings Bryan's last campaign. *Natural History, 96*(11), 16–26.

Hebb, D. O. (1955). Drives and the C.N.S. (conceptual nervous system). *Psychological Review, 62*, 243–254.

Hull, C. L. (1935). The conflicting psychologies of learning—A way out. *Psychological Review, 42,* 491–516.

Jones, E. E. (1985). History of social psychology. In G. A. Kimble & K. Schlesinger (Eds.), *Topics in the history of psychology* (Vol. 2, pp. 371–407). Hillsdale, NJ: Erlbaum.

Kendler, H. H. (1981). *Psychology: A science in conflict.* New York: Oxford University Press.

Kimble, G. A. (1984). Psychology's two cultures. *American Psychologist, 39,* 833–839.

Kimble, G. A., & Perlmuter, L. C. (1970). The problem of volition. *Psychological Review, 77,* 361–384.

Koch, S. (1981). The nature and limits of psychological knowledge. *American Psychologist, 36,* 257–269.

Kohn, A. (1988, April). You know what they say. *Psychology Today,* pp. 36–41.

Kuhn, T. S. (1970). *The structure of scientific revolutions.* Chicago: University of Chicago Press.

Lewin, K. (1931). Environmental forces in child behavior and development. In C. Murchison (Ed.), *A handbook of child psychology* (pp. 94–127). Worcester, MA: Clark University Press.

Matarazzo, J. D. (1987). There is only one psychology, no specialties, but many applications. *American Psychologist, 42,* 893–903.

Meehl, P. E. (1978). Theoretical risks and tabular asterisks: Sir Karl, Sir Ronald and the slow progress of soft psychology. *Journal of Consulting and Clinical Psychology, 46,* 806–834.

Selye, H. (1976). *The stress of life.* New York: McGraw-Hill.

Skinner, B. F. (1987). Whatever happened to psychology as the science of behavior? *American Psychologist, 42,* 780–786.

Spector, M. (1966). Theory and observation (I). *British Journal of the Philosophy of Science, 17,* 1–20.

Staats, A. W. (1981). Paradigmatic behaviorism, unified theory, unified theory construction methods, and the zeitgeist of separatism. *American Psychologist, 36,* 239–256.

Stroop, J. R. (1935). Studies of interference in serial verbal reactions. *Journal of Experimental Psychology, 18,* 643–662.

Tolman, E. C. (1938). The determiners of behavior at a choice point. *Psychological Review, 45,* 1–41.

Watson, J. B. (1913). Psychology as a behaviorist views it. *Psychological Review, 20,* 158–177.

DEVELOPING
RESEARCH IDEAS

2

GETTING OUT OF OUR CONCEPTUAL RUTS: STRATEGIES FOR EXPANDING CONCEPTUAL FRAMEWORKS

ALLAN W. WICKER

In 1879, Sir Francis Galton published an article describing a leisurely stroll he took in the interests of science—specifically to explore how the mind works. In the article, Galton told of walking down a London street and scrutinizing every object that came into his view. He recorded the first thought or two that occurred to him as he focused on each of about 300 objects. Galton reported that this method produced a great variety of associations, including memories of events that had occurred years earlier.

After several days, Galton repeated the walk and the recording procedure and again found a variety of associations. He also discovered a great deal of repetition or overlap in his thoughts on the two occasions. Galton likened his thoughts to actors in theater processions in which the players march off one side of the stage and reappear on the other. This recurrence of ideas

Reprinted from the *American Psychologist, 40,* 1094–1103. Copyright 1985 by the American Psychological Association.

piqued Galton's curiosity. He next devised some word association tasks that led him to the same conclusion as his walks, namely, that "the roadways of our minds are worn into very deep ruts" (Galton, 1879, cited by Crovitz, 1970, p. 35).

Although Galton's methods may have been faulty by present standards, he seems to have discovered a stable psychological principle: the recurrence of ideas (Crovitz, 1970). My comments here assume that Galton was right—that our thoughts flow in a limited number of channels and that our research efforts are thereby constrained.

This article sketches a variety of approaches for stimulating new insights on familiar research problems. Four sets of strategies, phrased as advice to researchers, are discussed as follows:

1. Researchers should play with ideas through a process of selecting and applying metaphors, representing ideas graphically, changing the scale, and attending to the process.
2. Researchers should consider contexts. They can place specific problems in a larger domain, make comparisons outside the problem domain, examine processes in the settings in which they naturally occur, consider the practical implications of research, and probe library resources.
3. It is important for researchers to probe and tinker with assumptions through such techniques as exposing hidden assumptions, making the opposite assumption, and simultaneously trusting and doubting the same assumption.
4. Finally, it is vital that researchers clarify and systematize their conceptual frameworks. They should scrutinize the meanings of key concepts, specify relationships among concepts, and write a concept paper.

The need for psychologists to attend to conceptual framing processes has been widely acknowledged (see, for example, Brinberg & McGrath, 1985; Campbell, Daft, & Hulin, 1982; Caplan & Nelson, 1973; Gergen, 1978, 1982; Jones, 1983; McGuire, 1973, in press; Tyler, 1983; Wachtel, 1980; Weick, 1979).

Several caveats are in order before we proceed:

1. Some readers may already be familiar with certain strategies and find them obvious. I have tried to include a diversity of heuristics in the hope that even seasoned investigators will find something of value.
2. Given the goal of presenting a range of strategies, only limited space is available for describing and illustrating each procedure. There is a risk that important and complex topics have been oversimplified—possibly even trivialized. I strongly rec-

ommend further reading on any strategy that seems promising; references are provided in the text.

3. These strategies are offered as heuristics. Most have not been systematically evaluated, although they have been useful to the scholars who proposed them and to others who have used them.

4. The substantial and important psychological literature on problem solving and critical and creative thinking has not been reviewed or even cited here. Much of that research addresses problems for which there are consensual solutions derived from mathematical or other logical systems. And some of that literature presumes that thinking habits developed from work on abstract puzzles or exercises are readily transferable to a wide range of other problems. The present concern is how to generate useful ideas whose "accuracy" cannot immediately be assessed. The following strategies draw upon, and in some cases expand, the researcher's existing knowledge structures (cf. Glaser, 1984). They are directly applicable to research problems in all areas of psychology.

PLAY WITH IDEAS

A playful, even whimsical, attitude toward exploring ideas is appropriate for the first set of strategies. These strategies include working with metaphors, drawing sketches, imagining extremes, and recasting entities as processes.

Select and Apply Metaphors

Playing with metaphors can evoke new perspectives on a problem. One strategy for exploiting metaphors is to identify some features from the research domain that are also discernible in another domain—perhaps another discipline or area of activity. Attention is shifted to this new area (the metaphor), which is then closely examined. From this examination, the researcher may discover some variables, relationships, or patterns that can usefully be translated back to the research problem.

A productive metaphor in social psychology is McGuire's inoculation theory of resistance to persuasion. The metaphor used was the medical procedure of stimulating bodily defenses against massive viral attacks by inoculating individuals with weakened forms of the virus. This procedure suggested the possibility of increasing resistance to persuasion by presenting weak arguments before strong arguments are encountered (McGuire, 1964). (The heuristic value of metaphors is discussed in Gowin, 1981b; Smith, 1981; and Weick, 1979. Leary, 1983, has analyzed the role of metaphor in the history of psychology. See Lakoff & Johnson, 1980, for a readable philosophical/linguistic analysis of metaphors.)

Exploring multiple, unusual metaphors may lead researchers to a greater awareness of the complexities and subtleties inherent in their domains (Weick, 1979). For example, likening interpersonal attraction to magnetic fields, a performance of Swan Lake, symbiosis, and hypnotism may reveal significant aspects of personal relationships that are not considered by such established perspectives as social exchange and equity theories.

Represent Ideas Graphically

A casual scan of such journals as *Science, American Scientist,* and *Scientific American* suggests that researchers in the physical and biological sciences make greater use of graphic presentations than do psychologists. We may be overlooking a powerful tool. In the development stages of a research problem, a pad of large drawing paper and a set of multicolored pens may be more useful than a typewriter. Visual images and sketches of problems can be liberating to researchers accustomed to representing their ideas only in linear arrangements of words, sentences, and paragraphs. Kurt Lewin, who used diagrams extensively, reportedly was ecstatic upon discovering a three-colored automatic pencil, which he carried everywhere to sketch his ideas (R. G. Barker, personal communications, April 10, 1983).

Many kinds of graphic schemes can be used to explore ideas and communicate them to others. Tabular grids, organization charts, flow diagrams, topological regions, and schematics are examples of abstract graphic languages. They have their own grammar and syntax and can be used to portray a variety of contents (McKim, 1972; Nelms, 1981). Figure 1 illustrates the flow diagram; it simply and clearly presents the three main approaches re-

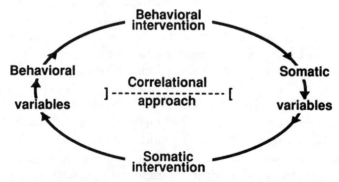

Figure 1. A graphic representation of three approaches to research on the relation between behavioral and somatic variables. *Note:* From "Experience, Memory, and the Brain" by M. R. Rosenzweig, 1983, *American Psychologist, 39,* p. 366. Copyright 1984 by American Psychological Association. Reprinted by permission.

searchers have taken in studying relations between behavioral and somatic variables.

In freehand idea sketching, there are no rules to be followed. With practice, researchers can fluently represent and explore their ideas and boldly experiment with relationships just as artists, composers, and urban planners have profitably done (McKim, 1972).

Change the Scale

Imagining extreme changes in proportion can stimulate our thinking. Mills (1959) gave this advice: "If something seems very minute, imagine it to be simply enormous, and ask yourself: What difference might that make? And vice versa, for gigantic phenomena" (p. 215). He then asked readers to imagine what preliterate villages might have been like with 30 million inhabitants. Or, to take another example, consider how childrearing would be different if at birth children had the motor ability and strength of adults. And if there were no memory loss, how would human information processing be different?

A variation of this procedure is to imagine what would be required for a perfect relationship to exist between two variables presumed to be linked. For example, psychologists have often assumed that a person's expressed attitudes determine how he or she will behave in daily affairs (Cohen, 1964). However, for people to act in complete accordance with their attitudes, they would have to be independently wealthy, to have unlimited time at their disposal, to have no regard for the opinions of others, to be unaffected by unforseen chance occurrences, to have a wide range of high-level skills, and even to be in several places at once (Wicker, 1969). Reflections on such factors can lead to more realistic theories and expectations.

Attend to Process

Research psychologists typically favor concepts that represent stable entities, perhaps because such concepts are easier to measure and to incorporate into theories than are processes. Yet it can be fruitful to view presumably stable concepts in dynamic terms. One systematic approach that can help us focus on process is the tagmemic method from the field of rhetoric: The same unit of experience is regarded alternatively as a "particle" (a thing in itself), a "wave" (a thing changing over time), and as part of a field (a thing in context; Young, Becker, & Pike, 1970).

A related strategy is changing nouns into verbs, or as Weick (1979) advised, "think'ing.'" Many concepts in our research vocabularies are nouns: perception, organization, social norm. Weick suggested imagining such concepts not as stable entities but as dynamic processes, constantly in flux, continually being reconstructed through accretion and erosion. Changing nouns to verbs may promote process imagery. Thus, one would speak of perceiving, organizing, and "norming."

In a recent application of this strategy, Wicker (in press) has recast the behavior setting concept from a relatively stable "given" to a more dynamic entity that develops over a series of life stages and in response to changing internal and external conditions.

CONSIDER CONTEXTS

The strategies in this section direct researchers' attention to the extended social world in which psychological events occur. These strategies are not theoretically neutral. They advance a viewpoint that has been expressed in ecological and environmental psychology (e.g., Barker, 1968; Stokols, 1982; Wicker, in press) and that has been stated more generally in terms of the implications for psychology of the new "realist" philosophy of science (e.g., Georgoudi & Rosnow, 1985; Manicas & Secord, 1983). The style of thought promoted here contrasts with much that is typical in psychology, but it can broaden our perspectives and suggest alternatives to traditional practices and ways of thinking.

Place Specific Problems in a Larger Domain

Researchers can use this strategy to decide where to begin work in a new area and to plan new research directions. The goal is to map out the broader domain of which an existing or contemplated study is only a part. Once the boundaries and features of a conceptual territory have been charted, judgments can be made about which areas are most promising for further exploration.

Such mapping of a research problem depends upon the researcher's current conceptual frame and upon a variety of information sources, such as intuition, theory, and research findings. An early step is to specify the boundaries of the broader domain at an appropriate level of abstraction. For example, in one of the several case studies cited by McGrath (1968) to illustrate this strategy, the domain was bounded by criteria for the mental health of emotionally disturbed patients.

Once the domain has been defined, the next step is to identify the major factors or influences that bear on the topic. Each of the major factors can then be analyzed into its components or attributes, and a systematic classification scheme can be developed. By examining all logical combinations of attributes, investigators can plan research to cover appropriate—perhaps neglected—aspects of the problem. In McGrath's (1968) example, three main factors were identified and analyzed into components: (a) sources of data on patients' mental health, whose components included self-reports, ratings by staff, and observations in standard and uncontrived situations; (b) modes of behavior, including motor, cognitive, emotional, and social; and (c) temporal frame of measurement, including measures of immediate treatments, overall hospital stay, and posthospital adjustment. This conceptual framework helped guide a study of how patients were affected by their move to a new hospital building.

A set of components applicable to most research domains consists of actors, behaviors, and contexts (Runkel & McGrath, 1972). Actors may be individuals, groups, organizations, or entire communities. Behaviors are actions that actors undertake toward objects. Contexts are immediate surroundings of actors and their behaviors, including time, place, and condition. Each component would be further subdivided into aspects appropriate to the research domain. Laying out the components and their subdivisions in a grid produces a domain "map" on which any particular investigation can be located. For example, the following factors could be used in a classification scheme for group problem solving: members' abilities and motives, type of tasks performed, relationships among members, group staffing levels, and type of settings in which groups perform.

Developing a comprehensive framework for a research domain contrasts with the more prevalent "up and out" strategy, in which investigators link their work on relatively narrow, focused topics with events outside their domain and then transpose their framework and findings to this new area. For example, research on students' verbal reactions to brief intervals of crowding has been extrapolated to prisons, homes, and transportation systems. An analysis of crowding using the three components metioned above would reveal many additional factors that could be considered and incorporated into subsequent research. Actors could be expanded to include prisoners and homemakers; behaviors could include social interaction and task performance; contexts could include living quarters, worksites, recreational settings, and time frames of months or years. Some research on crowding reflects these broader considerations (e.g., Cox, Paulus, & McCain, 1984).

Make Comparisons Outside the Problem Domain

We are familiar with the principle that knowledge is an awareness of differences—it is our rationale for using control groups. This principle can be invoked to generate new ideas: Comparisons can be made with actors, behaviors, or settings outside one's current problem domain. For example, Piotrkowski (1978) has provided insights into family interaction patterns by examining the nature of the work that family members perform both inside and outside the home. The emotional availability of family members to one another may depend less on their personalities than on the quality and timing of their work experiences, such as how stressful and fatiguing the work is and whether overtime and late shift work is involved.

More remote comparisons may also be fruitful. What we regard as basic social and cognitive processes are conditioned by cultural and historical factors (Gergen, 1982; Mills, 1959; Segall, Campbell, & Herskovitz, 1966). Researchers who focus on contemporary events in Western culture can profitably examine similar events in other periods and cultures. Guttentag and Secord's (1983) recent elaboration of social exchange theory to include social structural variables provides an illustration: Social exchange theorists have regarded participants in dyadic interactions as free agents capable of negotiating the most favorable outcomes for themselves. Using data from several cultures and historical periods, the investigators demonstrated that the demographic condition of disproportionate sex ratios (substantially more men than women in a particular population, or vice versa) directly affected the exchange process between man and women. For example, when men outnumbered women, men were less likely to enter or stay in a monogamous heterosexual relationship. Women might either cater to men or withdraw from them to express female independence (Guttentag & Secord, 1983; Secord, 1984). (More general treatments of theoretical and methodological issues in historical and cross-cultural research are found in Gergen & Gergen, 1984, and Malpass, 1977.)

We can also probe the structure of contemporary society for subtle influences on how we frame research topics. Sampson (1981) was concerned that psychologists interpret and present socially and historically limited events as fundamental properties of the human mind. He argued that the predominant psychological world view portrays people as independent agents whose primary functions are ruminations—cognitive activities such as planning, wishing, thinking, organizing, and problem solving—with little regard for the objective social world. Furthermore, he contended that such a view may not only be time bound, but may also serve to reaffirm present societal arrangements and values. Sampson's advocacy of a "critical study or psychology and society, a study that is self-conscious about its context, its values, and its relationship to human freedom (p. 741)" has numerous and profound implications for many specific research domains. Theories of work motivation, for example, may need to consider the worker's psychological state *and* the organizational, legal, economic, cultural, and even nutritional conditions under which work is performed (cf. Barrett & Bass, 1976).

Parenthetically, it is worth noting that academic disciplines and research specialties may also benefit from "outside" influences; for example, requirements in graduate programs for coursework outside the major field (Lawson, 1984), cross-disciplinary collaboration, and serious efforts to include perspectives of women, ethnic minorities, gays, and scholars from developing countries.

Examine Processes in the Settings in Which They Naturally Occur

Most psychological and behavioral processes unfold in behavior settings (taken-for-granted configurations of time, place, and objects where routine patterns of behavior occur) such as offices, workshops, hospital waiting rooms, parks, and worship services (Barker, 1968). These small-scale, commonsense units of social organization variously promote, afford, permit, encourage, and require behaviors that are part of or are compatible with the main activity, and they discourage or prohibit behaviors that interfere with it.

By contrast, much psychological research is conducted in contrived environments that lack the characteristics of behavior settings. Table 1 illustrates some differences between features of a typical laboratory study of small groups (see Miller, 1971) and a behavior setting.

In some psychological specialties, theories are formulated and may be revised on the basis of generations of studies conducted exclusively in the laboratory. Recognized experts may lack firsthand experience with the events and subjects that produce their data (cf. Jones, 1983). Yet the work of such seminal figures as Piaget and Lewin illustrates the benefits of direct observation of behaviors in context. (Observational strategies are discussed by Lofland, 1976, and Weick, 1968.)

Ideally, researchers who wish to consider contextual factors would first identify and then representatively sample settings where the behaviors of

TABLE 1
Contrast Between a Typical Small Group Study
and Behavior Setting Features

Typical small group study	Behavior setting features
Fixed duration, 1 hour or less	Indefinite duration, typically months or years
Group composed of college students	Staff composed of community members
No prior interaction among group members	Extensive prior interaction among staff members
Imposed task, often an intellectual problem to be solved	Endogenous tasks, typically involving behavior objects such as equipment and supplies
Casual interactions	Meaningful interactions
No enduring local culture	Established local culture
No hierarchical relationships among members	Hierarchical relationships among members
Closed system: no personnel changes, not part of a system network including suppliers, external information sources, and recipients of products	Open system: changes in personnel, part of a system network that includes suppliers, external information sources, and recipients of products.

interest regularly occur (cf. Brunswik, 1947; Petrinovich, 1979). But such an extensive effort may not be necessary to gain insights from behavioral contexts. Investigators might observe people in a few settings where the behaviors or processes of interest are a significant part of the program. For example, workers' adjustments to stress can be studied in police dispatcher worksites (Kirmeyer, 1984).

Ventures out of the laboratory can reveal neglected but significant influences on a behavior or process. For example, an environmental psychologist interested in personal space might, by observing people in medical office waiting rooms, discover that people's sense of what is a comfortable distance from others depends on how ill they feel, on whether the others may have contagious diseases, and on furniture arrangements and design, including whether chairs have armrests.

Consider Practical Implications of Research

Reflections on how research might be applied also can lead to expanded views of basic psychological processes. For example, theories and findings on human learning and memory can be used to design instructional materials. Though such efforts, previously unseen gaps in existing frameworks might become evident and could lead to broadened research procedures. Stimulus materials could be made more complex and more natural, response alternatives increased and made more meaningful, time frames expanded, and tasks and environments made more realistic (Mackie, 1974). Designed applications could be discussed with practitioners and then be implemented and evaluated.

Probe Library Resources

One of the most accessible vehicles for transcending narrow conceptual frames is the research library, whose extensive resources are scarcely considered by many researchers. As psychologists, we may limit our literature searches to work listed in the *Psychological Abstracts* or even to a few select journals. If so, we are ignoring enormous amounts of potentially useful information and sources of ideas from the larger social world.

The resources include both quantitative and qualitative data. Baseline data and other statistics relevant to most research topics can usually be found. For example, the *Statistical Abstract of the United States* (1985), published annually by the Bureau of the Census, includes national data on health, education, housing, social services, the labor force, energy, transportation, and many other topics. It also contains a guide to other statistical publications.

Statistics such as these can provide perspectives not generally available in the psychological literature. They can, for example, show trends in the frequency and distribution of events. Such data can suggest new research directions: A research might choose to give greater emphasis to cases that are more frequent, use more resources, have more beneficial or detrimental consequences, affect more people, or are on the leading edge of an important trend or development. Researchers of legal decision making might, for example, be influenced by the following facts: (a) In each of the past several years, less than 7% of civil cases before U.S. District Courts came to trial, and (b) from 1965 to 1983, the percentage of cases (civil and criminal cases combined) tried by jury in these courts declined from 51% to 40% (*Statistical Abstract of the United States*, 1985, pp. 178–179). Researchers of mock juries might profitably expand their work to include other aspects of legal decision making such as pretrial negotiations and the ways that judges consider and weigh evidence. (Bibliographies of useful statistical sources are found in Bart & Frankel, 1981; and Cottam & Pelton, 1977.)

Libraries are also a bountiful source of qualitative information on the range of human experience and behavior. These data take many forms: newspapers and magazines, popular nonfiction, oral histories, legal cases, ethnographies, diaries and letters, atlases, novels, and photographs, as well as the scholarly literature. Such materials can be sampled and analyzed much as a sociological field worker selects and studies people and events in a community. Qualitative information in libraries can be perused at the researcher's convenience, and it often covers extended time periods, allowing for analysis of trends. (The use of library data in theory building is discussed by Glaser & Strauss, 1967, chapter 7.)

The benefits of consulting a broad range of sources are evident in Heider's (1958/1983) influential book, *The Psychology of Interpersonal Relations*. In an attempt to document and systematize the layperson's knowledge of social relationships, Heider drew upon the works of philosophers, economists, novelists, humorists—and social scientists. For example, he credited the 17th century philosopher Spinoza for the insights that led to his statement of cognitive balance.

An illustration of the creative use of qualitative data in a psychological specialty where laboratory investigations predominate is Neisser's (1981) study of the memory of former presidential counsel John Dean. Neiser compared Dean's testimony before the Senate Watergate Investigating Committee with subsequently revealed manuscripts of the conversations Dean had testified about. Neisser's analysis drew upon memory theories and recent laboratory-based research to suggest a new term (*repisodic*) for memories that are accurate in the general substance but inaccurate in their detail (Neisser, 1981).

PROBE AND TINKER WITH ASSUMPTIONS

Virtually any conceptual framework, methodology, or perspective on a problem incorporates judgments that are accepted as true, even though they may not have been confirmed. Probing and tinkering with these assumptions can stimulate thinking in productive directions. Strategies considered here include making hidden assumptions explicit, making opposing assumptions, and simultaneously trusting and discrediting the same assumption.

Expose Hidden Assumptions

The task of revealing our own implicit assumptions is inherently difficult and can never be fully accomplished. Some assumptions may be imbedded in everyday or technical language, and others may be tied into our sensory and nervous systems. About all we can hope for is an increased awareness of a small portion of the assumptive network. And to probe any assumption, we must trust many others (Campbell, 1974).

The contrastive strategy—juxtaposing dissimilar elements from alternative or competing perspectives—is one way to uncover hidden assumptions. The juxtaposition can also lead to more precise statements of one or both conceptual frameworks. The conditions under which the alternative perspectives are most applicable may thus be clarified (McGuire, in press). To illustrate, two theories make contradictory predictions about how staff members respond when service settings such as child day care facilities and emergency medical services are understaffed. One theory (Barker, 1968) predicted a positive response: The staff will work harder, will assume additional responsibilities, and will have increased feelings of self-worth and competence. Another theory (Milgram, 1970) predicted such negative responses as disaffection with the work and disregard for clients' individual needs and low-priority claims for attention. Both theories are likely to be correct in certain circumstances. Positive responses may occur in settings where understaffing is infrequent and known to be temporary, whereas negative responses may characterize settings where there is a chronic shortage of staff members (Wicker, 1979/1983). In this case, the theorists apparently made different implicit assumptions about the frequency and duration of understaffing.

Allison's (1971) analysis of governmental decision making during the 1962 Cuban Missile Crisis illustrates the benefits of applying different conceptual perspectives to the same set of events. He demonstrated that certain actions were best explained by assuming that the various branches of the American and Soviet governments (such as the U.S. Navy and the Soviet KGB) followed their standard operating procedures. Other actions were better understood as "resultants" of pulling and hauling by political players within the governments. Both perspectives were contrasted with the more commonly accepted "rational actor model," which presumes that governmental actions are chosen after reviews of the costs and benefits of alternatives (Allison, 1971).

Make the Opposite Assumption

A more playful strategy is to recast an explicit assumption into its opposite and then to explore the implications of the reversal. A general procedure for recasting theoretical assumptions has been suggested by Davis (1971), who contended that theories are judged interesting when they challenge the assumption ground of an audience. He identified 12 general ways of recasting theoretical statements (see Table 2).

The following example illustrates the general–local contrast from Davis's list. Many research psychologists assume that if they empirically test a hypothesized relationship and the predicted result is obtained, they confirm not only that particular relationship but also the higher level conceptual hypothesis and general theory from which it was derived. An opposing assumption is that demonstrated effects are conceptually local, that is, limited to a subset of populations and/or conditions similar to those in the investigation. Researchers who seriously consider this latter assumption may become more sensitive to differences in populations and conditions and may even become interested in developing taxonomies that would be useful for specifying limits of generality.

An argument along these lines has been advanced by McKelvey (1982). He stated that management theorists and academic social scientists (notably social psychologists and sociologists) routinely advance principles that they assume are applicable to organizations in general. In a provocative challenge to this assumption, McKelvey drew upon evolutionary theory to

TABLE 2
Ways of Recasting Theoretical Statements

What something seems to be	What it is in reality (or vice versa)
Disorganized	Organized
Heterogeneous	Composed of a single element
A property of persons	A property of a larger social system
Local	General
Stable and unchanging	Unstable and changing
Ineffective	Effective
Bad	Good
Unrelated	Correlated
Coexisting	Incompatible
Positively correlated	Negatively correlated
Similar	Opposite
Cause	Effect

Note. Adapted from "That's Interesting: Toward a Phenomenology of Sociology and Sociology of Phenomenology" by M. S. Davis, 1971, *Philosophy of the Social Sciences, 1,* pp. 309–314. Copyright 1971 by Wilfred Laurier University Press. Adapted by permission.

propose an "organizational species" concept, "dominant competence," that he believed could be used to build a taxonomy of organizations.

Numerous recognized theoretical contributions in psychology can be viewed as articulated denials of existing assumptions. For example, Barker's (1963) classic article introducing behavior settings was essentially a rejection of the view that human environments are disordered, unstable, and without obvious boundaries. And Zajonc's (1965) analysis of social facilitation was a demonstration that seemingly incompatible research findings can coexist in a framework that distinguishes between responses that are high and low in the subject's response hierarchy.

Simultaneously Trust and Doubt the Same Assumption

Our thinking becomes more complicated when we devalue what we believe:

> Any person who has a view of the world and who also discredits part of that view winds up with two ways to examine a situation. Discrediting is a way to enhance a requisite variety and a way to register more of the variety that's present in the world. (Weick, 1979, p. 228)

Researchers can use this device to introduce flexibility and ambivalence into their conceptual framework—they can trust an assumption for some purposes and distrust it for others. The strategy has both theoretical and methodological applications. For example, when attempting to explain the behavior of people over their life span, a personality theorist might presume that actions are guided by a few enduring behavioral dispositions (traits), but when considering how people act on a specific occasion the theorist might doubt that traits are useful. Or a researcher might devise and administer a questionnaire or interview schedule on the assumption that people respond openly and freely, but interpret the responses in a way that assumes people respond primarily in guarded and self-serving ways.

CLARIFY AND SYSTEMATIZE THE CONCEPTUAL FRAMEWORK

Most of the above strategies will expand the researcher's conceptual framework. At some point the enlarged set of ideas should be reviewed to select the most provocative thoughts for further, more intensive analysis. The following procedures can be helpful in this sifting process as well as earlier in the conceptual framing process.

Scrutinize the Meanings of Key Concepts

Researchers should have and communicate a clear understanding of the concepts they use. One way to clarify meanings of key terms is to explore their roots, synonyms, and earliest known uses. Numerous sources are available, including dictionaries (etymological, unabridged, reverse, technical), technical books, handbooks, and encyclopedias. The nuances in meaning revealed by these sources can help researchers choose terms that precisely express their ideas. Consider, for example, the nuances implicit in the root meanings of these related words: *educate* (to rear or bring up), *instruct* (to construct or arrange), *teach* (to show, guide, or direct), and *train* (to pull, draw, or drag) (*Webster's Third New International Dictionary of the English Language, Unabridged,* 1969).

Theorists need to be sensitive to the different levels of generality that are implied by their concepts. Often it is advisable to examine terms at more than one level. Abstract terms can often be broken into components whose various meanings are worth exploring. For example, *health-promoting behavior* may include several types of actions, including habits like tooth brushing and infrequent voluntary activities like scheduling and taking a physical examination. More general terms may be sought for theoretical concepts currently defined in a limited domain. More abstract terms also may suggest other domains where the theory might be applied (Mills, 1959, pp. 212–213). For example, the concept "social loss of dying patients" can be expanded to "the social value of people" (Glaser & Strauss, 1967).

Concept analysis, a procedure developed by philosophers, can be used to clarify our thinking about terms we use in research. The first step is to identify cases or examples that clearly fit the intended meaning of the concept being analyzed. To illustrate, a clear example of my concept of job involvement might be working extra hours without pay when there is no external pressure to do so. Other examples—ones that are clearly outside the intended meaning and others that are borderline—are then evoked. From a careful review of such cases, the researcher can draw out the essential properties of the concept as he or she uses it. (Concept analysis is described and illustrated in Wilson, 1963, and in Gowin, 1981b, pp. 199–205.)

Specify Relationships Among Concepts

The most rigorous ways of expressing relationships among concepts, such as mathematical modeling and hypothetico-deductive systems, are well known to psychologists. Other procedures such as concept mapping can also be used to simplify and clarify a research domain. Figure 2 illustrates a concept map; it represents Gowin's (1981a) theory of educating. The first step in producing such a map is to list the major concepts that are part of a developing framework or theory. The concepts are then ranked in order of importance. This order is preserved in the concept map, with the most important concept at the top, and so on. Concepts are placed in boxes, and relationships among concepts are indicated by lines and brief verbal descriptions (Gowin, 1981a, pp. 93–95).

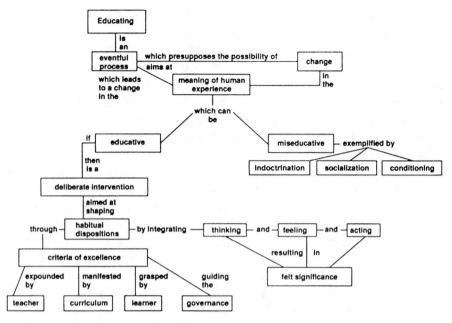

Figure 2. Concept map of Gowin's theory of educating. *Note:* From *Educating* (p. 94) by D. B. Gowin, 1981, Ithaca, NY: Cornell University Press. Copyright 1981 by Cornell University Press. Reprinted by permission.

In another variation of concept mapping, arrows are used to show a presumed direction of causality, and signs (+, −) are used to show whether the influence is positive or negative. From the pattern of such relationships, inferences can be drawn about the domain being considered; for example, whether a system is amenable to change, and if so, where change efforts might be directed (Maruyama, 1963; Weick, 1979, pp. 68–88).

Write a Concept Paper

Perhaps the most powerful tool for ordering and clarifying thinking is putting one's ideas into words. Writing is so familiar and often so burdensome that we often overlook or avoid it until we feel ready to communicate with an audience. Writing should be brought into play much earlier; it is an excellent medium for experimenting with conceptual meanings and relationships. Working papers can help researchers explore their thoughts and reveal gaps, inconsistencies, and faulty reasoning (Flower, 1981). In such papers researchers should address questions such as these: What is the core issue or question here? Why is it so important? What key concepts are imbedded in this topic and how are they related? What alternative methods can be used to answer the central question? What types of answers are desirable and feasible? (cf. Gowin, 1981a, pp. 86–107).

HOW TO BEGIN

Researchers who wish to explore these techniques should choose several strategies that seem appropriate to their problem and then consult the cited references for further details on each strategy. Any strategy explored should be given at least several hours of the researcher's "best time"—a period when he or she is alert, relaxed, and free from distractions and interruptions. Not every strategy attempted will prove fruitful for a given person or problem.

Devoting time to expanding and ordering one's conceptual frame can seem like a frivolous diversion from more pressing tasks. Yet the potential payoffs are substantial. A single new insight can go a long way, particularly in specialties in which theoretical and methodological traditions are strong and in which most published contributions are variations on familiar themes. Properly developed, a fresh idea can have a lasting impact.

REFERENCES

Allison, G. T. (1971). *Essence of decision*. Boston: Little, Brown.

Barker, R. G. (1963). On the nature of the environment. *Journal of Social Issues*, *19*(4), 17–38.

Barker, R. G. (1968). *Ecological psychology: Concepts and methods for studying the environment of human behavior*. Stanford, CA: Stanford University Press.

Barrett, G. V., & Bass, B. M. (1976). Cross-cultural issues in industrial and organizational psychology. In M. D. Dunnette (Ed.), *Handbook of industrial and organizational psychology* (pp. 1639–1686). Chicago: Rand-McNally.

Bart, P., & Frankel, L. (1981). *The student sociologist's handbook* (3rd ed.). Glenview, IL: Scott, Foresman.

Brinberg, D., & McGrath, J. E. (1985). *Validity and the research process*. Beverly Hills, CA: Sage.

Brunswik, E. (1947). *Systematic and representative design on psychological experiments*. Berkeley: University of California Press.

Campbell, D. T. (1974, September). *Qualitative knowing in action research*. Paper presented at the 82nd Annual Convention of the American Psychological Association, New Orleans.

Campbell, J. P., Daft, R. L., & Hulin, C. L. (1982). *What to study: Generating and developing research questions*. Beverly Hills, CA: Sage.

Caplan, N., & Nelson, S. D. (1973). On being useful: The nature and consequences of psychological research on social problems. *American Psychologist*, *28*, 199–211.

Cohen, A. R. (1964). *Attitude change and social influence*. New York: Basic Books.

Cottam, K. M., & Pelton, R. W. (1977). *Writer's research handbook*. New York: Barnes & Noble.

Cox, V. C., Paulus, P. B., & McCain, G. (1984). Prison crowding research: The relevance for prison housing standards and a general approach regarding crowding phenomena. *American Psychologist, 39*, 1148–1160.

Crovitz, H. F. (1970). *Galton's walk*. New York: Harper & Row.

Davis, M. S. (1971). That's interesting: Toward a phenomenology of sociology and a sociology of phenomenology. *Philosophy of the Social Sciences, 1*, 309–314.

Flower, L. (1981). *Problem-solving strategies for writing*. New York: Harcourt Brace Jovanovich.

Galton, F. (1879). Psychometric experiments. *Brain, 2*, 148–162.

Georgoudi, M., & Rosnow, R. L. (1985). Notes toward a contextualist understanding of social psychology. *Personality and Social Psychology Bulletin, 11*, 5–22.

Gergen, K. J. (1978). Toward generative theory. *Journal of Personality and Social Psychology, 36*, 1344–1360.

Gergen, K. J. (1982). *Toward transformation in social knowledge*. New York: Springer.

Gergen, K. J., & Gergen, M. M. (Eds.). (1984). *Historical social psychology*. Hillsdale, NJ: Erlbaum.

Glaser, B. G., & Strauss, A. L. (1967). *The discovery of grounded theory*. Hawthorne, NY: Aldine.

Glaser, R. (1984). Education and thinking: The role of knowledge. *American Psychologist, 39*, 93–104.

Gowin, D. B. (1981a). *Educating*. Ithaca, NY: Cornell University Press.

Gowin, D. B. (1981b). Philosophy. In N. L. Smith (Ed.), *Metaphors for evaluation* (pp. 181–209). Beverly Hills, CA: Sage.

Guttentag, M., & Secord, P. F. (1983). *Too many women? The sex ratio question*. Beverly Hills, CA: Sage.

Heider, F. (1983). *The psychology of interpersonal relations*. Hillsdale, NJ: Erlbaum. (Original work published 1958)

Jones, R. A. (1983, December). Academic insularity and the failure to integrate social and clinical psychology. *Society for the Advancement of Social Psychology Newsletter*, pp. 10–13.

Kirmeyer, S. L. (1984). Observing the work of police dispatchers: Work overload in service organizations. In S. Oskamp (Ed.), *Applied social psychology annual* (Vol. 5, pp. 45–66). Beverly Hills, CA: Sage.

Lakoff, G., & Johnson, M. (1980). *Metaphors we live by*. Chicago: University of Chicago Press.

Lawson, R. B. (1984). The graduate curriculum. *Science, 225*, 675.

Leary, D. E. (1983, April). *Psyche's muse: The role of metaphor in psychology*. Paper presented at the meeting of the Western Psychological Association, San Francisco.

Lofland, J. (1976). *Doing social life: The qualitative study of human interaction in natural settings*. New York: Wiley.

Mackie, R. R. (1974, September). *Chuckholes in the bumpy road from research to application*. Paper presented at the 82nd Annual Convention of the American Psychological Association, New Orleans.

Malpass, R. S. (1977). Theory and method in cross-cultural psychology. *American Psychologist, 32*, 1069–1079.

Manicas, P. T., & Secord, P. F. (1983). Implications for psychology of the new philosophy of science. *American Psychologist, 38*, 399–413.

Maruyama, A. J. (1963). The second cybernetics: Deviation-amplifying mutual casual processes. *American Scientist, 51*, 164–179.

McGrath, J. E. (1968). A multifacet approach to classification of individual group, and organization concepts. in B. P. Indik & F. K. Berrien (Eds.), *People, groups, and organizations* (pp. 192–215). New York: Teachers College Press.

McGuire, W. J. (1964). Inducing resistance to persuasion. In L. Berkowitz (Ed.), *Advances in experimental social psychology* (Vol. 1, pp. 192–229). New York: Academic Press.

McGuire, W. J. (1973). The yin and yang of progress in social psychology: Seven koan. *Journal of Personality and Social Psychology, 26*, 446–456.

McGuire, W. J. (in press). Toward psychology's second century. In S. Koch & D. E. Leary (Eds.), *A century of psychology as science*. New York: McGraw-Hill.

McKelvey, B. (1982). *Organizational systematics*. Berkeley: University of California Press.

McKim, R. H. (1972). *Experiences in visual thinking*. Monterey, CA: Brooks/Cole.

Milgram, S. (1970). The experience of living in cities. *Science, 167*, 1461–1468.

Miller, J. G. (1971). Living systems: The Group. *Behavioral Science, 16*, 302–398.

Mills, C. W. (1959). *The sociological imagination*. New York: Oxford University Press.

Neisser, U. (1981). John Dean's memory: A case study. *Cognition, 9*, 1–22.

Nelms, N. (1981). *Thinking with a pencil*. Berkeley: Ten Speed Press.

Petrinovich, L. (1979). Probabilistic functionalism: A conception of research method. *American Psychologist, 34*, 373–390.

Piotrkowski, C. S. (1978). *Work and the family system*. New York: Free Press.

Rosenzweig, M. R. (1984). Experience, memory, and the brain. *American Psychologist, 39*, 365–376.

Runkel, P. J., & McGrath, J. E. (1972). *Research on human behavior: A systematic guide to method*. New York: Holt, Rinehart & Winston.

Sampson, E. E. (1981). Cognitive psychology as ideology. *American Psychologist, 36*, 730–743.

Secord, P. F. (1984). Love misogyny, and feminism in selected historical periods. In K. J. Gergen & M. M. Gergen (Eds.), *Historical social psychology* (pp. 259–280). Hillsdale, NJ: Erlbaum.

Segall, M. H., Campbell, D. T., & Herskovitz, M. J. (1966). *The influence of culture on visual perception*. Indianapolis, IN: Bobbs-Merrill.

Smith, N. L. (1981). Metaphors for evaluation. In N. L. Smith (Ed.), *Metaphors for evaluation* (pp. 51–65). Beverly Hills, CA: Sage.

Statistical abstract of the United States. (1985). Washington, DC: U.S. Government Printing Office.

Stokols, D. (1982). Environmental psychology: A coming of age. In A. Kraut (Ed.), *G. Stanley Hall lecture series* (Vol. 2, pp. 155–205). Washington, DC: American Psychological Association.

Tyler, L. E. (1983). *Thinking creatively*. San Francisco: Jossey-Bass.

Wachtel, P. L. (1980). Investigation and its discontents: Some constraints on progress in psychological research. *American Psychologist, 35*, 399–408.

Webster's third new international dictionary of the English language, unabridged. (1969). Springfield, MA: Merriam-Webster.

Weick, K. E. (1968). Systematic observational methods. In G. Lindzey & E. Aronson (Eds.), *The handbook of social psychology* (2nd ed., pp. 357–451). Reading, MA: Addison-Wesley.

Weick, K. E. (1979). *The social psychology of organizing* (2nd ed.). Reading, MA: Addison-Wesley.

Wicker, A. W. (1969). Attitudes versus actions: The relationship of verbal and overt behavioral responses to attitude objects. *Journal of Social Issues, 25*(4), 41–78.

Wicker, A. W. (1983). *An introduction to ecological psychology*. New York: Cambridge University Press. (Original work published 1979)

Wicker, A. W. (in press). Behavior settings reconsidered: Temporal stages, resources, internal dynamics, context. In D. Stokols & I. Altman (Eds.), *Handbook of environmental psychology*. New York: Wiley.

Wilson, J. B. (1963). *Thinking with concepts*. Cambridge, England: Cambridge University Press.

Young, R. E., Becker, A. L., & Pike, K. L. (1970). *Rhetoric: Discovery and change*. New York: Harcourt Brace Jovanovich.

Zajonc, R. B. (1965). Social facilitation. *Science, 149*, 269–274.

DISCO
PSYCHOTI
RATIONALE

In their companion introductions to the special issues on psychotherapy research for the *American Psychologist* and the *Journal of Consulting and Clinical Psychology*, both VandenBos (1986) and Kazdin (1986a) flagged the accelerating breadth of development in this research field over the past four decades. One of these developments, mentioned both inside and outside these special issues, is a small but vigorous interest in what is coming to be known as discovery-oriented psychotherapy reaearch (Elliott, 1983a, 1983b, 1984; Gendlin, 1986; Glaser, 1978; Glaser & Strauss, 1967; Greenberg, 1986; Kazdin, 1986b; Mahrer, 1985, 1988; Rennie, Phillips, & Quartaro, 1988; Rice & Greenberg, 1984; Stiles, Shapiro, & Elliott, 1986; Strupp, 1986).

In this kind of research, the pivotal question is how to study psychotherapy to discover the discoverable, to learn the secrets of psychotherapy. If this question is kept centered, what begins to emerge is an increasing differentiation between research that is discovery-oriented and research that is

Reprinted from the *American Psychologist*, *43*, 694–702. Copyright 1988 by the American Psychological Association.

of hypotheses. The differentiation is across the
intent to do the research to the design and method-
from the framing of the research question to the sense
findings. The purpose of this article is to introduce
psychotherapy research as an alternative to hypothesis-
; to present the rationale, aims, and goals of this approach; to
methods in sufficient detail for adoption by psychotherapy re-
and thereby to stimulate research that is genuinely enthusiastic,
ing, practical, and conceptually challenging and that allows us to dis-
what is there to be discovered.

HYPOTHESIS-TESTING RESEARCH

The preponderance of mainstream psychotherapy research is designed
to test hypotheses. In the field of psychotherapy, there are at least two main
aims of this kind of research, and my thesis is that hypothesis testing is disappointingly ineffective for both.

The Confirmation or Disconfirmation of Theoretical Propositions

One of the major aims of hypothesis-testing research is to confirm or
disconfirm theoretical propositions. The rationale is that a network of theoretical assumptions is logically bound to a set of propositions that provides
the empirical basis for the testing of hypotheses (cf. Brodbeck & Feigl, 1968).
If the proposition is confirmed, the theory is a little more secure. If the
proposition is disconfirmed or refuted (Popper, 1968), the theory may be in
trouble.

A serious problem lies in going from the findings to the theoretical
proposition and from there to the network of theoretical assumptions, that
is, the theory of psychotherapy. Although theoretical propositions may bear
some degree of consistency or inconsistency with the findings, rarely if ever
does logical necessity include significant modification or abandonment of
the theoretical proposition. It is even rarer to find it necessary to significantly
modify or abandon the network of theoretical assumptions (Armstrong,
1982; Brush, 1974; Danziger, 1985; Feyerabend, 1975; Gould, 1981; Kuhn,
1962; Lakatos, 1976; Orne, 1969; Popper, 1968; Rosenthal, 1966). "No theory can be proven true by empirical data. And, just as it is impossible to prove
a theory, so also is it impossible to prove one false" (Greenwald, Pratkanis,
Leippe, & Baumgardner, 1986, p. 226). I know of no established theory of
psychotherapy that declared bankruptcy because of research that failed to
confirm, disconfirmed, or falsified its theoretical propositions and network of
theoretical assumptions; nor is there a logical necessity for that to occur.

60   ALVIN R. MAHRER

Theories of psychotherapy wax and wane because of considerations that have virtually nothing to do with the testing of hypotheses bearing on their theoretical propositions. "It is simply a sad fact that in soft psychology theories rise and decline, come and go, more as a function of baffled boredom than anything else" (Meehl, 1978, p. 807; cf. Feyerabend, 1975; Kuhn, 1962; Mahrer, 1978; Polanyi, 1958). The careers of theories of psychotherapy are under no logical necessity of being seriously affected by the results of hypothesis-testing research.

Indeed, there are solid reasons why no theory of psychotherapy need be in any genuinely grave danger from hypothesis-testing research. "One reason is that the usual use of null hypothesis testing in soft psychology as a means of 'corroborating' substantive theories does not subject the theory to grave risk of refutation *modus tollens*, but only to a rather feeble danger" (Meehl, 1978, p. 821; cf. Greenwald, 1975; Weimer, 1979). Meehl argued convincingly that the use of null hypotheses and significance tests leave the theoretical propositions in a state of virtual imperviousness to the findings.

Second, the space between a theory of psychotherapy and a derived or deduced testable hypothesis is so extensive, loose, and filled with implicit and explicit clauses and conditions that the theory is in no grave danger from whatever findings are obtained. Especially in the field of psychotherapy,

> no theory on its own ever gives rise to predictions of a testable sort. A theory itself is a set of general postulates together with their deductive consequences, and to obtain a testable prediction about a system we need to feed in both statements of the initial conditions of the system and auxiliary hypotheses. (Newton-Smith, 1981, p. 80)

When the findings are in, the theory of psychotherapy is in little danger.

Third, such research is rarely targeted on core theoretical propositions so that the theory of psychotherapy is in any real danger from the findings. Instead, the research is almost inevitably constrained to propositions that the theory of psychotherapy could easily live without.

Fourth, the propositions of theories of psychotherapy are generally so loose, floppy, and rarely, if ever, framed in explicit terms that they are safely immune from any attempts by researchers to disconfirm or refute what is not there to be disconfirmed or refuted (Grünbaum, 1979; Nagel, 1959). Furthermore, the case may be made that whereas there may be some qualified theories in the behavioral and social sciences, in the field of psychotherapy so-called theories are little more than loose collections of beliefs, ideologies, and second rate mythologies whose qualifications as scientific theories are amateur at best (Feyerabend, 1975; Mahrer, 1987, in press).

Fifth, it has probably never happened that the proponents of a theory of psychotherapy have spelled out the research grounds under which they would publicly foreswear their theory or renounce an important theoretical proposition (cf. Newton-Smith, 1981).

Sixth, rival theories are in no genuinely grave danger when pitted against one another by a researcher because it is rare that the rival theories agree that the contestants selected by the researcher are legitimate representatives of the theory. It is also rare that the proponents of rival theories accept the rules of the contest, that the theories agree on the consequences of losing, and especially that the theorists accept the referees and judges. The net result is that the contest is legitimate mainly in the eyes of the researcher while placing the losing theories at little risk.

Seventh, not only are firm believers easily able to refute and discount unfriendly findings of hypothesis-testing research, always managing to stay safely out of range, but their research lieutenants can inevitably be counted on to generate counterbalancing friendly studies.

Indeed, any theory that sponsors research can develop a methodology that ensures friendly results and pronounces alien research as dismissibly and discountably unscientific. The theory is "protected from the effects of contrary evidence because no evidence from outside the charmed methodological circle is accepted as valid . . . methods based on assumptions about the nature of the subject matter only produce observations which must confirm these assumptions" (Danziger, 1985, p. 10). Not only does the theory set the rules for what is to be accepted and rejected as scientific or unscientific, but the theory also can guarantee findings that are hypothesis-friendly by appropriate adjustments and readjustments of the research procedures, by continual reanalyses of the findings until they are friendly, and by persistent redoing of the study until it produces the right results (Armstrong, 1982; Brush, 1974; Gould, 1981; Greenwald et al., 1986; Lakatos, 1976; Orne, 1969; Rosenthal, 1966). "Putting it crudely, if you have enough cases and your measures are not totally unreliable, the null hypothesis will always be falsified, regardless of the truth of the substantive theory" (Meehl, 1978, p. 822). The net result is an increasingly successful partnership between theories of psychotherapy and the confirmatory empirical findings that their research produces. According to Feyerabend (1975), the theory

> is successful not because it agrees so well with the facts; it is successful because no facts have been specified that could constitute a test, and because some such facts have even been removed. Its "success" *is entirely man-made*. . . . This is how empirical "evidence" may be *created* by a procedure which quotes as its justification the very same evidence it has produced. (p. 44)

Behavioral theories of psychotherapy can justifiably claim to be supported by empirical research because they set their own rules for doing theory-friendly studies and for ensuring that they are in no danger from alien hypothesis-testing research.

To make matters even worse, reviewers engage in the confounding game of counting up the number of studies that are in favor and against, adding appropriate weights for carefulness and rigor, and then arriving at pronouncements about the research-supported status of the theoretical proposition.

> The writings of behavioral scientists often read as though they assumed—what is hard to believe anyone would explicitly assert if challenged—that successful and unsuccessful predictions are practically on all fours in arguing for and against a substantive theory . . . as if one could, so to speak, "Count noses," so that if a theory has somewhat more confirming than disconfirming instances, it is in pretty good shape evidentially. . . . We know that this is already grossly incorrect on purely formal grounds, it is a mistake a fortiori. (Meehl, 1967, p. 112; cf. Edelson, 1984; Smith & Glass, 1977)

All in all, theories of psychotherapy are safely impervious from the findings of hypothesis-testing research. Psychoanalysis is in no grave danger from the analysis of variance. I suggest that hypothesis testing is essentially unable to fulfill its self-assigned mission of confirming or disconfirming psychotherapeutic propositions or theories. Indeed, in the field of psychotherapy, the mission itself is fruitless. What is left for hypothesis-testing research in psychotherapy?

Contribution to the Cumulative Body of Knowledge in Psychotherapy

Hypothesis-testing research is justified as contributing to a supposed cumulative body of knowledge in psychotherapy. Picture a scientific body of knowledge containing at least two admissible classes of psychotherapeutic knowledge. One consists of scientifically stamped facts, hard and objective, empirical and tested, the tough data base of psychotherapeutic knowledge. The other class consists of psychotherapeutic laws and principles, canons and tenets. Hypothesis-testing research is apotheosized as the royal gatekeeper, guardian, and contributor to this cumulative body of psychotherapeutic knowledge. My thesis is that hypothesis-testing research is an inadequate means of contributing to an essentially nonexistent and mythical body of psychotherapeutic knowledge. The whole mission is both groundless and fruitless.

One of the problems is that precious little from outside the accepted body of knowledge is granted entry by hypothesis-testing research. Hypothesis testing contributes virtually nothing because most of the hypotheses are already in the body of knowledge, given their legitimacy by one lobby group or another. Nor is the hypothesis in any danger of exclusion by the findings of hypothesis-testing research provided that it is protected by a strong enough lobby.

Kiesler (1971) identified two major classes of hypotheses for psychotherapy researchers, both of which are already part and parcel of the cumulative body of knowledge because of powerful support groups. One class consists of the articulated clinical wisdom of the great thinkers in psychotherapy. "Here we find Freud, Sullivan, Rogers, Wolpe and the like—all originally practitioners of the art—attempting via explicit formulations to bring order out of chaos" (Kiesler, 1971, p. 39). Their followers already accept their formulations as entrenched landmarks in the body of knowledge. In contrast, the self-appointed role of psychotherapy researchers is to lend their weight of research confirmation or disconformation to the pieces of accepted knowledge and thereby to show that they either belong or do not belong. The problem is that proponents of these great clinical thinkers will continue to retain their formulated clinical wisdom in the body of psychotherapeutic knowledge, with the findings of hypothesis-testing research as lightweight irrelevancies.

The second class consists of the accepted knowledge base of such traditional academic fields as learning, perception, motivation, cognition, personality, biology, physiology, neurology, and social psychology (Kiesler, 1971). The problem here is that the factual knowledge and theories in these fields are already stamped as a legitimate part of the body of knowledge by powerful scientific lobbies. "The history of the social sciences reveals that whenever a theory showed itself to be promising, a conceptual leap was made from the empirical to the epistemological and the ontological" (Stigliano, 1986, p. 42). The aim of hypothesis-testing researchers is to convince psychotherapists to accept, cherish, respect, and apply to psychotherapy what is already firmly entrenched in the body of knowledge by the powerful lobbies of academic proponents of learning, perception, motivation, cognition, personality, biology, physiology, neurology, and social psychology. All in all, hypothesis-testing research does little more than confirm or fail to confirm the knowledge we already firmly believe we have, as supported by powerful lobby groups.

In fact, if hypothesis-testing research confirms the piece of knowledge, it is perhaps more firmly entrenched in the body of knowledge. If hypothesis-testing research fails to confirm the piece of knowledge, it should be on its way out of the body of knowledge, according to the research catechism, but it is typically unaffected as far as its proponents are concerned. The net result is that hypothesis-testing research either has no serious effect on the body of knowledge in psychotherapy, or far from contributing to a supposed cumulative body of knowledge, the research contributes to a shrinking body of knowledge that we hold with greater confidence. On the basis of hypothesis-testing research, we know less and less, but with higher and higher confidence.

The proof of the pudding is to take a look at the body of knowledge that all our hypothesis testing has produced. If we look at the larger body of knowledge in the social and behavioral sciences, the pantry is embarrassingly bare (Deutsch, Platt, & Senghors, 1971; Hesse, 1980; Kristol & Bell, 1981; MacIntyre, 1981; Stigliano, 1986); "The National Science Foundation was considering terminating funding for the social and behavioral sciences because no data base has emerged from the decades of studies which have been carried out" (Stigliano, 1986, p. 37).

When one takes a look at the corner of the cumulative body of knowledge that relates to psychotherapy, one finds a loosely conglomerated mixed bag. There are pieces of knowledge authoritatively contributed by the fields of learning, perception, motivation, cognition, personality, biology, physiology, neurology, and social psychology. There is also an even looser bag of psychotherapeutic truths, axioms, lore, tenets, laws, principles, canons, dictates, constructs, and firmly held beliefs. These vary all the way from the "law of effect" to the psychoanalytic "unconscious" and to such axiomatic truths as "in paranoia there are unconscious conflicts involving homosexual impulses." Even a moderately critical appraisal indicates that the body of scientific psychotherapeutic knowledge is bordering on nonexistent.

Instead of a single grand body of scientific psychotherapeutic knowledge, it is inviting to picture that each psychotherapeutic approach has its own package of cherished truths, dignified as a body of knowledge, with grossly varying weights attached to the findings of hypothesis-testing research, which stands relatively helpless in its assigned task of contributing to any cumulative body of knowledge in psychotherapy.

My conclusion is that hypothesis-testing research is poorly equipped for and disappointingly ineffective either in confirming or disconfirming theoretical propositions or in contributing to the supposed cumulative body of knowledge in psychotherapy. Yet hypothesis testing is just about all we do. My recommendation is that hypothesis testing be left in the hands of those who can see no alternative and that the balance of researchers adopt the rationale, aims, and methods of discovery-oriented psychotherapy research.

AN ALTERNATIVE APPROACH
TO PSYCHOTHERAPY RESEARCH

In the field of psychotherapy, the discovery-oriented approach is only a gleam in the eye of a few psychotherapy researchers (e.g., Elliott, 1983a, 1983b, 1984; Gendlin, 1986; Glaser, 1978; Glaser & Strauss, 1967; Mahrer, 1985; Rennie et al., 1988; Rice & Greenberg, 1984). Indeed, if one looks at the field of psychotherapy through the eyes of devout hypothesis-testers there is no such thing as discovery-oriented research as a distinctly viable alternative, for all good research can only be hypothesis testing in one form or another. When hypothesis testing is done properly it includes discovery. It can include discovery in the form of correlational investigations that may even study multidimensional and factorial relations among variables (Cronbach, 1957; Kiesler, 1971). Hypothesis testing graciously grants a measure of respectability to coming up with (i.e., discovery of) useful hypotheses from naturalistic or single case studies.

> Intensive study of the single case (either controlled or uncontrolled, with or without measurement) is a valuable *source of hypotheses*. . . . Discovery of hypotheses is a legitimate and essential scientific activity. But idiographic study has little place in the confirmatory aspect of scientific activity, which looks for laws applying to individuals generally. (Kiesler, 1971, p. 66)

Hypothesis-testing researchers tend to regard discovery-oriented methods as a somewhat useful secondary tool for the serious work of scientific hypothesis testing. In contrast, my aim is to nominate the discovery-oriented approach as a distinctly viable alternative for psychotherapy researchers, with its own rationale, aims, and methods. I submit that there are at least two aims and purposes of discovery-oriented research that are different from those of hypothesis-testing research (cf. Polkinghorne, 1983). One of these is to provide a closer, discovery-oriented look at psychotherapeutic phenomena, and the other is to discover the relations among psychotherapeutic conditions, operations, and consequences. The aims and purposes of discovery-oriented research thereby are distinct from the confirmation or disconfirmation of theoretical propositions or from contribution to a cumulative body of psychotherapeutic knowledge. Indeed, this "approach does not strive to contribute to any version of a bank of human data containing the cumulative record of eternal verities" (Kremer, 1986, p. 66). The whole basis for designing hypothesis-testing studies revolves around some predetermined, formulated idea or expectation or prediction or hypothesis that one then proceeds to test. "To design an experiment, one must first have an idea which he wishes to test" (Lathrop, 1969, p. 28). In contrast, the whole basis for designing discovery-oriented studies is the intention to learn more, to be surprised; to find out what one does not already expect, predict, or hypothesize; to answer a question whose answer provides something one wants to know but might not have expected, predicted, or hypothesized. To design a discovery-oriented investigation, one must first have a motivating interest in discovering what may be discovered by taking a closer look into psychotherapy or by inquiring into the interconnections among psychotherapeutic conditions, operations, and consequences. Accordingly, the purpose of the balance of this article is to show why and how to carry out this alternative approach to psychotherapy research.

66   ALVIN R. MAHRER

TAKING A CLOSER, DISCOVERY-ORIENTED LOOK

The aim is to take a closer, in-depth look at psychotherapy and to discover what is there to be discovered. There are five steps to be followed by the researcher.

Selecting the Target of the Investigation

The first step is to select some area in psychotherapy into which you want to take a closer look. What psychotherapeutic event or phenomenon excites you, piques your interest, or invites your taking a closer look? What is it that you would like to see in more detail, that you would like to investigate by getting down into it? Think of all the phenomena of psychotherapy, no matter how big and loose or small and tight. Think in terms of simple words rather that technical jargon constructs (such as locus of control, transference, self-efficacy, or ego alienness). Set aside general psychotherapeutic laws or principles or hypotheses. Just let yourself concentrate on whatever interests you enough so that you are drawn to taking a closer look into it.

Would you be interested in taking a closer look at what actually happened in Sigmund Freud's work with patients? If there were recordings of those sessions, I would be fascinated to discover what transpired. I am also interested in taking a closer look at what is going on when patients are in an extremely intense state of feeling and emotion or when patients are in the throes of genuinely impressive change or when patients are recounting incidents from very early childhood. Some of the targets may be small, such as a patient's erupting into a spontaneous outburst of strong, hearty laughter. In any case, the aim is to take a closer look in order to discover what may be there to be discovered.

Obtaining Instances of the Target of the Investigation

The second step is to obtain instances of the target of your investigation, of that area into which you want to take a closer look. Usually this means audiotapes or videotapes of your target. Try to obtain a large number of these tapes, particularly high-grade, fine instances of the target. Sometimes you are limited to one or only a few instances of your target. It would be fortunate to have even a single precious recording of one of Freud's sessions. Some targets are themselves rare or very hard to produce, such as instances of patients undergoing profoundly significant personality change. It is not easy to obtain 50 instances of patients erupting into sudden spontaneous outbursts of strong, hearty laughter. It might be easier to obtain a large number of instances of patients being in an extremely intense state of feeling and emotion, or of patients recounting incidents from very early childhood.

Whatever the selected target into which you want to take a closer look, it is helpful to obtain as many and as good instances as you can.

Obtaining an Instrument for Taking a Closer Look

The third step is to obtain (select or develop) an instrument that allows you to take a closer look at whatever target you selected. Some instruments may consist of a procedure. For example, you may get a closer look at moments in which patients have attained high levels of feeling and emotion by the procedure of interviewing the patients and therapists to find out more about those moments (e.g., Elliott, 1984). The instrument might be a tape recorder. Wouldn't it be wonderful to have audiotapes and videotapes of Freud's sessions? Audiotapes and videotapes are useful instruments for taking closer looks. You can use all sorts of technical instruments to get closer looks. For example, you need an instrument that records dreams so that you can get a closer look at the dreams by means of the video dream recorder. You need instruments to measure the exact body location and intensity of feeling as it occurs in both therapist and patient in the ongoing session.

I rely on category systems that are custom designed to provide a closer look at the selected target of investigation. Suppose that you wanted to take a closer look at what patients are saying and doing during spontaneous outbursts of strong, hearty laughter. Start with a search of the research and clinical literatures to provide some provisional hypotheses. Then obtain a large and representative number of audiotaped excerpts of such instances. With a group of judges, go through each of the excerpts one by one, slowly and carefully describing what the patient is saying and doing in each instance. Use terms that are close to the data and are simple, rather than using high-level constructs wrapped in the jargon of any therapeutic approach. With each succeeding instance, frame provisional categories, refine the categories you have already obtained, reorganize the system on the basis of each new instance against the backdrop of the developing category system complemented by the provisional hypotheses from the literature. In the serially progressive procedure, by the time you and the judges have completed your analysis of a large number of instances, you will have developed a category system that is generated from actual data and is increasingly rigorous and comprehensive. It is a category system of what patients are judged to be saying and doing during moments of spontaneous outbursts of strong, hearty laughter. My colleagues and I have followed this same procedure in developing category systems for taking closer looks at other targets of investigation. For example, one of the more robustly useful is a category system of good moments in psychotherapy—moments of patient change, progress, improvement, movement, and process—that are valued and prized from the perspectives of a broad range of therapeutic approaches (Mahrer, 1985, 1988; Mahrer & Nadler, 1986).

The instrument (e.g., category system) is the means for taking the closer look. It is careful and rigorous enough to keep the researcher honest, and it provides a better quality of data than trying to look into the target without the instrument. Nor is the instrument to be opposed to simple clinical study and analysis because it was born out of clinical study and analysis in the very process of its development.

On the other hand, the kind of instrument you use opens up a particular kind of closer look and reveals a particular class of data. A category system of what patients are saying and doing in moments of strong, hearty laughter will likely reveal nothing about changes in galvanic skin responses or heart rates. A category system of the good moments in psychotherapy sessions provides that kind of data and little else. Whatever instrument you use to take a closer look is limited to its own class of data.

Gathering the Data

The fourth step is to gather the data. Apply the instrument to all the instances of your selected target. If you have plenty of instances, apply the category system to instances that were not used in developing the category system. If you have only a limited number of instances, use a different set of judges and apply the category system to the instances used in constructing the category system. In any case, the application of the category system in a careful and rigorous way will yield the data for taking the closer look. Now you must make discovery-oriented sense of the data.

Making Discovery-Oriented Sense of the Data

It takes a particular attitude or perspective to see what there is to be discovered in the data. All the instrument can do is to organize and display the data in as hard and objective a manner as the instrument is able. Making discovery-oriented sense of the data is the job of the researcher. It calls for some helpful guidelines.

Welcoming Receptivity to the Discoverable

The clinical researcher is to be exceedingly open to what is new in the data, to what is of the ordinary, different, unexpected, exceptional, surprising, challenging, disconcerting. The researcher must be vigilant to what does not seem to fit, to what is hard to grasp, organize, explain. By taking this stance, the clinical researcher will be sensitive to the discoverable.

This way of seeing and listening to the data means that the investigator is to be a clinical researcher, with sufficient knowledge of what is ordinary, mainstream, or expected. Indeed, it helps to have a group of independent clinical researchers. The clinical researcher should also be passively naive in taking plenty of time to allow the data to show what is there to be discovered. This process involves a blend of passive naiveté and knowledgeable understanding in being sensitive to what is new, different, unexpected, exceptional, surprising, and discoverable.

You must scan the data, be open to cues and leads, try out various patternings, attend to repeated instances, organize and reorganize the data, and go back to the data again and again until you recieve the discoverable.

Declining Traps That Mask the Discoverable

There are several traps that tend to obfuscate the discoverable. Researchers should decline to mask the discoverable with easy explanations and rushed understandings, especially from their favorite psychotherapeutic approach. Another trap is to lose the discoverable by rising to higher levels of generalization that fit, make sense of, and manage to assimilate the discoverable. A third trap is to bypass the discoverable under central tendencies and normative schemas; statistical means and common themes easily hide the discoverable. Fourth, the researcher should decline the rush toward general laws, truths, and principles. All of these traps are easy and appealing, but they obfuscate the discoverable and are to be declined in the task of making discovery-oriented sense of the data.

By following these five steps, the clinical researcher can take a closer look into psychotherapy, a look that offers a good chance to discover something new. Researchers can take a closer, discovery-oriented look at Freud's actual work with patients, at what may be going on when patients are in an extremely intense state of feeling and emotion or are undergoing profoundly significant personality change, at what patients are saying and doing during spontaneous outbursts of strong, hearty laughter, or at any other events that are of genuine interest to researchers who want to see what may be discovered by taking a closer look into psychotherapy. However, this is only one way of doing discovery-oriented psychotherapy research.

DISCOVERING INTERCONNECTIONS AMONG CONDITIONS, OPERATIONS, AND CONSEQUENCES

There are lots of ways of carving up or imposing a schema or perspective on psychotherapy. The way that is selected in this research approach is to organize psychotherapy into conditions, operations, and consequences (Mahrer, 1985, in press). Furthermore, each of these three terms is taken as referring to more or less specific and concrete events rather than abstractions that are loose and general, and to events that occur in psychotherapy sessions rather than to anything occurring outside of these sessions.

Accordingly, *conditions* refer to the patient in session, to what the patient is doing and to how the patient is being. The condition is when the patient is on the verge of tears, says that his or her headache is starting to pound, begins to protest and complain in a loud voice, starts the session with a deep sigh, puts the therapist on the spot with a few well-aimed questions, or sinks into a conspicuous silence. Discovery-oriented reasearchers describe conditions in this way rather than identifying the patient as a borderline, phobic, or incest survivor or as being in the termination phase of treatment.

Operations refer to what the therapist does right here in these statements. The therapist gives an interpretation, tells the patient to say it with more feeling, or provides an empathic reflection. Operations do not refer to supportive therapy, assertion training, or desensitization.

Consequences refer to what the patient does and how the patient is subsequent to the therapist operation. Consequences refer to the patient's outburst of hearty laughter, expression of insightful understanding, or recounting of his or her first day at school. Consequences do not refer to Minnesota Multiphasic Personality Inventory (MMPI) profile or a post-therapy symptom checklist.

The aim of this research is to discover the interconnections among in-therapy conditions, operations, and consequences. In a way, this sounds somewhat like the bellwether question of psychotherapy research, which was nicely articulated by Paul (1967): "*What* treatment, by *whom*, is most effective for *this* individual with *that* specific problem, and under *which* set of circumstances" (p. 111; cf. Kiesler, 1971). This question is widely accepted as the solid foundation of what psychotherapy researchers should be investigating (Parloff, 1979). However, it is not the question asked by discovery-oriented researchers. The smaller difference is that discovery-oriented researchers are examining specifically concrete meanings of conditions, operations, and consequences whose referential meanings are in-session events. The larger difference is that they are engaged in a discovery-oriented search for the interconnections. If one begins with the more or less accepted psychotherapy research question, tightens it to include specifically concrete in-session referential meanings, and encases the modified traditional question in a discovery-oriented framework, one emerges with three general questions for discovering the interconnections among psychotherapeutic conditions, operations, and consequences.

1. Given this *operation*, carried out under this condition, what are the consequences? That is, if the therapist does this operation, when the patient is being this way, what will happen?
2. Given this *consequence*, what operations under what conditions can achieve this consequence? That is, what can the therapist do to effect this desired consequence?

3. Given this *condition*, what operation can achieve this consequence? That is, when the patient is this way, what does the
therapist want to achieve, and what does the therapist do to
achieve this consequence?

There are three steps in carrying out this research approach: (a) specifying the question, (b) obtaining data, and (c) examining the data.

Specifying the Discovery-Oriented Research Question

The first step is to start with one of the general research questions and
to frame a specific discovery-oriented research question.

*Given this operation, carried out under this condition, what are the conse-
quences?* This is B. F. Skinner's favorite discovery-oriented research question.
Skinner "had little use for making hypotheses or predictions about what the
effect of a manipulation *ought* to be. You can just make the manipulation and
see what its effect is" (Mook, 1982, p. 410).

How does the psychotherapy researcher select a manipulation (operation), carried out under some condition, to see what its effect (consequence)
is? One way is to begin with cherished therapeutic axioms and convert them
into discovery-oriented research questions. Consider this axiom, "When the
client focuses on meaningful material, and the therapist provides an empathic reflection, the consequence is enhanced self-exploration." This yields
the following research question: When the client focuses on meaningful material, and the therapist provides an empathic reflection, what are the consequences—including enhanced self-exploration? The axiom that "when
the patient talks about himself or herself, and the therapist self-discloses, the
consequence is enhanced self-disclosure" becomes the following research
question: "When the patient talks about himself or herself, and the therapist self-discloses, what are the consequences—including enhanced self-
disclosure?" Another axiom is that when there is an appropriate therapeutic
relationship, and the therapist offers interpretations, the cumulative consequence is increased insight and understanding. As a research question, this
becomes "When there is an appropriate therapeutic relationship, and the
therapist offers interpretations, what are the consequences—including increased insight and understanding?"

Another way of framing discovery-oriented research questions is by
asking reasonably appealing "what ifs." When a therapist is exasperated with
a patient, what if the therapist gives vent to his or her exasperation? When
the patient is perched on the scary edge of falling apart, what would the consequences be if the therapist encouraged the patient to go ahead? When the
therapist has private thoughts, what would the consequences be if the therapist disclosed them openly and freely?

Given this consequence, what operations under what conditions can achieve this consequence? Proceeding from this general research question to a particular and specific one calls for the researcher's selecting in-session consequences that are impressive, welcomed, desired, and significant, especially those that are taken as indicating therapeutic change, process, movement, progress, or improvement. Given that a patient's persistent headache has now cleared and is gone, what therapist operations under what conditions appear to have been instrumental in achieving this consequence? Given a patient's welcomed increase in self-assuredness, energy and enthusiasm, feeling level, or strength and toughness, what therapist operations under what conditions led to this desirable consequence? The researcher merely specifies a particular consequence, something the patient is or does that is welcomed and desired, and the discovery-oriented research question is in place.

Given this condition, what operation can achieve this consequence? The researcher turns this into a specific research question by identifying some concrete condition (or problem), figuring out the related consequence that is welcomed and desired, and looking for the right operations that can effect that consequence. For example, in the beginning of a session (condition), what therapist operations enable the patient to achieve a state of strong experiencing and feeling (consequence)? When the patient withdraws into an enveloping silence (condition), what therapist operations succeed in lifting the patient out of the silence and into providing useful therapeutic material (consequence)? Greenberg and his colleagues (Greenberg, 1984a) translated this general question into the following specific research question: When a client is in a condition regarded in gestalt therapy as a conflict split, what therapist–client operations are effective in achieving the desired consequence of a resolution of the conflict? Answering this question exemplifies the task analysis method (Greenberg, 1984b) wherein the discovery-oriented target is to identify therapist–client operations for moving from a designated in-therapy condition to a designated in-therapy consequence.

Obtaining the Data

Once the general research question is refined and put into a specific discovery-oriented question, the second step is to obtain the relevant data. Perhaps the best way of obtaining the data is from actual tapes and transcripts of therapists and patients. It is the step that punctuates the need for rich tape libraries in that each of the three general research questions yields specific discovery-oriented questions whose answers are best provided by a rich tape library (cf. Gendlin, 1986; Mahrer, in press).

Consider three specific questions, each taken from one of the three general questions: (a) When the client focuses on meaningful material, and the therapist provides an empathic reflection, what are the consequences? (b) Given that the patient's persistent headache was extinguished at this point in the session, what therapist operations under what conditions were instrumental in achieving this consequence? (c) In the beginning of a session, what therapist operations enable the patient to achieve a state of strong experiencing and feeling? It seems clear that the most appropriate data for each of the three questions call for a rich library of tapes, yet it is the rare researcher who has access to tapes offering ample instances of the right conditions, operations, and consequences.

One of the three general questions, however, lends itself to manufacturing the data by experimental manipulation. This is the first general question; that is, given this operation, carried out under this condition, what are the consequences? It is feasible, for example, to instruct therapists that when the patient focuses on meaningful material, the therapist is to provide an empathic reflection, or when the therapist is exasperated with the patient, the therapist is to give vent to his or her exasperation. Although data for this first general question may be obtained either by experimental manipulation or through selection from a research tape library, data for the other two questions are beyond experimental manipulation and are best obtained through a research tape library.

In this research, much of the carefulness and rigor lie in specifying the meanings of the terms used in defining the conditions, operations, and consequences. The researcher must be reasonably precise in defining conditions such as "when there is an appropriate therapeutic relationship" or "when a client is in a gestalt conflict split," in defining therapist operations such as self-disclosure or empathic reflections, and in defining consequences such as the extinguishing of a persistent headache or the achievement of a state of strong experience and feeling.

Examining the Data to Obtain a Discovery-Oriented Answer

The method of examining the data varies with the general research question. Consider the general research question: Given this consequence, what operations under what conditions can achieve this consequence? For each instance of the target consequence, the method is to examine the antecedent therapist and patient statements, opening the window progressively larger and larger. It is helpful to use a number of independent clinical researchers to examine the antecedent operations and conditions.

A different method is called for in examining the data for the second general question: Given this operation, carried out under this condition, what are the consequences? With a large number of instances, it is helpful to use a category system tailor-made for those consequences according to the guidelines described earlier. The third general question is: Given this condition, what operation can achieve this consequence? Once again, it is useful to have a large number of instances and to use another category system tailor-made from, and for, the therapist (and patient) operations intervening between the conditions and the consequences.

Each of these three methods enables the clinical researcher to examine the data and to answer the research question. However, as is required when the researcher takes a closer look into the psychotherapeutic phenomenon, it is important to examine the data so as to be exceedingly open to the discoverable, to what is new, out of the ordinary, different, unexpected, exceptional, or surprising. It is also important for the researcher to be sensitive to and avoid the common traps that bypass, hide, and lose the discoverable. By means of this third step, the clinical researcher examines the data to obtain a discovery-oriented answer to the research question and thereby to discover the interconnections among psychotherapeutic conditions, operations, and consequences.

CONCLUDING IMPLICATIONS

Hypothesis-testing research is essentially inadequate and unproductive for serious confirmation or disconfirmation of the propositions that make up theories of psychotherapy and also for contributing to a purportedly cumulative body of psychotherapeutic knowledge. Nor is hypothesis-testing research useful in discovering what is to be discovered in the field of psychotherapy. Hypothesis testing should be left in the hands of those who see no alternative way of doing psychotherapeutic research; otherwise, it should be abandoned.

Discovery-oriented research is a distinctive alternative whose rationale, aims, and methods contrast sharply with those of hypothesis-testing research. There are two approaches to this research. One consists of providing a closer, discovery-centered look into psychotherapeutic events and phenomena, and the other consists of the discovery of the interconnections among psychotherapeutic conditions, operations, and consequences. Each of these two kinds of discovery-oriented research has its own characteristic methodology and procedural steps. The challenge is that the development of the field of psychotherapy will benefit more from discovery-oriented than from hypothesis-testing research, and that rigorous and productive discovery-oriented research will unseat hypothesis testing as the specific means of inquiry in the field of psychotherapy research.

The findings of discovery-oriented research are of prime quality for (a) rigorously scientific theory building in the field of psychotherapeutic conceptualization, (b) generating advances throughout the field of psychotherapeutic practice, (c) opening up new avenues of psychotherapeutic research, and (d) integratively blending theory, practice, and research in the field of psychotherapy. Psychotherapy researchers are encouraged to develop the methodologies and procedures of discovery-oriented psychotherapy research and to adopt this way of discovering what is to be discovered in the field of psychotherapy.

These are two kinds of research that comprise the discovery-oriented approach to psychotherapy research. Although they both differ from the rationale, aims, and methods of hypothesis-testing research, each has its own characteristic rationale, aims, and steps. Some psychotherapy researchers will remain steadfast in their allegiance to hypothesis testing. Others may assert that discovery-oriented aims and methods are already in place in the larger program of hypothesis testing. Still others may hold that they already do discovery-oriented psychotherapy research, although it may be described in different words. However, for those who are willing to consider discovery-oriented research as a distinctly viable alternative to hypothesis testing, I submit that we are headed toward a new period of discovering what is discoverable in the field of psychotherapy.

REFERENCES

Armstrong, J. S. (1982). Research on scientific journals: Implications for editors and authors. *Journal of Forecasting, 1*, 83–104.

Brodbeck, M., & Feigl, H. (1968). *Readings in the philosophy of the social sciences.* New York: Macmillan.

Brush, S. G. (1974). Should the history of science be rated X? *Science, 183*, 1164–1172.

Cronbach, L. J. (1957). The two disciplines of scientific psychology. *American Psychologist, 12*, 671–684.

Danziger, K. (1985). The methodological imperative in psychology. *Philosophy of the Social Sciences, 15*, 1–13.

Deutsch, K., Platt, J., & Senghors, D. (1971). Predictability in the social sciences. *Science, 107*, 1113–1116.

Edelson, M. (1984). *Hypothesis and evidence in psychoanalysis.* Chicago: University of Chicago Press.

Elliott, R. (1983a). Fitting process research to the practicing psychotherapist. *Psychotherapy: Theory, Research, and Practice, 20*, 47–55.

Elliott, R. (1983b). "That in your hands": A comprehensive process analysis of a significant event in psychotherapy. *Psychiatry, 46*, 113–129.

Elliott, R. (1984). A discovery-oriented approach to significant change events in psychotherapy: Interpersonal process recall and comprehensive process analysis. In L. N. Rice & L. S. Greenberg (Eds.), *Patterns of change* (pp. 249–286). New York: Guilford.

Feyerabend, P. (1975). *Against method.* London: Verso.

Gendlin, E. T. (1986). What comes after traditional psychotherapy research? *American Psychologist, 41*, 131–136.

Glaser, B. G. (1978). *Theoretical sensitivity: Advances in the methodology of grounded theory.* Mill Valley, CA: Sociology Press.

Glaser, B. G., & Strauss, A. (1967). *The discovery of grounded theory: Strategies for qualitative research*. Chicago: Aldine.

Gould, S. J. (1981). *The mismeasure of man*. New York: Norton.

Greenberg, L. S. (1984a). A task analysis of interpersonal conflict resolution. In L. N. Rice & L. S. Greenberg (Eds.), *Patterns of change* (pp. 67–123). New York: Guilford.

Greenberg, L. S. (1984b). Task analysis: The general approach. In L. N. Rice & L. S. Greenberg (Eds.), *Patterns of change* (pp. 124–148). New York: Guilford.

Greenberg, L. S. (1986). Change process research. *Journal of Consulting and Clinical Psychology, 54*, 4–9.

Greenwald, A. G. (1975). Consequences of prejudice against the null hypothesis. *Psychological Bulletin, 82*, 1–20.

Greenwald, A. G., Pratkanis, A. R., Leippe, M. R., & Baumgardner, M. H. (1986). Under what conditions does theory obstruct research progress? *Psychological Review, 93*, 216–229.

Grünbaum, A. (1979). Is Freudian psychoanalytic theory pseudo-scientific by Karl Popper's criterion of demarcation? *American Philosophical Quarterly, 16*, 131–141.

Hesse, M. (1980). Theory and value in the social sciences. In P. Pettit & C. Hookway (Eds.), *Action and interpretation* (pp. 1–16). New York: Cambridge University Press.

Kazdin, A. E. (1986a). Editor's introduction to the special issue. *Journal of Consulting and Clinical Psychology, 54*, 3.

Kazdin, A. E. (1986b). Comparative outcome studies of psychotherapy: Methodological issues and strategies. *Journal of Consulting and Clinical Psychology, 54*, 95–105.

Kiesler, D. J. (1971). Experimental designs in psychotherapy research. In A. E. Bergin & S. L. Garfield (Eds.), *Handbook of psychotherapy and behavior change: An empirical analysis* (pp. 36–74). New York: Wiley.

Kremer, J. W. (1986). The human science approach as discourse. *Saybrook Review, 6*, 65–105.

Kristol, I., & Bell, D. (1981). *The crisis in economic theory*. New York: Basic Books.

Kuhn, T. (1962). *The structure of scientific revolutions*. Chicago: University of Chicago Press.

Lakatos, I. (1976). *Proofs and refutations*. London: Cambridge University Press.

Lathrop, R. G. (1969). *Introduction to psychological research: Logic, design, analysis*. New York: Harper & Row.

MacIntyre, A. (1981). *After virtue*. Notre Dame, IN: University of Notre Dame Press.

Mahrer, A. R. (1978). *Experiencing: A humanistic theory of psychology and psychiatry*. New York: Brunner/Mazel.

Mahrer, A. R. (1985). *Psychotherapeutic change: An alternative approach to meaning and measurement*. New York: Norton.

Mahrer, A. R. (1987). These are the components of any theory of psychotherapy. *Journal of Integrative and Eclectic Psychotherapy, 6,* 28–31.

Mahrer, A. R. (1988). Research and clinical applications of "good moments" in psychotherapy. *Journal of Integrative and Eclectic Psychotherapy, 1,* 81–93.

Mahrer, A. R. (in press). *The integration of psychotherapies: A guide for practicing psychotherapists.* New York: Human Sciences Press.

Mahrer, A. R., & Nadler, W. P. (1986). Good moments in psychotherapy: A preliminary review, a list, and some promising research avenues. *Journal of Consulting and Clinical Psychology, 54,* 10–16.

Meehl, P. E. (1967). Theory-testing in psychology and physics: A methodological paradox. *Philosophy of Science, 34,* 103–115.

Meehl, P. E. (1978). Theoretical risks and tabular asterisks: Sir Karl, Sir Ronald, and the slow process of soft psychology. *Journal of Consulting and Clinical Psychology, 46,* 806–834.

Mook, D. G. (1982). *Psychological research: Strategy and tactics.* New York: Harper & Row.

Nagel, E. (1959). Methodological issues in psychoanalytic theory. In S. Hook (Ed.), *Psychoanalysis, scientific method, and philosophy* (pp. 38–56). New York: Grove Press.

Newton-Smith, W. H. (1981). *The rationality of science.* London: Routledge & Kegan Paul.

Orne, M. T. (1969). Demand characteristics and the concept of quasi-controls. In R. Rosenthal & R. L. Rosnow (Eds.), *Artifact in behavioral research* (pp. 97–128). New York: Academic Press.

Parloff, M. B. (1979). Can psychotherapy research guide the policy-maker? *American Psychologist, 34,* 296–306.

Paul, G. L. (1967). Strategy of outcome research in psychotherapy. *Journal of Consulting Psychology, 31,* 109–118.

Polanyi, M. (1958). *Personal knowledge: Towards a post-critical philosophy.* Chicago: University of Chicago Press.

Polkinghorne, D. (1983). *Methodology for the human sciences.* Albany: State University of New York Press.

Popper, K. (1968). *The logic of scientific discovery.* London: Hutchinson.

Rennie, D. L., Phillips, J. R., & Quartaro, G. K. (1988). Grounded theory: A promising approach to conceptualization in psychology? *Canadian Psychology, 29,* 139–150.

Rice, L. N., & Greenberg, L. S. (1984). *Patterns of change.* New York: Guilford.

Rosenthal, R. (1966). *Experimenter effects in behavioral research.* New York: Appleton.

Smith, M. L., & Glass, G. V. (1977). Meta-analysis of psychotherapy outcome studies. *American Psychologist, 32,* 752–760.

Stigliano, A. (1986). An ontology for the human sciences. *Saybrook Review, 6,* 33–63.

Stiles, W. A., Shapiro, D. A., & Elliott, R. (1986). "Are all psychotherapies equivalent?" *American Psychologist, 41*, 165–180.

Strupp, H. H. (1986). Psychotherapy: Research, practice, and public policy (How to avoid dead ends). *American Psychologist, 41*, 120–130.

VandenBos, G. R. (1986). Psychotherapy research: A special issue. *American Psychologist, 41*, 111–112.

Weimer, E.B. (1979). *Notes on the methodology of scientific research*. Hillsdale, NJ: Erlbaum.

CONCEPTUALIZING
INDEPENDENT VARIABLES

4

TOWARD TERMINOLOGICAL, CONCEPTUAL, AND STATISTICAL CLARITY IN THE STUDY OF MEDIATORS AND MODERATORS: EXAMPLES FROM THE CHILD-CLINICAL AND PEDIATRIC PSYCHOLOGY LITERATURES

GRAYSON N. HOLMBECK

Despite the appearance of several useful discussions of differences between mediated and moderated effects (e.g., Aldwin, 1994; Baron & Kenny, 1986; James & Brett, 1984), there continue to be inconsistencies in the use of these terms. More specifically, several types of problems occur with some regularity: (a) vague or interchangeable use of the terms, (b) inconsistencies

Reprinted from the *Journal of Consulting and Clinical Psychology*, 65, 599–610. Copyright 1997 by the American Psychological Association.

Completion of this article was suported in part by Social and Behavioral Sciences Research Grants 12-FY93-0621 and 12-FY95-0496 from the March of Dimes Birth Defects Foundation and by Grant R01-MH50423 from the National Institute of Mental Health.

between terminology and the underlying conceptualization of the variables used, (c) use of data-analytic procedures that fail to test for mediated and moderated effects, and (d) a mismatch between written text and diagrammatic figures.

Frequently, terminological, conceptual, and statistical inconsistencies are all present in the same study, such as when investigators conceptualize a variable as a moderator (e.g., coping strategies are hypothesized to serve a protective or buffering function), use the term *mediator* (rather than *moderator*) to describe the impact of the variable, provide a figure where the variable is presented as a mediator (rather than a moderator), and conduct statistical analyses that test neither mediation nor moderation. When such mismatches among terminology, theory, figures, and statistical analyses exist, findings become particularly difficult to interpret.

A lack of conceptual and statistical clarity in the study of mediated and moderated effects has become particularly prevalent in mental health literatures where investigators seek to examine factors that mediate or moderate associations between selected predictors and adjustment outcomes. In the child-clinical and pediatric psychology literatures, for example, models of predictor–adjustment relationships have become quite complex (e.g., Grych & Fincham, 1990; Thompson, Gil, Burbach, Keith, & Kinny, 1993). Investigators working in these areas have found it necessary to invoke conceptual models that include mediated and moderated effects.

The purpose of this discussion is threefold: (a) the terms "mediator" and "moderator" are defined and differentiated, (b) statistical strategies for testing mediated and moderated effects are reviewed, and (c) examples of troublesome and appropriate uses of these terms in the child-clinical and pediatric psychology literatures are presented. Although examples have been drawn from only two literatures, the points made apply to any research area where mediated or moderated effects are of interest.

DEFINITION OF MEDIATED AND MODERATED EFFECTS

According to Baron and Kenny, a moderator specifies the conditions under which a given effect occurs, as well as the conditions under which the direction or strength of an effect vary. They describe a moderator variable as the following:

> a qualitative (e.g., sex, race, class) or quantitative . . . variable that affects the direction and/or strength of a relation between an independent or predictor variable and a dependent or criterion variable . . . a basic moderator effect can be represented as an interaction between a focal independent variable and a factor (the moderator) that specifies the appropriate conditions for its operation . . . Moderator variables are typically introduced when there is an unexpectedly weak or inconsistent

relation between a predictor and a criterion variable. (Baron & Kenny, 1986, pp. 1174, 1178)

In other words, a moderator variable is one that affects the relationship between two variables, so that the nature of the impact of the predictor on the criterion varies according to the level or value of the moderator (also see Saunders, 1956; Zedeck, 1971). A moderator interacts with a predictor variable in such a way as to have an impact on the level of a dependent variable.

A mediator, on the other hand, specifies how (or the mechanism by which) a given effect occurs (Baron & Kenny, 1986; James & Brett, 1984). More specifically, Baron and Kenny (1986) describe a mediator variable as the following:

> the generative mechanism through which the focal independent variable is able to influence the dependent variable of interest . . . (and) Mediation . . . is best done in the case of a strong relation between the predictor and the criterion variable. (pp. 1173, 1178)

Stated more simply, "the independent variable causes the mediator which then causes the outcome" (Shadish & Sweeney, 1991, p. 883). Although one may argue that the relationships among independent variable, mediator, and outcome may not necessarily be "causal," the nature of the mediated relationship is such that the independent variable influences the mediator which, in turn, influences the outcome. Also critical is the prerequisite that there be a significant association between the independent variable and the dependent variable before testing for a mediated effect.

Mediators and moderators can also be differentiated diagrammatically (see Figure 1; see also Baron & Kenny, 1986; Cohen & Cohen, 1983). A

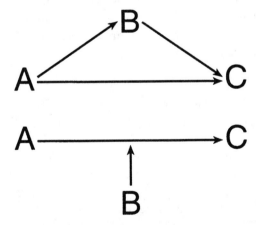

Figure 1. Models of mediated and moderated effects. In the top model, B mediates the relationship between A and C. In the bottom model, B moderates the relationship between A and C.

mediator (B in the top model in Figure 1) falls in the causal pathway between two variables (A and C in the top model in Figure 1; James & Brett, 1984); that is, if A is significantly associated with C, and if A influences B and B influences C, then B is a mediating variable between A and C (more detailed criteria are discussed later). On the other hand, if A is expected to be related to C, but only under certain conditions of B, then B is a moderator variable (see bottom model in Figure 1). The moderator (B) can be drawn to indicate that it has an impact on the relationship between A and C. Although some variables are more likely to be moderators than mediators (e.g., gender), some variables could serve either function, depending on the conceptual model under investigation (although not in the same analysis; see Lewis & Kliewer, 1996; Quittner, Glueckauf & Jackson, 1990; Sandler, Tein, & West, 1994, for examples where coping strategies or social support were tested as both mediators and moderators in competing models). Moreover, both moderators and mediators can be specified within the same model (e.g., moderated mediation; James & Brett, 1984; for examples of this strategy, see Harnish, Dodge, & Valente, 1995; Holmbeck, 1996; Simons, Lorenz, Wu, & Conger, 1993).

An example illustrates the distinction between moderated and mediated effects. This example is based on Fauber, Forehand, Thomas, and Wierson's (1990) study of marital conflict and adolescent adjustment in intact and divorced families. To examine the processes by which marital conflict has a negative influence on child adjustment, Fauber and his colleagues hypothesized that marital conflict has a negative impact on the quality of parenting to which a child is exposed which, in turn, has an impact on child adjustment. In this case, parenting quality is a potential mediator of the conflict → adjustment relationship and is predicted to account (at least partially) for this relationship. Alternatively, if one sought to test the hypothesis that the conflict → adjustment relationship would hold only for divorced families and would not hold for intact families, then one would be studying whether family structure (i.e., intact vs. divorced) moderates associations between marital conflict and child adjustment.

STATISTICAL STRATEGIES
FOR TESTING MODERATED EFFECTS

For both moderated and mediated effects, two types of statistical strategies are discussed: multiple regression (as reviewed by Baron & Kenny, 1986, and as used by several investigators) and structural equation modeling (SEM; see Tabachnick & Fidell, 1996, for a relatively straightforward discussion; also see Bollen, 1989; Byrne, 1994; Hoyle, 1995; Jaccard & Wan, 1996; Mueller, 1996). Although SEM is often considered the preferred method because of the information that it provides on the degree of "fit" for the entire model after controlling for measurement error (Peyrot, 1996), proper use of regression techniques can also provide meaningful tests of hypotheses. Moreover, for investigators working in the area of pediatric psychology, where sample Ns are often relatively small, use of regression techniques (as opposed to SEM) may be necessary because of power considerations (see Tabachnick & Fidell, 1996, for a discussion of sample size and SEM). Although regression strategies may be more familiar to many readers of this journal, user-friendly versions of SEM software are now available (e.g., EQS; Bentler, 1995; although Jaccard & Wan, 1996, argue that LISREL 8, Jöreskog & Sörbom, 1993, is currently the preferred software when attempting to analyze the significance of interaction effects because EQS does not permit nonlinear constraints among parameters).

Regression Approach to Testing Moderated Effects

Although the manner in which moderators are tested statistically varies somewhat depending on whether the predictor and moderator are continuous or dichotomous (Baron & Kenny, 1986; Mason, Tu, & Cauce, 1996), the general strategy is the same regardless of the nature of the variables involved. As noted earlier, a moderator effect is an interaction effect. The preferred strategy is to use the variables in their continuous form (if they are not dichotomies) and to use multiple regression techniques (Cohen & Cohen, 1983; Cohen & Wills, 1985; Jaccard, Turrisi, & Wan, 1990; James & Brett, 1984; Mason et al., 1996).

The predictor and moderator main effects (and any covariates, if applicable) are entered into the regression equation first, followed by the interaction of the predictor and the moderator (e.g., Fuhrman & Holmbeck, 1995). Depending on the investigator's conceptual framework, the main effects can be entered in a hierarchical, stepwise, or simultaneous fashion (Cohen & Cohen, 1983). For example, in analyses involving marital conflict as a predictor and family structure as a moderator, marital conflict and family structure could be entered in any order or simultaneously. The interaction term is represented by the product of the two main effects (e.g., Marital Conflict × Family Structure) and "only becomes the interaction when its constituent elements are partialled" (Cohen & Cohen, 1983, p. 305; see also Aiken & West, 1991; Evans, 1991; Friedrich, 1982; Holmbeck, 1989). Thus, although the main effects may be entered in any order, they must be entered before the interaction term for the product of these two terms to represent the interaction when it enters the equation.

Given the manner in which the interaction is computed, the main effects (i.e., the predictor and the moderator) will be highly correlated with the interaction term, which can produce "ill-conditioning" error messages when using some statistical software packages. To eliminate problematic multicollinearity effects between first-order terms (i.e., the independent variable and the moderator) and the higher order terms (i.e., the interaction terms), Aiken and West (1991) have recommended that the independent variable and the moderator be "centered" before testing the significance of the interaction term. To center a variable, scores are put into the deviation score form by simply subtracting the sample mean from all individuals' scores on the variable, thus producing a revised sample mean of zero. Such transformations have no impact on the level of significance of the interaction terms or the simple slopes of any plotted regression lines.

Statistically significant interactions are interpreted by plotting simple regression lines for high and low values of the moderator variable (Aiken & West, 1991; Cohen & Cohen, 1983; James & Brett, 1984; for recent examples with data tables or figures, see Brody, Stoneman, & Gauger, 1996; Colder, Lochman, & Wells, in press; Fuhrman & Holmbeck, 1995; Silverberg, Marczak, & Gondoli, 1996; Wagner, Cohen, & Brook, 1996). To plot regression lines, an equation is used that includes terms for the covariates (if applicable), the two main effects (e.g., marital conflict and family structure), and the interaction term (e.g., Marital Conflict × Family Structure), along with the corresponding unstandardized regression coefficients and the y intercept (Aiken & West, 1991; Cohen & Cohen, 1983; Holmbeck, 1989). By substituting into this equation all possible combinations of high (e.g., M + 1 SD) and low (e.g., M − 1 SD) values of the predictor and the moderator (i.e., high-high, low-low, high-low, and low-high), two regression lines can be generated where predicted values of the dependent variable are plotted (e.g., Fuhrman & Holmbeck, 1995). Also, as carefully explained by Aiken and West (1991), investigators can test the significance of the slopes for these simple regression lines (e.g., Colder, Lochman, & Wells, in press; Silverberg et al., 1996; Wagner et al., 1996; although, in some cases, associations between the predictor and the dependent variable may be curvilinear; Molina & Chassin, 1996). In the case of categorical moderator variables, high and low values are represented by the two dichotomous dummy values for this variable. With respect to covariates, the means can be substituted for these terms in the equation (which are multiplied by their corresponding regression weights). This strategy for including covariates should only be used, however, if the investigator has tested for the presence of significant interaction effects between the covariates and independent variables and found them to be nonsignificant.

As a caution to the reader, it is worth noting that significant moderator effects may be difficult to detect statistically. This difficulty is most likely to occur in studies where samples are relatively homogeneous because all high and low values of the moderator and predictor may not be adequately represented (see McClelland & Judd, 1993, for a complete discussion of this issue). Also, unreliability of measurement in the main effects is compounded once a multiplicative term is computed (see Jaccard & Wan, 1995, for suggestions on how to examine and take into account such unreliability when conducting statistical analyses).

SEM Approach to Testing Moderated Effects

Because of the problem of compounding of measurement error when computing interaction terms, several authors have maintained that SEM strategies provide a less biased assessment of the significance of moderator effects (e.g., Jaccard & Wan, 1996; Peyrot, 1996; Ping, 1996). In fact, regression strategies tend to underestimate the effect size of the interaction term, particularly as measurement error in the predictor and moderator variable increases (Jaccard & Wan, 1996; Peyrot, 1996). The SEM strategy is also preferred when the investigator has more than one measured variable for each of the constructs (or latent variables) assessed.

The logic behind testing the significance of interaction effects with SEM designs is relatively straightforward, particularly when the moderator is a dichotomous variable (Jaccard & Wan, 1996; Ping, 1996). Suppose that one is interested in whether the association between a latent predictor variable (which is assessed with more than one measured variable) and a latent criterion variable (which is also assessed with more than one measured variable) vary as a function of gender. To test for the presence of moderation, one assesses the overall fit of the model under two conditions: (a) when there are no constraints on the solution (i.e., when the relationship between the predictor and criterion variables can vary as a function of gender) and (b) when the association between the predictor and criterion variables is constrained to be equal (i.e., an equality constraint) for the two genders (see Farrell, 1994; Jaccard & Wan, 1996, for more in-depth treatments of this data-analytic technique; see Simons et al., 1993, for an empirical example). The effect of this constraint is to test a model where no Predictor × Gender interaction is present. One can then calculate and test the significance of the difference between the goodness-of-fit chi-square values for the two models. Unlike other data-analytic strategies, nonsignificant (i.e., lower) chi-square values are indicative of a better fit. The magnitude of the difference between chi-square values determines the degree to which an interaction effect is present; that is, if there is a significant deterioration in model fit when evaluating the model under the constraint of the second condition (an assumption of no interaction), this would indicate that a significant interaction is present.

When the predictor, criterion, and moderator are continuous, the analyses are more complex. On initial inspection, one may assume that all possible products of the measured indicators could be computed as indicators of a latent interaction variable (e.g., there would be 25 such interaction indicators if the moderator and predictor latent variables were each assessed with 5 indicators). On the other hand, Jöreskog and Yang (1996) and Jaccard and Wan (1996) have maintained that fewer terms are needed but that several constraints must be imposed to test the significance of the interaction effect (a complete discussion of interactions involving continuous variables is beyond the scope of this article; see Jaccard and Wan, 1996, for a discussion of these issues, as well as programming examples using LISREL 8).

STATISTICAL STRATEGIES FOR TESTING MEDIATED EFFECTS

As was done for moderated effects, both regression and SEM strategies for testing mediated effects are discussed here.

Regression Approach to Testing Mediated Effects

According to Baron and Kenny (1986), four conditions must be met for a variable to be considered a mediator: (a) the predictor, A, must be significantly associated with the hypothesized mediator, B (letters refer to variables in Figure 1), (b) the predictor, A, must be significantly associated with the dependent measure, C, (c) the mediator, B, must be significantly associated with the dependent variable, C, and (d) the impact of the predictor, A, on the dependent measure, C, is less after controlling for the mediator, B.[1] A corollary of the second condition is that there first has to be a significant relationship between the predictor and the dependent variable for a mediator to serve its mediating role. In other words, if A and C are not significantly associated, there is no significant effect to mediate. Such a bivariate association between A and C is not required in the case of moderated effects (nor is it required in the case on an indirect effect, as discussed later).

The four conditions can be tested with three multiple regression analyses (see Eckenrode, Rowe, Laird, & Brathwaite, 1995, for an example that includes figures as well as a complete explanation of this data-analytic strategy). This strategy is similar to that used when conducting a path analysis (Cohen & Cohen, 1983; Nie, Hull, Jenkins, Steinbrenner, & Bent, 1975). The significance of the A → B path (in the direction predicted; Condition 1 above) is examined in the first regression, after controlling for any covariates. The significance of the A → C path (Condition 2) is examined in the second regression. Finally, A and B are used as predictors in the third equation where C is the dependent variable. Baron and Kenny (1986) have recommended using simultaneous entry (rather than hierarchical entry) in this

---

[1] Although Baron and Kenny (1986) list three conditions of mediation (rather than four), their third condition actually contains two subconditions; the predictor (A) must be significantly associated with the outcome (C), and this association must be less after controlling for the mediator (B).

third equation, so that the effect of B on C is examined after A is controlled and the effect of A on C is examined after B is controlled (borrowing from path-analytic methodology; Nie et al., 1975). The significance of the B → C path in this third equation is a test of Condition 3. The relative effect of A on C in this equation (when B is controlled), in comparison with the effect of A on C in the second equation (when B is controlled), is the test of Condition 4. Specifically, A should be less highly associated with C in the third equation than was the case in the second equation. As Baron and Kenny (1986) discussed, it would be unusual in psychology for this A → C effect to be reduced from significance to zero. Thus, the degree to which the effect is reduced (e.g., the change in regression coefficients) is an indicator of the potency of the mediator. Moveover, significance of the indirect effect can be tested (Baron & Kenny, 1986). The reader should note, however, that Baron and Kenny's (1986) discussion of Sobel's (1982) significance test only includes an equation that determines the estimated standard error of the indirect effect. A recent article by Sobel (1988, p. 56) includes a more complete explanation of how to apply the significance test and compute confidence intervals for the indirect effect (see also Colder, Chassin, Stice, & Curran, in press; Ireys, Werthamer-Larsson, Kolodner, & Gross, 1994; Lustig, Ireys, Sills, & Walsh, 1996, for empirical examples).

SEM Approach to Testing Mediated Effects

The logic for using SEM to test for mediated effects is similar to that discussed earlier for moderated effects involving a dichotomous moderator. Again, the SEM strategy is particularly useful when one has multiple indicators for the latent variables under investigation.

Assuming that there is a latent predictor variable (A), an hypothesized latent mediator variable (B), and a latent outcome variable (C), one would first assess the fit of the direct effect (A → C) model (Hoyle & Smith, 1994). Assuming an adequate fit, the investigator than tests the fit of the overall A → B → C model. Assuming that the overall model provides an adequate fit, the A → B and B → C path coefficients are examined. At this point, the A → C, A → B, and B → C paths (as well as the A → B → C model) should all be significant in the directions predicted (which is analogous to the regression strategy discussed above).

The final step in assessing whether there is a mediational effect is to assess the fit of the A → B → C model under two conditions: (a) when the A → C path is constrained to zero, and (b) when the A → C path is not constrained. One then examines whether the second model provides a significant improvement in fit over the first model. As noted earlier, improvement in fit is assessed with a significance test on the basis of the difference between the two model chi-squares. If there is a mediational effect, the addition of the

A → C path to the constrained model should not improve the fit. In other words, the previously significant A → C path is reduced to nonsignificance (i.e., it does not improve the fit of the model) when the mediator is taken into account (which is, again, analogous to the regression approach). It is also useful at this point to report and compare the A → C path coefficients for when B is, versus when B is not, included in the model.

An additional consideration of using SEM to test for mediational effects is the important distinction between indirect and mediated effects. An example is used to highlight this distinction. Capaldi, Crosby, and Clark (1996) recently conducted an EQS-based longitudinal study, where they concluded that the effect of aggression in the family of origin on aggression in young adult intimate relationships was mediated by the level of boys' antisocial behaviors during adolescence. On the other hand, Capaldi and her colleagues appear to have found that the direct path between the predictor and criterion was not significant (i.e., all eight correlations between the measured variables for the predictor and the measured variables for the criterion were nonsignificant), despite the fact that the predictor → mediator and mediator → criterion paths were significant. Although there is evidence for an indirect effect between predictor and criterion, the findings suggest that the mediator does not (and cannot) significantly "account" for the predictor → criterion relationship (because there was not a significant relationship between predictor and criterion in the first place; Hoyle & Smith, 1994). Thus, Capaldi et al.'s (1996) findings fit the criteria for an indirect effect but do not fit the criteria for a mediated effect (as defined here). In the case of such an indirect effect, one must be conservative when discussing interpretations of links between predictor and criterion because one cannot claim that the predictor and criterion are significantly associated.

It is relatively commonplace for investigators who use SEM to claim support for a mediational model, when they have only tested the significance of and found support for an indirect pathway. Statistical textbooks (e.g., Tabachnick & Fidell, 1996) also use "mediational pathway" and "indirect pathway" interchangeably. As noted earlier, it is critical to test whether the direct path between predictor and criterion is significant (Holye & Smith, 1994) and, if so, whether this previously significant direct pathway fails to improve the fit of the mediational model.

INCONSISTENCIES IN THE TESTING OF MEDIATION AND MODERATION: EXAMPLES FROM THE PEDIATRIC AND CHILD-CLINICAL PSYCHOLOGY LITERATURES

Researchers in the area of pediatric psychology have noted that most chronic illnesses and physical disabilities require ongoing medical management and place considerable physical, psychological, and social demands on the individuals and families involved (e.g., Quittner, 1992). It is also the case, however, that there is considerable variability in the degree to which children and their families exhibit higher levels of adjustment difficulties (Thompson et al., 1993). The fact that there is such variability has led several investigators to suggest mechanisms that buffer (or exacerbate) the impact of illness on adjustment outcomes (e.g., coping resources, family functioning, illness appraisal; Thompson et al., 1993; Thompson & Gustafson, 1996; Wallander & Thompson, 1995). Similarly, child-clinical psychologists have long been interested in the child adjustment outcomes of various stressors as well as factors which account for such stressor → outcome associations. One such stressor, marital conflict, has received considerable theoretical and empirical attention (e.g., Cummings, Davies, & Simpson, 1994; Grych & Fincham, 1990; O'Brien, Margolin, & John, 1995).

Although the literatures on adjustment to illness and adjustment to marital conflict during childhood have advanced to the point where model development is now possible, several recent attempts to identify factors which are associated with adjustment have not taken full advantage of the terminological, conceptual, or statistical advances that would facilitate progress in the field. Many of these conceptual and statistical issues relate to use of the terms "mediating" and moderating." This section will highlight the following types of problems that have begun to emerge in these literatures as investigators have embarked on the study of moderated and mediated effects (see Appendix): (a) terminological inconsistencies, (b) inconsistencies between terminology and conceptualization, (c) inconsistencies between terminology and statistical analyses, (d) lack of diagrammatic clarity, and (e) lack of conceptual clarity when a proposed mediator represents a "response" to a predictor.

Terminological Inconsistencies

In this section, the following types of terminological inconsistencies will be discussed: (a) idiosyncratic definitions of terms, (b) lack of clarity in the labeling of variables, and (c) interchangeable use of terms.

An example of an idiosyncratic definition of the term mediator comes from the work of Thompson and his colleagues (Thompson, Kronenberger, Johnson, & Whiting, 1989), who have recently presented a transactional stress and coping model of psychological adjustment in children with chronic illness (e.g., Thompson et al., 1993; Thompson & Gustafson, 1996). In an earlier report on the role of central nervous system functioning and family relationships in the adjustment of children with myelodysplasia, Thompson et al. (1989) hypothesized the following:

> illness factors (e.g., type, age of onset, and severity), demographic factors
> (e.g., socioeconomic status), cognitive processes, and social support

mediate the relationship between the stress of chronic illness and psychosocial outcome. "Mediate" means that these factors and processes contribute to the variability in psychosocial outcome. In particular, there is theoretical and empirical evidence that family functioning is one type of social support that can lower the risk of poor psychosocial outcome in the face of the stress associated with chronic illness. (p. 243)

Thompson's definition of mediation is clearly at odds with that offered by several authors (e.g., Baron & Kenny, 1986; James & Brett, 1984), as well as standard dictionary definitions (e.g., to mediate is "to serve as a vehicle for bringing about a result . . . to occupy an intermediate or middle position"; *The American Heritage Dictionary of the American Language*, 1969, p. 814). Specifically, there is no specification of an A → B → C relationship. Although it is not the case that all investigators must adhere to the same definitions of all terms, it is likely that progress in the field will be hampered if the same term is used in different ways by different scholars.

The quote from Thompson et al. (1989) also demonstrates the second form of terminological inconsistency: a lack of clarity in the labeling of variables. Some of the variables that Thompson et al. (1989) list as potential mediators in the quote (e.g., age of onset, socioeconomic status) should probably have been listed as moderators. "Moderation" (rather than "mediation") appears to be what Thompson and his colleagues had in mind, given the last sentence in the quote (which is a clear description of a moderated effect). Variables such as age of onset and socioeconomic status presumably dictate conditions under which the stress of a chronic illness is (or is not) associated with problematic outcomes (i.e., these variables are more likely to serve a moderational than a mediational role; see Hackworth & McMahon, 1991, for a similar lack of clarity in the use of the term "mediating").

Finally, some investigators have, inappropriately, used the terms "mediating" and "moderating" interchangeably. Baron and Kenny (1986) provide some examples of this problem from the social psychology literature. More recently, Davies and Cummings (1995) appear to be using the terms interchangeably when discussing Grych and Fincham's (1990) model of child adjustment to marital conflict. On the one hand, Davies and Cummings (1995) maintain that Grych and Fincham (1990) "have proposed that intraindividual factors, including cognitive processes . . . and emotional states, interact with the characteristics of marital conflict to shape its impact" (p. 677), which implies that Grych and Fincham have proposed a moderational model. Later in the same article, Davies and Cummings (1995) argued that Grych and Fincham have emphasized "the delineation of cognitive processes mediating the impact of marital conflict on children . . ." (p. 678). Thus, Davies and Cummings have identified the same process as both a moderated effect and a mediated effect (see Hanson, Henggeler, & Burghen, 1987, and Mullins et al., 1991, for similar examples).

Inconsistencies Between Terminology and Conceptualization

Two types of inconsistencies are highlighted in this section: (a) the term "mediator" is used, but the variable in question is not conceptualized as a mediator or a moderator, and (b) the term "mediator" is used, but the variable is conceptualized as a moderator.

As an example of the first type of inconsistency, Thompson and colleagues present a diagrammatic model that includes "mediational processes" (e.g., cognitive processes, methods of coping, family functioning; Thompson, Gil, Abrams, & Phillips, 1992; Thompson et al., 1993; Thompson, Gustafson, & Gil, 1995; Thompson, Gustafson, Hamlett, & Spock, 1992), but the variables contained within these components of the model are not conceptualized as mediators, at least as the authors have described them in their published work.[2] Instead, Thompson et al. (1993) argued that "child cognitive processes, child pain-coping strategies, and maternal psychological adjustment will account for independent and significant increments in the variance in child adjustment over and above that accounted for by illness and demographic parameters" (p. 469). This is a statement of neither mediation nor moderation; rather, this hypothesis is a statement of relative predictive utility. In an example from the child-clinical literature, Cummings et al. (1994) used children's appraisals of marital conflict and perceived coping efficacy as mediators between marital conflict and child adjustment. Despite the use of the term "mediation," these investigators have not made a clear case for how their variables could serve a mediational function (i.e., they do not present a model in the A → B → C format, either in written or diagrammatic form).

As an example of the second type of inconsistency (i.e., the term "mediation" is used but the variable appears to be conceptualized as a moderator), Ireys et al. (1994) examined "perceived impact" as a variable that mediates associations between several illness parameters and psychological symptoms. Although the analyses appear to provide accurate tests of mediational effects, Ireys et al. (1994) have implied that perceived impact may serve a moderating function:

> Some young adults with a chronic health condition, for example, view their disorder as negatively affecting most aspects of their lives and may therefore report high levels of psychological symptomatology; others, with similar conditions, may view their condition in a less burdensome light ... . How a young adult perceives that a condition has influenced a

---

[2] Thompson and his colleagues have not used the phrase "mediational processes" in recent diagrammatic versions of their model (e.g., Thompson, Gil, Gustafson, et al., 1994; Thompson & Gustafson, 1996; Thompson, Gustafson, George, & Spock, 1994; Wallander & Thompson, 1995). On the other hand, the figure that they use continues to represent a mediational model, and they continue to use the term *mediate* in their writings (e.g., Thompson & Gustafson, 1996).

developmentally important task . . . appears to alter significantly some of the associations between specific condition characteristics and mental health status. (pp. 206, 219)

These statements appear to describe a moderated effect (rather than the intended mediational effect); an individual's condition is more likely to have a negative effect on outcome when the illness is perceived in a certain way (see Barakat & Linney, 1992, for a similar example).

In an example from the child-clinical literature, Grych and Fincham (1990) have provided a cognitive-contextual framework for understanding children's responses to marital conflict and emphasize "the role of cognitive factors in mediating the relationship between marital conflict and maladjustment" (p. 277). On the other hand, the examples they provide suggest that they are discussing a moderated effect. For example, in discussing causal attributions, they suggest that "a child who views him or herself as a cause of parental conflict is likely to experience more distress than a child who attributes the cause of conflict to one or both parents or to outside circumstances" (p. 282). This statement implies that the effect of marital conflict on adjustment is moderated by the child's attributions insofar as marital conflict is expected to have an impact on adjustment only under certain conditions (see O'Brien et al., 1995; Rudolph, Dennig, & Weisz, 1995, for similar examples).

Inconsistencies Between Terminology and Statistical Analyses

Three types of inconsistencies are highlighted in this section: (a) The term "mediation" is used, but the analyses test neither mediation nor moderation, (b) the term "moderation" is used, but the analyses test neither mediation nor moderation, and (c) a lack of clarity in discussing implications of statistical results.

Although Thompson and his colleagues use the term "mediator," their data analyses do not test for the presence of mediational effects (see also Varni, Wilcox, & Hanson, 1988). Consistent with the predictive utility hypothesis discussed above, Thompson et al. typically use hierarchical regression strategies to assess differential predictive utility rather than mediational effects (e.g., Thompson et al., 1993). On the other hand, Thompson et al. would probably not advance mediational hypotheses (as defined here), given their a priori expectation that disease parameters are not likely to be significantly associated with adjustment outcomes (Thompson et al., 1993). Similar inconsistencies have emerged in the child-clinical literature (Cummings et al., 1994; O'Brien et al., 1995).

A related statistical concern is that some investigators have not provided complete tests of moderated effects. To explain variability in the adjustment levels of children (and the parents of children) with chronic ill-nesses and handicapping conditions, Wallander proposed a disability–stress–coping model (Wallander & Varni, 1992). Risk factors are differenti-ated from resistance factors; the latter "are thought to influence the risk-adjustment relationship, both through a moderation process and via direct influence on adjustment" (Wallander & Varni, 1992, p. 282). Despite the clarity of this conceptualization, Wallander and Varni (1992) apparently have not examined whether their "resistance" factors serve a moderating function, even though it appears that they have the data to test this aspect of their model (although see Wallander & Bachanas, 1997, for an unpublished report). Wallander's strategy to date has been to examine direct (main) ef-fects with hierarchical regressions (e.g., Wallander, Varni, Babani, Banis, & Wilcox, 1989; Wallander, Varni, Babani, DeHaan, et al., 1989), which is similar to Thompson's predictive utility approach (see Barakat & Linney, 1992; Hamlett, Pellegrini, & Katz, 1992; Mullins et al., 1991; for other ex-amples of this approach).

Finally, some investigators demonstrate a lack of clarity when dis-cussing the implications of statistical findings. In Wallander, Pitt, and Mellins's (1990) study of the relationship between child functional indepen-dence and maternal adaptation, they argue that "the lack of even a weak re-lationship in this study suggests there is relatively little to be *moderated* [emphasis added] in this sample" (p. 823). Contrary to this statement, the strongest moderation effects occur (in a statistical sense) when there are no main effects present (i.e., when both independent variables are not associ-ated with the dependent measure; see Baron & Kenny, 1986, Footnote 1). When no main effects are present, a significant interaction would indicate that a pure moderated effect had emerged (i.e., a crossover interaction; Baron & Kenny, 1986).

Lack of Diagrammatic Clarity

Although moderational hypotheses are discussed in the text of Wallan-der's articles, it is not clear from his figures that moderated effects are pro-posed. Referring to the diagram of the model (which appears in several of Wallander's articles; Wallander & Varni, 1992; Wallander, Varni, Babani, Banis, & Wilcox, 1989; Wallander, Varni, Babani, DeHaan, et al., 1989), most variable clusters appear to have direct effects on other variable clusters. Moreover, some of the hypothesized moderating variable clusters (i.e., resis-tance factors) directly affect the predictors (e.g., psychosocial stressors) and the outcomes (e.g., adaptation). The connection between psychosocial stres-sors and adaptation appears to "pass through" the resistance factors, which appears to be Wallander's diagrammatic strategy for indicating a moderated effect. As it is, however, the model appears to be more mediational than moderational; the figure obscures the "moderating" aspects of the model.[3] As evidence of this lack of clarity, other investigators have had differing interpretations of this model. Lustig et al. (1996), for example, maintain that Wallander, Varni, Babani, DeHaan, et al.'s (1989) model suggests that associations between the functional severity of a child's medical condition and maternal adaptation are "mediated" by maternal appraisals and coping. Contrary to this statement, Wallander, Varni, Babani, DeHaan et al. (1989) suggest that "the impact of these risk factors on adaptation is . . . hypothesized to be moderated by social-ecological factors, intrapersonal factors, and coping" (p. 372; see Brown, Ievers, & Donegan, 1997; Mullins et al., 1991, for similar examples).

Lack of Conceptual Clarity When a Proposed Mediator (e.g., Coping) Represents a "Response" to a Predictor (e.g., Marital Conflict)

In many of the examples discussed thus far, a variable is included in a model that represents a response to another variable in the model. Variables such as coping strategies, cognitive appraisals, and causal attributions cannot exist in isolation; they only exist in relation to variables that have preceded them (e.g., marital conflict, a chronic illness). One cannot exhibit a coping strategy in response to marital conflict, for example, if there is no marital conflict in the first place. Some have also argued that such "response" variables are the mechanism through which the independent variable influences the dependent variable and are, therefore, best thought of as mediators (e.g., Folkman & Lazarus, 1991). In many investigations, such variables are included in a "box" that is placed, connected by arrows, between antecedent (e.g., stress) and outcome (e.g., adjustment) variables (e.g., Barakat & Linney, 1992; Thompson et al., 1993).

On the other hand, investigators who use variables such as coping strategies and cognitive appraisals as mediators rarely provide a complete rationale for how these variables could serve a mediational function (as defined in this article). For example, Thompson and his colleagues (e.g., Thompson & Gustafson, 1996) have not articulated how a child's illness parameters could influence the coping strategies used by the mother (the A → B portion of the model; top of Figure 1). To do so, they would need to select a specific coping strategy (e.g., denial) and propose how such a coping strategy is expected to be used with greater (or lesser) frequency when there are higher (or lower) levels of some illness parameter (e.g., severity of illness; Frese, 1986).

---

[3] To their credit, Wallander and his colleagues have recently provided a revised model that more clearly represents the hypothesized moderated effects (see Wallander & Thompson, 1995; Wallander & Varni, 1995). On the other hand, the moderational effects of the intrapersonal factors and social-ecological factors are still not clearly indicated. It appears that the moderational influence of these two factors is mediated by "stress processing," despite Wallander, Varni, Babani, DeHaan, et al.'s (1989) statements that all three of these resistance factors serve a moderational role.

They would also need to propose that higher (or lower) rates of certain maternal adjustment outcomes are expected when this particular coping strategy is used with greater (or lesser) frequency (B → C in Figure 1). Finally, they would need to propose that the illness parameters are expected to be associated with the maternal adjustment outcomes (A → C in Figure 1). Although Thompson and his colleagues do not provide this type of conceptualization (nor is such a conceptualization consistent with the types of predictions that are typically advanced by these investigators), it is possible to advance such hypotheses. One might predict, for example, that the higher the severity of childhood illness, the smaller a parent's family support network, which would, in turn, be associated with higher levels of maladjustment. Several investigators have conceptualized variables such as coping, appraisal, and social support as "mediational," although the degree to which a conceptual rationale is provided varies considerably (e.g., Blankfield & Holahan, 1996; Holahan, Valentiner, & Moos, 1995; Jose, Cafasso, & D'Anna, 1994; Lewis & Kliewer, 1996; Quittner, 1992; Quittner et al., 1990; Sandler et al., 1994).

Contrary to this "mediational" perspective, coping strategies and other "response" variables) can also be viewed as buffers or protective factors (i.e., moderators) of the stress → adjustment relationship (Aldwin, 1994; Cohen & Wills, 1985; Conrad & Hammen, 1993; Holmbeck, 1996; Jessor, Van Den Bos, Vanderryn, Costa, & Turbin, 1995; Rutter, 1990; see Frese, 1986, for a discussion of the mediational vs. moderational roles of coping strategies). From this perspective, high levels of stress are expected to produce poor outcomes only when the level of the protective factor is low. To examine such protective effects, one would test the significance of Stress × Protective Factor interactions after entering the main effects.

Why are variables such as coping and appraisal so frequently referred to as mediators and so often represented as mediators in diagrammatic versions of prediction or causal models, without the requisite rationale? Although it is probably impossible to trace the actual roots of this practice, some of the early work on coping and appraisal has been influential (see Thompson & Gustafson, 1996, for a review). Lazarus and Folkman (1984), for example, maintain the following:

> Under comparable conditions . . . one person responds with anger, another with depression, yet another with anxiety or guilt; and still others feel challenged rather than threatened . . . In order to understand variations among individuals under comparable conditions, we must take into account the cognitive processes that intervene between the encounter and the reaction, and the factors that affect the nature of this mediation. (pp. 22–23)

Although they use the term "mediation," Lazarus and Folkman (1984) appear to be describing a moderational process. In fact, they clearly endorse an individual differences perspective on coping and appraisal when they argue that there is considerable variability across individuals with respect to how they cope with and appraise stressors and that these individual differences influence the impact of the stressor on the outcome. Despite this perspective, their use of the term "mediation" and diagrams that include mediational causal pathways (e.g., Folkman & Lazarus, 1991) appear to have been more influential than the conceptualization, as is evidenced by the frequent references to Lazarus and Folkman's (1984) theory as an example of a mediational model (e.g., Thompson et al., 1993).

A key distinction in this lack of clarity seems to involve the difference between temporal antecedents and causal antecedents. From a temporal perspective, many of the diagrammatic versions of mediational models make sense. In a recent article by La Greca and her colleagues (La Greca, Vernberg, Silverman, & Prinstein, 1996), for example, a diagram of a mediational model is presented where "exposure to traumatic events" precedes "efforts to process and cope with events," which precedes "posttraumatic stress disorder symptomatology." From a temporal perspective, this figure is understandable insofar as the traumatic event precedes (temporally) the coping efforts which precede (temporally) the adjustment outcome.

On the other hand, a figure such as this lacks clarity as a causal model (also see Barakat & Linney, 1992; Folkman & Lazarus, 1991; Thompson et al., 1993; Thompson & Gustafson, 1996). Although the occurrence of a traumatic event will precede coping temporally and may (or may not) stimulate the individual to begin coping, whether the level of a stressor is high or low does not necessarily dictate what specific coping strategy will be chosen by a given individual or the degree to which this specific coping strategy will be used (i.e., coping strategies are individual differences variables; Lazarus & Folkman, 1984). As discussed above, a "response variable" model only becomes mediational when the investigator provides predictions that certain specific mediational "responses" (e.g., coping strategies) are expected to be more (or less) likely to be used when the level of a stressor is higher (or lower; see Quittner et al., 1990, for an example of such predictions where social support is used as a mediator). A corollary of this statement is that such models also require that the level of the stressor (e.g., marital conflict, severity of illness) vary across individuals in the study (i.e., one cannot assess the impact of a mediator when the predictor has no variability). Moreover, all individuals in the study should have been exposed to the stressor to some degree (otherwise coping and appraisal strategies are not necessary and become irrelevant for those individuals not exposed to the stressor; Rogers & Holmbeck, 1997).

It is my contention that many of the diagrammatic versions of these "response variable" models should probably be drawn as moderator models (see Figure 1) and should be analyzed as such. "Moderator" modeling and data-analytic strategies would probably be more consistent with the conceptualizations provided by most investigators (e.g., Aldwin, 1994). Moreover, those who advance predictive utility hypotheses should probably not provide figures that include mediated or moderated causal pathways. On the other hand, it is not my contention that variables such as coping, social support, and cognitive processes can never serve a mediational function (although, as discussed above, it is incumbent on the investigator to explain carefully how such mediation can occur; see Lewis & Kliewer, 1996; Quittner et al., 1990).

EXEMPLARY USES OF MEDIATION AND MODERATION

There are several instances in the pediatric and child-clinical literatures in which moderating or mediating effects have been hypothesized and tested in a manner consistent with the recommendations provided in this review.

Pediatric Psychology

Murch and Cohen (1989) were interested in buffers and exacerbators (i.e., moderators) of the relationship between life stress and psychological distress in adolescents with spina bifida. In this study, the conceptualization and statistical strategy are appropriate and clearly presented (also see Kager & Holden, 1992; Walker, Garber, & Greene, 1994; for other examples of moderator analyses with a pediatric sample). Varni and Setoguchi (1996) conducted a study of associations between perceived physical appearance and adjustment as mediated by general self-esteem in adolescents with congenital or acquired limb deficiencies. Their analyses were conducted in line with Baron and Kenny's (1986) recommendations and their mediational model was supported. Although their figure was useful, it may have been helpful for the reader if the results of the mediational analyses had been tabled (see Melnyk, 1995, for another example of mediator analyses with a pediatric example).

Finally, Quittner (1992; Quittner et al., 1990) tested for the presence of moderated and mediated effects within the same study. Mediated effects of social support in a study of families with deaf offspring, are presented diagrammatically and are fully tested. Similarly, moderated effects are discussed and tested as well. In another study that tested the significance of both mediated and moderated effects, Lewis and Kliewer (1996) examined associations between hope and adjustment as mediated or moderated by coping strategies in children with sickle cell disease. These investigators found support for the moderational model but not the mediational model. This study serves as a model for maintaining consistency between figures, written text, and tabled data. The tabled data for moderated effects (i.e., Lewis & Kliewer, 1996, Table 3) are particularly informative and well organized.

Child-Clinical Psychology

Allen, Leadbeater, and Aber (1994) examined moderators of associations between psychological factors (as well as other predictors) and problem behaviors in at-risk adolescents. In addition to testing for significance of interaction terms in their data analyses, they also tested for the significance of multiple moderated effects within a longitudinal design. By first controlling for earlier levels of the outcome when predicting later levels of the outcome, they were able to determine whether moderated effects were predictive of stability in the outcome (see Sandler et al., 1994, for another study of moderated effects within a longitudinal context; also see Colder, Lochman, & Wells, in press; Frank & Jackson, 1996; Fuhrman & Holmbeck, 1995; Jessor et al., 1995; Molina & Chassin, 1996; Rogers & Holmbeck, 1997; Silverberg et al., 1996; Wagner et al., 1996, for other examples of moderated effects within the child and adolescent adjustment literature).

Several studies of mediated effects in the literature on child adjustment have used the multiple regression strategy (e.g., Boivin, Hymel, & Bukowski, 1995; Campbell, Pierce, Moore, Marakovitz, & Newby, 1996; Eckenrode et al., 1995; Feldman & Weinberger, 1994; Felner et al., 1995; Lenhart & Rabiner, 1995; Taylor, 1996; Taylor, Casten, & Flickinger, 1993; Taylor & Roberts, 1995). Feldman and Weinberger (1994), for example, examined whether child self-restraint was a mediator of associations between parenting behaviors and child delinquent behavior. Baron and Kenny's (1986) strategy for assessing mediated effects was used. As was the case in the Allen et al. (1994) study, Feldman and Weinberger (1994) used a longitudinal design to assess associations among their variables. Although the study of mediated relationships has received relatively little attention in the child treatment literature (see Treadwell & Kendall, 1996, for an exception), some have suggested that such relationships could be incorporated into meta-analyses of treatment studies (Shadish & Sweeney, 1991).

Other mediational studies have used SEM (e.g., Blankfeld & Holahan, 1996; Colder, Chassin, et al., in press; Conger, Patterson, & Ge, 1995; Harnish et al., 1995; Holahan et al., 1995; Reynolds, Mavrogenes, Bezruczko, & Hagemann, 1996; Simons et al., 1993). Additionally, the Harnish et al. (1995) and Simons et al. (1993) studies examined both moderated and mediated effects, with Harnish et al. (1995) clearly assessing whether there was a mediational effect by examining the degree to which the direct effect between predictor and criterion was reduced after accounting for the mediator.

CONCLUSION

This discussion highlighted the need for consistency in the use of the terms "mediating" and "moderating" in the child-clinical and pediatric psychology literatures. It was recommended that care be taken in discussing these processes and that investigators be clear about what statistical approaches are appropriate for a given hypothesis. Because research in pediatric and child-clinical psychology has important treatment, prevention, and public policy implications, and given that the relationship between stress and adjustment is a complex one, appropriate modeling and statistical techniques are needed to move the field toward greater understanding.

REFERENCES

Aiken, L. S. & West, S. G. (1991), *Multiple regression: Testing and interpreting interactions*. Newbury Park, CA: Sage.

Aldwin, C. M. (1994). *Stress, coping, and development: An integrative perspective*. New York: Guilford.

Allen, J. P., Leadbeater, B. J., & Aber, J. L. (1994). The development of problem behavior syndromes in at-risk adolescents. *Development and Psychopathology, 6,* 323–342.

The American Heritage Dictionary of the English Language. (1969). New York: Houghton Mifflin.

Barakat, L. P., & Linney, J. A. (1992). Children with physical handicaps and their mothers: The interrelation of social support, maternal adjustment, and child adjustment. *Journal of Pediatric Psychology, 17,* 725–739.

Baron, R. M., & Kenny, D. A. (1986). The moderator–mediator variable distinction in social psychology research: Conceptual, strategic, and statistical considerations. *Journal of Personality and Social Psychology, 51,* 1173–1182.

Bentler, P. M. (1995). *EQS: Structural equations program manual*. Encino, CA: Multivariate Software.

Blankfeld, D. F., & Holahan, C. J. (1996). Family support, coping strategies, and depressive symptoms among mothers of children with diabetes. *Family Psychology, 10,* 174–179.

Boivin, M., Hymel, S., & Bukowski, W. M. (1995). The roles of social withdrawal, peer rejection, and victimization by peers in predicting loneliness and depressed mood in childhood. *Development and Psychopathology, 7,* 765–785.

Bollen, K. A. (1989). *Structural equations with latent variables*. New York: Wiley.

Brody, G. H., Stoneman, Z., & Gauger, K. (1996). Parent–child relationships, family problem-solving behavior, and sibling relationship quality: The moderating role of sibling temperament. *Child Development, 67,* 1289–1300.

Brown, R. T., Ievers, C. E., & Donegan, J. E. (1997, April). *Risk-resistance adaptation model for children with sickle cell syndromes*. Paper presented at the Florida Conference on Child Health Psychology, Gainesville, FL.

Byrne, B. M. (1994). *Structural equation modeling with EQS and EQS/Windows: Basic concepts, applications, and programming*. Thousand Oaks, CA: Sage.

Campbell, S. B., Pierce, E. W., Moore, G., Marakovitz, S., & Newby, K. (1996). Boys' externalizing problems at elementary school age: Pathways from early behavior problems, maternal control, and family stress. *Development and Psychopathology*, 8, 701–719.

Capaldi, D. M., Crosby, L., & Clark, S. (1996, March). *The prediction of aggression in young adult intimate relationships from aggression in the family of origin: A mediational model*. Paper presented at the sixth annual meeting of the Society for Research on Adolescence, Boston.

Cohen, J., & Cohen, P. (1983). *Applied multiple regression/correlation analysis for the behavior sciences* (2nd ed.). Hillsdale, NJ: Erlbaum.

Cohen, S., & Wills, T. A. (1985). Stress, social support, and the buffering hypothesis. *Psychological Bulletin*, 98, 310–357.

Colder, C. R., Chassin, L., Stice, E. M., & Curran, P. J. (in press). Alcohol expectancies as potential mediators of parent alcoholism effects on the development of adolescent heavy drinking. *Journal of Research on Adolescence*.

Colder, C. R., Lochman, J. E., & Wells, K. C. (in press). The moderating effects of children's fear and activity level on relations between parenting practices and childhood symptomatology. *Journal of Abnormal Child Psychology*.

Conger, R. D., Patterson, G. R., & Ge, X. (1995). It takes two to replicate: A mediational model for the impact of parents' stress on adolescent adjustment. *Child Development*, 66, 80–97.

Conrad, M., & Hammen, C. (1993). Protective and resource factors in high- and low-risk children: A comparison of children with unipolar, bipolar, medically ill, and normal mothers. *Developmental Psychopathology*, 5, 593–607.

Cummings, E. M., Davies, P. T., and Simpson, K. S. (1994). Marital conflict, gender, and children's appraisals and coping efficacy as mediators of child adjustment. *Journal of Family Psychology*, 8, 141–149.

Davies, P. T., & Cummings, E. M. (1995). Children's emotions as organizers of their reactions to interadult anger: A functionalist perspective. *Developmental Psychology*, 31, 677–684.

Eckenrode, J., Rowe, E., Laird, M., & Brathwaite, J. (1995). Mobility as a mediator of the effects of child maltreatment on academic performance. *Child Development*, 66, 1130–1142.

Evans, M. G. (1991). The problem of analyzing multiplicative composites: Interactions revisited. *American Psychologist*, 46, 6–15.

Farrell, A. D., (1994). Structural equation modeling with longitudinal data: Strategies for examining group differences and reciprocal relationships. *Journal of Consulting and Clinical Psychology*, 62, 477–487.

Fauber, R., Forehand, R., Thomas, A. M., & Wierson, M. (1990). A mediational model of the impact of marital conflict on adolescent adjustment in intact and divorced families: The role of disrupted parenting. *Child Development*, 61, 1112–1123.

Feldman, S. S., & Weinberger, D. A. (1994). Self-restraint as a mediator of family influences on boys' delinquent behavior: A longitudinal study. *Child Development, 65,* 195–211.

Felner, R. D., Brand, S., DuBois, D. L., Adan, A. M., Mulhall, P. F., & Evans, E. G. (1995). Socioeconomic disadvantage, proximal environmental experiences, and socioeconomic and academic adjustment in early adolescence: Investigation of a mediated effects model. *Child Development, 66,* 774–792.

Folkman, S., & Lazarus, R. S. (1991). Coping and emotion. In A. Monat & R. S. Lazarus (Eds.), *Stress and coping: An anthology* (3rd ed., pp. 207–227). New York: Columbia University Press.

Frank, S., & Jackson, S. (1996). Family experiences as moderators of the relationship between eating symptoms and personality disturbance. *Journal of Youth and Adolescence, 25,* 55–72.

Frese, M. (1986). Coping as a moderator and mediator between stress and work and psychosomatic complaints. In M. H. Appley & R. Trumball (Eds.), *Dynamics of stress: Physiological, psychological, and social perspectives* (pp. 183–206). New York: Plenum.

Friedrich, R. J. (1982). In defense of multiplicative terms in multiple regression equations. *American Journal of Political Science, 26,* 797–833.

Fuhrman, T., & Holmbeck, G. N. (1995). A contextual moderator analysis of emotional autonomy and adjustment in adolescence. *Child Development, 66,* 793–811.

Grych, J. H., & Finchman, F. D. (1990). Marital conflict and children's adjustment: A cognitive-contextual framework. *Psychological Bulletin, 108,* 267–290.

Hackworth, S. R., & McMahon, R. J. (1991). Factors mediating children's health care attitudes. *Journal of Pediatric Psychology, 16,* 69–85.

Hamlett, K. W., Pellegrini, D. S., & Katz, K. S. (1992). Childhood chronic illness as a family stressor. *Journal of Pediatric Psychology, 17,* 33–47.

Hanson, C. L., Henggeler, S. W., & Burghen, G. A. (1987). Social competence and parental support as mediators of the link between stress and metabolic control in adolescents with insulin-dependent diabetes mellitus. *Journal of Consulting and Clinical Psychology, 55,* 529–533.

Harnish, J. D., Dodge, K. A., & Valente, E. (1995). Mother–child interaction quality as a partial mediator of the roles of maternal depressive symptomatology and socioeconomic status in the development of child behavior problems. *Child Development, 66,* 739–753.

Holahan, C. J., Valentiner, D. P., & Moos, R. H. (1995). Parental support, coping strategies, and psychological adjustment: An integrative model with late adolescents. *Journal of Youth and Adolescence, 24,* 633–648.

Holmbeck, G. N. (1989). Masculinity, femininity, and multiple regression: Comment on Zeldow, Daugherty, and Clark's "Masculinity, femininity, and psychosocial adjustment in medical students: A 2-year follow-up." *Journal of Personality Assessment, 53,* 583–599.

Holmbeck, G. N. (1996). A model of family relational transformations during the transition to adolescence: Parent–adolescent conflict and adaptation. In J. A. Graber, J. Brooks-Gunn, & A. C. Petersen (Eds.), *Transitions through adolescence: Interpersonal domains and context* (pp. 167–199). Mahwah, NJ: Erlbaum.

Holye, R. H. (Ed.). (1995). *Structural equation modeling: Concepts, issues, and applications*. Thousand Oaks, CA: Sage.

Holye, R. H., & Smith, G. T. (1994). Formulating clinical research hypotheses as structural equation models: A conceptual overview. *Journal of Consulting and Clinical Psychology, 62*, 429–440.

Ireys, H. T., Werthamer-Larsson, Kolodner, K. B., & Gross, S. S. (1994). Mental health of young adults with chronic illness: The mediating effect of perceived impact. *Journal of Pediatric Psychology, 19*, 205–222.

Jaccard, J., Turrisi, R., & Wan, C. K. (1990). *Interaction effects in multiple regression*. Newbury Park, CA: Sage.

Jaccard, J., & Wan, C. K. (1995). Measurement error in the analysis of interaction effects between continuous predictors using multiple regression: Multiple indicator and structural equation approaches. *Psychological Bulletin, 17*, 348–357.

Jaccard, J., & Wan, C. K. (1996). *LISREL approaches to interaction effects in multiple regression*. Thousand Oaks, CA: Sage.

James, L. R., & Brett, J. M. (1984). Mediators, moderators, and tests for mediation. *Journal of Applied Psycholgy, 69*, 307–321.

Jessor, R., Van Den Bos, J., Vanderryn, J., Costa, F. M., & Turbin, M. S. (1995). Protective factors in adolescent problem behavior: Moderator effects and developmental change. *Developmental Psychology, 31*, 923–933.

Jöreskog, K., & Sörbom, D. (1993). *LISREL VIII*. Chicago: Scientific Software.

Jöreskog, K., & Yang, F. (1996). Nonlinear structural equation models: The Kenny–Judd model with interaction effects. In G. Marcoulides & R. Schumacker (Eds.), *Advanced structural equation modeling* (pp. 57–88). Hillsdale, NJ: Erlbaum.

Jose, P. E., Cafasso, L. L., & D'Anna, C. A. (1994). Ethnic group differences in children's coping strategies. *Sociological Studies of Children, 6*, 25–53.

Kager, V. A., & Holden, E. W. (1992). Preliminary investigation of the direct and moderating effects of family and individual variables on the adjustment of children and adolescents with diabetes. *Journal of Pediatric Psychology, 17*, 491–502.

La Greca, A. M., Vernberg, E. M., Silverman, W. K., & Prinstein, M. J. (1996). Symptoms of posttraumatic stress in children after Hurricane Andrew: A prospective study. *Journal of Consulting and Clinical Psychology, 64*, 712–723.

Lazarus, R. S., & Folkman, S. (1984). *Stress, appraisal, and coping*. New York: Springer.

Lenhart, L. A., & Rabiner, D. L. (1995). An integrative approach to the study of social competence in adolescence. *Development and Psychopathology, 7*, 543–561.

Lewis, H. A., & Kliewer, W. (1996). Hope, coping, and adjustment among children with sickle cell disease: Tests of mediator and moderator models. *Journal of Pediatric Psychology, 21*, 25–41.

Lustig, J. L., Ireys, H. T., Sills, E. M., & Walsh, B. B. (1996). Mental health of mothers of children with juvenile rheumatoid arthritis: Appraisal as a mediator. *Journal of Pediatric Psychology, 21,* 719–733.

Mason, C. A., Tu, S., & Cauce, A. M. (1996). Assessing moderator variables: Two computer simulation studies. *Educational and Psychological Measurement, 56,* 45–62.

McClelland, G. H., & Judd, C. M. (1993). Statistical difficulties of detecting interactions and moderator effects. *Psychological Bulletin, 114,* 376–390.

Melnyk, B. M. (1995). Coping with unplanned childhood hospitalization: The mediating functions of parental beliefs. *Journal of Pediatric Psychology, 20,* 299–312.

Molina, B. S. G., & Chassin, L. (1996). The parent–adolescent relationship at puberty: Hispanic ethnicity and parent alcoholism as moderators. *Developmental Psychology, 32,* 675–686.

Mueller, R. O. (1996). *Basic principles of structural equation modeling: An introduction to LISREL and EQS.* New York: Springer.

Mullins, L. L., Olson, R. A., Reyes, S., Bernardy, N., Huszti, H. C., & Volk, R. J. (1991). Risk and resistance factors in the adaptation of mothers of children with cystic fibrosis. *Journal of Pediatric Psychology, 16,* 701–715.

Murch, R. L., & Cohen, L. H. (1989). Relationships among life stress, perceived family environment, and the psychological distress of spina bifida adolescents. *Journal of Pediatric Psychology, 14,* 193–214.

Nie, N. M., Hull, C. H., Jenkins, J. G., Steinbrenner, K., & Bent, D. H. (1975). *SPSS: Statistical package for the social sciences* (2nd ed.). New York: McGraw-Hill.

O'Brien, M., Margolin, G., & John, R. S. (1995). Relation among marital conflict, child coping, and child adjustment. *Journal of Clinical Child Psychology, 24,* 346–361.

Peyrot, M. (1996). Causal analysis: Theory and application. *Journal of Pediatric Psychology, 21,* 3–24.

Ping, R. A. (1996). Latent variable interaction and quadratic effect estimation: A two-step technique using structural equation analysis. *Psychological Bulletin, 119,* 166–175.

Quittner, A. L. (1992). Re-examining research on stress and social support: The importance of contextual factors. In A. M. La Greca, L. J. Siegel, J. L. Wallander, & C. E. Walker (Eds.), *Stress and coping in child health* (pp. 85–115). New York: Guilford.

Quittner, A. L., Glueckauf, R. L., & Jackson, D. N. (1990). Chronic parenting stress: Moderating versus mediating effects of social support. *Journal of Personality and Social Psychology, 59,* 1266–1278.

Reynolds, A. J., Mavrogenes, N. A., Bezruczko, N., & Hagemann, M. (1996). Cognitive and family support mediators of preschool effectiveness: A confirmatory analysis. *Child Development, 67,* 1119–1140.

Rogers, M. J., & Holmbeck, G. N. (1997). Effects of interparental aggression on children's adjustment: The moderating role of cognitive appraisal and coping. *Journal of Family Psychology, 11*, 125–130.

Rudolph, K. D., Dennig, M. D., & Weisz, J. R. (1995). Determinants and consequences of children's coping in the medical setting: Conceptualization, review, and critique. *Psychological Bulletin, 118*, 328–357.

Rutter, M. (1990). Psychosocial resilience and protective mechanisms. In J. Rolf, A. S. Masten, D. Cicchetti, K. H. Nuechterlein, & S. Weintraub (Eds.), *Risk and protective factors in the development of psychopathology* (pp. 181–214). New York: Cambridge University Press.

Sandler, I. N., Tein, J. Y., & West, S. G. (1994). Coping, stress, and the psychological symptoms of children of divorce: A cross-sectional and longitudinal study. *Child Development, 65*, 1744–1763.

Saunders, D. R. (1956). Moderator variables in prediction. *Educational and Psychological Measurement, 16*, 209–222.

Shadish, W. R., & Sweeney, R. B. (1991). Mediators and moderators in meta-analysis: There's a reason we don't let dodo birds tell us which psychotherapies should have prizes. *Journal of Consulting and Clinical Psychology, 59*, 883–893.

Silverberg, S. B., Marczak, M. S., & Gondoli, D. M. (1996). Maternal depressive symptoms and achievement-related outcomes among adolescent daughters: Variations by family structure. *Journal of Early Adolescence, 16*, 90–109.

Simons, R. L., Lorenz, F. O., Wu, C. I., & Conger, R. D. (1993). Social network and marital support as mediators and moderators of the impact of stress and depression on parental behavior. *Developmental Psychology, 29*, 368–381.

Sobel, M. E. (1982). Asymptotic confidence intervals for indirect effects in structural equations models. In S. Leinhart (Ed.), *Sociological methodology 1982* (pp. 290–312). San Francisco: Jossey-Bass.

Sobel, M. E. (1988). Direct and indirect effects in linear structural equation models. In J. S. Long (Ed.), *Common problems/proper solutions: Avoiding error in quantitative research* (pp. 46–64). Beverly Hills, CA: Sage.

Tabachnick, B. G., & Fidell, L. S. (1996). *Using multivariate statistics* (3rd ed.). New York: Harper Collins.

Taylor, R. D., (1996). Adolescents' perceptions of kinship support and family management practices: Association with adolescent adjustment in African American families. *Developmental Psychology, 32*, 687–695.

Taylor, R. D., Casten R., & Flickinger, S. M. (1993). Influence of kinship support on the parenting experiences and psychosocial adjustment of African American adolescents. *Developmental Psychology, 29*, 382–388.

Taylor, R. D., & Roberts, D. (1995). Kinship support and maternal and adolescent well-being in economically disadvantaged African American families. *Child Development, 66*, 1585–1597.

Thompson, R. J., Gil, K. M., Abrams, M. R., & Phillips, G. (1992). Stress, coping, and psychosocial adjustment of adults with sickle cell disease. *Journal of Consulting and Clinical Psychology, 80*, 433–440.

Thompson, R. J., Gil, K. M., Burbach, D. J., Keith, B. R., & Kinney, T. R. (1993). Role of child and maternal processes in the psychological adjustment of children with sickle cell disease. *Journal of Consulting and Clinical Psychology, 61*, 468–474.

Thompson, R. J., Gil, K. M., Gustafson, K. E., George, L. K., Keith, B. R., Spock, A., & Kinney, T. R. (1994). Stability and change in the psychological adjustment of mothers of children and adolescents with cystic fibrosis and sickle cell disease. *Journal of Pediatric Psychology, 19*, 171–188.

Thompson, R. J., & Gustafson, K. E. (1996). *Adaptation to chronic childhood illness*. Washington, DC: American Psychological Association.

Thompson, R. J., Gustafson, K. E., George, L. K., & Spock, A. (1994). Change over a 12-month period in the psychological adjustment of children and adolescents with cystic fibrosis. *Journal of Pediatric Psychology, 19*, 189–203.

Thompson, R. J., Gustafson, K. E., & Gil, K. M. (1995). Psychological adjustment of adolescents with cystic fibrosis or sickle cell disease and their mothers. In J. L. Wallander & L. J. Siegel (Eds.), *Adolescent health problems: Behavioral perspectives* (pp. 232–247). New York: Guilford.

Thompson, R. J., Gustafson, K. E., Hamlett, K. W., & Spock, A. (1992). Psychological adjustment of children with cystic fibrosis: The role of child cognitive processes and maternal adjustment. *Journal of Pediatric Psychology, 17*, 741–755.

Thompson, R. J., Kronenberger, W. G., Johnson, D. F., & Whiting, K. (1989). The role of central nervous system functioning and family functioning in behavioral problems of children with myelodysplasia. *Developmental and Behavioral Pediatrics, 10*, 242–248.

Treadwell, K. R. H., & Kendall, P. C. (1996). Self-talk in youth with anxiety disorders: States of mind, content specificity, and treatment outcome. *Journal of Consulting and Clinical Psychology, 64*, 941–950.

Varni, J. W., & Setogouchi, Y. (1996). Perceived physical appearance and adjustment of adolescent with congenital/acquired limb deficiencies: A path-analytic model. *Journal of Clinical Child Psychology, 25*, 201–208.

Varni, J. W., Wilcox, K. T., & Hanson, V. (1988). Mediating effects of family social support on child psychological adjustment in juvenile rheumatoid arthritis. *Health Psychology, 7*, 421–431.

Wagner, B. M., Cohen, P., & Brook, J. S. (1996). Parent/adolescent relationships: Moderators of the effects of stressful life events. *Journal of Adolescent Research, 11*, 347–374.

Walker, L. S., Garber, J., & Green, J. W. (1994). Somatic complaints in pediatric patients: A prospective study of the role of negative life events, child social and academic competence, and parental somatic symptoms. *Journal of Consulting and Clinical Psychology, 62*, 1213–1221.

Wallander, J. L., & Bachanas, P. (1997). *A longitudinal investigation of stress as a risk factor for maladjustment in children with chronic physical conditions: Moderation or mediation by family variables*. Unpublished manuscript, University of Alabama at Birmingham.

Wallandar, J. L., Pitt, L. C., & Mellins, C. A. (1990). Child functional independence and maternal psychosocial stress as risk factors threatening adaptation in mother of physically or sensorially handicapped children. *Journal of Consulting and Clinical Psychology, 58,* 818–824.

Wallander, J. L., & Thompson R. J. (1995). Psychosocial adjustment of children with chronic physical conditions. In M. C. Roberts (Ed.), *Handbook of pediatric psychology* (pp. 124–141). New York: Guilford.

Wallander, J. L., & Varni, J. W. (1992). Adjustment in children with chronic physical disorders: Programmatic research on a disability-stress-coping model. In A. M. La Greca, L. J. Siegel, J. L. Wallander, & C. E. Walker (Eds.), *Stress and coping in child health* (pp. 279–298). New York: Guilford.

Wallandar, J. L., & Varni, J. W. (1995). Appraisal, coping, and adjustment in adolescents with a physical disability. In J. L. Wallandar & L. J. Siegel (Eds.), *Adolescent health problems: Behavioral perspectives* (pp. 209–231). New York: Guilford.

Wallander, J. L., Varni, J. W., Babani, L., DeHann, C. B., Wilcox, K. T., & Banis, H. T. (1989). The social environment and the adaptation of mothers of physically handicapped children. *Journal of Pediatric Psychology, 14,* 371–387.

Zedeck, S. (1971). Problems with the use of "moderator" variables. *Psychological Bulletin, 76,* 295–310.

APPENDIX

Examples of Terminological, Conceptual, and Statistical Inconsistencies in the Research Literature

A. Terminological inconsistencies

 1. Idiosyncratic definitions of terms
 2. Lack of clarity in the labeling of variables
 3. Interchangeable use of terms

B. Inconsistencies between terminology and conceptualization

 1. The term *mediator* is used, but the variable in question is not conceptualized as a mediator or a moderator
 2. The term *mediator* is used, but the variable is conceptualized as a moderator

C. Inconsistencies between terminology and statistical analyses

 1. The term *mediation* is used, but the analyses test neither mediation nor moderation

2. The term *moderation* is used, but the analyses test neither mediation nor moderation
3. Lack of clarity in discussing implications of statistical results

D. Lack of diagrammatic clarity

E. Lack of conceptual clarity when a proposed mediator (e.g., coping) represents a "response" to a predictor (e.g., marital conflict)

II

METHODS: PRINCIPLES AND PRACTICES

The theories, hypotheses, predictions, and ideas behind any study are obviously critical. Methodological issues emerge concretely at the stage where the idea is to be tested. Several decisions are required that affect the inferences that can be drawn. The articles in this section address several conditions of research that emerge when moving from the idea to implementation of research.

SAMPLING SUBJECTS AND CONDITIONS

The selection of research subjects and their assignment to conditions are central to experimentation. Among the many issues is the concern over biases that can emerge when subjects are identified and placed into various groups or conditions. An obvious initial goal is to form groups (e.g., experimental and control) with no pre-existing differences that could ultimately interfere with the conclusions. Investigators would like the groups to be equivalent before they are exposed to the different conditions, and they often believe that an unbiased method (e.g., random) of selecting subjects from an available subject pool and assigning them to conditions produces equivalent groups. *Equivalence* means that there are no differences on a host of "nuisance variables," or those variables that are not of interest to the investigator (e.g., social class, intelligence, various personality traits).

The article by Louis M. Hsu discusses how groups may differ if small samples are used, even when subjects are assigned randomly. Hsu elaborates pivotal concepts of randomization and identifies situations in which misleading conclusions about the intervention might be drawn. Psychotherapy research is used as a basis to illustrate several of the points and to make recommendations for minimal sample sizes in research. Small sample sizes (e.g., $ns <$ 20 per group) characterize a great deal of psychological research, well beyond the confines of psychotherapy. Consequently, points raised in this article warrant careful consideration in the design of studies.

Researchers are concerned with the generality of results from one set of subjects (e.g., college students) to another (e.g., clinic patients). A neglected feature of generality pertains to the stimulus conditions included in the investigation. The conditions presented to the subject reflect such features as the range, number, and characteristics of the experimenters, therapists, vignettes, stories, or other stimulus materials. Experimenters often include a narrow range of stimulus conditions (e.g., one therapist, one vignette) with the idea that this controls or holds constant the stimuli presented to the subject. Brendan A. Maher notes the importance of representing a broader range of stimulus conditions within an experiment. He discusses the concept of *representative design*, which refers to sampling the range of stimulus conditions to which the investigator wishes to generalize. Sampling of stimulus conditions is critically important as the basis for deciding the generality of results of a study and more fundamentally for separating the influence of the intervention or experimental manipulation from a restricted or single stimulus condition with which it may be confounded.

DESIGN OPTIONS AND APPROACHES

The set of articles in this section elaborates the conditions under which research is conducted, the implementation and evaluation of experimental manipulations, and the selection of research design strategies. A great deal of research in clinical psychology is conducted in laboratory settings to address questions that require special control conditions and procedures. Examples include research questions that focus on testing theory, understanding mechanisms and processes, and isolating variables that otherwise might be quite difficult to investigate. In such research, a concern is raised about the generality of the findings to individuals, situations, and circumstances of the "real world." This concern is more worrisome or relevant in some situations than others. The setting in which research is investigated cannot be evaluated in the abstract. Rather, one must speak to the goals of the investigation, and then the setting, sample, and other features can be evaluated in relation to those goals. At this point, it is critical to clarify key issues about the goals of research and how these relate to generality of the findings.

This section begins with an article by Douglas G. Mook, who discusses the purposes and importance of laboratory research. A central point is that research in the laboratory is often designed to convey what can happen and in so doing contributes significantly to the understanding of human functioning (i.e., to theory). Generality or applicability of the results is not always important or relevant. The role of laboratory research and its unique contribution to understanding are elaborated.

When investigators conduct research, it is obviously important to select experimental conditions that produce a strong effect. A strong effect is one that is likely to be detected in tests of statistical significance or to show a relatively large effect size. Indeed, when the results of an investigation show no differences between conditions, one interpretation is that the manipulation was not sufficiently strong. In the article by Deborah A. Prentice and Dale T. Miller, the importance of demonstrating *small* effects is elaborated. The article begins with a discussion of effect size and hence can give the impression that it may belong in the section of data analysis, later in the book. Yet, it is very important for researchers to have the concept of effect size in mind at the stage that they are designing the investigation because it influences all sorts of decisions (e.g., what conditions or groups ought to be included that would maximize an effect size, how many subjects should be included). The article conveys that small effects may have important implications for both theory and application. Indeed, small effects summed over time for an individual (e.g., Abelson, 1985) or spread across a large number of individuals (e.g., aspirin for treatment of heart disease) can have major applied consequences (Rosnow & Rosenthal, 1989). This article raises conceptual as well as methodological issues by prompting the reader to think about the conditions that could show an experimental effect, about whether the magnitude of the effect is important for what the investigator is trying to accomplish, and the relation between design and statistical concepts.

The *research design* refers to the arrangement or plan to evaluate the experimental conditions or interventions of interest. Among the many options is the decision of how to present the different conditions to the subjects. Anthony G. Greenwald discusses strategies in which subjects are assessed repeatedly and exposed to two or more experimental conditions (within-subject designs) or in which subjects are exposed to only one of the conditions (between-subject designs). The benefits, limitations, artifacts, and influences of different design approaches are discussed. The special advantages of within-subject designs are presented. In a given experiment, the benefits of both within- and between-subject strategies can be obtained in combined designs in which measures are administered on more than one occasion to the same subjects (e.g., pretreatment, midtreatment, and posttreatment) to assess performance of subjects in each group.

SAMPLING SUBJECTS
AND CONDITIONS

5

RANDOM SAMPLING, RANDOMIZATION, AND EQUIVALENCE OF CONTRASTED GROUPS IN PSYCHOTHERAPY OUTCOME RESEARCH

LOUIS M. HSU

Simple random sampling and random assignment (randomization) are some of the best and most popular methods of attaining the pretreatment equivalence of contrasted groups in psychological research (see Cook & Campbell, 1979), in medical research (see O'Fallon et al., 1978), and in the specialized area of psychotherapy efficacy studies (Huesmann, 1982; Kendall & Norton-Ford, 1982; D. A. Shapiro & Shapiro, 1983). In fact, in a recent meta-analysis of comparative psychotherapy outcome research that focused on some of the best studies in this area, D. A. Shapiro and Shapiro (1982, 1983) noted that unconstrained randomization was used in 57% of the client groups.

Reprinted from the *Journal of Consulting and Clinical Psychology*, 57, 131–137. Copyright 1989 by the American Psychological Association.

One of the most appealing characteristics of random sampling and randomization is that these methods can equate groups on several nuisance variables simultaneously and that these methods do not require the researcher to be aware of (a) how the important nuisance variables are related to the response measure, (b) the identities of the important nuisance variables, or even (c) the number of important nuisance variables (see Efron, 1971). These are, perhaps, the principal advantages of simple randomization and random sampling over alternative methods of controlling the effects of nuisance variables such as matching, stratification, analysis of covariance, analysis of covariance with reliability corrections, change score analysis, and standardized change score analysis. In all of these alternatives, the efficacy of control of the nuisance variables is contingent on the researcher's ability to identify the important nuisance variables or to develop a realistic model of how the contrasted groups would differ in the absence of different treatment effects (see Boruch, 1976; Kenny, 1975, 1979; Lord, 1967, 1969; McKinlay, 1977). Several authors have noted that, when sufficient information is available, these as well as other alternatives may be clearly preferable to simple random sampling and randomization (e.g., Fleiss, 1981, 1986; Pocock & Simon, 1975; Simon, 1979). Unfortunately, this information is often not available. (See Boruch, 1976, for an excellent discussion of this topic and for numerous real-world illustrations of problems associated with various alternatives to randomization.) Simple random sampling and randomization appear to be the methods of choice for controlling the effects of nuisance variables, especially the internal validity threats of maturation and selection and the selection–maturation interaction (see Cook & Campbell, 1979; Kirk, 1982), when information about the importance, the identities, and the number of variables is lacking.

However, as noted by Efron (1971), "complete randomization . . . suffers from the disadvantage that in experiments which are limited to a small number of subjects, the final distributions of treatments and controls [on the nuisance variables] can be very unbalanced" (p. 403). Similarly, Cook and Campbell (1979) warned that the "equivalence achieved by random assignment is probabilistic" (p. 341) and that it may not work with small samples. A related point was made by Keppel (1973): "Random assignment of subjects to treatments will ensure in the long run that there will be an equivalence of subjects across the different treatments" (p. 24). All of these statements indicate that random sampling and randomization can be expected to result in the equivalence of large samples but need not result in the equivalence of small samples.

It is generally recognized that clinical studies often involve small samples. Kraemer (1981), for example, pointed out that "a minority of clinical research studies report [as many as] 30–40 subjects" (p. 311). She further noted that "in recent psychiatric clinical research, 20 seems a generally acceptable sample size" (p. 311) but that "many studies with fewer than 20 subjects are published" (p. 311). The situation appears to be even worse in the specialized area of comparative therapy outcome studies (see Kazdin, 1986). More specifically, D. A. Shapiro and Shapiro (1983), whose meta-analysis focused on "an unbiased sample relatively well-designed, recently published comparative outcome studies" (p. 43) in this area, reported that "the 414 treated groups in our meta-analysis contained a mean of 11.98 ($SD = 7.12$) clients; the 143 control groups contained a mean of 12.12 ($SD = 6.64$) clients" (p. 44). They further indicated (a) that "forty-two (10%) of the treated groups contained six or fewer clients" (p. 44), (b) that 109 (26%) of these groups contained 7 to 9 clients, (c) that 148 (36%) contained between 10 and 12 clients, and (d) that only 115 (28%) contained 13 or more clients.

This article has five objectives related to the equivalence of contrasted groups in psychotherapy efficacy studies. The first objective is to investigate the relation of sample size and number of nuisance variables to the equivalence of groups in two popular models, a simple randomization model and a simple random sampling model. The second objective is to discuss the specific implications of these relations concerning the equivalence of groups described in D. A. Shapiro and Shapiro's (1982, 1983) recent meta-analyses of psychotherapy efficacy studies. The third objective is to illustrate how nonequivalence of contrasted groups can result in Simpson's paradox: The less beneficial treatment is estimated to be more beneficial. The fourth objective is to discuss the implications of Tversky and Kahneman's findings (1971) about belief in the law of small numbers concerning the interpretation of estimates of the relative efficacy of treatments in small psychotherapy efficacy studies. And the fifth objective is to compare the minimum sample sizes required for equivalence with the minimum sample sizes that have been recommended by Kraemer (1981) on the basis of other criteria.

FACTORS DETERMINING THE EQUIVALENCE OF GROUPS

Randomization

The efficacy of randomization as a method of equating groups on nuisance variables can be investigated in a variety of research designs. The single-factor independent-groups design was selected here because of the popularity of this design in comparative psychotherapy outcome research (see D. A. Shapiro & Shapiro, 1982). More specifically, this section focuses on a randomization (also called random assignment or permutation) version of this design. The next section focuses on a random sampling version of the same design.

Consider that N subjects are available for an experiment in which a treatment is to be contrasted with a control condition. Half of the subjects are randomly selected from the pool of N and are assigned to the treatment condition, whereas the remaining half are assigned to the control condition (the term *control* is a convenient term used, in this note, to refer to any condition other than the treatment condition, including other forms of treatment). Consider that the N subjects differ on K independent dichotomous variables and that the same fraction of the N subjects fall in one category of the dichotomy as in the other. It should be noted that this last characteristic does not exclude studies in which nuisance variables are continuous because continuous nuisance variables can be dichotomized at the median of the combined groups. For example, if a pool of 60 subjects is available for a study, we may think of 30 as scoring above (and 30 as scoring below) the median of the combined groups on a social desirability scale. In this example, we might define the treatment and control groups as non-equivalent in social desirability if the proportion of subjects who exceed the combined groups' median is at least twice as large in one group (say the treatment group) as it is in the other (the control group). More generally, in this section we will define the groups as nonequivalent on any nuisance variable (including pretreatment values of the dependent variable) if the proportion of subjects who fall in one category of the dichotomous nuisance variable in one group is at least twice that of the other group.[1]

The general term of the hypergeometric distribution was used to determine, for the class of experiments described previously, the probability of the nonequivalence of groups on any one nuisance variable for subject pool sizes ranging from 8 to 100. (see Table 1). The general term of binomial expansion was then used to estimate the probability that the groups would be nonequivalent on at least one of the K nuisance variables (for $K = 2$ and $K = 3$) for the same subject pool sizes.

Table 1 shows that the probability the equal-sized treatment and control groups will be nonequivalent (a) increases with an increase in the number of nuisance variables and (b) generally decreases, with one exception, with an increase in the size of the total subject pool. The exception reflects the fact that the minimum imbalance for the presence of nonequivalence, as defined in this article, cannot be obtained for all Ns: Note, more specifically, that when the total pool size is 12, it is possible for the proportion of above-median subjects (on the nuisance variable) in the treatment group (viz., 4/6)

---

[1] An anonymous reviewer noted that my definition of nonequivalence does not take into account non-equivalence with respect to interactions of nuisance variables. I acknowledge that this is an important limitation of my definition. It should be noted that a definition that takes interactions of nuisance variables into account would generally imply that larger sample sizes would be required for equivalence than the sample sizes implied by my definition. This makes sense, in the context of this article, if we conceive of interactions as additional dichotomous nuisance variables defined in terms of combinations of levels of the original nuisance variables. The same reviewer suggested that nonequivalence for interactions could be defined in terms of imbalance across treatment and control groups, within any combination of levels of the original dichotomous variables. This is a very interesting idea but, in my opinion, it would typically result in a very conservative view of equivalence because it would require labeling entire groups as nonequivalent if imbalance occurred in what would typically be a small fraction (related to the number of combinations of levels of the original dichotomous variables) of these groups.

TABLE 1
Estimated Probabilities That Groups Constructed by Random Assignment Will be Nonequivalent on at Least One Nuisance Variable as a Function of the Number of Nuisance Variables and the Total Sample Size (N)

N	Number of nuisance variables		
	1	2	3
8	.4857	.7355	.8640
12	.5671	.8126	.9189
18	.3469	.5735	.7214
24	.2203	.3921	.5260
32	.0756	.1455	.2101
40	.0256	.0505	.0749
64	.0055	.0110	.0164
80	.0034	.0068	.0102
100	.0006	.0012	.0018

Note. Nonequivalence was considered to occur for one nuisance variable in the randomization model if the proportion of subjects who belonged to one category of the dichotomous variable was at least twice as large in one group as in the other.

to be exactly twice that of the control group (2/4). But if $N = 8$, the smallest imbalance that fits the definition of nonequivalence is 3/4 for one group and 1/4 for the other. In that case, the ratio of the proportions is not 2.0 but rather 3.0.

The following example may be used to illustrate the meaning of the entries in Table 1. Suppose that a pool of 18 subjects is available for a comparative outcome study. Nine subjects randomly drawn from this pool are assigned to the treatment condition, whereas the remaining 9 are assigned to the control condition. Now consider that these 18 subjects are evenly split on two independent dichotomous nuisance variables. Note that it is necessary to have measurements of these nuisance variables, nor is it necessary even to know what these variables are, in order to use Table 1. The entry of .5735 corresponding to a row entry of 18 (the total pool size) and a column entry of 2 (the number of nuisance variables) indicates a probability of about .57 that the two groups are nonequivalent (as previously defined) on at least one of the two nuisance variables. Thus, in this situation, it is likely that randomization will not result in groups that can be considered equivalent on the nuisance variables.

Random Sampling

The random sampling version of the two independent groups design, considered in this article, differs from the randomization version in the following way. Instead of having a fixed number of subjects available for the study, the researcher has a very large pool of potential subjects. A random sample of (N/2) subjects is drawn from this pool and exposed to the treatment condition; another independent random sample of $(N/2)$ subjects is drawn from the same pool and is exposed to the control condition. Thus, in the random sampling model, the samples used in the study are viewed as independent random samples drawn from a very large pool of subjects. In the randomization model, all available subjects are used, and the two samples are not viewed as random samples from a large population. As in the case of the randomization model, we will assume in the random sampling model that subjects can be dichotomized into two equal-sized categories on each of K independent nuisance variables.[2] These categories may once more be defined in terms of median splits, but these splits are made in the population rather than in the combined samples. Nonequivalence in the random sampling model will be defined in a manner that is comparable to the definition of nonequivalence adopted in the randomization model: The groups will be viewed as nonequivalent on one nuisance variable if the proportion of one group falling in one category of the dichotomized variable differs from the corresponding proportion in the second group by at least 0.33333. For example, if 68% of one group is above the population median and only 33% of the second group is above the population median, then the groups would differ by .68 − .33 = .35 and, therefore, would be viewed as nonequivalent.

The exact probabilities of nonequivalence on at least one nuisance variable were determined for similar combinations of total sample sizes as those considered in the randomization model and for 1–10 nuisance variables. The algorithms used to determine these probabilities were similar to the algorithms that may be used to calculate exact probabilities in ridit analysis (see Fleiss, 1981, 1986). Figure 1 summarizes the findings for total sample sizes ranging from 6 to 84 and for numbers of nuisance variables ranging from 1 to 10. It is clear that these results, for the random sampling model, are very similar to the results obtained for the randomization model.

EQUIVALENCE OF GROUPS IN PSYCHOTHERAPY EFFICACY STUDIES

It may be recalled that in D.A. Shapiro and Shapiro's (1982, 1983) meta-analysis, (a) 10% of the treated groups contained 6 or fewer clients, (b) 26%

---

[2] An anonymous reviewer noted that the possible lack of independence of nuisance variables and the implications of nonindependence of nuisance variables should be mentioned. This reviewer indicated that if nuisance variables are nonindependent, then "the number of nuisance variables one has to worry about may not be as large as one thinks, because control of one variable may indirectly result in control of another." Consistent with this reviewer's comment, it should be noted that certain types of dependence between nuisance variables would imply that, as the number of nuisance variables increases, the probability of nonequivalence on at least one will not be as large as expected if these variables were independent. It should also be noted that other types of dependence imply the opposite: That is, that increasing the number of these nuisance variables would result in a greater increase in the probability of nonequivalence on at least one nuisance variable than would be expected if these variables were independent.

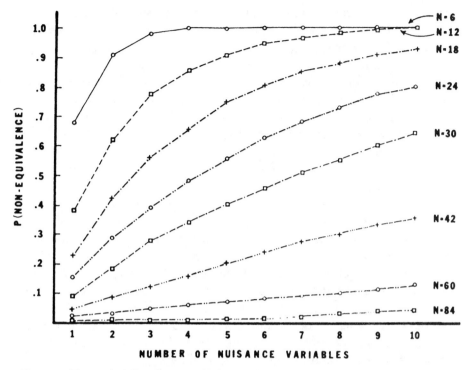

Figure 1. The probability of nonequivalence of randomly selected groups on at least one nuisance variable as a function of number of nuisance variables and total sample size.

contained 7–9 clients, (c) 36% contained 10–12 clients, and (d) only 28% contained 13 or more clients. An examination of the Table 1 entries relevant to groups with 6 or fewer clients indicates that if two contrasted groups in a design involving randomization each contained 6 clients, the probability would be greater than .5 that the groups would be nonequivalent following random assignment, even if the clients differed on only one nuisance variable. Figure 1 yields comparable findings if the clients differed on two nuisance variables. Similarly, entries relevant to groups with 7–9 clients suggest that groups containing 9 clients would probably be nonequivalent (i.e., the probability of nonequivalence would be greater than .5) if subjects in the pool differed on as few as two independent nuisance variables for the randomization model and on three nuisance variables for the sampling model. Entries relevant to groups with 10–12 clients indicate a better than even chance of nonequivalence of two randomly assigned groups containing 12 subjects each if subjects in the pool of 24 subjects differed on as few as three independent nuisance variables in the randomization model and on four or more independent nuisance variables in the random sampling model. It should be recalled, in relation to this finding, that the average sizes of client and control groups in D.A. Shapiro and Shapiro's (1982, 1983) meta-analyses were 11.98 and 12.12, respectively, and that only 28% of client groups were larger than 12. (The realism of considering that several important nuisance variables may be present in a variety of research settings has been clearly demonstrated by Boruch, 1976.) Thus, it appears that in more than half of the comparitive therapy outcome studies examined by D.A. Shapiro and Shapiro (1983), the samples were of small enough size to suggest (assuming that the models used in this article are realistic) a better than even chance of nonequivalence of the contrasted groups constructed by random assignment or random sampling.

It must be emphasized that the object of this article is not to argue against the use of simple randomization or random sampling in psychotherapy efficacy studies. Nor is the object to argue against the use of these methods for the purpose of creating equivalent contrasted groups (for that argument, see Luborsky, Singer, & Luborsky, 1975). Instead, the object is to draw attention to specific conditions under which it may be unrealistic (and to other conditions under which it may be realistic) to expect that these methods will result in the equivalence of contrasted groups and to point out some possible harmful consequences of nonequivalence on the estimation of the relative efficacy of different psychotherapeutic treatments.

CONSEQUENCES OF NONEQUIVALENCE: SIMPSON'S PARADOX

The major consequence of any specific degree of nonequivalence between contrasted groups is bias in the estimates of relative efficacy of treatment effects: That is, the difference in the effects of the treatments (or of the treatment versus the control condition) on the therapy outcome measure may be either overestimated or underestimated because of the nonequivalence of the contrasted groups on the nuisance variables (see Pocock & Simon, 1975, for a more detailed discussion of this topic).

Only the most serious type of bias will be described in this section: In the presence of nonequivalence on a dichotomous nuisance variable, it is possible that the control condition will result in a greater mean on the outcome measure than will the treatment condition, even though the treatment mean is greater than the control mean within each level of the nuisance variable. That is, the efficacy of the treatment is underestimated to the point that it is wrongly estimated to be less effective than the control condition. It is, of course, also possible for the opposite to happen—that the treatment mean will be greater than the control mean even though the control mean is greater than the treatment mean within each of the two levels of the nuisance variable. Occurrences of this type may be viewed as manifestations of

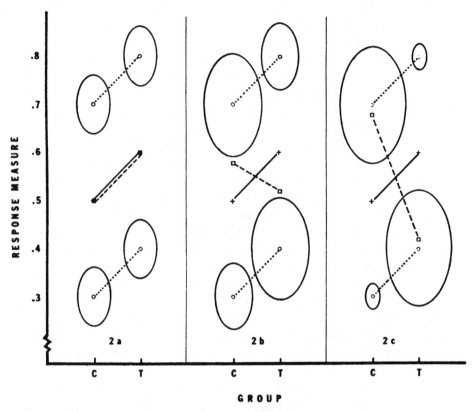

Figure 2. The biasing effects of three degrees of nonequivalence of groups (Figures 2a, 2b, 2c) on the estimate of differences between group means.

what has been described, in somewhat different contexts, as the reversal paradox (e.g., S. H. Shapiro, 1982; Simpson, 1951; Wagner, 1982). (See Messick and van de Geer, 1981, for an excellent discussion of the potential universality of the reversal paradox.)

Graphic methods proposed by Paik (1985) may be used to illustrate how the reversal paradox can be caused by the nonequivalence of the psychotherapy treatment and control groups on a dichotomous nuisance variable (see Figure 2). Figure 2 is divided into three parts (2a, 2b, and 2c). Each part represents a different degree of nonequivalence.

Each ellipse in each part corresponds to a subgroup of patients defined by a level of the dichotomous nuisance variable (e.g., say, the presence or absence of some condition) and a level of the independent variable (i.e., treatment or control). The sizes of the ellipses are proportional to subgroup sizes. The six ellipses in the upper portion of Figure 2 correspond to the presence of the nuisance variable, and the six ellipses in the lower portion correspond to the absence of the nuisance variable. Let us view the outcome measure as dichotomous for each patient: The patient manifests or does not manifest improvement. Each circle at the center of an ellipse represents the proportion of patients in the subgroup who show improvement.

It should be noted that this descriptive statistic (the proportion of members of a group who manifest improvement) appears to be consistent with several measures of clinical significance of the results of psychotherapy outcome studies (see Jacobson, Follette, & Revenstorf, 1984). This proportion may be viewed as a mean outcome measure for that subgroup if we assign a dummy variable value of 1 for improvement and of 0 for no improvement. We choose to do this in order to emphasize the generality of the reversal paradox with respect to psychotherapy response measures: That is, the reversal paradox is not limited to dichotomous response measures but is also observable with continuous response measures. Group (i.e., treatment and control) means are represented by the two small squares connected by the broken line in each part of Figure 2. It is clear that the slope of each broken line carries information about the relative efficacy of the treatment and control conditions. The solid straight lines are used to represent the relation of treatment and control means in a balanced design (i.e., the same fraction of control subjects show the presence of the nuisance variable as of the treatment subjects). Similarly, the slope of each dotted line carries information about the relative efficacy of the treatment and control conditions within a level of the nuisance variable.

It is apparent that only when the slope of the broken line is identical to the slope of both dotted lines in a part of Figure 2 is the estimate of the relative efficacy of the treatment and control conditions the same within levels of the nuisance variable as it is when we ignore the nuisance variable. Note that this happens only in Figure 2a, where the proportion of the control group that manifests the presence of the nuisance variable is equal to that of the treatment group (as reflected in the sizes of the ellipses). Figure 2b shows the effect of the minimum degree of imbalance that was considered to yield nonequivalence in both the randomization and the random sampling models discussed previously: The proportion of control subjects who show the presence of the nuisance variables (.67) is more than twice that of treatment subjects, or the difference between these proportions is at least .33. Note the influence of relative sizes of subgroups (reflected in the relative sizes of corresponding ellipses) within each group on the position of the group mean: In Figure 2a, the group mean is halfway between the subgroup means, reflecting the fact that these subgroups are of equal size. In Figure 2c, the group mean is 95% of the distance between the two subgroup means, reflecting the fact that one subgroup is 95% of the size of the group. In Figure 2b, the group mean is two thirds of the distance between subgroup means, reflecting the fact that one subgroup is twice as large as the other within that group.

An examination of Figure 2b indicates that, even when this minimum degree of imbalance is present, estimates of the relative efficacy of treatment and control not only will be different from the estimates obtained within levels of the nuisance variable but also will be reversed. That is, the mean outcome score (viz., 0 = *no improvement*, 1 = *improvement*) of all control subjects is greater than that of all treatment subjects even though the treatment mean is greater than the control mean within each level of the nuisance variable.

Figure 2c shows the effect of increasing the degree of imbalance: Now we consider that 95% of the control subjects and only 5% of the treatment subjects show the presence of the nuisance variable. The difference in the slopes of the dotted and broken lines illustrate a very large reversal: The means of outcome measures of treatment subjects are greater than those of control subjects within each level of the nuisance variable, whereas the mean of all control subjects is much larger than that of all treatment subjects. Note more specifically that 68% of control patients show improvement, whereas only 42% of treatment patients show improvement but that, within each level of the nuisance variable, a greater proportion of treatment patients show improvement than of control patients (80% vs. 70% for the presence of the nuisance variable and 40% vs. 30% for absence of that variable). There are two principal reasons for the large reversal in Figure 2c: First, the nuisance variable has a strong effect on the response measure, and, second, the degree of imbalance (or nonequivalence) is large. Researchers typically have little control over the first reason but can control the second reason by using sufficiently large samples.

NONEQUIVALENCE AND NONSIGNIFICANCE

Tversky and Kahneman (1971) found that both naive subjects and trained scientists tend to "view a sample randomly drawn from a population as highly representative, that is, similar to the population in all essential characteristics. Consequently, they expect any two samples drawn from a particular population to be more similar to one another . . . than sampling theory would predict, at least for small samples" (p. 105). Tversky and Kahneman (1971) described this expectation as a belief in the law of small numbers.

This belief, which is an unrealistic expectation of the equivalence of small groups constructed by random sampling, can result in misinterpretations of estimates of treatment efficacy obtained in individual studies. As was observed in Figure 2a, the equivalence of groups implies a lack of bias of the estimate of the relative efficacy of treatments. Consequently, one who believes in the law of small numbers is likely to consider the observed difference between group means a valid index of the relative efficacy of the treatments. As noted by Tversky and Kahneman (1971), "if [a scientist] believes in the law of small numbers, [he or she] will have exaggerated confidence in the validity of conclusions based on small samples" (p. 106).

Those who believe in the law of small numbers tend to ignore or downplay the influence of sampling error on estimates of treatment effects and, therefore, tend to downplay the importance of statistical significance tests, which evaluate estimates of treatment effects in relation to estimates of sampling error (see Tversky and Kahneman, 1971). However, these tests yield valid significance levels when groups have been constructed by randomization (see Efron, 1971, p. 404) or random sampling (Winer, 1971). The failure to obtain a statistically significant difference should be interpreted to mean that the difference can be conservatively explained in terms of sampling error rather than in terms of the effects of treatments.[3] As noted by Tversky and Kahneman (1971), "the computation of significance levels . . . forces the scientist to evaluate the obtained effect in terms of a valid estimate of sampling variance rather than in terms of his subjective biased estimate" (p. 106).

Tversky and Kahneman's (1971) points appear worth repeating because of the numerous criticisms of significance tests that have recently appeared in psychological journals (see Kupfersmid, 1988, for a summary). Cohen and Hyman (1979), for example, stated that "even if . . . results are not statistically significant, the magnitude or direction of the effect is often (more than just occasionally) most significant" (p. 14). Cohen and Hyman (1979) illustrated their point by noting that a statistically nonsignificant sample effect size of 1 (in a situation in which the predicted effect size was .5) obtained from small samples is a "dramatically significant difference" (p. 14). They also noted that "a researcher can not find that difference and then not accept it because of high alpha" (p. 14). Similarly, Carver (1978) argued that estimates of treatment effects "should be interpreted with respect to the research hypothesis regardless of its statistical significance" (p. 394). It is clear that following Cohen and Hyman's (1979) and Carver's (1978) advice, in the area of psychotherapy efficacy studies in which samples are small and nonequivalence is therefore highly probable (see Table 1 and Figure 1), could easily result in the misinterpretation of biased and misleading estimates of treatment efficacy. Clearly, the worst situations of this type occur when the reversal paradox in which the wrong treatment could be estimated to yield the better outcome.

---

[3] An anonymous reviewer noted that randomization and random sampling are sufficient to ensure the validity of statistical significance tests and that failure to use these methods raises questions about the validity of these tests. This reviewer also noted that "the probability of a significant result includes the probability of a false positive result arising from random variation (nonequivalence) between the two groups." An important implication of this statement is that the nonsignificance of a statistical test should be interpreted to mean that the observed difference between group means can reasonably be attributed to sampling error (which includes nonequivalence of groups).

MINIMUM SAMPLE SIZES:
AGREEMENT OF DIFFERENT CRITERIA

That there are certain combinations of total subject pool sizes and numbers of nuisance variables for which random sampling and randomization should not be expected to result in the equivalence of treatment and control groups is clearly demonstrated in Table 1 (for the randomization model) and Figure 1 (for the random sampling model). Also demonstrated in Table 1 and Figure 1 is the fact that, when samples are large (40 per group), randomization and random sampling appear to be effective methods of creating groups that are equivalent on the maximum number of nuisance variables examined in this article. Even when samples are of moderate size (20–40 per group), randomization and random sampling appear to work well provided the number of nuisance variables is small.

Kraemer (1981) noted that "a sample size of 20 [per group] which seems acceptable and feasible and which yields reasonable power in well-designed research (based on our own experience as well as evidence in published research . . .) . . . seems a reasonable base level for sample size" (p. 312). She also argued against using sample sizes less than 10 (p. 311). Her recommendations are based on criteria of "acceptability, feasibility, [statistical] power, and cost" (p. 311). The information in Table 1 and Figure 1 clearly supports her argument against using samples smaller than 10 and conditionally supports her recommendation of sample sizes of 20. The condition for recommendation of samples as small as 20, based on Table 1 and Figure 1 information, is that the number of important nuisance variables be small. Recommendations that sample size equal 20 or more, based on Kraemer's criteria and on the criteria of equivalence of this note, appear to be relevant to research in the area of comparative psychotherapy outcome studies because sample sizes of past studies in this area have generally been below 20 (Kazdin, 1986; D. A. Shapiro & Shapiro, 1982, 1983). It is an interesting coincidence that sample sizes that appear to be consistent with the criteria of acceptability, feasibility, statistical power, and cost (Kraemer's criteria) are about the same as the minimum sample sizes that appear to be consistent with the criteria of equivalence (as defined in this article) of contrasted groups on nuisance variables and on pre-existing values of the psychotherapy response variable.

REFERENCES

Boruch, R. F. (1976). On common contentions about randomized field experiments. In G. Glass (Ed.), *Evaluation studies: Review annual* (Vol. 1, pp. 158–194). Beverly Hills, CA: Sage.

Carver, R. P. (1978). The case against statistical significance testing. *Harvard Educational Review, 48*, 378–399.

Cohen, S. A., & Hyman, J. S. (1979). How come so many hypotheses in educational research are supported? *Educational Researcher, 8*, 12–16.

Cook, T. D., & Campbell, D. T. (1979). *Quasi-experimentation: Design and analysis issues for field settings*. Chicago: Rand McNally.

Efron, B. (1971). Forcing a sequential experiment to be balanced. *Biometrics, 58*, 403–417.

Fleiss, J. L. (1981). *Statistical analysis for rates and proportions*. New York: Wiley.

Fleiss, J. L. (1986). *The design and analysis of clinical experiments*. New York: Wiley.

Huesmann, L. R. (1982). Experimental methods in research in psychopathology. In P. C. Kendall & J. N. Butcher (Eds.), *Handbook of research methods in clinical psychology* (pp. 223–248). New York: Wiley.

Jacobson, N. S., Follette, W. C., & Revenstorf, D. (1984). Psychotherapy outcome research: Methods for reporting variability and evaluating clinical significance. *Behavior Therapy, 15*, 336–352.

Kazdin, A. E. (1986). Comparative outcome studies in psychotherapy: Methodological issues and strategies. *Journal of Consulting and Clinical Psychology, 54*, 95–105.

Kendall, P. C., & Norton-Ford, J. D. (1982). Therapy outcome research methods. In P. C. Kendall & J. N. Butcher (Eds.), *Handbook of research methods in clinical psychology* (pp. 429–460). New York: Wiley.

Kenny, D. A. (1975). A quasi-experimental approach to assessing treatment effects in the nonequivalent control group design. *Psychological Bulletin, 82*, 887–903.

Kenny, D. A. (1979). *Correlation and causality*. New York: Wiley.

Keppel, G. (1973). *Design and analysis: A researcher's handbook*. Englewood Cliffs, NJ: Prentice-Hall.

Kirk, R. (1982). *Experimental design* (2nd ed.). Belmont, CA: Brooks/Cole.

Kraemer, H. C. (1981). Coping strategies in psychiatric clinical research. *Journal of Consulting and Clinical Psychology, 49*, 309–319.

Kupfersmid, J. (1988). Improving what is published. *American Psychologist, 43*, 635–642.

Lord, F. M. (1967). A paradox in the interpretation of group comparisons. *Psychological Bulletin, 68*, 304–305.

Lord, F. M. (1969). Statistical adjustments when comparing pre-existing groups. *Psychological Bulletin, 72*, 336–337.

Luborsky, L., Singer, B., & Luborsky, L. (1975). Comparative studies of psychotherapies. *Archives of General Psychiatry, 32*, 995–1008.

McKinlay, S. (1977). Pair-matching—A reappraisal of a popular technique. *Biometrics, 33*, 725–735.

Messick, D. A., & van de Geer, J. P. (1981). A reversal paradox. *Psychological Bulletin, 90*, 582–593.

O'Fallon, J. R., Dubey, S. D., Salsburg, D. S., Edmonson, J. H., Soffer, A., & Colton, T. (1978). Should there be statistical guidelines for medical research papers? *Biometrics, 34,* 687–695.

Paik, M. (1985). A graphic representation of a three-way contingency table: Simpson's paradox and correlation. *American Statistician, 39,* 53–54.

Pocock, S. J., & Simon, R. (1975). Sequential treatment assignment with balancing for prognostic vactors in the controlled clinical trial. *Biometrics, 31,* 103–115.

Shapiro, D. A., & Shapiro, D. (1982). Meta-analysis of comparative therapy outcome studies: A replication and refinement. *Psychological Bulletin, 92,* 581–604.

Shapiro, D. A., & Shapiro, D. (1983). Comparative therapy outcome research: Methodological implications of meta-analysis. *Journal of Consulting and Clinical Psychology, 51,* 42–53.

Shapiro, S. H. (1982). Collapsing contingency tables—A geometric approach. *American Statistician, 36,* 43–46.

Simon, R. (1979). Restricted randomization designs in clinical trials. *Biometrics, 35,* 503–512.

Simpson, E. H. (1951). The interpretation of interaction in contingency tables. *Journal of the Royal Statistical Society, 13,* 238–241.

Strube, M. J., & Hartmann, D. P. (1982). A critical appraisal of meta-analysis. *British Journal of Psychology, 21,* 129–139.

Tversky, A., & Kahneman, D. (1971). Belief in the law of small numbers. *Psychological Bulletin, 76,* 105–110.

Wagner, C. H. (1982). Simpson's paradox in real life. *American Statistician, 36,* 46–48.

Winer, B. J. (1971). *Statistical principles in experimental design.* New York: McGraw-Hill.

6

STIMULUS SAMPLING IN CLINICAL RESEARCH: REPRESENTATIVE DESIGN REVIEWED

BRENDAN A. MAHER

More than 30 years ago, Egon Brunswik (1947) pointed out that if we wish to generalize the results of a psychological experiment to populations of subjects and to populations of stimuli, we must sample from both populations. This argument was elaborated by him in other articles and was summarized cogently in a short article by Hammond (1948). The purpose of this article is to review the issues that Brunswik raised and to examine some of their implications for contemporary research in clinical psychology.

Brunswik's thesis is very simple. When we conduct an experiment intended to investigate the effect of different values of an independent variable on a population, we always take care to draw a sample of subjects that is representative of the population in question. We do so, naturally, because we recognize the range of variation that exists in populations of individuals. We wish to make sure that deviant individual values do not distort our estimate

Reprinted from the *Journal of Consulting and Clinical Psychology, 46,* 643–647. Copyright 1978 by the American Psychological Association.

of the parameters of the population. If the stimuli that we use are defined in physical units, we are (or should be) careful to confine our generalizations to the range of values actually included in the study. When physical units are involved, we have relative confidence that the stimulus can be replicated by another investigator, provided that the detailed description of the stimulus is followed carefully. Should a subsequent investigator change one or more of these attributes, we are not surprised if there is a concomitant change in the responses that are made to the stimulus.

When the stimuli to which the subjects respond cannot be defined in physical units and are likely to vary within a population, a different situation arises. Outstanding examples are to be seen in research directed to the investigation of the effects of human beings as stimuli that elicit behavior from other human beings. Consider some instances drawn from recent volumes of this journal. Acosta and Sheehan (1976) reported that Mexican American subjects viewed an Anglo American professional therapist as more competent than a Mexican American professional when all other variables were matched. Babad, Mann, and Mar-Hayim (1975) reported that trainee clinicians who were told that a testee was a high-achieving upper-middle class child assigned higher scores to Wechsler Intelligence Scale for Children (WISC) responses than did another sample of clinicians who were led to believe that the same responses had been made by an underachieving deprived child. Research of this kind is generally cast in terms of a hypothesis that members of a specified population respond in discriminatory fashion to members of certain other populations. Thus, for example, we encounter such questions as, Do physicians give less adequate medical care to ex-mental patients than they do to normal medical patients? (Farina, Hagelauer, & Holzberg, 1976) and Are therapists with a behavioral orientation less affected by the label *patient* when evaluating observed behavior than are therapists of psychodynamic persuasion? (Langer & Abelson, 1974).

SINGLE-STIMULUS DESIGN

Human attributes are generally distributed in such a fashion that any one of them is likely to be found in conjunction with a wide variety of others. Let us consider an investigation of bias toward ex-mental patients. To belabor the obvious a little, we can note that the attribute *ex-mental patient* can be associated with any measure of intelligence, age, sex, education, socioeconomic status, physical attractiveness, and so forth. It is true that some of these attributes may have significant correlations with each other; a patient of upper socioeconomic status is quite likely to have had substantial education, for example. Nonetheless, even the largest of these correlations is quite modest, and the population of ex-mental patients to which we wish to generalize have a wide range of values on these attributes.

When we employ only one person as a stimulus, we are faced with the fact that the specific values of some of the other attributes possessed by this person will also have stimulus value that will be unknown and uncontrolled. Responses made by a sample of the normal population to an ex-mental patient who is female, young, attractive, articulate, and intelligent may well be different from those made to a normal control who is male, old, ugly, incoherent, and dull. These differences cannot be assigned to the patient/nonpatient status of the two stimulus persons, as many other unidentified differences were uncontrolled. At first sight it may appear that this problem is solved by the simple expedient of matching the patient and the control on all variables other than that of patient status. Unfortunately, this can only be achieved at the cost of further difficulties. We do not know the full range of variables that should be matched, and hence this solution necessarily involves resort to an actor and a script, barring the unlikely availability of discordant monozygotic twins for research purposes! Scripts bring with them some special problems, of which more will be said later. The main point to note here is that the use of a *single* human stimulus acting as his or her own control fails to deal with the problem of the *interaction* of the attribute under investigation with those that have been controlled by matching. Pursuing for a moment the example of responses to the label *ex-mental patient*, let us consider a hypothetical study using a male actor with athletic physique and vigorous movements. The willingness of a normal subject to accept this individual as a fellow worker, neighbor, or friend may well be influenced by the perception that the ex-patient, if violent, could be dangerous. Had the actor been older and visibly frail, the reaction might well be different. Under the first set of circumstances, the bias hypothesis would probably be confirmed, and under the second set, the null hypothesis might fail to be rejected.

An additional difficulty is incurred by the single-stimulus own-control strategy. We cannot determine whether a finding of no difference between group means is due to the weakness of the hypothesis, errors of method, or the inadvertent selection of an atypical stimulus person to represent one or both conditions. An example of the complexities of interpretation with this design can be found in Farina et al. (1976). These investigators hypothesized that physicians would provide less adequate medical care to former mental patients than to normal medical students. To test this hypothesis one stimulus person, a 23-year-old male graduate student, approached 32 medical practitioners. In each case he entered the doctor's office

> carrying a motorcycle helmet and a small knapsack. . . . The same symptoms were reported to all doctors. Stomach pains suggestive of ulcers were selected to be neither clearly psychiatric nor unrelated to the mind. . . . Every other practitioner was told the pains had first occurred 9 months earlier while the patient was traveling around the country. The remaining 16 doctors were also informed that the pain had appeared

9 months earlier, but at that time the patient reported being in a mental hospital. (Farina et al., 1976, p. 499)

No significant difference of any relevance was found in the kind of medical care given by the practitioners under either condition. In conclusion, the authors stated that "a former mental patient seems to receive the same medical treatment as anyone else" (p. 499).

Logically, several conclusions are compatible with this finding. One obviously valid conclusion is that a young male motorcyclist with the symptoms of ulcers receives a certain class of treatment whether or not he describes himself as a former mental patient. We cannot tell whether this treatment is the same, better, or worse than that typically given to a random sample of the normal population of patients who seek treatment for stomach pains, as no such sample was obtained. A substantial number of physicians may have had opinions about motorcyclists as unfavorable as those that they were hypothesized to have about former mental patients, and hence both conditions produced equally inadequate medical care. Alternatively, the physicians may have felt the necessity to be unusually careful in providing care to individuals who might be assumed to be irresponsible (such as motorcyclists and mental patients), and hence they provided better than average care. Finally, medical practice may be sufficiently precise about the adequate procedures to follow with patients who complain of stomach pains that no real room for bias exists, the treatment provided being the same as would be given to any sample of patients.

We can summarize the limitations of the single-stimulus design as follows:

1. Obtained differences may be due to the validity of the tested hypothesis or to the effect of uncontrolled stimulus variables in critical interaction with the intended independent variable. No method of distinguishing between these two explanations is possible.
2. Lack of difference may be due to the invalidity of the hypothesis, undiscovered methodological factors such as subject sampling error, or the presence of an uncontrolled stimulus variable operating to either counteract the effect of the intended independent variable or to raise this effect to a ceiling value in both experimental and control situations.

It is readily apparent that the problem of uncontrolled attributes occurring in a single stimulus person can only be solved by the provision of an adequate sample of stimulus persons, since they will tend to cancel each other out. No satisfactory solution is possible within the single-stimulus design.

SCRIPTS AND MANTICORES

Some investigators have attempted to solve the problems of the single-subject stimulus by fabricating scripts without the use of a human actor to present them. Case histories, dossiers, vignettes, audiotapes, or other devices have been used to reduce the effects of the uncontrolled aspects of a human stimulus. Thus, in a study by Babad et al. (1975), the trainee clinicians were given only the WISC protocol and did not see the child who was alleged to have been tested. These manufactured materials may be termed *scripts*. Scripts may be taken from existing sources of genuine material, such as clinical files; they may be created de novo in accordance with prior theoretical guidelines or in an attempt to present an ideal "typical" case.

When the script is drawn from original clinical files, the investigator is assured that at least one such case exists in nature. The limitations on the results obtained from such scripts are, in principle, the same as those that plague any single-stimulus design. Some minor advantage accrues to the method, however, in that the number of uncontrolled accidental attributes has been reduced by the elimination of those attributes associated with physical appearance, dress, and so forth. When the script is fabricated for research purposes, a new problem develops—namely that in devising material according to theoretical guidelines, a case is created that like the manticore, may never have existed in nature. We can imagine a hypothetical investigation of the attitudes of males toward females of varying degrees of power. Varying naval ranks with male and female gender of the occupant of each rank, we create the dossier of an imaginary female Fleet Admiral. Whatever our male subject's response to this dossier may be, we have no way of knowing whether it is due to the theoretically important combination of high rank with female gender or to the singularity of a combination that is, as yet, unknown to human experience.

For a recent illustration of this problem, we can turn to Acosta and Sheehan (1976). They presented groups of Mexican American and Anglo American undergraduates with a videotaped excerpt of enacted psychotherapy. Each group saw an identical tape, except that in one version the therapist spoke English with a slight Spanish accent and in the other version the accent was standard American English. Some subjects were told that the therapist was a highly trained professional; the others were told that the therapist was a para-professional of limited experience. There were thus four experimental conditions and two kinds of subjects. The Spanish-accent tape of a trained professional was introduced with a background vignette describing the therapist as American born of Mexican parentage and as having a Harvard doctorate in his field and a distinguished professional record. For the American-English-accent tape, the therapist was introduced with the same vignette but with an Anglo-Saxon name and parentage identified as

Northern European. Anglo American ratings of the therapist's competence were uninfluenced by the ethnic identification, whereas Mexican Americans rated the Mexican American therapist less favorably than the Anglo American therapist.

In their discussion of this somewhat surprising result, the authors noted that the number of Mexican American therapists actually in practice in the United States shortly before the study was done was 48 (28 psychologists and 20 psychiatrists). We do not know what characteristics would be typical of this population, and no attempt seems to have been made to ascertain them before preparing the script. There is, therefore, no way to be sure that the therapeutic style, choice of words, gesture, and so forth, were authentically typical of actual Mexican American therapists. Given that essentially the same script was used for both ethnic conditions, we must conclude that either one or the other version of the script was ethnically inaccurate or, less likely, that the only actual difference that would be seen in the comparative behaviors of Mexican American and Anglo American therapists would be their accent. In brief, we cannot ignore the possibility that the Mexican American subjects disapproved of the Mexican American therapist not because he was Mexican American but because his behavior was not representative of that of actual Mexican Americans. Like the woman admiral, he may have presented a combination of characteristics that is theoretically possible but unknown in the experience of the subjects responding to it. The only guarantee that a script is free from impossible or improbable combinations of variables is when it is directly drawn from an actual clinical case or other human transaction. We cannot produce a fictional script of a psychotherapeutic session with any confidence that it is as representative as a transcript of an actual session. The ideal or typical therapeutic interview may be as rare as the perfect textbook case of conversion hysteria or as a stereotypical Mexican American. This rarity or implausibility may well determine a subject's response far more than the attributes that were planned to make it appear typical. Our hesitation in generalizing from a single stimulus case to a population of cases is increased substantially by the prospect of generalizing from a case that is not known to have existed at all.

REPRESENTATIVE DESIGN

The moral to the foregoing review is simple. If we wish to generalize to populations of stimuli, we must sample from them. Only in this way can we be confident that the various attributes that are found in the population will be properly represented in the sample. Those attributes that are significantly correlated with membership in the population will appear in appropriate and better-than-chance proportions; those attributes that are uncorrelated with population membership will appear in chance proportions but will not affect the outcomes. If we intend to draw conclusions about the way in which physicians treat former mental patients, we must sample physicians and former mental patients. If we wish to know what Mexican American students think of Mexican American therapists, we must sample students and therapists. This is the essence of Brunswik's (1947) concept of representative design. There is no satisfactory alternative to it. Nonetheless, the use of representative design is rarely, if ever, seen in reported research. There are, in my opinion, three reasons for this. First, many clinical psychologists are unaware of Brunswik's work. The remedy for this is obvious and easy to apply. Second, there is a common failure to understand that the replication of single-stimulus studies with additional single-stimulus studies cannot create accumulated representative design unless the selection of single-stimulus persons was achieved by sampling.

Let us consider a hypothetical series of studies of the effect of examiner gender on children's test responses. In the population of examiners, there are likely to be attributes that distinguish males from females in addition to those that are inseparable from gender. Thus the proportions of married and single persons, prior experience with children, knowledge of various hobbies, mean age, prior locale of undergraduate education, and so forth, may differ between the two groups. In the first study we use one male examiner and one female examiner, each with 1 year of experience. Using samples of male and female children, we find differences in test responses attributable to examiner gender. Conscious of the fact that we included inexperienced examiners, we replicate the study with one male examiner and one female examiner each with 3 years of experience. Now we find no difference. Our series ends when we have made gender comparisons for examiners with 1, 3, 5, 7, 9, 11, 13, 15, 17, and 19 years of experience. We found significant examiner effects at every level of experience except 3 and 5 years. As 8 of our 10 students have found significant difference due to gender, we conclude that there is a generalizable finding. We might even treat the entire series as a single experiment comparing the group of 10 male examiners with the group of 10 female examiners and find a statistically significant difference between the mean test responses elicited by one group versus the other.

To accept this conclusion it is first necessary to know what the true proportion of the total population of examiners at each level of experience is. If the experience range of 3–5 years includes 65% of all examiners, our best conclusion is that gender differences have not been established. The reason is, of course, that the "sample" of examiners was not representative of the population to which it is intended to generalize, being underrepresented in the 3- to 5-year experience range. Note that we cannot handle this by some proportional weighing of the data obtained from the examiners with 3–5 years of experience, as the results obtained from those comparisons suffer from the limitations of single-stimulus design and might well be due to the effects of uncontrolled differences between examiners other than gender.

A third reason for the failure to use representative design is that it is laborious and expensive. Providing an adequate sample of stimulus persons, each of whom is to be observed by an adequate sample of subjects, necessarily involves large numbers and long hours. For some investigators it is, as one of my correspondents put it, "too hard to do it right."

There is however, no satisfactory alternative to doing it right. Clinical psychology is concerned with real people and not with hypothetical collections of attributes. Our research into the behavior of patients, therapists, diagnosticians, normal persons, and the like, must produce generalizations that are valid for actual populations of these people. Conclusions based on inadequate sampling may be worse than no conclusions at all if we decide to base our clinical decisions on them. If the patience and time that it takes to do it right create better science, our gratitude should not be diminished by the probability that fewer publications will be produced.

REFERENCES

Acosta, F. X., & Sheehan, J. G. (1976). Preferences toward Mexican American and Anglo American psychotherapists. *Journal of Consulting and Clinical Psychology*, *44*, 272–279.

Babad, E. Y., Mann, M., & Mar-Hayim, M. (1975). Bias in scoring WISC subtests. *Journal of Consulting and Clinical Psychology*, *43*, 268.

Brunswik, E. (1947). *Systematic and representative design of psychological experiments*. Berkeley: University of California Press.

Farina, A., Hagelauer, H. D., & Holzberg, J. D. (1976). Influence of psychiatric history on physician's response to a new patient. *Journal of Consulting and Clinical Psychology*, *44*, 499.

Hammond, K. (1948). Subject and object sampling—A note. *Psychological Bulletin*, *45*, 530–533.

Langer, E. J., & Abelson, R. P. (1974). A patient by any other name . . . : Clinician group of differences in labeling bias. *Journal of Consulting and Clinical Psychology*, *42*, 4–9.

DESIGN OPTIONS
AND APPROACHES

7

IN DEFENSE OF
EXTERNAL INVALIDITY

DOUGLAS G. MOOK

The greatest weakness of laboratory experiments lies in their artificiality.
Social processes observed to occur within a laboratory setting might not
necessarily occur within more natural social settings.
    —Babbie, 1975, p. 254

In order to behave like scientists we must construct situations in which
our subjects . . . can behave as little like human beings as possible and we
do this in order to allow ourselves to make statements about the nature
of their humanity.
    —Bannister, 1966, p. 24

Experimental psychologists frequently have to listen to remarks like
these. And one who has taught courses in research methods and experimental psychology, as I have for the past several years, has probably had no problem in alerting students to the "artificiality" of research settings. Students,
like laypersons (and not a few social scientists for that matter), come to us
quite prepared to point out the remoteness of our experimental chambers,
our preoccupation with rats and college sophomores, and the comic-opera
"reactivity" of our shock generators, electrode paste, and judgments of
lengths of line segments on white paper.

They see all this. My problem has been not to alert them to these considerations, but to break their habit of dismissing well-done, meaningful, informative research on grounds of "artificiality."

The task has become a bit harder over the last few years because a full-
fledged "purr" word has gained currency: *external validity*. Articles and mono-

Reprinted from the *American Psychologist, 38,* 379–387. Copyright 1983 by the American Psychological Association.

graphs have been written about its proper nurture, and checklists of specific threats to its well-being are now appearing in textbooks. Studies unescorted by it are afflicted by—what else?—*external invalidity*. That phrase has a lovely mouth-filling resonance to it, and there is, to be sure, a certain poetic justice in our being attacked with our own jargon.

WARM FUZZIES AND COLD CREEPIES

The trouble is that, like most "purr" and "snarl" words, the phrases *external validity* and *external invalidity* can serve as serious barriers to thought. Obviously, any kind of validity is a warm, fuzzy Good Thing; and just as obviously, any kind of invalidity must be a cold, creepy Bad Thing. Who could doubt it?

It seems to me that these phrases trapped even their originators, in just that way. Campbell and Stanley (1967) introduce the concept thus: "*External validity* asks the question of *generalizability*: To what populations, settings, treatment variables, and measurement variables can this effect be generalized?" (p. 5). Fair enough. External validity is not an automatic desideratum; it *asks a question*. It invites us to think about the prior questions: To what populations, settings, and so on, do we *want* the effect to be generalized? Do we want to generalize it at all?

But their next sentence is: "Both types of criteria are obviously important . . ." And ". . . the selection of designs strong in both types of validity is obviously our ideal" (Campbell & Stanley, 1967, p. 5).

I intend to argue that this is simply wrong. If it sounds plausible, it is because the word *validity* has given it a warm coat of downy fuzz. Who wants to be invalid—internally, externally, or in any other way? One might as well ask for acne. In a way, I wish the authors had stayed with the term *generalizability*, precisely because it does not sound nearly so good. It would then be easier to remember that we are not dealing with a criterion, like clear skin, but with a question, like "How can we get this sofa down the stairs?" One asks that question if, and only if, moving the sofa is what one wants to do.

But *generalizability* is not quite right either. The question of external validity is not the same as the question of generalizability. Even an experiment that is clearly "applicable to the real world," perhaps because it was conducted there (e.g., Bickman's, 1974, studies of obedience on the street corner), will have *some* limits to its generalizability. Cultural, historical, and age-group limits will surely be present; but these are unknown and no single study can discover them all. Their determination is empirical.

The external-validity question is a special case. It comes to this: Are the sample, the setting, and the manipulation so artificial that the class of "target" real-life situations to which the results can be generalized is likely to be trivially small? If so, the experiment lacks external validity. But that argument still begs the question I wish to raise here: Is such generalization our intent? Is it what we want to do? Not always.

THE AGRICULTURAL MODEL

These baleful remarks about external validity (EV) are not quite fair to its originators. In defining the concept, they had a particular kind of research in mind, and it was the kind in which the problem of EV is meaningful and important.

These are the applied experiments. Campbell and Stanley (1967) had in mind the kind of investigation that is designed to evaluate a new teaching procedure or the effects of an "enrichment" program on the culturally deprived. For that matter, the research context in which sampling theory was developed in its modern form—agricultural research—has a similar purpose. The experimental setting resembles, or is a special case of, a real-life setting in which one wants to know what to do. Does this fertilizer (or this pedagogical device) promote growth in this kind of crop (or this kind of child)? If one finds a significant improvement in the experimental subjects as compared with the controls, one predicts that implementation of a similar manipulation, in a similar setting with similar subjects, will be of benefit on a larger scale.

That kind of argument does assume that one's experimental manipulation represents the broader-scale implementation and that one's subjects and settings represent their target populations. Indeed, part of the thrust of the EV concept is that we have been concerned only with subject representativeness and not enough with representativeness of the settings and manipulations we have sampled in doing experiments.

Deese (1972), for example, has taken us to task for this neglect:

> Some particular set of conditions in an experiment is generally taken to be representative of all possible conditions of a similar type. . . . In the investigation of altruism, situations are devised to permit people to make altruistic choices. Usually a single situation provides the setting for the experimental testing. . . . [the experimenter] will allow that one particular situation to stand for the unspecified circumstances in which an individual could be altruistic. . . . the social psychologist as experimenter is content to let a particular situation stand for an indefinite range of possible testing situations in a vague and unspecified way. (pp. 59–60)

It comes down to this: The experimenter is generalizing on the basis of a small and biased sample, not of subjects (though probably those too), but of settings and manipulations.[1]

---

[1] In fairness, Deese goes on to make a distinction much like the one I intend here. "If the theory and observations are explicitly related to one another through some rigorous logical process, then the

The entire argument rests, however, on an applied, or what I call an "agricultural," conception of the aims of research. The assumption is that the experiment is *intended* to be generalized to similar subjects, manipulations, and settings. If this is so, then the broader the generalizations one can make, the more real-world occurrences one can predict from one's findings and the more one has learned about the real world from them. However, it may not be so. There are experiments—very many of them—that do not have such generalization as their aim.

This is not to deny that we have talked nonsense on occasion. We have. Sweeping generalizations about "altruism," or "anxiety," or "honesty" have been made on evidence that does not begin to support them, and for the reasons Deese gives. But let it also be said that in many such cases, we have seemed to talk nonsense only because our critics, or we ourselves, have assumed that the "agricultural" goal of generalization is part of our intent.

But in many (perhaps most) of the experiments Deese has in mind, the logic goes in a different direction. We are not *making* generalizations, but *testing* them. To show what a difference this makes, let me turn to an example.

A CASE STUDY OF A FLAT FLUNK

Surely one of the experiments that has had permanent impact on our thinking is the study of "mother love" in rhesus monkeys, elegantly conducted by Harlow. His wire mothers and terry-cloth mothers are permanent additions to our vocabulary of classic manipulations. And his finding that contact comfort was a powerful determinant of "attachment," whereas nutrition was small potatoes, was a massive spike in the coffin of the moribund, but still wriggling, drive-reduction theories of the 1950s.

As a case study, let us see how the Harlow wire- and cloth-mother experiment stands up to the criteria of EV.

The original discussion of EV by Campbell and Stanley (1967) reveals that the experimental investigation they had in mind was a rather complex mixed design with pretests, a treatment imposed or withheld (the independent variable), and a posttest. Since Harlow's experiment does not fit this mold, the first two of their "threats to external validity" do not arise at all: pretest effects on responsiveness and multiple-treatment interference.

The other two threats on their list do arise in Harlow's case. First, "there remains the possibility that the effects . . . hold only for that unique population from which the . . . [subjects were] selected" (Campbell & Stanley, 1967, p. 19). More generally, this is the problem of sampling bias, and it raises the

---

sampling of conditions may become completely unnecessary" (p. 60). I agree. "But a theory having such power is almost never found in psychology" (p. 61). I disagree, not because I think our theories are all that powerful, but because I do not think all that much power is required for what we are usually trying to do.

spectre of an unrepresentative sample. Of course, as every student knows, the way to combat the problem (and never mind that nobody does it) is to select a random sample from the population of interest.

Were Harlow's baby monkeys representative of the population of monkeys in general? Obviously not; they were born in captivity and then orphaned besides. Well, were they a representative sample of the population of lab-born, orphaned monkeys? There was no attempt at all to make them so. It must be concluded that Harlow's sampling procedures fell far short of the ideal.

Second, we have the undeniable fact of the "patent artificiality of the experimental setting" (Campbell & Stanley, 1967, p. 20). Campbell and Stanley go on to discuss the problems posed by the subjects' knowledge that they are in an experiment and by what we now call "demand characteristics." But the problem can be generalized again: How do we know that what the subjects do in this artificial setting is what they would do in a more natural one? Solutions have involved hiding from the subjects the fact that they are subjects; moving from a laboratory to a field setting; and, going further, trying for a "representative sample" of the field settings themselves (e.g., Brunswik, 1955).

What then of Harlow's work? One does not know whether his subjects knew they were in an experiment; certainly there is every chance that they experienced "expectations of the unusual, with wonder and active puzzling" (Campbell & Stanley, 1967, p. 21). In short, they must have been cautious, bewildered, reactive baby monkeys indeed. And what of the representatives of the setting? Real monkeys do not live within walls. They do not encounter mother figures made of wire mesh, with rubber nipples; nor is the advent of a terry-cloth cylinder, warmed by a light bulb, a part of their natural lifestyle. What can this contrived situation possibly tell us about how monkeys with natural upbringing would behave in a natural setting?

On the face of it, the verdict must be a flat flunk. On every criterion of EV that applies at all, we find Harlow's experiment either manifestly deficient or simply unevaluable. And yet our tendency is to respond to this critique with a resounding "So what?" And I think we are quite right to so respond.

Why? Because using the lab results to make generalizations about real-world behavior was no part of Harlow's intention. It was not what he was trying to do. That being the case, the concept of EV simply does not arise—except in an indirect and remote sense to be clarified shortly.

Harlow did not conclude, "Wild monkeys in the jungle probably would choose terry-cloth over wire mothers, too, if offered the choice." First, it would be a moot conclusion, since that simply is not going to happen. Second, who cares whether they would or not? The generalization would be trivial even if true. What Harlow did conclude was that the hunger-reduction interpretation of mother love would not work. If anything about his experiment has external validity, it is this theoretical point, not the findings themselves. And to see whether the theoretical conclusion is valid, we extend the experiments or test predictions based on theory.[2] We do not dismiss the findings and go back to do the experiment "properly," in the jungle with a random sample of baby monkeys.

The distinction between generality of findings and generality of theoretical conclusions underscores what seems to me the most important source of confusion in all this, which is the assumption that the purpose of collecting data in the laboratory is to *predict real-life behavior in the real world*. Of course, there are times when that is what we are trying to do, and there are times when it is not. When it is, then the problem of EV confronts us, full force. When it is not, then the problem of EV is either meaningless or trivial, and a misplaced preoccupation with it can seriously distort our evaluation of the research.

But if we are not using our experiments to predict real-life behavior, what are we using them for? Why else do an experiment?

There are a number of other things we may be doing. First, we may be asking whether something *can* happen, rather than whether it typically *does* happen. Second, our prediction may be in the other direction; it may specify something that ought to happen *in the lab*, and so we go to the lab to see whether it does. Third, we may demonstrate the power of a phenomenon by showing what happens even under unnatural conditions that ought to preclude it. Finally, we may use the lab to produce conditions that have no counterpart in real life at all, so that the concept of "generalizing to the real world" has no meaning. But even where findings cannot possibly generalize and are not supposed to, they can contribute to an understanding of the processes going on. Once again, it is that understanding which has external validity (if it does)—not the findings themselves, much less the setting and the sample. And this implies in turn that we cannot assess that kind of validity by examining the experiment itself.

ALTERNATIVES TO GENERALIZATION

"What Can" Versus "What Does"

"Person perception studies using photographs or brief exposure of the stimulus person have commonly found that spectacles, lipstick and untidy hair have a great effect on judgments of intelligence and other traits. It is suggested . . . that these results are probably exaggerations of any effect that

---

[2] The term *theory* is used loosely to mean, not a strict deductive system, but a conclusion on which different findings converge. Harlow's demonstration draws much of its force from the context of other findings (by Ainsworth, Bowlby, Spitz, and others) with which it articulates.

might occur when more information about a person is available" (Argyle, 1969, p. 19). Later in the same text, Argyle gives a specific example: "Argyle and McHenry found that targeted persons were judged as 13 points of IQ more intelligent when wearing spectacles and when seen for 15 seconds; however, if they were seen during 5 minutes of conversation spectacles made no difference" (p. 135).

Argyle (1969) offers these data as an example of how "the results [of an independent variable studied in isolation] may be exaggerated" (p. 19). Exaggerated with respect to what? With respect to what "really" goes on in the world of affairs. It is clear that on these grounds, Argyle takes the 5-minute study, in which glasses made no difference, more seriously than the 15-second study, in which they did.

Now from an "applied" perspective, there is no question that Argyle is right. Suppose that only the 15-second results were known; and suppose that on the basis of them, employment counselors began advising their students to wear glasses or sales executives began requiring their salespeople to do so. The result would be a great deal of wasted time, and all because of an "exaggerated effect," or what I have called an "inflated variable" (Mook, 1982). Powerful in the laboratory (13 IQ points is a lot!), eyeglasses are a trivial guide to a person's intelligence and are treated as such when more information is available.

On the other hand, is it not worth knowing that such a bias *can* occur, even under restricted conditions? Does it imply an implicit "theory" or set of "heuristics" that we carry about with us? If so, where do they come from?

There are some intriguing issues here. Why should the person's wearing eyeglasses affect our judgments of his or her intelligence under any conditions whatever? As a pure guess, I would hazard the following: Maybe we believe that (a) intelligent people read more than less intelligent ones, and (b) that reading leads to visual problems, wherefore (c) the more intelligent are more likely to need glasses. If that is how the argument runs, then it is an instance of how our person perceptions are influenced by causal "schemata" (Nisbett & Ross, 1980)—even where at least one step in the theoretical sequence ([b] above) is, as far as we know, simply false.

Looked at in that way, the difference between the 15-second and the 5-minute condition is itself worth investigating further (as it would not be if the latter simply "invalidated" the former). If we are so ready to abandon a rather silly causal theory in the light of more data, why are some other causal theories, many of them even sillier, so fiercely resistant to change?

The point is that in thinking about the matter this way, we are taking the results strictly as we find them. The fact that eyeglasses *can* influence our judgments of intelligence, though it may be quite devoid of real-world application, surely says something about us as judges. If we look just at that, then the issue of external validity does not arise. We are no longer concerned with generalizing from the lab to the real world. The lab (qua lab) has led us to ask questions that might not otherwise occur to us. Surely that alone makes the research more than a sterile intellectual exercise.

Predicting From and Predicting To

The next case study has a special place in my heart. It is one of the things that led directly to this article, which I wrote fresh from a delightful roaring argument with my students about the issues at hand.

The study is a test of the tension-reduction view of alcohol consumption, conducted by Higgins and Marlatt (1973). Briefly, the subjects were made either highly anxious or not so anxious by the threat of electric shock, and were permitted access to alcohol as desired. If alcohol reduces tension and if people drink it because it does so (Cappell & Herman, 1972), then the anxious subjects should have drunk more. They did not.

Writing about this experiment, one of my better students gave it short shrift: "Surely not many alcoholics are presented with such a threat under normal conditions."

Indeed. The threat of electric shock can hardly be "representative" of the dangers faced by anyone except electricians, hi-fi builders, and Psychology 101 students. What then? It depends! It depends on what kind of conclusion one draws and what one's purpose is in doing the study.

Higgins and Marlatt could have drawn this conclusion: "Threat of shock did not cause our subjects to drink in these circumstances. Therefore, it probably would not cause similar subjects to drink in similar circumstances either." A properly cautious conclusion, and manifestly trivial.

Or they could have drawn this conclusion: "Threat of shock did not cause our subjects to drink in these circumstances. Therefore, tension or anxiety probably does not cause people to drink in normal, real-world situations." That conclusion would be manifestly risky, not to say foolish; and it is that kind of conclusion which raises the issue of EV. Such a conclusion does assume that we can generalize from the simple and protected lab setting to the complex and dangerous real-life one and that the fear of shock can represent the general case of tension and anxiety. And let me admit again that we have been guilty of just this kind of foolishness on more than one occasion.

But that is not the conclusion Higgins and Marlatt drew. Their argument had an entirely different shape, one that changes everything. Paraphrased, it went thus: "Threat of shock did not cause our subjects to drink in these circumstances. Therefore, the tension-reduction hypothesis, which predicts that it should have done so, either is false or is in need of qualification." This is our old friend, the hypothetico-deductive method, in action. The important point to see is that the generalizability of the results, from lab to real life, is not claimed. It plays no part in the argument at all.

Of course, these findings may not require *much* modification of the tension-reduction hypothesis. It is possible—indeed it is highly likely—that there are tensions and tensions; and perhaps the nagging fears and self-doubts of the everyday have a quite different status from the acute fear of electric shock. Maybe alcohol does reduce these chronic fears and is taken, sometimes abusively, because it does so.[3] If these possibilities can be shown to be true, then we could sharpen the tension-reduction hypothesis, restricting it (as it is not restricted now) to certain kinds of tension and, perhaps, to certain settings. In short, we could advance our understanding. And the "artificial" laboratory findings would have contributed to that advance. Surely we cannot reasonably ask for more.

It seems to me that this kind of argument characterizes much of our research—much more of it than our critics recognize. In very many cases, we are not using what happens in the laboratory to "predict" the real world. Prediction goes the other way: Our theory specifies what subjects should do *in the laboratory*. Then we go to the laboratory to ask, Do they do it? And we modify our theory, or hang onto it for the time being, as results dictate. Thus we improve our theories, and—to say it again—it is these that generalize to the real world if anything does.

Let me turn to an example of another kind. To this point, it is artificiality of *setting* that has been the focus. Analogous considerations can arise, however, when one thinks through the implications of artificiality of, or bias in, the *sample*. Consider a case study.

A great deal of folklore, supported by some powerful psychological theories, would have it that children acquire speech of the forms approved by their culture—that is, grammatical speech—through the impact of parents' reactions to what they say. If a child emits a properly formed sentence (so the argument goes), the parent responds with approval or attention. If the utterance is ungrammatical, the parent corrects it or, at the least, withholds approval.

Direct observation of parent–child interactions, however, reveals that this need not happen. Brown and Hanlon (1970) report that parents react to the content of a child's speech, not to its form. If the sentence emitted is factually correct, it is likely to be approved by the parent; if false, disapproved. But whether the utterance embodies correct grammatical form has surprisingly little to do with the parent's reaction to it.

What kind of sample were Brown and Hanlon dealing with here? Families that (a) lived in Boston, (b) were well educated, and (c) were willing to have squadrons of psychologists camped in their living rooms, taping their

---

[3] I should note, however, that there is considerable doubt about that as a statement of the general case. Like Harlow's experiment, the Higgins and Marlatt (1973) study articulates with a growing body of data from very different sources and settings, but all, in this case, calling the tension-reduction theory into question (cf. Mello & Mendelson, 1978).

conversations. It is virtually certain that the sample was biased even with respect to the already limited "population" of upper-class-Bostonian-parents-of-young-children.

Surely a sample like that is a poor basis from which to generalize to any interesting population. But what if we turn it around? We start with the theoretical proposition: Parents respond to the grammar of their children's utterances (as by making approval contingent or by correcting mistakes). Now we make the prediction: Therefore, the *parents we observe* ought to do that. And the prediction is disconfirmed.

Going further, if we find that the children Brown and Hanlon studied went on to acquire Bostonian-approved syntax, as seems likely, then we can draw a further prediction and see it disconfirmed. If the theory is true, and if *these* parents do not react to grammaticality or its absence, then *these* children should not pick up grammatical speech. If they do so anyway, then parental approval is not necessary for the acquisition of grammar. And that is shown not by generalizing from sample to population, but by what happened *in the sample*.

It is of course legitimate to wonder whether the same contingencies would appear in Kansas City working-class families or in slum dwellers in the Argentine. Maybe parental approval/disapproval is a much more potent influence on children's speech in some cultures or subcultures than in others. Nevertheless, the fact would remain that the parental approval theory holds only in some instances and must be qualified appropriately. Again, that would be well worth knowing, and *this* sample of families would have played a part in establishing it.

The confusion here may reflect simple historical accident. Considerations of sampling from populations were brought to our attention largely by survey researchers, for whom the procedure of "generalizing to a population" is of vital concern. If we want to estimate the proportion of the electorate intending to vote for Candidate X, and if Y% of our sample intends to do so, then we want to be able to say something like this: "We can be 95% confident that Y% of the voters, plus or minus Z, intend to vote for X." Then the issue of representativeness is squarely before us, and the horror stories of biased sampling and wildly wrong predictions, from the *Literary Digest* poll on down, have every right to keep us awake at night.

But what has to be thought through, case by case, is whether that is the kind of conclusion we intend to draw. In the Brown and Hanlon (1970) case, nothing could be more unjustified than a statement of the kind, "We can be W% certain that X% of the utterances of Boston children, plus or minus Y, are true and are approved." The biased sample rules such a conclusion out of court at the outset. But it was never intended. The intended conclusion was not about a population but about a theory. That parental approval tracks content rather than form, in *these children*, means that the parental approval theory of grammar acquisition either is simply false or interacts in unsuspected ways with some attribute(s) of the home.

In yet other cases, the subjects are of interest precisely because of their unrepresentativeness. Washoe, Sarah, and our other special students are of interest because they are not representative of a language-using species. And with all the quarrels their accomplishments have given rise to, I have not seen them challenged as "unrepresentative chimps," except by students on examinations (I am not making that up). The achievements of mnemonists (which show us what *can* happen, rather than what typically *does*) are of interest because mnemonists are not representative of the rest of us. And when one comes across a mnemonist one studies that mnemonist, without much concern for his or her representativeness even as a mnemonist.

But what do students read? "Samples should always be as representative as possible of the population under study." "[A] major concern of the behavioral scientist is to ensure that the sample itself is a good representative [sic] of the population." (The sources of these quotations do not matter; they come from an accidental sample of books on my shelf.)

The trouble with these remarks is not that they are false—sometimes they are true—but that they are unqualified. Representativeness of sample is of vital importance for certain purposes, such as survey research. For other purposes it is a trivial issue.[4] Therefore, one must evaluate the sampling procedure in light of the purpose—separately, case by case.

Taking the Package Apart

Everyone knows that we make experimental settings artificial for a reason. We do it to control for extraneous variables and to permit separation of factors that do not come separately in Nature-as-you-find-it. But that leaves us wondering how, having stepped out of Nature, we get back in again. How do our findings apply to the real-life setting in all its complexity?

I think there are times when the answer has to be, "They don't." But we then may add, "Something else does. It is called understanding."

As an example, consider dark adaptation. Psychophysical experiments,

---

[4] There is another sense in which "generalizing to a population" attends most psychological research: One usually tests the significance of one's findings, and in doing so one speaks of sample values as estimates of population parameters. In this connection, though, the students are usually reassured that they can always define the population in terms of the sample and take it from there—which effectively leaves them wondering what all the flap was about in the first place.

Perhaps this is the place to note that some of the case studies I have presented may raise questions in the reader's mind that are not dealt with here. Some raise the problem of interpreting null conclusions; adequacy of controls for confounding variables may be worrisome; and the Brown and Hanlon (1970) study faced the problem of observer effects (adequately dealt with, I think; see Mook, 1982). Except perhaps for the last one, however, these issues are separate from the problem of external validity, which is the only concern here.

conducted in restricted, simplified, ecologically invalid settings, have taught us these things among others:

1. Dark adaptation occurs in two phases. There is a rapid and rather small increase in sensitivity, followed by a delayed but greater increase.
2. The first of these phases reflects dark adaptation by the cones; the second, by the rods.

Hecht (1934) demonstrated the second of these conclusions by taking advantage of some facts about cones (themselves established in ecologically invalid photochemical and histological laboratories). Cones are densely packed near the fovea; and they are much less sensitive than the rods to the shorter visible wavelengths. Thus, Hecht was able to tease out the cone component of the dark-adaptation curve by making his stimuli small, restricting them to the center of the visual field, and turning them red.

Now let us contemplate the manifest ecological invalidity of this setting. We have a human subject in a dark room, staring at a place where a tiny red light may appear. Who on earth spends time doing that, in the world of affairs? And on each trial, the subject simply makes a "yes, I see it/no, I don't" response. Surely we have subjects who "behave as little like human beings as possible" (Bannister, 1966)—We might be calibrating a photocell for all the difference it would make.

How then do the findings apply to the real world? They do not. The task, variables, and setting have no real-world counterparts. What does apply, and in spades, is the understanding of how the visual system works that such experiments have given us. That is what we apply to the real-world setting—to flying planes at night, to the problem of reading X-ray prints on the spot, to effective treatment of night blindness produced by vitamin deficiency, and much besides.

Such experiments, I say, give us understanding of real-world phenomena. Why? Because the *processes* we dissect in the laboratory also operate in the real world. The dark-adaptation data are of interest because they show us a process that does occur in many real-world situations. Thus we could, it is true, look at the laboratory as a member of a class of "target" settings to which the results apply, but it certainly is not a "representative" member of that set. We might think of it as a limiting, or even *defining*, member of that set. To what settings do the results apply? The shortest answer is: to any setting in which it is relevant that (for instance) as the illumination dims, sensitivity to longer visible wavelengths drops out before sensitivity to short ones does. The findings do not represent a class of real-world phenomena; they define one.

Alternatively, one might use the lab not to explore a known phenomenon, but to determine whether such and such a phenomenon exists or can be made to occur. (Here again the emphasis is on what can happen, not what usually does.) Henshel (1980) has noted that some intriguing and important phenomena, such as biofeedback, could never have been discovered by sampling or mimicking natural settings. He points out, too, that if a desirable phenomenon occurs under laboratory conditions, one may seek to make natural settings mimic the laboratory rather than the other way around. Engineers are familiar with this approach. So, for instance, are many behavior therapists.

(I part company with Henshel's excellent discussion only when he writes, "The requirement of 'realism,' or a faithful mimicking of the outside world in the laboratory experiment, applies only to . . . hypothesis testing within the logico-deductive model of research" [p. 470]. For reasons given earlier, I do not think it need apply even there.)

THE DRAMA OF THE ARTIFICIAL

To this point, I have considered alternatives to the "analogue" model of research and have pointed out that we need not intend to generalize our results from sample to population, or from lab to life. There are cases in which we do want to do that, of course. Where we do, we meet another temptation: We may assume that in order to *generalize* to "real life," the laboratory setting should *resemble* the real-life one as much as possible. This assumption is the force behind the cry for "representative settings."

The assumption is false. There are cases in which the generalization from research setting to real-life settings is made all the stronger by the lack of resemblance between the two. Consider an example.

A research project that comes in for criticism along these lines is the well-known work on obedience by Milgram (1974). In his work, the difference between a laboratory and a real-life setting is brought sharply into focus. Soldiers in the jungles of Viet Nam, concentration camp guards on the fields of Eastern Europe—what resemblance do their environments bear to a sterile room with a shock generator and an intercom, presided over by a white-coated scientist? As a setting, Milgram's surely is a prototype of an "unnatural" one.

One possible reaction to that fact is to dismiss the work bag and baggage, as Argyle (1969) seems to do: "When a subject steps inside a psychological laboratory he steps out of culture, and all the normal rules and conventions are temporarily discarded and replaced by the single rule of laboratory culture—'do what the experimenter says, no matter how absurd or unethical it may be'" (p. 20). He goes on to cite Milgram's work as an example.

All of this—which is perfectly true—comes in a discussion of how "laboratory research can produce the wrong results" (Argyle, 1969, p. 19). The wrong results! But that is the whole point of the results. What Milgram has shown is how easily we can "step out of culture" in just the way Argyle describes—and how, once out of culture, we proceed to violate its "normal rules and conventions" in ways that are a revelation to us when they occur. Remember, by the way, that most of the people Milgram interviewed grossly underestimated the amount of compliance that would occur *in that laboratory setting*.

Another reaction, just as wrong but unfortunately even more tempting, is to start listing similarities and differences between the lab setting and the natural one. The temptation here is to get involved in count-'em mechanics: The more differences there are, the greater the external invalidity. Thus:

> One element lacking in Milgram's situation that typically obtains in similar naturalistic situations is that the experimenter had no real power to harm the subject if the subject failed to obey orders. The subject could always simply get up and walk out of the experiment, never to see the experimenter again. So when considering Milgram's results, it should be borne in mind that a powerful source of obedience in the real world was lacking in this situation. (Kantowitz & Roediger, 1978, pp. 387–388)

"Borne in mind" to what conclusion? Since the next sentence is "Nonetheless, Milgram's results are truly remarkable" (p. 388), we must suppose that the remarks were meant in criticism.

Now the lack of threat of punishment is, to be sure, a major difference between Milgram's lab and the jungle war or concentration camp setting. But what happened? An astonishing two thirds obeyed anyway. The force of the experimenter's authority was sufficient to induce normal decent adults to inflict pain on another human being, even though they could have refused without risk. Surely the absence of power to punish, though a distinct difference between Milgram's setting and the others, only adds to the drama of what he saw.

There are other threats to the external validity of Milgram's findings, and some of them must be taken more seriously. There is the possibility that the orders he gave were "legitimized by the laboratory setting" (Orne & Evans, 1969, p. 199). Perhaps his subjects said in effect, "This is a scientific experiment run by a responsible investigator, so maybe the whole business isn't as dangerous as it looks." This possibility (which is quite distinct from the last one, though the checklist approach often confuses the two) does leave us with nagging doubts about the generalizability of Milgram's findings. Camp guards and jungle fighters do not have this cognitive escape hatch available to them. If Milgram's subjects did say "It must not be dangerous," then his conclusion—people are surprisingly willing to inflict danger under orders—is in fact weakened.

The important thing to see is that the checklist approach will not serve us. Here we have two differences between lab and life—the absence of punishment and the possibility of discounting the danger of obedience. The latter difference weakens the impact of Milgram's findings; the former strengthens it. Obviously we must move beyond a simple count of differences and think through what the effect of each one is likely to be.

VALIDITY OF WHAT?

Ultimately, what makes research findings of interest is that they help us understand everyday life. That understanding, however, comes from theory or the analysis of mechanism; it is not a matter of "generalizing" the findings themselves. This kind of validity applies (if it does) to statements like "The hunger-reduction interpretation of infant attachment will not do," or "Theory-driven inferences may bias first impressions," or "The Purkinje shift occurs because rod vision has *these* characteristics and cone vision has *those*." The validity of these generalizations is tested by their success at prediction and has nothing to do with the naturalness, representativeness, or even non-reactivity of the investigations on which they rest.

Of course there are also those cases in which one does want to predict real-life behavior directly from research findings. Survey research, and most experiments in applied settings such as factory or classroom, have that end in view. Predicting real-life behavior is a perfectly legitimate and honorable way to use research. When we engage in it, we do confront the problem of EV, and Babbie's (1975) comment about the artificiality of experiments has force.

What I have argued here is that Babbie's comment has force *only* then. If this is so, then external validity, far from being "obviously our ideal" (Campbell & Stanley, 1967), is a concept that applies only to a rather limited subset of the research we do.

A CHECKLIST OF DECISIONS

I am afraid that there is no alternative to thinking through, case by case, (a) what conclusion we want to draw and (b) whether the specifics of our sample or setting will prevent us from drawing it. Of course there are seldom any fixed rules about how to "think through" anything interesting. But here is a sample of questions one might ask in deciding whether the usual criteria of external validity should even be considered:

As to the sample: Am I (or is he or she whose work I am evaluating) trying to estimate from sample characteristics the characteristics of some population? Or am I trying to draw conclusions not about a population, but about a theory that specifies what *these* subjects ought to do? Or (as in linguistic apes) would it be important if *any* subject does, or can be made to do, this or that?

As to the setting: Is it my intention to predict what would happen in a real-life setting or "target" class of such settings? Our "thinking through" divides depending on the answer.

The answer may be no. Once again, we may be testing a prediction rather than making one; our theory may specify what ought to happen in *this* setting. Then the question is whether the setting gives the theory a fair hearing, and the external-validity question vanishes altogether.

Or the answer may be yes. Then we must ask, Is it therefore necessary that the setting be "representative" of the class of target settings? Is it enough that it be *a* member of that class, if it captures processes that must operate in all such settings? If the latter, perhaps it should be a "limiting case" of the settings in which the processes operate—the simplest possible one, as a psychophysics lab is intended to be. In that case, the stripped-down setting may actually *define* the class of target settings to which the findings apply, as in the dark-adaptation story. The question is only whether the setting actually preserves the processes of interest,[5] and again the issue of external validity disappears.

We may push our thinking through a set further. Suppose there are distinct differences between the research setting and the real-life target ones. We should remember to ask: So what? Will they weaken or restrict our conclusions? Or might they actually strengthen and extend them (as does the absence of power to punish in Milgram's experiments)?

Thinking through is of course another warm, fuzzy phrase, I quite agree. But I mean it to contrast with the cold creepies with which my students assault research findings: knee-jerk reactions to "artificiality"; finger-jerk pointing to "biased samples" and "unnatural settings"; and now, tongue-jerk imprecations about "external invalidity." People are already far too eager to dismiss what we have learned (even that biased sample who come to college and elect our courses!). If they do so, let it be for the right reasons.

REFERENCES

Argyle, M. (1969). *Social interaction*. Chicago: Atherton Press.

Babbie, E. R. (1975). *The practice of social research*. Belmont, CA: Wadsworth.

Bannister, D. (1966). Psychology as an exercise in paradox. *Bulletin of the British Psychological Society, 19*, 21–26.

Bickman, L. (1974, July). Social roles and uniforms: Clothes make the person. *Psychology Today*, pp. 49–51.

---

[5] Of course, whether an artificial setting does preserve the process can be a very real question. Much controversy centers on such questions as whether the operant-conditioning chamber really captures the processes that operate in, say, the marketplace. If resolution of that issue comes, however, it will depend on whether the one setting permits successful predictions about the other. It will not come from pointing to the "unnaturalness" of the one and the "naturalness" of the other. There is no dispute about that.

Brown, R., & Hanlon, C. (1970). Derivational complexity and order of acquisition in child speech. In J. R. Hayes (Ed.), *Cognition and the development of language*. New York: Wiley.

Brunswik, E. (1955). Representative design and probabilistic theory in a functional psychology. *Psychological Review, 62*, 193–217.

Campbell, D. T., & Stanley, J. C. (1967). *Experimental and quasi-experimental designs for research*. Chicago: Rand McNally.

Cappell, H., & Herman, C. P. (1972). Alcohol and tension reduction: A review. *Quarterly Journal of Studies on Alcohol, 33*, 33–64.

Deese, J. (1972). *Psychology as science and art*. New York: Harcourt Brace Jovanovich.

Hecht, S. (1934). Vision II: The nature of the photoreceptor process. In C. Murchison (Ed.), *Handbook of general experimental psychology*. Worcester, MA: Clark University Press.

Henshel, R. L. (1980). The purposes of laboratory experimentation and the virtues of deliberate artificiality. *Journal of Experimental Social Psychology, 16*, 466–478.

Higgins, R. L., & Marlatt, G. A. (1973). Effects of anxiety arousal on the consumption of alcohol by alcoholics and social drinkers. *Journal of Consulting and Clinical Psychology, 41*, 426–433.

Kantowitz, B. H., & Roediger, H. L., III. (1978). *Experimental psychology*. Chicago: Rand McNally.

Mello, N. K., & Mendelson, J. H. (1978). Alcohol and human behavior. In L. L. Iverson, S. D. Iverson, & S. H. Snyder (Eds.), *Handbook of psychopharmacology: Vol. 12. Drugs of abuse*. New York: Plenum Press.

Milgram, S. (1974). *Obedience to authority*. New York: Harper & Row.

Mook, D. G. (1982). *Psychological research: Strategy and tactics*. New York: Harper & Row.

Nisbett, R. E., & Ross, L. (1980). *Human inference: Strategies and shortcomings in social judgment*. New York: Century.

Orne, M. T., & Evans, T. J. (1965). Social control in the psychological experiment: Anti-social behavior and hypnosis. *Journal of Personality and Social Psychology, 1*, 189–200.

8

WHEN SMALL EFFECTS
ARE IMPRESSIVE

DEBORAH A. PRENTICE AND DALE T. MILLER

Psychologists are increasingly interested in statistical techniques that allow them to say something about the importance of their effects. This growing interest stems in large part from the realization that conventional significance-testing procedures provide an impoverished and possibly even misleading view of how seriously to take any particular result. Current wisdom regarding the use of statistics in psychological research holds that (a) the size of an effect is at least as informative as its statistical significance, if not more informative and (b) meta-analysis provides an important tool for assessing the reliability and magnitude of an effect across multiple studies (see, e.g., Cohen, 1990; Rosnow & Rosenthal, 1989). Underlying these points is the general argument that one should pay attention to size, as well as significance level, in deciding how impressed to be with an effect.

Whereas the use of effect size and other statistical measures of strength is relatively new in psychology, the goal of demonstrating the importance of an effect is not new at all. In this article, we examine the alternative ways in

Reprinted from *Psychological Bulletin*, *112*, 160–164. Copyright 1992 by the American Psychological Association.

which psychologists have approached this task and the implications of these approaches for questions of how much variance is accounted for. We argue that what makes some effects seem important is not their magnitude but rather the methodologies of the studies that produced them. The statistical size of an effect is heavily dependent on the operationalization of the independent variables and the choice of a dependent variable in a particular study. Thus, with sufficient ingenuity, a researcher can design an experiment so that even a small effect is impressive.

Our purpose here is to document these methodological strategies for demonstrating important effects. We consider effects to be important to the extent that they have had a major impact on thinking in the field (e.g., findings that are frequently cited, those that are featured in survey textbooks). Thus, our analysis is retrospective; we focus on examples of studies that have provided convincing demonstrations of the importance of certain psychological variables or processes, despite the fact that many of them have yielded small effects. Moreover, we make no assumptions about the motivations or intentions of the researchers whose work we cite but simply seek to make explicit the methodological approaches that they have used so successfully. We begin with a brief review of the rationale for using measures of effect size as an index of importance and then describe two alternative methodological strategies for demonstrating an important effect.

STATISTICAL STRENGTH OF AN EFFECT

One reasonable way to determine the importance of an effect is to compute it, using one of a family of effect-size measures (Cohen, 1977). The two most commonly used measures of effect size are the standardized mean difference (d) and the correlation coefficient (r), although there is an effect size index appropriate to any statistical test. These measures have many beneficial properties: (a) They indicate the degree to which a phenomenon is present in a population on a continuous scale, with zero always indicating that the phenomenon is absent (i.e., that the null hypothesis is true), (b) they come with conventions for what values constitute a small, medium, and large effect, (c) they provide some indication of the practical significance of an effect (which significance tests do not), (d) they can be used to compare quantitatively the results of two or more studies, and (e) they can be used in power analyses to guide decisions about how many subjects are needed in a study (see Cohen, 1977, 1990; Rosnow & Rosenthal, 1989). In short, effect size is a simple, easy-to-understand quantitative measure that provides one useful index of the importance of an effect.

An additional argument in favor of using effect size as a measure of importance is that effect sizes can be collected across studies. Most contemporary approaches to meta-analysis involve estimating effect sizes for each of a set of relevant studies or findings and then analyzing the mean and variability of these estimates (see Bangert-Drowns, 1986). Thus, effect size can serve as a measure of the importance of an effect not only in the context of a single study but also in a review of multiple studies conducted within a similar paradigm. For this reason, many researchers have suggested that effect sizes should be reported routinely for all significant and nonsignificant results (see Rosnow & Rosenthal, 1989).

ALTERNATIVE METHODS OF DEMONSTRATING THE IMPORTANCE OF AN EFFECT

Effect size and other measures of variance accounted for are unquestionably useful for assessing the magnitude of an effect and serve as an important supplement to conventional significance tests. One might question, in fact, why it has taken psychologists so long to discover these procedures (Cohen, 1990). One possible answer to this question is that in some areas of psychology, researchers have relied on alternative conceptions of what makes an effect seem important. Whether intentionally or unintentionally, these researchers have approached the problem of how to demonstrate the importance of an effect with more attention to design than to analysis: They have adopted methodological strategies that create impressive demonstrations, even though the studies often yield effects that are statistically small. We consider two of these strategies, along with their implications for statistical measures of strength.

Minimal Manipulations of the Independent Variable

One strategy for demonstrating important effects involves showing that even the most minimal manipulation of the independent variable still accounts for some variance in the dependent variable. A classic example of this approach is the so-called minimal group experiments of Tajfel and his colleagues (e.g., Billig & Tajfel, 1973; Tajfel, Billig, Bundy, & Flament, 1971). At the time these experiments were conducted, much research had already demonstrated that people favor members of their own group over members of other groups. But these investigators were interested in identifying the minimal conditions necessary to produce this ethnocentrism effect and thus conducted a series of studies using increasingly minimal manipulations of group membership. In one of the early studies in this series, boys were told that they tended either to overestimate or to underestimate the number of dots on briefly presented slides (Tajfel et al., 1971). When later given the opportunity to allocate points in a game, overestimators consistently allocated more points to other overestimators and underestimators to other underestimators. This effect was taken as strong evidence of ethnocentrism:

Even though the groups were based on a meaningless classification and members had no contact with each other, they still showed a preference for the in group.

Subsequent minimal group experiments provided still more convincing evidence of the importance of ethnocentrism without yielding effects of any greater magnitude. In the most minimal of the experiments, subjects were told that they were being assigned to groups at random and were even shown the lottery ticket that determined whether they were a member of the Phi group or the Gamma group (Locksley, Ortiz, & Hepburn, 1980). Even with explicit random assignment, subjects still showed a preference for members of their own group. The minimal group experiments, and this last study in particular, are impressive demonstrations of ethnocentrism, regardless of the size of the effects they produce. Indeed, the strength of these demonstrations derives not from the proportion of variance in allocations that group membership can account for but instead from the fact that such a slight manipulation of group membership can account for any variance in allocations at all.

Another example of this methodological tradition is provided by research on the effects of mere exposure on liking (see Harrison, 1977, for a review). Studies have demonstrated that exposure increases liking for stimuli as diverse as musical selections, Chinese-like characters, photographs of men's faces, and nonsense words, both in laboratory (Zajonc, 1968) and field (Zajonc & Rajecki, 1969) experiments. But just how mere an exposure is necessary to show increased liking? Additional investigations have focused on exploring the limits of this mere exposure effect. In one study, subjects listened to an audiotape of a prose passage in one ear while musical melodies played in their other, unattended ear. Even though they could not recognize the melodies later, subjects still liked them better than melodies to which they had not been exposed (Wilson, 1979). In another study, subjects were shown slides of geometric figures for durations too brief to permit recognition and still preferred these figures to those they had not previously seen (Kunst-Wilson & Zajonc, 1980). The minimal manipulations used in these studies did more than just provide yet another demonstration of the exposure–liking effect; they also showed how simply and subtly this effect could be produced.

The psychological literature (particularly the social psychological literature) offers many more examples of the minimalist approach to demonstrating an important effect. In these studies, the use of a minimal manipulation serves to demonstrate that even under the most inauspicious circumstances, the independent variable still has an effect. Consider, for example, a study by Isen and Levin (1972) that showed that putting people in a good mood leads them to be more helpful. They manipulated mood by giving some subjects cookies while they studied in the library (good mood) and giving other subjects nothing (control). There are clearly many stronger manipulations of mood that they might have used. They could, perhaps, have given good-mood subjects a free meal in a fancy restaurant or good grades in their courses or even a winning ticket in the lottery. These manipulations may very well have shown a stronger effect of mood on helping in terms of variance accounted for.[1] But Isen and Levin's cookie study still provides a convincing and memorable demonstration of the effect; the power of this demonstration derives in large part from the subtlety of the instigating stimulus. Indeed, this demonstration would become no less impressive if a meta-analysis on cookie studies showed that the manipulation accounted for little variance. Furthermore, although mood effects might be interesting however heavy-handed the manipulation that produced them, the cookie study was perhaps made more interesting by its reliance on the minimalist approach.

Choice of a Difficult-to-Influence Dependent Variable

A second approach to demonstrating important effects involves choosing a dependent variable that seems especially unlikely to yield to influence from the independent variable. A good example of this strategy comes from the literature on physical attractiveness. Many studies have shown that physically attractive people are seen as more intelligent, successful, sociable, kind, sensitive, and so on (see Berscheid & Walster, 1974 for a review). These findings suggest that physical attractiveness has a powerful effect on social perception. Even more convincing evidence of the importance of this effect comes from studies showing that physically attractive people receive more positive job recommendations, even when attractiveness could not possibly influence job performance (Cash, Gillen, & Burns, 1977). But could we imagine a still more impressive demonstration of the importance of physical attractiveness in social perception? Efran (1974) examined the effect of the physical attractiveness of a defendant on judgments of guilt and severity of punishment by a simulated jury. Even though legal judgments are supposed to be unaffected by such extraneous factors as attractiveness, in fact, Efran found that attractive defendants were judged less likely to be guilty and received less punishment than unattractive defendants (see also Sigall & Ostrove, 1975). This demonstration that physical attractiveness matters in the courtroom is impressive, despite the fact that it matters much less here than in other domains of interpersonal judgment. One is inclined to conclude from this study that if attractiveness can even affect legal judgments, then there is no domain of social perception that is immune to its influence.[2]

---

[1] We do not imply here that when a small manipulation produces a small effect, a large manipulation will always produce a large effect. Indeed, a linear relationship between the size of the manipulation and the size of the effect is not necessary to our claims about the importance of small effects. We argue that a result can be important regardless of its magnitude if it changes the way people think about a psychological variable or process.

[2] Sudnow (1967) has suggested that physical attractiveness may even influence the speed with which people are pronounced dead on arrival in emergency rooms. An empirical demonstration of this effect might well be the most impressive evidence for the importance of physical attractiveness yet!

Another example of achieving a convincing demonstration through selection of a resistant dependent variable is Asch's (1951) classic studies of conformity to group pressure. At the time that Asch undertook these studies, much research had already demonstrated the influence of group pressure on perceptual judgments when reality was ambiguous (e.g., Sherif, 1936). Asch believed that a truer test of the power of group pressure would require individuals to yield to a group judgment that they "perceived to be contrary to fact" (Asch, 1951, p. 177). In a prototypical study, a naive subject was asked to judge the length of a line after observing each of 8 other subjects (who were actually experimental confederates) give the same objectively incorrect answer. In this situation, one third of the judgments of naive subjects conformed with the erroneous judgment of the majority. This finding provides a striking demonstration of the importance of group pressure, regardless of whether one considers one third a large effect or a small effect. The fact that any subjects conformed to an obviously incorrect judgment is impressive.[3]

This strategy of showing that a psychological variable or process is important by demonstrating that it operates even in domains you would think were immune to its effects goes beyond the experimental tradition. For example, Durkheim's (1897/1951) finding of a relationship between social structure and suicide rates was impressive despite the fact that these macro variables surely cannot account for much of the variance. But the strength of the finding derives from the implication that if a behavior as individualistic and atomistic as suicide is correlated with social structure, we cannot assume that there is any microbehavior that is independent of it. Similarly, Freud's (1901/1971) analysis of the psychopathology of everyday life strongly suggested a pervasive influence of unconscious motives even though the incidence of slips of the tongue and lapses of memory is quite low. Again, the argument is that if the unconscious intrudes even in ordinary speech and memory, it must be quite powerful indeed.

Before leaving this section, we should note that judgments of the importance of an effect are, of course, highly subjective. Moreover, our arguments for the impressiveness of the demonstrations we have described apply primarily to researchers who focus on the independent variables or psychological processes under investigation, not to those who focus on the dependent variables. We would not, for example, expect a legal scholar to be impressed with the Efran study, nor would we necessarily expect a suicidologist to consider Durkheim's finding important. For investigators who define their research area in terms of a particular dependent variable or empirical relation-

---

[3] The Asch experiments also demonstrated how minimal a manipulation of group pressure was required to produce the effect by using an ad hoc group composed entirely of individuals unknown to the subject and by showing that even with only 3 members of the majority group (compared with 8 in the prototypical case), the effect still held.

ship (i.e., convergent researchers; see McGuire, 1983), variance accounted for may very well be the critical measure of the importance of an effect.

STATISTICAL VERSUS METHODOLOGICAL ROUTES TO AN IMPRESSIVE DEMONSTRATION

As we have suggested, statistical measures of variance accounted for are not the only tools researchers have to show that an effect is important. Despite the many virtues of these measures, in the context of particular studies, they can prove to be quite limited for conveying the importance of a finding. Declaring an effect to be important in effect-size terms is saying that a particular operationalization of the independent variable accounted for a lot of the variance in a particular dependent variable. This conception of importance makes sense if the experimenter is committed to the operations that were used to generate the data. If, however, the experimenter could easily have operationalized the independent variable differently or chosen a different dependent variable, the argument for using effect size, or more generally variance accounted for, as a measure of importance breaks down (see Mayo, 1978, for a similar argument).

In psychology, the utility of statistical versus methodological strategies for demonstrating the importance of an effect tends to divide along area lines. Statistical approaches are most useful in areas of psychology in which the operationalization of the independent variable and the choice of a dependent variable are clearly defined by the problem itself. For example, investigators interested in comparing the effectiveness of different methods of classroom teaching, the outcomes of different psychotherapeutic techniques, or the validity of different aptitude tests are typically committed to their operationalizations of these variables and to their choice of outcome measures. In these cases, effect size is a perfectly appropriate measure of importance, and indeed, meta-analyses have proven very useful for reviewing studies in these areas (see Bangert-Drowns, 1986).

By contrast, the problems addressed in other areas of psychology afford the investigator a great deal more latitude in decisions regarding experimental design. Investigators of the effects of ethnocentrism, stimulus exposure, or mood have many possible operationalizations of these variables at their disposal. Similarly, those interested in demonstrating the importance of physical attractiveness or group pressure can choose among a multitude of dependent measures. Social psychologists who study these problems often design their studies so as to explore the limits of the effects. Studies in this tradition are likely to result in some number of small effect sizes and skeptical meta-analyses. But although these effect sizes may force us to reconsider the strength of an operationalization or the choice of a dependent variable (both of which were, in fact, designed to yield small effects), they do not force us to reconsider the importance of an independent variable or a psychological process.

One difficulty raised by these methodological approaches to demonstrating an important effect is how to quantify them.[4] That is, how does one measure just how minimal a manipulation is or how unlikely a dependent variable is to yield to influence? Although we know of no simple metric on which to rely, one possible strategy is to argue, using Bayesian reasoning, that an effect is important to the extent that it increases the odds that a hypothesis is true compared with its alternatives (Abelson, 1990). For example, consider the hypothesis that a good mood increases helping. The odds that this hypothesis is true might be enhanced to a greater extent by an experiment showing that cookie recipients help more than by an experiment showing that lottery winners help more. Similarly, the hypothesis that physical attractiveness affects social perception might become relatively more likely given a demonstration that attractiveness affects judgments in the courtroom than that it affects judgments in the personnel office. This strategy works well in principle, but unfortunately, the practical difficulties of applying Bayes's theorem (e.g., estimating prior probabilities; see Abelson, 1990) limit its utility. Still, this Bayesian approach highlights the fact that the amount of variance an effect accounts for is just one of many ways to think about its importance and further suggests the possibility that alternative conceptions of importance can be quantified.

We are not the first to argue that small effects can, in fact, be important. Three major defenses of their potential importance have been offered previously: (a) Small effects may have enormous implications in a practical context, (b) small effects in ongoing processes may accumulate over time to become large effects, and (c) small effects may be quite important theoretically (see, e.g., Abelson, 1985; Mook, 1983; Rosenthal & Rubin, 1983; Yeaton & Sechrest, 1981). These arguments are well-taken, but they differ in both spirit and substance from what we are asserting here. In the types of studies we have described, small effects are important not because they have practical consequences nor because they accrue into large effects, nor because they lead to theory revision (indeed, in most of these cases, the effect or process under investigation was well established prior to the studies described). Instead, they are important because they show that an effect is so pervasive, it holds even under the most inauspicious circumstances.[5] More-

---

[4] In the examples in this article, we have set the criteria for a minimal manipulation of an independent variable and a difficult-to-influence dependent variable relative to other studies in the research area. For example, the minimal group studies use a minimal manipulation of group membership relative to other studies of ethnocentrism. However, one can conceive of these criteria more broadly in terms of people's expectations about whether a particular operationalization of an independent variable should have an effect or whether a particular dependent variable should be influenceable.

[5] Investigators have used a similar logic of showing that an effect holds even under inauspicious conditions by demonstrating an established effect on a population that seems very unlikely to be affected.

over, these methodological strategies for demonstrating importance underscore the fact that the size of an effect depends not just on the relationship between the independent and dependent variables but also on the operations used to generate the data. Many studies are not designed to account for a lot of variance and are no less impressive for the statistical size of the effects they produce.

SUMMARY AND CONCLUSIONS

In summary, we have argued here that although effect size can be a very useful measure of the strength of an effect, there are alternative ways to demonstrate that an effect is important. We have focused on two methodological approaches, in which importance is a function of how minor a manipulation of the independent variable or how resistant a dependent variable will still produce an effect. Our purpose has been to make explicit what experimenters who have used these methodologies have perhaps known implicitly: Showing that an effect holds even under the most unlikely circumstances possible can be as impressive as (or, in some cases, perhaps even more impressive than) showing that it accounts for a great deal of variance. Indeed, researchers might do well to consider these alternative goals (e.g., accounting for maximal variance, using the most minimal manipulation) when designing and reporting their studies.

The arguments we have made against the exclusive use of effect size as a means for evaluating the importance of empirical results apply equally well to regression analysis, path analysis, and all other techniques that are based on calculation of the proportion of variance accounted for. These techniques can tell us a lot about the strength of a particular operationalization, but their utility as measures of importance is limited by the relation of that operationalization to the independent variable or psychological process under investigation. In the studies we have described, investigators have minimized the power of an operationalization and, in so doing, have succeeded in demonstrating the power of the underlying process. Thus, a small effect size, low multiple correlation, or negligible path value will not lead these investigators to question their conclusions. On the contrary, they will be pleased that their effect survived the toughest test they could give it and will be more convinced than ever of its importance.

For example, showing that even physicians are overconfident about their diagnoses (Christensen-Szalanski & Bushyhead, 1981) or that even divinity students will not stop to help an emergency victim (Darley & Batson, 1973) provides impressive evidence for these psychological phenomena.

REFERENCES

Abelson, R. P. (1985). A variance explanation paradox: When a little is a lot. *Psychological Bulletin, 97,* 128–132.

Abelson, R. P. (1990). *Thinking about statistics.* Unpublished manuscript, Yale University.

Asch, S. (1951). Effects of group pressure upon the modification and distortion of judgments. In H. Guetzkow (Ed.), *Groups, leadership and men* (pp. 177–190). Pittsburgh, PA: Carnegie Press.

Bangert-Drowns, R. L. (1986). Review of developments in meta-analytic method. *Psychological Bulletin, 99,* 388–399.

Berscheid, E., & Walster, E. (1974). Physical attractiveness. In L. Berkowitz (Ed.), *Advances in experimental social psychology* (Vol. 7, pp. 157–215). San Diego, CA: Academic Press.

Billig, M., & Tajfel, H. (1973). Social categorization and similarity in intergroup behavior. *European Journal of Social Psychology, 3,* 27–52.

Cash, T., Gillen, B., & Burns, D. (1977). Sexism and "beautyism" in personnel consultant decision making. *Journal of Applied Psychology, 62,* 301–310.

Christensen-Szalanski, J., & Bushyhead, J. (1981). Physicians' use of probabilistic information in a real clinical setting. *Journal of Experimental Psychology: Human Perception and Performance, 7,* 928–935.

Cohen, J. (1977). *Statistical power analysis for the behavioral sciences.* San Diego, CA: Academic Press.

Cohen, J. (1990). Things I have learned (so far). *American Psychologist, 45,* 1304–1312.

Darley, J., & Batson, C. (1973). From Jerusalem to Jericho: A study of situational and dispositional variables in helping behavior. *Journal of Personality and Social Psychology, 27,* 100–108.

Durkheim, E. (1951). *Suicide* (J. Spaulding & G. Simpson, Trans.). Glencoe, IL: Free Press. (Original work published 1897)

Efran, M. (1974). The effect of physical appearance on the judgment of guilt, interpersonal attractiveness, and severity of recommended punishment in a simulated jury task. *Journal of Research in Personality, 8,* 45–54.

Freud, S. (1971). *The psychopathology of everyday life* (A. Tyson, Trans.). New York: Norton. (Original work published 1901)

Harrison, A. (1977). Mere exposure. In L. Berkowitz (Ed.), *Advances in experimental social psychology* (Vol. 10, pp. 39–83). San Diego, CA: Academic Press.

Isen, A. M., & Levin, P. F. (1972). The effect of feeling good on helping: Cookies and kindness. *Journal of Personality and Social Psychology, 21,* 384–388.

Kunst-Wilson, W., & Zajonc, R. (1980). Affective discrimination of stimuli that cannot be recognized. *Science, 207,* 557–558.

Locksley, A., Ortiz, V., & Hepburn, C. (1980). Social categorization and discriminatory behavior: Extinguishing the minimal intergroup discrimination effect. *Journal of Personality and Social Psychology, 39*, 773–783.

Mayo, R. J. (1978). Statistical considerations in analyzing the results of a collection of experiments. *Behavioral and Brain Sciences, 1*, 400–401.

McGuire, W. J. (1983). A contextualist theory of knowledge: Its implications for innovation and reform in psychological research. In L. Berkowitz (Ed.), *Advances in experimental social psychology* (Vol. 16, pp. 1–47). San Diego, CA: Academic Press.

Mook, D. G. (1983). In defense of external invalidity. *American Psychologist, 38*, 379–387.

Rosenthal, R., & Rubin, D. (1983). A note on percent of variance explained as a measure of the importance of effects. *Journal of Applied Social Psychology, 9*, 395–396.

Rosnow, R., & Rosenthal, R. (1989). Statistical procedures and the justification of knowledge in psychological science. *American Psychologist, 44*, 1276–1284.

Sherif, M. (1936). *The psychology of group norms*. New York: Harper & Row.

Sigall, H., & Ostrove, N. (1975). Beautiful but dangerous: Effects of offender attractiveness and nature of the crime on juridic judgments. *Journal of Personality and Social Psychology, 31*, 410–414.

Sudnow, D. (1967). Dead on arrival. *Transaction, 5*, 36–44.

Tajfel, H., Billig, M., Bundy, R., & Flament, C. (1971). Social categorization and intergroup behavior. *European Journal of Social Psychology, 1*, 149–178.

Wilson, W. (1979). Feeling more than we can know: Exposure effects without learning. *Journal of Personality and Social Psychology, 37*, 811–821.

Yeaton, W., & Sechrest, L. (1981). Meaningful measures of effect. *Journal of Consulting and Clinical Psychology, 49*, 766–767.

Zajonc, R. (1968). Attitudinal effects of mere exposure. *Journal of Personality and Social Psychology, Monograph Supplement, 9*(2, Pt. 2).

Zajonc, R., & Rajecki, D. (1969). Exposure and affect: A field experiment. *Psychonomic Science, 17*, 216–217.

9

WITHIN-SUBJECTS DESIGNS:
TO USE OR NOT TO USE?

ANTHONY G. GREENWALD

Frequently an investigator faces the choice of whether to examine the effects of two or more experimental treatments by exposing each subject to (a) only a single treatment (between-subjects design) or (b) several or all of the treatments (within-subjects or repeated-measures design). Grice (1966) has pointed out that the pattern of treatment effects obtained may vary considerably between the two types of designs. However, only rarely does an investigator make a choice of type of design after consideration of the appropriateness of each type to the problem being investigated. I attempt to assemble here several considerations that may often be appropriate to the decision between a within- or between-subjects design.

Although they are mentioned briefly, statistical considerations relating to choice of design are not of primary interest here. These statistical matters are well handled in standard statistical texts, as referenced below. My aim, rather, is to detail the *psychological* considerations that are critical to the

Reprinted from the *Psychological Bulletin, 83*, 314–320. Copyright 1976 by the American Psychological Association.

Preparation of this report was facilitated by support to the author from National Science Foundation Grant GS-42981 and National Institute of Mental Health Grant MH-20527.

choice of design. Some of these points are also covered in statistical texts, particularly insofar as they may affect the choice of statistical procedures. I have added only a few novel points to these earlier treatments and have aimed more at (a) putting the several points together in a single place and (b) observing that the prevailing cautions against the use of within-subjects designs need to be moderated without, however, being abandoned.

Poulton (1973, 1974; see also Rothstein, 1974) has recently issued a general warning against within-subjects designs, pointing out that the context provided by exposure to other treatments ("range effect") may often alter the effect of a given treatment. This point is certainly valid and is acknowledged here by considering (a) how procedures may serve to minimize or maximize such context effects and (b) when it may or may not be appropriate to allow the occurrence of context effects. The context effects that may be generated by a within-subjects design are discussed under three headings: Practice, Sensitization, and Carry-Over.

CONTEXT EFFECTS IN THE BETWEEN-SUBJECTS DESIGN

Poulton (1973) concluded that since context or range effects are to be expected in within-subjects designs, these designs should ordinarily be avoided or, if used, bolstered by between-subjects design results. Implicit in this conclusion is the principle that the between-subjects design provides a standard of validity against which results of a within-subject design must be evaluated. This may be questioned on three grounds. First, as Poulton (1973) noted, "The influence of range of stimuli cannot always be prevented by restricting each man to a single stimulus" (p. 115). This may be because extralaboratory experience leaves some residue of context. Second, even if the extralaboratory can be safely ignored, the presentation of a single treatment to each subject does not really achieve the *absence* of context, but rather the presence of the context provided by the single treatment. An example makes this clearer.

> Example 1: Researcher 1 uses two designs to study the effect of foreperiod duration on simple reaction time. In a between-subjects design, each subject is assigned to a single foreperiod treatment: 0, 200, 500, or 1,000 msec. In a parallel within-subjects design, each subject receives a series of trials in which the four treatments are randomly sequenced.

It is known that Researcher 1's results will be different for the two types of design. The within-subjects design may produce either an increasing or a decreasing function relating reaction time to foreperiod duration (see Poulton, 1973, Table 1). Which function will be obtained depends on whether the procedures are arranged to produce increasing or decreasing expectation of the response signal as the foreperiod grows. Thus, it may be said that the within-subjects design introduces an expectancy or readiness process that is affected by the context of other treatments (foreperiods).

Is this expectancy process absent from the between-subjects design? No—rather, readiness occurs and is focused at the end of the (single) expected foreperiod. Thus, the single treatment in the between-subjects design provides a very real context that influences performance. This context effect could be avoided by presenting each subject with only a single trial at the selected foreperiod duration, but this would be an impractical way of collecting data on the problem. Further, the researcher may well wish to *ignore* the first (or first several) trials, since these involve warm-up processes (effects due to lack of context!) that are not of interest.

These considerations raise the third basis for questioning the notion that between-subjects designs provide a standard of validity against which to evaluate within-subjects designs. In fact, the ecological or external validity (Campbell & Stanley, 1966) of a piece of research depends on the extent to which the research context approximates the context existing in the domain to which the researcher wishes to generalize the results. This point is considered further in the concluding section of this article.

STATISTICAL CONSIDERATIONS

No attempt is made here to detail the technical problems involved in statistics used to analyze the within- or between-subjects designs. However, a few general principles of a statistical nature must be considered as background. A more complete discussion of these points may be found in standard sources such as Myers (1972, especially chapter 7) and Winer (1971, especially chapter 4).

Power

When each subject provides data for two or more treatments, the subject may be said to serve "as his own control" in comparisons among treatment effects (i.e., treatment differences are not confounded with subject differences). To the extent that the *subjects* classification in the ensuing analysis of variance constitutes a substantial source of variance, this feature of the within-subjects design results in substantially more sensitivity to treatment effects (power) than would characterize a between-subjects design employing the same number of observations. Since a k-treatment between-subjects design would employ k times the number of subjects used in a within-subjects design with the same number of observations, it is apparent that a within-subjects design might often reach a desired level of power while using fewer than $1/k$ times the number of subjects in an equally powerful between-subjects design. The within-subjects design can therefore represent an immense experimental economy, particularly when per-subject costs are considerable in relation to per-treatment costs.

Violation of Assumptions

The standard analyses of within-subjects designs depend on an assumption of equality of the variances of differences between pairs of treatments (Winer, 1971, p. 272). It has been noted by statisticians that real data often violate this assumption and that the standard F ratio tests may be biased considerably by such violations. For this reason, within-subjects designs must be treated with a certain amount of special statistical care. Nonetheless, the techniques for dealing with violations of assumptions seem well enough established so that such violations can be tolerated but not ignored. The appropriate procedures include tests for extent of departure from assumptions, adjustments in degrees of freedom to correct for such departures, and the use of alternative statistical tests such as the multivariate analysis of variance (see Poor, 1973), which make less restrictive assumptions.

CONTEXT EFFECTS IN WITHIN-SUBJECTS DESIGNS

Practice

> Example 2: Researcher 2 is interested in assessing the effects of performance at a rotary pursuit task under three levels of distracting white noise: 75 db (A), 90 db (B), and 105 db (C). Should the effects of the three treatments be compared in a within- or between-subjects design?

A within-subjects design in which subjects were given Treatments A, B, C on Days 1, 2, 3 would suffer the obvious problem that the effects of treatments would be confounded with days. To the extent that performance on the motor skill task improves with practice, as is quite likely, this particular within-subjects procedure would yield seriously misleading results. There is a sometimes satisfactory remedy of *counterbalancing* the assignment of treatments to days in either (a) all possible combinations (six in this example) or (b) a balanced subset of combinations, as in a 3 × 3 Latin square design with *days* as the column factor, *groups of subjects* as the row factor, and *noise treatments* as the cell entries. This solution may not be satisfactory because the several treatments may be differently effective at different levels of practice. As a result, the observed treatment effects may be mixed inseparably with treatment-practice interactions.

At this point Researcher 2 should consider the relative interest of (a) treatment effects under minimum practice, (b) treatment effects under extensive practice, or (c) treatment effects across a range of practice levels (i.e., treatment–practice interaction). If the researcher is interested in treatment effects under minimum practice, the within-subjects design is inappropriate because subjects are providing data for two of the three treatments (more generally, $k - 1$ of k treatments) under more than minimum practice. A between-subjects design would be obligatory. If interest is in the treatment effect on the highly practiced skill, then a completely within-subjects design is possible, employing extensive practice to achieve a performance asymptote prior to administration of treatments in counterbalanced order. Finally, if interest is in the treatment effects across levels of practice, it may be best to use a combined between- and within-subjects design in which each subject provides data for performance at several levels of practice under only a single treatment condition.

The last design described above should be recognized as one of the most common instances of within-subjects designs—the learning experiment. Many psychologists would not think of studying practice effects with anything but a repeated-measurement assessment. Nonetheless, the decision to use a within-subjects design in a learning experiment should be made only after some thought. For a design with k different treatments and m levels of practice, it is possible to use km groups, each group being given a test of learning only once, after completion of the appropriate amount of practice. This might be advisable if the test for learning involves experiences that when applied repeatedly, might themselves affect performance. For example, paired-associate learning by passive exposure to word pairs could be tested after each passive exposure by presenting the first word of each pair and asking the subject to produce the second word that had been paired with each. For a variety of reasons, this type of test might affect later performance independently of what was learned during the exposure period. On the other hand, if an anticipation method is being used (learning trials consist of first-word presentation, after which the subject tries to produce the second before being shown it), then the researcher is able to obtain information on performance at various stages of practice without interfering in any way with the practice procedure. Here it would be folly to employ anything but a repeated-measurement procedure for the study of acquisition.

Summary

A within-subjects design should be avoided in studying effects of several treatments when the researcher is interested in the effects of the treatments in the absence of practice and practice is likely to affect performance (either a main effect of successive tests or an interaction of successive tests with treatments). For the purpose of using a within-subjects design, undesired practice effects may sometimes be controlled by counterbalancing the sequence of treatments, or may be avoided by providing extensive practice prior to administering any treatments. Choice among within- or between-subject procedures here should depend on the level(s) of practice at which it is appropriate to examine the treatment effects. Finally, the practice effect is often intended to be the direct object of study itself—in learning experiments. Here, within-subjects designs will often be appropriate, but only when performance information can be obtained (as it frequently can) without having an impact on the acquisition process.

Sensitization

> Example 3: Researcher 3 wishes to determine the effect of room illumination on worker productivity. Each subject is put to work on a well-learned task in a room in which the illumination is altered at periodic intervals in counterbalanced order across subjects, and the investigator determines the work rate under each illumination condition.

Researcher 3 should be concerned here with the possibility that the subject can readily discriminate the illumination differences and may thus be more sensitive and responsive to illumination than if there were exposure to only one of the several illumination level treatments. This sensitization to treatment variations may result in the subject's forming hypotheses about the treatment effects and responding to those perceived hypotheses rather than or in addition to the treatments themselves.

A variety of camouflaging strategies may be used to minimize the sensitization problem. The researcher in Example 3 may alter illumination from one treatment level to another so gradually that the subject will not notice it. In other circumstances, the experimenter may systematically alter several variables extraneous to the research design in order to draw attention away from a critical treatment variable (while, of course, not confounding the treatment with the extraneous variables).

The fact that perceptions of differences among treatments may be enhanced by their juxtaposition in a within-subjects design may be used to advantage in research when the experimenter is interested in observing the subject's capacity to discriminate such differences. Psychophysical studies constitute a large category of experiments in which the sensitization effect may be put to work for the researcher. In a brightness-judging experiment, for example, the experimenter is interested in the perceiver's sensitivity to brightness differences and wishes to optimize the conditions for observing such discrimination ability. By juxtaposing different treatments (brightnesses) in a within-subjects design, the limits of discrimination capacity can be assessed much more readily than in a between-subjects design.

Summary

A within-subjects design should be avoided when juxtaposition of treatments enhances perception of treatment variations *if* such perceptions can interfere with the processes the researcher desires to study. With ingenuity, it may often be possible to camouflage treatments so that this problem can be avoided. In quite a few experimental situations, particularly studies of perceptual discrimination, sensitization as a consequence of juxtaposing treatments (stimuli) in a within-subjects design will greatly facilitate the research.

Carry-Over

Example 4: Researcher 4 is interested in the effects of Drugs A, B, and C on performance on a single reaction time task. In order to employ a within-subjects design, Researcher 4 gives each subject four performance tests separated by 20 minutes, each test being preceded by the administration of a standard dosage injection of one of the three drugs or a placebo control and with the sequence of treatments being counterbalanced across subjects.

In general, a carry-over effect occurs when the effect of one treatment persists in some fashion at the time of measurement of the effect of another. In Example 4, there are two types of potential carry-over. One is due to practice at the performance task and has been discussed separately above. The second is that traces of prior drug treatments may be present at the time of testing the effects of a later treatment. Counterbalancing provides an only partially adequate solution of this problem, since the interference effects may not be bidirectional and, further, they may obscure the treatment effects of the drugs taken individually.[1]

The chief means of reducing carry-over effects is to separate the treatments in time. This would likely be an effective means of applying a within-subjects design to the problem given in Example 4, assuming that practice effects are not also involved. In general, the strategy of separating treatments in time will be effective in reducing intertreatment carry-over only to the extent that the effects of any treatment are not permanent.

In addition to the study of learning, there are several other major areas of study in which the target of study is some process that can be interpreted as an intertreatment carry-over in the framework of a within-subjects design. Perceptual assimilation and contrast, incentive contrast, violation of expectation, transfer of training, primacy–recency in persuasion, resistance to extinction, and various types of adaptation are some of these. The fact that intertreatment carry-overs are likely to be a major source of serendipitous findings should not be overlooked as one of the virtues of employing

---

[1] This inadequacy of counterbalancing involves the same considerations mentioned in discussing the possible inadequacy of counterbalancing in removing practice effects. Practice is certainly an instance of the general class of carry-over effects, but has been discussed separately because of the special status of learning effects in psychological research.

within-subjects designs in which treatments that would otherwise not be examined in near temporal proximity are juxtaposed.

Procedures that permit the occurrence of carry-over effects present special problems for statistical analysis. Cochran and Cox (1957, pp. 133–142) discussed a variety of means of estimating separately the direct and carry-over effects of experimental treatments.

Summary

When treatments have persistent effects, a within-subjects design may be unsatisfactory because the effect of one treatment may still be in force at the time of measuring another's effect. However, the within-subjects design may be salvaged in this case by increasing the separation of the treatments in time. Effects dependent on carry-over or, more generally, upon the sequence in which treatments are administered and their temporal proximity are frequently of psychological interest in and of themselves.

EXTERNAL VALIDITY

Several of the concerns already treated are appropriate to evaluating the internal validity of an experiment—that is, Does the within-subjects design permit the experimenter to test the hypothesis of interest, or will consequences of using the design in some way contaminate (by practice, sensitization, or carry-over) the hypothesis test? Now we take up a matter that may be at odds with some of these considerations and ask how the choice of design affects the external (or ecological) validity of the experiment (i.e., the ability of the researcher to account for the effects of treatment variations as they may occur in interesting nonresearch settings). (See Campbell & Stanley, 1966, for an exposition of internal and external validity.)

> Example 5: Researcher 5 is interested in the effects of source credibility on persuasion, and is considering two possible designs. In one, a between-subjects design, communications on two topics are attributed, for some subjects, to a trustworthy and expert source whereas, for other subjects, the same communications are attributed to an untrustworthy and inexpert source. In an alternate within-subjects design, each subject is exposed to the same two communications, but one is attributed to the high-credible source, the other to the low-credible source, with source-communication assignments being counterbalanced across subjects. Which design is preferable?[2]

---

[2] Both of the designs mentioned in this example are within-subjects or repeated-measurement designs in that the effects of two communications are studied on each subject. However, the treatment variation of credibility is a between-subjects variation in the first design and a within-subjects variation in the second.

Persons familiar with persuasion research will be aware that the be-tween-subjects design is most often chosen for the examination of source credibility effects (but not always—see Osgood & Tannenbaum, 1955). But this is perhaps the less justifiable choice if the researcher's primary interest is in predicting or characterizing source effects in the non-laboratory environment. Consider that people tend to be exposed to persuasive communications in clusters in many mass communication settings, these communications frequently being identified with different sources (e.g., columns in a newspaper editorial section, political or product advertisements in magazines, or on radio or television). Therefore, the within-subjects design for studying the consequences of communicator credibility may have greater external validity than does the between-subjects design.[3]

Similar considerations would lead to a preference for the between-subjects design for other problems. For example, a researcher may be interested in studying the effect of reinforcement-based versus psychoanalytically based therapies for phobia symptoms. In such a situation exposure of the same subjects to several different treatments would create a situation rather lacking in external validity.

Considerations of external validity should not necessarily be uppermost in the researcher's mind. The between-subjects design may be preferred even in some situations for which the within-subjects design would have greater external validity, because the between-subjects design may allow cleaner tests of theoretical hypotheses. Example 6 presents such a case, in which internal validity is of more concern to the investigator than is external validity.

> Example 6: Researcher 6 is interested in the effects of witnessing tele-vised violence on subsequent aggressive behavior of children. A within-subjects design would involve exposure of each subject to several different program sequences of varying degrees of violence, each followed by the provision of some opportunity to act aggressively in a play situation with other children. Should this design be employed?

In this case, the within-subjects design might not be preferable because the carry-overs among treatments (subjects still being under the influence of Program A at the time of Test B) might weaken the researcher's hypothesis test. Accordingly, the between-subjects design might be chosen even though the within-subjects design clearly has greater external validity in its correspondence to the mixture of types of programs the child would normally see on television.

---

[3] Poulton's (1973) concerns about range effects are quite relevant here. The investigator who is interested in generalizing to nonlaboratory settings should be concerned to see that the range and distribution of treatment variations in the experiment correspond to their range and distribution in the appropriate nonlaboratory setting. Otherwise, the experimental treatment effects may misrepresent the effects of their nonlaboratory analogs.

In many cases, a greater stress on internal validity than on external validity would lead to a choice of the within-subjects design. This might be particularly true in cases of basic research for which there is no readily apparent nonlaboratory setting for which the research is an analog. For example, a neuropsychologist studying functions of single cells in the central nervous system should almost certainly examine the consequences of the range of treatments in which he or she is interested on each of the research subjects.

Summary

Considerations of external or ecological validity may sometimes be at odds with considerations related to practice, sensitization, and carry-over effects. Thus, the within-subjects design may often have greater external validity because it contains these confounds, but these may also interfere with the researcher's ability to isolate the treatment effects.

CONCLUSIONS

A general force operating in the direction of selecting a within-subjects design is the statistical efficiency afforded by the removal of subject variance from error terms used to test treatment effects. However, context effects may often interfere with hypothesis tests and, therefore, should take precedence over considerations of statistical efficiency when choosing a design. Context effects may occur in either a between- or a within-subjects design, but the range of possible effects is much greater in the latter type of design and, correspondingly, the experimenter has greater potential control over them by selecting ranges of treatments to administer. In many situations a within-subjects design can be made more acceptable by appropriate counterbalancing of treatment sequences (to control practice effects), by camouflaging treatments (to reduce sensitization to the treatment dimensions), or by separating treatments in time (to reduce carry-over effects). In still other circumstances, the deliberate introduction of these context effects in a within-subjects design may have the desirable consequences of permitting the study of some interesting aspect of the context effect itself or of increasing the external (ecological) validity of the research.

REFERENCES

Campbell, D. T., & Stanley, J. C. (1966). *Experimental and quasi-experimental designs for research*. Chicago: Rand McNally.

Cochran, W. G., & Cox, G. (1957). *Experimental designs*. New York: Wiley.

Grice, G. R. (1966). Dependence of empirical laws upon the source of experimental variation. *Psychological Bulletin, 66*, 488–498.

Myers, J. L. (1972). *Fundamentals of experimental design* (2nd ed.). Boston: Allyn & Bacon.

Osgood, C. E., & Tannenbaum, P. H. (1955). The principle of congruity in the prediction of attitude change. *Psychological Review, 62*, 42–55.

Poor, D. D. S. (1973). Analysis of variance for repeated measures designs: Two approaches. *Psychological Bulletin, 80*, 204–209.

Poulton, E. C. (1973). Unwanted range effects from using within-subjects experimental designs. *Psychological Bulletin, 80*, 113–121.

Poulton, E. C. (1974). Range effects are characteristic of a person serving in a within-subjects experimental design—A reply to Rothstein. *Psychological Bulletin, 81*, 201–203.

Rothstein, L. D. (1974). Reply to Poulton. *Psychological Bulletin, 81*, 199–201.

Winer, B. J. (1971). *Statistical principles in experimental design* (2nd ed.). New York: McGraw-Hill.

III

ASSESSMENT

Researchers usually are interested in constructs (concepts) rather than measures. The exception, of course, is when they are focusing specifically on a particular measure they are evaluating or developing. A more concrete way of noting this is as follows: Individuals who are writing a proposal or article use the Introduction to the study to focus on concepts, their relation to one another, causes, mechanisms, and so on. When they move into the Method section, they describe ways of measuring those concepts. In the shift from concepts or constructs to measures, there is a special opportunity to be careless.

To assess the constructs of interest and the hypothesized relations in the study, one could select from an indefinite if not infinite number of measures, including those available and those that could be developed. Not all of the measures that reflect the construct would be expected to show the effects we predict. We already know that multiple measures of the "same" construct (e.g., multiple measures of psychopathology or of therapeutic change) are not perfectly correlated not only because of imperfect reliability of the individual measures but also because different measures often assess different facets of a construct. Stated differently, all measures of the construct of interest are not likely to support the hypotheses and predictions. A frequent recommendation in research is to use multiple measures of a given construct; indeed, a generally wise recommendation for researchers is to include in any given study few constructs and multiple measures of a given construct rather than multiple constructs and few measures (e.g., one measure per construct). This recommendation is based on efforts to evaluate constructs (concepts) better by representing each of them in multiple ways. The recommendation is methodologically sound, but it ignores a prior step to which much of this section is devoted. That prior step pertains to criteria to consider in the selection of measures for research. Often researchers select a measure for their research because it has been used previously. Wading through the literature to see if the measure has been used previously is important, but this is not the main, major, or most-informed criterion for deciding whether to include the measure in one's own study.

DESIGNING AND EVALUATING MEASURES

The first two articles in this section focus on scale development. The articles are relevant to developing a new measure but are included here for broader reasons. It is important to be aware of different ways in which scales are developed and to understand the conceptual model underlying the measure. That model is relevant because it may or may not be consistent with the model and hypotheses of the investigator who later puts the measure to a new use.

A discussion of scale development also conveys the criteria by which scales can be evaluated. All else being equal, investigators wish to select a measure that has gone through careful development, but what does that mean? Careful development is not a matter of using the measure and computing a few correlations that are consistent with what one might predict. The articles convey ways of developing a scale that will be useful when the occasion arises to devise a measure when one is not available or to weigh the strengths and likely utility of a given measure that is already available.

In the first article, René V. Dawis discusses the design and evaluation of measures that are developed for research. Different models of scale development are highlighted (e.g., Q-sort, Likert, Guttman, Rasch Methods) along with considerations that influence their selection. Critical issues are raised such as the development of unidimensional versus multidimensional scales, the role of factor analysis in scale evaluation, the relation of reliability and validity, and response bias. Each of these is important in the development of new scales and the evaluation of existing ones.

The next article, by Lee Anna Clark and David Watson, continues the discussion of scale development and relates this explicitly to construct validity and the role of theory in scale development. Key topics include conceptualization of the construct and its boundary conditions, item development, selection of the response format or scaling method, pilot testing, and criteria to select the final items on the basis of the initial data. The article conveys the importance of the investigator's conceptualization of the measure in the decision-making process of item selection and scale validation. Perhaps as valuable is the notion that, even when the investigator may not have an explicit model about the scale and the relation of the scale to the construct, the data analyses (e.g., solution used in factor analysis) to evaluate the measure may embrace a particular model. The article nicely integrates scale development, theory, and data analyses.

In the article by Samuel Messick, the concept of validity is elaborated more broadly. Construct validity is the unifying theme to which other validities contribute. The role of different types of studies in providing evidence for construct validity such as predicted changes in performance over time, differences between groups, and differences in response to experimental interventions or treatments play a central role. The different ways of validating a measure also convey research strategies that are important in their own right. Convergent and discriminant validity and other concepts in scale evaluation are presented. The article also discusses the value implications of test scores. That is, the construct, the underlying theory of the construct, and use of test scores have value implications and social consequences that are central to measurement development and validation. Illustrations are provided in the context of measuring psychopathology and intelligence in which the construct underlying the measure, the use to which the measure is put, and the limitations in interpreting the measure involve issues with significant social consequences.

MEASUREMENT AMONG DIFFERENT SAMPLES

Investigators often may consider an assessment device as an entity in its own right with properties (e.g., reliability, validity) that are established for that measure. That is, the evidence in behalf of the measure is considered somehow to inhere in the measure itself. Actually, the evidence in behalf of a measure is dependent on conditions of administration, that is, all those facets with which the validation evidence has been associated. Measures are often extended beyond the conditions in which they were originally developed. One of the common extensions is use of a measure with new populations. Such extensions are not inherently problematic. However, if the existing validation evidence does not include sampling data from the pertinent population, then use of the measure ought to include effects to support the meaning and interpretation of the measure in this new application. In principle, one could argue that any sample could be conceived as drawing from a "new" population because of some characteristics that were not part of the original validation sample. For example, one could say that even though the measure was validated with young adults, it was not used with the young adults in a particular study. These young adults were born later than those of the original sample and might, by growing up at a different time, behave differently. This concern may or may not be trivial, depending on the focus of the measure (e.g., on views of gender roles, politics, various substances such as alcohol or marijuana, which may change over time). The investigator's conceptualization of the measure, along with existing validation evidence, determine whether the application of the measure to a different sample warrants supplementary validity information to aid interpretation.

In applying measures to diverse populations, it is important to be sensitive to a variety of issues. Sumie Okazaki and Stanley Sue discuss assessment issues that emerge in extending measures to diverse ethnic groups. The article examines methodological issues, beyond assessment considerations, including what comparisons ought to be made to draw influences about ethnicity, what variables might be controlled, and what defines a population or subpopulation—that is, at what level of generality ought a particular group be studied (e.g., is it meaningful to study Asian Americans or American Indians as a group, given the many subdivisions and different cultures that can be distinguished within each group?). Apart from these critical issues, broader conceptual and methodological issues are raised about sampling, the importance of cross-validation of measures among samples, and the use of college students versus community samples. The equivalence of measures across samples is also raised and reflects the extent to which the underlying construct holds the same meaning among different samples and whether the measure reveals similar psychometric properties (e.g., reliability and validity) for these populations. These issues foster greater care in conceptualizing use of measurement techniques and underscore the importance of including within a study evidence that the measure behaves in a way that is consistent with prior uses or supports the construct and conceptualization the investigator has in mind. Moreover, studying constructs among different populations, groups, or cultures, represents an important line of work. One can theorize about population differences and in the process raise important substantive questions about culture, development, and values.

DESIGNING AND
EVALUATING MEASURES

10

SCALE CONSTRUCTION

RENÉ V. DAWIS

Scales are ubiquitous features of counseling psychology research. For instance, examination of a randomly chosen issue of the *Journal of Counseling Psychology* (1984, Vol. 31, No. 3) showed that all 12 major articles in the issue reported on studies that involved the use of scales.

As the term is used in counseling psychology research, a *scale* is a collection of items, the responses to which are scored and combined to yield a scale score. Scale scores can be categorized according to level of measurement. At the lowest, nominal level of measurement, scale scores are used to name or designate (identify) the classification categories to which the objects of measurement are grouped. At the ordinal level, scale scores rank order the measured objects along the classificatory dimension. At the interval level, scale scores reflect the relative distances between and among measured objects. At the ratio level, scale scores indicate the absolute distance of any measured object from a true-zero point on the scale. Few, if any, psychological scales are even-interval scales (Thomas, 1982).

Reprinted from the *Journal of Counseling Psychology, 34,* 481–489. Copyright 1987 by the American Psychological Association.

Scales can also be classified according to the source of scale score variation, following Torgerson (1958), as stimulus-centered, subject-centered, or response scales. Scale scores in stimulus-centered scales (also called judgment scales) reflect stimulus (item) differences along the measurement dimension. An example would be a life events scale, in which a respondent rates or ranks particular life events in terms of respondent rates or ranks particular life events in terms of how stressful they are to the respondent. In contrast, for subject-centered scales (also called individual differences scales), scale scores reflect differences among the subjects (respondents) in terms of their standing along the scale's dimension. Personality trait scales of the inventory or questionnaire variety are common examples of subject-centered scales. Lastly, response scales are those for which scale score variation is attributed to both stimuli (items) and subjects (respondents). Scales constructed according to the Rasch scaling methodology (Wright & Masters, 1982) are examples of response scales.

For the purposes of this article, the term *scale* will be limited to those instruments that are constructed by researchers in order to obtain quantitative data on variables for which appropriate standardized instruments are not available. Examples of such variables are counselee and counselor perceptions (cognitions), evaluations, feelings, attitudes, plans, and actions (behaviors) as these occur before, during, and after the counseling process. To instrument such variables, researchers have often had to construct their own scales. Typically, such scales rely on the research participant's verbal report, and response by the participant is structured, that is, limited to given choices. This article focuses, therefore, on the construction of verbal, structured scales of the rating, questionnaire, or inventory type. I do not discuss the construction of tests or what Cronbach (1984) calls measures of maximum performance (i.e., ability, aptitude, achievement, knowledge, or skill tests), for which a large literature is available.

The scale construction process may be divided into three stages: design, development, and evaluation. Each stage is discussed in turn.

SCALE DESIGN

Designing a scale requires, first of all, some theory of the scale that includes a well-articulated definition of the psychological variable to be measured and indications of how it is to be measured. Definition of the variable depends on the larger theory that impels the research. Definition includes distinctions (what the variable is and what it is not), dependencies (how the variable is a function of more basic or previously defined terms), and relations (how the variable is related to other variables). How the variable is to be measured depends on a number of considerations, such as how best to represent the variable, who the respondents will be, the context and conditions under which the measure is to be administered, and the research design of the study, especially the analyses planned. In short, the theory of the scale should give the scale constructor directions as to scale content (the writing of items) as well as scale format (the type of scale to construct).

Scale Content

A useful preliminary to item writing is to conduct open-ended interviews with representative subjects from the target respondent population. Skillful interviewing can elicit a wide range of statements about the variable in question. The interviewee's own words can then be used in writing the items. Such use can provide a degree of authenticity that in turn can contribute to the scale's validity. For example, a scale to be filled out by clients to describe the counselor's behavior would be much more acceptable and credible to the clients if it were expressed in their (lay) language rather than in the more technical (if more precise) language of theory. Use of respondents' own words will also mean that readability of the scale will be less of a problem. Whether respondents' own words are used or not, it is good practice to check on the readability level of the scale to make sure that it is appropriate to the level of the respondent population. Useful hints on writing readable items are given by Payne (1951) and Fiske (1981).

The initial pool of items can be written to be homogeneous or heterogeneous in content. The scale design should indicate what degree of content heterogeneity is desired, based on the theory of the scale. A useful aid in this regard is to look at the scale data matrix as a two-factor, completely crossed with no replication analysis of variance design, in which the two factors are items and respondents. One can then see that, depending on the researcher's purposes, the scale can be so constructed as to maximize item effect only, respondent effect only, or item-by-respondent interaction. Maximizing item effect will require heterogeneous items; minimizing it will require homogeneous item content.

If items are explicitly derived from hypotheses from the larger theory, it might be useful to do a "back translation" (Smith & Kendall, 1963). That is, competent judges who were not involved in the writing of the items could be asked to assign the items back to the hypotheses or hypothesized categories. Back translation can be a useful check on the coverage of the content domain as outlined by the design of the scale.

Scale Format

Items in structured verbal scales typically consist of a stimulus part (the item stem) and a response part (the response choices). Item stems may consist of full sentences, phrases, or even single words. They may describe some at-tribute of an object (e.g., "The counselor appears trustworthy"), or the state of the object ("The counselor is passive"), or some event involving the ob-ject ("The counselor is reflecting the client's feelings"), to varying degrees of specificity or generality. Item stems ordinarily consist of single components but may have two or more components (as in paired comparison or multiple rank-order scales).

Response choices in structured verbal scales vary in their underlying measurement dimension (e.g., agree–disagree, like–dislike, important–unimportant). They also vary in response format. Rating response formats differ in the number of scale points (choices) given the respondents (2-, 3-, or 5-point scales are the most common), and in the way scale points are an-chored. Anchors can be words (*yes–no*, *true–false*), phrases (*strongly agree–strongly disagree*), or more extended prose as in behaviorally anchored scales, (e.g., Campbell, Dunnette, Arvey, & Hellervik, 1973). Rating scales may be anchored at each scale point or only at selected scale points (e.g., at the ends and the middle of the scale). Response choices may be unweighted (scored with 0, 1 weights), or weighted using multiple weights. Rating response for-mats may be one-sided (zero to positive or to negative values) or two-sided (with both positive and negative sides of the continuum).

Ranking response formats are fewer in number, differing only in the number of elements ranked within an item (e.g., paired comparison, multiple rank orders such as triads and tetrads, or, at the extreme, a single ranking of all elements). Ranking response formats use ranks rather than weights as scores and by convention, ranks are ordered in a manner opposite that of weights in the racing response format, that is, the lower the number, the higher the rank.

In choosing a scale format, the general rule might be to choose the sim-pler format. However, there are other considerations: More complex formats might make the task of filling out the scale more interesting for the more ex-perienced or knowledgeable respondent. When rating response formats are used, more scale points are better than fewer, because once the data are in, one can always combine scale points to reduce their number, but one cannot increase that number after the fact. Also, more scale points can generate more variability in response, a desirable scale characteristic if the response is reliable. Inordinate use of the middlemost scale point can be avoided by eliminating that scale point, that is, by using an even number of scale points. This has the further advantage of ensuring that the underlying dimension will be linear or can be made linear. At times rank ordering may be easier to do than rating, but use of ranking response formats may place limits on the statistical analysis of the data. Finally, the amount of space available for the scale (e.g., in an extended questionnaire) might preclude the use of certain formats.

SCALE DEVELOPMENT

Scale development consists of collecting data with the use of a preliminary form and analyzing the data in order to select items for a more final form. ("More final" is intended to indicate that the process might have to undergo one or more iterations depending on the results of the evaluation stage.) It is always useful to conduct a small N pilot study before the main data collection effort. The pilot study can be used to check out such nuts-and-bolts points as how easily the scale instructions are followed, how well the scale format functions, how long the scale takes to complete, and especially, how appropriate the scale items are for the target respondent population.

As a rule, the development sample should be representative of the target respondent population. There can be exceptions, however; for example, in developing stimulus-centered scales, one could use a sample that is more homogeneous than samples from the target population.

At the heart of scale construction is the scaling method used to select items. Several methods are described, grouped according to the type of scale (stimulus-centered, subject-centered, or response) with which they are typically associated. A fourth group of methods, the external criterion methods, which select items on a different basis, are also described.

Stimulus-Centered Scale Methods

Because counseling psychology is concerned with the individual client, one might expect more frequent use of stimulus-centered scales than apparently is the case. How a particular client scales stimuli (e.g., stressfulness of life events, preference for occupations) regardless of how others do it should be just as significant for counseling as how the individual compares with others, if not more so. Stimulus-centered scales would appear to be particularly appropriate to use in monitoring the progress of the client during counseling.

The prototypic method for developing stimulus-centered scales was the Thurstone method (Thurstone & Chave, 1929). From this method developed the popular Q sort. Rank-order methods are also frequently used to construct stimulus-centered scales. Brief descriptions of these methods follow:

The Thurstone Method

Thurstone's groundbreaking insight was that questionnaires could be constructed as scales by the application of the methods of psychophysics. The Thurstone method proceeds as follows:

1. A large number of statements (say, 200 to 300) are written about the construct, to represent the range of the construct.

2. A number of judges (say, 20 to 30) are asked to sort the items with respect to the underlying measurement dimension and to assign an appropriate scale value (scale point on the numerical scale) to each item. An 11-point scale is typically used.
3. The central tendency and variability of scale values assigned to it are computed for each item.
4. On the basis of their average scale values, two or three items with the lowest variabilities are selected to represent each scale point. Thurstone scales typically have 22 items.

After the items have been selected, they are arranged in random fashion in a questionnaire. Respondents are instructed, for instance, in the case of an attitude scale, to identify those items that they endorse. (Similar instructions can be given for other types of scales, for example, identifying the items descriptive of self, or of another person being rated, or of the events being observed.) The scale score is calculated as the average of the scale values of the endorsed items.

The Thurstone method, although a historic methodological breakthrough, has not found much favor with scale constructors, and is practically unheard of in counseling psychology. Much better known is its derivative, the Q sort.

The Q-sort Method

The Q-sort method (Stephenson, 1953) has been used extensively in personality research, especially in research on the self-concept. The Q-sort method starts with a fixed set of stimuli (e.g., self-descriptive statements). The respondent is asked to sort the stimuli along a scale according to scale value (e.g., least to most descriptive). To ensure variability in the scores and to forestall response biases such as central tendency or leniency, the respondent might be asked to force the stimuli into a distribution, for example, for a 5-point scale, a 7%-24%-38%-24%-7% distribution.

The Q sort is useful in situations in which multiple response roles (positions) are taken with respect to the same set of stimuli (e.g., in self-concept research, "How I actually am," "How I would like to be," "How others see me," etc., are response roles that can be used with the same set of self-descriptors). Q-sort data are typically used in Q correlation (correlation between persons across variables) or in O correlation (correlation between occasions across variables). They may also be used in ordinary R correlation, unless the forced distribution method is used. In the latter case, the Q-sort scores will be ipsative. Ipsative scores (Clemans, 1966) are those in which the scores for an individual are distributed around that individual's mean and not around the population mean. Ipsative scores are not on a common scale for all individuals and therefore cannot be used in analyses that assume a common scale, for example, correlating variables across individuals, factor analysis, or analysis of variance. However, they would be appropriate in correlating individuals across variables (i.e., in Q correlation).

Rank-Order Methods

The two frequently used rank-order methods are the paired comparison method and the ranking method.

In the paired comparison method (Guilford, 1954), each stimulus (e.g., person, object, event, state, or condition) is paired with every other stimulus. The respondent's task is to select one stimulus from each pair on the basis of the scaling dimension, that is, the basis of comparison. From the number of times each stimulus is chosen, the stimuli can be rank ordered with more precise information than if all of the stimuli were just rank ordered in the usual way. (The additional information comes from circular triads, i.e., where A is chosen over B, B over C, and C over A. Such information is not obtained in ordinary ranking.)

Each stimulus' "score" (number of times chosen) can also be converted to a z score, using the normal curve table. Such z scores would be ipsative. The ipsative character of these z scores can be minimized by calibrating each individual's scores to that individual's zero point. This zero point can be ascertained (for each individual) by adding an absolute judgment scale (a two-categoried scale; see Guilford, 1954, pp. 171–173).

Because the number of pairs increases rapidly with increase in number of stimuli (for n stimuli, the total number of pairs equals $n[n - 1]/2$), the paired comparison method becomes impractical when more than 20 stimuli are involved. For such situations, the method of multiple rank orders (Gulliksen & Tucker, 1961) can be used, in which, instead of presenting stimuli in pairs, they are presented in blocks of threes (triads) or more, but in such a manner that each stimulus is paired only once with every other stimulus. (Special designs are necessary to accomplish this. See Guilliksen & Tucker, 1961.) If collected in this way, the data from the multiple rank orders can be reduced to paired comparisons, and then scaled as paired comparisons.

At the other extreme to paired comparisons is the ranking method. Ranking can be used with any number of stimuli. For small numbers, the instructions are straightforward. For large numbers of stimuli (i.e., more than 20), the reliability of the ranking can be improved by using the alternation ranking procedure, in which the respondent alternates between picking the highest and lowest ranks (i.e., first, the first ranked; next, the last ranked; then, the second ranked; then, the next to the last ranked; the third ranked, etc.). As with paired comparison data, ranking data can also be converted to z scores (Guilford, 1954).

Ranking data, that is, rank scores, whether obtained by the paired comparison, multiple rank orders, or ranking method, should be analyzed by using nonparametric statistics (Siegel, 1956), especially rank-order statistics.

When converted to z scores with a zero point, however, the data can be analyzed with the use of ordinary parametric statistics.

Subject-Centered Scale Methods

Subject-centered scales are probably the kind of scale in most frequent use in counseling psychology research. Individual differences in both the clients and the counselors are thought to account for significant portions of counseling outcome variance. Also, possibly because individual differences variables are among the most easily accessible to researchers, much effort has been put into constructing and developing subject-centered scales.

The classic method for developing subject-centered scales is the Likert method. Refinements in the method have been introduced via factor analysis. A variant of the method, the semantic differential, has proven quite useful. These methods are described below.

The Likert Method

Just as Thurstone saw the application of psychophysical methods to scaling nonsensory stimuli, so did Likert (1932) see the application of psychometric methods to scaling nonability-test items. The Likert procedure can be described as follows:

1. A number of items are written to represent the content domain. Five-point anchored rating scales are typically used as response choices for each item (hence, the mistaken use of *Likert* to refer to the 5-point-rating item format). Scoring weights from 1 to 5 assigned to the five rating-scale points. Direction of scoring (whether 1 or 5 is high) is immaterial provided it is consistent for all items.
2. The items are administered to a large group of respondents (N of at least 100). Each respondent's item rating choices are scored and the item scores summed to constitute the respondent's total score.
3. Items are selected according to their ability to discriminate between high and low scorers on total score. Likert used a group-difference procedure (difference in item means between high-scoring and low-scoring groups, e.g., uppermost 25% and lowermost 25%). One could also use an item-total-score correlation procedure, as is currently done in ability test construction. Maximizing item-total-score correlation will also maximize the scale's internal consistency reliability coefficient (coefficient alpha). Computer programs (e.g., the Statistical Package for the Social Sciences Reliability program) are available for use in this connection.

4. The best discriminating items are then selected to constitute the scale, and the scale score is obtained by summing the item scores for the selected items. At this point, scale scores can be treated as normative scores (i.e., transformed to standardized scores, used to determine percentile equivalents for specific populations, etc.).

Of all the scale construction methods, the most convenient for researchers is the Likert method because it can be employed with the use of ordinary SPSS programs. To implement the Likert method requires only (a) computing total score, (b) computing item-total-score correlations, and (c) computing alpha reliability for the final set of items. Incidentally, reliability should be computed for every research use of Likert scales, not just at scale development, because reliability is a function not only of the scale but also of the respondent sample.

Unfortunately, not all scales that are purported to be Likert-type scales are constructed according to the Likert procedure. They only look like Likert scales because of the use of the 5-point rating response format (Triandis, 1971). If, in such scales, the correlation of the items with total scale is not high, then the interpretation of the scale score is problematic.

Use of Factor Analysis

Factor analysis is a data reduction technique in which a large set of variables is reduced to a smaller set without much loss of information. The technique can be used to select items for Likert-type scales in the following way:

1. The items in the item pool are intercorrelated.
2. The item intercorrelation matrix is subjected to a principal components analysis. (This requires the use of the principal axis solution, with unities in the diagonal, and extracting only the first factor.)
3. The items with the highest loadings are selected for the scale. *Highest loading* can be defined in an absolute sense (e.g., at least .707 or .50, which would represent 50% and 25%, respectively, of the item variance) or in a relative sense (the loading squared, as a proportion of the communality, e.g., no less than 50%).
4. There may be instances in which certain items are essential to the definition of the scale but are not found among the highest loading ones, that is, are not selected by this procedure. In this case, the scale constructor can go back to the original item intercorrelation matrix and eliminate all items that correlate below a given level (e.g., .30) with the essential defining items. The reduced matrix can then be factor analyzed.

5. When a content domain represented in an item pool is thought or assumed to be multidimensional, factor analysis can be used to construct several scales at the same time. The procedure is the same as above, except that more than one factor (component) is extracted. An additional step, factor rotation, is usually required to find a best (simple structure) solution, the procedure most frequently preferred being orthogonal rotation to a varimax criterion. A scale is then constructed for each factor, with items selected as described above. If an item is selected for more than one scale, the researcher can choose (a) to assign it to the scale with the highest loading, (b) to assign it to all the scales for which it was selected, or (c) to leave it out altogether. Choices (a) and (c) waste some information, but choice (b) will contribute to an artifactual interscale correlation that is undesirable.

As with Likert scales, all scales developed via factor analysis should be evaluated for reliability each time they are used.

The Semantic Differential

The semantic differential (Osgood, Suci, & Tannenbaum, 1957), like the Likert, makes use of the rating response format. Unlike the Likert, which uses only one rating dimension for all items in a scale, the semantic differential uses several rating dimensions for rating the same item or stimulus object. Semantic differential rating dimensions are typically bipolar, anchored at both ends with contrasting adjectives, with a 7-point rating continuum. Provided that response distributions are not forced, semantic differential data can be treated like any other rating data.

Response Scale Methods

If stimuli can be assigned scale scores and subjects can be assigned scale scores, the next logical development should be to develop scale construction methods that assign scale scores to both subjects and stimuli. Such development has been going on (e.g., Coombs, 1964) but has been the province mainly of psychologists interested in scaling models and psychological modeling. Only relatively recently has response scale development had an impact on instrument construction in applied psychology (e.g., Lord & Novick, 1968). It has had practically no impact on counseling psychology research.

For the sake of completeness, however, and to illustrate the response scale approach, one of the earliest and more influential scaling methods—Guttman's scalogram technique—will be described. A more recently developed technique, the Rasch (1960) method, will also be briefly discussed.

The Guttman Method

Guttman's (1944) concern was the property of unidimensionality in a scale. With a unidimensional scale, according to Guttman, knowledge of the respondent's scale score should permit the reproduction of the respondent's item score pattern. In a unidimensional scale, the items can be arranged in order (of endorsement or descriptiveness or whatever the underlying dimension is) in such a way that positive response to an item (e.g., *agree*, in an attitude scale) should imply positive response to all other items lower down the scale, and conversely, negative response to an item should imply negative response to all other items higher up the scale. To ascertain unidimensionality, Guttman developed the scalogram technique.

Suppose we had a unidimensional attitude scale that was administered to a group of individuals. The scalogram technique would call for the data to be displayed as follows: Items are displayed as columns and ordered (from left to right) according to endorsement level from the most to the least endorsed item. Individuals are displayed as rows and ordered (from top to bottom) according to total score, from highest to lowest score. If the test were perfectly unidimensional, then the scalogram would show an orderly stepwise progression of endorsement for both the individuals and the items. Any exceptions to this expectation can be easily seen in a scalogram display, and the number of exceptions can be expressed as a proportion of the total matrix (N individuals $-$ m items). Guttman (1944) defines a *coefficient of reproducibility* as 1 minus the proportion of exceptions, where 1.00 means that the response pattern for any given scale score can be reproduced perfectly.

When the coefficient of reproducibility is not high (e.g., below .9 or .8), the scalogram display will reveal the items that do not conform to expectation. After removing these items, the coefficient of reproducibility is recalculated, and the process repeated until the desired level of the coefficient is attained. Sometimes it may also be necessary to eliminate some aberrant individuals whose responses do not conform to the expected pattern. (This underscores the fact that response is a function not just of the scale or instrument but also of the respondent population. Aberrant individuals might be hypothesized to belong to a different population insofar as the scale is concerned.)

The classic Bogardus (1928) social distance scale illustrates what Guttman had in mind. Respondents were asked whether they would be willing to admit members of a race or nationality group (a) to close kinship by marriage, (b) to membership in their club, (c) to their streets as neighbors, (d) to employment in their occupation, (e) to citizenship in their country, (f) only as visitors to their country, or (g) whether they would exclude them completely from their country. Admitting individuals at one level implies admitting them at lower levels but does not imply admitting them at higher levels.

The Rasch Method

The Rasch model, one of a group of models originating from item response theory, was initially developed in connection with the construction of ability tests. The model expresses Guttman's basic ideas in a probabilistic manner, as follows: (a) Given any item, a person of higher ability should have a higher probability of getting the item right than would a person of lower ability, and (b) given any person, an item of lower difficulty should be solved (gotten right) with a higher probability than would an item of higher difficulty. The model has since been extended to the construction of non-ability measures (e.g., attitude scales) by, among others, Wright and Masters (1982).

The Rasch model postulates that item response is a function of two parameters, an item parameter and a person parameter. As examples: For ability tests, the parameters would reflect item difficulty and person ability; for attitude scales, item endorsement, and person attitude; for interest measures, item liking (liking for an item) and person interest. The parameters are estimated from the item-by-score matrix (persons with the same scores are grouped together). Parameters are estimated from the data, given that the model is true (i.e., with the model as the premise). The data's fit to the model can be assessed, and if the fit is poor, one infers that the model's assumptions have not been met.

If the fit is acceptable, the data can be improved by eliminating the items that show a poor fit (and in theory, the persons that have a poor fit, as well). Thus, by eliminating poorly fitting items, the refined scale is assumed to be unidimensional. (The reader will note the similarity to the Guttman technique.)

Calculation of parameter estimates for the Rasch model is typically done via computer, although hand calculation methods are also available (Wright & Masters, 1982).

All of the scale development methods described thus far make use of the item-by-person data matrix in determining which items to retain in, or eliminate from, the scale. A final group of methods makes use of external criteria and the relation of items to external criteria in determining which items to select. These methods were developed in the context of the practitioner's problem of predicting outcomes (e.g., in vocational choice and personnel selection). For these methods, the choice of criterion (or criteria) is all-important because it preordains the items that are selected.

External Criterion Methods

Item selection, again, is the key question in scale construction by external criterion methods. The three most-used methods of item selection are (a) the group difference method, (b) the item validity method, and (c) the multiple regression method. It is assumed that the criterion variable has been selected and that an adequate measure of it is available. Criterion variables typically reflect whatever it is that psychologist-practitioners are trying to effect, for example, client satisfaction, client choice, client behavior. (To simplify discussion, a single criterion variable is assumed, although a scale can be constructed to predict to multiple criteria.)

In the group-difference method, items for the scale are selected according to the difference in mean item scores between two groups, a high criterion group and a low criterion group, or, alternatively, a criterion group (whose members meet one or more criteria) and a reference group (a baseline, or unselected, or typical-population group). The larger the mean difference, the more definitely the item should be selected for the scale. The size of the difference can be used to give differential weights to items and response choices (Strong, 1943), but when the number of items in the scale is large (20 or so), unit weights (0, 1) do just as well as differential weights (Clark, 1961).

Note that the group difference method is similar to Likert's original method. What differs is that Likert used an internal criterion (total score on the undeveloped scale), whereas the present method uses an external criterion. Otherwise, the statistical procedures are very much the same.

The item validity method is also similar to the Likert method except that instead of the Likert's item–total-score correlation, the external criterion method uses the correlation between item score and criterion score as the basis for item selection.

A more sophisticated external criterion method of item selection involves the use of multiple regression. The criterion variable is regressed on the items, with items being added to the regression equation one at a time, depending on the amount of explained variance the item contributes. This method tends to select items that correlate highly with the criterion and lowly or not at all with one another.

Scales developed by external criterion methods tend to be heterogeneous in content, because most criteria tend to be heterogeneous or multidimensional. If this is so, determining internal consistency reliability may not be appropriate for scales constructed by these methods. Rather, immediate test–retest or alternate-forms methods should be used to ascertain reliability.

Because external criterion methods tend to capitalize on chance (i.e., sample idiosyncrasies), three preventive steps should be taken: (a) The contrast groups (high vs. low, criterion vs. reference) should be large (Strong, 1943, used groups of at least 400); (b) the mean item score differences or item–total-score correlations should be practical, not just statistical, significance; and (c) the developed scale, after item selection, should be cross-validated, that is, tried out on new samples from the same population as the development sample. Cross-validation, to see if the group differences or correlations hold up, is of the utmost importance in scale construction by external criterion methods.

The fact that external criterion methods are designed to maximize the prediction of criteria is both their strength and their weakness. When the purpose of constructing a scale is to predict to a given criterion, an external criterion method is still unsurpassed as the method of choice. However, a scale that is developed to predict to an external criterion is only as good as the criterion at the time of scale development. If the criterion changes with time (e.g., a shift in emphasis in the criterion from quantity to quality), then the scale can become obsolete. If the criterion happens to be biased against one sex or one ethnic group, then the scale will also be biased. With new criteria, new scales may have to be constructed, although not before the old scales have been tried and found wanting. Otherwise, a seemingly never-ending series of new scale construction may result. For this reason, use of external criterion methods may require prior resolution of the criterion problem on theoretical as well as on practical grounds.

SCALE EVALUATION

Scales, as measuring instruments, are evaluated primarily on the basis of two criteria: reliability, or the proportion of scale score variance that is not error variance, and validity, or the proportion of scale score variance that accurately represents the construct or the proportion of criterion variance that is predicted by the scale. These two criteria are complex concepts, and a full discussion of them will not be attempted. However, certain points need to be made in connection with the evaluation of newly constructed scales. (A necessary reference for all scale constructors is the American Psychological Association's *Standards for Educational and Psychological Testing*, 1985.)

That different kinds of reliability estimates may be required for different kinds of scales has already been mentioned. For stimulus-centered scales, the reliability concern is whether on immediate retest the stimuli (items) will be rank ordered in the same way by the same person. The variance of the difference scores between test and retest would be indicative of error variance. For subject-centered scales, the concern is whether individuals are rank ordered in the same way on immediate retest. Variability in individuals' standing would be error variance. For trait scales, reliability refers to the stability of scores (or rank-order standing) over considerable lengths of time. This assumes that individuals are mature on the trait (i.e., developmentally in the stage when the trait is presumed to be stable). For state scales, reliability is the ability of the scale accurately to reflect changes in direction or intensity, or both, in the state being measured. For homogeneous scales, internal consistency reliability is appropriate; for heterogeneous scales, it is immediate test–retest or alternate-forms reliability.

Also, because reliability is a function of sample as well as of instrument, it should be evaluated on a sample from the intended target population—an obvious but sometimes overlooked point.

With respect to validity, although the concept continues to evolve (Messick, 1981; Embretson, 1983), certain practices have come to be accepted as mandatory. One of these is the use of the multitrait–multimethod design (Campbell & Fiske, 1959) to evaluate a scale. At the very least, the scale constructor should compare the new scale with the best competing scale and with a measure of a construct that clearly contrasts with the new scale (e.g., a positive affect scale against a negative affect scale).

It is also common—and good practice—to ascertain the correlates of the scale (e.g., age, sex, experience). It is even better if the expectations about correlates are given by theory. In ascertaining such theory-derived correlates, the *nomological net* (Cronbach & Meehl, 1955) that characterizes the construct is given concrete definition. However, such a network of correlations and other relations only delimits the scale's *nomothetic span* (Embretson, 1983). If the scale purported to be a measure of a construct, validation studies would have to identify the mechanisms that produce the scale scores and relate these mechanisms to the construct (i.e., do what Embretson calls *construct representation*).

The practical validity or utility (usefulness in professional practice) of a scale is still mainly a matter of predicting to criteria, either concurrently or subsequently measured. The number and range of criteria to which a scale can predict delineate its utility. The most useful scales in professional psychological practice (e.g., Minnesota Multiphasic Personality Inventory [MMPI], Strong–Campbell Interest Inventory [SCII]) are characterized by the large number and wide range of criteria for which the scales are valid predictors.

Prediction to a criterion can be evaluated in two ways: by correlation (proportion of criterion variance accounted for) or by hit rate (proportion of predicted positives who are true positives). The two are related in the Taylor-Russell tables (Taylor & Russell, 1939), which show what the hit rate would be as a function of the validity coefficient, the base rate, and the selection ratio. Hit rate data are much more concrete and much more useful to the counseling psychology practitioner than are correlation data.

Although reliability and validity concerns are of the essence, there are other less important (but nonetheless, important) considerations. Some of these have been mentioned, for example, administrative concerns. Another concern is the character of the score distribution generated by the scale—in part, a function of the respondent sample. Most users would prefer a scale that ordinarily produces a reasonably normally distributed set of scores. However, if the scale were to be used for diagnostic purposes, a user might prefer one that generates a skewed distribution, the direction of skew depending on whether low scores or high scores are diagnostic. Scales, like ability tests, can be so constructed as to produce the shape of score distribution that is desired, by selecting the appropriate items. Another concern is that the scale produce sufficient score variation to be useful, that is, produce unattenuated correlations. An old rule of thumb is that the coefficient of variation (standard deviation divided by the mean) should be between 5% and 15% (Snedecor, 1946, p. 47).

A final concern is a practical one: Is the scale necessary? That is, are there other, less expensive ways of getting the same information or the same measurements? This concern could also be a matter of social sensitivity: Are there other, less intrusive ways of getting the same information or measurements?

Other Issues

A number of other issues continue to be controversial or, at least, matters of concern for scale constructors.

1. *Measurement versus statistics.* This is an old and continuing debate that has recently been renewed (Gaito, 1980; Townsend & Ashby, 1984). In brief, the proponents of measurement hold that level of measurement (nominal, ordinal, interval, ratio) constrains the kinds of statistical procedures that can be applied to the numerical data. The proponents of statistics maintain that, "(t)he numbers do not know where they come from" (Lord, 1953, p. 751), that the level of measurement is not a constraining factor. Those who accept the latter view tolerate the use of parametric statistics with scores from quasi-interval scales that actually are at the ordinal level of measurement, a common practice that is criticized by proponents of the former view.

2. *Bandwidth versus fidelity (Cronbach & Gleser, 1965).* This is the scale constructor's dilemma that can be illustrated as follows: Suppose, for whatever reason, you are limited to 30 items. Do you construct a scale that yields a single, highly reliable score from 30 items or a scale that can yield three independent scores from three 10-item subscales, even if these subscale scores are of marginal reliability? The trade-off is reminiscent of an older one called the *attenuation paradox* (Loevinger, 1954), which identified a trade-off between reliability and validity. That is, high reliability is achieved at the expense of validity and high validity is achieved at the expense of reliability. Ways out of the paradox have been suggested (Humphreys, 1956).

3. *Empirical versus rational scales.* Conventional wisdom in applied psychology used to hold that empirical (external criterion) scales were the more valid, whereas rational (internal criterion,

intuitive) scales were the more reliable. The opinion—or at least the part about the superiority of empirical scales with respect to validity—has now been challenged (Ashton & Goldberg, 1973; Goldberg, 1972; Hase & Goldberg, 1967; Hornick, James, & Jones, 1977; Jackson, 1975).

4. *The reference group problem.* In the use of the external criterion method of scale construction, what should constitute a reference group? The answer to this question may seem obvious (i.e., a proportionately representative sample of the population), but more careful examination will show that the answer is not so obvious. What is the referent population? The general adult population? A particular age group or sex group? On what variables should there be proportionate representation? Is equal representation better? The constitution of the reference group is important because the scoring key (items selected, weights for response choices) can change with the change of the reference group (as Kuder, 1977, did) and use the criterion group's responses to develop the scoring key.

5. *Response bias.* Ratings—whether self- or other-descriptive, general (abstract) or specific (behavioral), or other kinds—are susceptible to certain response biases on the part of respondents. A response bias is a response tendency that operates in all rating situations, regardless of the context. At least three types of bias can be identified: (a) level bias, or the tendency to locate the mean of the ratings high on the scale (leniency or generosity), low on the scale (strictness or severity), or in the middle (central tendency); (b) dispersion bias, or the tendency to constrain or to expand the distribution of ratings (use of a small segment of the scale vs. use of the full range); and (c) correlation bias, which applies when several rating scales, dimensions, or items, i.e., variables, are involved. In such a situation, a common tendency called the *halo effect* results in the high correlation of variables. The opposite tendency, resulting in low or zero correlations, is rarely, if ever, observed. Most of the controversy concerns correlation bias, with some (e.g., Jackson & Messick, 1961) arguing for its removal in every case, and others (e.g., Block, 1965) arguing that such correlations are not necessarily bias and could be veridical. In any event, a large first principal component in rating data is a common finding, sometimes contrary to the expectations of the scale constructor.

6. *Multimethod measurement.* It is conventional wisdom nowadays to advocate the use of more than one method of measuring any construct. Such a recommendation may overlook the possibility that a change of method can change what it is that is being

measured. In other words, method of measurement should be an integral part of the definition and explication of a construct.

7. *Direction of measurement*. Seemingly bipolar variables sometimes pose problems for scale constructors in that scaling in one direction can result in a measure that does not correlate highly with another that is scaled in the opposite direction. Some constructs, such as masculinity–femininity and positive versus negative affectivity, initially construed as bipolar but unidimensional, have now been redefined as bidimensional. Others such as flexibility–rigidity, while still construed as unidimensional, nevertheless require two different scales for measurement at each pole. These phenomena underscore the need for an adequate theory of the construct to start with, but also for theory to be open to modification in the light of data.

8. *A final issue*. The demand for some quantitative measure of the multitude of process or outcome variables in counseling psychology research, coupled with the convenience of putting together a structured verbal scale, especially one of the Likert type, has led to the almost exclusive or even automatic use of such measures in our field. That researchers are quantifying their variables through the construction and use of such scales is laudable. That such scales have become the instrument of choice in our field is somehow worrisome. Just as we have been criticized for having developed a psychology of the college sophomore, may we not now be accused of having developed a psychology of the Likert scale response?

A Concluding Note

In scale construction, as in much of human endeavor, there can be no single "best" method. One method may be best for one research problem but not for another. Purpose, context, and limitations on the researcher have to be taken into account. Trade-offs in advantages and disadvantages seem to be the rule. A hybrid approach, tailored to the situation, might be better than any of the standard approaches discussed here. Researchers should not be reluctant to experiment with different scale construction approaches— and should report their results, so that the rest of us can find out what method is best.

REFERENCES

Ashton, S. G., & Goldberg, L. R. (1973). In response to Jackson's challenge: The comparative validity of personality scales constructed by the external (empirical) strategy and scales developed intuitively by experts, novices, and laymen. *Journal of Research in Personality, 7,* 1–20.

Block, J. (1965). *The challenge of response sets: Unconfounding meaning, acquiescence, and social desirability in the MMPI.* New York: Appleton-Century-Crofts.

Bogardus, E. S. (1928). *Immigration and race attitudes.* Lexington, MA: Heath.

Campbell, D. T., & Fiske, D. W. (1959). Convergent and discriminant validation by the multitrait-multimethod matrix. *Psychological Bulletin, 56,* 51–105.

Campbell, J. P., Dunnette, M. D., Arvey, R. D., & Hellervik, L. V. (1973). The development and evaluation of behaviorally based rating scales. *Journal of Applied Psychology, 57,* 15–22.

Clark, K. E. (1961). *The vocational interests of non-professional men.* Minneapolis: University of Minnesota Press.

Clemans, W. V. (1966). An analytical and empirical examination of some properties of ipsative measures. *Psychometric Monographs* (14).

Coombs, C. H. (1964). *A theory of data.* New York: Wiley.

Cronbach, L. J. (1984). *Essentials of psychological testing* (4th ed.). New York: Harper & Row.

Cronbach, L. J., & Gleser, G. C. (1965). *Psychological tests and personnel decisions.* Urbana: University of Illinois Press.

Cronbach, L. J., & Meehl, P. E. (1955). Construct validity in psychological tests. *Psychological Bulletin, 52,* 281–302.

Embretson (Whitely), S. (1983). Construct validity: Construct representation versus nomothetic span. *Psychological Bulletin, 93,* 179–197.

Fiske, D. W. (Ed.). (1981). *Problems with language imprecision.* San Francisco: Jossey-Bass.

Gaito, J. (1980). Measurement scales and statistics: Resurgence of an old misconception. *Psychological Bulletin, 87,* 564–567.

Goldberg, L. R. (1972). Parameters of personality inventory construction and utilization: A comparison of prediction strategies and tactics. *Multivariate Behavioral Research Monographs, 72*(2).

Guilford, J. P. (1954). *Psychometric methods* (2nd ed.). New York: McGraw-Hill.

Gulliksen, H., & Tucker, L. R. (1961). A general procedure for obtaining paired comparisons from multiple rank orders. *Psychometrika, 26,* 173–183.

Guttman, L. (1944). A basis for scaling qualitative data. *American Sociological Review, 9,* 139–150.

Hase, H. D., & Goldberg, L. R. (1967). Comparative validity of different strategies of constructing personality inventory scales. *Psychological Bulletin, 67,* 231–248.

Hornick, C. W., James, L. R., & Jones, A. P. (1977). Empirical item keying versus a rational approach to analyzing a psychological climate questionnaire. *Applied Psychological Measurement, 1,* 489–500.

Humphreys, L. G. (1956). The normal curve and the attenuation paradox in test theory. *Psychological Bulletin, 53,* 472–476.

Jackson, D. N. (1975). The relative validity of scales prepared by naive item writers and those based on empirical methods of personality scale construction. *Educational and Psychological Measurement, 35,* 361–370.

Jackson, D. N., & Messick, S. (1961). Acquiescence and desirability as response determinants on the MMPI. *Educational and Psychological Measurement, 21,* 771–790.

Kuder, F. (1977). *Activity interests and occupational choice.* Chicago: Science Research Associates.

Likert, R. (1932). A technique for the measurement of attitudes. *Archives of Psychology,* No. 140.

Loevinger, J. (1954). The attenuation paradox in test theory. *Psychological Bulletin, 51,* 493–504.

Lord, F. M. (1953). On the statistical treatment of football numbers. *American Psychologist, 8,* 750–751.

Lord, F. M. & Novick, M. (1968). *Statistical theories of mental test scores.* Reading, MA: Addison-Wesley.

Messick, S. (1981). Constructs and their vicissitudes in educational and pscyhological measurement. *Psychological Bulletin, 89,* 575–588.

Osgood, C. E., Suci, C. J., & Tannenbaum, P. H. (1957). *The measurement of meaning.* Urbana: University of Illinois Press.

Payne, S. L. (1951). *The art of asking questions.* Princeton, NJ: Princeton University Press.

Rasch, G. (1960). *Probabilistic models for some intelligence and attainment tests.* Copenhagen, Denmark: Danmarks Paedogogiske Institut. (Chicago: University of Chicago Press, 1980).

Siegel, S. (1956). *Nonparametric statistics for the behavioral science.* New York: McGraw-Hill.

Smith, P. C., & Kendall, L. M. (1963). Retranslation of expectations: An approach to the construction of unambiguous anchors for rating scales. *Journal of Applied Psychology, 47,* 149–155.

Snedecor, G. W. (1946). *Statistical methods.* Ames: Iowa State College Press.

Standards for educational and psychological testing. (1985). Washington, DC: American Psychological Association.

Stephenson, W. (1953). *The study of behavior.* Chicago: University of Chicago Press.

Strong, E. K., Jr. (1943). *Vocational interests of men and women.* Stanford, CA: Stanford University Press.

Taylor, H. C., & Russell, J. T. (1939). The relationship of validity coefficients to the practical effectiveness of tests in selection: Discussion and tables. *Journal of Applied Psychology, 23,* 565–578.

Thomas, H. (1982). IQ, interval scales, and normal distributions. *Psychological Bulletin, 91,* 198–202.

Thurstone, L. L., & Chave, E. (1929). *The measurement of attitude.* Chicago: University of Chicago Press.

Torgerson, W. S. (1958). *Theory and methods of scaling.* New York: Wiley.

Townsend, J. T., & Ashby, F. G. (1984). Measurement scales and statistics: The misconception misconceived. *Psychological Bulletin, 96,* 394–401.

Triandis, H. C. (1971). *Attitude and attitude change.* New York: Wiley.

Wright, B. D., & Masters, G. N. (1982). *Rating scale analysis.* Chicago: Mesa Press.

11

CONSTRUCTING VALIDITY: BASIC ISSUES IN OBJECTIVE SCALE DEVELOPMENT

LEE ANNA CLARK AND DAVID WATSON

Scale development remains a growth industry within psychology. A PsycLIT database survey of articles published in the 6-year period from 1989 through 1994 revealed 1,726 articles with the key words "test construction" or "scale development" published in English-language journals, 270 in other-language journals, and 552 doctoral dissertations. During this same period (i.e., beginning with its inception), 50 articles addressing scale development or test construction were published in *Psychological Assessment* alone. The majority of these articles reported the development of one or more new measures (82%); most of the rest presented new scales derived from an existing instrument (10%). We use these 41 scale-development articles as a reference set for our discussion. Clearly, despite the criticism leveled at psychological testing in recent years, assessment retains a central role within the field.

Given that test construction remains a thriving activity, it is worthwhile

Reprinted from *Psychological Assessment*, 7, 309–319. Copyright 1995 by the American Psychological Association.

to reconsider the scale development process periodically to maintain and enhance the quality of this enterprise. The goal of this article is to articulate some basic principles that we believe anyone developing a scale should know and follow. Many of these principles have been stated before, but we repeat them here both because they are sufficiently important to bear repetition and because a review of the recent literature indicates that they are still not universally honored.

We focus on verbally mediated measures; thus, for example, we do not address the development of behavioral observation scales. Moreover, our primary focus is on self-report measures, because these constitute the majority (67%) of our reference sample. Nonetheless, most of the basic principles we articulate are applicable to interview-based measures and rating scales designed to be completed by clinicians, parents, teachers, spouses, peers, and so forth.

Before proceeding further, it is interesting to examine the new measures comprising our *Psychological Assessment* sample. This examination sample offers a glimpse at why scale development continues unabated, as well as the nature of the unmet needs these scale developers are seeking to fill. First, not surprisingly given this journal's focus, more than half (61%) of the scales assess some aspect of psychopathology, personality, or adjustment. The next most common categories are measures of attitudes and interpersonal relations (20% and 15%, respectively). The remaining scales assess a miscellany of behaviors, abilities, response validity, trauma experience, and so forth. In all categories, most new scales apparently tap relatively narrow constructs, such as suicidality, fear of intimacy, postpartum adjustment, drug-use expectancies, or parent–teenager relations, that have a focused range of utility. However, the extent to which the score variance of such scales is, in fact, attributable to the named target construct is an important issue that we will consider.

THE CENTRALITY OF PSYCHOLOGICAL MEASUREMENT

It has become axiomatic that (publishable) assessment instruments are supposed to be reliable and valid; indeed, every article in the *Psychological Assessment* set addresses these qualities. However, it appears that many test developers do not fully appreciate the complexity of these concepts. As this article is being prepared, the *Standards for Educational and Psychological Testing* (American Psychological Association, 1985) are undergoing intensive review and revision for the first time in a decade. Strong and conflicting pressures regarding the *Standards'* revision are being brought to bear on the Joint Committee on the Standards for Educational and Psychological Testing by diverse groups, and major changes in the *Standards* are expected. Whatever else it may do, however, the Joint Committee intends to emphasize the centrality of construct validity in testing even more than in previous versions, according to Co-Chair C. D. Spielberger (personal communication, February 15, 1995). And yet, widespread misunderstanding remains regarding precisely what construct validity is and what establishing construct validity entails.

Cronbach and Meehl (1955) argued that investigating the construct validity of a measure necessarily involves at least the following three steps: (a) articulating a set of theoretical concepts and their interrelations, (b) developing ways to measure the hypothetical constructs proposed by the theory, and (c) empirically testing the hypothesized relations among constructs and their observable manifestations. This means that without an articulated theory (which Cronbach and Meehl termed "the nomological net"), there is no construct validity. The Joint Committee's emphasis on the centrality of construct validity is therefore highly appropriate because the process of establishing construct validity represents a key element in differentiating psychology as a science from other, nonscientific approaches to the analysis of human behavior.

Construct validity cannot be inferred from a single set of observations, whether these pertain to a measure's factor structure, correlations with other measures, differentiation between selected groups, or hypothesized changes over time or in response to an experimental manipulation. Clearly, a series of investigations is required even to begin the process of identifying the psychological construct that underlies a measure. Nonetheless, Cronbach and Meehl's (1955) dictum that "One does not validate a test, but only a principle for making inferences" (p. 297) is often ignored, as scale developers speak lightly—sometimes in a single sentence—of establishing the construct validity of a scale. Even the more straightforward concept of reliability is widely mistreated, as we discuss in a later section.

It also should be noted that construct validity is important from the standpoint of practical utility as well as science. That is, for economic reasons, practitioners increasingly are being asked to justify the use of specific assessment procedures to third-party payers. Clear documentation of the precision and efficiency of psychological measures will be required in the near future. The most precise and efficient measures are those with established construct validity; they are manifestations of constructs in an articulated theory that is well supported by empirical data. Thus, construct validity lies at the heart of the clinical utility of assessment and should be respected by scale developers and users alike.

A THEORETICAL MODEL FOR SCALE DEVELOPMENT

Loevinger's (1957) monograph arguably remains the most complete exposition of theoretically based psychological test construction. Like any great work, however, her monograph requires exegesis, and in this article we assume this role. Specifically, we offer practical guidance for applying Loevinger's theoretical approach to the actual process of scale development. We limit ourselves to that portion of her article that details the "three components of construct validity," which she labels *substantive*, *structural*, and *external*. More specifically, because our topic is initial scale development, we focus primarily on the first two of these components, which together address a measure's "internal validity" (Loevinger, 1957, p. 654). Smith and McCarthy's (1995) article in this special issue addresses the external component more thoroughly.

SUBSTANTIVE VALIDITY: CONCEPTUALIZATION AND DEVELOPMENT OF AN INITIAL ITEM POOL

Conceptualization

Our PsycLIT database search suggests that human psychology is sufficiently complex that there is no limit to the number of psychological constructs that can be operationalized as scales. One now widely recognized reason for this is that psychological constructs are ordered hierarchically at different levels of abstraction or breadth (see Comrey, 1988; John, 1990; Watson, Clark, & Harkness, 1994). In the area of personality, for example, one can conceive of the narrow traits of talkativeness and physical expressiveness, the somewhat broader concepts of gregariousness and assertiveness, and the still more general disposition of extraversion. Scales can be developed to assess constructs at each of many levels of abstraction. Consequently, a key issue to be resolved in the initial developmental stage is the scope or generality of the target construct.

As mentioned, our *Psychological Assessment* sample consists primarily of scales that assess narrow-band (e.g., Cocaine Expectancy Questionnaire; Jaffe & Kilbey, 1994) or midlevel (Social Phobia and Anxiety Inventory; Turner, Beidel, Dancu, & Stanley, 1989) constructs. It is noteworthy, therefore, that Loevinger (1957) argued that, even when relatively narrow measurements are desired, those scales based on a "deeper knowledge of psychological theory" (p. 641) will be more helpful in making specific pragmatic decisions than those developed using a purely "answer-based" technology. Accordingly, even narrow-band measures should be embedded in a theoretical framework, and even measures of the same basic phenomenon will vary with the theoretical perspective of the developer.

A critical first step is to develop a precise and detailed conception of the target construct and its theoretical context. We have found that writing out a brief, formal description of the construct is very useful in crystallizing one's conceptual model. For example, in developing the Exhibitionism scale of the Schedule for Nonadaptive and Adaptive Personality (SNAP; Clark, 1993), the initial target construct was defined as a continuum ranging from normal adaptive functioning to potentially pathological behavior of which the high end was defined by overly dramatic, reactive, and intensely expressed behavior; an exaggerated expression of emotions; excessive attention-seeking behavior; an inordinate need for admiration; vanity; and a demanding interpersonal style.

This emphasis on theory is not meant to be intimidating. That is, we do not mean to imply that one must have a fully articulated set of interrelated theoretical concepts before embarking on scale development. Our point, rather, is that thinking about these theoretical issues prior to the actual process of scale construction increases the likelihood that the resulting scale will make a substantial contribution to the psychological literature.

Literature Review

To articulate the basic construct as clearly and thoroughly as possible, it is necessary to review the relevant literature to see how others have approached the same problem. Initially, the review should include previous attempts to conceptualize and assess both the same construct and closely related constructs. For instance, in developing a new measure of hopelessness, a thorough literature search would encompass measures of related constructs at various levels of the hierarchy in which the target construct is embedded—for example, depression and optimism–pessimism—in addition to existing measures of hopelessness.

Subsequently, the review should be broadened to encompass what may appear to be less immediately related constructs to articulate the conceptual boundaries of the target construct. That is, in the initial stages one investigates existing scales and concepts to which the target is expected to be related. Then, one also must examine entities from which the target is to be distinguished. In other words, a good theory articulates not only what a construct is, but also what it is not. Continuing with the hopelessness example, a thorough review would reveal that various measures of negative affect (depression, anxiety, hostility, guilt and shame, dissatisfaction, etc.) are strongly intercorrelated, so that it is important to articulate the hypothesized relation of hopelessness to other negative affects. Similarly, a good measure will have a predicted convergent and discriminant correlational pattern (Smith & McCarthy, 1995), and it is important to consider this aspect of measurement at the initial as well as later stages of development.

The importance of a comprehensive literature review cannot be overstated. First, such a review will serve to clarify the nature and range of the content of the target construct. Second, a literature review may help to identify problems with existing measures (e.g., unclear instructions or problematic response formats) that then can be avoided in one's own scale. Finally, and perhaps most importantly, a thorough review will indicate whether the proposed scale is actually needed. If reasonably good measures of the target construct already exist, why create another? Unless the prospective test developer can clearly articulate ways in which the proposed scale will represent either a theoretical or an empirical improvement over existing measures, it is preferable to avoid contributing to the needless proliferation of assessment instruments.

Creation of an Item Pool

Once the scope and range of the content domain have been tentatively identified, the actual task of item writing can begin. No existing data-analytic technique can remedy serious deficiencies in an item pool. Accordingly, the creation of the initial pool is a crucial stage in scale construction. The fundamental goal at this stage is to sample systematically all content that is potentially relevant to the target construct. Loevinger (1957) offered the classic articulation of this principle: *"The items of the pool should be chosen so as to sample all possible contents which might comprise the putative trait according to all known alternative theories of the trait"* (p. 659, emphasis in original).

Two key implications of this principle are that the initial pool (a) should be broader and more comprehensive than one's own theoretical view of the target construct and (b) should include content that ultimately will be shown to be tangential or even unrelated to the core construct. The logic underlying this principle is simple: Subsequent psychometric analyses can identify weak, unrelated items that should be dropped from the emerging scale but are powerless to detect content that should have been included but was not. Accordingly, in creating the item pool one always should err on the side of overinclusiveness. The importance of the initial literature review becomes quite obvious in this connection.

In addition to sampling a sufficient breadth of content, the scale developer must ensure that there is an adequate sample of items within each of the major content areas comprising the broadly conceptualized domain; failure to do so may mean that one or more of these areas will be underrepresented in the final scale. To ensure that each important aspect of the construct is assessed adequately, some test developers have recommended that formal subscales be created to assess each major content area. Hogan (1983), for instance, identified 10 content areas (e.g., anxiety, guilt, and somatic complaints) that make up the more general dimension of Adjustment versus Maladjustment and created 4- to 10-item "homogeneous item composites" to assess each of them. Similarly, Comrey (1988) has championed the use of "factored homogeneous item dimensions" to assess individual content areas within a specified domain.

The important point here is not that a particular procedure must be followed, but that scale developers need to ensure that each content area is well represented in the initial item pool. If only one or two items are written to cover a particular content area, then the chances of that content being represented in the final scale are much reduced. Loevinger (1957) recommended that the proportion of items devoted to each content area be proportional to the importance of that content in the target construct. This is a worthy goal, although in most cases the theoretically ideal proportions will be unknown. However, broader content areas should probably be represented by more items than narrower content areas.

Many of the procedures that we are discussing are traditionally described as the *theoretical–rational* or *deductive* method of scale development. We consider this approach to be an important initial step in a more extensive process rather than a scale development method to be used by itself. Similarly, Loevinger (1957) affirmed that content issues must always be considered in defining the domain, but emphasized that alone they are insufficient. That is, empirical validation of content (as distinguished from "blind empiricism") is important: "If theory is fully to profit from test construction . . . every item [on a scale] must be accounted for" (Loevinger, 1957, p. 657). This obviously is a very lofty goal and clearly is articulated as an ideal to be striven for rather than an absolute requirement (for a very similar view, see Comrey, 1988). For further discussion of content validity issues, see Haynes, Richard, and Kubany (1995) in this special issue.

In this context, we emphasize that good scale construction typically is an iterative process involving several periods of item writing, followed in each case by conceptual and psychometric analysis. These analyses serve to sharpen one's understanding of the nature and structure of the target domain as well as to identify deficiencies in the initial item pool. For instance, a factor analysis might establish that the items can be subdivided into several subscales but that the initial pool does not contain enough items to assess each of these content domains reliably. Accordingly, new items need to be written and again subjected to psychometric analyses. Alternatively, analyses may suggest that conceptualization of the target construct as, for example, a single bipolar dimension is countermanded by evidence that the two poles actually represent separate and distinct entities. In this case, revision of one's theoretical model may be in order.

An examination of the *Psychological Assessment* sample of scale development articles indicates that most test developers did start with a large item pool that was reduced to a smaller final set. However, it is not clear whether this finding reflects the broad and systematic domain sampling that we advocate or, alternatively, the mere elimination of items that were psychometrically weak for any number of reasons. That is, we saw little evidence of an iterative process through which the conceptualization of the target construct was itself affected by the process of scale development (see Smith & McCarthy, 1995, and Tellegen & Waller, in press, for discussions of this issue).

Basic Principles of Item Writing

In addition to sampling well, it also is essential to write "good" items. When developing a scale it is worth the time to consult the available literature on item writing (e.g., Angleitner & Wiggins, 1985; Comrey, 1988; Kline, 1986). What constitutes a good item? First, the language should be simple, straightforward, and appropriate for the reading level of the scale's target population. For instance, scales intended for use in general clinical samples need to be readily understandable by respondents with only a modest education. In addition, one should avoid using trendy expressions that quickly may become dated, as well as colloquialisms and other language for which the familiarity (and thus utility) will vary widely with age, ethnicity, region, gender, and so forth. Finally, there is little point in writing items that virtually everyone (e.g., "Sometimes I am happier than at other times") or no one (e.g., "I am always furious") will endorse, unless they are intended to assess invalid responding. For this and other reasons we discuss later, items should be written to ensure variability in responding.

Item writers also should be careful to avoid complex or "double-barreled" items that actually assess more than one characteristic. At best, such items are ambiguous; at worst, they may leave respondents with no viable response alternative. Consider, for example, the true–false item, "I would never drink and drive for fear that I might be stopped by the police," which confounds the occurrence versus nonoccurrence of a behavior (drinking and driving) with a putative motive for that behavior (fear of legal complications). As such, it may leave respondents who avoid drinking and driving—but who do so for other reasons (e.g., because it is dangerous or morally wrong)—puzzled as to how they should respond. Of equal or greater concern is the fact that respondents will interpret complex items in different ways; accordingly, their responses will reflect the heterogeneity of their interpretations, and the item likely will show very poor psychometric properties as a result.

Furthermore, the exact phrasing of items can exert a profound influence on the construct that is actually measured. This is well illustrated by the example of the general personality trait of neuroticism (negative affectivity; Watson & Clark 1984). Over the years, it has been demonstrated repeatedly that attempts to assess a specific construct (such as hardiness or pessimism) have yielded instead yet another measure that is strongly saturated with this pervasive dimension. Indeed, items must be worded very carefully to avoid tapping into the broad individual differences in affect and cognition that characterize neuroticism. For instance, our own experience has shown that the inclusion of almost any negative mood term (e.g., "I worry about . . . ," or "I am upset [or bothered or troubled] by . . .") virtually guarantees that an item will have a substantial neuroticism component; the inclusion of several such affect-laden items, in turn, ensures that the resulting scale—regardless of its intended construct—will be primarily a marker of neuroticism.

Choice of Format

Finally, in creating the initial item pool, the test developer also must decide on the response format to be used. Clearly, the two dominant response formats in contemporary personality assessment are dichotomous responding (e.g., true–false and yes–no) and Likert-type rating scales with three or more options. Checklists, forced-choice, and visual analog measures also have been used over the years, but for various reasons have fallen out of favor. *Checklists*—scales that permit respondents to scan a list and check only the applicable items—proved to be problematic because they are more prone to response biases than formats that require a response to every item (Bentler, 1969; D. P. Green, Goldman, & Salovey, 1993). Most *forced-choice* formats, in which respondents must choose between alternatives that represent different constructs, are limited in that the resulting scores are ipsative; that is, they reflect only the relative intraindividual strength of the assessed constructs and do not provide normative, interindividual information. Finally, *visual analog* scales provide a free range of response options along a defined continuum, usually anchored at the two endpoints (e.g., *No pain at all* vs. *Excruciating pain; worst I can imagine*). This scale type is rarely used for multi-item scales because they are extremely laborious to score, although this may change with increased use of computer administration. Thus, they are most useful when a single (or few) measurements are desired and the target construct is either very simple (e.g., a single mood term) or represents a summary judgment (e.g., bodily pain).[1]

There are several considerations in choosing between dichotomous and Likert-type formats; furthermore, in the latter case, one also has to decide the number of response options to offer and how to label the response options. Comrey (1988) has criticized dichotomous response formats extensively, arguing that "multiple-choice item formats are more reliable, give more stable results, and produce better scales" (p. 758). Comrey's points are cogent and should be taken very seriously, especially his valid assertion that dichotomous items with extremely unbalanced response distributions (i.e., those in which virtually everyone answers either true or false) can lead to distorted correlational results. However, this problem can be avoided by carefully inspecting individual item frequencies during scale development and eliminating items with extreme response rates (one often-used cutoff is any item on which more than 95% of all respondents give the same response). Furthermore, dichotomous response formats offer an important advantage over rating scales:

---

[1] We are grateful to an anonymous reviewer for providing additional information regarding visual analog scales.

Other things being equal, respondents can answer many more items in the same amount of time. Consequently, if assessment time is limited, dichotomous formats can yield significantly more information. Moreover, Loevinger (1957) has argued that response biases are more problematic with Likert-type scales and that the assumption of equal-interval scaling often is not justified.

Likert-type scales are used with a number of different response formats: among the most popular are the frequency (*never* to *always*), degree or extent (*not at all* to *very much*), similarity (*like me* or *not like me*), and agreement (*strongly agree* to *strongly disagree*) formats. Obviously, the nature of the response option constrains item content in an important way (see Comrey, 1988). For example, the item "I often lose my temper" would be inappropriate if used with a frequency format. Note also that with an odd number of response options (typically, five or seven), the label for the middle option must be considered carefully; for example, *cannot say* confounds possible uncertainty about item meaning with a midrange rating of the attribute. An even number of response options (typically, four or six) eliminates this problem but forces respondents to "fall on one side of the fence or the other," which some may find objectionable. In a related vein, it must be emphasized also that providing more response alternatives (e.g., a 9-point rather than a 5-point scale) does not necessarily enhance reliability or validity. In fact, increasing the number of alternatives actually may reduce validity if respondents are unable to make the more subtle distinctions that are required. That is, having too many alternatives can introduce an element of random responding that renders scores less valid.

Finally, we emphasize that dichotomous and rating scale formats typically yield very similar results. For example, neuroticism scales using various formats (including true–false, yes–no, and rating scales) are all highly intercorrelated and clearly define a single common factor (Watson, Clark, & Harkness, 1994). In light of these considerations, we cannot conclude that one type of format is generally preferable to the other. Used intelligently, both formats can yield highly reliable and valid scales. To ensure such intelligent usage, we strongly recommend that a proposed format be pilot-tested on a moderately sized sample to obtain preliminary information about both respondent reactions and response option distributions.

STRUCTURAL VALIDITY: ITEM SELECTION AND PSYCHOMETRIC EVALUATION

Test Construction Strategies

The choice of a primary test construction or item selection strategy is as important as the compilation of the initial item pool. In particular, the item selection strategy should be matched to the goal of scale development and to the theoretical conceptualization of the target construct. In this regard, Loevinger (1957) described three main conceptual models: (a) quantitative (dimensional) models that differentiate individuals with respect to degree or level of the target construct, (b) class models that seek to categorize individuals into qualitatively different groups, and (c) more complex dynamic models.

It is beyond the scope of this article to discuss either dynamic or class models; however, we note with concern that some of the articles in the *Psychological Assessment* sample applied methods more appropriate for quantitative models (e.g., factor analysis) to constructs that appeared to reflect class models (such as diagnoses). Of course, some theoreticians have argued that the empirical data do not strongly support class models even in the case of psychiatric diagnoses (e.g., Clark, Watson, & Reynolds, 1995) and, therefore, that dimensional or quantitative models are more appropriate. Thus, these aforementioned *Psychological Assessment* scale developers may have implicitly accepted this stance in selecting their test construction method. In any case, analytic methods appropriate for class model constructs do exist and should be used to develop measures of such constructs (e.g., Gangestad & Snyder, 1991; Meehl & Golden, 1982).

Loevinger (1957) advanced the concept of structural validity, that is, the extent to which a scale's internal structure (i.e., the interitem correlations) parallels the external structure of the target trait (i.e., correlations among nontest manifestations of the trait). She also emphasized that items should reflect the underlying (latent) trait variance. These three concerns parallel the three main item selection strategies in use for quantitative model constructs: empirical (primarily reflecting concern with nontest manifestations), internal consistency (concerned with the interitem structure), and item response theory (focused on the latent trait). The fact that structural validity encompasses all three concerns demonstrates that these methods may be used in conjunction with one another and that exclusive reliance on a single method is neither required nor necessarily desirable.

Criterion-based Methods

Meehl's (1945) "empirical manifesto" ushered in the heyday of empirically keyed test construction. Backed by Meehl's cogent arguments that a test response could be considered verbal behavior in its own right—with nontest correlates to be discovered empirically—test developers embraced criterion keying as a method that permitted a wide range of practical problems to be addressed in an apparently straightforward manner. With widespread use, however, the limitations of this approach quickly became evident. From a technical viewpoint, major difficulties arose in cross-validating and generalizing instruments to new settings and different populations. More fundamentally, the relative inability of the method to advance psychological theory was a severe disappointment. With the advent of construct validity (Cronbach & Meehl, 1955), it became difficult to advocate exclusive reliance on pure "blind empiricism" in test construction. Yet, empirical approaches are still in use; in fact, 17% of the *Psychological Assessment* sample relied primarily on criterion groups for item selection.

Certainly, it is important not to throw the baby out with the bathwater. Correlations of a test with theoretically relevant criteria still constitute crucial evidence of validity, and there is no reason to avoid examining these correlations even in the early stages of scale development. One very strong approach would be to administer the initial item pool to a large heterogeneous sample (e.g., one encompassing both normal range and clinical levels of the target construct). Then, one basis (among several) for selecting items would be the power of the items to differentiate appropriately between subgroups in the sample (e.g., normal vs. clinical, or between individuals with different behavioral patterns or diagnoses within the clinical range).

Internal Consistency Methods

Currently, the single most widely used method for item selection in scale development is some form of internal consistency analysis. For example, 32% of the *Psychological Assessment* sample used factor analysis, and an additional 17% used another variant of the internal consistency method. These non–factor-analytic analyses typically used corrected item–total correlations to eliminate items that did not correlate strongly with the assessed construct. Appropriately, factor analytic methods were used most frequently when the target construct was conceptualized as multidimensional and, therefore, subscales were desired. Indeed, whenever factor analysis was used, the resulting instrument had subscales, although subscales sometimes were developed without benefit of factor analysis, usually through some combination of rational and internal consistency analyses. Because Floyd and Widaman's (1995) article in this special issue examines the role of factor analysis in scale development in detail, we focus here on only a few basic issues.

First, put simply, factor analytic results provide information, not answers or solutions. That is, factor analysis is a tool that can be used wisely or foolishly. Naturally, the better one understands the tool the more likely it is to be used wisely, so we strongly recommend that scale developers either educate themselves about the technique or consult with a psychometrician at each stage of the development process. The power of the technique is such that blind adherence to a few simple rules is not likely to result in a terrible scale, but neither is it likely to be optimal.

Second, there is no substitute for good theory and careful thought when using these techniques. To a considerable extent, internal consistency is always had at the expense of breadth, so simply retaining the 10 or 20 "top" items may not yield the scale that best represents the target construct. That is, the few items correlating most strongly with the assessed or (in the case of factor analysis) latent construct may be highly redundant with one another; consequently, including them all will increase internal consistency estimates but also will create an overly narrow scale that likely will not assess the construct optimally. We consider this "attenuation paradox" (Loevinger, 1954) in more detail later.

Similarly, if items that reflect the theoretical core of the construct do not correlate strongly with it in preliminary analyses, it is not wise simply to eliminate them without consideration of why they did not behave as expected. Other explanations (e.g., Is the theory inadequate? Is the item poorly worded? Is the sample nonrepresentative in some important way? Is the item's base rate too extreme? Are there too few items representing the core construct?) should be considered before such items are eliminated.

Item Response Theory (IRT)

Although IRT is by no means new, it has only recently begun to capture general attention. IRT is based on the assumption that test responses reflect an underlying trait (or set of traits, although most users assume that a single dominant trait can explain most of the response variance) and, moreover, that the relation between response and trait can be described for each test item by a monotonically increasing function called an *item characteristic curve* (ICC). Individuals with higher levels of the trait have higher expected probabilities for answering an item correctly (in the case of an ability) or in the keyed direction (for traits related to personality or psychopathology), and the ICC provides the precise value of these probabilities for each level of the trait.

Once the item parameters have been established (actually, estimated) by testing on a suitably large and heterogeneous group, IRT methods offer several advantages to scale developers. First, the methods provide a statistic indicating the precision with which an individual respondent's trait level is estimated. Thus, for example, the user can know whether the scale provides more precise estimates of the trait at the lower, middle, or upper end of the distribution. Second, trait-level estimates can be made independent of the particular set of items administered, thus providing greater flexibility and efficiency of assessment than is afforded by tests in which the ICCs are unknown. This property permits the development of computer-adaptive tests, in which assessment is focused primarily on those items for which maximum discriminative ability lies close to the respondent's trait level.

Standard intelligence tests make use of this IRT feature in a basic way. That is, older individuals are not administered the first, very easy items for each subtest unless they fail on the first few items tested. Rather, it is assumed that they would pass these items and they are given credit for them. Similarly, when examinees fail a sufficient number of items on a subtest, they are not administered the remaining, more difficult items under the assumption that they would fail them also. Scales developed using IRT simply apply these same features in a more comprehensive and precise manner. Interested readers are referred to Hambleton, Swaminathan, and Rogers (1991) for a relatively nontechnical presentation of IRT principles and applications and to King, King, Fairbank, Schlenger, and Surface (1993), Reise and Waller (1993), and Reise, Widaman, and Pugh (1993) for recent discussions.

Initial Data Collection

Inclusion of Comparison (Anchor) Scales

In the initial round of data collection, it is common practice to administer the preliminary item pool without any additional items or scales. This practice is regrettable, however, because it does not permit examination of the boundaries of the target construct; as we discussed earlier, exploring these boundaries is absolutely critical to understanding the construct from both theoretical and empirical viewpoints. Just as the literature was reviewed initially to discover existing scales and concepts to which the target is expected to be related and from which it must be differentiated, marker scales assessing these other constructs should be included in the initial data collection. Too often test developers discover late in the process that their new scale correlates .85 with an existing measure.

Sample Considerations

It can be very helpful to do some preliminary pilot-testing on moderately sized samples of convenience (e.g., 100–200 college students for testing item formats) before launching a major scale development project. However, it is likely that some basic item content decisions will be made after the first full round of data collection, decisions that will shape the future empirical and conceptual development of the scale. Therefore, after initial pilot-testing, it is very important to use a large and appropriately heterogeneous sample for the first major stage of scale development. On the basis of existing evidence regarding the stability and replicability of structural analyses (Guadagnoli & Velicer, 1988), we recommend that a minimum of 300 respondents be assessed at this stage. Moreover, if the scale is to be used in a clinical setting it is critical to obtain data on patient samples early on, rather than rely solely on college students until relatively late in the development process. One reason for obtaining data on patient samples early on is because the target construct may have rather different properties in different samples. If this fact is not discovered until late in the development process, the utility of the scale may be seriously compromised.

Psychometric Evaluation

Analysis of Item Distributions

Before conducting more complex structural analyses, scale developers should examine the response distributions of the individual items. In inspecting these distributions, two considerations are paramount. First, it is important to identify and eliminate items that have highly skewed and unbalanced distributions. In a true–false format, these are items that virtually everyone (e.g., 95% or more) either endorses or denies: with a Likert rating format, these are items to which almost all respondents respond similarly (e.g., "slightly agree"). Highly unbalanced items are undesirable for several reasons. First, when most respondents answer similarly, items convey little information. Second, owing to their limited variability, these items are likely to correlate weakly with other items in the pool and therefore will fare poorly in subsequent structural analyses. Third, as noted earlier, items with extremely unbalanced distributions can produce highly unstable correlational results. Comrey (1988), for instance, pointed out that if one individual answers false to two items, whereas the remaining 199 all answer true, the items will correlate 1.0 with one another. With a more normal distribution, a high correlation would indicate that the items are redundant and that one of them probably should be eliminated. However, in this case, if that one individual changed just one of those responses to true, the 1.0 correlation would disappear. Clearly, the normal decision-making rules cannot be applied in this situation.

However, before excluding an item on the basis of an unbalanced distribution, it is essential to examine data from diverse samples representing the entire range of the scale's target population. Most notably, many items will show very different response distributions across clinical and nonclinical samples. For instance, the item "I have things in my possession that I can't explain how I got" likely would be endorsed by very few undergraduates and, therefore, would show a markedly unbalanced distribution in a student sample. In an appropriate patient sample, however, this item may be useful in assessing clinically significant levels of dissociative pathology. Thus, it may be desirable to retain items that assess important construct-relevant information in one type of sample, even if they have extremely unbalanced distributions (and relatively poor psychometric properties) in others.

This brings us to the second consideration, namely, that it is desirable to retain items showing a broad range of distributions. In the case of true–false items, this means keeping items with widely varying endorsement percentages. The reason for this is that most constructs are conceived to be—and, in fact, are empirically shown to be—continuously distributed dimensions, and scores can occur anywhere along the entire dimension.

Consequently, it is important to retain items that discriminate at different points along the continuum. For example, in assessing the broad personality dimension of extraversion, it clearly would be undesirable to retain only those items that discriminated extreme introverts from everyone else; rather, one should include at least some items that differentiate extreme introverts from mild introverts, mild introverts from mild extraverts, and mild extraverts from extreme extraverts. Similarly, returning to an earlier example, the item "I have things in my possession that I can't explain how I got" may be useful precisely because it serves to define the extreme upper end of the dissociative continuum (i.e., those who suffer from dissociative identity disorder).

This is, in fact, one of the key advantages offered by IRT (King et al., 1993; Reise & Waller, 1993; Reise et al., 1993). As noted earlier, IRT yields parameter estimates that specify the point in a continuum at which a given item is maximally informative. These estimates, then, can be used as a basis for choosing an efficient set of items that yield precise assessment across the entire range of the continuum. Naturally, this almost invariably leads to the retention of items with widely varying distributions.

Unidimensionality, Internal Consistency, and Coefficient Alpha

The next crucial stage is to conduct structural analyses to determine which items are to be eliminated from or retained in the item pool. This stage is most critical when the test developer is seeking to create a theoretically based measure of a target construct, so that the goal is to measure one thing (i.e., the target construct)—and only this thing—as precisely as possible. This goal may seem relatively straightforward, but it is readily apparent from the recent literature that it remains poorly understood by test developers and users. The most obvious problem is the widespread misapprehension that the attainment of this goal can be established simply by demonstrating that a scale shows an acceptable level of internal consistency reliability, as estimated by an index such as coefficient alpha (Cronbach, 1951) or K-R 20 (Kuder & Richardson, 1937). A further complication is the fact that there are no longer any clear standards regarding what level of reliability is considered acceptable. For instance, although Nunnally (1978) recommended minimum standards of .80 and .90 for basic and applied research, respectively, it is not uncommon for contemporary researchers to characterize reliabilities in the .60s and .70s as good or adequate (e.g., Dekovic, Janssens, & Gerris, 1991; Holden, Fekken, & Cotton, 1991).

More fundamentally, psychometricians long have disavowed the practice of using reliability indices to establish the homogeneity of a scale (see Boyle, 1991; Cortina, 1993; S. B. Green, Lissitz, & Mulaik, 1977). To understand why this is so, it is necessary to distinguish between internal consistency on the one hand and homogeneity or unidimensionality on the other. *Internal consistency* refers to the overall degree to which the items that make up a scale are intercorrelated, whereas *homogeneity* and *unidimensionality* indicate whether the scale items assess a single underlying factor or construct (Briggs & Cheek, 1986; Cortina, 1993; S. B. Green et al., 1977). As such, internal consistency is a necessary but not sufficient condition for homogeneity or unidimensionality. In other words, a scale cannot be homogeneous unless all of its items are interrelated, but as we illustrate later, a scale can contain many interrelated items and still not be unidimensional. Because theory-driven assessment seeks to measure a single construct systematically, the test developer ultimately is pursuing the goal of homogeneity or unidimensionality rather than internal consistency per se.

Unfortunately, K-R 20 and coefficient alpha are measures of internal consistency rather than homogeneity and so are of limited utility in establishing the unidimensionality of a scale. Furthermore, they are ambiguous and imperfect indicators of internal consistency because they essentially are a function of two parameters: the number of test items and the average intercorrelation among the items (Cortina, 1993; Cronbach, 1951). That is, one can achieve a high internal consistency reliability estimate by having either many items or highly intercorrelated items (or some combination of the two). Whereas the degree of item intercorrelation is a straightforward indicator of internal consistency, the number of items is entirely irrelevant. In practical terms, this means that as the number of items becomes quite large, it is exceedingly difficult to avoid achieving a high reliability estimate. Cortina (1993), in fact, suggested that coefficient alpha is virtually useless as an index of internal consistency for scales containing 40 or more items.

Accordingly, the average interitem correlation (which is a straightforward measure of internal consistency) is a much more useful index than coefficient alpha per se (which is not). Thus, test developers should work toward a target mean interitem correlation rather than try to achieve a particular level of alpha. As a more specific guideline, we recommend that the average interitem correlation fall in the range of .15–.50 (see Briggs & Cheek, 1986). This rather wide range is suggested because the optimal value necessarily will vary with the generality versus specificity of the target construct. If one is measuring a broad higher order construct such as extraversion, a mean correlation as low as .15–.20 probably is desirable; by contrast, for a valid measure of a narrower construct such as talkativeness, a much higher mean intercorrelation (perhaps in the .40–.50 range) is needed.

As suggested earlier, however, the average interitem correlation alone cannot establish the unidimensionality of a scale; in fact, a multidimensional scale actually can have an acceptable level of internal consistency. Cortina (1993, Table 2), for instance, reported the example of an artificially constructed 18-item scale composed of two distinct 9-item groups. The items that made up each cluster were highly homogeneous and in each case had an average interitem correlation of .50. However, the two groups were made to be orthogonal, such that items in different clusters correlated zero with one another. Obviously, the scale was not unidimensional, but instead reflected two distinct dimensions; nevertheless, it had a coefficient alpha of .85 and a moderate mean interitem correlation of approximately .24.

This example clearly illustrates that one can achieve a seemingly satisfactory mean interitem correlation by averaging many high coefficients with many low ones. Thus, unidimensionality cannot be ensured simply by focusing on the mean interitem correlation; rather, it is necessary to examine the range and distribution of these correlations as well. Consequently, we must amend our earlier guideline to state that virtually all of the individual interitem correlations should fall somewhere in the range of .15 to .50. Put another way, to ensure unidimensionality, almost all of the interitem correlations should be moderate in magnitude and should cluster narrowly around the mean value. B. F. Green (1978) articulated this principle most eloquently, stating that the item intercorrelation matrix should appear as "a calm but insistent sea of small, highly similar correlations" (pp. 665–666).

The "Attenuation Paradox"

Some readers may be puzzled by our assertion that all of the interitem correlations should be moderate in magnitude. As we have seen, estimates of internal consistency will increase as the average interitem correlation increases; obviously, therefore, one can maximize internal consistency estimates by retaining items that are very highly correlated with others in the pool. It is not desirable, therefore, to retain highly intercorrelated items in the final scale?

No, it is not. This is the essence of the classic attenuation paradox in psychometric theory (see Boyle, 1991; Briggs & Cheek, 1986; Loevinger, 1954, 1957). Simply put, the paradox is that increasing the internal consistency of a test beyond a certain point will not enhance its construct validity and, in fact, may occur at the expense of validity. One reason for this is that strongly intercorrelated items are highly redundant: Once one of them is included in the scale, the other(s) contribute virtually no incremental information. For instance, it is well known that a test developer can achieve a highly reliable scale simply by writing several slightly reworded versions of the same basic item. Consider, for example, the three items "I often feel uncomfortable at parties," "Large social gatherings make me uneasy," and "I usually feel anxious at big social events." Because virtually everyone will respond to these variants in the same way (e.g., they either will endorse or deny them all), the items together will yield little more construct-relevant information than any one item individually. Accordingly, a scale will yield far more information—and, hence, be a more valid measure of a construct—if it contains more differentiated items that are only moderately intercorrelated.

Note, moreover, that maximizing internal consistency almost invariably produces a scale that is quite narrow in content; if the scale is narrower than the target construct, its validity is compromised. For instance, imagine two investigators each developing measures of general negative affect. The first chooses terms reflecting a wide array of negative mood states (scared, angry, guilty, sad, and scornful), whereas the second selects various indicators of fear and anxiety (scared, fearful, anxious, worried, and nervous). The latter scale will yield a higher reliability estimate, in that it consists of more semantically similar (and, therefore, more strongly intercorrelated) items; clearly, however, the former scale is a more valid measure of the broad construct of general negative affect.

In light of this paradox, it becomes clear that the goal of scale construction is to maximize validity rather than reliability. This is not to say that internal consistency estimates are useless or inappropriate. Indeed, coefficient alpha and other indices of internal consistency convey very important information regarding the proportion of error variance contained in the scale (see Cortina, 1993), and it is always desirable to demonstrate that a scale possesses an adequate level of reliability. Following the general guidelines of Nunnally (1978), we recommend that scale developers always strive for a coefficient alpha of at least .80; if a new scale or subscale falls below this mark, then revision should be undertaken to try to raise reliability to an acceptable level. This may involve writing additional items for a too-brief scale or eliminating weaker items from a longer one. Nevertheless, an overconcern with internal consistency per se can be counterproductive: Once this benchmark of .80 has been secured with an appropriate number of items (as low as 4 or 5 items for very narrow constructs up to about 35 items for broad dimensions), there is no need to strive for any substantial increases in reliability.

Structural Analyses in Scale Construction

Given that internal consistency estimates are untrustworthy guides, how can one achieve the desired goal of a unidimensional scale? How does one produce a "calm sea of highly similar correlations?" It is conceivable that this could be accomplished through a careful inspection of the item intercorrelation matrix, perhaps in conjunction with a standard reliability program (such as those contained in SAS and SPSS). However, as the pool of candidate items increases, this process becomes unwieldy. Note, for instance, that a pool of only 30 items generates 435 individual intercorrelations to be inspected and evaluated, and that a pool of 40 items produces nearly 800 item intercorrelations.

Consequently, psychometricians strongly recommend that the test developer begin by factor-analyzing the items (Briggs & Cheek, 1986; Comrey, 1988; Cortina, 1993; Floyd & Widaman, 1995). Unfortunately, many test developers are hesitant to use factor analysis, either because it requires a relatively large number of respondents or because it involves several perplexing decisions. Both these concerns are unwarranted. First, it is true that factor analysis requires a minimum of 200–300 respondents (Comrey, 1988; Guadagnoli & Velicer, 1988), but this ultimately is no more than is needed for any good correlational or reliability analysis. Second, although the factor analyst must make a number of tactical decisions (e.g., methods of factor extraction and rotation), these decisions typically have much less effect on the resulting factor structures than is commonly believed; in fact, factor structures have been shown to be highly robust across different methods of factor extraction and rotation (see Guadagnoli & Velicer, 1988; Snook & Gorsuch, 1989; Watson et al., 1994). Hence, there is no reason to avoid using factor techniques in the initial stages of item selection. Nevertheless, as we stated earlier, the more one knows about this technique, the greater the probability that it will be used wisely; therefore, it is important that test developers either learn about the technique or consult with a psychometrician during the scale development process.

A thorough discussion of factor analysis is beyond the scope of this article (see especially Floyd & Widaman, 1995), but we will offer a very brief sketch of how it can be used in item selection. For the sake of simplicity, we consider the case of constructing a single unidimensional measure. First, subject the items to either a principal factor analysis (strongly preferred by Comrey, 1988) or a principal components analysis (recommended by Cortina, 1993) and extract the first few factors (say, four or five); in this simplified case, there is no need to be concerned with rotation. Next, examine the loadings of items on the first unrotated factor or component, which can be viewed as a direct measure of the common construct defined by the item pool. Items that load weakly on this first factor (below .35 in a principal factor analysis or below .40 in a principal components analysis) tend to be modestly correlated with the others and are leading candidates for removal from the scale. Similarly, items that have stronger loadings on later factors also are likely candidates for deletion. Conversely, items that load relatively strongly on the first factor and relatively weakly on subsequent factors are excellent candidates for retention. Thus, factor analysis quickly enables one to generate testable hypotheses regarding which items are good indicators of the construct and which are not. These predictions then can be evaluated in subsequent correlational and reliability analyses, which also can be used to identify pairs of redundant, highly correlated items.

A well-designed factor analysis also can play a crucial role in enhancing the discriminant validity of a new measure. For instance, we noted earlier that many new scales are not clearly differentiable from the broad trait of neuroticism (negative affectivity), thereby lacking discriminant validity. The easiest way to avoid creating yet another neuroticism measure is to subject the items of the provisional scale—together with a roughly equal number of neuroticism items—to a joint factor analysis. In this instance, one would extract two factors and rotate them to "simple structure" (e.g., using varimax or promax). Ideally, the target scale items (but often only a subset thereof) will load strongly on one factor, whereas the neuroticism items will load highly on the other. If not, then the new scale apparently is indistinguishable from neuroticism and the situation is likely to be hopeless. If so, then items that load strongly on the provisional scale factor—but quite weakly on the neuroticism factor—are excellent candidates for retention; conversely, items with relatively high loadings on the neuroticism factor have poor discriminant validity and probably should be dropped. This procedure can be followed for any construct that needs to be differentiated from the target scale, as long as marker items assessing the construct have been included in the initial data collection. At this stage of development, confirmatory factor analytic techniques also can be used to evaluate interrelations among scale items and their discriminant validity in comparison with related measures (see Floyd & Widaman, 1995, for an expanded discussion of the role of confirmatory factor analytic techniques in scale construction).

Creating Subscales

We conclude this section with a brief consideration of subscales. In using the term *subscales*, we are referring to a situation in which a set of related measures are designed both to be assessed and analyzed separately and also to be combined into a single overall score. In other words, subscales are hypothesized to be specific manifestations of a more general construct. Defined in this way, subscales are a popular and important feature of test construction, as illustrated by the fact that approximately 70% of the *Psychological Assessment* sample included subscale development.

Creating valid subscales is an exceptionally tricky process, so much so that it is difficult to believe that it can be accomplished without some variant of factor analysis.[2] Indeed, the test constructor resembles the legendary hero Odysseus, who had to steer a narrow course between the twin terrors of Scylla and Charybdis. On the one hand, it makes no psychometric sense to combine unrelated items or subscales into a single overall score (although many scales developed by criterion keying do, in fact, show this property; see Carver, 1989). Accordingly, the scale developer must establish that all of the items—regardless of how they are placed in the various subscales—define a single general factor. If they do not, then the items need to be split off into separate, distinct scales. On the other hand, it also makes no psychometric sense to take a homogeneous pool of substantially intercorrelated items and arbitrarily divide it into separate subscales (e.g., on the basis of apparent differences in content). Accordingly, the scale developer must demonstrate

---

[2] We acknowledge that this statement reflects a modern prejudice. Loevinger, Gleser, and DuBois (1953) developed a technique for "maximizing the discriminating power of a multiple-score test" (p. 309) that achieves the same end. This technique also has the practical advantage of treating items as all-or-none units, thereby paralleling the way they typically are used in scoring scales; by contrast, factor analysis apportions the item variance among the extracted factors, which necessitates decisions regarding factor-loading cutoffs to retain or eliminate items.

that the intrasubscale item correlations (i.e., among the items that make up each subscale) are systematically higher than the intersubscale item correlations (i.e., between the items of different subscales). If this condition cannot be met, then the subscales should be abandoned in favor of a single overall score.

To illustrate the test developer's dilemma, consider the example of a test composed of two 10-item subscales. Let us further assume that the average intercorrelation of the items that make up Subscale A is .40, whereas that for Subscale B is .35. If, on the one hand, the average correlation between the A items and the B items is near zero—such that the two subscales also are essentially uncorrelated—then there is no justification for combining them into a single overall score; rather, they simply should be analyzed as two distinct constructs. On the other hand, if the average correlation between the A items and the B items is much above .30, there is no justification for dividing the items into two arbitrary subscales; instead, they simply should be summed into a single 20-item score. In this hypothetical case, the test developer's task is to have the mean correlation between the A items and B items be significantly greater than zero but substantially less than the average within-subscale values (say, .20). Without the assistance of a sophisticated structural technique such as factor analysis, this truly is a formidable task. Finally, we emphasize again that in making the decision of whether subscales are warranted, both theoretical and empirical considerations should be brought to bear, and data from diverse samples representing the entire range of the scale's target population should be considered.

EXTERNAL VALIDITY: THE ONGOING PROCESS

Just as graduation is properly called *commencement* to emphasize that it signals a beginning as well as an end, the process that we have described represents the initial rather than the final steps in scale development, refinement, and validation. However, the quality of the initial stages has clear ramifications for those stages that follow. For example, if the target concept is clearly conceptualized and delineated initially, then the resulting scale more likely will represent a novel contribution to the assessment armamentarium. If a widely relevant range of content is included in the original item pool, then the scale's range of clinical utility will be more clearly defined. Similarly, if the scale has been constructed with a focus on unidimensionality and not just internal consistency, then the scale will identify a more homogeneous clinical group, rather than a heterogeneous group requiring further demarcation. Finally, if issues of convergent and discriminant validity have been considered from the outset, then it will be far easier to delineate the construct boundaries precisely and to achieve the important goal of knowing exactly what the scale measures and what it does not.

Previously, Jackson (1970) has written extensively about the role of external validity in scale development. Moreover, in this issue, Smith and McCarthy (1995) describe the later refinement stages in some detail, so we conclude by noting simply that both the target of measurement and measurement of the target are important for optimal scale development. That is, later stages will proceed more smoothly if the earlier stages have been marked by both theoretical clarity (i.e., careful definition of the construct) and empirical precision (i.e., careful consideration of psychometric principles and procedures). Thus, we leave the aspiring scale developer well begun but far less than half done.

REFERENCES

American Psychological Association. (1985). *Standards for educational and psychological testing*. Washington, DC: Author.

Angleitner, A., & Wiggins, J. S. (1985). *Personality assessment via questionnaires*. New York: Springer-Verlag.

Bentler, P. M. (1969). Semantic space is (approximately) bipolar. *Journal of Psychology, 71*, 33–40.

Boyle, G. J. (1991). Does item homogeneity indicate internal consistency or item redundancy in psychometric scales? *Personality and Individual Differences, 3*, 291–294.

Briggs, S. R., & Cheek, J. M. (1986). The role of factor analysis in the development and evaluation of personality scales. *Journal of Personality, 54*, 106–148.

Carver, C. S. (1989). How should multifaceted personality constructs be tested? Issues illustrated by self-monitoring, attributional style, and hardiness. *Journal of Personality and Social Psychology, 56*, 577–585.

Clark, L. A. (1993). *Schedule for Nonadaptive and Adaptive Personality (SNAP)*. Minneapolis: University of Minnesota Press.

Clark, L. A., Watson, D., & Reynolds, S. (1995). Diagnosis and classification in psychopathology: Challenges to the current system and future directions. *Annual Review of Psychology, 46*, 121–153.

Comrey, A. L. (1988). Factor-analytic methods of scale development in personality and clinical psychology. *Journal of Consulting and Clinical Psychology, 56*, 754–761.

Cortina, J. M. (1993). What is coefficient alpha? An examination of theory and applications. *Journal of Applied Psychology, 78*, 98–104.

Cronbach, L. J. (1951). Coefficient alpha and the internal structure of tests. *Psychometrika, 16*, 297–334.

Cronbach, L. J., & Meehl, P. E. (1955). Construct validity in psychological test. *Psychological Bulletin, 52*, 281–302.

Dekovic, M., Janssens, J. M. A. M., & Gerris, J. R. M. (1991). Factor structure and construct validity of the Block Child Rearing Practices Report (CRPR). *Psychological Assessment, 3*, 182–187.

Floyd, F. J., & Widaman, K. F. (1995). Factor analysis in the development and refinement of clinical assessment instruments. *Psychological Assessment, 7*, 286–299.

Gangestad, S. W., & Snyder, M. (1991). Taxonomic analysis redux: Some statistical considerations for testing a latent class model. *Journal of Personality and Social Psychology, 61*, 141–161.

Green, B. F., Jr. (1978). In defense of measurement. *American Psychologist, 33*, 664–670.

Green, D. P., Goldman, S. L., & Salovey, P. (1993). Measurement error masks bipolarity in affect ratings. *Journal of Personality and Social Psychology, 64*, 1029–1041.

Green, S. B., Lissitz, R. W., & Mulaik, S. A. (1977). Limitations of coefficient alpha as an index of test unidimensionality. *Educational and Psychological Measurement, 37*, 827–838.

Guadagnoli, E., & Velicer, W. F. (1988). Relation of sample size to the stability of component patterns. *Psychological Bulletin, 103*, 265–275.

Hambleton, R. K., Swaminathan, H., & Rogers, H. J. (1991). *Fundamentals of item response theory*. Newbury Park, CA: Sage.

Haynes, S. N., Richard, D. C. S., & Kubany, E. S. (1995). Content validity in psychological assessment. A functional approach to concepts and methods. *Psychological Assessment, 7*, 238–247.

Hogan, R. T. (1983). A socioanalytic theory of personality. In M. Page (Ed.), *1982 Nebraska Symposium on Motivation* (pp. 55–89). Lincoln: University of Nebraska Press.

Holden, R. R., Fekken, G. C., & Cotton, D. H. G. (1991). Assessing psychopathology using structured test-item response latencies. *Psychological Assessment, 3*, 111–118.

Jackson, D. N. (1970). A sequential system for personality scale development. In C. D. Spielberger (Ed.), *Current topics in clinical and community psychology* (Vol. 2, pp. 61–96). New York: Academic Press.

Jaffe, A., & Kilbey, M. M. (1994). The Cocaine Expectancy Questionnaire (CEQ): Construction and predictive utility. *Psychological Assessment, 6*, 18–26.

John, O. P. (1990). The "Big Five" factor taxonomy: Dimensions of personality in the natural language and in questionnaires. In L. A. Pervin (Ed.), *Handbook of personality: Theory and research* (pp. 66–100). New York: Guilford Press.

King, D. W., King, L. A., Fairbank, J. A., Schlenger, W. E., & Surface, C. R. (1993). Enhancing the precision of the Mississippi Scale for Combat-Related Posttraumatic Stress Disorder: An application of item response theory. *Psychological Assessment, 5*, 457–471.

Kline, P. (1986). *A handbook of test construction: Introduction to psychometric design*. New York: Methuen.

Kuder, G. F., & Richardson, M. W. (1937). The theory of the estimation of test reliability. *Psychometrika, 2*, 151–160.

Loevinger, J. (1954). The attenuation paradox in test theory. *Psychological Bulletin, 51*, 493–504.

Loevinger, J. (1957). Objective tests as instruments of psychological theory. *Psychological Reports, 3*, 635–694.

Loevinger, J., Gleser, G. C., & DuBois, P. H. (1953). Maximizing the discriminating power of a multiple-score test. *Psychometrika, 18*, 309–317.

Meehl, P. E. (1945). The dynamics of structured personality tests. *Journal of Clinical Psychology, 1*, 296–303.

Meehl, P. E., & Golden, R. R. (1982). Taxometric methods. In P. C. Kendall & J. N. Butcher (Eds.), *Handbook of research methods in clinical psychology* (pp. 127–181). New York: Wiley.

Nunnally, J. C. (1978). *Psychometric theory* (2nd ed.). New York: McGraw-Hill.

Reise, S. P., & Waller, N. G. (1993). Traitedness and the assessment of response pattern scalability. *Journal of Personality and Social Psychology, 65*, 143–151.

Reise, S. P., Widaman, K. F., & Pugh, R. H. (1993). Confirmatory factor analysis and item response theory: Two approaches for exploring measurement invariance. *Psychological Bulletin, 114*, 552–566.

Smith, G. T., & McCarthy, D. M. (1995). Methodological considerations in the refinement of clinical assessment instruments. *Psychological Assessment, 7*, 300–308.

Snook, S. C., & Gorsuch, R. L. (1989). Component analysis versus common factor analysis: A Monte Carlo study. *Psychological Bulletin, 106*, 148–154.

Tellegen, A., & Waller, N. G. (in press). Exploring personality through test construction: Development of the Multidimensional Personality Questionnaire. In S. R. Briggs & J. M. Cheek (Eds.), *Personality measures: Development and evaluation* (Vol. 1). Greenwich, CT: JAI Press.

Turner, S., Beidel, D. C., Dancu, C. V., & Stanley, M. A. (1989). An empirically derived inventory to measure social fears and anxiety: The Social Phobia and Anxiety Inventory. *Psychological Assessment, 1*, 35–40.

Watson, D., & Clark, L. A. (1984). Negative affectivity: The disposition to experience aversive emotional states. *Psychological Bulletin, 96*, 465–490.

Watson, D., Clark, L. A., & Harkness, A. R. (1994). Structures of personality and their relevance to psychopathology. *Journal of Abnormal Psychology, 103*, 18–31.

12

VALIDITY OF PSYCHOLOGICAL ASSESSMENT: VALIDATION OF INFERENCES FROM PERSONS' RESPONSES AND PERFORMANCES AS SCIENTIFIC INQUIRY INTO SCORE MEANING

SAMUEL MESSICK

Validity is an overall evaluative judgment of the degree to which empirical evidence and theoretical rationales support the adequacy and appropriateness of interpretations and actions on the basis of test scores or other modes of assessment (Messick, 1989b). Validity is not a property of the test or assessment as such, but rather of the meaning of the test scores. These scores are a function not only of the items or stimulus conditions, but also of the persons responding as well as the context of the assessment. In particular, what needs to be valid is the meaning or interpretation of the score; as well as any implications for action that this meaning entails (Cronbach,

Reprinted from *American Psychologist, 50,* 741–749. Copyright 1995 by the American Psychological Association.

1971). The extent to which score meaning and action implications hold across persons or population groups and across settings or contexts is a persistent and perennial empirical question. This is the main reason that validity is an evolving property and validation a continuing process.

THE VALUE OF VALIDITY

The principles of validity apply not just to interpretive and action inferences derived from test scores as ordinarily conceived, but also to inferences based on any means of observing or documenting consistent behaviors or attributes. Thus, the term *score* is used generically in its broadest sense to mean any coding or summarization of observed consistencies or performance regularities on a test, questionnaire, observation procedure, or other assessment devices such as work samples, portfolios, and realistic problem simulations.

This general usage subsumes qualitative as well as quantitative summaries. It applies, for example, to behavior protocols, to clinical appraisals, to computerized verbal score reports, and to behavioral or performance judgments or ratings. Scores in this sense are not limited to behavioral consistencies and attributes of persons (e.g., persistence and verbal ability). Scores may also refer to functional consistencies and attributes of groups, situations or environments, and objects or institutions, as in measures of group solidarity, situational stress, quality of artistic products, and such social indicators as school dropout rate.

Hence, the principles of validity apply to all assessments, including performance assessments. For example, student portfolios are often the source of inferences—not just about the quality of the included products but also about the knowledge, skills, or other attributes of the student—and such inferences about quality and constructs need to meet standards of validity. This is important because performance assessments, although long a staple of industrial and military applications, are now touted as purported instruments of standards-based education reform because they promise positive consequences for teaching and learning. Indeed, it is precisely because of such politically salient potential consequences that the validity of performance assessment needs to be systematically addressed, as do other basic measurement issues such as reliability, comparability, and fairness. The latter reference to fairness broaches a broader set of equity issues in testing that includes fairness of test use, freedom from bias in scoring and interpretation, and the appropriateness of the test-based constructs or rules underlying decision making or resource allocation, that is, distributive justice (Messick, 1989b).

These issues are critical for performance assessment—as they are for all educational and psychological assessment—because validity, reliability, comparability, and fairness are not just measurement principles, they are social

Samuel Messick. Photo by William
Monachan, Educational Testing Service,
Princeton, NJ.

values that have meaning and force outside of measurement whenever evaluative judgments and decisions are made. As a salient social value, validity assumes both a scientific and a political role that can by no means be fulfilled by a simple correlation coefficient between test scores and a purported criterion (i.e., classical criterion-related validity) or by expert judgments that test content is relevant to the proposed test use (i.e., traditional content validity).

Indeed, validity is broadly defined as nothing less than an evaluative summary of both the evidence for and the actual—as well as potential—consequences of score interpretation and use (i.e., construct validity conceived comprehensively). This comprehensive view of validity integrates considerations of content, criteria, and consequences into a construct framework for empirically testing rational hypotheses about score meaning and utility. Therefore, it is fundamental that score validation is an empirical evaluation of the meaning and consequences of measurement. As such, validation combines scientific inquiry with rational argument to justify (or nullify) score interpretation and use.

COMPREHENSIVENESS OF CONSTRUCT VALIDITY

In principle as well as in practice, construct validity is based on an integration of any evidence that bears on the interpretation or meaning of the test scores—including content- and criterion-related evidence—which are thus subsumed as part of construct validity. In construct validation the test score is not equated with the construct it attempts to tap, nor is it considered to define the construct, as in strict operationalism (Cronbach & Meehl, 1955). Rather, the measure is viewed as just one of an extensible set of indicators of the construct. Convergent empirical relationships reflecting communality among such indicators are taken to imply the operation of the construct to the degree that discriminant evidence discounts the intrusion of alternative constructs as plausible rival hypotheses.

A fundamental feature of construct validity is construct representation, whereby one attempts to identify through cognitive-process analysis or research on personality and motivation the theoretical mechanisms underlying task performance, primarily by decomposing the task into requisite component processes and assembling them into a functional model or process theory (Embretson, 1983). Relying heavily on the cognitive psychology of information processing, construct representation refers to the relative dependence of task responses on the processes, strategies, and knowledge (including metacognitive or self-knowledge) that are implicated in task performance.

Sources of Invalidity

There are two major threats to construct validity: In the one known as *construct underrepresentation*, the assessment is too narrow and fails to include important dimensions or facets of the construct. In the threat to validity known as *construct-irrelevant variance*, the assessment is too broad, containing excess reliable variance associated with other distinct constructs as well as method variance such as response sets or guessing propensities that affects responses in a manner irrelevant to the interpreted construct. Both threats are operative in all assessments. Hence a primary validation concern is the extent to which the same assessment might underrepresent the focal construct while simultaneously contaminating the scores with construct-irrelevant variance.

There are two basic kinds of construct-irrelevant variance. In the language of ability and achievement testing, these might be called *construct-irrelevant difficulty* and *construct-irrelevant easiness*. In the former, aspects of the task that are extraneous to the focal construct make the task irrelevantly difficult for some individuals or groups. An example is the intrusion of undue reading comprehension requirements in a test of subject matter knowledge. In general, construct-irrelevant difficulty leads to construct scores that are invalidly low for those individuals adversely affected (e.g., knowledge scores of poor readers or examinees with limited English proficiency). Of course, if concern is solely with criterion prediction and the criterion performance requires reading skill as well as subject matter knowledge, then both sources of variance would be considered criterion-relevant and valid. However, for score interpretations in terms of subject matter knowledge and for any score uses based thereon, undue reading requirements would constitute construct-irrelevant difficulty.

Indeed, construct-irrelevant difficulty for individuals and groups is a major source of bias in test scoring and interpretation and of unfairness in test use. Differences in construct-irrelevant difficulty for groups, as distinct from construct-relevant group differences, is the major culprit sought in analyses of differential item functioning (Holland & Wainer, 1993).

In contrast, construct-irrelevant easiness occurs when extraneous clues in item or task formats permit some individuals to respond correctly or appropriately in ways irrelevant to the construct being assessed. Another instance occurs when the specific test material, either deliberately or inadvertently, is highly familiar to some respondents, as when the text of a reading comprehension passage is well-known to some readers or the musical score for a sight reading exercise invokes a well-drilled rendition for some performers. Construct-irrelevant easiness leads to scores that are invalidly high for the affected individuals as reflections of the construct under scrutiny.

The concept of construct-irrelevant variance is important in all educational and psychological measurement, including performance assessments. This is especially true of richly contextualized assessments and so-called "authentic" simulations of real-world tasks. This is the case because "paradoxically, the complexity of context is made manageable by contextual clues" (Wiggins, 1993, p. 208). And it matters whether the contextual clues that people respond to are construct-relevant or represent construct-irrelevant difficulty or easiness.

However, what constitutes construct-irrelevant variance is a tricky and contentious issue (Messick, 1994). This is especially true of performance assessments, which typically invoke constructs that are higher order and complex in the sense of subsuming or organizing multiple processes. For example, skill in communicating mathematical ideas might well be considered irrelevant variance in the assessment of mathematical knowledge (although not necessarily vice versa). But both communication skill and mathematical knowledge are considered relevant parts of the higher-order construct of mathematical power, according to the content standards delineated by the National Council of Teachers of Mathematics (1989). It all depends on how compelling the evidence and arguments are that the particular source of variance is a relevant part of the focal construct, as opposed to affording a plausible rival hypothesis to account for the observed performance regularities and relationships with other variables.

A further complication arises when construct-irrelevant variance is deliberately capitalized upon to produce desired social consequences, as in score adjustments for minority groups, within-group norming, or sliding band procedures (Cascio, Outtz, Zedeck, & Goldstein, 1991; Hartigan & Wigdor, 1989; Schmidt, 1991). However, recognizing that these adjustments distort the meaning of the construct as originally assessed, psychologists should distinguish such controversial procedures in applied testing practice (Gottfredson, 1994; Sackett & Wilk, 1994) from the valid assessment of focal constructs and from any score uses based on that construct meaning. Construct-irrelevant variance is always a source of invalidity in the assessment of construct meaning and its action implications. These issues portend the substantive and consequential aspects of construct validity, which are discussed in more detail later.

Sources of Evidence in Construct Validity

In essence, construct validity comprises the evidence and rationales supporting the trustworthiness of score interpretation in terms of explanatory concepts that account for both test performance and score relationships with other variables. In its simplest terms, construct validity is the evidential basis for score interpretation. As an integration of evidence for score meaning, it applies to any score interpretation—not just those involving so-called "theoretical constructs." Almost any kind of information about a test can contribute to an understanding of score meaning, but the contribution becomes stronger if the degree of fit of the information with the theoretical rationale underlying score interpretation is explicitly evaluated (Cronbach, 1988; Kane, 1992; Messick, 1989b). Historically, primary emphasis in construct validation has been placed on internal and external test structures—that is, on the appraisal of theoretically expected patterns of relationships among item scores or between test scores and other measures.

Probably even more illuminating in regard to score meaning are studies of expected performance differences over time, across groups and settings, and in response to experimental treatments and manipulations. For example, over time one might demonstrate the increased scores from childhood to young adulthood expected for measures of impulse control. Across groups and settings, one might contrast the solution strategies of novices versus experts for measures of domain problem-solving or, for measures of creativity, contrast the creative productions of individuals in self-determined as opposed to directive work environments. With respect to experimental treatments and manipulations, one might seek increased knowledge scores as a function of domain instruction or increased achievement motivation scores as a function of greater benefits and risks. Possibly most illuminating of all, however, are direct probes and modeling of the processes underlying test responses, which are becoming both more accessible and more powerful with continuing developments in cognitive psychology (Frederiksen, Mislevy, & Bejar, 1993; Snow & Lohman, 1989). At the simplest level, this might involve querying respondents about their solution processes or asking them to think aloud while responding to exercises during field trials.

In addition to reliance on these forms of evidence, construct validity, as previously indicated, also subsumes content relevance and representativeness as well as criterion-relatedness. This is the case because such information about the range and limits of content coverage and about specific criterion behaviors predicted by the test scores clearly contributes to score interpretation. In the latter instance, correlations between test scores and criterion measures—viewed within the broader context of other evidence supportive of score meaning—contribute to the joint construct validity of both predictor and criterion. In other words, empirical relationships between predictor scores and criterion measures should make theoretical sense in terms of what the predictor test is interpreted to measure and what the criterion is presumed to embody (Gulliksen, 1950).

An important form of validity evidence still remaining bears on the social consequences of test interpretation and use. It is ironic that validity theory has paid so little attention over the years to the consequential basis of test validity, because validation practice has long invoked such notions as the functional worth of the testing—that is, a concern over how well the test does the job for which it is used (Cureton, 1951; Rulon, 1946). And to appraise how well a test does its job, one must inquire whether the potential and actual social consequences of test interpretation and use are not only supportive of the intended testing purposes, but also at the same time consistent with other social values.

With some trepidation due to the difficulties inherent in forecasting, both potential and actual consequences are included in this formulation for two main reasons: First, anticipation of likely outcomes may guide one where to look for side effects and toward what kinds of evidence are needed to monitor consequences; second, such anticipation may alert one to take timely steps to capitalize on positive effects and to ameliorate or forestall negative effects.

However, this form of evidence should not be viewed in isolation as a separate type of validity, say, of "consequential validity." Rather, because the values served in the intended and unintended outcomes of test interpretation and use both derive from and contribute to the meaning of the test scores, appraisal of the social consequences of the testing is also seen to be subsumed as an aspect of construct validity (Messick, 1964, 1975, 1980). In the language of the Cronbach and Meehl (1955) seminal manifesto on construct validity, the intended consequences of the testing are strands in the construct's nomological network representing presumed action implications of score meaning. The central point is that unintended consequences, when they occur, are also strands in the construct's nomological network that need to be taken into account in construct theory, score interpretation, and test use. At issue is evidence for not only negative but also positive consequences of testing, such as the promised benefits of educational performance assessment for teaching and learning.

A major concern in practice is to distinguish adverse consequences that stem from valid descriptions of individual and group differences from adverse consequences that derive from sources of test invalidity such as construct underrepresentation and construct-irrelevant variance. The latter adverse consequences of test invalidity present measurement problems that need to be investigated in the validation process, whereas the former consequences of valid assessment represent problems of social policy. But more about this later.

Thus, the process of construct validation evolves from these multiple sources of evidence a mosaic of convergent and discriminant findings supportive of score meaning. However, in anticipated applied test use, this mosaic of general evidence may or may not include pertinent specific evidence of (a) the relevance of the test to the particular applied purpose and (b) the utility of the test in the applied setting. Hence, the general construct validity evidence may need to be buttressed in applied instances by specific evidence of relevance and utility.

In summary, the construct validity of score interpretation comes to undergird all score-based inferences—not just those related to interpretive meaningfulness but also the content- and criterion-related inferences specific to applied decisions and actions based on test scores. From the discussion thus far, it should also be clear that test validity cannot *rely* on any one of the supplementary forms of evidence just discussed. However, neither does validity *require* any one form, granted that there is defensible convergent and discriminant evidence supporting score meaning. To the extent that some form of evidence cannot be developed—as when criterion-related studies must be forgone because of small sample sizes, unreliable or contaminated criteria, and highly restricted score ranges—heightened emphasis can be placed on other evidence, especially on the construct validity of the predictor tests and on the relevance of the construct to the criterion domain (Guion, 1976; Messick, 1989b). What *is* required is a compelling argument that the available evidence justifies the test interpretation and use, even though some pertinent evidence had to be forgone. Hence, validity becomes a unified concept, and the unifying force is the meaningfulness or trustworthy interpretability of the test scores and their action implications, namely, construct validity.

ASPECTS OF CONSTRUCT VALIDITY

However, to speak of validity as a unified concept does not imply that validity cannot be usefully differentiated into distinct aspects to underscore issues and nuances that might otherwise be downplayed or overlooked, such as the social consequences of performance assessments or the role of score meaning in applied use. The intent of these distinctions is to provide a means of addressing functional aspects of validity that help disentangle some of the complexities inherent in appraising the appropriateness, meaningfulness, and usefulness of score inferences.

In particular, six distinguishable aspects of construct validity are highlighted as a means of addressing central issues implicit in the notion of validity as a unified concept. These are content, substantive, structural, generalizability, external, and consequential aspects of construct validity. In effect, these six aspects function as general validity criteria or standards for all educational and psychological measurement (Messick, 1989b). Following a capsule description of these six aspects, some of the validity issues and sources of evidence bearing on each are highlighted:

- The content aspect of construct validity includes evidence of content relevance, representativeness, and technical quality (Lennon, 1956; Messick, 1989b);
- The substantive aspect refers to theoretical rationales for the observed consistencies in test responses, including process models of task performance (Embretson, 1983), along with empirical evidence that the theoretical processes are actually engaged by respondents in the assessment tasks;
- The structural aspect appraises the fidelity of the scoring structure to the structure of the construct domain at issue (Loevinger, 1957; Messick, 1989b);
- The generalizability aspect examines the extent to which score properties score properties and interpretations generalize to and across population groups, settings, and tasks (Cook & Campbell, 1979; Shulman, 1970), including validity generalization of test criterion relationships (Hunter, Schmidt, & Jackson, 1982);
- The external aspect includes convergent and discriminant evidence from multitrait–multimethod comparisons (Campbell & Fiske, 1959), as well as evidence of criterion relevance and applied utility (Cronbach & Gleser, 1965);
- The consequential aspect appraises the value implications of score interpretation as a basis for action as well as the actual and potential consequences of test use, especially in regard to sources of invalidity related to issues of bias, fairness, and distributive justice (Messick, 1980, 1989b).

Content Relevance and Representativeness

A key issue for the content aspect of construct validity is the specification of the boundaries of the construct domain to be assessed—that is, determining the knowledge, skills, attitudes, motives, and other attributes to be revealed by the assessment tasks. The boundaries and structure of the construct domain can be addressed by means of job analysis, task analysis, curriculum analysis, and especially domain theory, in other words, scientific inquiry into the nature of the domain processes and the ways in which they combine to produce effects or outcomes. A major goal of domain theory is to understand the construct-relevant sources of task difficulty, which then serves as a guide to the rational development and scoring of performance tasks and other assessment formats. At whatever stage of its development, then, domain theory is a primary basis for specifying the boundaries and structure of the construct to be assessed.

However, it is not sufficient merely to select tasks that are relevant to the construct domain. In addition, the assessment should assemble tasks that are representative of the domain in some sense. The intent is to insure that all important parts of the construct domain are covered, which is usually described as selecting tasks that sample domain processes in terms of their functional importance, or what Brunswik (1956) called *ecological sampling*. Functional importance can be considered in terms of what people actually do in the performance domain, as in job analyses, but also in terms of what characterizes and differentiates expertise in the domain, which would usually emphasize different tasks and processes. Both the content relevance and representativeness of assessment tasks are traditionally appraised by expert professional judgment, documentation of which serves to address the content aspect of construct validity.

Substantive Theories, Process Models, and Process Engagement

The substantive aspect of construct validity emphasizes the role of substantive theories and process modeling in identifying the domain processes to be revealed in assessment tasks (Embretson, 1983; Messick, 1989b). Two important points are involved: One is the need for tasks providing appropriate sampling of domain processes in addition to traditional coverage of domain content; the other is the need to move beyond traditional professional judgment of content to accrue empirical evidence that the ostensibly sampled processes are actually engaged by respondents in task performance.

Thus, the substantive aspect adds to the content aspect of construct validity the need for empirical evidence of response consistencies or performance regularities reflective of domain processes (Loevinger, 1957). Such evidence may derive from a variety of sources, for example, from "think aloud" protocols or eye movement records during task performance; from correlation patterns among part scores; from consistencies in response times for task segments; or from mathematical or computer modeling of task processes (Messick, 1989b, pp. 53–55; Snow & Lohman, 1989). In summary, the issue of domain coverage refers not just to the content representativeness of the construct measure but also to the process representation of the construct and the degree to which these processes are reflected in construct measurement.

The core concept bridging the content and substantive aspects of construct validity is representativeness. This becomes clear once one recognizes that the term *representative* has two distinct meanings, both of which are applicable to performance assessment. One is in the cognitive psychologist's sense of representation or modeling (Suppes, Pavel, & Falmagne, 1994); the other is in the Brunswikian sense of ecological sampling (Brunswik, 1956; Snow, 1974). The choice of tasks or contexts in assessment is a representative sampling issue. The comprehensiveness and fidelity of simulating the construct's realistic engagement in performance is a representation issue. Both issues are important in educational and psychological measurement and especially in performance assessment.

Scoring Models As Reflective of Task and Domain Structure

According to the structural aspect of construct validity, scoring models should be rationally consistent with what is known about the structural relations inherent in behavioral manifestations of the construct in question (Loevinger, 1957; Peak, 1953). That is, the theory of the construct domain should guide not only the selection or construction of relevant assessment tasks but also the rational development of construct-based scoring criteria and rubrics.

Ideally, the manner in which behavioral instances are combined to produce a score should rest on knowledge of how the processes underlying those behaviors combine dynamically to produce effects. Thus, the internal structure of the assessment (i.e., interrelations among the scored aspects of task and subtask performance) should be consistent with what is known about the internal structure of the construct domain (Messick, 1989b). This property of construct-based rational scoring models is called *structural fidelity* (Loevinger, 1957).

Generalizability and the Boundaries of Score Meaning

The concern that a performance assessment should provide representative coverage of the content and processes of the construct domain is meant to insure that the score interpretation not be limited to the sample of assessed tasks but be broadly generalizable to the construct domain. Evidence of such generalizability depends on the degree of correlation of the assessed tasks with other tasks representing the construct or aspects of the construct. This issue of generalizability of score inferences across tasks and contexts goes to the very heart of score meaning. Indeed, setting the boundaries of score meaning is precisely what generalizability evidence is meant to address.

However, because of the extensive time required for the typical performance task, there is a conflict in performance assessment between time-intensive depth of examination and the breadth of domain coverage needed for generalizability of construct interpretation. This conflict between depth and breadth of coverage is often viewed as entailing a trade-off between validity and reliability (or generalizability). It might better be depicted as a trade-off between the valid description of the specifics of a complex tax and the power of construct interpretation. In any event, such a conflict signals a design problem that needs to be carefully negotiated in performance assessment (Wiggins, 1993).

In addition to generalizability across tasks, the limits of score meaning are also affected by the degree of generalizability across time or occasions and across observers or raters of the task performance. Such sources of measurement error associated with the sampling of tasks, occasions, and scorers underlie traditional reliability concerns (Feldt & Brennan, 1989).

Convergent and Discriminant Correlations With External Variables

The external aspect of construct validity refers to the extent to which the assessment scores' relationships with other measures and nonassessment behaviors reflect the expected high, low, and interactive relations implicit in the theory of the construct being assessed. Thus, the meaning of the scores is substantiated externally by appraising the degree to which empirical relationships with other measures—or the lack thereof—are consistent with that meaning. That is, the constructs represented in the assessment should rationally account for the external pattern of correlations. Both convergent and discriminant correlation patterns are important, the convergent pattern indicating a correspondence between measures of the same construct and the discriminant pattern indicating a distinctness from measures of other constructs (Campbell & Fiske, 1959). Discriminant evidence is particularly critical for discounting plausible rival alternatives to the focal construct interpretation. Both convergent and discriminant evidence are basic to construct validation.

Of special importance among these external relationships are those between the assessment scores and criterion measures pertinent to selection, placement, licensure, program evaluation, or other accountability purposes in applied settings. Once again, the construct theory points to the relevance of potential relationships between the assessment scores and criterion measures, and empirical evidence of such links attests to the utility of the scores for the applied purpose.

Consequences As Validity Evidence

The consequential aspect of construct validity includes evidence and rationales for evaluating the intended and unintended consequences of score interpretation and use in both the short- and long-term. Social consequences of testing may be either positive, such as improved educational policies based on international comparisons of student performance, or negative, especially when associated with bias in scoring and interpretation or with unfairness in test use. For example, because performance assessments in education promise potential benefits for teaching and learning, it is important to accrue evidence of such positive consequences as well as evidence that adverse consequences are minimal.

The primary measurement concern with respect to adverse consequences is that any negative impact on individuals or groups should not derive from any source of test invalidity, such as construct underrepresentation or construct-irrelevant variance (Messick, 1989b). In other words, low scores should not occur because the assessment is missing something relevant to the focal construct that, if present, would have permitted the affected persons to display their competence. Moreover, low scores should not occur because the measurement contains something irrelevant that interferes with the affected persons' demonstration of competence.

Validity As Integrative Summary

These six aspects of construct validity apply to all educational and psychological measurement, including performance assessments. Taken together, they provide a way of addressing the multiple and interrelated validity questions that need to be answered to justify score interpretation and use. In previous writings, I maintained that it is "the relation between the evidence and the inferences drawn that should determine the validation focus" (Messick, 1989b, p. 16). This relation is embodied in theoretical rationales or persuasive arguments that the obtained evidence both supports the preferred inferences and undercuts plausible rival inferences. From this perspective, as Cronbach (1988) concluded, validation is evaluation argument. That is, as stipulated earlier, validation is empirical evaluation of the meaning and consequences of measurement. The term *empirical evaluation* is meant to convey that the validation process is scientific as well as rhetorical and requires both evidence and argument.

By focusing on the argument or rationale used to support the assumptions and inferences invoked in the score-based interpretations and actions of a particular test use, one can prioritize the forms of validity evidence needed according to the points in the argument requiring justification or support (Kane, 1992; Shepard, 1993). Helpful as this may be, there still remain problems in setting priorities for needed evidence because the argument may be incomplete or off target, not all the assumptions may be addressed, and the need to discount alternative arguments evokes multiple priorities. This is one reason that Cronbach (1989) stressed cross-argument criteria for assigning priority to a line of inquiry, such as the degree of prior uncertainty, information yield, cost, and leverage in achieving consensus.

Kane (1992) illustrated the argument-based approach by prioritizing the evidence needed to validate a placement test for assigning students to a course in either remedial algebra or calculus. He addressed seven assumptions that, from the present perspective, bear on the content, substantive, generalizability, external, and consequential aspects of construct validity. Yet the structural aspect is not explicitly addressed. Hence, the compensatory property of the usual cumulative total score, which permits good performance on some algebra skills to compensate for poor performance on others, remains unevaluated in contrast, for example, to scoring models with multiple cut scores or with minimal requirements across the profile of prerequisite skills. The question is whether such profile scoring models might yield not only useful information for diagnosis and remediation but also better student placement.

The structural aspect of construct validity also received little attention in Shepard's (1993) argument-based analysis of the validity of special education placement decisions. This was despite the fact that the assessment referral system under consideration involved a profile of cognitive, biomedical, behavioral, and academic skills that required some kind of structural model linking test results to placement decisions. However, in her analysis of selection uses of the General Aptitude Test Battery (GATB), Shepard (1993) did underscore the structural aspect because the GATB within-group scoring model is both salient and controversial.

The six aspects of construct validity afford a means of checking that the theoretical rationale or persuasive argument linking the evidence to the inferences drawn touches the important bases; if the bases are not covered, an argument that such omissions are defensible must be provided. These six aspects are highlighted because most score-based interpretations and action inferences, as well as the elaborated rationales or arguments that attempt to legitimize them (Kane, 1992), either invoke these properties or assume them, explicitly or tacitly.

In other words, most score interpretations refer to relevant content and operative processes, presumed to be reflected in scores that concatenate responses in domain-appropriate ways and are generalizable across a range of tasks, settings, and occasions. Furthermore, score-based interpretations and actions are typically extrapolated beyond the test context on the basis of presumed relationships with nontest behaviors and anticipated outcomes or consequences. The challenge in test validation is to link these inferences to convergent evidence supporting them and to discriminant evidence discounting plausible rival inferences. Evidence pertinent to all of these aspects needs to be integrated into an overall validity judgment to sustain score inferences and their action implications, or else provide compelling reasons why there is not a link, which is what is meant by validity as a unified concept.

MEANING AND VALUES IN TEST VALIDATION

The essence of unified validity is that the appropriateness, meaningfulness, and usefulness of score-based inferences are inseparable and that the integrating power derives from empirically grounded score interpretation. As seen in this article, both meaning and values are integral to the concept of validity, and psychologists need a way of addressing both concerns in validation practice. In particular, what is needed is a way of configuring validity evidence that forestalls undue reliance on selected forms of evidence as opposed to a pattern of supplementary evidence, that highlights the important yet subsidiary role of specific content- and criterion-related evidence in support of construct validity in testing applications. This means should formally bring consideration of value implications and social consequences into the validity framework.

A unified validity framework meeting these requirements distinguishes two interconnected facets of validity as a unitary concept (Messick, 1989a, 1989b). One facet is the source of justification of the testing based on appraisal of either evidence supportive of score meaning or consequences contributing to score valuation. The other facet is the function or outcome of the testing—either interpretation or applied use. If the facet for justification (i.e., either an evidential basis for meaning implications or a consequential basis for value implications of scores) is crossed with the facet for function or outcome (i.e., either test interpretation or test use), a four-fold classification is obtained, highlighting both meaning and values in both test interpretation and test use, as represented by the row and column headings of Figure 1.

These distinctions may seem fuzzy because they are not only interlinked but overlapping. For example, social consequences of testing are a form of evidence, and other forms of evidence have consequences. Furthermore, to interpret a test is to use it, and all other test uses involve interpretation either explicitly or tacitly. Moreover, utility is both validity evidence and a value consequence. This conceptual messiness derives from cutting through what indeed is a unitary concept to provide a means of discussing its functional aspects.

Each of the cells in this four-fold crosscutting of unified validity are

	Test Interpretation	Test Use
Evidential Basis	Construct Validity (CV)	CV + Relevance/Utility (R/U)
Consequential Basis	CV + Value Implications (VI)	CV + R/U + VI + Social Consequences

Figure 1. Facets of validity as a progressive matrix.

briefly considered in turn, beginning with the evidential basis of test interpretation. Because the evidence and rationales supporting the trustworthiness of score meaning are what is meant by construct validity, the evidential basis of test interpretation is clearly construct validity. The evidential basis of test use is also construct validity, but with the important proviso that the general evidence supportive of score meaning either already includes or becomes enhanced by specific evidence for the relevance of the scores to the applied purpose and for the utility of the scores in the applied setting, where utility is broadly conceived to reflect the benefits of testing relative to its costs (Cronbach & Gleser, 1965).

The consequential basis of test interpretation is the appraisal of value implications of score meaning, including the often tacit value implications of the construct label itself, of the broader theory conceptualizing construct properties and relationships that undergirds construct meaning, and of the still broader ideologies that give theories their perspective and purpose—for example, ideologies about the functions of science or about the nature of the human being as a learner or as an adaptive or fully functioning person. The value implications of score interpretation are not only part of score meaning, but a socially relevant part that often triggers score-based actions and serves to link the construct measured to questions of applied practice and social policy. One way to protect against the tyranny of unexposed and unexamined values in score interpretation is to explicitly adopt multiple value perspectives to formulate and empirically appraise plausible rival hypotheses (Churchman, 1971; Messick, 1989b).

Many constructs such as competence, creativity, intelligence, or extraversion have manifold and arguable value implications that may or may not be sustainable in terms of properties of their associated measures. A central issue is whether the theoretical or trait implications and the value implications of the test interpretation are commensurate, because value implications are not ancillary but, rather, integral to score meaning. Therefore, to make clear that score interpretation is needed to appraise value implications and vice versa, this cell for the consequential basis of test interpretation needs to comprehend both the construct validity as well as the value ramifications of score meaning.

Finally, the consequential basis of test use is the appraisal of both potential and actual social consequences of the applied testing. One approach to appraising potential side effects is to pit the benefits and risks of the proposed test use against the pros and cons of alternatives or counterproposals. By taking multiple perspectives on proposed test use, the various (and sometimes conflicting) value commitments of each proposal are often exposed to open examination and debate (Churchman, 1971; Messick, 1989b). Counterproposals to a proposed test use might involve quite different assessment technique, such as observations or portfolios when educational performance standards are at issue. Counterproposals might attempt to serve the intended purpose in a different way, such as through training rather than selection when productivity levels are at issue (granted that testing may also be used to reduce training costs, and that failure in training yields a form of selection).

What matters is not only where the social consequences of test interpretation and use are positive or negative, but how the consequences came about and what determined them. In particular, it is not that adverse social consequences of test use render the use invalid but, rather, that adverse social consequences should not be attributable to any source of test invalidity, such as construct underrepresentation or construct-irrelevant variance. And once again, in recognition of the fact that the weighing of social consequences both presumes and contributes to evidence of score meaning, of relevance, of utility, and of values, this cell needs to include construct validity, relevance, and utility, as well as social and value consequences.

Some measurement specialists argue that adding value implications and social consequences to the validity framework unduly burdens the concept. However, it is simply not the case that values are being *added* to validity in this unified view. Rather, values are intrinsic to the meaning and outcomes of the testing and have always been. As opposed to adding values to validity as an adjunct or supplement, the unified view instead exposes the inherent value aspects of score meaning and outcome to open examination and debate as an integral part of the validation process (Messick, 1989a). This makes explicit what has been latent all along, namely, that validity judgments *are* value judgments.

A salient feature of Figure 1 is that construct validity appears in every cell, which is fitting because the construct validity of score meaning is the integrating force that unifies validity issues into a unitary concept. At the same time, by distinguishing facets reflecting the justification and function of the testing, it becomes clear that distinct features of construct validity need to be emphasized, in addition to the general mosaic of evidence, as one moves from the focal issue of one cell to that of the others. In particular, the forms of evidence change and compound as one moves from appraisal of evidence for the construct interpretation per se, to appraisal of evidence supportive of a rational basis for test use, to appraisal of the value consequences of score interpretation as a basis for action, and finally, to appraisal of the social consequences—or, more generally, of the functional worth—of test use.

As different foci of emphasis are highlighted in addressing the basic construct validity appearing in each cell, this movement makes what at first glance was a simple four-fold classification appear more like a progressive matrix, as portrayed in the cells of Figure 1. From one perspective, each cell represents construct validity, with different features highlighted on the basis of the justification and function of the testing. From another perspective, the entire progressive matrix represents construct validity, which is another way of saying that validity is a unified concept. One implication of this progressive-matrix formulation is that both meaning and values, as well as both test interpretation and test use, are intertwined in the validation process. Thus, validity and values are one imperative, not two, and test validation implicates both the science and the ethics of assessment, which is why validity has force as a social value.

REFERENCES

Brunswik, E. (1956). *Perception and the representative design of psychological experiments* (2nd ed.). Berkeley: University of California Press.

Campbell, D. T., & Fiske, D. W. (1959). Convergent and discriminant validation by the multitrait−multimethod matrix. *Psychological Bulletin, 56,* 81−105.

Cascio, W. F., Outtz, J., Zedeck, S., & Goldstein, I. L. (1991). Statistical implications of six methods of test score use in personnel selection. *Human Performance, 4,* 233−264.

Churchman, C. W. (1971). *The design of inquiring systems: Basic concepts of systems and organization.* New York: Basic Books.

Cook, T. D., & Campbell, D. T. (1979). *Quasi-experimentation: Design and analysis issues for field settings.* Chicago: Rand McNally.

Cronbach, L. J. (1971). Test validation. In R. L. Thorndike (Ed.), *Educational measurement* (2nd ed., pp. 443−507). Washington, DC: American Council on Education.

Cronbach, L. J. (1988). Five perspectives on validation argument. In H. Wainer & H. Braun (Eds.), *Test validity* (pp. 34−35). Hillsdale, NJ: Erlbaum.

Cronbach, L. J. (1989). Construct validation after thirty years. In R. L. Linn (Ed.), *Intelligence: Measurement, theory, and public policy* (pp. 147−171). Chicago: University of Illinois Press.

Cronbach, L. J., & Gleser, G. C. (1965). *Psychological tests and personnel decisions* (2nd ed.). Urbana: University of Illinois Press.

Cronbach, L. J., & Meehl, P. E. (1955). Construct validity in psychological tests. *Psychological Bulletin, 52,* 281−302.

Cureton, E. E. (1951). Validity. In E. F. Lindquist (Ed.), *Educational measurement* (1st ed., pp. 621−694). Washington, DC: American Council on Education.

Embretson, S. (1983). Construct validity: Construct representation versus nomothetic span. *Psychological Bulletin, 93,* 179−197.

Feldt, L. S., & Brennan, R. L. (1989). Reliability. In R. L. Linn (Ed.), *Educational measurement* (3rd ed., pp. 105−146). New York: Macmillan.

Frederiksen, N., Mislevy, R. J., & Bejar, I. (Eds.). (1993). *Test theory for a new generation of tests.* Hillsdale, NJ: Erlbaum.

Gottfredson, L. S. (1994). The science and politics of race-norming. *American Psychologist, 49,* 955−963.

Guion, R. M. (1976). Recruiting, selection, and job placement. In M. D. Dunnette

(Ed.), *Handbook of industrial and organizational psychology* (pp. 777–828). Chicago: Rand McNally.

Gulliksen, H. (1950). Intrinsic validity. *American Psychologist, 5*, 511–517.

Hartigan, J. A., & Wigdor, A. K. (Eds.). (1989). *Fairness in employment testing: Validity generalization, minority issues, and the General Aptitude Test Battery*. Washington, DC: National Academy Press.

Holland, P. W., & Wainer, H. (Eds.). (1993). *Differential item functioning*. Hillsdale, NJ: Erlbaum.

Hunter, J. E., Schmidt, F. L., & Jackson, C. B. (1982). *Advanced meta-analysis: Quantitative methods of cumulating research findings across studies*. San Fransisco: Sage.

Kane, M. T. (1992). An argument-based approach to validity. *Psychological Bulletin, 112*, 527–535.

Lennon, R. T. (1956). Assumptions underlying the use of content validity. *Educational and Psychological Measurement, 16*, 294–304.

Loevinger, J. (1957). Objective tests as instruments of psychological theory [Monograph]. *Psychological Reports, 3*, 635–694 (Pt. 9).

Messick, S. (1964). Personality measurement and college performance. In *Proceedings of the 1963 Invitational Conference on Testing Problems* (pp. 110–129). Princeton, NJ: Educational Testing Service.

Messick, S. (1975). The standard problem: Meaning and values in measurement and evaluation. *American Psychologist, 30*, 955–966.

Messick, S. (1980). Test validity and the ethics of assessment. *American Psychologist, 35*, 1012–1027.

Messick, S. (1989a). Meaning and values in test validation: The science and ethics of assessment. *Educational Researcher, 19(2)*, 5–11.

Messick, S. (1989b). Validity. In R. L. Linn (Ed.), *Educational measurement* (3rd ed., pp. 13–103). New York: Macmillan.

Messick, S. (1994). The interplay of evidence and consequences in the validation of performance assessments. *Educational Researcher, 23(2)*, 13–23.

National Council of Teachers of Mathematics. (1989). *Curriculum and evaluation standards for school mathematics*. Reston, VA: Author.

Peak, H. (1953). Problems of observation. In L. Festinger & D. Katz (Eds.), *Research methods in the behavioral sciences* (pp. 243–299). Hinsdale, IL: Dryden Press.

Rulon, P. J. (1946). On the validity of educational tests. *Harvard Educational Review, 16*, 290–296.

Sackett, P. R., & Wilk, S. L. (1994). Within-group norming and other forms of score adjustment in preemployment testing. *American Psychologist, 49*, 929–954.

Schmidt, F. L. (1991). Why all banding procedures are logically flawed. *Human Performance, 4*, 265–278.

Shepard, L. A. (1993). Evaluating test validity. *Review of research in education, 19*, 405–450.

Shulman, L. S. (1970). Reconstruction of educational research. *Review of Educational Research, 40,* 371–396.

Snow, R. E. (1974). Representative and quasi-representative designs for research on teaching. *Review of Educational Research, 44,* 265–291.

Snow, R. E., & Lohman, D. F. (1989). Implications of cognitive psychology for educational measurement. In R. L. Linn (Ed.), *Educational measurement* (3rd ed., pp. 263–331). New York: Macmillan.

Suppes, P., Pavel, M., & Falmagne, J.-C. (1994). Representations and models in psychology. *Annual Review of Psychology, 45,* 517–544.

Wiggins, G. (1993). Assessment: Authenticity, context, and validity. *Phi Delta Kappan, 75,* 200–214.

MEASUREMENT AMONG
DIFFERENT SAMPLES

13

METHODOLOGICAL ISSUES IN ASSESSMENT RESEARCH WITH ETHNIC MINORITIES

SUMIE OKAZAKI AND STANLEY SUE

Assessment research on ethnic minority groups has had a controversial history. For example, comparisons of intellectual abilities and cognitive skills, of self-esteem and self-hatred, of personality patterns, and of prevalence rates and degrees of psychopathology among different ethnic and racial groups have generated considerable controversy regarding the validity of findings. It is our belief that conducting valid assessment research with ethnic minority groups is particularly problematic because of methodological, conceptual, and practical difficulties that arise in such research. This article addresses common methodological problems that have plagued assessment research on ethnic minorities. Our intent here is not to provide definitive solutions to methodological problems but rather to raise issues that many researchers may not have otherwise considered, so that informed decisions can be made about how to handle variables related to ethnicity. We also pose

Reprinted from *Psychological Assessment*, 7, 367–375. Copyright 1995 by the American Psychological Association.

some guidelines for future assessment research with ethnic minorities to improve the knowledge base not only for ethnic minorities but also for the field of psychological assessment. In doing so, we will closely examine fundamental problems such as sample heterogeneity, measurement of culture, and underlying assumptions about ethnicity, all of which make assessment research with ethnic minorities inherently challenging. Because our work involves Asian Americans, many of the cited examples deal with this population, although the point behind the examples may apply to other ethnic groups.

We refer to assessment research in a broad sense and use examples from extant literature on cognitive, personality, and clinical psychodiagnostic assessment with various ethnic minority groups. The focus is not on particular assessment instruments but on underlying conceptual and methodological issues with respect to ethnicity.

ETHNICITY AND RACE

Use of Terms

From the outset, let us address some definitional issues. It must be noted that the notions of race and ethnic minority status are highly charged with potential political ramifications. A prevailing example of a classification system with vast political consequences is the use of the terms race and Hispanic origin by the U.S. Bureau of the Census, whose population count influences each region's allotment of federal funds as well as possible district realignment for voting purposes. The U.S. Bureau of the Census uses the following categories: White; Black; American Indian, Eskimo, or Aleut; Asian or Pacific Islanders; Hispanic origin (of any race); and Other. The use of the term "race" appears to imply biological factors, as races are typically defined by observable physiognomic features such as skin color, hair type and color, eye color, stature, facial features, and so forth. However, some researchers have argued that designation of race is often arbitrary and that within-race differences in even the physiognomic features are greater than between-race differences (Zuckerman, 1990), and this topic continues to be hotly debated (e.g., Yee, Fairchild, Weizmann, & Wyatt, 1993).

There is no one definition of ethnicity, race, and culture that is agreed on by all. Indeed, it is common for both researchers and others to refer to ethnicity, culture, and race interchangeably when identifying and categorizing people by background (Betancourt & Lopez, 1993). Granted, these terms are closely related, as illustrated by a definition of ethnic status provided by Eaton (1980, p. 160):

> Ethnic status is defined as an easily identifiable characteristic that implies a common cultural history with others possessing the same charac-

teristic. The most common ethnic "identifiers" are race, religion, country of origin, language, and/or cultural background.

It is quite obvious that various characteristics serving as ethnic identifiers do not usually occur as independent features but appear in interrelated patterns and configurations (Dahlstrom, 1986), thus the common practice of interchanging the terms is understandable to a degree. However, confusion or a lack of differentiation among race, ethnicity, and culture at the terminology level likely reflects confusion at the conceptual level. That is, is the research concerned with race as a biological variable, ethnicity as a demographic variable, or some aspect of subjective cultural experience as a psychological variable?

Often, the implicit rationale behind grouping together individuals of the same racial or ethnic background and conducting assessment research using ethnicity as an independent or predictor variable is based on the assumptions that (a) these individuals share some common psychological characteristics associated with culture and (b) such shared cultural–psychological characteristics are related to personality or psychopathology. However, ethnicity is a demographic variable that is relatively distal to the variable of psychological or clinical interest. In many research studies, the participants' ethnicity may be serving as a proxy for psychological variables such as cultural values, self-concept, minority status, and so forth. Nonetheless, communications of findings (in the form of journal reports) often fail to clarify what assumptions were made about psychological characteristics of the particular sample in research studies. We believe that imprecisely using race and ethnicity to categorize individuals and then conducting studies on such population groups have contributed to the problems in assessment research with ethnic minorities. In the absence of each research study explicating the assumptions underlying the use of such categorical variables, we cannot assume that researchers are studying and communicating about the same constructs. Therefore, we echo the assertions made by Clark (1987) and by Betancourt and Lopez (1993) that research involving individuals from different ethnic and cultural backgrounds must specify and directly measure the underlying psychological variables associated with culture that are hypothesized to produce cultural or ethnic group differences.

Individual Differences Versus Group Characteristics

Some have argued that grouping together individuals based on ethnicity or race perpetuates unnecessary stereotyping or useless categorizations. Although we will, in the next section, point to the pitfalls of underestimating within-group heterogeneity, we still uphold the value of conducting research on broad groups of individuals classified into ethnic minority groups to the extent that as previously discussed, certain sets of characteristics covary with racial, ethnic, or cultural groups. After all, what is culture, if not a set of values and attitudes, a world view, and so forth that are shared by a large number of people who also share, to a greater or lesser extent, other demographic and physical characteristics? One caveat in examining characteristics of a broad group rests on a basic principle, namely, the greater the heterogeneity, the less precise the prediction is apt to be. Thus, although we may conclude that in general, White Americans are more individualistic than are Mexican Americans, we cannot predict with any certainty the level of individualism of a particular person. It is obvious that the confounding of an individual with the individual's culture results in stereotyping. Furthermore, an awkwardness exists when terms such as *Asian Americans* or *African Americans* are used because within-group heterogeneity cannot be conveyed by such terms. By making explicit the meaning of the terms and the context in which they are used, one can reduce some of the awkwardness.

COMMON METHODOLOGICAL PROBLEMS

Methodological problems with respect to ethnic minorities can occur at all stages of assessment research. We will examine salient issues in the stages of design (with respect to the population focus), sampling, measure selection and establishing equivalence of measures, method of assessment, and interpretation of data.

Population Focus

Selecting Participants

In the initial design of assessment research, a salient dilemma confronting researchers may be which ethnic groups to include in the design and for what purpose. Let us examine two scenarios, one case in which the primary research question does not involve ethnicity or culture and another case in which the research question does concern ethnic minorities. In the scenario in which the main investigation does not involve ethnicity, a researcher must decide which ethnic minority group(s), if any, to include in the design. If ethnic minority individuals comprise a subsample that is too small with which to run separate or comparative analyses with the majority ethnic group, a researcher may choose to exclude them from analyses altogether. This certainly simplifies the problem, but it does not contribute to the much needed knowledge of whether the findings may be generalized to ethnic minorities. If a subsample of ethnic minorities is too small for meaningful analyses but large enough not to be discarded, a researcher must contend with the knowledge that observed variance in the variables of interest may contain some unmeasured or unanalyzed factors related to ethnicity. On the other hand, a well-intentioned researcher may collect data from sizable ethnic minority groups but without a sound conceptual basis or a planned course of analyses for handling the ethnicity variable. A common outcome in such a case may be that ethnicity is relegated to the status of an extraneous variable, to be dealt with as an afterthought in the analysis.

In the second scenario, where the primary research question is concerned with ethnic minorities (e.g., establishing psychometric properties of an established assessment measure for an ethnic minority group), a frequent dilemma involves deciding whether to collect data solely from the target ethnic minority group or to compare the ethnic minorities with a control group. It is a common practice to compare one or more ethnic minority groups with Whites on a psychological characteristic of empirical interest. A part of this practice is rooted in the existing research paradigm that emphasizes differences (with "statistical significance") across groups. And because many assessment measures and methods have been developed and normed on largely, if not exclusively, White populations (e.g., the original Minnesota Multiphasic Personality Inventory; MMPI), researchers are taken to task to assess whether these measures and methods are psychometrically and practically valid with ethnic minorities. However, the rare comparison paradigm should not go unquestioned. The comparative approach has been criticized for potentially reinforcing racial stereotypes or the interpretation of non-White behavior as deviant as well as underestimating or overlooking within-ethnic group variations (Azibo, 1988; Campbell, 1967; Graham, 1992). The question often posed is, Are within-group differences as important or as valid as between-group differences? An example of the dilemma was presented by Korchin (1980). Korchin wanted to assess the determinants of personality competence among two groups of African American men—those demonstrating exceptional and average competence. Results of the study were analyzed, and a paper on the study was submitted to a major journal. One of the paper's reviewers criticized the study as being "grievously flawed," because no White control group was employed. Korchin raised several questions. Why should a White control group have been employed when the purpose of the study was to analyze within-group differences? What would happen if someone submitted a study identical in all respects except that all participants were White? Would it be criticized because it lacked an African American control group? There are no easy answers to these questions. As suggested by Korchin, assumptions concerning the appropriateness of comparisons should be guided by the purpose of a particular study.

Ethnic Comparisons

Once the question of population focus (i.e., inclusion or exclusion of specific ethnic minority groups) has been resolved, the next issue to consider is "matching" two or more ethnic groups for comparison purposes. Group comparisons are commonly achieved through two methods: (a) matching the participants a priori on the relevant but secondary variables or (b) controlling for those variables post hoc in analyses. With respect to matching, ethnic groups are typically matched on demographic characteristics such as age, sex, and possibly socioeconomic status, as well as defining characteristics such as psychiatric diagnoses. However, it may be difficult to match two or more ethnic groups on all relevant characteristics, as it has been well documented that various sectors of ethnic minority populations differ in the nature and distribution of characteristics. For example, American Indians have a much higher rate of unemployment, a larger number of individuals living under the poverty level, a higher school dropout rate, and a shorter life expectancy than other ethnic groups (LaFromboise, 1988). Graham (1992) noted the paramount importance of controlling for group differences in socioeconomic status when comparing African Americans and Whites, given overrepresentation of African Americans in economically disadvantaged segments of the population.

In deciding which variables need to be controlled for in the ethnic group comparisons, again, there is no agreed list of variables that are considered as essential control variables for each ethnic group. It is advised that variability in social and demographic characteristics (e.g., educational attainment, income level, language fluency, etc.) be statistically controlled in the analysis when ethnic differences exist on such variables and when the researcher has a reason to believe such differences may moderate the relationship between the variables of interest. A potential problem that remains in matching participants or controlling for differences in social characteristics is that a researcher may assume, given similar demographics of two ethnic groups, that individuals constituting the study are similar on a number of other unmeasured variables. Some have argued that similar demographics may have different effects for ethnic minorities, such as the interactive effect of ethnicity and social class on stress and distress (Cervantes & Castro, 1985; Kessler & Neighbors, 1986). A more sophisticated understanding of psychological correlates of demographic characteristics, including ethnicity, is needed.

Sampling

The design problem over inclusion or exclusion of ethnic minorities in assessment research is closely tied to problems in sampling. In this section we review specific sampling techniques used to identify and solicit participation of ethnic minority participants. Some of the examples for obtaining ethnic minority samples are not from personality assessment research but from epidemiological and community studies targeting subclinical or nonclinical ethnic minority populations. They are used here as illustrations of methods for obtaining difficult-to-reach samples.

Identifying Participants

Foremost in the sampling problem is identifying the ethnicity of participants. Self-identification of ethnicity by participants' self-report is the most common method, and this is most often accomplished by a limited categorical listing of ethnic groups, as defined by the investigator. Ethnicity may be defined at a broad level (e.g., Latino or Hispanic) or at a more specific level (e.g., Puerto Rican, Mexican American, etc.). Researchers are also faced with the decision of how to classify persons of mixed racial or ethnic backgrounds (see Hall, 1992; Root, 1992). Another method for identifying potential participants' ethnicity is through the surname identification method. Some ethnic groups such as Asians and Hispanics have unequivocally ethnic surnames (e.g., "Kim" for Koreans, "Nguyen" for Vietnamese, and "Gutierrez" for Latino), which enables surname-based community sampling methodology. Indeed some studies have used surnames or other key characteristics as the sole basis for determining participants' ethnicity (e.g., Dion & Giordano, 1990; Dion & Toner, 1988). This method for ascertaining the ethnicity of participants (i.e., without cross-validation from the participants) is sometimes the only option, particularly when working with archival data, but this obviously limits the certainty with which the results may be interpreted. There are further issues with respect to identification of ethnicity. Sasao and Sue (1993) pointed to the faulty but commonly made assumption that once individuals are identified as belonging to a certain ethnic–cultural group, they share a common understanding of their own ethnicity or culture and identify with the ethnic–cultural group. To illustrate, in a high school drug abuse survey conducted in multicultural communities in Southern California (Sasao, 1992), approximately 20% of the Chinese American students indicated their primary cultural identification was Mexican, though the self-perceived ethnicity of these Chinese students was Chinese.

Small Sample Size

Collecting data from a large enough sample of ethnic minorities has long posed a challenge, partly because of the small overall population size. Let us take the example of American Indians (technically categorized as American Indians, Eskimo, or Aleut by the U.S. Bureau of the Census), who comprised only 0.8% of the total U.S. population according to the 1990 U.S. Census (U.S. Bureau of the Census, 1991). American Indian populations tend to be geographically much more concentrated than does the general U.S. population, as the majority of American Indians lived in just six states in 1990. The American Indian population was highest in Alaska, where it comprised about 16% of that state's total population, but there were 35 states in which American Indians represented less than 1% of the total population of each state in 1990 (U.S. Bureau of the Census, 1991). About half of the

American Indian population lives in urban areas and about half lives in rural areas or areas on or adjacent to reservations that are located in the Plains States (Bureau of Indian Affairs, 1991). Thus, locating an adequate sample size of American Indian participants is difficult, if not impractical, in many states and regions.

The problem of small sample size often results in researchers combining the data from a number of ethnic–cultural groups with some common origin (e.g., combining Chinese Americans, Japanese Americans, and Korean Americans into one group), or in the case of American Indians, across tribal groups (e.g., combining Hopis, Lakotas, and Navahos into one group). However, broadening the ethnic grouping increases heterogeneity. Again, taking the case of American Indians, there are over 510 federally recognized tribes, including more than 200 Alaskan Native villages (Bureau of Indian Affairs, 1991). American Indian tribes vary enormously in customs, language, and type of family structure, so much so that Tefft (1967) argued that differences between certain tribal groups are greater than those between Indians and Whites on some variables. American Indian individuals also vary in their degree of acculturation and exposure to tribal or White American cultures, whether they live on or off a reservation, ethnic or tribal identification, experience with racism, and so forth. Given such a list of even the most basic sources of sample heterogeneity, a researcher is inevitably faced with the decision of which sources of variability can or cannot be overlooked in aggregating individuals into an ethnic group classification. This discussion is not to underestimate the cultural diversity within the White American population; in fact, it is intended to stimulate a more refined treatment of ethnicity and culture in psychological research.

Recruiting Participants

In efforts to recruit ethnic minority participants, researchers must consider possible ethnic and cultural differences in participants' likelihood to participate in psychological assessment research. Are ethnic minorities less likely to cooperate with research? Are the rates of attrition from research studies equal across ethnic groups? For some ethnic groups, cultural values may influence their participation or response patterns in research. Ying (1989) analyzed the cases of nonresponse to Center for Epidemiological Studies-Depression scale (CES-D) items in a community sample of Chinese Americans. The original study was conducted as a telephone interview study with randomly selected Chinese-surnamed households listed in the San Francisco public telephone directory. Ying found that demographic factors such as age, sex, and education as well as item content were related to the rates of nonresponse to CES-D items. Ying explained that older Chinese women were less likely to be familiar with telephone surveys, the methodology which, in and of itself, may reflect a middle-class American lifestyle and set of values. Older Chinese women may experience being questioned by a stranger about mood and somatic symptoms as foreign and intrusive yet refrain from directly refusing to participate because such behavior would be too assertive and impolite. For other Chinese community cohorts such as middle-aged Chinese men, endorsement of positive feelings (e.g., feeling good about self or feeling happy and enjoying life) may be regarded as indicative of immodesty and frivolousness in Chinese culture, thus such values may also contribute to nonresponse. This type of in-depth analysis of nonresponse illustrates the importance of considering the potential influence of cultural and social norms in responding to and participating in psychological research.

Use of College Samples

For ethnic minority groups for which it is extremely difficult to obtain a large community sample of participants, sampling from college populations is a particularly attractive and viable option because of the ease of access to a relatively large captive pool of potential participants. For example, a significant portion of Asian American personality and psychopathology literature has been conducted with college students (Leong, 1986; Uba, 1994). This sampling strategy clearly impacts the question of representativeness of the sample. Sears (1985) argued that a significant portion of psychological research is conducted with college sophomores, and he pointed to the hazards of basing much of what we know about human processes on a sample not representative of the larger population. Sears named a number of differences between American college undergraduates and the general population, such as education, test-taking experience, and restricted age range, which in turn are associated with intrapsychic characteristics such as a less than fully formulated sense of self, less crystallized social and political attitudes, highly unstable peer relationships, and so forth. The same criticisms apply to assessment research with ethnic minorities, and the representativeness of ethnic minority college students must be carefully assessed, not only with respect to socioeconomic and educational attainment of student participants in relation to their age cohorts who do not attend college but also with respect to a correspondent set of values and attitudes, a limited range of political awareness of self-identification, and an American education. For language minority groups such as some American Indians, immigrant Asian Americans, and immigrant Latinos (and some would argue African Americans; see Helms, 1992), good or adequate English language skills are necessary to gain entrance into colleges and universities. However, those with university-level English skills may not be representative of a significant portion of immigrant ethnic minorities. Ethnic minority college samples tend to underestimate both the demographic and the psychosocial diversity of the larger ethnic minority populations. Consequently, sample heterogeneity, as high as it may be in college samples, may still be an underestimate of true population heterogeneity.

Use of Community Samples

Given the questionable generalizability of research studies with ethnic minority college students to the ethnic community population at large, it is often desirable, although also extremely challenging, to sample from ethnic minority communities. Many research studies conducted with ethnic minorities in the community rely on systematic or captive sampling or snowball sampling (a method in which one starts with a known group of participants, and recruits more participants through contacts) in intact ethnic groups or organizations such as churches, temples, professional associations, political organizations, social clubs, kinship associations, and so forth. It is clear that each of these organizations attracts a subsample of the target ethnic community, and the results cannot be easily generalized to the entire group. Sasao and Sue (1993) criticized psychological research with ethnic minorities for its lack of ecological and contextual considerations. Specifically, Sasao and Sue argued that too often, research ignores the societal context in relation to other relevant ethnic–cultural community groups. Many psychological characteristics of clinical interest may be greatly influenced by the target community group's geographical and political context in which ethnic minority individuals function, such that psychological research on African Americans in South Central Los Angeles must take into account the community's relation to Korean Americans and the contemporary political climate. When the research question involves the assessment of psychopathology, studies may be conducted with those ethnic minority participants who utilize clinical services. There is some evidence to indicate differential patterns of mental health services utilization among different ethnic minority groups (Sue, Fujino, Hu, Takeuchi, & Zane, 1991), thereby making it difficult to assess the generalizability of the findings. Clearly, the procurement of representative and adequately sized samples of ethnic minorities poses a considerable methodological challenge.

Establishing Equivalence of Measures

One goal of assessment research with ethnic minorities is to conduct reliable and valid assessment while minimizing cultural or ethnic bias. Use of assessment measures in research with ethnic minorities presents several problems, primarily with respect to equivalence. Brislin (1993) discussed three types of equivalence (translation, conceptual, and metric) as being of foremost concern in cross-cultural research methodology. To the extent that assessment research is concerned with effects of culture on assessed psychological characteristics among ethnic minorities, the cross-cultural principles apply to research with ethnic minorities.

Although some of the frequently used assessment instruments such as the Wechsler scales, the SCL-90-R, the Zung Self-Rating Depression Scale, and the MMPI have been translated into languages such as Spanish, Japanese, and Chinese, researchers and clinicians are often faced with the sheer lack of relevant assessment measures in the language of the target ethnic minority populations that also have established translation equivalence. Importantly, linguistic equivalence issues also cannot be ignored for ethnic minority participants who are functionally English-speaking. For example, Helms (1992) argued that most African Americans in the United States are probably exposed to some versions of both Black and White English, yet commonly used standardized tests are in White standard English. A recent study examining Spanish–English bilingualism among Hispanic immigrants (Bahrick, Hall, Goggin, Bahrick, & Berger, 1994) indicated a complex interaction among language dominance, the assessment task (e.g., oral comprehension, vocabulary recognition, category generation, etc.), age at immigration, and other factors. Such findings suggest that the type of language skills used to assess bilingual participants in either English or their first language may influence some results.

In the absence of appropriate assessment measures for which the translated versions' psychometric properties have been established, a researcher may choose to translate and adopt the instrument to the ethnic minority group of research interest. In order to ensure that a newly translated measure has achieved translation equivalence, a multistep method has been recommended, in which translation (e.g., from English to Spanish) is followed by back translation (from Spanish to English), comparison of the two versions (e.g., English and English), revisions in the translation, and so forth (Brislin, 1993). Geisinger (1994) has outlined a set of rigorous methodological steps for translating an assessment instrument and adopting it to a new culture. However, it must be acknowledged that carefully following the methodological steps suggested by Geisinger and performing psychometric analyses would require multiple, adequately sized samples of ethnic minorities, leaving the researcher once again with dilemmas in obtaining large sample sizes.

Conceptual equivalence is concerned with whether the psychological construct under investigation (e.g., depression, intelligence, or assertiveness) holds the same meanings in two or more cultural groups. Conceptual equivalence of a construct may be highly dependent on the context in which the assessment takes place. Although this may be true for any participant population, researchers must be aware that for ethnic minorities, variability of and sensitivity to contextual factors may be increased as they move between a traditional cultural setting (e.g., family and ethnic communities) and a more mainstream American cultural setting (e.g., work, school, etc.). For example, in assessing the meaning of aggressiveness in youths, an assessment may be conducted in a school setting, in which Latinos, Asians, and Whites share the same environmental space, and to a large extent, the same ecological context. If the construct is found to be equivalent in this setting, it may not necessarily translate into conceptual equivalence in other settings, such as the family or the street culture.

Metric equivalence refers to the assumption that the same metric can be used to measure the same concept in two or more cultures. For example, the test score of 100 for a White participant is assumed to be interpretable in the same manner as the test score of 100 for a Mexican American partici-pant. Metric equivalence is often overlooked or assumed without empirical validation in research with ethnic minorities, particularly if the measure does not involve translation. The danger of assuming equivalence of translated measures was illustrated by an analysis comparing the Wechsler Adult Intel-ligence Scale (WAIS) and its Spanish adaptation, Escala de Inteligencia Wechsler para Adultos (EIWA; Lopez & Romero, 1988), in which major dif-ferences between the two instruments were found with respect to the con-version of raw scores to scale scores, administration, and content. Lopez and Romero pointed to the importance of noting the rural, less educated charac-teristics of the Puerto Rican sample on which the EIWA was normed, and concluded that "psychologists should not expect the scores of the EIWA to be comparable with those of the WAIS, and perhaps even with the scores of the WAIS-R" (Lopez & Romero, 1988, p. 269). It is also critical to note here the heterogeneity within an ethnic minority group (e.g., rural Puerto Rican vs. urban Mexican American), which may be underestimated or overlooked because of a common language (in this case, Spanish) when a translated ver-sion is available.

In research, psychometric statistical analyses are often performed in or-der to address equivalence problems of a measure across ethnic groups. For example, Ben-Porath (1990) advocated the use of replicatory factor analysis (i.e., using the same factor analytic method to examine the factor structure of a newly translated or adopted instrument that was used in the original measure) to establish cross-cultural validity of the instrument. Ben-Porath also suggested that prior to conducting factor analyses, it is important to ex-amine the distribution of the scale items across ethnic and cultural groups in order to detect possible range restrictions and outliers. This is particularly vital to the assessment studies involving ethnic minorities, as Helms (1992) cautioned that cultural and interethnic factors may compromise the basic assumptions underlying statistics, such as independence of ethnic groups with respect to culture or equal range and variance between ethnic groups. Regression analyses have also been used to study instrument or test bias, specifically to examine whether tests make predictions that are similar, and similarly accurate, to those of a criterion measure. If, for example, regression slopes for a test or evaluation procedure and a criterion differ for different groups, test bias exists. Such studies require that fairly clear-cut criteria can be found on which to judge the adequacy of predictors. An example of this approach was provided by Timbrook and Graham (1994), who examined ethnic differences between African Americans and Whites in the restandardization sample of the MMPI-2. The researchers used ratings of interpersonal behavior and personality characteristics of the participants made by their partners as external criteria against which the accuracy of predictions of five MMPI-2 clinical scales could be examined. Regression equations were developed to predict the partner rating scale scores, and no ethnic differences were found on the accuracy of the MMPI-2 scale predictions.

Methods of Assessment

Thus far, our discussion of methodological issues in measure selection for use with ethnic minorities has been primarily focused on standardized objective personality assessment measures (with the exception of the Wechsler scales), most often of the self-report variety. However, it is debatable whether some methods of assessment may be more likely to result in cultural or ethnic bias than others. There are at least three approaches to assessment that have been understudied with respect to ethnic minorities: (a) behavioral observations, (b) qualitative assessment, and (c) projective tests. One may question for ethnic minorities whether behavioral observation methods are more prone to bias than self-report instruments, whether qualitative assessment is more prone to bias than quantitative data, or whether projective tests are more prone to bias than objective tests.

Surveying the assessment research on ethnic minorities, there is a shortage of assessment methodology using observational data. Behavioral observation methodologies often involve in-depth, microlevel analysis of behavior. Although largescale surveys are necessary in order to obtain some normative information on ethnic minorities, the field is ripe for a contribution in microlevel analysis as well. The behavioral observation methods also have the advantage of requiring relatively small sample sizes that are necessary to conduct analyses, although generalizability to the larger population is likely to be compromised with potential self-selection of ethnic or cultural minority participants who are willing to participate in such in-depth assessment research.

Psychological assessment research, which is heavily rooted in psychometric tradition, has favored quantitative research. Although the limitations of qualitative methodologies must be acknowledged, little empirical work has examined the relative advantages and disadvantages of collecting qualitative data from ethnic minorities. Brink (1994) argued that purely quantitative measurement methodologies used to assess ethnic minority populations (e.g., elderly Hispanics) are insufficiently sensitive to cultural factors and recommended integrating psychometric data with qualitative methodologies (e.g., in-depth interviews and life histories).

Finally, some have argued that cross-cultural (and by extension, ethnic minority) research may have prematurely dismissed the usefulness of projective measures of assessment because of the assumption that such instruments are too rooted in Western culture (Draguns, 1990). The problem here is the lack of empirical evidence to argue for or against the notion that ambiguous stimuli used in projective tests are less culturally bound but that clinical interpretations are more prone to bias by the interpreter's cultural background. Research on the use of projective tests with Asian Americans is notably absent (Okazaki & Sue, 1995), but a body of research exists on the use of the Rorschach and picture-story tests (e.g., the Thematic Apperception Test) with African Americans, Latinos, and several American Indian tribes (see Gray-Little, 1995; Rogler, Malgady, & Rodriguez, 1989; Velasquez, 1995). Increased attention in ethnic minority assessment research to various methods of assessment is consistent with recommendations made by cross-cultural methodologists to use multiple assessment measures to establish convergent validity of cultural constructs.

Interpretation of Data

A common problem in conducting ethnic comparison research is that differences tend to be evaluated in disfavor of ethnic minorities. For example, Rogler, Malgady, and Rodriguez (1989) argued that ethnic differences on personality measures are often interpreted negatively from the Western perspective. In the case of Latinos, their scores on personality measures are often interpreted as indicating low verbal fluency, less emotional responsiveness, and more pathology, all of which are considered as undesirable characteristics in American society. However, the same scores may be interpreted as reflecting appropriate restraint and respect for authority. In a study comparing clinical evaluations by Chinese American and White therapists of the same clients (either Chinese American or White), therapists' ratings of client functioning have been found to vary as a function of the interaction of therapist and client ethnicity (Li-Repac, 1980), which suggests interpretive bias. At the same time, one must also be aware of the danger of underestimating pathology for culturally different clients through overattribution of bizarre behavior or thought patterns to that person's culture (Lopez, 1989). It is essential to be aware of possible cultural bias, either in overpathologizing or underpathologizing ethnic minorities when interpreting ethnic differences on assessment measures.

GUIDELINES

Based on the various methodological issues we have raised with respect to assessment research with ethnic minorities, we summarize several guidelines for considering ethnicity and related variables below.

1. Assumptions underlying the use of ethnicity should be made explicit. A researcher must ask, Is the research concerned with ethnicity as a demographic variable, or is it being used as a proxy for a psychological construct hypothesized to covary with ethnicity?

2. Research reports should contain more elaborated, fuller discussions of the sample and the sampling methodology used. That is, rather than merely indicating the number of African Americans, Asian Americans, Latinos, and American Indians included in the sample, details should be made explicit on variables such as generalized status, acculturation, self-identification, ethnic and cultural composition of the neighborhoods or communities, and so forth. Such discussions will help promote better communication among researchers and focus future research efforts by identifying what we know about whom.

3. Given inherent problems with small sample size in ethnic minority research, we suggest the following strategies to maximize the significance of each study: (a) For studies examining ethnic differences on various assessment instruments, enough details regarding the sampling methodology, data analyses, and statistical findings should be reported to allow meta-analyses and cross-study comparisons and (b) individual studies with small samples of ethnic minorities should test specific cultural hypotheses that may contribute to ethnic variance on assessment processes or instruments, with increased attention on whether statistically significant ethnic differences are also clinically significant (see Timbrook and Graham, 1994, for an example of this approach).

4. Individual studies should consider using multiple measures and multiple methods of assessments. Given that many assessment tools and instruments have not been widely used or cross-culturally validated with ethnic minority groups, it is advisable to use several different measures in order to test convergent validity. To the extent that results converge, there is incremental validity.

5. Expert cultural or ethnic consultants should be involved in evaluating the translation and conceptual equivalence of the measures prior to data collection or in interpreting the results of studies. These consultants can often provide the cultural context for anticipating and interpreting the responses of ethnic minorities.

6. Findings from assessment tools pertinent to ethnic and cultural variables should generate hypotheses for further testing or con-

firmation rather than routine assumptions that the findings are valid.

CONCLUSION

Little attention in the past has been paid to the relevance of ethnicity and cultural issues in psychological research. Graham (1992) recently conducted a content analysis of empirical articles concerned with African Americans that were published in six top psychology journals between 1970 and 1989. The results, which indicated a decline in the amount of African American research over the years and a relative lack of methodological rigor of existing research, were a sobering indictment of the scientific psychological community's level of sophistication in examining ethnic and cultural factors. Lack of research, training, or both in cross-cultural assessment often leads to misdiagnosis, overestimation, underestimation, or neglect of psychopathology, which in turn has grave consequences, such as treatment failure, at individual levels (Westermeyer, 1987).

However, assessment research with ethnic minorities should not be encouraged merely because of a potential for negative consequences in neglecting ethnic minorities. As noted by proponents of cross-cultural psychology, studies of cultural variations are good for both psychology and science (Triandis & Brislin, 1984). For one, the inclusion of ethnicity and culture-related variables increases the range of human behavior variables to explore and understand. For instance, an examination of the collectivism–individualism dimension of interpersonal orientation within the middle-class White American college student population will yield a fairly narrow and skewed range. By including ethnic minorities and individuals from other cultures, the full range of this construct as well as its relationship to other personality and clinical variables can be fruitfully examined. Another advantage to including ethnic and cultural variables in research is that it provides a better test of theories. Establishing the generalizability or limitations of personality theories and of assessment tools through systematic testing with a broad range of individuals benefits the field (Ben-Porath, 1990). And lastly, the American Psychological Association (APA) Board of Ethnic Minority Affairs in 1991 developed a set of guidelines for providers of psychological services to ethnically, linguistically, and culturally diverse populations (APA, 1933), which parallels the APA Ethical Standards guidelines. It is clearly stated in this guideline (APA, 1993, p. 46) that:

> Psychologists consider the validity of a given instrument or procedure and interpret resulting data, keeping in mind the cultural and linguistic characteristics of the person being assessed. Psychologists are aware of

the test's reference population and possible limitations of such instruments with other populations.

Hence, it is crucial that research on the validity of various assessment tools and procedures for ethnic minority population continue to add to the necessary database in order for the psychological community to responsibly carry out these guidelines.

There are many methodological challenges to conducting assessment research with ethnic minorities, but this is not a cause for throwing out the baby with the bath water. By making explicit the assumptions underlying the use of ethnicity as a predictor variable, the collective scientific community will begin to differentiate between racial stereotypes and legitimate uses of ethnic or cultural generalizations.

REFERENCES

American Psychological Association (1993). Guidelines for providers of psychological services to ethnic, linguistic, and culturally diverse populations. *American Psychologist, 48*, 45–48.

Azibo, D. A. (1988). Understanding the proper and improper usage of the comparative research framework. *Journal of Black Psychology, 15*, 81–91.

Bahrick, H. P., Hall, L. K., Goggin, J. P., Bahrick, L. E., & Berger, S. A. (1994). Fifty years of language maintenance and language dominance in bilingual Hispanic immigrants. *Journal of Experimental Psychology: General, 123*, 264–283.

Ben-Porath, Y. S. (1990). Cross-cultural assessment of personality: The case for replicatory factor analysis. In J. N. Butcher & C. D. Spielberger (Eds.), *Advances in personality assessment* (Vol. 8, pp. 27–48). Hillsdale, NJ: Erlbaum.

Betancourt, H., & Lopez, S. R. (1993). The study of culture, ethnicity, and race in American psychology. *American Psychologist, 48*, 629–637.

Brink, T. L. (1994). The need for qualitative research on mental health elderly Hispanics. *International Journal of Aging and Human Development, 38*, 279–291.

Brislin, R. W. (1993). *Understanding culture's influence on behavior.* New York: Harcourt Brace Jovanovich.

Bureau of Indian Affairs. (1991). *American Indians today* (3rd ed.). Washington, DC: U.S. Department of the Interior.

Campbell, D. T. (1967). Stereotypes and the perception of group differences. *American Psychologist, 22*, 817–829.

Cervantes, R. C., & Castro, F. G. (1985). Stress, coping, and Mexican American mental health: A systematic review. *Hispanic Journal of Behavioral Sciences, 7*, 1–73.

Clark, L. A. (1987). Mutual relevance of mainstream and cross-cultural psychology. *Journal of Consulting and Clinical Psychology, 55*, 461–470.

Dahlstrom, W. G. (1986). Ethnic status and personality measurement. In W. G. Dahlstrom, D. Lacher, & L. E. Dahlstrom (Eds.), *MMPI patterns of American minorities* (pp. 3–23). Minneapolis: University of Minnesota Press.

Dion, K. L., & Giordano, C. (1990). Ethnicity and sex as correlates of depression symptoms in a Canadian university sample. *International Journal of Social Psychiatry, 36*, 30–41.

Dion, K. L., & Toner, B. B. (1988). Ethnic differences in test anxiety. *Journal of Social Psychology, 128*, 165–172.

Draguns, J. G. (1990). Applications of cross-cultural psychology in the field of mental health. In R. W. Brislin (Ed.), *Applied cross-cultural psychology* (pp. 302–324). Newbury Park, CA: Sage.

Eaton, W. W. (1980). *The sociology of mental illness.* New York: Praeger.

Geisinger, K. F. (1994). Cross-cultural normative assessment: Translation and adaptation issues influencing the normative interpretation of assessment instruments. *Psychological Assessment, 6*, 304–312.

Graham, S. (1992). "Most of the subjects were White and middle class": Trends in published research on African Americans in selected APA journals, 1970–1989. *American Psychologist, 47*, 629–639.

Gray-Little, B. (1995). The assessment of psychopathology in racial and ethnic minorities. In J. N. Butcher (Ed.), *Clinical personality assessment: Practical approaches* (pp. 140–157). New York: Oxford University Press.

Hall, C. C. I. (1992). Please choose one: Ethnic identity choices for biracial individuals. In M. P. P. Root (Ed.), *Racially mixed people in America* (pp. 250–264). Newbury Park, CA: Sage.

Helms, J. E. (1992). Why is there no study of cultural equivalence in standardized cognitive ability testing? *American Psychologist, 47*, 1083–1101.

Kessler, R. C., & Neighbors, H. W. (1986). A new perspective on the relationships among race, social class and psychological distress. *Journal of Health and Social Behavior, 27*, 107–115.

Korchin, S. J. (1980). Clinical psychology and minority problems. *American Psychologist, 35*, 262–269.

LaFromboise, T. D. (1988). American Indian mental health policy. *American Psychologist, 43*, 388–397.

Leong, F. T. L. (1986). Counseling and psychotherapy with Asian-Americans: Review of the literature. *Journal of Counseling Psychology, 33*, 196–206.

Li-Repac, D. (1980). Cultural influences on clinical perception: A comparison between Caucasian and Chinese-American therapists. *Journal of Cross-Cultural Psychology, 11*, 327–342.

Lopez, S. R. (1989). Patient variable biases in clinical judgment: Conceptual overview and methodological considerations. *Psychological Bulletin, 106*, 184–204.

Lopez, S., & Romero, A. (1988). Assessing the intellectual functioning of Spanish-speaking adults: Comparison of the EIWA and the WAIS. *Professional Psychology: Research and Practice, 19*, 263–270.

Okazaki, S., & Sue, S. (1995). Cultural considerations in psychological assessment of Asian Americans. In J. N. Butcher (Ed.), *Clinical personality assessment: Practical approaches* (pp. 107–119). New York: Oxford University Press.

Rogler, L. H., Malgady, R. G., & Rodriguez, O. (1989). *Hispanics and mental health: A framework for research.* Malabalar, FL: Krieger.

Root, M. P. P. (1992). Back to the drawing board: Methodological issues in research on multiracial people. In M. P. P. Root (Ed.), *Racially mixed people in America* (pp. 181–189). Newbury Park, CA: Sage.

Sasao, T. (1992). *Correlates of substance use and problem behaviors in multiethnic high school settings.* Unpublished manuscript, University of California, Los Angeles.

Sasao, T., & Sue, S. (1993). Toward a culturally anchored ecological framework of research in ethnic-cultural communities. *American Journal of Community Psychology, 21,* 705–727.

Sears, D. O. (1985). College sophomores in the laboratory: Influences of a narrow data base on psychology's view of human nature. *Journal of Personality and Social Psychology, 51,* 515–530.

Sue, S., Fujino, D. C., Hu, L., Takeuchi, D., & Zane, N. W. S. (1991). Community mental health services for ethnic minority groups: A test of cultural responsive hypothesis. *Journal of Consulting and Clinical Psychology, 59,* 533–540.

Tefft, S. K. (1967). Anomie, values, and culture change among teen-age Indians: An exploratory study. *Sociology of Education, 40,* 145–157.

Timbrook, R. E., & Graham, J. R. (1994). Ethnic differences on the MMPI-2? *Psychological Assessment, 6,* 212–217.

Triandis, H. C., & Brislin, R. W. (1984). Cross-cultural psychology. *American Psychologist, 39,* 1006–1016.

Uba, L. (1994). *Asian Americans: Personality patterns, identity, and mental health.* New York: Guilford.

U.S. Bureau of the Census. (1991). Race and Hispanic origin. *1990 Census Profile (No. 2).* Washington, DC: U.S. Department of Commerce.

Velasquez, R. J. (1995). Personality assessment of Hispanic clients. In J. N. Butcher (Ed.), *Clinical personality assessment: Practical approaches* (pp. 120–139). New York: Oxford University Press.

Westermeyer, J. (1987). Cultural factors in clinical assessment. *Journal of Consulting and Clinical Psychology, 55,* 471–478.

Yee, A. H., Fairchild, H. H., Weizmann, F., & Wyatt, G. E. (1993). Addressing psychology's problems with race. *American Psychologist, 48,* 1132–1140.

Ying, Y. (1989). Nonresponse on the Center for Epidemiological Studies-Depression scale in Chinese Americans. *International Journal of Social Psychiatry, 35,* 156–163.

Zuckerman, M. (1990). Some dubious premises in research and theory on racial differences: Scientific, social, and ethical issues. *American Psychologist, 45,* 1297–1303.

IV

DATA ANALYSIS, EVALUATION, AND INTERPRETATION

Data analysis refers to systematic evaluation of the information that has been collected, usually to summarize or codify the information and to draw inferences about the relations between the independent and dependent variables. For most researchers, data analysis is synonymous with quantitative evaluation of the results (the application of statistical tests). In contemporary scientific research, quantitative evaluation—and within this tradition statistical significance testing—clearly dominates. There are many other data-analytic options such as graphical methods to present and describe the data, qualitative evaluation of data that systematize narrative descriptions, and visual inspection to draw inferences about change; some of these methods are discussed in later sections. The different methods are useful to mention, if only to convey that what is often taken as a given or the essence of data evaluation is, in the scheme of scientific research, one approach to identify whether effects are reliable, important, and likely to be replicable. In this section, I focus on statistical evaluation because it is central in contemporary research.

The nightmare of methodologists and statisticians is having a colleague or student convene a meeting that begins with the statement, "I have finished collecting the data and was wondering what analyses I ought to do." A general view inadvertently fostered by academicians during training is that statistics are merely a tool to evaluate the results and as such are not really part of the design. Yet the methods used to analyze the data are central to the design of the study and to the conceptualization of the phenomenon that is studied. How well, and indeed whether, the hypotheses are well tested depend on strategies and the plan for the data analyses. Decisions about the data analyses depend on how many different measures will be combined or evaluated; the relation of independent variables (predictors) and outcomes (criteria) to one another; whether the hypotheses focus on mediators, moderators, and direct or indirect causal paths; and other issues, many of which emerge before the first subject is tested. The need to address questions about the data analysis begins at the point that the hypothesis or prediction is first formulated. With that hypothesis or prediction, one can ask, How will the data be analyzed to test this hypothesis? What are the chances that the results would support the prediction, if in fact the prediction were true? If there are potential confounding influences, can suitable controls (experimental or statistical) be used?

Articles in this section emphasize fundamental issues about statistical evaluation that emerge both in the planning and in the data-analytic stages of the study. The articles discuss the meaning of referring to a finding as statistically significant. Key concepts are raised, including alpha (α) or the probability level used to determine whether an effect is statistically significant, sample size (N), the magnitude of an effect (effect size), and statistical power (the extent to which a study can detect a statistically significant difference when one exists). Although the interrelations of these concepts are often discussed and are well known, the knowledge is rarely translated into the design of a study by individual investigators (Sedlmeier & Gigerenzer, 1989).

It is critical to begin the study with a clear idea of how the data will be analyzed and the likelihood that an effect, if present, can readily be detected. This does not mean that all data analyses that eventually will be completed need to be specified in advance. Many data analyses elaborate specific findings and pursue interesting tributaries that flow from the main findings; some of these can be determined only once the pattern of data is revealed. Yet, the primary hypotheses and predictions are not of this form, and how they will be tested statistically ought to be specified in advance. This is not a complex requirement or process, but it has not been inculcated in training.

BACKGROUND AND UNDERPINNINGS OF DATA ANALYSES

The vast majority of psychological research focuses on null hypothesis testing and statistical significance. *Statistical significance* refers to conventions regarding when to consider a particular finding or difference as reliable or unlikely to be due to "chance." Most statisticians within psychology probably would say that as a criterion for knowledge, statistical significance is relied on too heavily. Significance and the p level on which it is based are not a magical threshold for calling an effect *veridical*. Unfortunately, researchers tend to consider a finding that meets the criterion of $p < .05$ as real and that effects above this level likely to be due to chance (Rosenthal & Gaito, 1963). In fact, some instances will always narrowly miss any criterion (p level) that is adopted. Perhaps a criterion will always have the problem of seeming or being arbitrary at the cut-off point. The problem is not only in specifying a criterion but also the use of that criterion for binary decisions, namely, to reject or accept the null hypothesis. Thus, the null hypothesis is rejected at $p = .04$ or .05 but not at .059 or .06. This does not sound very reasonable. Indeed, as Rosenthal and Rosnow (1989) noted, "surely, God loves the .06 nearly as much as the .05" (p. 1277).

Any particular level of significance is a useful guideline and may provide a screening device or filter for making some decisions, but it is hardly a level to be worshipped. In their article, Michael Cowles and Caroline Davis discuss the origins of the use of $p < .05$ as a criterion for deciding statistical significance. The foundations of the criterion for statistical significance are important to understand because of the marked influence of this convention and how the criterion for significance relates to believability. Moreover, the use, abuse, and misinterpretation of findings that meet the criterion of $p < .05$ are elaborated in subsequent articles and so a very useful beginning to see what the Founding Mothers and Fathers of statistical significance had in mind.

Statistical tests are conducted in the service of the substantive ideas that underlie the investigation. In the general case, this is well known. However, the connection between the design and the statistical evaluation often is neglected at the design stage. When they plan research, investigators often focus on the rationale for the study and several procedural decisions (Introduction and Method section material). Indeed, in graduate training, master's degree or doctoral research proposals may consist of Introduction and Method sections without further material regarding the methods of statistical evaluation. However, the types of data analyses, characteristics of the data that are likely to emerge, and limitations of interpretation at the end of the study can be greatly aided by considering statistical evaluation before the design of the study is finalized.

The importance of considering statistical evaluation in planning the study is recognized in many contexts outside of graduate training. For example, in preparing grant applications, a key section in the research plan is a description of what data analyses will be conducted, how the hypotheses will be tested in relation to these analyses, and whether the key statistical tests are sufficiently powerful to detect differences. At another level, developing a clear plan of the strategies for data analyses at the design stage also conveys how much and how carefully the investigator has thought about the study.

Whether in a proposal or a final article, the connection between the predictions and the statistical analyses ought to be explicit. That is, the reader of the article should be able at all times to see why a particular statistical analysis was conducted; what it was designed to accomplish; and how the analysis reflects a prediction, hypothesis, or critical issue. Bruce E. Wampold, Betsy Davis, and Roland H. Good introduce the notion of *hypothesis validity* to refer to the connections between the theory, hypotheses, and statistical evaluation. With examples from clinical research, the authors note the importance of specifying predictions and hypotheses and the relation of the specific analyses to these predictions. Several statistical evaluation issues are raised, including the use of multiple statistical tests within a given study and the use and limits of omnibus tests.

In the article that follows, Jacob Cohen discusses in an informal and highly engaging style critical issues related to conducting research and data analyses. Among the key points are the importance of keeping research "simple" in the sense of limiting the number of independent and dependent variables, emphasizing few variables and many subjects (rather than the reverse), looking closely at the data, and simplifying the data analyses and reporting when possible. The article also begins the discussion on null hypothesis testing and power, which are covered further in the next section.

NULL HYPOTHESES AND STATISTICAL SIGNIFICANCE TESTING

In this section, fundamental issues about statistical significance tests are confronted directly. The section begins with another article by Jacob Cohen that focuses more specifically on power and its relation to α, N, and effect size. Power, of course, refers to the likelihood of detecting a difference in an investigation when in fact there is a genuine difference between conditions or, stated another way, the likelihood of rejecting the null hypothesis (no difference) when that hypothesis is false. Almost 40 years ago, Cohen (1962) published an article that evaluated the extent to which studies in abnormal and social psychology had sufficient power to detect differences if such differences existed. The main conclusion was that power is very weak in most studies. Since that time, many evaluations of research have been completed, spanning multiple areas of research within psychology and other disciplines as well (e.g., Sedlmeier & Gigerenzer, 1989). Alas, the conclusions are quite similar to those reached by Cohen in 1962, namely, that the power of studies is rather weak, except when there are very strong effects (effect sizes). Studies continue to be designed and reported with weak power, and there are no genuine signs that conditions are improving. In this article, Cohen provides useful tables for estimating power and sample sizes needed for an investigation given different effect sizes. Because significance testing continues to dominate contemporary research, it is essential to master concepts such as power on which such testing depends.

The tradition of statistical significance testing itself has been challenged. When statistical tests and null hypothesis testing first emerged (Fisher, 1925; Neyman & Pearson, 1928), significant objections were raised regarding their use (Berkson, 1938). At the most extreme level, the objection is that the use of significance tests retards the development of knowledge and actually harms science (see Meehl, 1978; Shrout, 1997). The article by Frank L. Schmidt elaborates the bases of the objection and the uses and misinterpretations of statistical significance testing. The article calls for abandoning statistical significance testing. Much of the confusion in the literature and seeming inconsistencies is the direct result of the way the data are analyzed and inferences are drawn from these analyses rather than of the differences obtained in the studies themselves. Schmidt argues for estimates of effect size and confidence intervals as a way to make the research literature less confusing and contradictory than it seems. He discusses the role of meta-analysis as a means of developing cumulative knowledge. Among the strengths of meta-analysis is the ability to integrate findings from multiple studies. He shows with a detailed example how conclusions from multiple studies are much more likely to converge using meta-analysis and effect size rather than using statistical significance. There has been a long tradition of challenging significance testing; Schmidt underscores positive alternatives and what they could mean for our science more generally.

Many statisticians clearly oppose current statistical significance and null hypothesis testing and are frustrated at the widespread misuse and misinterpretation of the results from such tests. Others place the role of such tests in perspective in terms of what such tests can and cannot do. Rather than abandoning such tests, these statisticians focus on more appropriate and restricted uses. The article by Robert W. Frick begins with a summary of key concerns and objections to significance testing and elaborates the situations in which null hypothesis testing is particularly useful. Emphasis is placed on use of null hypothesis testing to evaluate the ordering of conditions (i.e., which one is greater than the other or under what conditions are effects in one direction rather than another). There are conditions in which knowing the effect size is not a goal of research, and these are discussed in the article. Among the excellent features of this article are discussions of the relation of null hypothesis testing to theory and the criteria for deciding what ought to be believed. Although this article presents views that are different from those in the prior article by Schmidt, there are also points of agreement regarding the misinterpretation of significant tests and what the results of such tests provide. Furthermore, both authors suggest other strategies than those in current use as a way to improve analysis and presentation of the results of research.

BACKGROUND AND UNDERPINNINGS OF DATA ANALYSES

14

ON THE ORIGINS OF THE .05 LEVEL
OF STATISTICAL SIGNIFICANCE

MICHAEL COWLES AND CAROLINE DAVIS

It is generally understood that the conventional use of the 5% level as the maximum acceptable probability for determining statistical significance was established, somewhat arbitrarily, by Sir Ronald Fisher when he developed his procedures for the analysis of variance.

Fisher's (1925) statement in his book, *Statistical Methods for Research Workers*, seems to be the first specific mention of the $p = .05$ level as determining statistical significance.

> It is convenient to take this point as a limit in judging whether a deviation is to be considered significant or not. Deviations exceeding twice the standard deviation are thus formally regarded as significant. (p. 47)

Cochran (1976), commenting on a slightly later, but essentially similar, statement by Fisher (1926), says that, "Students sometimes ask, 'how

Reprinted from the *American Psychologist*, 37, 553–558. Copyright 1982 by the American Psychological Association.

did the 5 per cent significance level or Type I error come to be used as a standard?' . . . I am not sure but this is the first comment known to me on the choice of 5 per cent" (p. 15).

In the 1926 article Fisher acknowledges that other levels may be used:

> If one in twenty does not seem high enough odds, we may, if we prefer it, draw the line at one in fifty (the 2 per cent point), or one in a hundred (the one per cent point). Personally, the writer prefers to set a low standard of significance at the 5 per cent point, and ignore entirely all results which fail to reach this level. A significant fact should be regarded as experimentally established only if a properly designed experiment *rarely fails* to give this level of significance. (p. 504)

Cochran feels that Fisher was fairly casual about the choice, "as the words *convenient* and *prefers* have indicated" (p. 16). However, the statement quoted above leaves no doubt about Fisher's acceptance of the level as the critical cutoff point, once he had decided upon it.

Other writers, well-versed in the history and development of probability, have also fostered the attitude that the level is an arbitrary one. Yule and Kendall (1950), in the 14th edition of a book first published by Yule in 1911, state,

> In the examples we have given . . . our judgment whether P was small enough to justify us in suspecting a significant difference . . . has been more or less intuitive. Most people would agree . . . that a probability of .0001 is so small that the evidence is very much in favour . . . Suppose we had obtained $P = 0.1$. . . . Where, if anywhere, can we draw the line? The odds against the observed event which influence a decision one way or the other depend to some extent on the caution of the investigator. Some people (not necessarily statisticians) would regard odds of ten to one as sufficient. Others would be more conservative and reserve judgment until the odds were much greater. It is a matter of personal taste. (pp. 471–472)

Cramer (1955), in a completely rewritten version of a Swedish text first published in 1926, tells his readers,

> a value of t . . . will be denoted as *almost significant* if t exceeds the 5% value, but falls short of the 1% . . . called *significant* if t lies between the 1% and 0.1% values and *highly significant* if t exceeds the 0.1% value. This is, of course, a purely conventional terminology. (p. 202)

The issue to be considered is whether the choice of the 5% value was as arbitrary and casual as is so often implied. An examination of the history of probability and statistical theory, however, indicates that the choice was far from arbitrary and was influenced by previous scientific conventions that themselves were based on the notion of "chance" and the unlikelihood of an event occurring.

ORIGINS

As David (1962) has so articulately and elegantly described, the first glimmerings of an appreciation of long-run relative frequencies, randomness, and the unlikelihood of rare events being merely fortuitous go back at least to the Greek mathematicians and the Roman philosophers. Later, however, the spread of Christianity and the collapse of the Roman Empire made the Church the sole haven for scholars. This religious philosophy that accepted a universe in which every event, no matter how trivial, as being caused by an omnipotent God left no place for the investigation of random events. This is very likely the reason why the seeds of mathematical probability theory were not sown until late in 17th-century France. The opportunities had always been there: Because both the archaelogical and the written records show that gambling has been an ever-popular pastime, informal and relatively unsystematic "systems" for calculating "odds" were undoubtedly developed.

The questions posed by Antoine Gombauld, the Chevalier de Méré, related to certain gaming problems, sparked off the correspondence between Blaise Pascal and Pierre Fermat in 1654. Here are the beginnings of combinatorial algebra and mathematical probability theory (again see David, 1962).

In a slightly later (1662) development, John Graunt, a London haberdasher, constructed tables from the Bills of Mortality, parish accounts regularly recorded from early in the 17th century and, most importantly, used these tables for a series of statistical, actuarial inferences.

Graunt was, for example, able to reassure readers of his quite remarkable, unassuming, and refreshing work that,

> This *casualty* [Lunacy] being so uncertain, I shall not force myself to make any inference from the numbers, and proportions we finde in our Bills concerning it: onely I dare ensure any man at this present, well in his Wits, for one in the thousand, that he shall not die a *Lunatick* in *Bedlam,* within these seven years, because I finde not above one in about one thousand five hundred have do so. (Graunt, 1662/1956, p. 1430)

Here is a statement based on numerical data and couched in terms not so very far removed from those in reports in the modern literature.

In 1657, Huygens (1657/1970) published a tract, *On Reasoning in Games of Dice,* that was based upon the exchanges between Pascal and Fermat, and in 1713 Jacques Bernoulli's (1713/1970) book, *The Art of Conjecture,* developed a theory of games of chance. De Moivre's (1756/1967) *The Doctrine of Chances* was the most important of the gambling manuals; it appeared in three editions in 1718, 1738, and 1756. In the two later editions De Moivre presents a method, which he had first published in 1733, of approximating the sum of a very large number of binomial terms. It is safe to say that no other theoretical mathematical abstraction has had such an important influence on psychology and the social sciences as that method, for it generates the bell-shaped curve now commonly known by the name Karl Pearson gave it: the normal distribution.

The law of frequency of errors is often attributed to Laplace (1749–1827) and Gauss (1777–1855). Both men developed the use of the distribution outside of gaming and in particular demonstrated its utility in evaluating the variable results of measurements and observations in astronomy and in geodetic surveying. With the introduction of this distribution into the field of the biological and social sciences, we may start to trace the path that leads to the $p = .05$ level.

THE NORMAL DISTRIBUTION

The credit for the extension of the use of calculations used to assess observational error or gaming expectancies into the organization of human characteristics goes to Lambert Adolphe Quetelet (1796–1874), a Belgian astronomer.

Quetelet (1849) found, for example, that the frequency distribution of the chest girths of 5,738 Scottish soldiers closely approximated the normal curve. Moreover, he used the curve to infer what he took to be a non-chance occurrence. In examining the distribution of the heights of 100,000 French army conscripts, he observed a discrepancy between the calculated and reported frequencies of men falling at the minimum height for military service. "Is it not a fair presumption that the . . . men who constitute the difference of these numbers have been fraudulently rejected?" (p. 97).

Sir Francis Galton (1822–1911) eagerly adopted the curve in the organization of the anthropometric data that he collected and introduced the concept of percentiles.

> All persons conversant with statistics are aware that this supposition brings Variability within the grasp of the laws of Chance, with the result that the relative frequency of Deviations of different amounts admits of being calculated, when these amounts are measured in terms of any self-contained unit of variability, such as our Q. (Galton, 1889, pp. 54–55)

Q is the symbol for the semi-interquartile range, defined as one half of the difference between the score at the 75th percentile (the third quartile) and the 25th percentile (the first quartile). This means that in a distribution of scores, one half of the deviations fall within ± Q of the mean, which in the normal distribution falls at the 50th percentile (the second quartile). This measure of variability is equivalent to the *probable error*.

PROBABLE ERROR

The unit of measure of the abscissa of the normal distribution has had many forms. Today the *standard deviation* is the unit of choice, but for many years the probable error (*PE*) was in common use, and it is still used occasionally in the physical sciences. Fundamentally, probable error defines the deviation from a central measure between whose positive and negative values one half of the cases may be expected to fall by chance.

The term appeared in the early 19th century among German mathematical astronomers. Although De Moivre refers to the concept on which *PE* is based, Bessel used the term (*der wahrscheinliche Fehler*) for the first time in 1818. It was subsequently adopted by Gauss, who developed several methods of computing it (Walker, 1929). It was first used with the normal distribution in instances where it was necessary to determine the best possible value of the true position of a point from a series of measurements or observations all of which involved an element of error.

It remained for Karl Pearson (1894) to coin the term *standard deviation*, but the calculation of an equivalent value had existed since De Moivre. Simple calculation shows that the *PE* is equivalent to 0.674560, or roughly ⅔ of a standard deviation.

It was apparently normal practice for Quetelet and Galton to express values in a normal distribution as a function of *PE*, and it seems reasonable to assume that their preference was the overriding influence in its being used in subsequent statistical practice. It should be noted in passing that Galton (1889) objected to the name probable error, calling it a "cumbrous, slipshod, and misleading phrase."

The probable error is, quite clearly, not the most probable of all errors, and the use of the term *error* in describing the variation of human characteristics perhaps carries the analogy with measurement error distribution a shade too far.

STATISTICAL TESTS

In 1893 Pearson began his investigations into the general problem of fitting observed distributions to theoretical curves. The work led eventually to the formulation of the χ^2 test of "goodness of fit" in 1900, one of the most important developments in the history of statistics.

Weldon, the co-founder with Pearson of the biometric school (both men, of course, being much influenced by Galton), approached the problem of discrepancies between theory and observation in a much more empirical way, tossing coins and dice and comparing the outcomes with the binomial model.

In a letter written to Galton in 1894, Weldon asks for a comment on the results of some 7,000 throws of 12 dice collected for him by a clerk at University College, London.

> A day or two ago Pearson wanted some records of the kind in a hurry, in order to illustrate a lecture, and I gave him the record of the clerk's 7,000 tosses . . . on examination he rejects them because he thinks the deviation from the theoretically most probable result is so great as to make the record intrinsically incredible. (E. S. Pearson, 1965/1970, p. 331)

This incident set off a good deal of correspondence and discussion among the biometricians. These interchanges contain various references to odds and probabilities beyond which one would be ready to assert that the outcome was unlikely to be chance. Certainly it seems to have been agreed that what we now call the alpha level should have a relatively low value.

But only with the publication of the χ^2 test, the first test that enabled us to determine the probability of occurrence of discrepancies between expected and measured frequencies in a distribution, are indications of specific criteria to be found. Here we see the beginnings of standard rejection levels (i.e., points at which the probability of occurrence is so small as to make it difficult, perhaps impossible, for one to regard the observed distribution as a random variation on the theoretical distribution).

Pearson did not choose one particular value as the point of rejection. However, from an examination of the various examples of χ^2 calculations presented, with their corresponding probability values, one can see the range within which what might be described as a mixture of intuitive and statistical rejection occurred. The following remarks are from Pearson's paper: $p = .5586$ ("thus we may consider the fit remarkably good" [p. 170]); $p = .28$ ("fairly represented" [p. 174]); $p = .1$ ("not very improbable that the observed frequencies are compatible with a random sampling" [p. 171]); $p = .01$ ("this very improbable result" [p. 172]).

From Pearson's comments, it appears that he began to have some doubts about the goodness of fit at the .1 level ("not very improbable" implies that the results were perhaps *a little* improbable); however, he was convinced of the unlikelihood of the fit at the .01 level. The midpoint between the two is, of course, the .05 level.

William Gosset (who wrote under the pen name of "Student") began his employment with the Guinness Brewery in Dublin in 1899. Scientific methods were just starting to be applied to the brewing industry. Among Gossett's tasks was the supervision of what were essentially quality control experiments. The necessity of using small samples meant that his results were, at best, only approximations to the probability values derived from the normal curve. Therefore the circumstances of his work led Gosset to formulate the small-sample distribution that is called the *t* distribution.

With respect to the determination of a level of significance, Student's

(1908) article, in which he published his derivation of the *t* test, stated that "three times the probable error in the normal curve, for most purposes, would be considered significant" (p. 13).

A few years later, another important article was published under the joint authorship of an agronomist and an astronomer (Wood & Stratton, 1910). This paper was essentially to provide direction in the use of probability in interpreting experimental results. These authors endorse the use of *PE* as a measure: "The astronomer . . . has devised a method of estimating the accuracy of his averages . . . the agriculturist cannot do better than follow his example" (p. 425). They recommend "taking 30 to 1 as the lowest odds which can be accepted as giving practical certainty that a difference is significant" (p. 433). Such odds applied to the normal probability curve correspond to a difference from the mean of 3.2 *PE* (for practical purposes this was probably rounded to 3 *PE*).

What specifically determined the adoption of this convention is largely a matter of speculation. Perhaps it was a combination of the preferred use of the *PE* as a measure by early statisticians like Galton and the influence of Pearson and his statements about the unlikelihood of particular results. In any case, it is clear that as early as 1908 X $\pm$ 3 *PE* was accepted as a useful rule of thumb for rejecting differences occurring as the result of chance fluctuations.

Certainly by the time Fisher published his first book on statistical methods 17 years later, 3PE was a frequently used convention for determining statistical significance in a variety of sciences that employed statistical tests as experimental tools. For example, an article in the 1925 volume of the *British Journal of Psychology* reports that the chance occurrence of all calculated correlations is "greater than 3 times the *PE*" (Flugel, 1925).

McGaughy (1924) uses the term *critical ratio* for the expression X/3PE, where X represents a difference. This, he says, is "the accepted standard for the undoubted significance of an obtained difference between averages" and cites Jones (1921).

Having examined the events preceding Fisher's 1925 publication and remembering the context of his discussion, consideration of his first reference to $p = .05$ quite clearly indicates nothing startling or new, or for that matter arbitrary, about what he was suggesting.

A fact that would have been no surprise to most of those reading his book (and which, indeed, Fisher pointed out) is that "a deviation of three times the probable error is effectively equivalent to one of twice the standard error" (Fisher, 1925, pp. 47–48).

Fisher then cannot be credited with establishing the value of the significance level. What he can perhaps be credited with is the beginning of a trend to express a value in a distribution in terms of its own standard deviation instead of its probable error. Fisher was apparently convinced of the advantages of using standard deviation (*SD*), as evidenced by his remark that "The common use of the probable error is its only recommendation" (p. 48).

Fisher provided calculations for a "probability integral table," from which for any value (described as a function of its *SD*), one could find what proportion of the total population had a larger deviation. Therefore, when conducting any critical test, use of this table necessitated expressing the deviation of a value in terms of its *SD*.

Although, strictly speaking, the conventional rejection level of 3*PE* is equivalent to two times the *SD* (in modern terminology, a z score of 2), which expressed as a percentage is about 4.56%, one may hazard a guess that Fisher simply rounded off this value to 5% for ease of explanation. Furthermore, it seems reasonable to assume that as the use of statistical analysis was extended to the social sciences, the tendency to report experimental results in terms of their associated probability values rather than transforming them to z score values provided a broader base for general understanding by those not thoroughly grounded in statistical theory. In other words, the statement that the probability of obtaining a particular result by chance was less than 5% could be more easily digested by the uninitiated than the report that the result represented a z score of approximately 2.

SUBJECTIVE PROBABILITY

How the 5% significance level came to be adopted as a standard has been considered. However, *why* this level seemed appropriate to early statisticians, or why it has continued to prevail in statistical analysis for so long, must be approached not so much from a historical point of view, but from a consideration of the concept of *probability*.

Definitions of the term are most frequently based on expositions of the formal mathematical theory of probability. This may reflect the need to bridge the reality of events in everyday life and the philosophy of logic. Probability in this sense is an objective exercise that uses numerical calculations based on the mathematical theories of arrangements and frequency for the purpose of estimation and prediction.

What often eludes precise definition is the idea that, fundamentally, probability refers to the personal cognition of individuals whereby their knowledge of past experience aids in the formation of a system of expectations with which they face future events. This has been called *subjective probability* to distinguish this notion from its more formal mathematical counterpart.

Alberoni (1962a, 1962b) has conceptualized the intellectual processes that underlie the operation of subjective probability. When individuals cannot find a cause or a regular pattern to explain some differences or variation in the real world, they arrive at the idea of *chance*. This, in turn, forms their expectations for future events. If, however, at some point the events begin to contradict the expectations they have formed, they introduce *cause* and abandon the idea of chance. The point at which this rejection occurs depends largely on the degree of discrepancy and how it is interpreted by each individual. Alberoni refers to this point as the "threshold of dismissal of the idea of chance."

The fundamental questions that remain are straightforward and simple: Do people, scientists and nonscientists, generally feel that an event which occurs 5% of the time or less is a rare event? Are they prepared to ascribe a cause other than mere chance to such infrequent events?

If the answer to both these questions is "Yes," or even "Generally speaking, yes," then the adoption of the level as a criterion for judging outcomes is justifiable.

There is no doubt that the "threshold of dismissal of the idea of chance" depends on a complex set of factors specific to each individual, and therefore varies among individuals.[1] As a formal statement, however, the level has a longer history than is generally appreciated.

REFERENCES

Alberoni, F. (1962a). Contribution to the study of subjective probability. Part I. *Journal of General Psychology*, 66, 241–264.

Alberoni, F. (1962b). Contribution to the study of subjective probability. Prediction. Part II. *Journal of General Psychology*, 66, 265–285.

Bernoulli, J. (1970). *The art of conjecture* (F. Maseres, Ed. & Trans.). New York: Redex Microprint. (Original work published 1795)

Bessel, F. W. (1818). *Ueber den Ort des Polarsterns*. Berlin: Berliner Astronomische Jahrbuch für 1818.

Cochran, W. G. (1976). Early development of techniques in comparative experimentation. In D. B. Owen (Ed.), *On the history of statistics and probability*. New York: Dekker.

Cramer, H. (1955). *The elements of probability theory*. New York: Wiley.

David, F. N. (1962). *Games, gods and gambling*. New York: Hafner.

De Moivre, A. (1967). *The doctrine of chances* (3rd ed.). New York: Chelsea. (Original work published 1756)

Fisher, R. A. (1925). *Statistical methods for research workers*. Edinburgh: Oliver & Boyd.

Fisher, R. A. (1926). The arrangement of field experiments. *Journal of the Ministry of Agriculture*, 33, 503–513.

Flugel, J. C. (1925). A quantitative study of feeling and emotion in everyday life. *British Journal of Psychology*, 15, 318–355.

---

[1] We have some evidence, based on both formal and informal data, that people, on average, do indeed approach this threshold when the odds reach about 1 in 10 and are pretty well convinced when the odds are 1 in 100. The midpoint of the two values is close to .05, or odds of 1 in 20. One is reminded that these subjective probability norms are congruent with the ideas expressed in Pearson's 1900 publication.

Galton, F. (1889). *Natural inheritance*. London: Macmillan.

Graunt, J. (1956). Natural and political observations made upon the bills of mortality, 1662. In J. R. Newman (Ed.), *The world of mathematics*. New York: Simon & Schuster. (Original work published 1662)

Huygens, C. (1970). On reasoning in games. In J. Bernoulli (F. Maseres, Ed. & Trans.), *The art of conjecture*. New York: Redex Microprint. (Original work published 1657)

Jones, D. C. (1921). *A first course in statistics*. London: Bell.

McGaughy, J. R. (1924). *The fiscal administration of city school systems*. New York: Macmillan.

Pearson, E. S. (1970). Some incidents in the early history of biometry and statistics, 1890–94. In E. S. Pearson & M. G. Kendall (Eds.), *Studies in the history of statistics and probability*. London: Griffin. (Original work published 1965)

Pearson, K. (1894). Contributions to the mathematical theory of evolution: I. On the dissection of asymmetrical frequency curves. *Philosophical Transactions*, Part I, pp. 71–110.

Pearson, K. (1990). On the criterion that a given system of deviations from the probable in the case of a correlated system of variables is such that it can be reasonably supposed to have arisen from random sampling. *Philosophical Magazine, 50*, 150–175.

Quetelet, L. A. (1849). *Letters on the theory of probabilities* (O. G. Downes, Trans). London: Layton.

Student [W. S. Gossett]. (1908) The probable error of a mean. *Biometrika, 6*, 1–25.

Walker, H. M. (1929). *Studies in the history of statistical method*. Baltimore, MD: Williams & Wilkins.

Wood, T. B., & Stratton, F. J. M. (1910). The interpretation of experimental results. *Journal of Agricultural Science, 3*, 417–440.

Yule, G. U., & Kendall, M. G. (1950). *An introduction to the theory of statistics* (14th ed.). London: Griffin.

15

HYPOTHESIS VALIDITY OF
CLINICAL RESEARCH

BRUCE E. WAMPOLD, BETSY DAVIS, AND ROLAND H. GOOD III

Clinical research spans a wide range of applied areas. To varying degrees, the basis of this research emanates from principles of behavior and behavior change. On the more technological side are treatment studies that answer the questions of whether a treatment works or which treatment is more effective (Kazdin, 1980, 1986), and status studies, which are designed to identify differences between populations. Yet certainly even these studies rely heavily on principles of behavior and behavior change to design the treatments, select measures, and interpret the results. For example, it is important to know whether maternal depression is associated with childhood problems; however, the curious investigator will soon seek to understand the nature of the relation between these two constructs (e.g., Dumas, Gibson, & Albin, 1989; Forehand, Lautenschlager, Faust, & Graziano, 1986; Hops et al., 1987). The link between theory and constructs in applied research is discussed by Cook and Campbell (1979):

Reprinted from the *Journal of Consulting and Clinical Psychology*, 58, 360–367. Copyright 1990 by the American Psychological Association.

Researchers would like to be able to give their presumed cause and effect operations names which refer to theoretical constructs. The need for this is most explicit in theory-testing research where the operations are explicitly derived to represent theoretical notions. But applied researchers also like to give generalized abstract names to their variables, for it is hardly useful to assume that the relationship between the two variables is causal if one cannot summarize these variables other than by describing them in exhaustive operational detail. (p. 38)

Although the importance of theory for the design of interpretation of clinical research is apparent, the mechanics of designing research in such a way that the results will be theoretically interesting are far from clear. The purpose of our article is to explore some of the aspects of clinical research that relate to theory. We have designated the term *hypothesis validity* to refer to the extent to which research results reflect theoretically derived predictions about the relations between or among constructs. If a study has adequate hypothesis validity, the results will be informative about the nature of the relation between constructs; that is, the study will inform theory. If a study has inadequate hypothesis validity, ambiguity about the relation between constructs will result, and indeed less certainty about the relation may exist than before the research was conducted. Hypothesis validity involves the development and statement of research hypotheses, the match of statistical hypotheses to research hypotheses, and the focus of statistical tests.

THE ROLE OF HYPOTHESES IN THEORY TESTING

Some important points from the philosophy of science as it relates to hypotheses supply the language to discuss and the base from which to develop hypothesis validity. Adopting the notation of Chow (1988), the crucial concepts needed for this discussion are illustrated in Table 1 and discussed below. Consider a theory T_1. Implication I_{11} of theory T_1 specifies an outcome that should occur given the mechanisms of the theory. $A.I_{11}$ represents the implication plus the auxiliary assumptions (e.g., normality of scores). X is an experimental expectation given $A.I_{11}$ (under the proper experimental conditions). Deductively, if the theory implies that X will occur (given the implication and the auxiliary assumptions, i.e., $A.I_{11}$) and if an experimental outcome D that is dissimilar to X is obtained, then the theory T_1 must be false. This approach to testing theory, which has been labeled the *falsificationist approach* (Popper, 1968), has bothered many philosophers of science, especially when used in conjunction with statistical tests (Folger, 1989; Mahoney, 1978; Meehl, 1978; Serlin, 1987; Serlin & Lapsley, 1985).

In the context of statistical hypothesis testing, falsification occurs when the null hypothesis is not rejected because the obtained result D is contrary to the expected result X. However, there are many ways that failure to reject

TABLE 1
Deductive Logic of Hypothesis Testing

Theory Implication	T_1 I_{11} Falsification	T_1 I_{11} Corroboration
Major premise	If $A.I_{11}$ then X under EFG	If $A.1_{11}$ then X under EFG
Minor premise	D is dissimilar to X.	D is similar to X.
Experimental conclusion	$A.I_{11}$ is false.	$A.I_{11}$ could be true.
Theoretical conclusion	T_1 is false.	T_1 could be true.

Note. T_1 = theory of interest; I_{11} = one implication of T_1; EFG = control and independent variables of the experiment; X = experimental expectation; A = set of auxiliary assumptions underlying the experiment; D = experimental outcomes (i.e., the pattern shown by the dependent variable in various conditions of the experiment). From "Significance Test or Effect Size?" by S. L. Chow, 1988, *Psychological Bulletin, 103,* p. 107. Copyright 1988 by the American Psychological Association. Adapted by permission. See also Folger, 1989.

the null hypothesis can result other than the fact that the theory is false, ruining the clean deductive nature of falsification (Folger, 1989). The obtained findings may be due to chance (Type II error), incorrect formulation of the implication of the theory, misspecification of the expected outcome X, low power, poor experimental methods, unreliable variables, or violated assumptions (Cook & Campbell, 1979; Folger, 1989).

Besides being epistemologically troublesome, falsification is not the modus operandi of research in the social sciences. If anything, there is a prejudice against research that fails to reject the null hypothesis, especially in clinically related areas (Atkinson, Furlong, & Wampold, 1982; Fagley, 1985; Greenwald, 1975; Mahoney, 1977). The alternative hypothesis holds the upper hand in psychological research; that is, researchers usually hope to reject the null hypothesis and lend support to a particular point of view. Furthermore, journal editors and reviewers look to significant results to inform the field (Atkinson et al., 1982). However, there are epistemological problems with this approach as well. The fact that the obtained pattern of results D is similar to the predicted pattern X does not imply that the theory T_1 is true, because other theories may also imply a predicted pattern X. Claiming the truth of a theory on the basis of the appearance of the expected pattern of results is a deductive error called *affirming the consequent*. The problems with affirming the consequent in psychological research have been acknowledged previously (e.g., Folger, 1989; Mahoney, 1978). Nevertheless, an experiment that produces the theoretically expected pattern of results has survived an attempt at falsification. In such a case, the theory is said to be *corroborated*; corroboration implies that the theory has been tested and has survived, which is quite different from implying that it has been confirmed (see Mahoney, 1978).

There is another problem with statistical testing and theory that is more subtle, and yet more troublesome, than the deductive problems we have discussed. In the hard sciences, as methods are refined (e.g., better measurement of phenomena), theories are winnowed, leaving fewer theories that are ascribed to with more confidence. Just the opposite is true in many areas of social science research. It is reasonable to believe that the null hypothesis is not literally true; that is, all constructs are related, even if to some small degree. As methods are refined, error variance will be reduced and statistical tests will be more powerful. As a consequence, it will be more likely that theories will be corroborated and less likely that they will be falsified and rejected. Instead of winnowing, theories will proliferate (Serlin, 1987; Serlin & Lapsley, 1985).

Several remedies to the philosophical problems of hypothesis testing have been suggested. An omnipresent suggestion involves the use of effect-size measures, confidence intervals, statements about power, measures of clinical significance, or other measures that reflect the degree to which the obtained results differ from that hypothesized under the null hypothesis (e.g., Cohen, 1988; Cook & Campbell, 1979; Fagley, 1985; Folger, 1989; Haase, Waechter, & Solomon, 1982; Jacobson, Follette, & Revenstorf, 1984; Rosnow & Rosenthal, 1988; Wampold, Furlong, & Atkinson, 1983). These measures are useful because they provide information in addition to the binary decision of whether the null hypothesis is rejected, although their use is controversial logically and statistically (Chow, 1988, 1989; Hollon & Flick, 1988; Mitchell & Hartmann, 1981; Murray & Dosser, 1987; O'Grady, 1982).

Another remedy to the traditional hypothesis-testing strategy is to use alternative statistical paradigms or to use no statistics at all. The Bayesian approach readjusts prior estimates of the probabilities of events with information provided by new samples (Schmitt, 1969). Serlin and Lapsley (1985) have promulgated the *good-enough principle*, which embodies a hypothesis-testing strategy in which, instead of hypothesizing a null effect, the researcher hypothesizes the magnitude of the effect that is sufficient to corroborate the theory or that is clinically significant. Of course, the researcher may eschew the use of statistical tests entirely; a significant body of knowledge has been accumulated in experimental and applied areas by the visual analysis of data generated by single-subject designs (Barlow & Hersen, 1984).

Hypothesis validity addresses the interrelations of theory, research hypotheses, and statistical hypotheses. Research hypotheses are derived from theory and can be characterized as statements about the presumed relations among constructs. In Chow's (1988) framework, the research hypotheses represent an implication of the theory. Research hypotheses should be stated in such a way that a theory is falsifiable and that competing theories can be winnowed. Clarity of a research hypothesis is vital to determine whether an obtained outcome is similar or dissimilar to the outcome predicted by theory.

Certain properties of statistical hypotheses are needed in order to assure adequate hypothesis validity. First, statistical hypotheses should be congruent with the research hypotheses. If the research hypotheses posit a relation between constructs on the basis of means, then the statistical hypotheses should be phrased in terms of μ, the population mean. However, a statistical hypothesis regarding μ would be inappropriate if the implication of the theory was phrased in terms of differences in variances. Second, statistical hypotheses must be sufficiently specific to determine whether the obtained result is similar or dissimilar to the predicted experimental outcome.

The relations among theory, research hypotheses, statistical hypotheses, and results are presented in Figure 1. The design of experiments involves deriving research hypotheses from theory, matching statistical hypotheses to research hypotheses, and creating the experiment in order to obtain the results. It is interesting to note that design texts and courses often focus on the last operation (i.e., design of the experiment rather than design of the research). Inference proceeds in the opposite direction. The results are used to make decisions about the statistical hypotheses (e.g., reject the null hypothesis), and these decisions indicate whether the predicted patterns stipulated in the research hypotheses have been verified, determining whether the theory is corroborated or falsified. Traditional statistics texts concentrate on making inferences from sample data (i.e., the results) to statements about population parameters (i.e., statistical hypotheses). Hypothesis validity involves

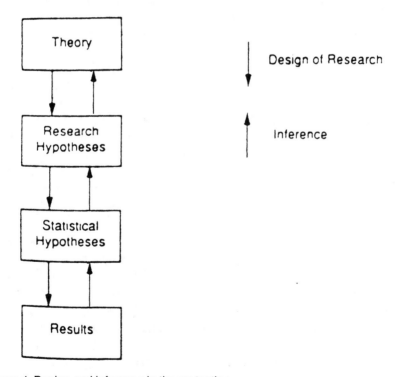

Figure 1. Design and inference in theory testing.

both the design of research and the inferences made from the results of studies.

In the spirit of Campbell and Stanley (1966), Bracht and Glass (1968), and Cook and Campbell (1979), we discuss hypothesis validity in more detail by posing threats to hypothesis validity.

THREATS TO HYPOTHESIS VALIDITY

Inconsequential Research Hypotheses

In Chow's (1988) framework, I_{11} was an implication of theory T_1. There are many other implications from theory T_1 that could be made (i.e., I_{12}, I_{13}, etc.). An important question is whether I_{11} represents a crucial issue. That is, from the set of possible implications (some of which may not have been entertained by the researcher), is I_{11} central to determining the veridicality of the theory T_1 in comparison with T_2, T_3, and so forth? Implication I_{11} is suboptimal to the extent that competing theories would have implications similar to I_{11}. For example, if theory T_2 implied I_{21}, which was identical to I_{11}, then any experimental result corroborating T_1 would also corroborate T_2. The hypothesis validity of a study is strengthened when the number of tenable theories that have implications similar to I_{11} is small. Ideally, corroborating T_1 should simultaneously falsify a large number of competing theories.

In his discussion of strong inference, Platt (1964) discussed the importance of determining the crucial question and devising research so that various explanations for observed phenomena can be ruled out. Implication I_{11} is superior to other implications to the extent that research that is based on this implication will result in a clearer understanding of the relation between constructs than would research that is based on other implications, and to the extent that this understanding is important to understanding the psychological phenomena of interest. Thus, strong inference is based, in part, on inductive reasoning about the implications of the theory under scrutiny.

Framing the discussion of research questions notationally should not be construed to indicate that this process is necessarily formal or deductive. Essentially the researcher surveys existing knowledge relating to his or her problems and attempts to pose the important unanswered question. Examining crucial hypotheses leads to the extension of knowledge, the winnowing of theories, the clarification of discrepancies, the identification of active ingredients of treatments, and so on. Inconsequential research hypotheses, on the other hand, do not produce resolution because they do not lead to a convergence of knowledge.

Platt (1964) addressed the issue of inconsequential research hypotheses by advocating multiple hypotheses. He has claimed that sciences that progress rapidly are characterized by experimentation that tests one theory against another. In that way, the results simultaneously corroborate one theory while falsifying another. For example, in particle physics, two models might be postulated; one model cannot explain the appearance of a certain particle in an experiment, whereas the other can explain it. If the particle appears (reliably), the first model is abandoned, and the second is tentatively adopted until a competing model is developed and tested against the tentatively adopted model.

This multiple hypothesis idea has implications for the manner in which models are tested in psychological research, especially with the advent of modeling techniques such as LISREL (Jöreskog & Sörbom, 1988). Typically, a model is proposed (one that is based on theory, it is hoped), and its compatibility with sample data is assessed. If the sample data are not consistent with the model proposed, the model is rejected (e.g., a significant chi-square goodness-of-fit test is obtained). On the other hand, if the goodness of fit is not significant, the model is retained. However, it is not proved, because this conclusion would be affirming the consequent (Cliff, 1983); there may be other models that fit the data as well (or better) than the model proposed. According to the multiple-hypothesis concept, stronger inferences can be made by contrasting competing models. For example, using a LISREL analysis of attitudes, Kerlinger (1980) demonstrated that a model with separate conservative and liberal dimensions was superior to a model with conservatism and liberalism as poles on a single dimension.

Ambiguous Research Hypotheses

Ambiguous research hypotheses make it difficult to ascertain how the results of a study influence our theoretical understanding. If the experimental expectation (X in Chow's [1988] notation) is not specified sufficiently, it may well be impossible to determine whether the obtained results D are similar or dissimilar to what was expected. Ambiguity with regard to research hypotheses results in the inability to falsify a theory, a particularly troublesome state of affairs from a philosophy of science perspective (Mahoney, 1978; Platt, 1964; Popper, 1968).

Ambiguous research hypotheses are often stated in journal articles with phrases such as "the purpose of the present study is to explore the relation between . . ." or "the purpose is to determine the relation between. . . ." In one sense, such research cannot fail, because some relation between variables will be "discovered," even if the relation is null (i.e., no relation). In another sense, the research will always fail because the results do not falsify or corroborate any theory about the true state of affairs.

As an example of ambiguous research hypotheses, consider the following purpose of a study (Webster-Stratton, 1988) on parents' perceptions of child deviance:

> The present study attempted to determine (a) the relation of parental adjustment measures of such variables as depression, marital satisfaction, parenting stress, and other negative life stressors to mothers' and fathers' perceptions of their children's deviant behaviors; (b) the relation of teachers' independent perceptions of the children's behaviors to mothers' and fathers' perceptions; (c) the relation of mother, father, and teacher perceptions of child behaviors to observed mother, father, and child behaviors; and (d) the relation of parent measures to observed mother, father, and child behaviors. (pp. 909–910)

Interpretation of the results of this study was problematic because there was no predicted experimental outcome of result with which to compare the obtained pattern of results. It is not surprising that this research discovered some patterns that confirmed previous research (e.g., mothers' perceptions of their children's deviant behaviors were affected by mothers' personal adjustment) and some patterns that contradicted other previous research (e.g., that teacher reports were better than maternal depression for the prediction of mothers' reports of child deviance).

Although careful observation is an important step in the development of hypotheses in any science, reliance on exploratory research can result only in confusion, if for no other reason than that some of the observed patterns are due to chance. A preponderance of studies with ambiguous research hypotheses will tend not to converge on important principles of behavior but will result in post hoc attempts to reconcile discrepant findings. As a result, weak theories will proliferate.

An example of clear hypotheses is provided by Borkovec and Mathews (1988) in a study of nonphobic anxiety disorders: "Clients with predominantly cognitive symptoms might be expected to respond better to techniques addressing this symptom domain, whereas clients with predominantly somatic symptoms might improve more under coping desensitization" (p. 878). This hypothesis is specific enough that, if other aspects of the study are valid (including other aspects of hypothesis validity discussed later), the results can clearly corroborate or fail to support the Borkovec and Mathews prediction.

As a hypothetical example to illustrate research hypotheses (and later statistical tests), consider a treatment study contrasting a behavioral intervention and a cognitive intervention. To answer Paul's (1967) question about which treatments work with which type of clients, further suppose the differential effects of the treatment on two types of persons—cognitively oriented and noncognitively oriented. Suppose five dependent variables were used to operationally define the construct targeted for change (e.g., marital satisfaction). A reasonable and specific hypothesis would be that the behav-

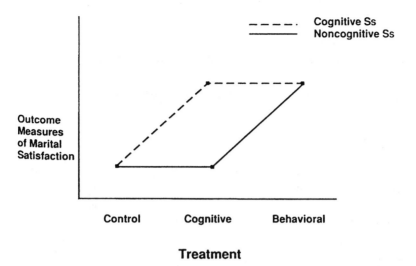

Figure 2. Predicted pattern for outcome variables for Type of Subject × Treatment. (Higher scores indicate more satisfaction.)

ior therapy would be effective with both types of subjects (i.e., cognitively oriented and noncognitively oriented), whereas the cognitive therapy would be effective only with the cognitively oriented subjects. The anticipated pattern of results is presented in Figure 2.

The argument for specificity in research hypotheses has been made in the context of traditional hypothesis testing. However, our points are as pertinent, if not more so, for many alternative strategies. For example, in the Bayesian approach, specificity is important because one has to stipulate prior probabilities. According to the good-enough principle, the minimal effect size that represents importance must be specified (Serlin & Lapsley, 1985).

Noncongruence of Research Hypotheses and Statistical Hypotheses

To determine whether the obtained outcome D is similar or dissimilar to the experimental expectation X, the statistical hypothesis must correspond to the research hypothesis. When the research and statistical hypotheses are incongruent, even persuasive statistical evidence (small alpha levels, high power, large effect sizes) will not allow valid inferences to be made about the research hypotheses.

Although the problems of noncongruence seem obvious, consider the case in which the research hypothesis addresses differences in variances; that is, a treatment is expected to increase the variance (and quite possibly leave the mean unchanged). For example, a treatment for autoimmune deficiency syndrome could possibly prolong the lives of one half of the subjects and hasten the death of the other half. In such a case, it would be inappropriate to hypothesize mean differences à la an analysis of variance (ANOVA; viz., $\mu_1 = \mu_2 = \ldots \mu_j$) when the question of interest is whether the variances are equal (viz., $\sigma^2_1 = \sigma^2_2 = \ldots = \sigma^2_j$). A perusal of the statistical tests used in clinical research convincingly demonstrates, we believe, that differences among groups are expressed as differences among means by default.

Diffuse Statistical Hypotheses and Tests

Statistical tests are used to evaluate the extent to which an observed experimental outcome D is similar or dissimilar to the experimental expectation X. If the research hypothesis is translated into one set of statistical hypotheses (a null and an alternative), then, if the statistical test is valid and is congruent to the research hypothesis, the results of the statistical test will provide information so that the researcher can decide whether D is similar to X. If the null hypothesis for this test is rejected in favor of an alternative hypothesis that is consistent with X, then the conclusion is made that D is similar to X. If the null hypothesis is not rejected, then the conclusion is made that D is dissimilar to X (Chow, 1988). Of course, the decisions made could be incorrect (viz., Type I and Type II error).

Diffusion of statistical tests is created in one of three ways: First, a specific research hypothesis can be (and often is) translated into many statistical hypotheses and tests. Second, the statistical test used may be an omnibus test that does not focus on a specific research question. Third, extraneous independent variables may be included.

Multiple Statistical Tests

When more than one set of statistical hypotheses is tested per research hypothesis, theoretical ambiguity can result because it is not clear what pattern of results will corroborate or falsify the conjecture embodied in the research hypothesis. Specifically, many statistical tests per research hypothesis are problematic for two reasons. First, there is uncertainty with regard to the interpretation of many statistical tests because the results may not be consistent. Suppose that the researcher conducts two statistical tests. One yields a result consistent with the theory, and the other yields a result that is inconsistent with the theory, as might be the case when two dependent variables are used. Is this evidence for or against the theory?

The interpretation of multiple statistical tests is further compounded by the fact that some of the statistically significant results will have occurred by chance when there was no effect (Type I error), and some of the nonsignificant results will have occurred even though the expected effect was present (Type II error). Control of experimentwise Type I error will minimize the Type I errors but will lead to greater experimentwise Type II error. In any event, the question remains, "Which results were due to Type I and Type II errors?"

TABLE 2
Pattern of Predicted Significant *T* Tests

Test	Significant
Control/cognitive Ss vs. control/noncognitive Ss	No
Cognitive Tx/cognitive Ss vs. cognitive Tx/noncognitive Ss	Yes
Behavioral Tx/cognitive Ss vs. behavioral Tx/noncognitive Ss	No
Control/cognitive Ss vs. cognitive Tx/cognitive Ss	Yes
Control/cognitive Ss vs. behavioral Tx/cognitive Ss	Yes
Control/noncognitive Ss vs. cognitive Tx/noncognitive Ss	No
Control/noncognitive Ss vs. behavioral Tx/noncognitive Ss	Yes
Cognitive Tx/cognitive Ss vs. behavioral Tx/cognitive Ss	No
Cognitive Tx/noncognitive Ss vs. behavioral Tx/noncognitive Ss	Yes

Note. S = subject. Tx = treatment.

The problem with many statistical tests is illustrated by the Borkovec and Mathews (1988) study of nonphobic anxiety. For the specific hypothesis with regard to clients with cognitive and with somatic symptoms, several statistical tests were used. Predictably the outcome was ambiguous, giving rise to difficulties in interpretation: "Such an ambiguous outcome is open to a variety of interpretations" (Borkovec & Mathews, p. 882).

To further illustrate the ambiguity created by many statistical tests, consider the example presented earlier with regard to the behavioral and cognitive treatments for cognitively and noncognitively oriented subjects. To test the research hypothesis embodied in Figure 2, a series of *t* tests for each dependent variable could be conducted in which several tests would be expected to be significant and others nonsignificant. These *t* tests are presented in Table 2; 45 tests would be needed (9 for each dependent variable). Clearly such an approach is questionable because it is unclear what degree of correspondence with the expected pattern of results in Table 2 would be required to corroborate the research hypothesis. Suppose that 1 of the *t*-test outcomes was not as expected; would that still be strong enough evidence to decide that the results were consistent with the prediction? What about 2 or 3, 35 or 40? As mentioned previously, this question is complicated by the fact that the probability of a Type I error has escalated dramatically. One could, of course, control the experimentwise Type I error rate with a Bonferroni type procedure, although this would be a very conservative approach, resulting in unacceptable experimentwise Type II error rates (Hays, 1988; Rosenthal & Rubin, 1984).

Omnibus Tests

Omnibus tests are problematic because they contain effects, contrasts, or combinations that do not reflect solely the research hypothesis. Hence, several different research hypotheses can lead to a significant omnibus test. For example, an omnibus *F* test in an ANOVA for a treatment study with several treatments may be due to the treatments' being superior to the control group, or may be due to one treatment's being superior to the other treatments and to the control group. Although differences may be explored post hoc, planned comparisons are advantageous for theory testing. The interpretation given to the results of a planned comparison (or any other focused test[1]) is a direct test of a specific hypothesis. On the other hand, if the omnibus F test is significant at a given level, then some possible post hoc comparison must be significant at that level (Hays, 1988; Wampold & Drew, 1990); however, there is no assurance that this comparison will be interpretable. Even if the comparison is interpretable, the interpretation is made post hoc, and correspondence to a predicted pattern is precluded.

There are problems with omnibus tests other than their questionable relation to theory. Omnibus tests (and post hoc follow-up tests) are statistically less powerful means to detect effects than are focused tests (Hays, 1988; Rosnow & Rosenthal, 1988). Furthermore, calculation and interpretation of effect sizes for omnibus tests are problematic (Rosnow & Rosenthal, 1988).

Returning to the marital satisfaction example, we could conduct a 3 (two treatments plus control group) × 2 (type of subject) ANOVA for each dependent variable, a less diffuse choice than conducting the 45 t tests. However, this approach also suffers from multiple tests because it yields 15 F tests, 2 tests of main effects, and 1 test of the interaction effect for each of the five dependent variables. However, the omnibus F test for the ANOVA is particularly pernicious because it does not directly address the pattern of expected results. The research hypothesis embodied in Figure 1 combines a main effect and an interaction effect.

The expected pattern of results for this problem can be neatly expressed as a planned comparison (see display below). However, even though this comparison tests the research hypothesis directly, testing this comparison for each dependent variable maintains the multiple statistical test problem.

Tx:	Control	Control	Cognitive	Cognitive	Behavioral	Behavioral
Ss:	Cognitive	Noncognitive	Cognitive	Noncognitive	Cognitive	Noncognitive
Comparison:	−1	−1	+1	−1	+1	+1

The most focused test would be a multivariate planned comparison. This one test would answer the question of whether the expected pattern of means was reflected in the sample data and thus would avoid multiple statistical tests as well as omnibus tests. There would be no need to conduct follow-up tests because the research hypothesis did not specify differential

---

[1] Focused tests have been defined by Rosnow and Rosenthal (1988) to be "significance tests that address precise questions, such as any t test, any F test with 1 df in the numerator, and any $1-df$ χ^2 test" (p. 204). However, there are tests with more than 1 df that answer specific questions. For example, a general linear model F test that all higher order interaction effects are zero could be used to show that a number of independent variables do not interact with a treatment variable.

effects for individual outcome variables; presumably the variables were measuring the same construct.

In this example, the focused test was one multivariate test. However, this example should not be taken to indicate that multivariate tests are necessarily less diffuse than univariate tests. A common practice is to conduct omnibus multivariate analyses of variance (MANOVAs) followed by omnibus univariate ANOVAs. This practice is diffuse because of the omnibus nature of the tests and because it is not clear which pattern of the univariate tests corroborates the research hypothesis. In fact, it is possible to reject the multivariate null hypothesis while not being able to reject any of the univariate null hypotheses (Huberty & Morris, 1989). It has been recommended that significant multivariate tests be followed by discriminant analyses so that the linear combination of variables that best differentiate the groups can be examined (e.g., Bray & Maxwell, 1982). Although this may be an improvement over univariate Fs, without hypothesizing linear combinations, it remains difficult to link the statistical results to the research hypotheses.

The choice of a multivariate test should depend on the research hypothesis. Multivariate tests often are advocated for the express purpose of controlling experimentwise Type I error (e.g., Leary & Altmaier, 1980). Although controlling Type I error is beneficial, consideration of hypothesis validity of the study should be the primary criterion in the choice of a statistical procedure. For example, when the dependent variables are conceptually independent and result in multiple research questions, multiple ANOVAs may be the appropriate procedures to answer specific research questions (Huberty & Morris, 1989).

Generally, the less diffuse the statistical tests (and hence statistical hypotheses), the greater the hypothesis validity of the study. To the extent possible, one statistical test should be focused on one research hypothesis. Accordingly, planned comparisons would be preferable to omnibus F tests in the ANOVA context, a test of a hypothesized curvilinear relation would treat other curvilinear relations as residual, higher order interactions with no theoretical relevance would not be tested, parameters would be contrasted rather than tested individually (e.g., tests of differences between correlations), and so forth.

The importance of focusing a few specific tests on research questions rather than using diffuse tests has long been emphasized. Serlin (1987) has succinctly summarized the theoretical problems associated with omnibus tests:

> But one still sees omnibus F tests performed in analysis of variance, even though almost all the contrasts subsumed by the omnibus null hypothesis have *no possibility of interpretation* [italics added]. In a similar fashion, the omnibus null hypothesis in multivariate analysis of variance subsumes

an even larger set of mostly *uninterpretable* [italics added] contrasts performed on mostly *uninterpretable* [italics added] linear combinations of the dependent variables. Finally, the omnibus null hypothesis in regression analysis examines whether any of an infinite set of linear combinations of the predictor variables is related to the dependent variable. In each of these cases, *a consideration of the theoretically derived research questions under examination in the experiment would obviate the use of the omnibus hypothesis test* [italics added]. (p. 370)

Extraneous Independent Variables

Often independent variables are included in a study to increase the external validity of a study, that is, to increase the generalizability of the results across persons, settings, or time (Cook & Campbell, 1979). For example, to determine whether the results apply equally to men and women, gender may be added to a design as an independent variable. Of course, the set of possible independent variables related to persons, settings, or time is very large. With regard to persons, the most widely used variables include gender, ethnicity, socioeconomic status, and intelligence, although there are many other variables that could be included. Furthermore, each of these variables very likely glosses over other important distinctions. For example, gender ignores sex role orientation, and ethnicity ignores level of acculturation.

The choice of independent variables related to generalizability is difficult. We contend that this choice should be driven by theory to the extent possible. If there is good reason to believe that the results of a study will differ for men and women, then there is a good rationale to include gender in the study. However, if the theory implies that sex role orientation is the critical variable, then sex role orientation should be included.

Inclusion of extraneous variables inflates the number of hypotheses tested, increasing the diffusion of the statistical tests. In the typical factorial design, each independent variable added to the design introduces another main effect as well as interaction effects with the other independent variables. Additional independent variables also increase the likelihood that omnibus tests will be used because it becomes more difficult and less appropriate (without theory) to make specific predictions with regard to the main and, particularly, the interaction effects.

One could suggest another caution about additional independent variables. If an additional independent variable is important enough to be included in the study, it should be treated as a legitimate part of the design, and predictions should be made about the outcome for this variable. The irrelevance of independent variables is demonstrated when researchers conduct a preliminary test for differences on a variable such as gender and then collapse over this factor when no significant differences are found. This process rules out the possibility of detecting an interaction effect as well, which is often the most interesting of results from an external validity point of view.

CONCLUSIONS

The purpose of our article is to call attention to the connection between theory and results of individual studies. The concept of hypothesis validity has been introduced to emphasize the importance of drawing crucial implications from theory, stating clear research hypotheses, matching statistical hypotheses with research hypotheses, and focusing the statistical tests on the research hypotheses. We hope that the presentation of hypothesis validity provides a framework that is useful for the design and critique of clinical research.

Any conceptual framework is somewhat arbitrary; hypothesis validity is no exception. Hypothesis validity borders on both construct validity of putative causes and effects and statistical conclusion validity, as discussed by Cook and Campbell (1979). Construct validity of putative causes and effects involves determining the degree to which the variables included in a study reflect theoretical constructs. Clearly, construct validity plays an important role in the theoretical relevance of studies. However, hypothesis validity differs from construct validity by focusing on the relation between the constructs; construct validity focuses on the operationalization of the constructs.

Hypothesis validity is also related to statistical conclusion validity. Multiple statistical tests pose threats to statistical conclusion validity because of fishing and error rate problems (Cook & Campbell, 1979). However, even if these problems are attenuated by statistical means (e.g., using the Bonferroni inequality), ambiguity is present because of the difficulty in comparing the obtained pattern of results with the predicted pattern of results. Focused tests are advantageous primarily because they provide an explicit test of a specific hypothesis, although they are also desirable from a statistical point of view (e.g., increased power under certain circumstances).

Hypothesis validity applies most directly to theoretically driven clinical research. What about purely exploratory research or technological research? In any field of empirical inquiry, exploration is important. Most researchers enjoy searching through data to discover unanticipated relations among variables. Nevertheless, the search is guided by knowledge and understanding of theory, and interpretation of the discoveries is made within a theoretical context. Although the tenets of hypothesis validity do not apply as directly to purely exploratory research, they are critical to testing the conjectures that emanate from the exploratory phase.

Examples of purely technological research in clinical psychology are difficult to find. At first glance, comparative treatment studies may appear to answer the atheoretical question about the relative efficacy of two or more treatments (Kazdin, 1980, 1986). However, development of the treatment will most likely rely on principles of behavior change, selection of the dependent measures will be based on the intended outcome, and interpretation of the results will be explained within a theoretical context. Regardless of the degree to which such studies rely on theory, the principles of hypothesis validity are valuable. One still wants to conduct a study crucial to establishing the relative efficacy of a treatment, to state clearly the research hypotheses about relative efficacy, to match the statistical hypotheses to the research hypotheses, and so on.

We hope that describing the threats to hypothesis validity will result in more thought about the research hypotheses and how they can be tested elegantly. If a researcher uses a strong rope to lower himself or herself from theory to research hypotheses to statistical hypotheses and finally to the results of a study, then he or she will be able to climb back with the results so that a valid statement about theory can be made. If the rope is fatally frayed at some point, the results picked up at the bottom will be of little value (and may become burdensome weight) for the return journey.

REFERENCES

Atkinson, D. R., Furlong, M. J., & Wampold, B. E. (1982). Statistical significance, reviewer evaluations, and the scientific process: Is there a (statistically) significant relationship? *Journal of Counseling Psychology, 29,* 189–194.

Barlow, D. H., & Hersen, M. (1984). *Single case experimental designs: Strategies for studying behavior change* (2nd ed.). New York: Pergamon Press.

Borkovec, T. D., & Mathews, A. M. (1988). Treatment of nonphobic anxiety disorders: A comparison of nondirective, cognitive, and coping desensitization. *Journal of Consulting and Clinical Psychology, 56,* 877–884.

Bracht, G. H., & Glass, G. V. (1968). The external validity of experiments. *American Educational Research Journal, 5,* 437–474.

Bray, H. J., & Maxwell, S. E. (1982). Analyzing and interpreting significant MANOVAS. *Review of Educational Research, 52,* 340–367.

Campbell, D. T., & Stanley, J. C. (1966). *Experimental and quasi-experimental designs for research.* Chicago: Rand McNally.

Chow, S. L. (1988). Significance test or effect size? *Psychological Bulletin, 103,* 105–110.

Chow, S. L. (1989). Significance tests and deduction: Reply to Folger. (1989). *Psychological Bulletin, 106,* 161–165, 778.

Cliff, N. (1983). Some cautions concerning the application of causal modeling methods. *Multivariate Behavioral Research, 18,* 115–126.

Cohen, J. (1988). *Statistical power analysis for the behavioral sciences* (2nd ed.). Hillsdale, NJ: Erlbaum.

Cook, T. D., & Campbell, D. T. (1979). *Quasi-experimentation: Design and analysis for field settings.* Chicago: Rand McNally.

Dumas, J. E., Gibson, J. A., & Albin, J. B. (1989). Behavioral correlates of maternal depressive symptomatology in conduct-disordered children. *Journal of Consulting and Clinical Psychology, 57*, 516–521.

Fagley, N. S. (1985). Applied statistical power analysis and the interpretation of nonsignificant results by research consumers. *Journal of Counseling Psychology, 32*, 391–396.

Folger, R. (1989). Significance tests and the duplicity of binary decisions. *Psychological Bulletin, 106*, 155–160.

Forehand, R., Lautenschlager, G. J., Faust, J., & Graziano, W. G. (1986). Parent perceptions and parent–child interaction in clinic-referred children: A preliminary investigation of the effects of maternal depressive moods. *Behaviour Research and Therapy, 24*, 73–75.

Greenwald, A. G. (1975). Consequences of prejudice against the null hypothesis. *Psychological Bulletin, 82*, 1–20.

Haase, R. F., Waechter, D. M., & Solomon, G. S. (1982). How significant is a significant difference? Average effect size of research in counseling psychology. *Journal of Counseling Psychology, 29*, 58–65.

Hays, W. L. (1988). *Statistics* (4th ed.). New York: Holt, Rinehart & Winston.

Hollon, S. D., & Flick, S. N. (1988). On the meaning and methods of clinical significance. *Behavioral Assessment, 10*, 197–206.

Hops, H., Biglan, A., Sherman, L., Arthur, J., Friedman, L., & Osteen, V. (1987). Home observations of family interactions of depressed women. *Journal of Consulting and Clinical Psychology, 55*, 341–346.

Huberty, C. J., & Morris, J. D. (1989). Multivariate analysis versus multiple univariate analyses. *Psychological Bulletin, 105*, 302–308.

Jacobson, N. S., Follette, W. C., & Revenstorf, D. (1984). Psychotherapy outcome research: Methods for reporting variability and evaluating clinical significance. *Behavior Therapy, 17*, 336–352.

Jöreskog, K. G., & Sörbom, D. (1988). LISREL VII: *A guide to the program and applications* [Computer program manual]. Chicago: SPSS.

Kazdin, A. E. (1980). *Research design in clinical psychology*. New York: Harper & Row.

Kazdin, A. E. (1986). The evaluation of psychotherapy: Research design and methodology. In S. L. Garfield & A. E. Bergin (Eds.), *Handbook of psychotherapy and behavior change* (3rd ed., pp. 23–68). New York: Wiley.

Kerlinger, F. N. (1980). Analysis of covariance structures test of a criterial referents theory of attitudes. *Multivariate Behavioral Research, 15*, 403–422.

Leary, M. R., & Altmaier, E. M. (1980). Type I error in counseling research: A plea for multivariate analyses. *Journal of Counseling Psychology, 27*, 611–615.

Mahoney, M. J. (1977). Publication prejudices: An experimental study of confirmatory bias in the peer review system. *Cognitive Therapy and Research, 1*, 161–175.

Mahoney, M. J. (1978). Experimental methods and outcome evaluation. *Journal of Consulting and Clinical Psychology, 46*, 660–672.

Meehl, P. (1978). Theoretical risks and tabular asterisks: Sir Karl, Sir Ronald, and the slow progress of soft psychology. *Journal of Consulting and Clinical Psychology, 46,* 806–834.

Mitchell, C., & Hartmann, D. P. (1981). A cautionary note on the use of omega squared to evaluate the effectiveness of behavioral treatments. *Behavioral Assessment, 3,* 93–100.

Murray, L. W., & Dosser, D. A., Jr. (1987). How significant is a significant difference? Problems with the measurement of magnitude of effect. *Journal of Counseling Psychology, 34,* 68–72.

O'Grady, K. E. (1982). Measures of explained variance: Caution and limitations. *Psychological Bulletin, 92,* 766–777.

Paul, G. L. (1967). Strategy of outcome research in psychotherapy. *Journal of Consulting Psychology, 31,* 104–118.

Platt, J. R. (1964). Strong inference. *Science, 146,* 347–353.

Popper, K. (1968). *Conjectures and refutations.* London: Routledge & Kegan Paul.

Rosenthal, R., & Rubin, D. B. (1984). Multiple contrasts and ordered Bonferroni procedures. *Journal of Educational Psychology, 76,* 1028–1034.

Rosnow, R. L., & Rosenthal, R. (1988). Focused tests of significance and effect size estimation in counseling psychology. *Journal of Counseling Psychology, 35,* 203–208.

Schmitt, S. A. (1969). *Measuring uncertainty: An elementary introduction to Bayesian statistics.* Reading, MA: Addison-Wesley.

Serlin, R. C. (1987). Hypothesis testing, theory building, and the philosophy of science. *Journal of Counseling Psychology, 34,* 365–371.

Serlin, R. C., & Lapsley, D. K. (1985). Rationality in psychological research: The good-enough principle. *American Psychologist, 40,* 73–83.

Wampold, B. E., Furlong, M. J., & Atkinson, D. R. (1983). Statistical significance, power, and effect size: A response to the reexamination of reviewer bias. *Journal of Counseling Psychology, 30,* 459–463.

Wampold, B. E., & Drew, C. J. (1990). *Theory and application of statistics.* New York: McGraw-Hill.

Webster-Stratton, C. (1988). Mothers' and fathers' perceptions of child deviance: Roles of parent and child behaviors and parent adjustment. *Journal of Consulting and Clinical Psychology, 56,* 909–915.

16

THINGS I HAVE LEARNED (SO FAR)

JACOB COHEN

What I have learned (so far) has come from working with students and colleagues, from experience (sometimes bitter) with journal editors and review committees, and from the writings of, among others, Paul Meehl, David Bakan, William Rozeboom, Robyn Dawes, Howard Wainer, Robert Rosenthal, and more recently, Gerd Gigerenzer, Michael Oakes, and Leland Wilkinson. Although they are not always explicitly referenced, many of you will be able to detect their footprints in what follows.

SOME THINGS YOU LEARN AREN'T SO

One of the things I learned early on was that some things you learn aren't so. In graduate school, right after World War II, I learned that for doctoral dissertations and most other purposes, when comparing groups, the proper sample size is 30 cases per group. The number 30 seems to have arisen from the understanding that with fewer than 30 cases, you were dealing with "small" samples that required specialized handling with "small-sample

Reprinted from the *American Psychologist*, 45, 1304–1312. Copyright 1990 by the American Psychological Association.

statistics" instead of the critical-ratio approach we had been taught. Some of us knew about these exotic small-sample statistics—in fact, one of my fellow doctoral candidates undertook a dissertation, the distinguishing feature of which was a sample of only 20 cases per group, so that he could demonstrate his prowess with small-sample statistics. It wasn't until some years later that I discovered (mind you, not invented) power analysis, one of whose fruits was the revelation that for a two-independent-group-mean comparison with $n = 30$ per group at the sanctified two-tailed .05 level, the probability that a medium-sized effect would be labeled as significant by the most modern methods (a t test) was only .47. Thus, it was approximately a coin flip whether one would get a significant result, even though, in reality, the effect size was meaningful. My $n = 20$ friend's power was rather worse (.33), but of course he couldn't know that, and he ended up with nonsignificant results— with which he proceeded to demolish an important branch of psychoanalytic theory.

LESS IS MORE

One thing I learned over a long period of time that *is* so is the validity of the general principle that *less is more*, except of course for sample size (Cohen & Cohen, 1983, pp. 169–171). I have encountered too many studies with prodigious numbers of dependent variables, or with what seemed to me far too many independent variables, or (heaven help us) both.

In any given investigation that isn't explicitly exploratory, we should be studying few independent variables and even fewer dependent variables, for a variety of reasons.

If all of the dependent variables are to be related to all of the independent variables by simple bivariate analyses or multiple regression, the number of hypothesis tests that will be performed willy-nilly is at least the product of the sizes of the two sets. Using the .05 level for many tests escalates the experimentwise Type 1 error rate—or in plain English, greatly increases the chances of discovering things that aren't so. If, for example, you study 6 dependent and 10 independent variables and should find that your harvest yields 6 asterisks, you know full well that if there were no real associations in any of the 60 tests, the chance of getting one or more "significant" results is quite high (something like $1 - .95^{60}$, which equals, coincidentally, .95), and that you would expect three spuriously significant results on the average. You then must ask yourself some embarrassing questions, such as, Well, which three are real?, or even, Is six significant *significantly* more than the chance-expected three? (It so happens that it isn't.)

And of course, as you've probably discovered, you're not likely to solve your multiple tests problem with the Bonferroni maneuver. Dividing .05 by

60 sets a per-test significance criterion of $.05/60 = 0.00083$, and therefore a critical two-sided t value of about 3.5. The effects you're dealing with may not be large enough to produce any interesting ts that high, unless you're lucky.

Nor can you find salvation by doing six stepwise multiple regressions on the 10 independent variables. The amount of capitalization on chance that this entails is more than I know how to compute, but certainly more than would a simple harvest of asterisks for 60 regression coefficients (Wilkinson, 1990, p. 481).

In short, the results of this humongous study are a muddle. There is no solution to your problem. You wouldn't, of course, write up the study for publication as if the unproductive three quarters of your variables never existed. . . .

The irony is that people who do studies like this often start off with some useful central idea that, if pursued modestly by means of a few highly targeted variables and hypotheses, would likely produce significant results. These could, if propriety or the consequences of early toilet training deemed it necessary, successfully withstand the challenge of a Bonferroni or other experimentwise-adjusted alpha procedure.

A special case of the too-many-variables problem arises in multiple regression-correlation analysis with large numbers of independent variables. As the number of independent variables increases, the chances are that their redundancy in regard to criterion relevance also increases. Because redundancy increases the standard errors of partial regression and correlation coefficients and thus reduces their statistical significance, the results are likely to be zilch.

I have so heavily emphasized the desirability of working with few variables and large sample sizes that some of my students have spread the rumor that my idea of the perfect study is one with 10,000 cases and no variables. They go too far.

A less profound application of the less-is-more principle is to our habits of reporting numerical results. There are computer programs that report by default four, five, or even more decimal places for all numerical results. Their authors might well be excused because, for all the programmer knows, they may be used by atomic scientists. But we social scientists should know better than to repeat our results to so many places. What, pray, does an $r = .12345$ mean? or, for an IQ distribution, a mean of 105.6345? For $N = 100$, the standard error of the r is about .1 and the standard error of the IQ mean about 1.5. Thus, the 345 part of $r = .12345$ is only 3% of its standard error, and the 345 part of the IQ mean of 105.6345 is only 2% of its standard error. These superfluous decimal places are no better than random numbers. They are actually worse than useless because the clutter they create, particularly in tables, serves to distract the eye and mind from the necessary comparisons among the meaningful leading digits. Less is indeed more here.

SIMPLE IS BETTER

I've also learned that simple is better, which is a kind of loose generalization of less is more. The simple-is-better idea is widely applicable to the representation, analysis, and reporting of data.

If, as the old cliché has it, a picture is worth a thousand words, in describing a distribution, a frequency polygon or, better still, a Tukey (1977, pp. 1–26) stem and leaf diagram is usually worth more than the first four moments, that is, the mean, standard deviation, skewness, and kurtosis. I do not question that the moments efficiently summarize the distribution or that they are useful in some analytic contexts. Statistics packages eagerly give them to us and we dutifully publish them, but they do not usually make it possible for most of us or most of the consumers of our products to see the distribution. They don't tell us, for example, that there are no cases between scores of 72 and 90, or that this score of 24 is somewhere in left field, or that there is a pile-up of scores of 9. These are the kinds of features of our data that we surely need to know about, and they become immediately evident with simple graphic representation.

Graphic display is even more important in the case of bivariate data. Underlying each product–moment correlation coefficient in an acre of such coefficients there lies a simple scatter diagram that the r presumes to summarize, and well it might. That is, it does so if the joint distribution is more-or-less bivariate normal—which means, among other things, that the relationship must be linear and that there are no wild outlying points. We know that least squares measures, like means and standard deviations, are sensitive to outliers. Well, Pearson correlations are even more so. About 15 years ago, Wainer and Thissen (1976) published a data set made up of the heights in inches and weights in pounds of 25 subjects, for which the r was a perfectly reasonable .83. But if an error in transcription were made so that the height and weight values for one of the 25 subjects were switched, the r would become $-.26$, a rather large and costly error!

There is hardly any excuse for gaps, outliers, curvilinearity, or other pathology to exist in our data unbeknownst to us. The same computer statistics package with which we can do very complicated analyses like quasi-Newtonian nonlinear estimation and multidimensional scaling with Guttman's coefficient of alienation also can give us simple scatter plots and stem and leaf diagrams with which we can see our data. A proper multiple regression/correlation analysis does not begin with a matrix of correlation coefficients, means, and standard deviations, but rather with a set of stem and leaf diagrams and scatter plots. We sometimes learn more from what we see than from what we compute; sometimes what we learn from what we see is that we shouldn't compute, at least not on those data as they stand.

Computers are a blessing, but another of the things I have learned is that they are not an unmixed blessing. Forty years ago, before computers

(B.C., that is), for my doctoral dissertation, I did three factor analyses on the 11 subtests of the Wechsler-Bellevue, with samples of 100 cases each of psychoneurotic, schizophrenic, and brain-damaged patients. Working with a pad and pencil, 10-to-the-inch graph paper, a table of products of two-digit numbers, and a Friden electromechanical desk calculator that did square roots "automatically," the whole process took the better part of a year. Nowadays, on a desktop computer, the job is done virtually in microseconds (or at least lickety-split). But another important difference between then and now is that the sheer laboriousness of the task assured that throughout the entire process I was in intimate contact with the data and their analysis. There was no chance that there were funny things about my data or intermediate results that I didn't know about, things that could vitiate my conclusions.

I know that I sound my age, but don't get me wrong—I love computers and revel in the ease with which data analysis is accomplished with a good interactive statistics package like SYSTAT and SYGRAPH (Wilkinson, 1990). I am, however, appalled by the fact that some publishers of statistics packages successfully hawk their wares with the pitch that it isn't necessary to understand statistics to use them. But the same package that makes it possible for an ignoramus to do a factor analysis with a pull-down menu and the click of a mouse also can greatly facilitate with awesome speed and efficiency the performance of simple and informative analyses.

A prime example of the simple-is-better principle is found in the compositing of values. We are taught and teach our students that for purposes of predicting a criterion from a set of predictor variables, assuming for simplicity (and as the mathematicians say, "with no loss of generality"), that all variables are standardized, we achieve maximum linear prediction by doing a multiple regression analysis and forming a composite by weighting the predictor z scores by their betas. It can be shown as a mathematical necessity that with these betas as weights, the resulting composite generates a higher correlation with the criterion in the sample at hand than does a linear composite formed using any other weights.

Yet as a practical matter, most of the time, we are better off using unit weights: $+1$ for positively related predictors, -1 for negatively related predictors, and 0, that is, throw away poorly related predictors (Dawes, 1979; Wainer, 1976). The catch is that the betas come with guarantees to be better than the unit weights only for the sample on which they were determined. (It's almost like a TV set being guaranteed to work only in the store.) But the investigator is not interested in making predictions for that sample—he or she *knows* the criterion values for those cases. The idea is to combine the predictors for maximal prediction for *future* samples. The reason the betas are not likely to be optimal for future samples is that they are likely to have large standard errors. For the typical 100 or 200 cases and 5 or 10 correlated predictors, the unit weights will work as well or better.

Let me offer a concrete illustration to help make the point clear. A running example in our regression text (Cohen & Cohen, 1983) has for a sample of college faculty their salary estimated from four independent variables: years since PhD, sex (coded in the modern manner—1 for female and 0 for male), number of publications, and number of citations. The sample multiple correlation computes to .70. What we want to estimate is the correlation we would get if we used the sample beta weights in the population, the cross-validated multiple correlation, which unfortunately shrinks to a value smaller than the shrunken multiple correlation. For $N = 100$ cases, using Rozeboom's (1978) formula, that comes to .67. Not bad. But using unit weights, we do better: .69. With 300 or 400 cases, the increased sampling stability pushes up the cross-validated correlation, but it remains slightly smaller than the .69 value for unit weights. Increasing sample size to 500 or 600 will increase the cross-validated correlation in this example to the point at which it is larger than the unit-weighted .69, but only trivially, by a couple of points in the *third* decimal! When sample size is only 50, the cross-validated multiple correlation is only .63, whereas the unit weighted correlation remains at .69. The sample size doesn't affect the unit weighted correlation because we don't estimate unstable regression coefficients. It is, of course, subject to sampling error, but so is the cross-validated multiple correlation.

Now, unit weights will not always be as good or better than beta weights. For some relatively rare patterns of correlation (suppression is one), or when the betas vary greatly relative to their mean, or when the ratio of sample size to the number of predictors is as much as 30 to 1 and the multiple correlation is as large as .75, the beta weights may be better, but even in these rare circumstances, probably not much better.

Furthermore, the unit weights work well outside the context of multiple regression where we have criterion data—that is, in a situation in which we wish to measure some concept by combining indicators, or some abstract factor generated in a factor analysis. Unit weights on standardized scores are likely to be better for our purposes than the factor scores generated by the computer program, which are, after all, the fruits of a regression analysis for that sample of the variables on the factor as criterion.

Consider that when we go to predict freshman grade point average from a 30-item test, we don't do a regression analysis to get the "optimal" weights with which to combine the item scores—we just add them up, like Galton did. Simple is better.

We are, however, *not* applying the simple-is-better principle when we "simplify" a multivalued graduated variable (like IQ, or number of children, or symptom severity) by cutting it somewhere along its span and making it into a dichotomy. This is sometimes done with a profession of modesty about the quality or accuracy of the variable, or to "simplify" the analysis. This is not an application, but rather a perversion of simple is better, because this practice is one of willful discarding of information. It has been shown that when you so mutilate a variable, you typically reduce its squared correlation with other variables by about 36% (Cohen, 1983). Don't do it. This kind of simplification is of a piece with the practice of "simplifying" a factorial design ANOVA by reducing all cell sizes to the size of the smallest by dropping cases. They are both ways of throwing away the most precious commodity we deal with: information.

Rather more generally, I think I have begun to learn how to use statistics in the social sciences.

The atmosphere that characterizes statistics as applied in the social and biomedical sciences is that of a secular religion (Salsburg, 1985), apparently of Judeo–Christian derivation, as it employs as its most powerful icon a six-pointed cross, often presented multiply for enhanced authority. I confess that I am an agnostic.

THE FISHERIAN LEGACY

When I began studying statistical inference, I was met with a surprise shared by many neophytes. I found that if, for example, I wanted to see whether poor kids estimated the size of coins to be bigger than did rich kids, after I gathered the data, I couldn't test this research hypothesis, but rather the null hypothesis that poor kids perceived coins to be the same size as did rich kids. This seemed kind of strange and backward to me, but I was rather quickly acculturated (or, if you like, converted, or perhaps brainwashed) to the Fisherian faith that science proceeds only through inductive inference and that inductive inference is achieved chiefly by rejecting null hypotheses, usually at the .05 level. (It wasn't until much later that I learned that the philosopher of science, Karl Popper, 1959, advocated the formulation of falsifiable *research* hypotheses and designing research that could falsify *them*.)

The fact that Fisher's ideas quickly became *the* basis for statistical inference in the behavioral sciences is not surprising—they were very attractive. They offered a deterministic scheme, mechanical and objective, independent of content, and led to clear-cut yes–no decisions. For years, nurtured on the psychological statistics text books of the 1940s and 1950s, I never dreamed that they were the source of bitter controversies (Gigerenzer & Murray, 1987).

Take, for example, the yes–no decision feature. It was quite appropriate to agronomy, which was where Fisher came from. The outcome of an experiment can quite properly be the decision to use this rather than that amount of manure or to plant this or that variety of wheat. But we do not deal in manure, at least not knowingly. Similarly, in other technologies—for example, engineering quality control or education—research is frequently designed to produce decisions. However, things are not quite so clearly decision-oriented in the development of scientific theories.

Next, consider the sanctified (and sanctifying) magic .05 level. This basis for decision has played a remarkable role in the social sciences and in the lives of social scientists. In governing decisions about the status of null hypotheses, it came to determine decisions about the acceptance of doctoral dissertations and the granting of research funding, and about publication, promotion, and whether to have a baby just now. Its arbitrary unreasonable tyranny has led to data fudging of varying degrees of subtlety from grossly altering data to dropping cases where there "must have been" errors.

THE NULL HYPOTHESIS TESTS US

We cannot charge R. A. Fisher with all of the sins of the last half century that have been committed in his name (or more often anonymously but as part of his legacy), but they deserve cataloging (Gigerenzer & Murray, 1987; Oakes, 1986). Over the years, I have learned not to make errors of the following kinds:

When a Fisherian null hypothesis is rejected with an associated probability of, for example, .026, it is *not* the case that the probability that the null hypothesis is true is .026 (or less than .05, or any other value we can specify). Given our framework of probability as long-run relative frequency—as much as we might wish it to be otherwise—this result does not tell us about the truth of the null hypothesis, given the data. (For this we have to go to Bayesian or likelihood statistics, in which probability is not relative frequency but degree of belief.) What it tells us is the probability of the data, given the truth of the null hypothesis—which is not the same thing, as much as it may sound like it.

If the p value with which we reject the Fisherian null hypothesis does not tell us the probability that the null hypothesis is true, it certainly cannot tell us anything about the probability that the *research* or alternate hypothesis is true. In fact, there *is* no alternate hypothesis in Fisher's scheme: Indeed, he violently opposed its inclusion by Neyman and Pearson.

Despite widespread misconceptions to the contrary, the rejection of a given null hypothesis gives us no basis for estimating the probability that a replication of the research will again result in rejecting that null hypothesis.

Of course, everyone knows that failure to reject the Fisherian null hypothesis does not warrant the conclusion that it is true. Fisher certainly knew and emphasized it, and our textbooks duly so instruct us. Yet how often do we read in the discussion and conclusions of articles now appearing in our most prestigious journals that "there is no difference" or "no relationship"? (This is 40 years after my $N = 20$ friend used a nonsignificant result to demolish psychoanalytic theory.)

The other side of this coin is the interpretation that accompanies results that surmount the .05 barrier and achieve the state of grace of "statistical significance." "Everyone" knows that all this means is that the effect is not nil, and nothing more. Yet how often do we see such a result to be taken to mean, at least implicitly, that the effect is *significant*, that is, *important*, *large*. If a result is *highly* significant, say $p < .001$, the temptation to make this misinterpretation becomes all but irresistible.

Let's take a close look at this null hypothesis—the fulcrum of the Fisherian scheme—that we so earnestly seek to negate. A null hypothesis is any precise statement about a state of affairs in a population, usually the value of a parameter, frequently zero. It is called a "null" hypothesis because the strategy is to nullify it or because it means "nothing doing." Thus, "the difference in the mean scores of U.S. men and women on an Attitude Toward the U.N. scale is zero" is a null hypothesis. "The product–moment r between height and IQ in high school students is zero" is another. "The proportion of men in a population of adult dyslexics is .50" is yet another. Each is a precise statement—for example, if the population r between height and IQ is in fact .03, the null hypothesis that it is zero is false. It is also false if the r is .01, .001, or .000001!

A little thought reveals a fact widely understood among statisticians: The null hypothesis, taken literally (and that's the only way you can take it in formal hypothesis testing), is *always* false in the real world. It can only be true in the bowels of a computer processor running a Monte Carlo study (and even then a stray electron may make it false). If it is false, even to a tiny degree, it must be the case that a large enough sample will produce a significant result and lead to its rejection. So if the null hypothesis is always false, what's the big deal about rejecting it?

Another problem that bothered me was the asymmetry of the Fisherian scheme: If your test exceeded a critical value, you could conclude, subject to the alpha risk, that your null was false, but if you fell short of that critical value, you couldn't conclude that the null was true. In fact, all you could conclude is that you *couldn't* conclude that the null was false. In other words, you could hardly conclude anything.

And yet another problem I had was that if the null were false, it had to be false to some degree. It had to make a difference whether the population mean difference was 5 or 50, or whether the population correlation was .10 or .30, and this was not taken into account in the prevailing method. I had stumbled onto something that I learned after awhile was one of the bases of the Neyman–Pearson critique of Fisher's system of statistical induction.

In 1928 (when I was in kindergarten), Jerzy Neyman and Karl Pearson's boy Egon began publishing papers that offered a rather different perspective on statistical inference (Neyman & Pearson, 1928a, 1928b). Among other things, they argued that rather than having a single hypothesis that one either rejected or not, things could be so organized that one could choose between two hypotheses, one of which could be the null hypothesis and the other an alternate hypothesis. One could attach to the precisely defined null an alpha risk, and to the equally precisely defined alternate hypothesis a beta risk. The rejection of the null hypotheses when it was true was an error of the first kind, controlled by the alpha criterion, but the failure to reject it when the alternate hypothesis was true was also an error, an error of the second kind, which could be controlled to occur at a rate beta. Thus, given the magnitude of the difference between the null and the alternate (that is, given the hypothetical population effect size), and setting values for alpha and beta, one could determine the sample size necessary to meet these conditions. Or, with the effect size, alpha, and the sample size set, one could determine the beta, or its complement, the probability of rejecting the null hypothesis, the power of the test.

Now, R. A. Fisher was undoubtedly the greatest statistician of this century, rightly called "the father of modern statistics," but he had a blind spot. Moreover, he was a stubborn and frequently vicious intellectual opponent. A feud with Karl Pearson had kept Fisher's papers out of *Biometrika*, which Karl Pearson edited. After old-man Pearson retired, efforts by Egon Pearson and Neyman to avoid battling with Fisher were to no avail. Fisher wrote that they were like Russians who thought that "pure science" should be "geared to technological performance" as "in a five-year plan." He once led off the discussion on a paper by Neyman at the Royal Statistical Society by saying that Neyman should have chosen a topic "on which he could speak with authority" (Gigerenzer & Murray, 1987, p. 17). Fisher fiercely condemned the Neyman–Pearson heresy.

I was of course aware of none of this. The statistics texts on which I was raised and their later editions to which I repeatedly turned in the 1950s and 1960s presented null hypothesis testing à la Fisher as a done deal, as *the* way to do statistical inference. The ideas of Neyman and Pearson were barely or not at all mentioned, or dismissed as too complicated.

When I finally stumbled onto power analysis, and managed to overcome the handicap of a background with no working math beyond high school algebra (to say nothing of mathematical statistics), it was as if I had died and gone to heaven. After I learned what noncentral distributions were and figured out that it was important to decompose noncentrality parameters into their constituents of effect size and sample size, I realized that I had a framework for hypothesis testing that had four parameters: the alpha significance criterion, the sample size, the population effect size, and the power of the test. For any statistical test, any one of these was a function of the other three. This meant, for example, that for a significance test of a product–moment correlation, using a two-sided .05 alpha criterion and a sample size of 50 cases, if the population correlation is .30, my long-run probability of rejecting the null hypothesis and finding the sample correlation to be significant was .57, a coin flip. As another example, for the same $\alpha = .05$ and population $r = .30$, if I want to have .80 power, I could determine that I needed a sample size of 85.

Playing with this new toy (and with a small grant from the National Institute of Mental Health) I did what came to be called a meta-analysis of the articles in the 1960 volume of the *Journal of Abnormal and Social Psychology* (Cohen, 1962). I found, among other things, that using the nondirectional .05 criterion, the median power to detect a medium effect was .46—a rather abysmal result. Of course, investigators could not have known how underpowered their research was, as their training had not prepared them to know anything about power, let alone how to use it in research planning. One might think that after 1969, when I published my power handbook that made power analysis as easy as falling off a log, the concepts and methods of power analysis would be taken to the hearts of null hypothesis testers. So one might think. (Stay tuned.)

Among the less obvious benefits of power analysis was that it made it possible to "prove" null hypotheses. Of course, as I've already noted, everyone knows that one can't actually prove null hypotheses. But when an investigator means to prove a null hypothesis, the point is not to demonstrate that the population effect size is, say, zero to a million or more decimal places, but rather to show that it is of no more than negligible or trivial size (Cohen, 1988, pp. 16–17). Then, from a power analysis at, say, $\alpha = .05$, with power set at, say, .95, so that $\beta = .05$, also, the sample size necessary to detect this negligible effect with .95 probability can be determined. Now if the research is carried out using that sample size, and the result is *not* significant, as there had been a .95 chance of detecting this negligible effect, and the effect was *not* detected, the conclusion is justified that no nontrivial effect exists, at the $\beta = .05$ level. This does, in fact, probabilistically prove the intended null hypothesis of no more than a trivially small effect. The reasoning is impeccable, but when you go to apply it, you discover that it takes enormous sample sizes to do so. For example, if we adopt the above parameters for a significance test of a correlation coefficient and $r = .10$ is taken as a negligible effect size, it requires a sample of almost 1,300 cases. More modest but still reasonable demands for power of course require smaller sample sizes, but not sufficiently smaller to matter for most investigators—even .80 power to detect a population correlation of .10 requires almost 800 cases. So it generally takes an impractically large sample size to prove the null hypothesis as I've redefined it; however, the procedure makes clear what it takes to say or imply from the failure to reject the null hypothesis that there is no nontrivial effect.

A salutary effect of power analysis is that it draws one forcibly to consider the magnitude of effects. In psychology, and especially in soft psychology, under the sway of the Fisherian scheme, there has been little consciousness of how big things are. The very popular ANOVA designs yield F ratios, and it is these whose size is of concern. First off is the question of whether they made the sanctifying .05 cut-off and are thus significant, and then how far they fell below this cut-off: Were they perhaps *highly significant* (*p* less than .01) or *very highly significant* (less than .001)? Because science is inevitably about magnitudes, it is not surprising how frequently *p* values are treated as surrogates for effect sizes.

One of the things that drew me early to correlation analysis was that it yielded an *r*, a measure of effect size, which was then translated into a *t* or *F* and assessed for significance, whereas the analysis of variance or covariance yielded only an *F* and told me nothing about effect size. As many of the variables with which we worked were expressed in arbitrary units (points on a scale, trials to learn a maze), and the Fisherian scheme seemed quite complete by itself and made no demands on us to think about effect sizes, we simply had no language with which to address them.

In retrospect, it seems to me simultaneously quite understandable yet also ridiculous to try to develop theories about human behavior with *p* values from Fisherian hypothesis testing and no more than a primitive sense of effect size. And I wish I were talking about the long, long ago. In 1986, there appeared in the *New York Times* a UPI dispatch under the headline "Children's Height Linked to Test Scores." The article described a study that involved nearly 14,000 children 6 to 17 years of age that reported a *definite* link between height (age- and sex-adjusted) and scores on tests of both intelligence and achievement. The relationship was described as significant, and persisting, even after controlling for other factors, including socioeconomic status, birth order, family size, and physical maturity. The authors noted that the effect was small, but *significant*, and that it didn't warrant giving children growth hormone to make them taller and thus brighter. They speculated that the effect might be due to treating shorter children as less mature, but that there were alternative biological explanations.

Now this was a newspaper story, the fruit of the ever-inquiring mind of a science reporter, not a journal article, so perhaps it is understandable that there was no effort to deal with the actual size of this small effect. But it got me to wondering about how small this significant relationship might be. Well, if we take significant to mean $p < .001$ (in the interest of scientific tough-mindedness), it turns out that a correlation of .0278 is significant for 14,000 cases. But I've found that when dealing with variables expressed in units whose magnitude we understand, the effect size in linear relationships is better comprehended with regression than with correlation coefficients. So, accepting the authors' implicit causal model, it works out that raising a child's IQ from 100 to 130 would require giving the child enough growth hormone to increase his or her height by 14 ft (more or less). If the causality goes the other way, and one wanted to create basketball players, a 4-in. increase in height would require raising the IQ about 900 points. Well, they said it was a small effect. (When I later checked the journal article that described this research, it turned out that the correlation was much larger than .0278. It was actually about .11, so that for a 30-point increase in IQ it would take only enough growth hormone to produce a 3.5-ft increase in height, or with the causality reversed, a 4-in. increase in height would require an increase of only 233 IQ points.)

I am happy to say that the long neglect of attention to effect size seems to be coming to a close. The clumsy and fundamentally invalid box-score method of literature review based on p values is being replaced by effect-size-based meta-analysis as formulated by Gene Glass (1977). The effect size measure most often used is the standardized mean difference d of power analysis. Several book-length treatments of meta-analysis have been published, and applications to various fields of psychology are appearing in substantial numbers in the *Psychological Bulletin* and other prestigious publications. In the typical meta-analysis, the research literature on some issue is surveyed and the effect sizes that were found in the relevant studies are gathered. Note that the observational unit is the study. These data do not only provide an estimate of the level and variability of the effect size in a domain based on multiple studies and therefore on many observations, but by relating effect size to various substantive and methodological characteristics over the studies, much can be learned about the issue under investigation and how best to investigate it. One hopes that this ferment may persuade researchers to explicitly report effect sizes and thus reduce the burden on meta-analysts and others of having to make assumptions to dig them out of their inadequately reported research results. In a field as scattered (not to say anarchic) as ours, meta-analysis constitutes a welcome force toward the cumulation of knowledge. Meta-analysis makes me very happy.

Despite my career-long identification with statistical inference, I believe, together with such luminaries as Meehl (1978), Tukey (1977), and Gigerenzer (Gigerenzer & Murray, 1987), that hypothesis testing has been greatly overemphasized in psychology and in the other disciplines that use it. It has diverted our attention from crucial issues. Mesmerized by a single all-purpose, mechanized, "objective" ritual in which we convert numbers into other numbers and get a yes–no answer, we have come to neglect close scrutiny of where the numbers came from. Recall that in his delightful parable about averaging the numbers of football jerseys, Lord (1953) pointed out that "the numbers don't know where they came from." But surely *we* must know where they came from and should be far more concerned with why and what and how well we are measuring, manipulating conditions, and selecting our samples.

We have also lost sight of the fact that the error variance in our observations should challenge us to efforts to reduce it and not simply to thoughtlessly tuck it into the denominator of an F or t test.

HOW TO USE STATISTICS

So, how would I use statistics in psychological research? First of all, descriptively. John Tukey's (1977) *Exploratory Data Analysis* is an inspiring account of how to effect graphic and numerical analyses of the data at hand so as to understand *them*. The techniques, although subtle in conception, are simple in application, requiring no more than pencil and paper (Tukey says if you have a hand-held calculator, fine). Although he recognizes the importance of what he calls confirmation (statistical inference), he manages to fill 700 pages with techniques of "mere" description, pointing out in the preface that the emphasis on inference in modern statistics has resulted in a loss of flexibility in data analysis.

Then, in planning research, I think it wise to *plan* the research. This means making tentative informed judgments about, among many other things, the size of the population effect or effects you're chasing, the level of alpha risk you want to take (conveniently, but not necessarily .05), and the power you want (usually some relatively large value like .80). These specified, it is a simple matter to determine the sample size you need. It is then a good idea to rethink your specifications. If, as is often the case, this sample size is beyond your resources, consider the possibility of reducing your power demand or, perhaps the effect size, or even (heaven help us) increasing your alpha level. Or, the required sample may be smaller than you can comfortably manage, which also should lead you to rethink and possibly revise your original specifications. This process ends when you have a credible and viable set of specifications, or when you discover that no practicable set is possible and the research as originally conceived must be abandoned. Although you would hardly expect it from reading the current literature, failure to subject your research plans to power analysis is simply irrational.

Next, I have learned and taught that the primary product of a research inquiry is one or more measures of effect size, not *p* values (Cohen, 1965). Effect-size measures include mean differences (raw or standardized), correlations and squared correlation of all kinds, odds ratios, kappas—whatever conveys the magnitude of the phenomenon of interest appropriate to the research context. If, for example, you are comparing groups on a variable measured in units that are well understood by your readers (IQ points, or dollars, or number of children, or months of survival), mean differences are excellent measures of effect size. When this isn't the case, and it isn't the case more often than it is, the results can be translated into standardized mean differences (*d* values) or some measure of correlation or association (Cohen, 1988). (Not that we understand as well as we should the meaning of a given level of correlation [Oakes, 1986, pp. 88–92]. It has been shown that psychologists typically overestimate how much relationship a given correlation represents, thinking of a correlation of .50 not as its square of .25 that its proportion of variance represents, but more like its cube root of about .80, which represents only wishful thinking! But that's another story.)

Then, having found the sample effect size, you can attach a p value to it, but it is far more informative to provide a confidence interval. As you know, a confidence interval gives the range of values of the effect-size index that includes the population value with a given probability. It tells you incidentally whether the effect is significant, but much more—it provides an estimate of the range of values it might have, surely a useful piece of knowledge in a science that presumes to be quantitative. (By the way, I don't think that we should routinely use 95% intervals: Our interests are often better served by more tolerant 80% intervals.)

Remember that throughout the process in which you conceive, plan, execute, and write up a research, it is on your informed judgment as a scientist that you must rely, and this holds as much for the statistical aspects of the work as it does for all the others. This means that your informed judgment governs the setting of the parameters involved in the planning (alpha, beta, population effect size, sample size, confidence interval), and that informed judgment also governs the conclusions you will draw.

In his brilliant analysis of what he called the "inference revolution" in psychology, Gerd Gigerenzer showed how and why no single royal road of drawing conclusions from data is possible, and particularly not one that does not strongly depend on the substantive issues concerned—that is, on everything that went into the research besides the number crunching. An essential ingredient in the research process is the judgment of the scientist. He or she must decide by how much a theoretical proposition has been advanced by the data, just as he or she decided what to study, what data to get, and how to get it. I believe that statistical inference applied with informed judgment is a useful tool in this process, but it isn't the most important tool: It is not as important as everything that came before it. Some scientists, physicists for example, manage without the statistics, although to be sure not without the informed judgment. Indeed, some pretty good psychologists have managed without statistical inference: There come to mind Wundt, Kohler, Piaget, Lewin, Bartlett, Stevens, and if you'll permit me, Freud, among others. Indeed, Skinner (1957) thought of dedicating his book *Verbal Behavior* (and I quote) "to the statisticians and scientific methodologists with whose help this book would never have been completed" (p. 111). I submit that the proper application of statistics by sensible statistical methodologists (Tukey, for example) would not have hurt Skinner's work. It might even have done it some good.

The implications of the things I have learned (so far) are not consonant with much of what I see about me as standard statistical practice. The prevailing yes–no decision at the magic .05 level from a single research is a far cry from the use of informed judgment. Science simply doesn't work that way.

A successful piece of research doesn't conclusively settle an issue, it just makes some theoretical propositions to some degree more likely. Only successful future replication in the same and different settings (as might be found through meta-analysis) provides an approach to settling the issue. How much more likely this single research makes the proposition depends on many things, but not on whether p is equal to or greater than .05; .05 is not a cliff but a convenient reference point along the possibility–probability continuum. There is no ontological basis for dichotomous decision making in psychological inquiry. The point was neatly made by Rosnow and Rosenthal (1989) last year in the *American Psychologist*. They wrote "surely, God loves the .06 nearly as much as the .05" (p. 1277). To which I say amen!

Finally, I have learned, but not easily, that things take time. As I've already mentioned, almost three decades ago, I published a power survey of the articles in the 1960 volume of the *Journal of Abnormal and Social Psychology* (Cohen, 1962) in which I found that the median power to detect a medium effect size under representative conditions was only .46. The first edition of my power handbook came out in 1969. Since then, more than two dozen power and effect-size surveys have been published in psychology and related fields (Cohen, 1988, pp. xi–xii). There have also been a slew of articles on power-analytic methodology. Statistics textbooks, even some undergraduate ones, give some space to power analysis, and several computer programs for power analysis are available (e.g., Borenstein & Cohen, 1988). They tell me that some major funding entities require that their grant applications contain power analyses, and that in one of those agencies my power book can be found in every office.

The problem is that, as practiced, current research hardly reflects much attention to power. How often have you seen any mention of power in the journals you read, let alone an actual power analysis in the methods sections of the articles? Last year in *Psychological Bulletin*, Sedlmeier and Gigerenzer (1989) published an article entitled "Do Studies of Statistical Power Have an Effect on the Power of Studies?". The answer was no. Using the same methods I had used on the articles in the 1960 *Journal of Abnormal and Social Psychology* (Cohen, 1962), they performed a power analysis on the 1984 *Journal of Abnormal Psychology* and found that the median power under the same conditions was .44, a little worse than the .46 I had found 24 years earlier. It was worse still (.37) when they took into account the occasional use of an experimentwise alpha criterion. Even worse than that, in some 11% of the studies, research hypotheses were framed as null hypotheses and their nonsignificance interpreted as confirmation. The median power of these studies to detect a medium effect at the two-tailed .05 level was .25! These are not isolated results: Rossi, Rossi, and Cottrill (in press), using the same methods, did a power survey of the 142 articles in the 1982 volumes of the *Journal of Personality and Social Psychology* and the *Journal of Abnormal Psychology* and found essentially the same results.

A less egregious example of the inertia of methodological advance is set correlation, which is a highly flexible realization of the multivariate general linear model. I published it in an article in 1982, and we included it in an appendix in the 1983 edition of our regression text (Cohen, 1982; Cohen & Cohen, 1983). Set correlation can be viewed as a generalization of multiple correlation to the multivariate case, and with it you can study the relationship between anything and anything else, controlling for whatever you want in either the anything or the anything else, or both. I think it's a great method; at least, my usually critical colleagues haven't complained. Yet, as far as I'm aware, it has hardly been used outside the family. (The publication of a program as a SYSTAT supplementary module [Cohen, 1989] may make a difference.)

But I do not despair. I remember that W. S. Gosset, the fellow who worked in a brewery and appeared in print modestly as "Student," published the t test a decade before we entered World War I, and the test didn't get into the psychological statistics textbooks until after World War II.

These things take time. So, if you publish something that you think is really good, and a year or a decade or two go by and hardly anyone seems to have taken notice, remember the t test, and take heart.

REFERENCES

Borenstein, M., & Cohen, J. (1988). *Statistical power analysis: A computer program.* Hillsdale, NJ: Erlbaum.

Children's height linked to test scores. (1986, October 7). *New York Times*, p. C4.

Cohen, J. (1962). The statistical power of abnormal-social psychological research: A review. *Journal of Abnormal and Social Psychology, 65*, 145–153.

Cohen, J. (1965). Some statistical issues in psychological research. In B. B. Wolman (Ed.), *Handbook of clinical psychology* (pp. 95–121). New York: McGraw-Hill.

Cohen, J. (1982). Set correlation as a general multivariate data-analytic method. *Multivariate Behavioral Research, 17*, 301–341.

Cohen, J. (1983). The cost of dichotomization. *Applied Psychological Measurement, 7*, 249–253.

Cohen, J. (1988). *Statistical power analysis for the behavioral sciences* (2nd ed.). Hillsdale, NJ: Erlbaum.

Cohen, J. (1989). *SETCOR: Set correlation analysis, a supplementary module for SYSTAT and SYGRAPH.* Evanston, IL: SYSTAT.

Cohen, J., & Cohen, P. (1983). *Applied multiple regression/correlation analysis for the behavioral sciences* (2nd ed.). Hillsdale, NJ: Erlbaum.

Dawes, R. M. (1979). The robust beauty of improper linear models in decision making. *American Psychologist, 34*, 571–582.

Gigerenzer, G., & Murray, D. J. (1987). *Cognition as intuitive statistics*. Hillsdale, NJ: Erlbaum.

Glass, G. V. (1977). Integrating findings: The meta-analysis of research. In L. Shulman (Ed.), *Review of research in education* (Vol. 5, pp. 351–379). Itasca, IL: Peacock.

Lord, F. M. (1953). On the statistical treatment of football numbers. *American Psychologist, 8,* 750–751.

Meehl, P. E. (1978). Theoretical risks and tabular asterisks: Sir Karl, Sir Ronald, and the slow progress of soft psychology. *Journal of Consulting and Clinical Psychology, 46,* 806–834.

Neyman, J., & Pearson, E. (1928a). On the use and interpretation of certain test criteria for purposes of statistical inference: Part I. *Biometrika, 20A,* 175–240.

Neyman, J., & Pearson, E. (1928b). On the use and interpretation of certain test criteria for purposes of statistical inference: Part II. *Biometrika, 20A,* 263–294.

Oakes, M. (1986). *Statistical inference: A commentary for the social and behavioral sciences*. New York: Wiley.

Popper, K. (1959). *The logic of scientific discovery*. New York: Basic Books.

Rosnow, R. L., & Rosenthal, R. (1989). Statistical procedures and the justification of knowledge in psychological science. *American Psychologist, 44,* 1276–1284.

Rossi, J. S., Rossi, S. R., & Cottrill, S. D. (in press). Statistical power in research in social and abnormal psychology. *Journal of Consulting and Clinical Psychology.*

Rozeboom, W. W. (1978). Estimation of cross-validated multiple correlation: A clarification. *Psychological Bulletin, 85,* 1348–1351.

Salsburg, D. S. (1985). The religion of statistics as practiced in medical journals. *American Statistician, 39,* 220–223.

Sedlmeier, P., & Gigerenzer, G. (1989). Do studies of statistical power have an effect on the power of studies? *Psychological Bulletin, 105,* 309–316.

Skinner, B. F. (1957). *Verbal behavior*. New York: Appleton-Century-Crofts.

Tukey, J. W. (1977). *Exploratory data analysis*. Reading, MA: Addison-Wesley.

Wainer, H. (1976). Estimating coefficients in linear models: It don't make no nevermind. *Psychological Bulletin, 83,* 213–217.

Wainer, H., & Thissen, D. (1976). When jackknifing fails (or does it?). *Psychometrika, 41,* 9–34.

Wilkinson, L. (1990). *SYSTAT: The system for statistics*. Evanston, IL: SYSTAT.

NULL HYPOTHESES
AND STATISTICAL
SIGNIFICANCE TESTING

17

A POWER PRIMER

JACOB COHEN

The preface to the first edition of my power handbook (Cohen, 1969) begins:

> During my first dozen years of teaching and consulting on applied statistics with behavioral scientists, I became increasingly impressed with the importance of statistical power analysis, an importance which was increased an order of magnitude by its neglect in our textbooks and curricula. The case for its importance is easily made: What behavioral scientist would view with equanimity the question of the probability that his investigation would lead to statistically significant results, i.e., its power? (p. vii)

This neglect was obvious through casual observation and had been confirmed by a power review of the 1960 volume of the *Journal of Abnormal and Social Psychology*, which found the mean power to detect medium effect sizes to be .48 (Cohen, 1962). Thus, the chance of obtaining a significant result was about that of tossing a head with a fair coin. I attributed this disregard of

Reprinted from *Psychological Bulletin, 112*, 155–159. Copyright 1992 by the American Psychological Association.

power to the inaccessibility of a meager and mathematically difficult literature, beginning with its origin in the work of Neyman and Pearson (1928, 1933).

The power handbook was supposed to solve the problem. It required no more background than an introductory psychological statistics course that included significance testing. The exposition was verbal–intuitive and carried largely by many worked examples drawn from across the spectrum of behavioral science.

In the ensuing two decades, the book has been through revised (1977) and second (1988) editions and has inspired dozens of power and effect-size surveys in many areas of the social and life sciences (Cohen, 1988, pp. xi–xii). During this period, there has been a spate of articles on power analysis in the social science literature, a baker's dozen of computer programs (reviewed in Goldstein, 1989), and a breakthrough into popular statistics textbooks (Cohen, 1988, pp. xii–xiii).

Sedlmeier and Gigerenzer (1989) reported a power review of the 1984 volume of the *Journal of Abnormal Psychology* (some 24 years after mine) under the title, "Do Studies of Statistical Power Have an Effect on the Power of Studies?" The answer was no. Neither their study nor the dozen other power reviews they cite (excepting those fields in which large sample sizes are used, e.g., sociology, market research) showed any material improvement in power. Thus, a quarter century has brought no increase in the probability of obtaining a significant result.

Why is this? There is no controversy among methodologists about the importance of power analysis, and there are ample accessible resources for estimating sample sizes in research planning using power analysis. My 2-decades-long expectation that methods sections in research articles in psychological journals would invariably include power analyses has not been realized. Indeed, they almost invariably do not. Of the 54 articles Sedlmeier and Gigerenzer (1989) reviewed, only 2 mentioned power, and none estimated power or necessary sample size or the population effect size they posited. In 7 of the studies, null hypotheses served as research hypotheses that were confirmed when the results were nonsignificant. Assuming a medium effect size, the median power for these tests was .25! Thus, these authors concluded that their research hypotheses of no effect were supported when they had only a .25 chance of rejecting these null hypotheses in the presence of substantial population effects.

It is not at all clear why researchers continue to ignore power analysis. The passive acceptance of this state of affairs by editors and reviewers is even more of a mystery. At least part of the reason may be the low level of consciousness about effect size: It is as if the only concern about magnitude in much psychological research is with regard to the statistical test result and its accompanying p value, not with regard to the psychological phenomenon under study. Sedlmeier and Gigerenzer (1989) attribute this to the accident of the historical precedence of Fisherian theory, its hybridization with the contradictory Neyman–Pearson theory, and the apparent completeness of Fisherian null hypothesis testing: objective, mechanical, and a clear-cut go– no-go decision straddled over $p = .05$. I have suggested that the neglect of power analysis simply exemplifies the slow movement of methodological advance (Cohen, 1988, p. xiv), noting that it took some 40 years from Student's publication of the t test to its inclusion of psychological statistics textbooks (Cohen, 1990, p. 1311).

An associate editor of this journal suggests another reason: Researchers find too complicated, or do not have at hand, either my book or other reference material for power analysis. He suggests that a short rule-of-thumb treatment of necessary sample size might make a difference. Hence this article.

In this bare bones treatment, I cover only the simplest cases, the most common designs and tests, and only three levels of effect size. For readers who find this inadequate, I unhesitatingly recommend *Statistic Power Analysis for the Behavioral Sciences* (Cohen, 1988; hereafter SPABS). It covers special cases, one-sided tests, unequal sample sizes, other null hypotheses, set correlation and multivariate methods and gives substantive examples of small, medium, and large effect sizes for the various tests. It offers well over 100 worked illustrative examples and is as user friendly as I know how to make it, the technical material being relegated to an appendix.

METHOD

Statistical power analysis exploits the relationships among the four variables involved in statistical inference: sample size (N), significance criterion (α), population effect size (ES), and statistical power. For any statistical model, these relationships are such that each is a function of the other three. For example, in power reviews, for any given statistical test, we can determine power for given α, N, and ES. For research planning, however, it is most useful to determine the N necessary to have a specified power for given α and ES; this article addresses this use.

The Significance Criterion, α

The risk of mistakenly rejecting the null hypothesis (H_o) and thus of committing a Type I error, α, represents a policy: the maximum risk attending such a rejection. Unless otherwise stated (and it rarely is), it is taken to equal .05 (part of the Fisherian legacy; Cohen, 1990). Other values may of course be selected. For example, in studies testing several H_0s, it is recommended that $\alpha = .01$ per hypothesis in order that the experimentwise risk (i.e., the risk of any false rejections) not become too large. Also, for tests whose parameters may be either positive or negative, the α risk may be defined as two sided or one sided. The many tables in SPABS provide for both kinds, but the sample sizes provided in this note are all for two-sided tests at $\alpha = .01, .05,$ and $.10,$ the last for circumstances in which a less rigorous standard for rejection is desired, as, for example, in exploratory studies. For unreconstructed one tailers (see Cohen, 1965), the tabled sample sizes provide close approximations for one-sided tests at $\frac{1}{2}\alpha$ (e.g., the sample sizes tabled under $\alpha = .10$ may be used for one-sided tests at $\alpha = .05$).

Power

The statistical power of a significance test is the long-term probability, given the population ES, α, and N of rejecting H_0. When the ES is not equal to zero, H_0 is false, so failure to reject it also incurs an error. This is a Type II error, and for any given ES, α, and N, its probability of occurring is β. Power is thus $1 - \beta$, the probability of rejecting a false H_0.

In this treatment, the only specification for power is .80 (so $\beta = .20$), a convention proposed for general use. (SPABS provides for 11 levels of power in most of its N tables.) A materially smaller value than .80 would incur too great a risk of a Type II error. A materially larger value would result in a demand for N that is likely to exceed the investigator's resources. Taken with the conventional $\alpha = .05$, power of .80 results in a $\beta:\alpha$ ratio of 4:1 (.20 to .05) of the two kinds of risks. (See SPABS, pp. 53–56.)

Sample Size

In research planning, the investigator needs to know the N necessary to attain the desired power for the specified α and hypothesized ES. N increases with an increase in power desired, a decrease in the ES, and a decrease in α. For statistical tests involving two or more groups, N as here defined is the necessary sample size for *each* group.

Effect Size

Researchers find specifying the ES the most difficult part of power analysis. As suggested above, the difficulty is at least partly due to the generally low level of consciousness of the magnitude of phenomena that characterizes much of psychology. This in turn may help explain why, despite the stricture of methodologists, significance testing is so heavily preferred to confidence interval estimation, although the wide intervals that usually result may also play a role (Cohen, 1990). However, neither the determination of power or necessary sample size can proceed without the investigator having some idea about the degree to which the H_0 is believed to be false (i.e., the ES).

In the Neyman–Pearson method of statistical inference, in addition to the specification of H_0, an alternate hypothesis (H_1) is counterpoised against H_0. The degree to which H_0 is false is indexed by the discrepancy between H_0 and H_1 and is called the ES. Each statistical test has its own ES index. All the indexes are scale free and continuous, ranging upward from zero, and for all, the H_0 is that ES = 0. For example, for testing the product–moment correlation of a sample for significance, the ES is simply the population r, so H_0 posits that $r = 0$. As another example, for testing the significance of the departure of a population proportion (P) from .50, the ES index is $g = P - .50$, so the H_0 is that $g = 0$. For the tests of the significance of the difference between independent means, correlation coefficients, and proportions, the H_0 is that the difference equals zero. Table 1 gives for each of the tests the definition of its ES index.

To convey the meaning of any given ES index, it is necessary to have some idea of its scale. To this end, I have proposed as conventions or operational definitions small, medium, and large values for each that are at least approximately consistent across the different ES indexes. My intent was that medium ES represent an effect likely to be visible to the naked eye of a careful observer. (It has since been noted in effect-size surveys that it approxi-

TABLE 1
ES Indexes and Their Values for Small, Medium, and Large Effects

Test	ES Index	Small	Medium	Large
1. m_A vs. m_B for independent means	$d = \dfrac{m_A - m_B}{\sigma}$	.20	.50	.80
2. Significance of product-moment r	r	.10	.30	.50
3. r_A vs. r_B for independent rs	$q = z_A - z_B$ where $z = $ Fisher's z	.10	.30	.50
4. $P = .5$ and the sign test	$g = P - .50$	.05	.15	.25
5. P_A vs. P_B for independent proportions	$h\,\phi_A - \phi_B$ where $\phi = $ arcsine transformation	.20	.50	.80
6. Chi-square for goodness of fit and contingency	$w = \sqrt{\displaystyle\sum_{j=1}^{k} \dfrac{(P_{1i} - P_{0i})^2}{P_{0i}}}$	.10	.30	.50
7. One-way analysis of variance	$f = \dfrac{\sigma_m}{\sigma}$	.10	.25	.40
8. Multiple and multiple partial correlation	$f^2 = \dfrac{R^2}{1 - R^2}$	.02	.15	.35

Note. ES = population effect size.

mates the average size of observed effects in various fields.) I set small ES to be noticeably smaller than medium but not so small as to be trivial, and I set large ES to be the same distance above medium as small was below it. Although the definitions were made subjectively, with some early minor adjustments, these conventions have been fixed since the 1977 edition of SPABS and have come into general use. Table 1 contains these values for the tests considered here.

In the present treatment, the H_1s are the ESs that operationally define small, medium, and large effects as given in Table 1. For the test of the significance of a sample r, for example, because the ES for this test is simply the alternate-hypothetical population r, small, medium, and large ESs are respectively .10, .30, and .50. The ES index for the t test of the difference between independent means is d, the difference expressed in units of (i.e., divided by) the within-population standard deviation. For this test, the H_0 is that $d = 0$ and the small, medium, and large ESs (or H_1s) are $d = .20, .50$, and .80. Thus, an operationally defined medium difference between means is half a standard deviation; concretely, for IQ scores in which the population standard deviation is 15, a medium difference between means is 7.5 IQ points.

STATISTICAL TESTS

The tests covered here are the most common tests used in psychological research:

1. The t test for the difference between two independent means, with $df = 2 (N - 1)$.
2. The t test for the significance of a product-moment correlation coefficient r, with $df = N - 2$.
3. The test for the difference between two independent rs, accomplished as a normal curve test through the Fisher z transformation of r (tabled in many statistical texts).
4. The binomial distribution or, for large samples, the normal curve (or equivalent chi-square, 1 df) test that a population proportion $(P) = .50$. This test is also used in the nonparametric sign test for differences between paired observations.
5. The normal curve test for the difference between two independent proportions, accomplished through the arcsine transformation ϕ (tabled in many statistical texts). The results are effectively the same when the test is made using the chi-square test with 1 degree of freedom.
6. The chi-square test for goodness of fit (one way) or association in two-way contingency tables. In Table 1, k is the number of

TABLE 2
N For Small, Medium, and Large ES at Power = .80 for α = .01, .05, and .10

		α							
	.01			.05			.10		
Test	Sm	Med	Lg	Sm	Med	Lg	Sm	Med	Lg
1. Mean dif	586	95	38	393	64	26	310	50	20
2. Sig r	1,163	125	41	783	85	28	617	68	22
3. r dif	2,339	263	96	1,573	177	66	1,240	140	52
4. P = .5	1,165	127	44	783	85	30	616	67	23
5. P dif	584	93	36	392	63	25	309	49	19
6. χ^2									
1df	1,168	130	38	785	87	26	618	69	25
2df	1,388	154	56	964	107	39	771	86	31
3df	1,546	172	62	1,090	121	44	880	98	35
4df	1,675	186	67	1,194	133	48	968	108	39
5df	1,787	199	71	1,293	143	51	1,045	116	42
6df	1,887	210	75	1,362	151	54	1,113	124	45
7. ANOVA									
2g[a]	586	95	38	393	64	26	310	50	20
3g[a]	464	76	30	322	52	21	258	41	17
4g[a]	388	63	25	274	45	18	221	36	15
5g[a]	336	55	22	240	39	16	193	32	13
6g[a]	299	49	20	215	35	14	174	28	12
7g[a]	271	44	18	195	32	13	159	26	11
8. Mult R									
2k[b]	698	97	45	481	67	30			
3k[b]	780	108	50	547	76	34			
4k[b]	841	118	55	599	84	38			
5k[b]	901	126	59	645	91	42			
6k[b]	953	134	63	686	97	45			
7k[b]	998	141	66	726	102	48			
8k[b]	1,039	147	69	757	107	50			

Note. ES = population effect size, Sm = small, Med = medium, Lg = large, diff = difference, ANOVA = analysis of variance. Tests numbered as in Table 1.
[a] Number of groups.   [b] Number of independent variables.

cells and P_{0i} and P_{1i} are the null hypothetical and alternate hypothetical population proportions in cell i. (Note that w's structure is the same as chi-square's for cell sample frequencies.) For goodness-of-fit tests, the $df = k - 1$, and for contingency tables, $df = (a - 1)(b - 1)$, where a and b are the number of levels in the two variables. Table 2 provides (total) sample sizes for 1 through 6 degrees of freedom.

7. One-way analysis of variance. Assuming equal sample sizes (as we do throughout), for g groups, the F test has $df = g - 1$, $g(N - 1)$. The ES index is the standard deviation of the g population means divided by the common within-population standard deviation. Provision is made in Table 2 for 2 through 7 groups.

8. Multiple and multiple partial correlation. For k independent variables, the significance test is the standard F test for $df = k$, $N - k - 1$. The ES index, f^2, is defined for either squared multiple or squared multiple partial correlations (R^2). Table 2 provides for 2 through 8 independent variables.

Note that because all tests of population parameters that can be either positive or negative (Tests 1–5) are two-sided, their ES indexes here are absolute values.

In using the material that follows, keep in mind that the ES posited by the investigator is what he or she believes holds for the population and that the sample size that is found is conditional on the ES. Thus, if a study is planned in which the investigator believes that a population r is of medium size (ES $= r = .30$ from Table 1) and the t test is to be performed with two-sided $\alpha = .05$, then the power of this test is .80 if the sample size is 85 (from Table 2). If, using 85 cases, t is not significant, then either r is smaller than .30 or the investigator has been the victim of the .20 (β) risk of making a Type II error.

EXAMPLES

The necessary N for power of .80 for the following examples are found in Table 2.

1. To detect a medium difference between two independent sample means ($d = .50$ in Table 1) at $\alpha = .05$ requires $N = 64$ in each group. (A d of .50 is equivalent to a point-biserial correlation of .243; see SPABS, pp. 22–24.)
2. For a significance test of a sample r at $\alpha = .01$, when the population r is large (.50 in Table 2), a sample size $= 41$ is required. At $\alpha = .05$, the necessary sample size $= 28$.
3. To detect a medium-sized difference between two population rs ($q = .30$ in Table 1) at $\alpha = .05$ requires $N = 177$ in each group. (The following pairs of rs yield $q = .30$: .00, .29; .20, .46; .40, .62; .60, .76; .80, .89; .90, .94; see SPABS, pp. 113–116.)
4. The sign test tests the H_0 that .50 of a population of paired differences are positive. If the population proportion's departure from .50 is medium ($q = .15$ in Table 1), at $\alpha = .10$, the necessary $N = 67$; at $\alpha = .05$, it is 85.
5. To detect a small difference between two independent population proportions ($h = .20$ in Table 1) at $\alpha = .05$ requires $N = 392$ cases in each group. (The following pairs of Ps yield approximate values of $h = .20$: .05, .10; .20, .29; .40, .50; .60, .70; .80, .87; .90, .95; see SPABS, p. 184f.)

6. A 3×4 contingency table has 6 degrees of freedom. To detect a medium degree of association in the population ($w = .30$ in Table 1) at $\alpha = .05$ required $N = 151$. ($w = .30$ corresponds to a contingency coefficient of .287, and for 6 degrees of freedom, a Cramèr ϕ of .212; see SPABS, pp. 220–227).

7. A psychologist considers alternate research plans involving comparisons of the means of either three or four groups in both of which she believes that the ES is medium ($f = .25$ in Table 1). She finds that at $\alpha = .05$, the necessary sample size per group is 52 cases for the three-group plan and 45 cases for the four-group plan, thus, total sample sizes of 156 and 180. (When $f = .25$, the proportion of variance accounted for by group membership is .0588; see SPABS, pp. 280–284.)

8. A psychologist plans a research in which he will do a multiple regression/correlation analysis and perform all the significance tests at $\alpha = .01$. For the F test of the multiple R^2, he expects a medium ES, that is, $f^2 = .15$ (from Table 1). He has a candidate set of eight independent variables for which Table 2 indicates that the required sample size is 147, which exceeds his resources. However, from his knowledge of the research area, he believes that the information in the eight variables can be effectively summarized in three. For three variables, the necessary sample size is only 108. (Given the relationship between f^2 and R^2, the values for small, medium, and large R^2 are respectively .0196, .1304, and .2592, and for R, .14, .36, and .51; see SPABS, pp. 410–414.)

REFERENCES

Cohen, J. (1962). The statistical power of abnormal–social psychological research: A review. *Journal of Abnormal and Social Psychology, 65*, 145–153.

Cohen, J. (1965). Some statistical issues in psychological research. In B. B. Wolman (Ed.), *Handbook of clinical psychology* (pp. 95–121). New York: McGraw-Hill.

Cohen, J. (1969). *Statistical power analysis for the behavioral sciences.* San Diego, CA: Academic Press.

Cohen, J. (1988). *Statistical power analysis for the behavioral sciences* (2nd ed.). Hillsdale, NJ: Erlbaum.

Cohen, J. (1990). Things I have learned (so far). *American Psychologist, 45*, 1304–1312.

Goldstein, R. (1989). Power and sample size via MS/PC-DOS computers. *American Statistician, 43*, 253–260.

Neyman, J., & Pearson, E. S. (1928). On the use and interpretation of certain test criteria for purposes of statistical inference. *Biometrika, 20A,* 175–240, 263–294.

Neyman, J., & Pearson, E. S. (1933). On the problem of the most efficient tests of statistical hypotheses. *Transactions of the Royal Society of London Series A, 231,* 289–337.

Sedlmeier, P., & Gigerenzer, G. (1989). Do studies of statistical power have an effect on the power of studies? *Psychological Bulletin, 105,* 309–316.

18

STATISTICAL SIGNIFICANCE TESTING AND CUMULATIVE KNOWLEDGE IN PSYCHOLOGY: IMPLICATIONS FOR TRAINING OF RESEARCHERS

FRANK L. SCHMIDT

In 1990, Aiken, West, Sechrest, and Reno published an important article surveying the teaching of quantitative methods in graduate psychology programs. They were concerned about what was not being taught or was being inadequately taught to future researchers and the harm this might cause to research progress in psychology. For example, they found that new and important quantitative methods such as causal modeling, confirmatory factor analysis, and meta-analysis were not being taught in the majority of graduate programs. This is indeed a legitimate cause for concern. But in this article, I am concerned about the opposite: what is being taught and the harm that this is doing. Aiken et al. found that the vast majority of programs were

Reprinted from *Psychological Methods*, 1, 115–129. Copyright 1996 by the American Psychological Association.

teaching, on a rather thorough basis, what they referred to as "the old standards of statistics"; traditional inferential statistics. This includes the t test, the F test, the chi-square test, analysis of variance (ANOVA), and other methods of statistical significance testing. Hypothesis testing based on the statistical significance test has been the main feature of graduate training in statistics in psychology for over 40 years, and the Aiken et al. study showed that it still is.

Methods of data analysis and interpretation have a major effect on the development of cumulative knowledge. I demonstrate in this article that reliance on statistical significance testing in the analysis and interpretation of research data has systematically retarded the growth of cumulative knowledge in psychology (Hunter & Schmidt, 1990b; Schmidt, 1992). This conclusion is not new. It has been articulated in different ways by Rozeboom (1960), Meehl (1967), Carver (1978), Guttman (1985), Oakes (1986), Loftus (1991, 1994), and others, and most recently by Cohen (1994). Jack Hunter and I have used meta-analysis methods to show that these traditional data analysis methods militate against the discovery of the underlying regularities and relationships that are the foundation for scientific progress (Hunter & Schmidt, 1990b). Those of us who are the keepers of the methodological and quantitative flame for the field of psychology bear the major responsibility for this failure because we have continued to emphasize significance testing in the training of graduate students despite clear demonstrations of the deficiencies of this approach to data analysis. We correctly decry the fact that quantitative methods are given inadequate attention in graduate programs, and we worry that this signals a future decline in research quality. Yet it was our excessive emphasis on so-called inferential statistical methods that caused a much more serious problem. And we ignore this fact.

My conclusion is that we must abandon the statistical significance test. In our graduate programs we must teach that for analysis of data from individual studies, the appropriate statistics are point estimates of effect sizes and confidence intervals around these point estimates. We must teach that for analysis of data from multiple studies, the appropriate method is meta-analysis. I am not the first to reach the conclusion that significance testing should be replaced by point estimates and confidence intervals. Jones stated this conclusion as early as 1955, and Kish in 1959. Rozeboom reached this conclusion in 1960. Carver stated this conclusion in 1978, as did Hunter in 1979 in an invited American Psychological Association (APA) address, and Oakes in his excellent 1986 book. So far, these individuals (and others) have all been voices crying in the wilderness.

Why then is the situation any different today? If the closely reasoned and logically flawless arguments of Kish, Rozeboom, Carver, and Hunter have been ignored all these years—and they have—what reason is there to believe that this will not continue to be the case? There is in fact a reason to be optimistic that in the future we will see reform of data analysis methods in psychology. That reason is the development and widespread use of meta-analysis methods. These methods have revealed more clearly than ever before the extent to which reliance on significance testing has retarded the growth of cumulative knowledge in psychology. These demonstrations based on meta-analysis methods are what is new. As conclusions from research literature come more and more to be based on findings from meta-analysis (Cooper & Hedges, 1994; Lipsey & Wilson, 1993; Schmidt, 1992), the significance test necessarily becomes less and less important. At worst, significance tests will become progressively deemphasized. At best, their use will be discontinued and replaced in individual studies by point estimation of effect sizes and confidence intervals.

The reader's reaction to this might be that this is just one opinion and that there are defenses of statistical significance testing that are as convincing as the arguments and demonstrations I present in this article. This is not true. As Oakes (1986) stated, it is "extraordinarily difficult to find a statistician who argues explicitly in favor of the retention of significance tests" (p. 71). A few psychologists have so argued. But Oakes (1986) and Carver (1978) have carefully considered all such arguments and shown them to be logically flawed and hence false. Also, even these few defenders of significance testing (e.g., Winch & Campbell, 1969) agree that the dominant usages of such tests in data analysis in psychology are misuses, and they hold that the role of significance tests in data analysis should be greatly reduced. As you read this article, I want you to consider this challenge: Can you articulate even one legitimate contribution that significance testing has made (or makes) to the research enterprise (i.e., any way in which it contributes to the development of cumulative scientific knowledge?) I believe you will not be able to do so.

TRADITIONAL METHODS VERSUS META-ANALYSIS

Psychology and the other social sciences have traditionally relied heavily on the statistical significance test in interpreting the meaning of data, both in individual studies and in research literature. Following the fateful lead of Fisher (1932), null hypothesis significance testing has been the dominant data analysis procedure. The prevailing decision rule, as Oakes (1986) has demonstrated empirically, has been this: If the statistic (t, F, etc.) is significant, there is an effect (or a relation); if it is not significant, then there is no effect (or relation). These prevailing interpretational procedures have focused heavily on the control of Type I errors, with little attention being paid to the control of Type II errors. A Type I error (alpha error) consists of concluding that there is a relation or an effect when there is not. A Type II error (beta error) consists of the opposite, concluding that there is no relation or effect when there is. Alpha levels have been controlled at the .05 or

.01 levels, but beta levels have by default been allowed to climb to high levels, often in the 50% to 80% range (Cohen, 1962, 1988, 1990, 1994; Schmidt, Hunter, & Urry, 1976). To illustrate this, let us look at an example from a hypothetical but statistically typical area of experimental psychology.

Suppose the research question is the effect of a certain drug on learning, and suppose the actual effect of a particular dosage is an increase of one half of a standard deviation in the amount learned. An effect size of .50 is considered medium-sized by Cohen (1988) and corresponds to the difference between the 50th and 69th percentiles in a normal distribution. With an effect size of this magnitude, 69% of the experimental group would exceed the mean of the control group, if both were normally distributed. Many reviews of various literatures have found relations of this general magnitude (Hunter & Schmidt, 1990b). Now suppose that a large number of studies are conducted on this dosage, each with 15 rats in the experimental group and 15 in the control group.

Figure 1 shows the distribution of effect sizes (d values) expected under the null hypothesis. All variability around the mean value of zero is due to sampling error. To be significant at the .05 level (with a one-tailed test), the effect size must be .62 or larger. If the null hypothesis is true, only 5% will be that large or larger. In analyzing their data, researchers in psychology typically focus only on the information in Figure 1. Most believe that their significance test limits the probability of an error to 5%.

Actually, in this example the probability of a Type I error is zero, not 5%. Because the actual effect size is always .50, the null hypothesis is always false, and therefore there is no possibility of a Type I error. One cannot falsely conclude that there is an effect when in fact there is an effect. When the null hypothesis is false, the only kind of error that can occur is a Type II error: failure to detect the effect that is present (and the total error rate for the study

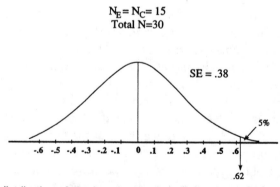

$N_E = N_C = 15$
Total N=30

SE = .38

5%

-.6 -.5 -.4 -.3 -.2 -.1 0 .1 .2 .3 .4 .5 .6

.62

Figure 1. Null distribution of d values in a series of experiments. Required for significance: $d_c = 0.62$; $d_c = [1.645(0.38)] = 0.62$ (one-tailed test, $\alpha = .05$).

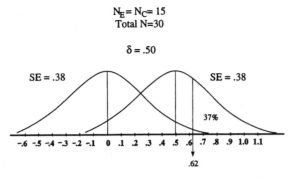

$N_E = N_C = 15$
Total $N = 30$

$\delta = .50$

SE = .38   SE = .38

37%

-.6 -.5 -.4 -.3 -.2 -.1 0 .1 .2 .3 .4 .5 .6 .7 .8 .9 1.0 1.1

.62

Figure 2. Statistical power in a series of experiments. Required for significance: $d_c =$ 0.62 (one-tailed test, $\alpha = .05$); statistical power = 0.37; Type II error rate = 63%; Type I error rate = 0%.

is therefore the Type II error rate). The only type of error that can occur is the type that is not controlled.

Figure 2 shows not only the irrelevant null distribution but also the actual distribution of effect sizes across these studies. The mean of this distribution is the true value of .50, but because of sampling error, there is substantial variation in observed effect sizes. Again, to be significant, the effect size must be .62 or larger. Only 37% of studies conducted will obtain a significant effect size; thus statistical power for each of these studies is only .37. That is, the true (population) effect size of the drug is always .50; it is never zero. Yet it is only detected as significant in 37% of the studies. The error rate in this research literature is 63%, not 5%, as many would mistakenly believe.

In actuality, the error rate would be even higher. Most researchers in experimental psychology would traditionally have used F tests from an ANOVA to analyze these data. This means the significance test would be two-tailed rather than one-tailed as in our example. With a two-tailed test (i.e., one-way ANOVA), statistical power is even lower: .26 instead of .37. The Type II error rate (and hence the overall error rate) would be 74%. Also, this example assumes use of a z test; any researchers not using an ANOVA would probably use a t test. For a one-tailed t test with $\alpha = .05$ and $df = 28$, the effect size (d value) must be .65 to be significant. (The t value must be at least 1.70, instead of the 1.645 required for the z test.) With the t test, statistical power would also be lower: .35 instead of .37. Thus both commonly used alternative significance tests would yield even lower statistical power and produce even higher error rates.

Also, note in Figure 2 that the studies that are significant yield distorted estimates of effect sizes. The true effect size is always .50; all departures from .50 are due solely to sampling error. But the minimum value required for significance is .62. The obtained d value must be .12 above its true value—24% larger than its real value—to be significant. The average of the significant d values is .89, which is 78% larger than the true value of .50.

In any study in this research literature that by chance yields the correct value of .50, the conclusion under the prevailing decision rule is that there is no relationship. That is, it is only the studies that by chance are quite inaccurate that lead to the correct conclusion that a relationship exists.

How would this body of studies be interpreted as a research literature? There are two interpretations that would have traditionally been accepted. The first is based on the traditional voting method (critiqued by Light & Smith, 1971, and by Hedges & Olkin, 1980). Using this method, one would note that 63% of the studies found "no relationship." Since this is a majority of the studies, the conclusion would be that no relation exists. This conclusion is completely false, yet many reviews in the past have been conducted in just this manner (Hedges & Olkin, 1980).

The second interpretation is as follows: In 63% of the studies, the drug had no effect. However, in 37% of the studies, the drug did have an effect. (Moreover, when the drug did have an effect, the effect was quite large, averaging .89.) Research is needed to identify the moderator variables (interactions) that cause the drug to have an effect in some studies but not in others. For example, perhaps the strain of rat used or the mode of injecting the drug affects study outcomes. This interpretation is also completely erroneous. In addition, it leads to wasted research efforts to identify nonexistent moderator variables.

Both traditional interpretations fail to reveal the true meaning of the studies and hence fail to lead to cumulative knowledge. In fact, the traditional methods based on significance testing make it impossible to reach correct conclusions about the meaning of these studies. This is what is meant by the statement that traditional data analysis methods militate against the development of cumulative knowledge.

How would meta-analysis interpret these studies? Different approaches to meta-analysis use somewhat different quantitative procedures (Bangert-Drowns, 1986; Glass, McGaw, & Smith, 1981; Hedges & Olkin, 1985; Hunter, Schmidt, & Jackson, 1982; Hunter & Schmidt, 1990b; Rosenthal, 1984, 1991). I illustrate this example using the methods presented by Hunter, Schmidt, and Jackson (1982) and Hunter and Schmidt (1990b). Figure 3 shows that meta-analysis reaches the correct conclusion. Meta-analysis first computes the variance of the observed d values (using the ordinary formula for the variance of any set of numbers). Next, it uses the standard formula for the sampling error variance of d values (e.g., see Hunter & Schmidt, 1990b, chap. 7) to determine how much variance would be expected in observed d values from sampling error alone. The amount of real variance in population d values (δ values) is estimated as the difference between the two. In our example, this difference is zero, indicating correctly that there is only one

I.   **Compute Actual Variance of Effect Sizes**

     1. $S_d^2 = .1444$ (Observed Variance of d Values)

     2. $S_e^2 = .1444$ (Variance Predicted from Sampling Error)

     3. $S_\delta^2 = S_d^2 - S_e^2$

     4. $S_\delta^2 = .1444 - .1444 = 0$ (True Variance of δ Values)

II.   **Compute Mean Effect Size**

     1. $\overline{d} = .50$ (Mean Observed d Value)

     2. $\delta = .50$

     3. $SD_\delta = 0$

III.   **Conclusion**:   There is only one effect size, and its value is .50 standard deviation.

Figure 3. Meta-analysis of drug studies.

population value. This single population value is estimated as the average observed value, which is .50 here, the correct value. If the number of studies is large, the average d value will be close to the true (population) value, because sampling errors are random and hence average out to zero.[1]

Note that these meta-analysis methods do not rely on statistical significance tests. Only effect sizes are used, and significance tests are not used in analyzing the effect sizes. Unlike traditional methods based on significance tests, meta-analysis leads to correct conclusions and hence leads to cumulative knowledge.

The data in this example are hypothetical. However, if one accepts the validity of basic statistical formulas for sampling error, one will have no reservations about this example. But the same principles do apply to real data, as shown next by an example from research in personnel selection. Table 1 shows observed validity coefficients (correlations) from 21 studies of a single clerical test and a single measure of job performance. Each study has $n = 68$ (the median n in the literature in personnel psychology), and every study is a random draw (without replacement) from a single larger validity study with

---

[1]Actually the d statistic has a slight positive (upward) bias as the estimator of δ, the population value. Formulas are available to correct observed d values for this bias and are given in Hedges and Olkin (1985, p. 81) and Hunter and Schmidt (1990b, p. 262). This example assumes that this correction has been made. This bias is trivial if the sample size is 10 or greater in both the experimental and control groups.

TABLE 1
21 Validity Studies,
$N = 68$ for Each

Study	Observed validity correlation
1	.04
2	.14
3	.31*
4	.12
5	.38*
6	.27*
7	.15
8	.36*
9	.20
10	.02
11	.23
12	.11
13	.21
14	.37*
15	.14
16	.29*
17	.26*
18	.17
19	.39*
20	.22
21	.21

* $p < .05$ (two tailed).

1,428 subjects. The correlation in the large study (uncorrected for measurement error, range restriction, or other artifacts) is .22 (Schmidt, Ocasio, Hillery, & Hunter, 1985).

The validity is significant in 8 (or 38%) of these studies, for an error rate of 62%. The traditional conclusion would be that this test is valid in 38% of the organizations, and invalid in the rest, and that in organizations in which it is valid, its mean observed validity is .33 (which is 50% larger than its real value). Meta-analysis of these validities indicates that the mean is .22 and that all variance in the coefficients is due solely to sampling error. The meta-analysis conclusions are correct; the traditional conclusions are false.

In these examples, the only type of error that is controlled—Type I error—is the type that cannot occur. In most areas of research, as time goes by, researchers gain a better and better understanding of the processes they are studying; as a result, it is less and less frequently the case that the null hypothesis is "true" and more and more likely that the null hypothesis is false. Thus Type I error decreases in importance, and Type II error increases in importance. This means that as time goes by, researchers should be paying increasing attention to Type II error and to statistical power and increasingly less attention to Type I error. However, a recent review in *Psychological Bul-*

letin (Sedlmeier & Gigerenzer, 1989) concluded that the average statistical power of studies in one APA journal had declined from 46% to 37% over a 22-year period (despite the earlier appeal in that journal by Cohen in 1962 for attention to statistical power). Only 2 of the 64 experiments reviewed even mentioned statistical power, and none computed estimates of power. The review concluded that the decline in power was due to increased use of alpha-adjusted procedures (such as the Newman–Keuls, Duncan, and Scheffé procedures). That is, instead of attempting to reduce the Type II error rate, researchers had been imposing increasingly stringent controls on Type I errors, which probably cannot occur in most studies. The result is a further increase in the Type II error rate, an average increase of 17%. This trend illustrates the deep illogic embedded in the use of significance tests.

These examples have examined only the effects of sampling error. There are other statistical and measurement artifacts that cause artifactual variation in effect sizes and correlations across studies, for example, differences between studies in amount of measurement error, in degree of range restriction, and in dichotomization of measures. Also, in meta-analysis, *d* values and correlations must be corrected for downward bias due to such research artifacts as measurement error and dichotomization of measures. These artifacts are beyond the scope of this presentation but are covered in detail elsewhere (Hunter & Schmidt, 1990a, 1990b; Schmidt & Hunter, 1996). My purpose here is to demonstrate only that traditional data analysis and interpretation methods logically lead to erroneous conclusions and to demonstrate that meta-analysis solves these problems at the level of aggregate research literatures.

For almost 50 years, reliance on statistical significance testing in psychology and the other social sciences has led to frequent serious errors in interpreting the meaning of data (Hunter & Schmidt, 1990b, pp. 29–42 and 483–484), errors that have systematically retarded the growth of cumulative knowledge. Despite the best efforts of such individuals as Kish (1959), Rozeboom (1960), Meehl (1967), Carver (1978), Hunter (1979), Guttman (1985), and Oakes (1986), it has not been possible to wean researchers away from their entrancement with significance testing. Can we now at least hope that the lessons from meta-analysis will finally stimulate change? I would like to answer in the affirmative, but later in this article I present reasons why I do not believe these demonstrations alone will be sufficient to bring about reform. Other steps are also needed.

In my introduction, I state that the appropriate method for analyzing data from multiple studies is meta-analysis. These two examples illustrate that point dramatically. I also state that the appropriate way to analyze data in a single study is by means of point estimation of the effect size and use of a confidence interval around this point estimate. If this had been done in the studies in these two examples, what would these two research literatures have looked like prior to application of meta-analysis?

In the first example, from the experimental psychology literature, the traditional practice would have been to report only the F statistic values and their associated significance levels. Anyone looking at this literature would see that 26% of these F ratios are significant and 74% are nonsignificant. This would create at best the impression of a contradictory set of studies. With appropriate data analysis methods, the observed d value is computed in each study; this is the point estimate of the effect size. Anyone looking at this literature would quickly see that the vast majority of these effect sizes— 91%—are positive. This gives a very different and much more accurate impression than does the observation that 74% of the effects are nonsignificant. Next, the confidence interval around each effect size is computed and presented. A glance at these confidence intervals would reveal that almost all of them overlap with almost all of the other confidence intervals. This again correctly suggests that the studies are in substantial agreement, contrary to the false impression given by the traditional information that 26% are significant and 74% are nonsignificant. (These studies use simple one-way ANOVA designs; however, d values and confidence intervals can also be computed when factorial ANOVA designs or repeated measures designs are used.)

To see this point more clearly, let us consider again the observed correlations in Table 1. The observed correlation is an index of effect size, and therefore in a truly traditional analysis it would not be reported; only significance levels would be reported. So all we would know is that in 62% of the studies there was "no significant relationship," and in 38% of the studies there was a significant relationship. Table 2 shows the information that would be provided by use of point estimates of effect size and confidence intervals. In Table 2, the observed correlations are arranged in order of size with their 95% confidence intervals.

The first thing that is obvious is that all the correlations are positive. It can also be seen that every confidence interval overlaps every other confidence interval, indicating that these studies could all be estimating the same population parameter, which indeed they are. This is true for even the largest and smallest correlations. The confidence interval for the largest correlation (.39) is .19 to .59. The confidence interval for the smallest correlation (.02) is −.22 to .26. These confidence intervals have an overlap of .07. Thus in contrast to the picture provided by null hypothesis significance testing, point estimates and confidence intervals provide a much more correct picture, a picture that correctly indicates substantial agreement among the studies.[2]

---

[2] The confidence intervals in Table 2 have been computed using the usual formula for the standard error of the sample correlation: $SE = (1 - r^2)/\sqrt{N - 1}$. Hence these confidence intervals are symmetrical. Some would advocate the use of Fisher's Z transformation of r in computing confidence intervals for r. This position is typically based on the belief that the sampling distribution of Fisher's Z transformation of r is normally distributed, while r itself is skewed. Actually, both are skewed and both approach normality as N increases, and the Fisher's Z transformation approaches normality only marginally faster than r as N increases. For a population correlation of .22 and sample sizes in the ranges considered here, the differences are trivial.

TABLE 2

95% Confidence Intervals for Correlations From Table 1, $N = 68$ for Each

Study	Observed correlation	95% confidence interval	
		Lower	Upper
1	.39	.19	.59
2	.38	.18	.58
3	.37	.16	.58
4	.36	.15	.57
5	.31	.09	.53
6	.29	.07	.51
7	.27	.05	.49
8	.26	.04	.48
9	.23	.00	.46
10	.22	−.01	.45
11	.21	−.02	.44
12	.21	−.02	.44
13	.20	−.03	.43
14	.17	−.06	.40
15	.15	−.08	.38
16	.14	−.09	.37
17	.14	−.09	.37
18	.12	−.12	.36
19	.11	−.13	.35
20	.04	−.20	.28
21	.02	−.22	.26

There are also other reasons for preferring confidence intervals (see Carver, 1978; Hunter & Schmidt, 1990b, pp. 29–33; Kish, 1959; Oakes, 1986, p. 67; and Rozeboom, 1960). One important reason is that, unlike the significance test, the confidence interval does hold the overall error rate to the desired level. In the example from experimental psychology, we saw that many researchers believed that the error rate for the significance test was held to 5% because the alpha level used was .05, when in fact the error rate was really 63% (74% if F tests from an ANOVA are used). However, if the 95% confidence interval is used, the overall error rate is in fact held to 5%. Only 5% of such computed confidence intervals will be expected to not include the population (true) effect size and 95% will.

To many researchers today, the idea of substituting point estimates and confidence intervals for significance tests might seem radical. Therefore it is important to remember that prior to the appearance of Fisher's 1932 and 1935 texts, data analysis in individual studies was typically conducted using point estimates and confidence intervals (Oakes, 1986). The point estimates were usually accompanied by estimates of the "probable error," the 50% confidence interval. Significance tests were rarely used (and confidence intervals were not interpreted in terms of statistical significance). Most of us rarely look at the psychological journals of the 1920s and early 1930s, but if we did, this is what we would see. As can be seen both in the psychology research journals and in psychology statistics textbooks, during the latter half of the 1930s and during the 1940s, under the influence of Fisher, psychological researchers adopted en masse Fisher's null hypothesis significance testing approach to analysis of data in individual studies (Huberty, 1993). This was a major mistake. It was Sir Ronald Fisher who led psychological researchers down the primrose path of significance testing. All the other social sciences were similarly deceived, as were researchers in medicine, finance, marketing, and other areas.

Fisher's influence not only explains this unfortunate change, it also suggests one reason why psychologists for so long gave virtually no attention to the question of statistical power. The concept of statistical power does not exist in Fisherian statistics. In Fisherian statistics, the focus of attention is solely on the null hypothesis. No alternative hypothesis is introduced. Without an alternative hypothesis, there can be no concept of statistical power. When Neyman and Pearson (1932, 1933) later introduced the concepts of the alternate hypothesis and statistical power, Fisher argued that statistical power was irrelevant to statistical significance testing as used in scientific inference (Oakes, 1986). We have seen in our two examples how untrue that statement is.

Thus it is clear that even if meta-analysis had never been developed, use of point estimates of effect size and confidence intervals in interpreting data in individual studies would have made our research literatures far less confusing, far less apparently contradictory, and far more informative than those that have been produced by the dominant practice of reliance on significance tests. Indeed, the fact of almost universal reliance on significance tests in data analysis in individual studies is a major factor in making meta-analysis absolutely essential to making sense of research literatures (Hunter & Schmidt, 1990b, chap. 1).

However, it is important to understand that meta-analysis would still be useful even had researchers always relied only on point estimates and confidence intervals, because the very large numbers of studies characteristic of many of today's literatures create information overload even if each study has been appropriately analyzed. Indeed, we saw earlier that applying meta-analysis to the studies in Table 1 produces an even clearer and more accurate picture of the meaning of these studies than the application of point estimates and confidence intervals shown in Table 2. In our example, meta-analysis tells us that there is only one population correlation and that that value is .22. Confidence intervals tell us only that there may be only one population value; they do not specify what that value might be. In addition, in more complex applications, meta-analysis makes possible corrections for the effects of other artifacts—both systematic and unsystematic—that bias effect size estimates and cause false variation in such estimates across studies (Hunter & Schmidt, 1990b).

CONSEQUENCES OF TRADITIONAL SIGNIFICANCE TESTING

As we have seen, traditional reliance on statistical significance testing leads to the false appearance of conflicting and internally contradictory research literatures. This has a debilitating effect on the general research effort to develop cumulative theoretical knowledge and understanding. However, it is also important to note that it destroys the usefulness of psychological research as a means for solving practical problems in society.

The sequence of events has been much the same in one applied research area after another. First, there is initial optimism about using social science research to answer socially important questions that arise. Do government-sponsored job-training programs work? One will do studies to find out. Does integration increase the school achievement of Black children? Research will provide the answer. Next, several studies on the question are conducted, but the results are conflicting. There is some disappointment that the question has not been answered, but policymakers—and people in general—are still optimistic. They, along with the researchers, conclude that more research is needed to identify the interactions (moderators) that have caused the conflicting findings. For example, perhaps whether job training works depends on the age and education of the trainees. Maybe smaller classes in the schools are beneficial only for lower IQ children. Researchers may hypothesize that psychotherapy works for middle-class patients but not lower-class patients.

In the third phase, a large number of research studies are funded and conducted to test these moderator hypotheses. When they are completed, there is now a large body of studies, but instead of being resolved, the number of conflicts increases. The moderator hypotheses from the initial studies are not borne out. No one can make much sense out of the conflicting findings. Researchers conclude that the phenomenon that was selected for study in this particular case has turned out to be hopelessly complex, and so they turn to the investigation of another question, hoping that this time the question will turn out to be more tractable. Research sponsors, government officials, and the public become disenchanted and cynical. Research funding agencies cut money for research in this area and in related areas. After this cycle has been repeated enough times, social and behavioral scientists themselves become cynical about the value of their own work, and they begin to express doubts about whether behavioral and social science research is capable in principle of developing cumulative knowledge and providing general answers to socially important questions (e.g., see Cronbach, 1975; Gergen, 1982; Meehl, 1978). Cronbach's (1975) article "The Two Disciplines of Scientific Psychology Revisited" is a clear statement of this sense of hopelessness.

Clearly, at this point the need is not for more primary research studies but for some means of making sense of the vast number of accumulated study findings. This is the purpose of meta-analysis. Applications of meta-analysis to accumulated research literatures have generally shown that research findings are not nearly as conflicting as we had thought and that useful general conclusions can be drawn from past research. I have summarized some of these findings in a recent article (Schmidt, 1992; see also Hunter & Schmidt, in press). Thus, socially important applied questions can be answered.

Even more important, it means that scientific progress is possible. It means that cumulative understanding and progress in theory development is possible after all. It means that the behavioral and social sciences can attain the status of true sciences; they are not doomed forever to the status of quasi-sciences or pseudosciences. One result of this is that the gloom, cynicism, and nihilism that have enveloped many in the behavioral and social sciences is lifting. Young people starting out in the behavioral and social sciences today can hope for a much brighter future.

These are among the considerable benefits of abandoning statistical significance testing in favor of point estimates of effect sizes and confidence intervals in individual studies and meta-analysis for combining findings across multiple studies.

IS STATISTICAL POWER THE SOLUTION?

So far in this article, the deficiencies of significance testing that I have emphasized are those stemming from low statistical power in typical studies. Significance testing has other important problems, and I discuss some of these later. However, in our work on meta-analysis methods, John Hunter and I have repeatedly been confronted by researchers who state that the only problem with significance testing is low power and that if this problem could be solved, there would be no problems with reliance on significance testing in data analysis and interpretation. Almost invariably, these individuals see the solution as larger sample sizes. They believe that the problem would be solved if every researcher before conducting each study would calculate the number of subjects needed for "adequate" power (usually taken as power of .80), given the expected effect size and the desired alpha level, and then use that sample size.

What this position overlooks is that this requirement would make it impossible for most studies ever to be conducted. At the inception of research in a given area, the questions are often of the form, "Does Treatment

A have an effect?" If Treatment A indeed has a substantial effect, the sample size needed for adequate power may not be prohibitively large. But as research develops, subsequent questions tend to take the form, "Does Treatment A have a larger effect than does Treatment B?" The effect size then becomes the difference between the two effects. A similar progression occurs in correlational research. Such effect sizes will often be much smaller, and the required sample sizes are therefore often quite large, often 1,000 or more (Schmidt & Hunter, 1978). This is just to attain power of .80, which still allows a 20% Type II error rate when the null hypothesis is false. Many researchers cannot obtain that many subjects, no matter how hard they try; either it is beyond their resources or the subjects are just unavailable at any cost. Thus the upshot of this position would be that many—perhaps most—studies would not be conducted at all.

People advocating the position being critiqued here would say this would be no loss at all. They argue that a study with inadequate power contributes nothing and therefore should not be conducted. But such studies do contain valuable information when combined with others like them in a meta-analysis. In fact, very precise meta-analysis results can be obtained on the basis of studies that all have inadequate statistical power individually. The information in these studies is lost if these studies are never conducted.

The belief that such studies are worthless is based on two false assumptions: (a) the assumption that each individual study must be able to support and justify a conclusion, and (b) the assumption that every study should be analyzed with significance tests. In fact, meta-analysis has made clear that any single study is rarely adequate by itself to answer a scientific question. Therefore each study should be considered as a data point to be contributed to a later meta-analysis, and individual studies should be analyzed using not significance tests but point estimates of effect sizes and confidence intervals.

How, then, can we solve the problem of statistical power in individual studies? Actually, this problem is a pseudoproblem. It can be "solved" by discontinuing the significance test. As Oakes (1986, p. 68) noted, statistical power is a legitimate concept only within the context of statistical significance testing. If significance testing is no longer used, then the concept of statistical power has no place and is not meaningful. In particular, there need be no concern with statistical power when point estimates and confidence intervals are used to analyze data in studies and when meta-analysis is used to integrate findings across studies.[3] Thus when there is no significance testing, there are no statistical power problems.

---

[3] Some state that confidence intervals are the same as significance tests, because if the lower bound of the confidence interval does not include zero, that fact indicates that the effect size estimate is statistically significant. But the fact that the confidence interval can be interpreted as a significance test does not mean that it must be so interpreted. There is no necessity for such an interpretation, and as noted earlier, the probable errors (50% confidence intervals) popularly used in the literature up until the mid 1930s were never interpreted as significance tests.

WHY ARE RESEARCHERS ADDICTED
TO SIGNIFICANCE TESTING?

Time after time, even in recent years, I have seen researchers who have learned to understand the deceptiveness of significance testing sink back into the habit of reliance on significance testing. I have occasionally done it my-self. Why is it so hard for us to break our addiction to significance testing? Methodologists such as Bakan (1966), Meehl (1967), Rozeboom (1960), Oakes (1986), Carver (1978), and others have explored the various possible reasons why researchers seem to be unable to give up significance testing.

Significance testing creates an illusion of objectivity, and objectivity is a critical value in science. But objectivity makes a negative contribution when it sabotages the research enterprise by making it impossible to reach correct conclusions about the meaning of data.

Researchers conform to the dominant practice of reliance on signifi-cance testing because they fear that failure to follow these conventional practices would cause their studies to be rejected by journal editors. But the solution to this problem is not conformity to counterproductive practices but education of editors and reviewers.

There is also a feeling that, as bad as significance testing is, there is no satisfactory alternative; just looking at the data and making interpretations will not do. But as we have seen, there is a good statistical alternative: point estimates and confidence intervals.

However, I do not believe that these and similar reasons are the whole story. An important part of the explanation is that researchers hold false be-liefs about significance testing, beliefs that tell them that significance testing offers important benefits to researchers that it in fact does not. Three of these beliefs are particularly important.

The first is the false belief that the significance level of a study indicates the probability of successful replication of the study. Oakes (1986, pp. 79–82) empirically studied the beliefs about the meaning of significance tests of 70 research psychologists and advanced graduate students. They were pre-sented with the following scenario:

> Suppose you have a treatment which you suspect may alter performance on a certain task. You compare the means of your control and experi-mental groups (20 subjects in each). Further, suppose you use a simple independent means t test and your result is $t = 2.7$, d.f. $= 38$, $p = .01$. (Oakes, 1986, p. 79)

He then asked them to indicate whether each of several statements were true or false. One of these statements was this:

> You have a reliable experimental finding in the sense that if, hypotheti-cally, the experiment were repeated a great number of times, you would obtain a significant result in 99% of such studies. (Oakes, 1986, p. 79)

Sixty percent of the researchers indicated that this false statement is true. The significance level gives no information about the probability of replication. This statement confuses significance level with power. The probability of replication is the power of the study; the power of this study is not .99, but rather .43.[4] If this study is repeated many times, the best estimate is that less than half of all such studies will be significant at the chosen alpha level of .01. Yet 60% of the researchers endorsed the belief that 99% of such studies would be significant. This false belief may help to explain the traditional indifference to power among researchers. Many researchers believe a power analysis does not provide any information not already given by the significance level. Furthermore, this belief leads to the false conclusion that statistical power for every statistically significant finding is very high, at least .95.

That many researchers hold this false belief has been known for decades. Bakan criticized this error in 1966, and Lykken discussed it at some length in 1968. The following statement from an introductory statistics textbook by Nunnally (1975) is a clear statement of this belief:

> If the statistical significance is at the .05 level, it is more informative to talk about the *statistical confidence* as being at the .95 level. This means that the investigator can be confident with odds of 95 out of 100 that the observed difference will hold up in future investigations. (p. 195)

Most researchers, however, do not usually explicitly state this belief. The fact that they hold it is revealed by their description of statistically significant findings. Researchers obtaining a statistically significant result often refer to it as "a reliable difference," meaning one that is replicable. In fact, a false argument frequently heard in favor of significance testing is that we must have significance tests in order to know whether our findings are reliable or not. As Carver (1978) pointed out, the popularity of statistical significance testing would be greatly reduced if researchers could be made to realize that the statistical significance level does not indicate the replicability of research data. So it is critical that this false belief be eradicated from the minds of researchers.

A second false belief widely held by researchers is that statistical significance level provides an index of the importance or size of a difference or relation (Bakan, 1966). A difference significant at the .001 level is regarded as theoretically (or practically) more important or larger than a difference significant at only the .05 level. In research reports in the literature, one sees statements such as the following: "Moreover, this difference is

---

[4] The statistical power for future replications of this study is estimated as follows. The best estimate of the population effect size is the effect size (d value) observed in this study. This observed d value is $2t/\sqrt{N}$ (Hunter & Schmidt, 1990b, p. 272), which is .85 here. With 20 subjects each in the experimental and control groups, an alpha level of .01 (two tailed), and a population d value of .85, the power of the t test is .43.

highly significant ($p < .001$)," implying that the difference is therefore large or important. This belief ignores the fact that significance level depends on sample size; highly significant differences in large sample studies may be smaller than even nonsignificant differences in smaller sample studies. This belief also ignores the fact that even if sample sizes were equal across studies compared, the p values would still provide no index of the actual size of the difference or effect. Only effect size indices can do that.

Because of the influence of meta-analysis, the practice of computing effect sizes has become more frequent in some research literatures, thus mitigating the pernicious effects of this false belief. But in other areas, especially in many areas of experimental psychology, effect sizes are rarely computed, and it remains the practice to infer size or importance of obtained findings from statistical significance levels. In an empirical study, Oakes (1986, pp. 86–88) found that psychological researchers infer grossly overestimated effect sizes from significance levels. When the study p values were .01, they estimated effect sizes as five times as large as they actually were.

The size or importance of findings is information important to researchers. Researchers who continue to believe that statistical significance levels reveal the size or importance of differences or relations will continue to refuse to abandon significance testing in favor of point estimates and confidence intervals. So this is a second false belief that must be eradicated.

The third false belief held by many researchers is the most devastating of all to the research enterprise. This is the belief that if a difference or relation is not statistically significant, then it is zero, or at least so small that it can safely be considered to be zero. This is the belief that if the null hypothesis is not rejected, then it is to be accepted. This is the belief that a major benefit from significance tests is that they tell us whether a difference or effect is real or "probably just occurred by chance." If a difference is not significant, then we know that it is probably just due to chance. The two examples discussed earlier show how detrimental this false operational decision rule is to the attainment of cumulative knowledge in psychology. This belief makes it impossible to discern the real meaning of research literatures.

Although some of his writings are ambiguous on this point, Fisher himself probably did not advocate this decision rule. In his 1935 book he stated,

> It should be noted that this null hypothesis is never proved or established, but is possibly disproved in the course of experimentation. Every experiment may be said to exist only in order to give the facts a chance of disproving the null hypothesis. (p. 19)

If the null hypothesis is not rejected, Fisher's position was that nothing could be concluded. But researchers find it hard to go to all the trouble of conducting a study only to conclude that nothing can be concluded. Oakes (1986) has shown empirically that the operational decision rule used by researchers is indeed "if it is not significant, it is zero." Use of this decision rule amounts to an implicit belief on the part of researchers that the power of significance tests is perfect or nearly perfect. Such a belief would account for the surprise typically expressed by researchers when informed of the low level of statistical power in most studies.

The confidence of researchers in a research finding is not a linear function of its significance level. Rosenthal and Gaito (1963) studied the confidence that researchers have that a difference is real as a function of the p value of the significance test. They found a precipitous decline in confidence as the p value increased from .05 to .06 or .07. There was no similar "cliff effect" as the p value increased from .01 to .05. This finding suggests that researchers believe that any finding significant at the .05 level or beyond is real and that any finding with a larger p value—even one only marginally larger—is zero.

Researchers must be disabused of the false belief that if a finding is not significant, it is zero. This belief has probably done more than any of the other false beliefs about significance testing to retard the growth of cumulative knowledge in psychology. Those of us concerned with the development of meta-analysis methods hope that demonstrations of the sort given earlier in this article will effectively eliminate this false belief.

I believe that these false beliefs are a major cause of the addiction of researchers to significance tests. Many researchers believe that statistical significance testing confers important benefits that are in fact completely imaginary. If we were clairvoyant and could enter the mind of a typical researcher, we might eavesdrop on the following thoughts:

> Significance tests have been repeatedly criticized by methodological specialists, but I find them very useful in interpreting my research data, and I have no intention of giving them up. If my findings are not significant, then I know that they probably just occurred by chance and that the true difference is probably zero. If the result is significant, then I know I have a reliable finding. The p values from the significance tests tell me whether the relationships in my data are large enough to be important or not. I can also determine from the p value what the chances are that these findings would replicate if I conducted a new study. These are very valuable things for a researcher to know. I wish the critics of significance testing would recognize this fact.

Every one of these thoughts about the benefits of significance testing is false. I ask the reader to ponder this question: Does this describe your thoughts about the significance test?

ANALYSIS OF COSTS AND BENEFITS

We saw earlier that meta-analysis reveals clearly the horrendous costs in failure to attain cumulative knowledge that psychology pays as the price for its addiction to significance testing. I expressed the hope that the appreciation of these massive costs will do what 40 years of logical demonstrations of the deficiencies of significance testing have failed to do: convince researchers to abandon the significance test in favor of point estimates of effect sizes and confidence intervals. But it seems unlikely to me that even these graphic demonstrations of costs will alone lead researchers to give up statistical significance testing. We must also consider the perceived benefits of significance testing. Researchers believe that significance testing confers important imaginary benefits. Many researchers may believe that these "benefits" are important enough to outweigh even the terrible costs that significance testing extracts from the research enterprise. It is unlikely that researchers will abandon significance testing unless and until they are educated to see that they are not getting the benefits they believe they are getting from significance testing. This means that quantitative psychologists and teachers of statistics and other methodological courses have the responsibility to teach researchers not only the high costs of significance testing but also the fact that the benefits typically ascribed to them are illusory. The failure to do the latter has been a major oversight for almost 50 years.

CURRENT SITUATION IN DATA ANALYSIS IN PSYCHOLOGY

There is a fundamental contradiction in the current situation with respect to quantitative methods. The research literatures and conclusions in our journals are now being shaped by the results and findings of meta-analyses, and this development is solving many of the problems created by reliance on significance testing (Cooper & Hedges, 1994; Hunter & Schmidt, 1990b). Yet the content of our basic graduate statistics courses has not changed (Aiken et al., 1990); we are training our young researchers in the discredited practices and methods of the past. Let us examine this anomaly in more detail.

Meta-analysis has explicated the critical role of sampling error, measurement error, and other artifacts in determining the observed findings and the statistical power of individual studies. In doing so, it has revealed how little information there typically is in any single study. It has shown that, contrary to widespread belief, a single primary study can rarely resolve an issue or answer a question. Any individual study must be considered a data point to be contributed to a future meta-analysis. Thus the scientific status and value of the individual study is necessarily lower than has typically been imagined in the past.

As a result, there has been a shift of the focus of scientific discovery in our research literatures from the individual primary study to the meta-analysis, creating a major change in the relative status of reviews. Journals that formerly published only primary studies and refused to publish reviews are now publishing meta-analytic reviews in large numbers. Today, many discoveries and advances in cumulative knowledge are being made not by those who do primary research studies but by those who use meta-analysis to discover the latent meaning of existing research literatures. This is apparent not only in the number of meta-analyses being published but also—and perhaps more important—in the shifting pattern of citations in the literature and in textbooks from primary studies to meta-analyses. The same is true in education, social psychology, medicine, finance, accounting, marketing, and other areas (Hunter & Schmidt, 1990a, chap. 1).

In my own substantive area of industrial/organizational psychology there is even some evidence of reduced reliance on significance testing in analyses of data within individual studies. Studies are much more likely today than in the past to report effect sizes and more likely to report confidence intervals. Results of significance tests are usually still reported, but they are now often sandwiched into parentheses almost as an afterthought and are often given appropriately minimal attention. It is rare today in industrial/organizational psychology for a finding to be touted as important solely on the basis of its p value.

Thus when we look at the research enterprise being conducted by the established researchers of our field, we see major improvements over the situation that prevailed even 10 years ago. However—and this is the worrisome part—there have been no similar improvements in the teaching of quantitative methods in graduate and undergraduate programs. Our younger generations of upcoming researchers are still being inculcated with the old, discredited methods of reliance on statistical significance testing. When we teach students how to analyze and interpret data in individual studies, we are still teaching them to apply t tests, F tests, chi-square tests, and ANOVAS. We are teaching them the same methods that for over 40 years made it impossible to discern the real meaning of data and research literatures and have therefore retarded the development of cumulative knowledge in psychology and the social sciences. We must introduce the reforms needed to solve this serious problem.

It will not be easy. At Michigan State University, John Hunter and Ralph Levine reformed the graduate statistics course sequence in psychology over the last 2 years along the general lines indicated in this article. The result was protests from significance testing traditionalists among the faculty. These faculty did not contend that the new methods were erroneous; rather, they were concerned that their graduate students might not be able to get their research published unless they used traditional significance testing-based methods of data analysis. They did not succeed in derailing the reform, but it has not been easy for these two pioneers. But this must be done and done everywhere. We can no longer tolerate a situation in which our upcoming generation of researchers are being trained to use discredited data analysis methods while the broader research enterprise of which they are to become a part has moved toward improved methods.

REFERENCES

Aiken, L. S., West, S. G., Sechrest, L., & Reno, R. R. (1990). Graduate training in statistics, methodology, and measurement in psychology: A survey of PhD programs in North America. *American Psychologist, 45,* 721–734.

Bakan, D. (1966). The test of significance in psychological research. *Psychological Bulletin, 66,* 423–437.

Bangert-Drowns, R. L. (1986). Review of developments in meta-analytic method. *Psychological Bulletin, 99,* 388–399.

Carver, R. P. (1978). The case against statistical significance testing. *Harvard Educational Review, 48,* 378–399.

Cohen, J. (1962). The statistical power of abnormal-social psychological research: A review. *Journal of Abnormal and Social Psychology, 65,* 145–153.

Cohen, J. (1988). *Statistical power analysis for the behavioral sciences* (2nd ed.) Hillsdale, NJ: Erlbaum.

Cohen, J. (1990). Things I have learned (so far). *American Psychologist, 45,* 1304–1312.

Cohen, J. (1994). The earth is round ($p < .05$). *American Psychologist, 49,* 997–1003.

Cooper, H. M., & Hedges, L. V. (1994). *Handbook of research synthesis.* New York: Russell Sage Foundation.

Cronbach, L. J. (1975). The two disciplines of scientific psychology revisited. *American Psychologist, 30,* 116–127.

Fisher, R. A. (1932). *Statistical methods for research workers* (4th ed.). Edinburgh, Scotland: Oliver & Boyd.

Fisher, R. A. (1935). *The design of experiments.* Edinburgh, Scotland: Oliver & Boyd.

Gergen, K. J. (1982). *Toward transformation in social knowledge.* New York: Springer-Verlag.

Glass, G. V., McGaw, B., & Smith, M. L. (1981). *Meta-analysis in social research.* Beverly Hills, CA: Sage.

Guttman, L. (1985). The illogic of statistical inference for cumulative science. *Applied Stochastic Models and Data Analysis, 1,* 3–10.

Hedges, L. V., & Olkin, I. (1980). Vote counting methods in research synthesis. *Psychological Bulletin, 88,* 359–369.

Hedges, L. V., & Olkin, I. (1985). *Statistical methods for meta-analysis.* Orlando, FL: Academic Press.

Huberty, C. J. (1993). Historical origins of statistical testing practices. *Journal of Experimental Education, 61*, 317–333.

Hunter, J. E. (1979, September). *Cumulating results across studies: A critique of factor analysis, canonical correlation, MANOVA, and statistical significance testing.* Invited address presented at the 86th Annual Convention of the American Psychological Association, New York, NY.

Hunter, J. E., & Schmidt, F. L. (1990a). Dichotomization of continuous variables: The implications for meta-analysis. *Journal of Applied Psychology, 75*, 334–349.

Hunter, J. E., & Schmidt, F. L. (1990b). *Methods of meta-analysis: Correcting error and bias in research findings.* Newbury Park, CA: Sage.

Hunter, J. E., & Schmidt, F. L. (in press). Cumulative research knowledge and social policy formulation: The critical role of meta-analysis. *Psychology, Public Policy, and Law.*

Hunter, J. E., Schmidt, F. L., & Jackson, G. B. (1982). *Meta-analysis: Cumulating research findings across studies.* Beverly Hills, CA: Sage.

Jones, L. V. (1955). Statistics and research design. *Annual Review of Psychology, 6*, 405–430.

Kish, L. (1959). Some statistical problems in research design. *American Sociological Review, 24*, 328–338.

Light, R. J., & Smith, P. V. (1971). Accumulating evidence: Procedures for resolving contradictions among different research studies. *Harvard Educational Review, 41*, 429–471.

Lipsey, M. W., & Wilson, D. B. (1993). The efficacy of psychological, educational, and behavioral treatment. *American Psychologist, 48*, 1181–1209.

Loftus, G. R. (1991). On the tyranny of hypothesis testing in the social sciences. *Contemporary Psychology, 36*, 102–105.

Loftus, G. R. (1994, August). *Why psychology will never be a real science until we change the way we analyze data.* Address presented at the American Psychological Association 102nd Annual Convention, Los Angeles, CA.

Lykken, D. (1968). Statistical significance in psychological research. *Psychological Bulletin, 70*, 151–159.

Meehl, P. E. (1967). Theory testing in psychology and physics: A methodological paradox. *Philosophy of Science, 34*, 103–115.

Meehl, P. E. (1978). Theoretical risks and tabular asterisks: Sir Karl, Sir Ronald and the slow process of soft psychology. *Journal of Consulting and Clinical Psychology, 46*, 806–834.

Neyman, J., & Pearson, E. S. (1932). The testing of statistical hypotheses in relation to probabilities a priori. *Proceedings of the Cambridge Philosophical Society, 29*, 492–516.

Neyman, J., & Pearson, E. S. (1933). On the problem of the most efficient tests of statistical hypotheses. *Philosophical Transactions of the Royal Society of London, A231*, 289–337.

Nunnally, J. C. (1975). *Introduction to statistics for psychology and education*. New York: McGraw-Hill.

Oakes, M. L. (1986). *Statistical inference: A commentary for the social and behavioral sciences*. New York: Wiley.

Rosenthal, R. (1984). *Meta-analytic procedures for social research*. Beverly Hills, CA: Sage.

Rosenthal, R. (1991). *Meta-analytic procedures for social research* (2nd ed.). Newbury Park, CA: Sage.

Rosenthal, R., & Gaito, J. (1963). The interpretation of levels of significance by psychological researchers. *Journal of Psychology, 55*, 33–38.

Rozeboom, W. W. (1960). The fallacy of the null hypothesis significance test. *Psychological Bulletin, 57*, 416–428.

Schmidt, F. L. (1992). What do data really mean? Research findings, meta-analysis, and cumulative knowledge in psychology. *American Psychologist, 47*, 1173–1181.

Schmidt, F. L., & Hunter, J. E. (1978). Moderator research and the law of small numbers. *Personnel Psychology, 31*, 215–232.

Schmidt, F. L., & Hunter, J. E. (1996). Measurement error in psychological research; Lessons from 26 research scenarios. *Psychological Methods, 1*, 199–223.

Schmidt, F. L., Hunter, J. E., & Urry, V. E. (1976). Statistical power in criterion-related validation studies. *Journal of Applied Psychology, 61*, 473–485.

Schmidt, F. L., Ocasio, B. P., Hillery, J. M., & Hunter, J. E. (1985). Further within-setting empirical tests of the situational specificity hypothesis in personnel selection. *Personnel Psychology, 38*, 509–524.

Sedlmeier, P., & Gigerenzer, G. (1989). Do studies of statistical power have an effect on the power of studies? *Psychological Bulletin, 105*, 309–316.

Winch, R. F., & Campbell, D. T. (1969). Proof? No. Evidence? Yes. The significance of tests of significance. *American Sociologist, 4*, 140–143.

19

THE APPROPRIATE USE OF NULL HYPOTHESIS TESTING

ROBERT W. FRICK

Null hypothesis testing is a statistical procedure used by most experimenters. Roughly speaking, an experimenter constructs a null hypothesis, such as there is no difference between conditions or no association between two variables, then calculates a value of p, which is conventionally defined as the probability of achieving the observed outcome or larger, given the null hypothesis. When p is less than some criterion, which is almost always .05, the experimenter "rejects" the null hypothesis and concludes that (a) one condition is better than another, (b) there is an association between two variables, or (c) some particular pattern exists in the data (Johnstone, 1987; Kaiser, 1960).

Null hypothesis testing has received severe criticism; among many it is taken as obvious that it should be abandoned (Cohen, 1994). For example, Oakes (1986, p. vii) wrote, "Many researchers retain an infatuation with

Reprinted from *Psychological Methods, 1*, 379–390. Copyright 1996 by the American Psychological Association.

significance tests despite the formidable arguments that have been presented against them. In Chapters 1–3 I marshal these arguments . . . in an attempt to kill the beast—but I suspect the headless corpse will continue to flail through journal pages for years to come." Or, "There is a long and honorable tradition of blistering attacks on the role of significance testing in the behavioral sciences, a tradition reminiscent of knights in shining armor bravely marching off, one by one, to slay a rather large and stubborn dragon. . . . Given the cogency, vehemence and repetition of such attacks, it is surprising to see that the dragon will not stay dead" (Harris, 1991, p. 375).

Despite these attacks, null hypothesis testing still dominates the social sciences (Loftus & Masson, 1994). Its continued use is typically attributed to experimenters' ignorance, misunderstanding, laziness, or adherence to tradition (Falk & Greenbaum, 1995; Johnstone, 1988; Nunnally, 1960; Oakes, 1986; Weitzman, 1984). However, as an anonymous reviewer put it, "A way of thinking that has survived decades of ferocious attacks is likely to have some value."

This article explains the value of null hypothesis testing. The attacks on null hypothesis testing point out its limitations but do not rule out its appropriate use. This article also builds on previous attempts to defend null hypothesis testing (e.g., Chow, 1988, 1991; Cox, 1977; Giere, 1972; Greenwald, Gonzalez, Harris, & Guthrie, 1996; Kalbfleisch & Sprott, 1976).

First, this article will consider the issue of the type of claim experimenters should be making, comparing what I will call *quantitative* to *ordinal* claims. For quantitative claims, null hypothesis testing is not sufficient and perhaps not the statistic of choice, but for ordinal claims it is ideal. Next, this article considers the role of null hypothesis testing in establishing these ordinal claims. Null hypothesis testing is not sufficient for establishing beliefs or estimating the probability that these ordinal claims are correct. Instead, it establishes that sufficient evidence has been presented to support a claim, with *sufficient* defined as $p < .05$. This is one criterion for a finding entering the corpus of psychology. Finally, reasons are presented for why experimenters are not allowed to choose their own value of alpha.

This article will be concerned with the use of null hypothesis testing when an effect is found, which is to say, when statistical significance is achieved. It is well agreed that null hypothesis testing by itself does not provide sufficient evidence for accepting the null hypothesis. (The issue of accepting the null hypothesis is addressed in Frick, 1995.)

When there is an effect, but the experiment does not have sufficient power to detect that effect using null hypothesis testing, the outcome is unfortunate. However, the problem is insufficient power, not the use of null hypothesis testing, and the only solution is to increase power (e.g., test more subjects or perform a meta-analysis across experiments).

SUPPORTING ORDINAL CLAIMS

One common criticism of null hypothesis testing begins with the assumption that experimenters should be interested in the size of an effect. If a drug impairs IQ 6 points, it is natural and appropriate to think of 6 as being a measure of "effect size" (Cohen, 1988, p. 10; Hunter & Schmidt, 1990, p. 233; Richardson, 1996), though there are a variety of other measures of effect size (cf. the American Psychological Association's *Publication Manual*, 1994, p. 18; Richardson, 1996). I call all claims about size of effect quantitative claims.

The assertions that conventional statistical testing actually slows or impedes science (Cohen, 1994; Loftus, 1994; Oakes, 1986) probably are based on the belief that estimating effect size is the ultimate goal of science. Cohen (1988) wrote, "A moment's thought suggests that it [effect size] is, after all, what science is all about. For sure, it's not about significance testing" (p. 532). If the goal of an experiment was to make a claim concerning size of effect, one could simply report the observed size of effect. If it was desirable to express the precision of this estimate, a confidence interval around this observed size of effect could also be reported. Null hypothesis testing would not be needed, and in fact would draw attention away from the size of the effect.

Instead of claiming the drug increases IQ 6 points, one could claim merely that the drug improves IQ. For convenience in exposition, I will refer to this type of claim as ordinal. An *ordinal claim* can be defined as one that does not specify the size of effect; alternatively, it could be defined as a claim that specifies only the order of conditions, the order of effects, or the direction of a correlation. The statistical operations used to justify these claims usually assume more than an ordinal scale, so an ordinal claim is ordinal only in the sense that the final claim is about order. In a factorial design, the ordinal claim of an interaction would be, for example, that an effect is larger in one situation than in another, without specifying the size of the difference between the two situations. In a correlational study, for example, obtaining a correlation between smoking and lung cancer, the value of r is a measure of the size of effect and the ordinal claim would be that smoking has a positive correlation with lung cancer.

Null hypothesis testing is used to provide support for ordinal claims, because establishing a pattern of order requires ruling out equivalence. The problem is that an observed effect in the data could have been caused by chance fluctuations, not by some "real" effect. Null hypothesis testing addresses whether or not there is sufficient evidence to support the existence of an effect. For example, to claim that a drug improved IQ, the experimenter would need statistical significance for the null hypothesis that the drug had no effect on IQ; to claim a correlation between smoking and lung cancer, the experimenter would need statistical significance for the null hypothesis that

$r = 0$. This explains the common use of 0 as a null hypothesis: The value of 0 neatly divides the space of possible effect sizes into the three relevant categories of no effect (the drug does not influence IQ), effect in one direction (the drug increases IQ), and effect in the other direction (the drug impairs IQ; Cox, 1977).

Knowing the exact size of effect would imply the direction of effect. However, no experiment ever establishes the exact size of an effect; all the experiment can do is establish the approximate size of effect, and knowing the approximate size of effect does not necessarily establish the direction of effect. Therefore, the two are different goals. For example, consider the confidence interval for a drug's effect on IQ. An experiment producing a confidence interval of $(-3, 7)$ establishes the size of effect just as well as an experiment producing a confidence interval of $(10, 20)$, but only the latter establishes the ordinal claim that the drug improves IQ.

A critical issue for the value of null hypothesis testing, hence, is whether the goal of experimenting always is determining the size of effect. I will consider three different statistical niches, formed by three different uses for the finding of an experiment: (a) testing a model making quantitative predictions, (b) supporting or disconfirming a law or theory, and (c) directly applying the finding to a practical situation. The argument will be that for one of these niches null hypothesis testing is inappropriate, for one it is insufficient but potentially useful, and for one it is ideal.

Models Making Quantitative Predictions

It is useful to think of theories as being statements about the workings of an underlying reality. As such, theories do not make quantitative predictions about the values that will be observed in the world. For example, Newton's theory includes statements about the force of gravity and the conservation of energy and momentum. Newton's theory, by itself, makes no predictions about the path of Mars (or any other object). However, with estimates of the mass of the sun and Mars, and the current position and velocity of Mars (with respect to the sun), Newton's theory can be used to model the path of Mars around the sun. Thus, models can be built with the purpose of making quantitative predictions. Models can also be based on regression estimates of potentially relevant variables.

For the purpose of testing the model, the issue might seem to be the accuracy of its predictions. However, as is well-accepted, quantitative predictions are never perfectly accurate. One problem is that the input variables are rarely perfectly accurate. A second problem is that a model usually ignores factors that might be having small effects. Third, when a model is based on regression estimates of potentially relevant variables, it might assume linear relationships, which is rarely correct.

For example, the model of the path of Mars presented here will necessarily be wrong, independent of any problems in Newton's theory. First, the estimates concerning the Sun and Mars will not be perfectly accurate. Second, this model ignores the influence of other heavenly bodies. The fact that the model is not perfect is hence uninteresting and does not disconfirm Newton's theory.

Null hypothesis testing could be used to compare the model's prediction to the observed value. However, because the fallibility of the model is known in advance, a statistically significant discrepancy from the model's prediction is not informative. This test will always be statistically significant, given enough power (Grant, 1962). Conversely, a lack of statistical significance does not mean the model is correct, it just means that not enough observations were made.

Thus, null hypothesis testing is not useful for testing a model (Berkson, 1938; Grant, 1962). Similarly, in comparing two models, it would be inappropriate to conclude that one model is correct just because another has been shown to be wrong by statistical testing.

Testing Laws and Theories

A second statistical niche is formed by experiments supporting or disconfirming a law or theory. To start, consider laws, which can be defined as claims relating the changes in two (or more) variables. A law is supported by demonstrating that it holds in a particular experiment.

An examination of any textbook will reveal that the laws in psychology are usually stated in an ordinal form, not quantitatively. For example, one law in psychology is that frustration increases the tendency to aggression. To test this law experimentally, the question for statistics would be whether frustration increased the amount of observed aggression, with the size of increase being irrelevant. Null hypothesis testing is ideal for supporting these ordinal laws. The size of the effect is irrelevant for supporting the law, and scientists seem to be interested in laws whether the effect size is large or small.

The size of effect is not completely irrelevant. First, the size of effect might signal the importance of the manipulated variable in the process being studied. Second, the robustness of the effect is important for purposes of further experimentation, with larger effect sizes being easier to replicate. However, for these two purposes, the exact size of effect is not important. For example, a classic experiment by Sperling (1960) compared whole report to partial report for brief visual presentations. Whole report capacity was about 4.5 and partial report suggested a capacity of about 9. It is important that the difference between these two conditions was 4.5 rather than .5. However, a difference of 3.5 or 13.5 would have had essentially the same meaning.

The point of disagreement with regard to null hypothesis testing is not whether the current laws in psychology are ordinal; the disagreement is whether experiments should be trying to support ordinal laws. With everything else being equal, a quantitative law contains more information than an ordinal law and hence would be preferred.

The problem for quantitative laws, however, is generality. It is easy to form a quantitative law on the basis of an experimental finding—one simply reports the size of the effect. However, a law holding for just one very narrow situation is not very useful and cannot be usefully added to the collection of laws comprising the science of psychology. Therefore, for a law to be of any value, it must generalize across different situations.

As examples will suggest, there are substantial and perhaps insurmountable obstacles to forming quantitative laws with generality. Consider the law that frustration increases the tendency to aggression. The exact size of the effect would depend on a very large number of different factors. First, there are a variety of different ways of measuring aggression. Second, the amount of increase in aggression depends on the size of the manipulation of frustration. These are a variety of ways of manipulating frustration, and the effectiveness of each will vary. The ordinal law would be expected to generalize to new methods of producing frustration and new methods of measuring tendency to aggression; it is difficult to imagine how any quantitative expression of this law would generalize to new manipulations of frustration or new measures of aggression.

Third, it would be unlikely that any scale of aggression would be an interval scale, which would be needed to make quantitative predictions with any economy. For example, if a given amount of frustration is going to increase aggression by 2, it must increase the level of aggression from 1 to 3, from 2 to 4, and from 3 to 5, which implies an interval scale. With just an ordinal scale, there is no simple relationship between increase in frustration and increase in aggression—instead, the relationship between aggression and frustration would have to be plotted for each level of frustration.

Fourth, the ordinal law that frustration increases aggression presumably applies to a wide variety of people and situations. However, a law claiming a specific size of increase in aggression will apply only to the sample and situation used in the experiment supporting that law. For example, the effect might be larger in less emotionally mature people, or it might depend on intelligence, age, or amount of schooling. Sears (1986) noted that the size of effect for social phenomena in college students does not generalize well to noncollege students, but the ordinal pattern does.

Thus, examples suggest several reasons why psychology does not contain quantitative laws with generality. One exception is in psychophysics. Psychophysicists have interval scales for their manipulations (e.g., brightness), they use a common scale for measurement (e.g., probability of detection), and they try to control for the effect of all extraneous variables (such as amount of adaptation to light). As a result, they can and do attempt to construct quantitative conclusions, with Weber's Law standing as a good example. Nonetheless, examination of a sensation and perception textbook

(Levine & Shefner, 1991) reveals a presentation of more ordinal than quantitative claims, suggesting a small range for quantitative laws.

The story is the same for theories. Theories can be roughly defined as one or more statements (a) about underlying and often unobservable constructs that (b) together make predictions. Currently, most theories in psychology yield predictions about ordinal patterns, not size of effect. For example, the existence of iconic memory predicts that, for brief visual presentations, partial report can be superior to full report. Thus, testing theories requires testing ordinal predictions, so null hypothesis testing is ideal for this niche.

Physics has had great success with theories that make quantitative predictions, and many people hope that the theories in psychology will eventually make quantitative predictions. However, again there seems to be possibly insurmountable problems in constructing theories that by themselves make quantitative predictions. Consider the prediction of better partial report of a brief visual presentation. The existence of iconic memory makes no prediction about the size of this effect, because the size of effect depends on many factors completely extraneous to the theory. First, the size of increase depends on details concerning the stimulus array. Second, it depends on the rate of decay from iconic memory versus the time at which subjects process the cue and focus on the relevant part of the display. For example, Sperling used tones to cue subjects as to which row would be reported; subject's performance was influenced by how perceivable and discriminable the tones were.

Therefore, prior to performing the experiment, it would have been impossible to make a quantitative prediction. After the experiment was performed, a quantitative prediction would be possible for the particular situation tested in the experiment. However, this would not be an example of the theory making a quantitative prediction.

Sometimes a theory will predict that one effect is larger than another. This is a prediction about effect size, but it is still an ordinal prediction: Is there a difference in effect sizes, and if so, which is larger? Similarly, with regard to laws, one can ask if an effect in one situation is the same, larger, or smaller in a new situation. Conventional statistical testing can address the comparison of sizes of effect in two ways. If the exact size of the original effect was already known, it could be used as the null hypothesis. If the size of the first effect is also being measured, an F test can be performed for the presence of an interaction, comparing the effect size in one condition to the effect size in another condition.

Thus, the current status of psychology is that theories and laws are tested by ordinal patterns. Null hypothesis testing is then used to support these laws and theories. A goal of many is that the laws and theories in psychology be quantitative. Physics obviously has had great success with quantitative laws, so it is natural to hope that psychology could have the same success. However, the goal of quantitative laws is old, and it has not proved very successful. Some people are still working toward this goal, and perhaps they will eventually succeed. However, it is at least possible that the long-standing goal to found psychology as a quantitative science might be impossible and that psychology perhaps should take pride in its successes as an ordinal science. In any case, current experimenters have to deal with the current condition, which is laws and theories making ordinal predictions.

Practical Applications

The third statistical niche is formed by experiments intending to use the results for immediate practical application. For example, an experiment might find that Treatment A is more effective than Treatment B, then use this finding to support the use of Treatment A.

If everything else is constant, then this ordinal claim is enough to decide that Treatment A should be used over Treatment B. However, it is rare for everything else to be held constant. For example, the treatments might differ in their cost or side effects. Whenever a decision must be made balancing costs and benefits, it is important to consider the size of the costs and benefits. Therefore, the size of effect is always important in the practical application experiment.

Because size of effect is important, exclusive reliance on null hypothesis testing is inappropriate. Instead, it is important to distinguish statistical significance from "clinical significance" or "practical significance" (Cohen, 1965; Edwards, 1950; Grant, 1962; Tyler, 1931)—just because a result is statistically significant does not mean that it is clinically significant.

However, although null hypothesis testing is insufficient, that does not mean that null hypothesis testing cannot play a role. Some experimenters apparently use null hypothesis testing in the following manner. First, a difference is shown to be statistically significant. Then the obtained effect size is used as an estimate of the actual effect size. Finally, either the experimenter or consumer judges whether or not the obtained effect size is clinically significant. Another possibility is to first determine the minimal size of a clinically significant effect. This minimally relevant size can be used as a null hypothesis. Rejecting this null hypothesis would suggest that the true difference is clinically significant (Fowler, 1985).

Confidence Intervals

Two different functions of confidence intervals should be distinguished. First, confidence intervals can be used to indicate the precision of the estimate of effect size. For example, the 95% confidence interval of 6 ± 2 shows more precision than the 95% confidence interval of 6 ± 5. This function of the confidence interval is appropriate whenever size of effect is the issue.

Technically, whether or not 0 is part of the confidence interval is not an issue.

Second, a 95% confidence interval can function to indicate which values could not be rejected by a two-tailed test with alpha at .05. In this function, the confidence interval could replace the report of null hypothesis for just one value, instead communicating the outcome of the tests of all values as null hypotheses (e.g., Cohen, 1994). This function does not avoid the logic of null hypothesis testing, however—Cohen (1994) was being illogical when he criticized the logic of null hypothesis testing and then advocated using the confidence interval because it reported the results of all statistical tests.

Usually there is one particular value of interest as a null hypothesis, because rejecting this value establishes an ordinal pattern the experimenter wishes to claim. The value of p for this null hypothesis contains important information, as is discussed later in this article, so it should be reported (Greenwald et al., 1996). It would be inappropriate to replace this report of p with a confidence interval (Spjotvoll, 1977). Therefore, replacing the report of the test of one null hypothesis with a confidence interval is inappropriate when null hypothesis testing is being used to support an ordinal claim.

Evaluation

As critics have long noted, not all experimenters can mindlessly perform null hypothesis testing, achieve statistical significance, and be done. Instead, null hypothesis testing is sometimes of little value (when testing models making quantitative predictions) and sometimes insufficient (for the practice application experiment). However, null hypothesis testing is ideal for supporting ordinal claims. Examples suggest that psychology might always have laws and theories making ordinal predictions, and in any case this is the situation most experimenters currently face.

DEMONSTRATING SUFFICIENT EVIDENCE

A second major attack on null hypothesis testing begins with the assumption that the goal in science is to establish the degree to which a claim warrants belief. For example, in his criticism of null hypothesis testing, Rozeboom (1960) wrote, "The primary aim of a scientific experiment is not to precipitate decisions, but to make an appropriate adjustment in the degree to which one accepts, or believes, the hypothesis or hypotheses being tested" (p. 420).

It is useful to distinguish personal belief from warranted belief. *Personal belief* is what a person actually believes. *Warranted belief* is what a person should believe, given the available information. Thus, warranted belief is rational. If a personal belief was formed rationally, it would also be a warranted belief, but obviously personal beliefs are not always formed rationally.

Personal beliefs are obviously relevant to the pursuit of science, but they presumably should not be a part of formal science. For example, whether or not a manuscript is accepted for publication presumably should depend on the strength of evidence, the importance of the finding, and so on, not whether the conclusion matches the reviewer's personal beliefs. Therefore, the suggestions that beliefs should play a role in formal science presumably refer to warranted belief.

Degree of warranted belief in a claim would be quantified as the rationally estimated probability that a claim is correct. Therefore, the terms *warranted belief* and *probability correct* are interchangeable in the following discussions.

Null Hypothesis Testing: Not a Method of Supporting Beliefs

Null hypothesis testing is not a good method of estimating the probability that a claim is correct. First, according to the traditional interpretation, p is the probability of the observed results or larger given the null hypothesis, not the probability that the null hypothesis is correct. Therefore, null hypothesis testing does not determine the probability that a claim is correct (Bakan, 1966; Cohen, 1994; Oakes, 1986; Wilson, 1961).

Second, the overall probability that a claim is correct should take into account not only the evidence from a single experiment, but also evidence from previous experiments and the plausibility of the claim given other knowledge (Cox, 1958). Suppose one experimenter claims that eating Jell-O increases weight and another claims that eating Jell-O increases IQ, and both have evidence for their claim at $p = .04$. The former claim is more likely to be correct, because it is a priori plausible and the latter claim is not.

Third, null hypothesis testing has a "cliff" at .05. The value of p is compared to alpha, which is almost always set at .05. Success is then achieved when p is less than .05, creating a cliff: The value $p = .04$ is treated the same as $p = .001$, even though the two are very different; .06 is treated the same as .80, even though these two are also very different; and $p = .04$ is treated differently from $p = .06$, even though the two are nearly the same.

This cliff has often been criticized (e.g., Eysenck, 1960; Kempthorne, 1971; Morrison & Henkel, 1969; Oakes, 1986; Rozeboom, 1960). In fact, this cliff makes no sense from the standpoint of modifying beliefs. For example, $p = .001$ is a much better reason to modify a belief than $p = .04$, and $p = .04$ does not provide much more reason for modifying a belief than $p = .06$. Therefore, null hypothesis testing would not be the tool of choice if the goal in science was to determine the probability of a claim being correct.

Establishing Sufficient Evidence

If null hypothesis testing does not determine beliefs, what does it accomplish? It begins with the calculation of a test statistic, such as t or F. The size of this statistic is a monotonically increasing function of the strength of evidence for an ordinal claim. For example, if two experimenters have identical experiments, the one with the higher value of t has the stronger evidence.

The value of p is defined as the probability of obtaining this value of the test statistic or larger if the null hypothesis is true. Converting this test statistic to a value of p creates a common measure of strength of evidence across statistical tests (Greenwald et al., 1996). Thus, $p = .04$ is equally strong evidence for a t test, F test, Mann-Whitney, or whatever statistical test is being used.

Finally, the obtained value of p is compared to a criterion alpha, which is conventionally set at .05 (for reasons to be explained later in this article). When p is less than .05, the experimenter has sufficient empirical evidence to support a claim. Thus, statistical testing functions to establish sufficient evidence to support a claim, with the criterion held constant across experiments.

Establishing a Corpus of Findings

Rozeboom (1960) suggested that scientists should not be making decisions about claims, they should be calculating and updating the probability of these claims. However, this does not seem practical. If there were only a handful of potential claims in any given area of psychology, it would be feasible to assign them probabilities, to be constantly updating the probabilities, and to expect experimenters to keep track of these ever-changing probabilities. In fact, just the number of claims in psychology is overwhelming. It would probably be impossible for human beings to keep track of the probability for each claim, especially if these probabilities were constantly changing. In any case, scientists do not assign probabilities to claims. Instead, scientists act like the goal of science is to collect a corpus of claims that are considered to be established (Giere, 1972).

It is useful to divide this corpus into two types of claims. The first type is general laws and theories, such as the law that frustration increases the tendency to aggression. These general laws and theories are essentially the knowledge of psychology. The second type of claim is experimental findings. For example, an experimental finding might be that, for these subjects in this experiment, frustration led to increased aggression, or a drug caused an improvement in IQ (as opposed to a difference between conditions being caused by just chance fluctuations). (The interpretation needed to allow null hypothesis testing to support this type of finding is presented in Frick, 1996.)

This corpus of findings provides the support for laws and theories. A scientist asserting some law or theory will often provide his or her own experimental finding as support. However, the scientist can cite other findings to support the law or theory, and there should not be any experimental findings that contradict the law or theory. Thus, using this corpus is both an opportunity and an obligation.

According to Cook and Campbell (1979), there are four steps to establishing validity. The first step, achieving statistical conclusion validity, is demonstrating that an effect is statistically significant. The second and third steps, achieving internal and construct validity, are verifying that there are no confounds. Experimental findings that pass these steps apparently are accepted as part of the corpus of psychology. Before publication, an experimental finding is examined by reviewers. If it does not meet these requirements it will not be published. Publication is then taken as certification by experts that the finding has passed these requirements. However, a finding's legitimacy (which is to say, its membership in the corpus of acceptable findings) can be later challenged by noting a confound or something inappropriate about the statistical test. If a finding is not published in a journal, it still can be accepted as a legitimate finding when these requirements are met.

This role of null hypothesis testing—as one of the criteria for a finding entering the corpus of psychology—explains the cliff (Chow, 1991). Cliffs are created by the need to make categorical decisions. For example, to be directly elected to the baseball hall of fame, a player must receive 75% of the votes of the baseball writers. A player either receives sufficient votes to be elected or does not. With regard to assessing worthiness to enter the hall of fame, there is no cliff at 75%. However, with regard to eligibility to enter the hall of fame, there is a huge cliff at 75%. In null hypothesis testing, the categorical decision is between sufficient and insufficient evidence to support a finding. The line between the two is currently set at $p = .05$.

The Bayesian Alternative

The need for a categorical decision—about whether or not a claim should enter the corpus of psychology—does not rule out warranted belief as a criterion. In addition to other criteria, should the criterion for entering the corpus of psychology be warranted belief or strength of evidence? If the answer is warranted belief, the next question is, What statistical test would be best for determining warranted belief?

A Bayesian statistical analysis (e.g., Edwards, Lindman, & Savage, 1963; Jeffreys, 1961; Oakes, 1986) takes into account the prior probabilities of the possible hypotheses, combines them with the available evidence, and yields (with suitable integration) the probability of the given claim being correct. One study found that, with any reasonable assumption about prior probabilities, a Bayesian analysis would outperform conventional statistical testing (Samaniego & Reneau, 1994). Therefore, if the goal was to estimate the probability that a claim was correct, a Bayesian analysis would be a very attractive alternative to null hypothesis testing.

However, there are several problems with a Bayesian analysis. First, the estimate of prior probabilities is subjective and somewhat arbitrary. As will be discussed, it is undesirable for the outcome of a statistical test to depend on subjective, arbitrary, or possibly biased choices by the experimenter. Of course, the current practice of forming beliefs is also subjective. Null hypothesis testing is used to evaluate the strength of evidence, and then combined subjectively with the results of other experiments and available theories, which would be presented along with the experimental finding. It is not clear which of these procedures is more subjective.

Second, it is not clear that a Bayesian analysis is more accurate than the current subjective practice. Oakes (1986) noted that constructing prior probabilities is not easy. It is somewhat contradictory to expect people to be able to intuitively construct good prior probabilities and yet require statistical testing to avoid the intuitive construction of final probabilities. Oakes also noted that there have been suggestions to adjust the prior probability so that the conclusion matches the user's expectations. This would undermine the rationale of a Bayesian analysis. Moreover, this suggestion implies that people can more accurately construct final beliefs than prior beliefs.

A third problem is the transient nature of the answer produced by the Bayesian analysis. The factor that would influence the prior probabilities would change across time, so the results of a Bayesian analysis would change across time. Thus, any Bayesian analysis would apply to only a short period of time. In contrast, the results of the null hypothesis test are an unchanging record of the amount of evidence supporting the finding. Obviously, it is more valuable to publish an unchanging statistic than one that quickly becomes outdated.

Thus, there are problems with using a Bayesian analysis. If beliefs should be the criterion, it is not clear that a Bayesian analysis would be better than the current practice.

Should Beliefs Be the Criterion?

The next question is, Should warranted belief be the criterion for a claim entering the corpus of psychology? For general laws and theories, the answer seems to be yes: Laws and theories presumably should be part of the corpus of psychology if and only if they are well-supported by all of the findings, not just the particular finding being presented by the experimenter.

However, there is a critical disadvantage to making warranted belief a criterion for findings entering the corpus of psychology (Oakes, 1986). Suppose the finding of one experiment would be consistent with current theories and expectations in psychology and the finding of a second experiment would contradict current theories and expectations. Suppose also that both findings achieve the same value of p, say $p = .02$. The first finding is more likely to be correct, which is to say warranted belief is higher for the first finding than the second. If warranted belief was the criterion for entering the corpus of psychology, the first finding would have an advantage over the second, and it is plausible that the second finding might not generate sufficient warranted belief to meet the criterion.

However, the second finding is the more valuable of the two. Findings that are consistent with current theories and expectations as a general rule do not advance a field of knowledge; the field is advanced by unexpected findings and findings that contradict current laws and theories. Therefore, if everything else is equal, unexpected findings are preferred over expected findings. The problem with using warranted belief as a criterion is that it gives a substantial advantage to expected findings over unexpected findings.

For example, consider Garcia's difficulties (described in Garcia, 1981) publishing his finding of learned taste aversion, which contradicted the dominant learning theory of the time. It is reasonable that psychologists of the time might not immediately believe Garcia's finding. However, it would have been unfortunate if his finding had not been published. More generally, science would not work well if the acceptance of a theory led to repression of findings inconsistent with the theory and facilitation of findings consistent with the theory. Therefore, warranted belief would not be a good criterion for a finding entering the corpus of psychology.

Evaluation

Thus, psychology seems to work by having a corpus of claims. The criterion for belief in laws and theories probably should be warranted belief, but warranted belief would not be a good criterion for findings. The criterion for findings, which seems appropriate, is a lack of confounds and sufficient evidential support. Null hypothesis testing is then used to demonstrate sufficient evidential support, giving it an important and appropriate role in psychology.

SETTING ALPHA

In practice, the general rule is that alpha is set at .05 (Sterling, Rosenbaum, & Weinkam, 1995). However, many people believe that experimenters should be allowed to set their own value of alpha. For example, the APA *Publication Manual* (American Psychological Association, 1994) asks experimenters to report alpha, implying that they have a choice. The claim that experimenters should set their own value of alpha is not an attack on null hypothesis testing as described in textbooks, but it is an attack on null hypothesis testing as it is practiced in current psychology.

There are two reasons for adjusting alpha in statistical testing. The issue is whether they apply to the use of null hypothesis testing to demonstrate sufficient evidence for a finding.

Adjusting Alpha to Reflect Costs and Benefits

If a statistical test is being used to decide between actions, the decisions' costs (when wrong) and benefits (when correct) should be incorporated into alpha (Neyman & Pearson, 1933b; Oakes, 1986; Skipper, Guenther, & Nass, 1967). For example, if someone has a cold, it is relatively harmless to take vitamin C if it doesn't help and relatively valuable to take vitamin C if it does help. Thus, despite apparently uncertain evidence concerning the efficacy of vitamin C, many people take it for a cold.

However, suppose an experimenter wanted to publish a claim that taking vitamin C reduced the duration of a cold. Obviously, that experimenter should not be allowed to use a high value of alpha just because the action supported by that claim might be useful and cannot hurt. Instead, the claim should be backed by standard levels of evidence. Science is in the business of providing knowledge, not making decisions for people. The users of a finding can incorporate their own cost-benefit analysis into their decision.

The only action science takes is to publish a claim. Some claims are more important than others, which is to say they will attract more attention and use. Therefore, they have a higher benefit when correct. However, these claims also have a higher cost when wrong. Therefore, there is no obvious cost–benefit reason for why important claims should deserve a higher or lower value of alpha than any other claim.

Thus, it is important to consider costs and benefits when deciding between actions. However, there is little or no reason with respect to costs and benefits for adjusting alpha from one experiment to another.

Minimizing Error

A second reason for adjusting alpha is to minimize the total probability of error (Cohen, 1965; Neyman & Pearson, 1933a; Oakes, 1986; Winer, 1962). Suppose an experimenter is in the situation of choosing between two well-defined point hypotheses. For example, the experimenter might be trying to decide if a drug has (a) no effect on IQ or (b) raises IQ 6 points. In this situation, the experimenter can calculate the power of the experiment, which is defined as the likelihood of achieving statistical significance if the drug actually does increase IQ 6 points. The probability of making a Type II error (not rejecting the null hypothesis when the null hypothesis is incorrect) is equal to $1 -$ power. The total probability of making an error (the probability of making a Type 1 error plus the probability of making a Type II error) will be minimized by choosing a value of alpha that equalizes the two types of errors.

For example, suppose a very large number of subjects were being tested, such that, with alpha at .05, there would be 5% chance of making a Type I error and much less than a 1% chance of making a Type II error. The total probability of error would be between 5% and 6%. If alpha was lowered to .01, there would be only a 1% chance of making a Type I error and, assuming enough power, possibly still less than a 1% chance of making a Type II error, creating a total probability of error between 1% and 2%. Thus, adjusting alpha would lower the total probability of error. Similarly, if power was low, alpha could be raised to equalize the probability of Type I and Type II errors and lower the total probability of error.

However, experimenters usually are not in the situation of choosing between two well-defined point hypotheses (as noted by Neyman, 1950, p. 324). Instead, null hypothesis testing is used by experimenters to choose between the null hypothesis and some ordinal conclusion. Within this framework, there is no basis for determining the probability of a Type II error, hence no basis for adjusting alpha to lower total probability of error.

More important, the total probability of error is not the issue. First, when the null hypothesis is rejected, there is no chance of a Type II error. Second, null hypothesis testing is being used to demonstrate a sufficient amount of evidence. It would be inappropriate to choose a high value of alpha just to compensate for the fact that one was running an experiment with low power. It would similarly be inappropriate to ignore a finding at p less than .05 just because an experiment had high power.

Thus, when power can be known and when the goal is to reduce the total probability of error, it is useful to be able to adjust alpha. However, experimenters are not in this position—they are not choosing between two well-defined point hypotheses and they are not using null hypothesis testing to minimize the probability of error.

Objectivity

Thus, despite claims to the contrary (e.g., Labovitz, 1968), there is little reason for experimenters to choose different levels of alpha. On the other hand, allowing experimenters to choose their own alpha would inject a subjective element into statistical testing, which would be undesirable (Glass, McGaw, & Smith, 1981; Rozeboom, 1960). As Hick (1952) noted, the results of statistical testing should be determined only by the data, not the experimenter's opinion. Or, as Cox (1977) put it, two different experimenters should not reach different statistical conclusions given the same data.

Put another way, the question is, Should the experimenter decide what amount of evidence is sufficient for a finding to enter the corpus of psychology? Obviously not. In addition to being subjective and arbitrary, one might worry that experimenters would be biased in the selection of alpha for their own experiment. Furthermore, it would not work well if the experimenter could choose one value of alpha and other people citing the finding could choose a different level of alpha and come to a different conclusion. Therefore, to avoid the influence of the experimenter's opinions, judgments, and biases, it is desirable that experimenters not choose their own value of alpha. Instead, it is appropriate that alpha is set by the enterprise of psychology.

SUMMARY

Null hypothesis testing can be easily criticized (a) assuming that it should be accomplishing something it does not, (b) assuming that experimenters should be accomplishing goals that do not require null hypothesis testing, or (c) not appreciating the situation in which null hypothesis testing is used. These criticisms usefully point out the limitations of null hypothesis testing. It is inappropriate for testing the quantitative predictions of models, it is insufficient for the practical application experiment, it is insufficient for the practical application experiment, it is insufficient for determining warranted belief given all of the evidence, and an inflexible alpha is inappropriate when costs and benefits change or when the goal is to minimize overall error.

However, these restrictions do not rule out its use—null hypothesis testing is useful for demonstrating sufficient empirical evidence to support an ordinal claim. Because this is a common function in psychology, null hypothesis testing is appropriately used often. Experimenters commonly use a finding to test an ordinal law or the ordinal prediction of theory, findings are categorized as being acceptable or not to enter the corpus of claims in psychology, and sufficient evidence is an appropriate criterion for a claim being acceptable and warranted belief is not. The cost-benefit ratio does not change, the goal is not to minimize overall error, and subjective judgments by the experimenter are undesirable, so allowing the experimenter to select alpha is unneeded and inappropriate.

This article has not attempted to defend much of the philosophical justification typically associated with null hypothesis testing. Instead, it considered the practice of null hypothesis testing, justifying it only as an optimal procedure for assessing whether there is sufficient evidence in an experiment to support an ordinal finding.

REFERENCES

American Psychological Association. (1994). *Publication manual*. Washington, DC: Author.

Bakan, D. (1966). The test of significance in psychological research. *Psychological Bulletin, 66*, 423–437.

Berkson, J. (1938). Some difficulties of interpretation encountered in the application of the chi-square test. *Journal of the American Statistical Association, 33,* 526–542.

Chow, S. L. (1988). Significance test or effect size? *Psychological Bulletin, 103,* 105–110.

Chow, S. L. (1991). Conceptual rigor versus practical impact. *Theory & Psychology, 1,* 337–360, 389–400.

Cohen, J. (1965). Some statistical issues in psychological research. In B. B. Wolman (Ed.), *Handbook of clinical psychology* (pp. 95–121). New York: McGraw-Hill.

Cohen, J. (1988). *Statistical power analysis for the behavioral sciences* (2nd ed.). Hillsdale, NJ: Erlbaum.

Cohen, J. (1994). The earth is round (*p* < .05). *American Psychologist, 49,* 997–1003.

Cook, T. D., & Campbell, D. T. (1979). *Quasi-experimentation: Design and analysis issues for field settings.* Chicago: Rand McNally.

Cox, D. R. (1958). Some problems connected with statistical inference. *Annals of Mathematical Statistics, 29,* 357–372.

Cox, D. R. (1977). The role of significance tests. *Scandinavian Journal of Statistics, 4,* 49–70.

Edwards, A. L. (1950). *Experimental design in psychological research.* New York: Rinehart.

Edwards, W., Lindman, H., & Savage, L. (1963). Bayesian statistical inference for psychological research. *Psychological Review, 70,* 193–242.

Eysenck, H. J. (1960). The concept of statistical significance and the controversy about one-tailed tests. *Psychological Review, 67,* 269–271.

Falk, R., & Greenbaum, C. W. (1995). Significance tests die hard: The amazing persistence of a probabilistic misconception. *Theory & Psychology, 5,* 75–98.

Fowler, R. L. (1985). Testing for substantive significance in applied research by specifying nonzero effect null hypotheses. *Journal of Applied Psychology, 70,* 215–218.

Frick, R. W. (1995). Accepting the null hypothesis. *Memory and Cognition, 23,* 132–138.

Frick, R. W. (1996). *Interpreting statistical testing: Not random sampling from a population.* Submitted for publication.

Garcia, J. (1981). Tilting at the windmills of academe. *American Psychologist, 36,* 149–158.

Giere, R. N. (1972). The significance test controversy. *The British Journal for the Philosophy of Science, 23,* 170–181.

Glass, G. V., McGraw, B., & Smith, M. L. (1981). *Meta-analysis in social research.* Beverly Hills, CA: Sage.

Grant, D. A. (1962). Testing the null hypothesis and the strategy and tactics of investigating theoretical models. *Psychological Review, 69,* 54–61.

Greenwald, A. G., Gonzalez, R., Harris, R. J., & Guthrie, D. (1996). Effect sizes and p-values: What should be reported and what should be replicated? *Psychophysiology, 33,* 175–183.

Harris, M. J. (1991). Significance tests are not enough: The role of effect-size estimation in theory corroboration. *Theory & Psychology, 1,* 375–382.

Hick, W. E. (1952). A note on one-tailed and two-tailed tests. *Psychological Review, 59,* 316–318.

Hunter, J. E., & Schmidt, F. L. (1990). *Methods of meta-analysis: Correcting error and bias in research findings.* Newbury Park, CA: Sage.

Jeffreys, H. (1961). *Theory of probability.* Oxford: Clarendon Press.

Johnstone, D. J. (1987). Tests of significance following R. A. Fisher. *The British Journal for the Philosophy of Science, 38,* 481–499.

Johnstone, D. J. (1988). Comments on Oakes on the foundations of statistical inference in the social and behavioral sciences: The market for statistical significance. *Psychological Reports, 63,* 319–331.

Kaiser, H. F. (1960). Directional statistical decision. *Psychological Review, 67,* 160–167.

Kalbfleisch, J. G., & Sprott, D. A. (1976). On test of significance. In W. L. Harper & C. A. Hooker (Eds.), *Foundations of probability theory, statistical inference, and statistical theories of science* (Vol. 2, pp. 259–272). Dordrecht, Holland: Reidel.

Kempthorne, O. (1971). Probability, statistics, and the knowledge business. In V. P. Godambe & D. A. Sprott (Eds.), *Foundations of statistical inferences* (pp. 470–490). Toronto: Holt, Rinehart, & Winston.

Labovitz, S. (1968). Criteria for selecting a significance level: A note on the sacredness of .05. *American Sociologist, 3,* 200–222.

Levine, M. W., & Shefner, J. M. (1991). *Fundamentals of sensation and perception* (2nd ed.). Pacific Grove, CA: Brooks-Cole.

Loftus, G. R. (1994, August). *Why psychology will never be a real science until we change the way we analyze data.* Paper presented at the 102nd Annual Convention of the American Psychological Association, Los Angeles, CA.

Loftus, G. R., & Masson, M. J. (1994). Using confidence intervals in within-subject designs. *Psychonomic Bulletin & Review, 1,* 476–490.

Morrison, D. E., & Henkel, R. E. (1969). Significance tests reconsidered. *American Sociologist, 4,* 131–140.

Neyman, J. (1950). *First course in probability and statistics.* New York: Holt.

Neyman, J., & Pearson, E. S. (1933a). On the problem of the most efficient tests of statistical inference. *Biometrika, 20A,* 175–240, 263–294.

Neyman, J., & Pearson, E. S. (1933b). The testing of statistical hypotheses in relation to probabilities a priori. *Proceedings of the Cambridge Philosophical Society, 29,* 492–510.

Nunnally, J. C. (1960). The place of statistics in psychology. *Educational and Psychological Measurement, 20,* 641–650.

Oakes, M. (1986). *Statistical inference: A commentary for the social and behavioral sciences*. New York: Wiley.

Richardson, J. T. E. (1996). Measures of effect size. *Behavior Research Methods, Instruments, & Computers, 28*, 12–22.

Rozeboom, W. W. (1960). The fallacy of the null hypothesis significance test. *Psychological Bulletin, 57*, 416–428.

Samaniego, F. J., & Reneau, D. M. (1994). Toward a reconciliation of the Bayesian and frequentist approaches to point estimation. *Journal of the American Statistical Association, 89*, 947–957.

Sears, D. O. (1986). College sophomores in the laboratory: Influences of a narrow data base on social psychology's view of human nature. *Journal of Personality and Social Psychology, 51*, 515–530.

Skipper, Jr., J. K., Guenther, A. L., & Nass, G. (1967). The sacredness of .05: A note concerning the uses of statistical levels of significance in social science. *American Sociologist, 2*, 16–18.

Sperling, G. (1960). The information available in brief visual presentations. *Psychological Monographs, 74*, 1–29.

Spjotvoll, E. (1977). Discussion of D. R. Cox's paper. *Scandinavian Journal of Statistics, 4*, 63–66.

Sterling, T. D., Rosenbaum, W. L., & Weinkam, J. J. (1995). Publication decisions revisited: The effect of the outcome of statistical tests on the decision to publish and vice versa. *American Statistician, 49*, 108–112.

Tyler, R. W. (1931). What is statistical significance? *Educational Research Bulletin, 10*, 115–118, 142.

Weitzman, R. A. (1984). Seven treacherous pitfalls of statistics, illustrated. *Psychological Reports, 54*, 355–363.

Wilson, K. V. (1961). Subjectivist statistics for the current crisis. *Contemporary Psychology, 6*, 229–231.

Winer, B. J. (1962). *Statistical principles in experimental design*. New York: McGraw Hill.

V

SPECIAL TOPICS IN CLINICAL RESEARCH

A variety of special circumstances, methods, and problems emerge in clinical research. Articles in this section illustrate special situations and methods for research and evaluation and hence supplement more traditional methods covered previously.

CASE STUDY AND SMALL SAMPLE RESEARCH

There has been little systematic evaluation of psychotherapy as it is administered in clinical practice, either through the use of measures of client change or documentation that treatment is responsible for change. Instead of systematic assessment, clinical judgment is used as the basis of measurement. Indeed, clinical judgment is usually the basis to decide what the client "needs," what treatment ought to be applied, whether therapeutic changes have been achieved, and when to stop or alter treatment. Clinical judgment and clinicians have been roundly criticized because judgment has not fared very well when compared to the use of more systematic data to make decisions (see Dawes, 1994). It is important to move beyond the criticism and to ask, How can we extend knowledge from research to aid clinical care, and how can clinical care be conducted in a way that is systematic and of optimal benefit to the client? Occasionally, innovative practitioners develop means of systematic evaluation in clinical practice (e.g., Clement, 1996), but they are stark exceptions.

Some methodologies can be used in clinical work with individuals in the context of treatment or other intervention programs (e.g., Alter & Evens, 1990; Barlow, Hayes, & Nelson, 1984; Kazdin, 1993). These vary markedly in the experimental constraints and control they place on the client. The articles in this section focus on evaluation of the individual case to conduct clinically sensitive but methodologically informed evaluations of treatment. A goal of clinical work, as research, is to draw valid inferences. In the case of clinical work, the usual inference one wishes to draw is whether change has occurred and whether the intervention is likely to be responsible for the change. The articles present methods for evaluating the single case and offer illustrations in several different contexts.

In the first article, I discuss ways to improve the quality of inferences that can be drawn from case studies over traditional anecdotal methods. Key to case evaluation is assessment over time (i.e., on multiple occasions). In addition, patterns in the data can be used to evaluate change and to help rule out or make implausible rival hypotheses about what factors are responsible for change. A critical priority of case studies is patient care, that is, improvement of the patient's condition. The challenge is ensuring that this priority is maintained and that inferences can be drawn about change. Several case examples are provided that vary in the strength of conclusions that can be drawn about the intervention effects.

In the second article, Steven C. Hayes provides an overview of single-case experimental designs and their applicability to clinical practice. These designs, rarely taught in research programs in clinical psychology, can greatly enhance conclusions that can be drawn about the effects of treatment. This article presents core elements of single-case designs and how they compare with traditional group designs. Replication of effects within single-case designs, creative variations of design options, and the flexibility of the designs during the course of treatment are elaborated. The designs not only present planned experimental arrangements but also convey a way of thinking about case studies that emphasizes systematic evaluation over time and flexibility of the design in response to changing patterns in the data.

The previous articles suggest that a variety of single-case methods can be used to evaluate clinical work. In the next article, authors Karla Moras, Leslie A. Telfer, and David H. Barlow use single-case designs to evaluate treatments for two patients with anxiety and mood disorders. Separate cases are treated and evaluated individually using variations of design and assessment strategies. Noteworthy features include using multiple measures of outcome, evaluating treatment integrity, and using a manual to guide the therapy. The article nicely conveys the applicability of theory, hypothesis testing, and questions about the effectiveness of different treatments with the individual case. Moreover, this article shows that methodological features of research (e.g., using treatment manuals, monitoring treatment integrity) may be very applicable to clinical work.

EVALUATING TREATMENT OR OTHER INTERVENTIONS

Evaluating the impact of treatment (e.g., psychotherapy, medication) or other interventions (e.g., prevention, rehabilitation) makes special methodological demands. Over the years, studies have improved in relation to how intervention research is conducted and evaluated. In this section, articles address key areas where methodological practices and standards have improved.

The first issue to consider is *treatment integrity*, which refers to the extent to which the intervention was carried out or delivered as intended. In the broader context of research, treatment integrity refers to checking on the experimental manipulation and in this sense is applicable to many areas of research well beyond clinical psychology. For many years, published research reports merely noted in the Method section that treatment X or Y was provided. Details of the procedures (e.g., what transpired in the sessions) and whether the therapist adhered to the procedures and administered them well or competently were not presented. Studies clearly might vary considerably in the extent to which a given intervention was administered as intended. The results from many studies would be very difficult to interpret without information regarding how well or carefully the intervention was implemented.

The importance of checking on implementation of the intervention was evident from many lines of work. Among the more dramatic illustrations was a major review and evaluation of the effectiveness of intervention programs for the rehabilitation of criminals, that is, providing treatments that altered their future criminal behavior (Lipton, Martinson, & Wilks, 1975). The reviewers concluded that, after hundreds of studies, essentially no intervention was effective in rehabilitating criminals. A further evaluation of this review and the extensive research on which it was based confirmed that the interventions had not been shown to be effective, as originally stated, but neither had they been well tested (Sechrest, White, & Brown, 1979). There was little evidence that interventions were implemented correctly or in a way that would be expected to produce change. In some cases, integrity of the interventions had been sacrificed because none of the intended treatment sessions was actually held with the clients. Obviously, treatment integrity is critically important. The hypothesis that one treatment is effective or that two treatments vary in their effectiveness presumes that the treatments were delivered as intended.

Within the past decade, special efforts have been made to improve treatment evaluation. Treatment manuals have been developed to help identify the key ingredients of treatments that are to be delivered. There is some controversy about the extent to which treatment manuals capture all critical elements of treatment and to which all treatments can be manualized. Even so, there is little question that guidelines of some sort are needed to operationalize the intervention and to permit evaluation of how the intervention was implemented (see Addis, 1997; Wilson, in press). Data have been gathered as part of treatment studies to show that the treatments, as specified in the manuals, have been adhered to by the therapists, and hence treatment was reasonably tested.

In the first article, Jennifer Waltz, Michael E. Addis, Kelly Koerner, and Neil S. Jacobson focus on multiple issues that are raised by the assessment and evaluation of treatment integrity. They discuss the multiple purposes of assessing treatment integrity, different assessment strategies, and the relevance of treatment integrity for clinical training. Examples of the assessment of integrity are drawn from key studies in the field such as the National Institute of Mental Health Treatment of Depression Collaborative Research Program, a multisite study of cognitive therapy, interpersonal psychotherapy, and pharmacotherapy for the treatment of depression in adults. Recommendations are provided to assess the extent to which therapists adhere to the treatment program as intended. Although the article focuses on methodological improvements in treatment research, it is not a far leap to consider the implicit challenges the key points make for clinical practice. What is the treatment delivered in clinical work, and are there any assurances that treatment was delivered faithfully? Advances in methods to specify treatment and to assess treatment adherence, as suggested by this article, might enhance clinical practice.

In therapy outcome research, a central task is to understand the impact of treatment. The impact of treatment is likely to depend on a variety of factors and influences including the specific intervention, characteristics of clients and therapists, processes that emerge within treatment, and other conditions of treatment administration. To say that treatment depends on multiple factors means that treatment is moderated by or interacts with these other factors. (Moderators are discussed in the article by Holmbeck in the first section of this book.) If we as psychologists understood these moderators, we could match clients to treatments much better than we do, that is, we could provide clients those treatments from which they are most likely to benefit. To do this, of course, requires research that focuses on what types of clients respond to what types of treatments.

The article by Bradley Smith and Lee Sechrest discusses the study of Aptitude × Treatment interactions in therapy research. In this context, *aptitude* refers to those variables (client or therapist characteristics, setting, and other factors) that may moderate the impact or outcome. (This use of the term *aptitude*, of course, is different from the more familiar cognitive or intellectual ability to which the term is often applied in educational or vocational settings and psychological testing.) The article addresses substantive, methodological, and data-analytic issues in examining interactions of treatment with other variables. Many of the points also apply well beyond therapy research. For example, the different patterns of interaction that can emerge and difficulties in studying interactions rather than main effects are widely applicable well beyond treatment studies. Comments in this article on the role of theory, statistical modeling, and exemplary methodological practices (use of manualized treatment, ensuring strong tests of treatment) make this article a rich contribution to methodology more generally.

Treatment research, by definition, focuses on producing improvements in clients over the course of the intervention. Evaluation of the change is usually based on statistical criteria (statistical significance). In clinical psychology and other areas with applied interests, interventions are intended to have an impact that is important and that makes a difference. Statistically significant changes on one or more measures do not necessarily reflect important differences in terms of client functioning. *Clinical significance* reflects the extent to which changes make a difference to the individual in everyday life. Clinical significance can be evaluated in many ways, and options continue to develop (see Kazdin, 1998). Among the salient methods of assessing clinical significance is to evaluate whether or the extent to which

- the individual seen in treatment is returned to normative levels of functioning at the end of treatment;
- the problem that precipitated seeking treatment has been completely eliminated;
- the degree of improvement of the individual's symptoms make the scores obtained at posttreatment depart markedly from the pretreatment scores, as measured in prespecified standard deviation units;
- the individual no longer meets diagnostic criteria for the disorder(s) that he or she met at pretreatment; and
- other persons in contact with the client (e.g. spouse, peers) subjectively view the client as noticeably improved.

As any other outcome, no single measure is definitive in showing that the change is clinically significant, perhaps, except for a demonstration that the problem (e.g., tics, obsessions, panic attacks) has been completely eliminated. What is critical in intervention research is an effort to use one or more measures of clinical significance.

The article by Neil S. Jacobson and Paula Truax discusses clinical significance and the many issues it raises. The article conveys how clinical significance differs from statistical significance and effect size. Moreover, the authors provide a statistic referred to as the *reliability of change index* as a measure to evaluate whether the change is clinically important. The measure and what it is trying to accomplish are important. In section 4, articles convey that statistical significance and null hypothesis testing are useful in testing theory and establishing directions of relations. Clinical significance introduces another dimension of data evaluation and is essential for intervention research.

DESIGNING RESEARCH TO BE RELEVANT TO PRACTICE AND POLICY

There has been a perennial concern in relation to psychotherapy research regarding the extent to which research findings can be generalized to clinical settings. Many methodological practices in psychotherapy research are standard and are viewed as essential for careful evaluation of treatment. These practices pertain to treatment implementation (e.g., well controlled, relatively fixed in duration, carefully monitored), therapist training (e.g., special training regimen, use of training manuals, close supervision), and subject characteristics (e.g., carefully screened and relatively homogeneous clients). Such research is recognized to be well controlled and internally valid, but can the results be extended to clinical work, that is, to "real" treatments, therapists, and clients (e.g., Borkovec & Rachman, 1979; Kazdin, 1978)?

In psychotherapy, a distinction has been made between efficacy and effectiveness research. *Efficacy research* consists of well-controlled trials under conditions that tend to depart from those in clinical work. *Effectiveness research* consists of studies in clinical settings in which many of those characteristics of experimental settings are not available. The distinction is considered to reflect a continuum (see Hoagwood & Hibbs, 1995) because research can vary along many dimensions (e.g., who serves as subjects and therapists, how treatment is implemented and monitored, what the setting is in which treatment is delivered). These dimensions vary in degree to which a study may be more toward the efficacy side or more toward the effectiveness side of the multidimensional continuum.

Recent attention to the generality of therapy research has been fueled in part from results of meta-analyses of psychotherapy. Such analyses have consistently shown that psychotherapy "works," that is, it produces change and is better than not receiving therapy (for reviews of meta-analyses, see Matt & Navarro, 1997; Roth & Fonagy, 1996; Weisz & Weiss, 1993), although there are many qualifications (e.g., most therapies in use have never been investigated, these results apply to statistically significant change rather than to clinically significant changes). Occasionally, meta-analyses have examined studies that are completed in clinical settings and more toward the effectiveness, rather than efficacy, side of the continuum. Authors have reached different conclusions, namely, that treatment is less effective in clinical settings (effectiveness studies) than when evaluated in research (efficacy studies; Weisz, Weiss, & Donenberg, 1992) or that treatment is equally effective in both contexts (see Shadish et al., 1997). There is agreement that too few effectiveness studies are available.

The distinction between efficacy and effectiveness studies is important in contemporary research and clinical application (i.e., the practice of therapy). Many of the characteristics of well-controlled therapy research may limit generality of the results. Yet, many features of research, such as the careful specification of treatment, evaluation of treatment integrity, and systematic assessment of outcome, might be used more routinely by therapists in clinical work. In the article by Gregory N. Clarke, the author carefully describes the differences between efficacy and effectiveness research. Those characteristics that make research an efficacy study and are exemplary of well-controlled treatment research are described. Several methodological practices are examined, including the care with which treatments are implemented and monitored, the use of various control conditions, and the selection of samples for research. The article raises issues relevant to both efficacy and effectiveness research and the transition between them. Moreover, the comments have implications for clinical practice and training individuals for such practice.

In the article by Wolfgang Linden and Frances K. Wen, the relevance and applicability of therapy outcome research is extended beyond considerations of clinical practice. Research often does not influence clinicians, consumers, and policy makers. This raises fundamental questions about how research is conducted and what might be done to make findings more cumulative, disseminable, and relevant. Linden and Wen survey therapy research to examine the extent to which key characteristics are included that are likely to make research relevant to a range of consumers, beyond other researchers. Recommendations are made that will improve the quality of individual research studies, the comparability of multiple studies, the accumulation of knowledge about treatment, and the clinical relevance of research. The article conveys how methodology is critically important to the social relevance and disseminability of research findings.

A central issue related to dissemination of research results pertains to the assessment of treatment effects. Researchers are usually quite content to show that the domain that served as the clinical focus (e.g., substance abuse, depression, panic disorder) improved in the treatment group(s) but not at all, or to a lesser extent, in the control group(s). Researchers heap even greater self-praise when they evaluate outcome in terms of clinical significance, in addition to the usual statistical significance. Yet, even so, to the world at large, many of the measures are not clearly relevant to decisions that need to be made about treatment. For decision making, consumers and policy makers are more concerned with measures of social impact, that is, measures that can be shown to have an impact on everyday outcomes (e.g., number of days of missing work, arrest or rehospitalization rates, utilization of health services, number of emergency room visits). Many of these measures are occasionally incorporated into research because they represent constructs of interest to researchers. For example, frequency of arrest for driving while under the influence of alcohol, clearly a social impact measure, may be of interest to a researcher because it is another measure of how well treatment affected alcohol use.

A key measure of interest to society is the cost of the intervention (treatment and prevention) and the benefits that result from the intervention in terms of cost reduction. Indeed, even if effectiveness is demonstrated, decision making about whether to adopt, use, or implement that intervention is driven in part by cost. The article by Brian T. Yates conveys the importance of measuring costs in clinical research. Cost is a key dimension for evaluating treatment in part because it sensitizes individuals to other features of research (e.g., who is providing treatment, what are the relevant or most important outcomes, what are suitable control or comparison conditions). Key concepts and their measurement such as cost-effectiveness and cost–benefit analyses are presented. Recommendations are provided on ways to assess, report, and evaluate data on cost.

CASE STUDY AND
SMALL SAMPLE
RESEARCH

20

DRAWING VALID INFERENCES
FROM CASE STUDIES

ALAN E. KAZDIN

The case study has played a central role in clinical psychology. Indeed, understanding the individual person is occasionally considered to be a distinguishing characteristic of clinical psychology relative to other branches of the field (Korchin, 1976; Watson, 1951). The intensive study of the individual has contributed to clinical research and practice by providing a rich source of hypothesis about the bases of personality and behavior and by serving as a place to develop and apply intervention techniques (Bolgar, 1965; Garfield, 1974; Kazdin, 1980; Lazarus & Davison, 1971).

Despite its recognized heuristic value, the case study is usually considered to be inadequate as a basis for drawing valid scientific inferences. Relationships between independent and dependent variables are difficult to discern in a typical case study because of the ambiguity of the factor(s) responsible for performance. For example, treatment for a particular clinical case may be associated with therapeutic change. However, the basis for the

Reprinted from the *Journal of Consulting and Clinical Psychology*, 49, 183–192. Copyright 1981 by the American Psychological Association.

Preparation of this manuscript was facilitated by Grant MH31047 from the National Institute of Mental Health.

change cannot be determined from an uncontrolled case study. Even if treatment were responsible for change, several alternative interpretations of the case might be proposed. These alternative interpretations have been catalogued under the rubric of "threats to internal validity" (Campbell & Stanley, 1963).[1]

The case study has been discounted as a potential source of scientifically validated inferences, because threats to internal validity cannot be ruled out in the manner achieved in experimentation. Even though the case study is not experimental research, under several circumstances it can lead to knowledge about treatment effects for a given client that approximates the information achieved in experimentation. The present article examines the case study and its variations as a research tool. Alternative ways in which case studies are conducted and reported have important implications for drawing scientifically validated information. The present article discusses what can be done with the clinical case to improve the scientific inferences that can be drawn.

The case study as a potential source of scientifically valid information warrants careful scrutiny for several reasons. First, the case study has had tremendous impact on psychotherapy. Individual cases (e.g., Little Hans, Anna O., Little Albert) and series of cases (e.g., Masters & Johnson, 1970; Wolpe, 1958) have exerted remarkable influence on subsequent research and practice. Second, the case study draws attention to the frequently lamented hiatus between clinical practice and research. Clinicians have access to the individual case as their most convenient and feasible investigative tool, but inadequacies of the case study as a research strategy limit the inferences that can be drawn. Researchers often rigorously investigate psychotherapy but may sacrifice clinical relevance in the populations, therapeutic conditions, and standardization of treatment that research may require. Hence, investigation of psychotherapy often obscures aspects of the phenomenon of interest (Strupp & Hadley, 1979), and even under the best conditions, treatment may only be an "analogue" of the clinical situation (Kazdin, 1978).

One suggestion to help bring research and practice of psychotherapy closer together is to encourage clinicians to utilize single case experimental designs (Hersen & Barlow, 1976). The designs permit experimental investigation of the single case. The designs have been applied successfully and often dramatically in case reports where the effects of treatment have been

---

[1] The threats to internal validity refer to classes of variables that might produce effects mistaken for the effects of treatment. The major threats include the influence of (a) history (specific events occurring in time), (b) maturation (processes within the person), (c) testing (repeated exposure to the assessment procedures), (d) instrumentation (changes in the scoring procedures or criteria over time), (e) statistical regression (reversion of scores toward the mean or toward less extreme scores), (f) selection (differential composition of subjects among the groups), (g) mortality (differential attrition among groups), and (h) selection-maturation (and other) interactions (where differential changes occur as a function of other threats with selection). For additional threats, see Cook and Campbell (1979) and Kazdin (1980).

carefully documented with complex clinical problems seen in individual treatment. However, single-case experimental designs often impose special requirements (e.g., withdrawing or withholding treatment at different points in the designs) that are not always feasible in the clinical situation. Hence, some authors have suggested that the designs have not really been applied as widely as they should (Barlow, 1980) and perhaps often cannot be applied, because of the ethical, methodological, and practical obstacles inherent in clinical settings (Kazdin & Wilson, 1978).

Apart from the merits of single-case experimentation, nonexperimental alternatives need to be examined carefully. Indeed, in other areas of psychology, experimentation is not always possible. In such instances, important alternatives have been provided by elaborating the requirements for quasi-experiments (Campbell & Stanley, 1963), which can achieve some if not all of the goals of experimentation. Similarly, in the context of clinical practice, experiments are to be encouraged when opportunities exist. However, it is very important to elaborate the conditions that can be invoked to achieve several goals of experiments when rigorous investigations are not possible. The uncontrolled case study is a widely available investigative tool, and its methodological limitations, advantages, and alternatives need to be elaborated.

CHARACTERISTICS OF THE CASE STUDY

The case study has been defined in many different ways. Traditionally, the case study has referred to intensive investigation of the individual client. Case reports often include detailed descriptions of individual clients. The descriptions rely heavily on anecdotal accounts of the therapist to draw inferences about factors that contributed to the client's plight and changes over the course of treatment. Aside from the focus on the individual, the case study has come to refer to a methodological approach in which a person or group is studied in such a fashion that inferences cannot be drawn about the factors that contribute to performance (Campbell & Stanley, 1963; Paul, 1969). Thus, even if several persons are studied, the approach may still be that of a case study. Often cases are treated on an individual basis, but the information that is reported is aggregated across cases, for example, as in reports about the efficacy of various treatments (e.g., Lazarus, 1963; Wolpe, 1958). Hence, there is some justification for not delimiting the case study merely to the report of an individual client.

In general, the case study has been defined heterogeneously to denote several different things, including the focus on the individual, reliance on anecdotal information, and the absence of experimental controls. A central feature of the diverse definitions is that case studies differ from experimental demonstrations. Texts on methodology usually discount the case study as a preexperimental design and use it as a point of departure to show that experimentation is the alternative means for obtaining scientifically validated knowledge (Campbell & Stanley, 1963; Hersen & Barlow, 1976; Kazdin, 1980). However, the purpose of the present article is to suggest that case studies and experiments fall on a continuum that reflects the degree to which scientifically adequate inferences can be drawn. More importantly, several types of uncontrolled case studies can be identified that vary in the extent to which they permit valid conclusions.

The purpose of experimentation is to rule out threats to internal validity, which serve as alternative rival hypotheses of the results. For example, in clinical treatment research, single-case or between-groups experimental designs are required to rule out the impact of extraneous factors that might account for the findings. Case studies do not provide the arrangements that permit conclusions that are as clear as those available from experimentation. However, many of the threats to internal validity can be ruled out in case studies so that conclusions can be reached about the impact of treatment.

DIMENSIONS FOR EVALUATING CASE STUDIES

Case studies have been loosely and heterogeneously defined to include a variety of uncontrolled demonstrations aimed at showing that treatment produces therapeutic change. However, case studies may vary in how they are conducted and reported. The distinctions that can be made among case studies have important implications for drawing unambiguous conclusions. Major dimensions that can distinguish case studies insofar as they relate to internal validity, are presented below.

Type of Data

The main criterion that distinguishes case studies is the basis for claiming that a change has been achieved. At one extreme, anecdotal information may be relied on and include narrative accounts by the client and/or therapist regarding how client functioning has improved. Anecdotal reports are subject to a variety of limitations and sources of bias that need not be elaborated here. Suffice it to say that the anecdotal reports usually are not sufficient to conclude that changes really occurred in client behavior.

Case studies can include objective information, which refers to the large category of measurement strategies in which systematic and quantitative data are obtained. The specific measures encompass the gamut of assessment modalities and techniques (e.g., self-reports, ratings by others, overt behavior). Depending on other dimensions discussed below, objective information is a basic condition of a case study that has important implications for drawing inferences about the effects of treatment. The type of data obtained in a case study, that is, anecdotal or objective information, perhaps is the most important precondition for drawing inferences from a case study. Without some systematic data collection, other dimensions that might be applied to evaluate the case become almost irrelevant. Scientific inferences are difficult if not impossible to draw from anecdotal information. Indeed, it is the anecdotal information that is the problem rather than the fact that an individual case is studied. Even a rigorously designed experiment would be completely uninterpretable if anecdotal reports rather than objective assessment procedures served as the dependent measures.[2]

Assessment Occasions

Other dimensions that can distinguish case studies are the number and timing of assessment occasions. The occasions in which this objective information is collected have extremely important implications for drawing inferences from the case. Major options consist of collecting information on a one- or two-shot basis (e.g., posttreatment only, pre- and posttreatment, respectively) or continuously over time (e.g., every day or a few times per week) for an extended period.

When information is collected on one or two occasions, say before or after treatment, difficulties arise in inferring that change has occurred as a result of treatment. Other interpretations of the change might be proposed (e.g., testing, instrumentation, statistical regression). With continuous assessment over time conducted before or after treatment, artifacts associated with the assessment procedures become less plausible. That is, changes as a function of the measurement instrument, if evident, normally would be detected prior to treatment and would not necessarily obscure the pattern of data relied on to infer changes associated with treatment.

Continuous assessment provides an additional advantage that can strengthen the internal validity of the case study. Data from continuous assessment prior to treatment can serve as a basis for making predictions about likely performance in the future. Extrapolations about the likely direction of performance provide implicit predictions about what performance would be like. The effects of treatment can be judged by the extent to which departures in the data are evident from the previously projected performance.

---

[2] The absence of quantitative information may not necessarily rule out drawing causal inferences. Occasionally, intervention effects are so powerful that qualitative changes appear to be produced, and the certainty of change and the reason for this change are relatively unambiguous. These effects, occasionally referred to as "slam bang" effects (Gilbert, Light, & Mosteller, 1975), are evident throughout the history of medicine and psychology. For example, Shapiro (1963) described a case of a patient with terminal cancer who showed a dramatic remission of symptoms on separate occasions as a function of receiving inert substances (an inactive drug and water). In this case, the changes were so strong and immediate ("slam bang" effects) that the absence of careful measurement did not pose as serious a problem for drawing inferences that the administration of treatment led to change. Apart from occasional examples, in most instances, quantitative information is required to attest to the fact that changes have in fact occurred and that these changes can be assessed with procedures that are replicable.

Past and Future Projections

The extent to which valid inferences can be drawn about treatment effects is influenced by past and future projections of performance. The past and future projections may derive from continuous assessment which shows that the problem is stable and has not changed for an extended period. As noted above, continuous assessment can provide information extrapolated to the future that may serve as an implicit but testable prediction. If behavior appears stable for an extended period, changes that coincide with treatment suggest that the intervention may have led to change.

Past and future projections of performance also may be derived from understanding the course of a particular clinical problem. For some problems (e.g., obesity, social withdrawal), an extended history may be evident. The extended history is important from the standpoint of drawing inferences when change occurs. When change has occurred for a client whose problem has been evident for a long period, the plausibility that treatment caused the change is greatly increased. On the other hand, an acute clinical problem that has emerged relatively recently or is associated with a clear precipitating event may make evaluation of treatment slightly more difficult than it would be for a chronic problem. The acute or even episodic problem might be more amenable to the influence of extraneous (i.e., nontreatment) factors. Hence, it will be relatively difficult to rule out factors other than treatment that may account for the changes.

Projections of what the problems would be like in the future derived from understanding the particular clinical problem are also very relevant to drawing inferences about treatment. Research may suggest that a particular clinical problem is very likely to improve, worsen, or remain the same over a period of time. These alternative prognoses may be important when drawing inferences about treatment effects in a given case. For example, knowledge about the disorder may suggest that the problem will deteriorate over time (e.g., terminal cancer). The likely future for such a problem is highly relevant for evaluating whether treatment may be responsible for change. In the case of a patient with a terminal disease, improvements associated with a highly experimental treatment provide a strong inferential basis. Patient improvement strongly attests to the efficacy of treatment as the important intervention, because change in the disorder controverts the expected prediction.[3] Of course, with some clients and clinical problems, the future projections may

---

[3] This, of course, is not to say that the component the investigator believes to be important in the treatment was the one actually responsible for change, but only that the treatment and all that the treatment encompassed was the important event. The aspect(s) of treatment that caused change in experimentation is not a question of internal validity but rather one of construct validity (Cook & Campbell, 1976, 1979). In experimental research, the particular aspect of treatment may still be debated (construct validity), even though the experiment has ruled out the impact of extraneous influences (internal validity).

indicate that improvements are likely even if no treatments are provided. For example, in treatment of children who have specific fears, conclusions about the short-term or long-term effects of treatment in a clinical case may be difficult to reach, because the projection for the future is for improvement (Agras, Chapin, & Oliveau, 1972). In general, inferences about the effects of treatment in a given case are more easily made to the extent that predictions can be made on the basis of extraneous information that the problem, if untreated, will follow a particular course. The plausibility that the changes are a result of treatment depend in part on the extent to which changes in client performance depart from the expected and predicted pattern of performance.

Type of Effect

The degree to which inferences can be drawn about the causal agent in the treatment of a clinical case also depends on the kinds of changes that occur. The immediacy and magnitude of changes contribute to judgments that treatment may have caused the change. Usually, the more immediate the therapeutic changes after the onset of treatment, the stronger a case can be made that treatment was responsible for the change. Of course, as any other of the dimensions discussed, showing that the conditions are met, in this case an immediate change, does not by itself mean that treatment was responsible for the change. But the more immediate the change, the less likely alternative sources of influence coincident with treatment account for the change. Alternatively, when change is gradual or delayed rather than immediate, the plausibility of associating the change with a particular event in the past (i.e., treatment) decreases. As the latency between treatment administration and behavior change increases, the number of extraneous experiences that could account for the change increases as well.

Aside from the immediacy of change, the magnitude of change also contributes to the extent to which treatment can be accorded a causal role. More confidence might be placed in the causal role of treatment when relatively large changes are achieved. Of course, the magnitude and immediacy of change when combined increase the confidence that one can place in according treatment a causal role. Rapid and dramatic changes provide a strong basis for attributing the effects to treatment than more gradual and relatively small changes. A rapid and large change suggests that a particular intervention rather than randomly occurring extraneous influences accounts for the pattern of results.

Number and Heterogeneity of Subjects

Dimensions related to the subjects may influence the confidence that can be placed in conclusions about treatment effects. The number of cases included is important. Obviously, a stronger basis for inferring the effects of treatment stems from demonstrations with several cases rather than one case. The more cases that show changes associated with treatment, the more unlikely an extraneous event is responsible for change. An extraneous event that covaries with treatment and leads to therapeutic change is an unlikely rival hypothesis of the results, because the event must be common to all of the cases. The sheer number of cases obviously can contribute to the extent to which conclusions about treatment can be drawn by making implausible other explanations.

Aside from the number of cases, the heterogeneity of the cases may also contribute to drawing inferences about the cause of therapeutic change. If change is demonstrated across several clients who differ in various subject and demographic characteristics and the time that they are treated, the inferences that can be drawn are much stronger than if this diversity does not exist. Essentially, different persons have different histories and rates of maturation. As the diversity and heterogeneity of the clients and the conditions of treatment increase, it becomes increasingly implausible that the common experience shared by the clients (i.e., treatment) accounts for the changes.

APPLICATION OF THE DIMENSIONS

The above dimensions do not necessarily exhaust all of the factors that contribute to drawing firm conclusions from case studies. Also, each of the dimensions is discussed separately. Yet, any particular case can be examined in terms of where it lies on each of the dimensions. Precisely where a particular case falls on all of the dimensions determines the extent to which particular threats to internal validity or rival alternative hypotheses can be ruled out in interpreting the results.

All of the possible combinations of the dimensions would yield a large number of types of case studies that cannot be presented here. Many of the dimensions represent continua where an indefinite number of gradations are possible so a large set of types of cases could be enumerated. However, it is important to look at selected types of cases that vary on the dimensions mentioned earlier to show how internal validity can be addressed.

Table 1 illustrates a few types of cases that differ in their standing on the dimensions mentioned earlier. The extent to which each type of case rules out the specific threats to internal validity is also presented using a format that parallels similar analyses for true and quasi-experiments (Campbell & Stanley, 1963). For each case type, the collection of objective data was included. As noted earlier, the absence of objective or quantifiable data usually precludes drawing firm conclusions about whether change occurred. Drawing conclusions about the basis for change is premature, because the change

TABLE 1
Examples of Types of Cases and the Threats
to Internal Validity That They Address

	Case example		
Measure	1	2	3
Characteristic of Case			
Objective data	+	+	+
Continuous Assessment	−	+	+
Stability of problem	−	−	+
Immediate and marked effects	−	+	−
Multiple cases	−	−	+
Major threats to internal validity			
History	−	?	+
Maturation	−	?	+
Testing	−	+	+
Instrumentation	−	+	+
Statistical regression	−	+	+

Note: + indicates that the threat to internal validity is probably controlled, − indicates that the threat remains a problem, and ? indicates that the threat may remain uncontrolled. In preparation of the table, selected threats (mortality, selection, and others; see Footnote 1) were omitted because they arise primarily in the comparison of different groups in experiments and quasi-experiments. They are not usually a problem for a case study, which of course does not rely on group comparisons.

itself has not been carefully documented. In the case types illustrated in Table 1, the assumption will be made that some form of assessment was completed, even if only one or two occasions to measure performance before and after treatment.

Case Example Type 1: With Pre- and Postassessment

A case study where a client is treated may utilize pre- and posttreatment assessment. The inferences that can be drawn from a case with such assessment are not necessarily increased by the assessment alone. Whether specific threats to internal validity are ruled out depends on characteristics of the case with respect to the other dimensions. Table 1 illustrates a case with pre- and postassessment but without other optimal features that would address and rule out threats to internal validity.

If changes occur in the case from pre- to posttreatment assessment, one cannot draw valid inferences about whether the treatment led to change. It is quite possible that events occurring in time (history), processes of change within the individual (maturation), repeated exposure to assessment (testing), changes in the scoring criteria (instrumentation), or reversion of the score to the mean (regression) rather than treatment led to change. Hence, even though the case included objective assessment, the conclusion that can be drawn about the basis for change is not greatly improved over an anecdotal report.

Case Example Type 2: With Repeated Assessment and Marked Changes

If the case study includes assessment on several occasions before and after treatment, and the changes that occur at the time or over the course of treatment are relatively marked, then the inferences that can be drawn about treatment are vastly improved. Table 1 illustrates the characteristics of the case along with the extent to which specific threats to internal validity are addressed.

The fact that continuous assessment is included is important in ruling out the specific threats to internal validity that are related to assessment. First, the changes that coincide with treatment are not likely to result from exposure to repeated testing or changes in the instrument. When continuous assessment is utilized, changes due to testing or instrumentation could have been evident before treatment began. Similarly, regression to the mean from one data point to another, a special problem with assessment conducted only at two points in time, is eliminated. Repeated observation over time shows a pattern in the data. Extreme scores may be a problem for any particular assessment occasion in relation to the immediately prior occasion. However, these changes cannot account for the pattern of performance for an extended period.

Aside from continuous assessment, this case illustration was proposed to include relatively marked treatment effects, that is, changes that are relatively immediate and large. These types of changes produced in treatment help rule out the influence of history and maturation as plausible rival hypotheses. Maturation in particular may be relatively implausible, because maturational changes are not likely to be abrupt and large. However, a "?" was placed in the table, because maturation cannot be ruled out completely. In this case example, information on the stability of the problem in the past and future was not included. Hence, it is not known whether the clinical problem might ordinarily change on its own and whether maturational influences are plausible. Some problems that are episodic in nature conceivably could show marked changes that have little to do with treatment. With immediate and large changes in behavior, history is also not likely to account for the results. However, a "?" was placed in the table here too. Without a knowledge of the stability of the problem over time, one cannot be too confident about the impact of extraneous events.

For this case overall, much more can be said about the impact of treatment than in the previous case. Continuous assessment and marked changes help to rule out specific rival hypotheses. In a given instance, history and maturation may be ruled out too, although these are likely to depend on other dimensions in the table that specifically were not included in this case.

Case Example Type 3: With Multiple Cases, Continuous Assessment, and Stability Information

Several cases rather than only one may be studied where each includes continuous assessment. The cases may be treated one at a time and accumulated into a final summary statement of treatment effects or treated as a single group at the same time. In this illustration as characterized, assessment information is available on repeated occasions before and after treatment as in the last type of case. Also, the stability of the problem is known in this example. Stability refers to the dimension of past–future projections and denotes that information is available from other research that the problem does not usually change over time. When the problem is known to be highly stable or follows a particular course without treatment, the clinician has an implicit prediction of the effects of no treatment. The results can be compared to this predicted level of performance.

As evident in Table 1, the threats to internal validity are addressed by a case report meeting the specified characteristics. History and maturation are not likely to interfere with drawing conclusions about the causal role of treatment, because several different cases are included. All cases are not likely to have a single historical event or maturational process in common that could account for the results. Knowledge about the stability of the problem in the future also helps to rule out the influence of history and maturation. If the problem is known to be stable over time, this means that ordinary historical events and maturational processes do not provide a strong enough influence in their own right. Because of the use of multiple subjects and the knowledge about the stability of the problem, history and maturation are considered to be implausible explanations of therapeutic change.

The threats to internal validity related to testing are handled largely by the assessment over time. Repeated testing, changes in the instrument, and reversion of scores toward the mean may influence a comparison of performance from one occasion to another. Problems associated with testing are not likely to influence the pattern of data over a large number of occasions. Also, information about the stability of the problem helps to further make implausible changes due to testing. The fact that the problem is known to be stable means that it probably would not change merely as a function of assessment.

In general, the case study of the type illustrated in this example provides a strong basis for drawing valid inferences about the impact of treatment. The manner in which the multiple case report is designed does not constitute an experiment, as usually conceived, because each case represents an uncontrolled demonstration. However, characteristics of the type of case study can rule out specific threats to internal validity in a manner approaching that of true experiments.

General Comments

From the standpoint of experimentation, all of the above types of cases share a similar methodological status by being preexperimental and by not providing a sufficient basis for drawing scientifically valid inferences. The results that may emerge are usually rejected, because the data are from case studies. However, it is extremely important to shift the focus from the type of demonstration (i.e., case study versus experiment) to the specific threats to internal validity that interfere with drawing valid inferences. The focus on rival alternative hypotheses that may be proposed draws attention to characteristics of the case reports that can be altered to improve the scientific yield.

The purpose of experimentation is to make as implausible as possible alternative explanations of the results. At the end of an experimental investigation, the effects of the treatment should be the most plausible and parsimonious interpretation of the results. Case studies can also rule out alternative explanations that might compete with drawing inferences about the impact of treatment.

Specific procedures that can be controlled by the clinical investigator can influence the strength of the case demonstration. First, the investigator can collect objective data in place of anecdotal report information. Clear measures are needed to attest to the fact that change has actually occurred. Second, client performance can be assessed on several occasions, perhaps before, during, and after treatment. The continuous assessment helps rule out important rival hypotheses related to testing, which a simple pre- and post-treatment assessment strategy does not accomplish.

Third, the clinical investigator can accumulate cases that are treated and assessed in a similar fashion. Large groups are not necessarily needed but only the systematic accumulation of a number of clients. As the number and heterogeneity of clients increase and receive treatment at different points in time, history and maturation become less plausible as alternative rival hypotheses. If treatment is given to several clients on different occasions, one has to propose an intricate explanation showing how different historical events or maturational processes intervened to alter performance. As in ordinary experimentation, in such cases, treatment effects become the more likely interpretation.

Some features of the case study that can help rule out threats to internal validity are out of control of the clinical investigator. For example, knowledge about the stability of the problem over time comes from information extraneous to a particular client. Knowledge about the course of the disorder is required. However, even though this is not controllable by the clinical investigator, he or she can bring available information to bear when interpreting results. This is already implicit in some instances where, for example, the problem in treatment is known to have a high remission rate (e.g., childhood fears). Remission of the problem, which may normally occur over time, requires special care for interpreting the long-term effects of treatment with any particular case or intervention.

The clinical investigator cannot easily control whether the changes in treatment are immediate rather than marginal. However, the data pattern that does result should be examined specifically in light of other rival hypotheses that might explain the results. Could any historical events (e.g., family processes, job experiences) or maturational processes (e.g., decreased depression as a function of the passage of time since divorce or death of a relative) be brought to bear that might explain the pattern of results? Perhaps the pattern of the data can help rule out specific rival hypotheses.

It is not merely how we conduct case studies that might warrant reconsideration but how we conceptualize them as well. Much can be done in carrying out case studies to increase the strength of the inferences about causal events. The well-known criticism of case studies as research tools has fostered a methodological learned helplessness about what can be done. In fact, much can be done to rule out specific threats to internal validity within case studies, such as the use of assessment on multiple occasions and the accumulation of several cases.

Some of the dimensions that help rule out threats to internal validity are out of the control of the clinical investigator. For example, one cannot by fiat achieve immediate and marked therapeutic changes nor be sure of the stability of the problem over the past and future. However, the clinical investigator can bring to bear the available research on the nature of the problem and evaluate the likelihood that historical events and maturational processes could achieve the sorts of changes evident in treatment. It is not necessarily the lack of control over the clinical situation that is a problem. Within the limits of the situation, the clinical investigator might keep in mind some of the specific alternative rival hypotheses that need to be ruled out or made less plausible.

CONCLUSION

The case study occupies an extremely important place in clinical work both in inpatient and outpatient care. Case studies are widely recognized to serve as an important place to develop hypotheses about clinical problems and to explore innovative treatments. However, cases are usually considered to be completely inadequate as a basis for drawing scientifically validated inferences.

Case studies encompass several types of demonstrations that may differ in the extent to which inferences can be drawn. The issue is not whether a particular report is a case study. The focus on classifying reports on the basis of their lack of experimental design detracts from the more pertinent issue.

Drawing inferences, whether in case studies, quasi-experiments, or experiments, is a matter of ruling out rival hypotheses that could account for the results. In case studies, by definition, the number of rival hypotheses and their plausibility are likely to present greater problems than they would in experiments. However, it is possible to include features in the case study that help decrease the plausibility of specific rival hypotheses.

The present article discusses several possibilities for assessing performance that rule out selected threats to internal validity. The purpose in adopting this approach is not to legitimize the case study as a replacement for experimental research. Experiments based on intra- and intersubject methodology can uniquely rule out threats to internal validity and can provide relatively clear information about the impact of treatment. Although the case study is not a substitute for experimentation, it has and probably will continue to contribute greatly to the information available in the field. Hence, it is important to consider the case study as a potential source of scientifically useful information and to adopt procedures, where they exist, to increase the strength of case demonstrations in clinical situations when true or quasi-experiments are not viable options.

REFERENCES

Agras, W. S., Chapin, H. H., & Oliveau, D. C. (1972). The natural history of phobia. *Archives of General Psychiatry, 26,* 315–317.

Barlow, D. H. (1980). Behavior therapy: The next decade. *Behavior Therapy, 11,* 315–328.

Bolgar, H. (1965). The case study method. In B. B. Wolman (Ed.), *Handbook of clinical psychology.* New York: McGraw-Hill.

Campbell, D. T., & Stanley, J. C. (1963). *Experimental and quasi-experimental designs for research.* Chicago: Rand McNally.

Cook, T. D., & Campbell, D. T. (1976). The design and conduct of quasi-experiments and true experiments in field settings. In M. D. Dunnette (Ed.), *Handbook of industrial and organizational psychology.* Chicago: Rand McNally.

Cook, T. D., & Campbell, D. T. (Eds.). (1979). *Quasi-experimentation: Design and analysis issues for field settings.* Chicago: Rand McNally.

Garfield, S. L. (1974). *Clinical psychology: The study of personality and behavior.* Chicago: Aldine.

Gilbert, J. P., Light, R. J., & Mosteller, F. (1975). Assessing social innovations: An empirical base for policy. In C. A. Bennett & A. A. Lumsdaine (Eds.), *Evaluation and experiment.* New York: Academic Press.

Hersen, M., & Barlow, D. H. (1976). *Single-case experimental designs: Strategies for studying behavior change.* New York: Pergamon Press.

Kazdin, A. E. (1978). Evaluating the generality of findings in analogue therapy research. *Journal of Consulting and Clinical Psychology, 46,* 673–686.

Kazdin, A. E. (1980). *Research design in clinical psychology.* New York: Harper & Row.

Kazdin, A. E., & Wilson, G. T. (1978). *Evaluation of behavior therapy: Issues, evidence, and research strategies.* Cambridge, MA: Ballinger.

Korchin, S. J. (1976). *Modern clinical psychology.* New York: Basic Books.

Lazarus, A. A. (1963). The results of behaviour therapy in 126 cases of severe neurosis. *Behaviour Research and Therapy, 1,* 69–79.

Lazarus, A. A., & Davison, G. C. (1971). Clinical innovation in research and practice. In A. E. Bergin & S. L. Garfield (Eds.), *Handbook of psychotherapy and behavior change: An empirical analysis.* New York: Wiley.

Masters, W. H., & Johnson, V. E. (1970). *Human sexual inadequacy.* Boston: Little, Brown.

Paul, G. (1969). Behavior modification research: Design and tactics. In C. M. Franks (Ed.), *Behavior therapy: Appraisal and status.* New York: McGraw-Hill.

Shapiro, A. K. (1963). Psychological aspects of medication. In H. I. Lief, V. F. Lief, & N. R. Lief (Eds.), *The psychological basis of medical practice.* New York: Harper & Row.

Strupp, H. H., & Hadley, S. W. (1979). Specific vs. nonspecific factors in psychotherapy. *Archives of General Psychiatry, 36,* 1125–1137.

Watson, R. I. (1951). *The clinical method in psychology.* New York: Harper & Row.

Wolpe, J. (1958). *Psychotherapy by reciprocal inhibition.* Stanford, CA: Stanford University Press.

21

SINGLE CASE EXPERIMENTAL DESIGN AND EMPIRICAL CLINICAL PRACTICE

STEVEN C. HAYES

The progress of research in clinical psychology presents something of a paradox. The social need for clinical research can hardly be overestimated; the field incorporates many of the most serious social and personal ills of the day. Further, tremendous resources are available to the field in the numbers of professionals, training programs, employment opportunities, and (compared with many disciplines) funding patterns. Yet data abound that these needs and resources have not yet been fully combined to produce maximum research progress (Garfield & Kurtz, 1976; Kelly, Goldberg, Fiske, & Kilkowski, 1978; Levy, 1962).

This paradox has often been noted, especially in the well-worn discussion of the research/practice split (e.g., Leitenberg, 1974; Meehl, 1971; Peterson, 1976; Raush, 1969, 1974; Rogers, 1973; Shakow, 1976). Some psychologists have rationalized the split, pointing to the irrelevance of the

Reprinted from the *Journal of Consulting and Clinical Psychology*, 49, 193–211. Copyright 1981 by the American Psychological Association.

traditional research enterprise to clinical practice (Holt, 1971; Meehl, 1971; Peterson, 1976; Raush, 1974). Others have denied the split, defending the scientist-practitioner model (e.g., Shakow, 1976) and calling for better, more controlled, and even more intricate clinical research (e.g., Meltzoff & Kornreich, 1970; Paul, 1969; cf. Thelen & Ewing, 1970). A third reaction has begun to receive some attention (e.g., Barlow, 1980). It attempts to dissolve the split, claiming that practicing clinicians may not be lacking a dedication to research, just tools for the task. If single case (or time series) methodology[1] would be taught in a manner that fits demands of the clinical environment (the thinking goes), practicing clinicians could produce more research data and make consumption of clinical research more worthwhile for the practitioner.

This view has been advanced periodically over the years (e.g., Barlow & Hersen, 1973; Browning & Stover, 1971; Chassan, 1967, 1979; Hersen & Barlow, 1976; Kazdin, 1978, 1980; Leitenberg, 1973; Svenson & Chassan, 1967). Most of the conceptual work to date, however, has been oriented toward the full-time clinical researcher, not the practicing clinician. Clinical researchers and academic clinicians have not been unresponsive to single case methodology, but group comparison approaches are often equally attractive and valuable. It is in the on-line clinical environment that the unique value of time series experimentation truly becomes apparent, yet little has been done to advance its use there.

The goodness of fit between clinical decision making and time series methodology is remarkable. As will be shown, good clinical practice seems often to be a type of single subject experimentation in that the logic of the two enterprises is so similar. The present article will argue that good practicing clinicians are already doing evaluations of potential scientific value with most clients they see. They need only (a) take systematic repeated measurements, (b) specify their own treatment, (c) recognize the design strategies they are already using, and (d) at times use existing design elements deliberately to improve clinical decision making.

---

[1] The terminological diversity surrounding this research strategy is enormous. These designs have been termed single subject, $N = 1$, or single case (e.g., Hersen & Barlow, 1976); intrasubject replication (Kazdin, 1980); intensive (Chassan, 1967, 1979); own control (e.g., Millon & Diesenhaus, 1972); and time series (e.g., Campbell & Stanley, 1963; Glass, Wilson, & Gottman, 1975), among other names (Jayaratne & Levy, 1979). I have chosen to use two terms somewhat interchangeably. The first is *time series experimentation*. It emphasizes the critical component of these designs. Its drawback is possible confusion with time series analysis, a statistical technique used to analyze time series data (e.g., Box & Jenkins, 1976; Gottman, McFall, & Barnett, 1969), or confusion with specific designs, such as Campbell and Stanley's name for an A/B design. The other term, *single case designs*, emphasizes the number of subjects as the central issue. For clinical work, analyzing the individual is a desirable end in and of itself (Bernard, 1865), and this is the most popular name for these designs. Nevertheless, many of these designs (e.g., multiple baseline across subjects) require several subjects, and all can be done with entire groups as the unit of analysis. Other terms are more problematic. "Intensive" carries an evaluative connotation. "Intrasubject replication" and "own control" wrongly assert that all control strategies in these designs are within subject when many of them (e.g., baseline-only control, multiple baseline across subjects) are not.

If this argument can be shown to be correct, then it is worth considering why single case experimentation, hardly a newcomer on the methodological scene, is so underutilized in applied settings. Several reasons might be suggested:

1. It is undertaught. In most training programs, methodological courses are taught by nonclinicians (e.g., statisticians, general experimental psychologists). With some notable exceptions (e.g., the experimental analysis of behavior), most of these other subfields are heavily committed to group comparison research.

2. It has not been aimed at the practicing clinician. Perhaps in order to show that time series methodology can be just as scientific as group comparison approaches, methodological niceties have often been overemphasized. Individual clinicians cannot be expected to distinguish between the core essentials and simple issues of degree, and it may be rejected because it is seemingly impractical to do it right.

3. It is associated with behaviorism. Historically, single case methodology has been most heavily developed and used by behaviorists (e.g., Sidman, 1960) and may often be rejected because of it. This is unfortunate, however, because the methodology is theory free. One can use time series experimentation to answer questions about self-disclosure as readily as behavioral indicants of anxiety, and about insight-oriented procedures as successfully as assertiveness training.

4. Clinicians may fail to distinguish between research methodology and group comparison approaches. To most clinicians, group comparison research is research. Individual clinicians (and clinical training programs) are likely to throw the single case baby out with the group comparison bathwater.

5. There are few outlets for on-line clinical research. On-line single case evaluations, modified as they frequently are by realities of clinical practice, may meet a severe reception in most clinical journals. Reviewers of such articles are themselves unlikely to be practicing clinicians, and appropriate standards for evaluations of actual clinical practice are still unformed.

6. Clinical agencies often provide little support for scientific work. Everything from case loads to secretarial help to agency policies concerning research may hinder on-line use of single case methodology. Fortunately, third-party payments are beginning to create counter pressures for clinical evaluation.

In the past few years, a whole host of professional developments have indicated the possible beginning of an empirical clinical movement based on the combination of single case methodology with the resources of the practicing clinician. These include books (e.g., Jayaratne & Levy, 1979), articles (Barlow, 1980; Levy & Olson, 1979; in fact the present series of articles), conferences (e.g., the Association for Advancement of Behavior Therapy adopted this issue as the theme of its 1980 convention), special issues of journals (e.g., a 1979 issue of the *Journal of Social Service Research*; an upcoming issue of *Behavioral Assessment*), workshops, and the like.

The present article will outline the nature of times series experimentation and underline ways it can fit into routine clinical practice. I have assumed that the clinician is working with actual paying clients (individuals, groups, agencies, etc.) who have given consent to routine clinical evaluation and treatment. No willingness to endure a significant increase in risk, cost, or time to the client beyond that required by good clinical decision making is assumed. Finally, I have not attempted to analyze in detail the many fine points and issues raised by single case experimentation (for that, the interested reader is referred elsewhere, e.g., Hersen & Barlow, 1976; Jayaratne & Levy, 1979; Kratochwill, 1978; Sidman, 1960), and general, noncontroversial recommendations drawn from such sources have not been referenced separately.

THE ESSENTIALS OF SINGLE CASE METHODOLOGY

All time series work is based on combining essential core elements into logical designs. In this section, the general rules of approach will be described. In the following sections, specific design elements will be detailed.

Repeated Measurement

The absolute core of time series methodology, as denoted by the very name, is repeated measurement of the client's behavior, including thoughts, feelings, and so forth. Because estimates of the stability, level, and trend of the data (against which treatment effects might be seen) are drawn within subject, the clinician must have a record of client progress across time (see Nelson, 1981). Repeated measurement also parallels rules of clinical practice. Practical clinical guides often exhort clinicians to "examine regularly and consistently whether therapy is being helpful" (Zaro, Barach, Nedelmann, & Dreiblatt, 1977, p. 157).

In clinical practice, repeated measurement should start early, using several measures if possible. An experienced clinician often has a good idea of several of the client's problems even before the end of the first session. If measurement is begun immediately, then when normal assessments ends, the clinician will often have a systematically collected baseline. Early collection of systematic measures will also often contribute to clinical assessment itself.

Some problems, when measured repeatedly, will turn out not to be real difficulties. Measures should also be practical. It is better to collect measures of medium quality than to collect none because excessively high standards of measurement are set. Finally, they should be taken under reasonably consistent conditions to avoid variability caused by inconsistent measurement procedures.

Establishment of the Degree of Intraclient Variability

An estimate of the degree of variability in the client's behavior (as repeatedly measured) is critical in single case methodology. In the context of this estimate, determinations are made about the level and trend in the behavior, and predictions are drawn about the future course of the behavior. Measures need only be stable enough to see effects, should they occur. The target problem and probable effects of intervention bear heavily on issues of stability, the question is always, Stable in terms of what? For example, if a total reduction of a behavior is anticipated, extreme variability would present no problem. Conversely, if measurement variability could not allow any treatment effect to be seen, then it would be foolish to proceed. This methodological advice dovetails nicely with clinical realities, however. For example, a client showing infrequent nondestructive outbursts of anger would probably not be treated for anger control if their frequency would be indistinguishable from that expected after treatment.

When the client's behavior is excessively variable, several actions can be taken. First, the clinician can simply wait until patterns become clearer. Often variability is temporary (for example, it may be caused by the initial effect of entering treatment), and it is frequently better to wait than to plunge ahead unnecessarily.

Second, if at times the client is behaving well and at times badly, the practicing clinician will probably begin to search for factors that account for these differences. For example, if a client's self-esteem (as measured, say, by a brief paper-and-pencil instrument before each therapy session) is high some weeks and very low others, the clinician may search for reasons accounting for it. Finding that the client's self-esteem is low only on weeks following rejection by potential dates might lead to a treatment program of social skills training or therapy around the issue of rejection. Further, the previously unstable measures might now be quite stable when organized into times following or not following instances of rejection.

A third strategy is to examine the temporal unit of analysis. Often measures are collected in particular units for convenience (e.g., clients are often asked to self-record in daily blocks). If the actual phenomena may be better seen in larger units, then the data may be blocked (or intraclient averaged). For example, a clinician working with a marital couple might find that daily records of arguments reveal extremely variable behavior, some days there are no arguments, and on others there are several. This may be expected, since all couples have some good days and some bad. More clinically important may be, for example, the average number of arguments in a week. When the data are blocked by weeks, stability may emerge. Some of the detail is lost, but this is always true: Organizing events by day disguises hourly variability; organizing them by hour disguises minute-by-minute effects. Part of good clinical skill seems to involve knowing when to ignore individual trees in order to see the forest.

A final strategy is to proceed anyway. If the effects are very strong, they may be seen. If not, enough may be learned that the next client may benefit.

Specification of Conditions

All research requires clear specification of the independent variable. In the clinic, true "technological" (Baer, Wolf, & Risley, 1968) specificity is sometimes difficult. Even when the therapist cannot specify the intervention, however, it may be possible to measure therapist behavior using some of the same within-clinic procedures for measuring client behavior (Nelson, 1981; e.g., see Becker & Rosenfeld, 1976).

Replication

The logic of all time series designs requires replication of effects. In the clinic, this requirement is increased because of the methodological compromises often forced there. In addition, the external validity of single case research depends on systematic replications of effects in many clients.

An Attitude of Investigative Play

Undoubtedly the biggest difference between group comparison research and time series methodology is the overall approach that they encourage. Single case research should be a dynamic, interactive enterprise in which the design is always tentative, always ready to change if significant questions arise in the process. The data should be graphed frequently and in various forms so that apparent patterns can emerge and leads can be followed. Group comparison research, however, is usually planned out in detail beforehand and then simply carried out.

One of the common mistake made by researchers in time series research is their approaching these tools as they would approach group comparison research (e.g., deciding beforehand on a sequence of phases or setting specific phase length). Unfortunately, clients' data often do not conform to the preset mold; these data often do not confirm preset hypotheses. When unanticipated effects are seen, the clinician must be ready to abandon previous

424   STEVEN C. HAYES

design decisions and to let the client's data be the guide. This is also good clinical practice. For example, clinical guides advise clinicians to "be prepared to alter your style of dealing with a client in response to new information" and "be prepared to have many of your hypotheses disproved" (Zaro et al., 1977, p. 28).

Other Suggested Requirements

Many other rules about single case methodology are not essential but are issues of degree. One rule is to keep phases about the same length (Hersen & Barlow, 1976). Widely different phase lengths can produce errors in interpretation, but changing phases based on time alone can also produce unclear comparisons. This is a matter of degree, and its importance can be minimized by clear effects and systematic replication. Another rule is, "Change one variable at a time" (Hersen & Barlow, 1976). This rule is often a good one, but it can be easily misinterpreted (e.g., Thomas, 1978). The meaning of "variable" here is better conveyed by the phrase "condition you wish to analyze." Thus, entire packages may be varied when it is the package that is being evaluated.

Creative Use of the Design Elements

The creative use of time series designs may have been inadvertently hindered by the literature's emphasis on complete designs rather than on design elements. For example, designs such as an A/B/A or B/C/B/C have often been described as separate designs even though their logical structures are identical (e.g., Hersen & Barlow, 1976; Mahoney, 1978; indeed, virtually the entire literature in the area has followed this course). All single case designs are built from a small set of building blocks. There are potentially as many specific single case designs as there are designs for brick buildings, and the core elements of each are comparably simple.

The present article distills all time series work into a few core elements, organized by the nature of their estimates of stability and the logic of their data comparisons. These core elements can then be creatively combined to contribute to good clinical decision making. There are three general types of strategies used: within, between, and combined series. All current single case design elements can be readily organized into these three types.

WITHIN-SERIES STRATEGIES

The best known types of time series rely on changes seen within a series of data points (in a single measure or homogeneous set of measures).

There are two subtypes of within-series strategies: the simple phase change and the complex phase change. Each of these will be described, and their use in clinical practice will be detailed.

The Simple Phase Change

The cornerstone of many of the most popular single case designs is the simple phase change. This element consists of (a) the establishment of stability, level, and trend within a series of data points across time, taken under similar conditions; (b) a change in the conditions impinging on the client; and (c) examination of concomitant changes in the stability, level, or trend in a series of data points taken under the law conditions. It is a within-series strategy in the sense that it is systematic changes seen within a series of data points across time that are examined.

A common example of the simple phase change is the A/B design. If the stability, level, or trend shown in A suddenly changes when B is implemented, our confidence increases that B is responsible for that change. Often there are possible alternative explanations for the effect (e.g., maturation, the effect of measurement, coincidental external events; see Campbell & Stanley, 1963; Hersen & Barlow, 1976; Kratochwill, 1978), and usually the effect must be replicated before our confidence in the effect is sufficiently high. One way is to repeat the phase change in reverse order (the A/B/A design). If the behavior tracks the change once again, our confidence increases further. This simple phase change process can be repeated indefinitely, each sequence forming a new completed design (e.g., A/B/A/B; B/A/B). Two treatments can be compared in the same manner (e.g., B/C/B; C/B/C/B). All of these are merely specific applications of the logic of the simple phase change, allowing us to ask questions such as, Does treatment work? or Which treatment is better?

Complex Phase Changes

The simple phase change can be coordinated into a more complex series of phases. Each of the complex phase change strategies specifies an overall integrative logic.

Interaction Element

This is a series of phase changes in which a treatment or treatment component (B) is alternately added or subtracted from another treatment or treatment component (C). A number of specific sequences are possible (e.g., B/B+C/B; C/C+B/C; B+C/C/B+C). Its logic is essentially identical to the simple phase change. This can be easily seen if instead of writing

A/B/A one were to write the equally correct A/A+B/A. The question, however, seems a bit more complex, namely, What is the combined effect of two treatment components compared to one alone? As an example, suppose a clinician wonders if the empty-chair technique is really helpful in the treatment of unresolved grief. In the first place, a specified set of techniques (B+C) might be used, including empty-chair exercises involving the lost loved one. This technique (C) might then be withdrawn and reinstituted, forming a B+C/B/B+C design. If the client's functioning tracks these changes, the role of this procedure in the overall package could be determined.

Combining Does B Work? And Does C Work? Elements

A simple phase change comparing two treatments does not make sense unless it is known that either works relative to baseline. If this is not known, the design must compare them with baseline as well as with each other by combining simple phase change strategies for determining their effectiveness. For example, the sequence A/B/A/C/A combines an A/B/A with an A/C/A. This allows us to ask if B and if C are effective. It also allows a comparison of the two treatments, but it is weak, because order effects are possible and noncontiguous data are being compared (the data in the B phase with those in the C phase). To strengthen this comparison, other subjects might receive an A/C/A/B/A sequence. If the conclusions are the same, then the believability of the treatment comparison is strengthened.

Changing Criterion

This element (see Hartmann & Hall, 1976) is usually based on the following line of reasoning: If you arbitrarily specify the level that a given behavior must reach to achieve an outcome, and the behavior repeatedly and closely tracks these criteria, then the criteria are probably responsible. Typically, this element is used when the behavior can only change in one direction, either for ethical or practical reasons. The logic of the maneuver, however, allows for criterion reversals when the behavior is reversable.

The weakness of the procedure is that it is not always clear when observed behavior is tracking criterion shifts. This problem can be alleviated by altering the length and magnitude of criterion shifts (or, if possible, their direction), as shown in Figure 1.

Other Strategies

Several other complex phase change strategies exist, although they are used infrequently in the applied literature. For example, an ascending/descending design element (see Sidman, 1960) is a popular research tool in basic operating psychology.

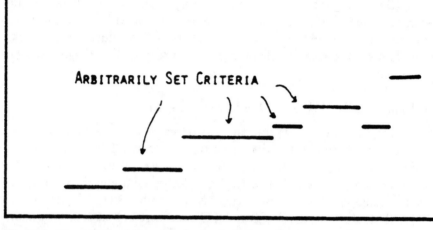

Figure 1. An example of the arbitrary manipulation of the length, depth, and direction of criterion shifts, making any behavioral correspondence with the criteria more obvious.

Using Within-Series Strategies

When a clinician begins to work with a client, be it an individual, group, or agency, it is rare that an elaborate clinical question springs forth in whole cloth. Clinical work usually involves a gradual process of investigation. The use of within-series strategies provides a good example of how single case methodology suits itself to this clinical reality. In the sections that follow, the sequence of events faced by a clinician doing a within-series evaluation will be described. The choice points and design options in this process will be given particular emphasis.

Establishing the First Phase

The clinician typically begins a therapeutic relationship with a period of assessment. If the advice offered earlier has been followed, when this period ends, a baseline is already in hand or nearly so. Several rules have been offered as to the adequacy of obtained baselines.

A first consideration is the length of the first phase. To establish estimates of stability, level, and trend, at least three measurement points seem to be needed (e.g., see Hersen & Barlow, 1976), though more are desirable. If fewer have been obtained, and the needs of the client are clear, then the practicing clinician must push ahead anyway. To do otherwise would be to delay treatment for research, not clinical, reasons. Short baselines are not necessarily lethal. There may be other information available about the problem being measured. For example, the disorder may have a known history and course (e.g., the social withdrawal of a chronic schizophrenic), or archival baselines may be available (e.g., records from previous therapists). Also, the clinician can often make up for short baselines by using other design elements later (e.g., withdrawals) or by replicating the effects with others (e.g., multiple baselines across subjects).

A second consideration is the stability of baseline. The earlier recommendations regarding stability all apply here, with one addition. If first-phase data are unavailable or excessively variable, and if treatment must begin, a design might be used that does not require a baseline (e.g., an alternating treatments design).

A final consideration is the trend in baseline. When the following phase is expected to produce increases in the data, as falling or flat baseline is desirable. When deceleration is expected, rising or flat trends are beneficial. These are not rigid rules, however. A slowly rising baseline may be adequate if treatment is expected to increase it substantially. Again, these methodological suggestions coincide closely with good clinical judgment. If the client is already improving maximally, then the therapist should wait before beginning treatment.

Once again, these considerations actually apply to any phase in a within-series strategy. The logic of simple and complex phase changes is the same whether one is going from A to B or from C to D.

Implementing the Second Phase

To begin with, is there a variable that needs to be controlled first? For example, could any effects be due simply to, say, encouragement to change and not to the specific treatment? If this is highly plausible, and especially if treatment is costly, difficult, aversive, or restrictive, the alternative treatment (e.g., encouragement) might be implemented first. This parallels good clinical decision making and may fit in with legal requirements, such as the initial use of the least restrictive alternative. If the less restrictive treatment does not work, there is still the option of implementing the full treatment (see below).

Another consideration in implementing treatment or any new phase is that it should begin in full force if possible. Gradual implementation might minimize apparent differences between phases. This is a difficult issue (Thomas, 1978), but violating this rule only makes positive findings less likely. Once found, clear results are not jeopardized.

When the second phase is implemented, only three outcomes are possible: no improvement, deterioration, or improvement. If there is no improvement, the clinician has three reasonable paths open, both clinically and methodologically. One is to wait to see if there is a delayed effect. A second option, also a common clinical step, is to try another treatment strategy. It is typically assumed that a phase producing no change can be with caution considered part of the previous phase (e.g., A=B/C). As phases are added, the plausibility of equivalence is jeopardized (e.g., an A=B=C=D=E/F/E/F design seems weak.) The solution is to be had in systematic replication across clients (e.g., several A/F/A/F designs could be added to the one above). Finally, treatment can be altered by adding or subtracting components (e.g., A=B/B+C/B), also a common clinical step.

If treatment produces deterioration, the clear course is to withdraw treatment. If the behavior once again improves, the clinician will have documented an iatrogenic effect of treatment, often itself a significant contribution to the field.

The final possible effect of the second phase is improvement, which opens three possible paths. First, the clinician can continue treatment through to a successful conclusion and store the resulting A/B design. When a similar case presents itself, a multiple baseline across persons can be attempted. This is an extremely useful option and will be discussed at length later in the article. Second, if the client has other similar problems or problem situations, apply the same treatment to them (again, a multiple baseline). A final course of action is to withdraw the treatment or implement a treatment placebo. If improvement then slows, a treatment effect is more likely.

The use of withdrawal is so popular that many confuse this design option with all of single case methodology, so a more extended discussion is warranted. There are potential problems with the withdrawal of an apparently effective treatment. It raises ethical issues, client fee issues, potential client morale problems, and possible neutralization of subsequent treatment effects. Few data exist on the actual likelihood of these problems, however, and there are many important counterarguments to be made (e.g., Hersen & Barlow, 1976).

The issue of withdrawal relates in special ways to the practicing clinical environment. First, if the treatment is of unknown benefit, a withdrawal can avoid the unnecessary use of ineffective treatment. Physicians recognize this issue in the common practice of drug holidays (i.e., withdrawals) to assess the continued need for treatment. Second, withdrawals often present themselves naturally in treatment in the form of vacations, holidays, sickness, temporary treatment dropouts, and the like. These can then be incorporated into ongoing clinical evaluations by examining measurements taken during or after these periods but before reintervention. Unlike withdrawals determined by the clinician, however, natural withdrawals are more likely to reflect variables of importance to these measures. For example, deterioration following treatment dropout may be due to factors producing that very decision rather than to the withdrawal of treatment per se. Therefore, clinicians should specify reasons for natural withdrawals and stress greater caution and need for replication when presenting cases with natural withdrawals. Third, withdrawals need not be long and drawn out. The slight delay in treatment that they impose should be weighed against their clinical value. Fourth, a good rationale that will minimize client morale problems can usually be given. The rationale can be either absolutely honest (e.g., "You've been rather successful so far with this approach, but I'm not sure we still need to be following this course, so let's take a little breather and see where things go"), or they can be somewhat deceptive (e.g., giving the client the expectation that treatment is normally stopped now and that this often leads to even greater improvement). Such placebo rationales must be handled with care, of course, just as a placebo drug might be in medical practice. Fifth, withdrawals are often produced when turning to other issues. For example, the clinician may wish to spend a few weeks in reassessment of the client. While clinically valuable, this might constitute an attention placebo for a specific problem under treatment. This is a type of withdrawal, just as data taken during an initial assessment phase (which involves much more than mere baseline measurement) is thought of as baseline. Finally, withdrawals often have clear clinical benefit to the client. If behavior worsens, the client may become convinced that treatment is necessary and successful. If not, the client may see that the problem is now under control.

After Withdrawal

If the clinician returns to the first condition following improvement on the second, three possible outcomes once again occur: deterioration, no change, or continued improvement. If the behavior deteriorates, the clinical and methodological course is clear: Reimplement the effective treatment (e.g., an A/B/A/B). If the behavior shows continued and further improvement, several options are available. One option is simply to wait. As in any situation in which the behavior is already improving, there may be little reason to further intervene. Sometimes the behavior will soon stop improving or deteriorate, perhaps due to a short-lived carry-over effect from the second phase. If, however, the behavior keeps improving significantly, the clinician can allow the case to continue to a successful conclusion and store these data, waiting for a similar case. This sequence can then be repeated but with a longer or shorter initial phase as part of a multiple baseline across subjects. If the effect is subsequent replicated and order effects eliminated, nonreversible improvement due to treatment will have been documented. If improvement continues in the withdrawal phase, the same sequence can be followed with another of the client's problem behaviors or the problem behavior in another situation, again producing multiple baselines. If the continued improvement is not maximal, treatment can be reimplemented anyway. A subsequent increase in the rate of improvement would establish greater confidence in the treatment.

If no change is seen when the second phase is withdrawn (the behavior shows neither deterioration nor continued improvement), the options described above are open. The reimplementation option is particularly attractive. Some methodologists might be concerned over this advice, since the level of the behavior shown in baseline was not reattained in the return to baseline phase. This is a difficult argument for the clinician, since it implies that lack of maintenance of behavior change is a requirement in order to show treatment effects when using a withdrawal. Essentially, this would have clinicians document success by showing failure. Fortunately, it is the history of single case methodology, not its logic, that enables such a problematic argument to be made. For example, animal operant researchers (especially historically) have often seemed to assume that current behavior is primarily a function of immediately present environmental variables. Thus, behavior should be in one steady state when these variables are present and in another when they are not. This type of assumption pervades much of single case methodology, often to the detriment of its clinical uses.

The assumptions of the clinician are quite different. The clinician usually assumes that the current level of behavior is often a function of historical variables as much as current conditions. Greater improvement may be expected to be associated with treatment, but the actual level of behavior hopefully is maintained even when treatment is withdrawn (cf. Sidman, 1960, on transition states).

When these assumptions are applied to the logic of within-series strategies, it is apparent that deteriorating (return to the previous level) is not required during withdrawal. If behavior improves faster during treatment than not, an effect is shown. It may be useful to regraph some data to underscore this. The top half of Figure 2, for example, shows an A/B/A/B sequence in which withdrawal produces less improvement but no clean reversals. The bottom half of the figure shows the same data calculated as difference scores from the trend in the previous phase (or same phase in the case of the first phase). When plotted in terms of improvement, a more classical pattern emerges.

There are many other ways in which the assumptions of the typical clinician overturn nonessentials of time series methodology as developed by operantly oriented psychologists and lead to new design options. For example, the notion of treatment phases as easily identifiable entities is jeopardized. A good deal of clinical work is done under 1 hour per week outpatient conditions. Sometimes, it is true, clinicians use this time to set up treatments that are obviously present throughout a specifiable time (e.g., a token economy for a noncompliant child). However, other clinicians (e.g., especially

432   STEVEN C. HAYES

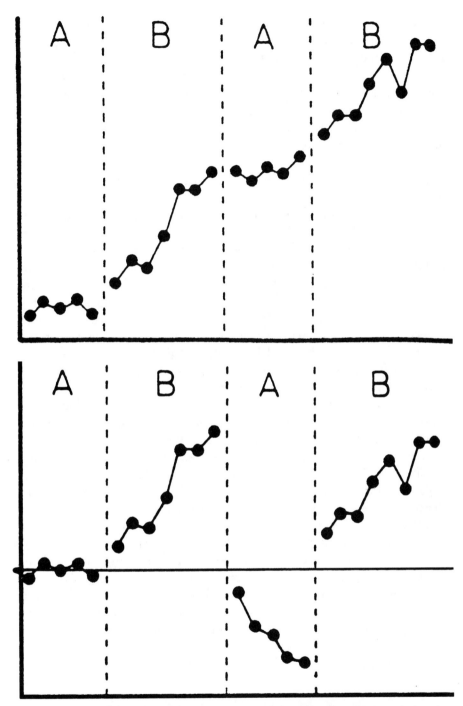

Figure 2. An example of the nondeterioration of behavior in the withdrawal phase of a within-series design, hypothetical data. (The lower graph is calculated in terms of improvement to highlight the control shown over the transitional state of behavior. The upper graph and lower graph both demonstrate experimental control despite nonreversibility; the lower is merely more obvious.)

those working with adults) do not change obvious aspects of the client's environment outside of the clinical session itself. When, then, can treatment be said to be present? During that hour? That day? That week?

Ambiguity about the meaning of the word *phase* is not lethal to the clinical use of within-series strategies, but it does help open up new design options. It is not lethal, because (a) the effects of treatment often last well beyond the actual therapy hours, (b) any ambiguity about the nature of phases (e.g., Thomas, 1978) makes only robust effects visible, and (c) phases usually incorporate considerable lengths of time. Thus, ambiguity about what is in one phase or in another is not a major threat to the internal validity of any clear effects actually obtained.

The design element opened up by this issue is the periodic treatments element (Hayes & Nelson, Note 1). The notion is that a consistent relationship between the periodicity of treatment and the periodicity of behavior change can demonstrate therapeutic effects. This relationship can only be shown when the frequency of behavioral measurement far exceeds the frequency of treatment sessions. An example may show the principle. The top half of Figure 3 shows the hypothetical record of positive social interactions self-recorded daily by a client. Arrows on the abscissa show days when the client saw a psychotherapist for 1-hr insight-oriented therapy sessions. Since the treatment sessions occur at varying intervals, and periods of improvement only follow them, these changes are likely due to treatment. The bottom half of the figure presents the data in difference score form, which draws this out even further. These data do not show what about the treatment produced the change (any more than an A/B/A design would). It may be therapist concern or the fact that the client attended a session of any kind. These possibilities would then need to be eliminated. For example, one could manipulate both the periodicity and nature of treatment. If the periodicity of behavior change was shown only when a particular type of treatment was in place, this would provide evidence for a more specific effect.

The periodic treatments element has apparently not be used in a published study (this is the first published description of the design element), although some of my own cases have shown clear examples of such periodicity (e.g., Hayes, Note 2). The major point is that clinical assumptions seem to lead to different design elements than those generated by the animal laboratory. It is possible that new developments in single case designs will occur as the needs and assumptions of practicing clinicians have more of an effect on the methodology itself.

BETWEEN-SERIES STRATEGIES

In contrast with the within-series elements, in which changes within a series of data points are compared, the between-series strategies compare two

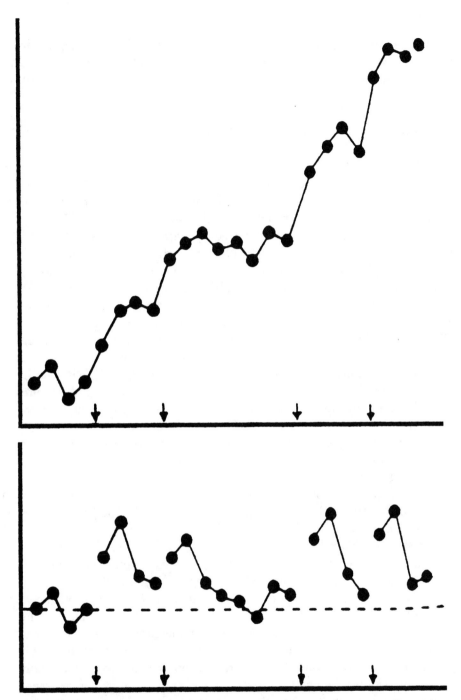

Figure 3. The periodic treatments effect is shown on hypothetical data. (Data are graphed in raw data form in the top graph. Arrows on the abscissa indicate treatment sessions. This apparent B-only graph does not reveal the periodicity of improvement and treatment as well as the bottom graph, where each two data points are plotted in terms of the difference from the mean of the two previous data points. Significant improvement occurs only after treatment. Both graphs show an experimental effect; the lower is merely more obvious.)

or more series of data points across time. The comparisons are repeatedly made between these series. There are two basic types of pure between-series elements: the alternating treatments design and the simultaneous treatments design.

The Alternating Treatments Design Element

The logic of the alternating treatments design (Barlow & Hayes, 1979) is based simply on the rapid and random (or semi-random) alternation of two or more conditions, in which there is one potential alternation of condition per measurement opportunity. Since a single data point associated with one condition may be preceded and followed by measurements associated with other conditions, there is no opportunity to estimate stability, level, and trend within phases. Rather, these estimates are obtained within conditions, by collecting each into a separate series. If there is a clear separation between such series, differences among conditions are inferred. For example, suppose a clinician wishes to examine the relationship of therapist self-disclosure to client self-disclosure. At the beginning of some sessions (randomly determined), the therapist self-discloses; in the other sessions, no self-disclosure is seen. Tape recordings of the sessions are rated (see Figure 4), with results demonstrating that therapist self-disclosure increases client self-disclosure. Note that the comparison is made purely between series. The general upward trend in each condition is not analyzed and may be due to extraneous factors, but the major comparison is still sound. Thus, the alternating treatments strategy is viable even if within-series trends are extreme or are changing rapidly (e.g., in learning situations or with maturational phenomena).

One could think of this as an extremely rapid A/B/A (cf. Campbell & Stanley's, 1963, discussion of an "equivalent time samples" design), but they differ significantly. Not only are the estimates of variability and source of treatment comparisons different, but this design also minimizes order effects (by random sequencing) and can incorporate three or even more conditions into a single comparison sequence (see Barlow & Hayes, 1979).

This design strategy is often combined with other design elements (e.g., a baseline), though it is not required. It is particularly useful for the comparison of two or more treatments or when measurement is cumbersome or lengthy (e.g., an entire MMPI). Only four data points are absolutely needed (two in each condition). Each data point may incorporate many treatment sessions; the rapid alternation refers only to the rate of treatment alternation relative to the rate of measurement. On the other extreme, alternations might be made several times per session (e.g., Hayes, Hussian, Turner, Grubb, & Anderson, Note 3).

This design is also valuable when difficult assessment decisions are presented. Suppose, for example, that a client is presenting with social deficits. The clinician may have a difficult time determining if the client is more

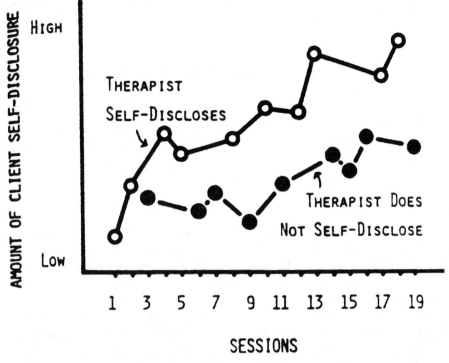

Figure 4. An example, using hypothetical data, of the alternating treatments design element. (The clear difference between the two conditions shows that more client self-disclosure is produced when the therapist self-discloses. The overall increase across time is not analyzed without the addition of other design elements; e.g., A phases before and after.)

likely to respond to anxiety management procedures or social skills training procedures. Rather than guess, the clinician might do both in an alternating treatments fashion. The better treatment may quickly be revealed, and all treatment effort could then go in this direction.

The Simultaneous Treatment Design Element

The only other true between-series element is the simultaneous treatment design (Browning, 1967). It requires the simultaneous presence of two or more treatments. Since the treatments are truly available simultaneously, the client controls which treatment is actually applied (much as in a concurrent schedule design in animal operant work). Thus, a true instance of this design can only measure treatment preference, not treatment effectiveness. Apparently only one example (Browning, 1967) exists in the applied literature. (As for Kazdin & Hartmann, 1978, and McCullough, Cornell, McDaniel, & Meuller, 1974, see Barlow & Hayes, 1979.) However, many current applied questions (e.g., about the relative aversiveness or restrictiveness of treatments) are issues of preference, and the simultaneous treatments design might be of real use in these situations.

COMBINED-SERIES STRATEGIES

Several design elements in time series experimentation borrow from both of the previously described strategies. The combined-series elements utilize coordinated sets of comparisons made both between and within series of measurements.

The Multiple Baseline

Undoubtedly the most familiar combined-series element is the multiple baseline. Its logic is intended to correct for major deficiencies of a simple phase change (say, an A/B). In an A/B, any changes between the two phases could be due to coincidental extraneous events: maturation, cyclical behavior, baseline assessment, and so on. The multiple baseline solves these problems by replicating the A/B but with different lengths of baseline for each replication (a strategy that controls for the amount of baseline assessment or mere maturation) and with the actual time of the phase change arbitrarily altered (to reduce the possibility of correlated extraneous events).

As is shown in Figure 5, a typical multiple baseline allows several comparisons. Some are identical to those made in a simple phase change, whereas others are between-series comparisons, examining patterns within an unchanged series compared to phase changes in other series.

A multiple baseline can be done with a similar behavior in two or more clients (across people), two or more behaviors in one client (across behaviors), or with a behavior in two or more settings in one person (across settings). The specific phase changes, however, must be the same—the same first condition must yield to the same second condition—since it is alternative explanations for a specific phase change effect that are being controlled.

The label *multiple baseline* is something of a misnomer. The logic of the comparison applies to any set of phase changes so arranged, whether or not there is a baseline present. For example, a series of B/C phase changes could easily be arranged into a multiple baseline (*multiple phase change* would actually be a clearer term). Sometimes it is used sequentially; for example, the sequence A/B/C (with A/C/B to control for order effects) can be put into a type of multiple baseline, as shown in the top half of Figure 6. This arrangement is problematic, since the third phase is introduced after equal second-phase lengths in each series (not controlling for sudden maturational or for phase length effects in the B/C comparison). A better sequential multiple baseline is shown in the bottom half of Figure 6.

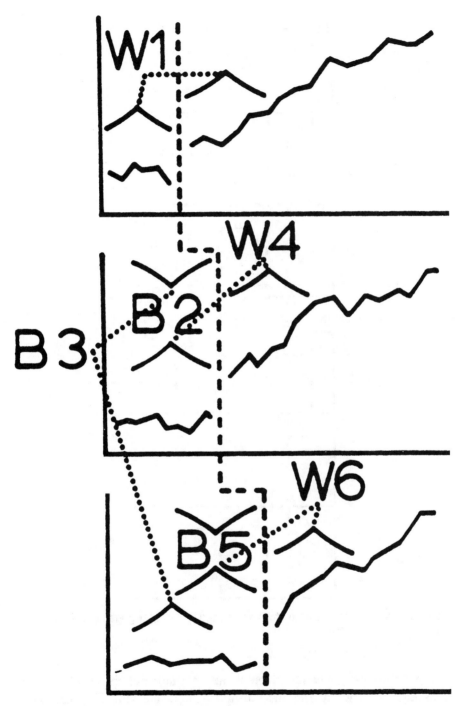

Figure 5. The types of comparisons made in a multiple baseline. (W = a within-series comparison, and B = a between-series comparison. The numbers show the usual sequence of comparisons.)

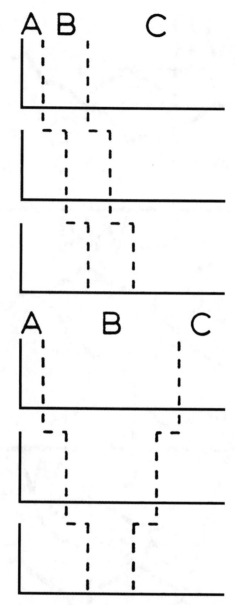

Figure 6. An example of a weak (top) and strong (bottom) arrangement in a sequential multiple baseline.

No absolute rule can be given about the number of phase shift replications required between series in a multiple baseline element. The logic of the maneuver applies as well to a single replication as to several; it is simply that each additional series strengthens our confidence that much more. Thus, the clinician should not feel as though the element is useless when only two series are compared, though more are desirable. The same can be said about the differences in initial phase length. If one series has an initial phase only slightly longer or shorter than the other, this is less satisfactory than if there are large differences.

Much has been made of the need to avoid the multiple baseline when the specific sites are interdependent (e.g., Kazdin & Kopel, 1975). If a phase shift in a multiple baseline is accompanied by behavior change not only within series but also between series, it is difficult to distinguish uncontrolled effects from true treatment effects. For example, in a multiple baseline across behaviors, changes in one behavior may produce changes in another, because of actual processes of response generalization caused by treatment. Typically, this is not a problem in the use of multiple baseline elements so much as it is an opportunity to study generalization effects. Thus, the clinician in this situation could immediately embark on a new design (e.g., withdraw treatment and see if both behaviors stop improving), which would document that the multiple effects are actually being caused by treatment, an important contribution. Further, if several series are being compared, some interdependence can be tolerated (e.g., Hayes & Barlow, 1977; Hersen & Bellack, 1976) without undoing the design (Kazdin, 1980).

The opportunity to use the multiple baseline element in clinical practice is very large. Multiple baselines often form naturally across behaviors due to the tendency for practicing clinicians to tackle subsets of problems sequentially rather than all at once. Multiple baselines across settings are less common but also naturally occur when clinicians treat problem behavior shown in one specific condition first rather than treating the problem all at once (e.g., Hayes & Barlow, 1977).

The multiple baseline across people is probably one of the clearest examples of natural design elements that arise in clinical practice. Nothing could be more natural to clinical work than an A/B. To form a multiple baseline, all the clinician need do is save several of these with similar problems and the same treatment. Individual clients will inevitably have differing lengths of baseline, often widely so, due to case complexities or to matters of convenience. Thus, sequential cases usually lead to multiple baseline across people.

Some of the earliest applied literature on the multiple baseline (e.g., Baer, Wolf, & Risley, 1968) stated that multiple baselines across persons should always be done at the same time in the same setting with the same behavior. Saving cases, with perhaps periods of months or even years separating each, violates this rule, but fortunately the logic of the strategy does not really require it. If the time of the phase shift differs in real time from client to client, it is unlikely that important external events could repeatedly coincide with the phase changes. The control exerted by the different lengths of baseline remain.[2]

---

[2] A minor weakness is the fact that the events in real time that might have produced the phase change are not present in the other series. If effects are clear, this need not be a concern, since a series of such coincidences is still unlikely.

There is a potential difficulty, which was touched on in the earlier discussion of natural withdrawals. If the clinician is allowing the case itself to determine the exact length of baseline, there is the danger that the same factor which indicated that it is time to change phases is correlated with processes that produce behavior change. The main practical protections against this difficulty are replication (including several cases in natural multiple baselines) and information (reporting why the phase was changed for each client). If reasons for changing phases vary from client to client, it is unlikely that a third variable consistently produced changes in the second phase.

It is also essential that clinicians report all cases attempted, not just those showing the desired effect. If the effect is not seen in some of the cases, the clinician should attempt to find out why; indeed this seems required by good clinical practice. A careful examination of possible differences between individuals accounting for variable results may lead to treatment solutions for nonresponsive clients. Data showing subsequent response would increase our knowledge about mechanisms producing change and about boundary conditions of a given treatment.

The multiple baseline across cases also provides a home for those cases in which just treatment is given (B only) and in which treatment is never given (baseline-only control; see below). As anchors in a series of cases arranged into a multiple baseline across subjects, such cases can provide evidence of the effectiveness of treatment even when no baseline is taken (B only), thus controlling for an unlikely order effect due to A or of the likelihood of change when no treatment is given (baseline-only control).

Crossovers

This maneuver (drawn from similar group-comparison approaches; see Kazdin, 1980) is based on two concurrent phase changes, one in reverse order of the other. For example, one subject may experience a B/C sequence; the other, a C/B. By changing phases at the same time, this strategy equalizes alternative sources of control that might have produced an apparent phase change effect (e.g., maturation, phase length). Since these sources are equalized, consistent within-series effects in the two series (e.g., if B > C in both cases) provide evidence for the comparison. The controls are not strong, however (e.g., order effects are weakly dealt with), so the entire crossover should be replicated at least once with other clients. Some of these same issues apply to the true reversal, which also is a combined series element (see Leitenberg, 1973).

The Baseline-Only Control

Many times problems are repeatedly assessed but never treated. This may be done deliberately (e.g., assessing those on a waiting list) or serendipitously (e.g., assessing a problem behavior that is never treated, because the client moves away). Whatever else has been done, these data can be examined as a type of combined- or between-series comparison (e.g., Brownell, Hayes, & Barlow, 1977; Hayes & Cone, 1977). The logic of this comparison is identical to the between-series comparisons made in a multiple baseline design (see Figure 5). Changes occurring elsewhere and not in the baseline-only control series are more likely to have been produced by treatment (cf. Campbell & Stanley's, 1963, equivalent time samples design).

ISSUES IN THE USE OF TIME SERIES DESIGN TOOLS

The purpose of the present article is to provide an overall framework for present single-case design tools and to point out how they might fit into evaluations of actual clinical practice. If these tools are to be used by large numbers of practicing clinicians, many specific problems need to be solved (e.g., development of practical measurement tools, methods of specifying of treatment activities), but the most important problem is one of overall approach. By repeatedly emphasizing design elements rather than complete designs, the present organization is meant to encourage creative evaluations in actual clinical decision making. These are not static tools. It is quite possible to devise designs without names, designs in which many of the elements mentioned in the article are combined. As the clinician approaches each case, questions arise that require answers on clinical grounds. If the clinician is aware of available design options, some time series strategy is almost always available that fits closely with the logic of clinical decision making itself.

Table 1 presents some clinically important questions and examples of the various design elements useful in that situation. Within any row of this table, various elements can be combined to address a given clinical question. As different questions arise, different elements can be used (draw from different rows).

Another major stumbling block in the use of time series design tools in clinical practice is the historical status of the division between practice and research. At first glance, the distinction between research and treatment is clear cut and easily applied. Clinicians who have not used the type of approach advocated here often very easily define research and treatment in terms of their apparent structure (Hayes, Note 4), such as (a) Did the clinician collect systematic data? (b) Were the variables producing the impact systematically analyzed? (c) Were the results of this endeavor presented or published? The presence of any one of these is likely to lead to the endeavor's being termed "research." The consequences of this can be dramatic. We have generated a large number of protections in research with human subjects. It is possible, however, to use the structure of research to perform the function

TABLE 1
Examples of the Use of Design Elements to Answer Specific Types of Clinical Questions

Clinical Question	Design type		
	Within series	Between series	Combined series
Does a treatment work?	A/B/A/B/ ... B/A/B/A/ ... A/B (see combined designs) Periodic treatments design Changing criterion design	Alternating treatments (comparing A and B)	Multiple baseline across settings, behaviors, or persons comparing A and B Replicated crossovers (comparing A and B)
Does one treatment work better than another, given that we already know they work?	B/C/B/C/ ... C/B/C/B/ ...	Alternating treatments (comparing B and C)	Replicated crossovers (comparing B and C) Multiple baselines (comparing B and C and controlling for order)
Does one treatment work, does another work, and which works better?	A/B/A/C/A combined with A/C/A/B/A	Alternating treatments (comparing A and B and C)	Multiple baseline (comparing A and B and C and controlling for order)
	Or combine any element from Row A with any element from Row B		
Are there elements within a successful treatment that make it work?	B/B +C/B B+C/B/B+C C/B+C/C B+C/C/B+C	Alternating treatments (comparing, for example, B and B+C)	Multiple baseline (comparing B and B+C, and C and B+C) Replicated crossovers (comparing B and B+C, and C and B+C)
Does the client prefer one treatment over another?		Simultaneous treatments (comparing B and C)	
Does a treatment work, and if it does, what part of it makes it work?	Combine any elements from Rows A or C with any element from Row D		
What level of treatment is optimal?	Ascending/descending design A/B'/B/B'	Alternating treatments (comparing B and B')	Multiple baseline (comparing B and B' and controlling for order) Replicated crossovers (comparing B and B')

of treatment. This is treatment evaluation or empirical clinical practice (Jayaratne & Levy, 1979).

The ethical questions posed by treatment as opposed to treatment evaluation seem very similar. Indeed, the effects of evaluations of the sort described here seem beneficial on two grounds (Levy & Olson, 1979). First, the attempt to evaluate treatment is likely to contribute to clinical effectiveness by increasing feedback to the clinician and client alike, by increasing the clinician's involvement in the case, and by increasing information available about the client's response to treatment. Second, by increasing the knowledge base in the field more generally, such an approach would make successful treatment of others more likely.

Nevertheless, practicing clinicians (and society more generally) often make a distinction between treatment and evaluation based on mere appearance. In particular, evaluation is often grouped with research rather than with treatment per se. The effect of this is to discourage empirical clinical practice, since it leads to a number of additional protections beyond that required in the treatment environment itself. Unless this process is resisted (e.g., by not submitting routine clinical evaluation to human-subjects committees), strong negative pressure is put on the practicing clinician to avoid systematic evaluation.

Additional problems remain (Hayes, 1980; Levy & Olson, 1979; Thomas, 1978). For example, if the approach advocated here were adopted, a flood of information could emerge from the many thousands of practicing clinicians. Where would it be put? Who would publish it? Would it be simple-minded research anyway? Multiple case manuscripts might be a partial solution; a clearing-house-type arrangement might also be of aid, but it clearly would strain current information-handling systems.

Another problem is the importance of compromises forced by the clinical environment. There are a number of them (Thomas, 1978), although most seem soluble. The major solution is the same as that for most difficulties in time series designs more generally: replication. Only with the enormous resources provided by practicing clinicians does this advice seem practical. Without them, the external validity of single case work, which emerges only from replication (Hersen & Barlow, 1976), has little chance of full demonstration or analysis.

This, then, is the situation. Practicing clinicians are essential to the development of our knowledge base in clinical psychology, and time series experimentation seems fully applicable to the clinical environment. Indeed, the resources needed to repeatedly replicate single case experimentation are available only by including practicing clinicians. If combined, these needs, abilities, and resources could create a true revolution in clinical psychology. The question is, will they be?

REFERENCE NOTES

1. Hayes, S. C., & Nelson, R. O. *Realistic research strategies for practicing clinicians*. Workshop presented at the meeting of the Association for Advancement of Behavior Therapy, San Francisco, December 1979.
2. Hayes, S. C. *A component analysis of flooding relief*. Paper presented at the meeting of the American Psychological Association, Washington, DC, September 1976.
3. Hayes, S. C., Hussian, R., Turner, A. E., Grubb T., & Anderson, N. *The nature, effect, and generalization of coping statements in the treatment of clinically significant anxiety*. Paper presented at the meeting of the Association for Advancement of Behavior Therapy, San Francisco, December 1979.
4. Hayes, S. C. *Ethical dilemmas of the empirical clinician*. Paper presented at the meeting of the Association for Behavior Analysis, Dearborn, Michigan, May 1979.

REFERENCES

Baer, D. M., Wolf, M. M., & Risley, T. R. (1968). Some current dimensions of applied behavior analysis. *Journal of Applied Behavior Analysis, 1*, 91–97.

Barlow, D. H. (1980). Behavioral therapy: The next decade. *Behavior Therapy, 11*, 315–328.

Barlow, D. H., & Hayes, S. C. (1979). Alternating treatments design: One strategy for comparing the effects of two treatments in a single subject. *Journal of Applied Behavior Analysis, 12*, 199–210.

Barlow, D. H., & Hersen, M. (1973). Single-case experimental designs: Uses in applied clinical research. *Archives of General Psychiatry, 29*, 319–325.

Becker, I. M., & Rosenfeld, J. G. (1976). Rational–emotive therapy—A study of initial therapy sessions of Albert Ellis. *Journal of Clinical Psychology, 76*, 12–26.

Bernard, C. (1865). *An introduction to the study of experimental medicine*. New York: Dover.

Box, G. E. P., & Jenkins, G. M. (1976). *Time series analysis: Forecasting and control*. San Francisco: Holden-Day.

Brownell, K. E., Hayes, S. C., & Barlow, D. H. (1977). Patterns of appropriate and deviant arousal: The behavioral treatment of multiple sexual deviations. *Journal of Consulting and Clinical Psychology, 45*, 1144–1155.

Browning, R. M. (1967). A same-subject design for simultaneous comparison of three reinforcement contingencies. *Behaviour Research and Therapy, 5*, 237–243.

Browning R. M., & Stover, D. O. (1971). *Behavior modification in child treatment: An experimental and clinical approach*. Chicago: Aldine-Atherton.

Campbell, D. T., & Stanley, J. C. (1963). *Experimental and quasi-experimental designs for research*. Chicago: Rand McNally.

Chassan, J. B. (1967). *Research design in clinical psychology and psychiatry*. New York: Appleton-Century-Crofts.

Chassan, J. B. (1979). *Research design in clinical psychology and psychiatry* (2nd ed.). New York: Irvington.

Garfield, S. L., & Kurtz, R. (1976). Clinical psychologists in the 1970s. *American Psychologist, 31*, 1–9.

Glass, G. V., Wilson, V. L., & Gottmann, J. M. (1975). *Design and analysis of time-series experiments*. Boulder: University of Colorado Press.

Gottmann, J. M., McFall, R. M., & Barnett, J. T. (1969). Design and analysis of research using time series. *Psychological Bulletin, 72*, 299–306.

Hartmann, D. P., & Hall, R. V. (1976). The changing criterion design. *Journal of Applied Behavior Analysis, 9*, 527–532.

Hayes, S. C. (1980). A review of Jayaratne & Levy's "Empirical clinical practice." *Behavioral Assessment, 2*, 306–308.

Hayes, S. C., & Barlow, D. H. (1977). Flooding relief in a case of public transportation phobia. *Behavior Therapy, 8*, 742–746.

Hayes, S. C., & Cone, J. D. (1977). Reducing residential electrical energy use: Payments, information, and feedback. *Journal of Applied Behavior Analysis, 10*, 425–435.

Hersen, M., & Barlow, D. H. (1976). *Single case experimental designs: Strategies for studying behavior change*. New York: Pergamon Press.

Hersen, M., & Bellack, A. S. (1976). A multiple baseline analysis of social skills training in chronic schizophrenics. *Journal of Applied Behavior Analysis, 9*, 527–532.

Holt, R. R. (Ed). (1971). *New horizons for psychotherapy: Autonomy as a profession*. New York: International Universities Press.

Jayaratne, S., & Levy, R. L. (1979). *Empirical clinical practice*. New York: Columbia University Press.

Kazdin, A. E. (1978). Methodological and interpretive problems of single-case experimental designs. *Journal of Consulting and Clinical Psychology, 46*, 629–642.

Kazdin, A. E. (1980). *Research design in clinical psychology*. New York: Harper & Row.

Kazdin, A. E., & Hartmann, D. P. (1978). The simultaneous-treatment design. *Behavior Therapy, 9*, 912–922.

Kazdin, A. E., & Kopel, S. A. (1975). On resolving ambiguities of the multiple-baseline design: Problems and recommendations. *Behavior Therapy, 6*, 601–608.

Kelly, E. L., Goldberg, L. R., Fiske, D. W., & Kilkowski, J. M. (1978). Twenty-five years later. *American Psychologist, 33*, 746–755.

Kratochwill, T. F. (1978). *Single subject research: Strategies for evaluating change*. New York: Academic Press.

Leitenberg, H. (1973). The use of single case methodology in psychotherapy research. *Journal of Abnormal Psychology, 82,* 87–101.

Leitenberg, H. (1974). Training clinical researchers in psychology. *Professional Psychology, 5,* 59–69.

Levy, L. H. (1962). The skew in clinical psychology. *American Psychologist, 17,* 244–249.

Levy, R. L., & Olson, D. G. (1979). The single subject methodology in clinical practice: An overview. *Journal of Social Service Research, 3,* 25–49.

Mahoney, M. J. (1978). Experimental methods and outcome evaluation. *Journal of Consulting and Clinical Psychology, 42,* 660–672.

McCullough, J. P., Cornell, J. E., McDaniel, M. H., & Meuller, R. K. (1974). Utilization of the simultaneous treatment design to improve student behavior in a first-grade classroom. *Journal of Consulting and Clinical Psychology, 42,* 288–292.

Meehl, P. E. (1971). A scientific, scholarly, non-research doctorate for clinical practitioners: Arguments pro and con. In R. R. Holt (Ed.), *New horizons for psychotherapy: Autonomy as a profession*. New York: International Universities Press.

Meltzoff, J., & Kornreich, M. (1970). *Research in a psychotherapy*. New York: Atherton.

Millon, T., & Diesenhaus, H. I. (1972). *Research methods in psychopathology*. New York: Wiley.

Nelson, R. O. (1981). Realistic dependent measures for clinical use. *Journal of Consulting and Clinical Psychology, 49,* 168–182.

Paul, G. L. (1969). Behavior modification research: Design and tactics. In C. M. Franks (Ed.), *Behavior therapy: Appraisal and status*. New York: McGraw-Hill.

Peterson, D. R. (1976). Need for the doctor of psychology degree in professional psychology. *American Psychologist, 31,* 792–798.

Raush, H. L. (1969). Naturalistic method and the clinical approach. In E. P. Willems & H. L. Raush (Eds.), *Naturalistic viewpoints in psychological research*. New York: Holt, Rinehart & Winston.

Raush, H. L. (1974). Research, practice, and accountability. *American Psychologist, 29,* 678–681.

Rogers, C. R. (1973). Some new challenges. *American Psychologist, 28,* 379–387.

Shakow, D. (1976). What is clinical psychology? *American Psychologist, 31,* 553–560.

Sidman, M. (1960). *Tactics of scientific research*. New York: Basic Books.

Svenson, S. E., & Chassan, J. B. (1967). A note on ethics and patient consent in single-case design. *Journal of Nervous and Mental Disease, 145*(3), 206–207.

Thelen, M. H., & Ewing, D. R. (1970). Roles, functions, and training in clinical psychology: A survey of academic clinicians. *American Psychologist, 25,* 550–554.

Thomas, E. J. (1978). Research and service in single-case experimentation: Conflicts and choices. *Social Work Research and Abstracts, 14,* 20–31.

Zaro, J. S., Barach, R., Nedelmann, D. J., & Dreiblatt, I. S. (1977). *A guide for beginning psychotherapists.* Cambridge, England: Cambridge University Press.

22

EFFICACY AND SPECIFIC EFFECTS DATA ON NEW TREATMENTS: A CASE STUDY STRATEGY WITH MIXED ANXIETY–DEPRESSION

KARLA MORAS, LESLIE A. TELFER, AND DAVID H. BARLOW

This article illustrates a case study research strategy that can yield preliminary efficacy data on psychotherapeutic treatments, as well as examine theorized mechanisms of action of treatments. Preliminary efficacy data on new treatments are a critical link to conducting controlled trials of potentially important psychotherapeutic interventions. However, as psychotherapy researchers have noted, a handicap to psychosocial treatment outcome research is that evidence for a treatment's efficacy is needed to support grant applications (e.g., to the National Institute of Mental Health [NIMH]) to study the treatment's efficacy. Furthermore, essentially no funding sources are

Reprinted from the *Journal of Consulting and Clinical Psychology, 61*, 412–420. Copyright 1993 by the American Psychological Association.

This work was supported in part by a National Alliance for Research on Schizophrenia and Depression Young Investigator Award to Karla Moras, Grant RO1 M-39096 from the National Institute of Mental Health (NIMH) to David H. Barlow, and by NIMH Clinical Research Center Grant P50 MH45178 to Paul Crits-Christoph.

available for preliminary efficacy studies of psychosocial treatments. The situation is a paradoxical one that differs from the circumstances affecting psychopharmacological treatment research, in which drug companies financially support and actively recruit investigators to do preliminary drug trials. The results of such trials are often subsequently used by investigators to support NIMH grant applications on drug treatments.

Using single-case designs to develop and study new treatments is not a novel idea. Wolpe's (1958) pioneering and broadly influential work on the technique of systematic desensitization, based on a series of 210 cases, is one notable example (Barlow, Hayes, & Nelson, 1984). Historically, however, single-case experimental designs have been used almost exclusively to study treatments derived from behavioral theories and principles, as illustrated by the examples used in major textbooks on single-case design (e.g., Barlow & Hersen, 1984; Hersen & Barlow, 1976; Kazdin, 1982). Thus, our goal in this article is to illustrate the application of single-case methodology to a treatment that is not primarily behavioral and to thereby attend investigators to the utility of such methods for preliminary studies of diverse forms of psychotherapy. In addition, one of our primary interests in conducting the case studies described here is to test a specific effects model of the therapeutic action of treatments for anxiety and for depression.

We used a single-case experimental design strategy to study a treatment for patients who have both an anxiety and a mood disorder as described in the *Diagnostic and Statistical Manual of Mental Disorders* (3rd ed., rev.; DSM–III–R; American Psychiatric Association, 1987). The strategy was developed to test the hypothesis that two existing treatment approaches, one for panic disorder (Barlow & Craske, 1989) and one for major depression (Klerman, Weissman, Rounsaville, & Chevron, 1984), could be modified and combined to create a useful treatment for patients with coexisting DSM–III–R generalized anxiety disorder (GAD) and major depression (MD). We further hypothesized that, because the combined treatment would focus on both anxiety and depression, it would be more effective for such patients than a treatment that targeted only one of the disorders. The foregoing hypothesis implied the additional hypothesis that each of the treatments would show some specific effect on the symptoms for which the treatment was developed; that is, the anxiety treatment component would have relatively more impact on symptoms of anxiety than depression, and the reverse would be true for the depression treatment component. The hypothesis is presented in schematic form in Figure 1.

The essence of our research strategy is to apply the same case study protocol in a replication series of cases, each of which is designed to provide data on outcome and on the pattern of symptom change associated with administration of each component of the treatment. The strategy was tailored to certain features of our situation, but it can be modified for other situations. A

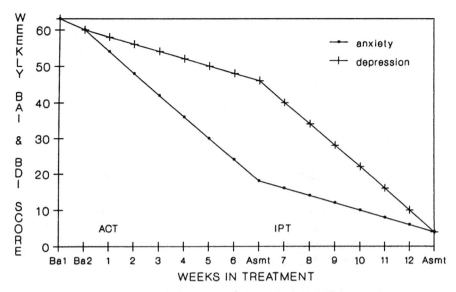

Figure 1. Hypothesized differential rates of change of symptoms of anxiety and depression during the anxiety control (ACT) component of the treatment and the Interpersonal Psychotherapy of Depression (IPT) component of the treatment. (BAI = Beck Anxiety Inventory; BDI = Beck Depression Inventory; Ba1 = Baseline Week 1; Ba2 = Baseline Week 2; Asmt = assessment week.)

"skeleton" strategy is presented that can be enhanced with more patients per therapist or with more therapists, when such resources are available. The elements of the strategy are listed next. References indicate where more extensive discussions of relevant aspects of case study methodology can be found.

1. Hypotheses were generated that the case study protocol was designed to examine, either statistically (e.g., by pooling data from a series of case studies) or by visual inspection (Barlow & Hersen, 1984; Kazdin, 1982). The hypotheses determined the design of the case study protocol.
2. An A/B/A/C/A/A single-case design was used in which A = assessment (2-week baseline); B = treatment for GAD; A = assessment (after six sessions of anxiety treatment); C = treatment for MD; A = assessment (after six sessions of depression treatment); and A = assessment (6-month and 1-year follow-ups). Depending on the hypotheses, when two treatments are administered, as they were in our cases, counterbalancing the order of the treatments across cases might be the optimal design because it controls for the influence of order effects on the dependent variables.

3. Patients were matched on intake diagnoses and on other potentially outcome-relevant demographic features. Patients in our case studies were required to meet *DSM–III–R* criteria for both GAD and MD; have about equally severe symptoms of GAD and MD; have no other clinically significant diagnoses; and be of similar age and marital, parental, and employment status.[1] The matching strategy is the "conservative approach" described by Barlow and Hersen (1984).

4. An assessment battery was used that included continuous self-report assessment (Kazdin, 1982) of dependent variables and diagnosticians' assessments of dependent variables by means of a structured interview. The main dependent variables in our cases were diagnostic and symptom measures of anxiety and depression. Patients made global ratings of their anxiety and depression daily, starting from the baseline assessment period. They also completed the Beck Anxiety Inventory (Beck, Epstein, & Brown, 1988) and the Beck Depression Inventory (Beck, Steer, & Garbin, 1988) weekly, starting from the baseline period. Therapist measures were not used because two of the investigators (Moras and Telfer) were the therapists and we assumed that measures we completed would be biased. Ideally, the therapists would be neither the investigators nor the developers of the treatment.

5. All assessments for a case were performed by the same diagnostician. To reduce error variance across the repeated clinical ratings on each case, the same diagnostician performed each assessment on any one patient, but different diagnosticians were used across cases.

6. Two therapists were used, each of whom treated an equal number of patients of each gender. A clinical replication strategy was used in which a series of case studies are completed, using the same design (Barlow et al., 1984; Barlow & Hersen, 1984; Hersen & Barlow, 1976). In a clinical replication strategy, more than one therapist participates, and an equal number of patients of each gender are treated by each therapist, to obtain data on the generalizability of findings. Two female therapists

---

[1] When a primary goal is to obtain generalizable outcome findings from a series of case studies, heterogeneity of cases on demographic variables is preferable to matching (Hersen & Barlow, 1976). Our interest in a process question (the relationship between changes in anxiety and depression over the course of treatment) led us to match on demographic variables. We thought that a person's typical environmental stressors caused by basic social responsibilities (e.g., employment, parenting, or marriage) would affect day-to-day fluctuations in anxiety and depression; therefore, we controlled for marital, parental, and employment status and for age group.

were a given in our situation. Ideally, with only two therapists available, one would have been male and one female, and each would treat an equal number of patients of each gender.

7. A treatment manual was created that specifies the conduct of the treatment. A treatment manual is required to teach the therapists how to conduct the treatment that is studied, help standardize each therapist's administration of the treatment across the case studies, and describe the treatment intervention to facilitate replication by other investigators.

8. Treatment sessions were audiotaped. Audiotapes are needed to evaluate the extent to which the designated treatment approach is adhered to by each therapist.

9. Outcome data from another treatment were compared with outcome data from the case studies to evaluate the efficacy of the new treatment. Case study outcome data were compared with outcome data on diagnostically similar cases who received only an anxiety-focused treatment for GAD (Barlow, Rapee, & Brown, 1992). The comparison was done to evaluate the efficacy of the new treatment, specifically its impact on anxiety and depression, compared with a treatment for anxiety only. This component of the research strategy is similar to Sidman's (1960) method of independent verification.

METHOD

This section describes how the foregoing strategy was applied in two completed case studies.

Patients

Patients were selected from those evaluated at an anxiety disorders specialty clinic. The main inclusion criterion was meeting diagnostic criteria for DSM–III–R GAD and MD, based on a structured diagnostic interview, the Anxiety Disorders Interview Schedule–Revised (ADIS–R; Di Nardo & Barlow, 1988). The ADIS–R includes a 9-point severity rating scale (0–8) that is used to indicate the clinical severity of each diagnosis assigned. Any case that had comorbid GAD and MD of approximately equal clinical severity and no other clinically significant disorder could be selected.

Two cases were selected and treated, each by a different therapist. The patients were well matched diagnostically as well as on potentially relevant sociodemographic characteristics (e.g., marital and parental status, age, and employment).

Case 1

The patient was a woman in her early 40s who had three children (ranging in age from 7 to 15). She held a medically oriented job. Her complaints were waking up and not feeling like getting out of bed, palpitations, poor appetite, and low energy level. She also reported symptoms consistent with excessive worry about financial matters and about inadvertently harming someone by making mistakes in her job. When asked about relationships in her life, she said that her husband was hard to live with and that she felt that she was suppressing anger, although he did not realize that anything was wrong. Her complaints had been going on for about 3 months, but she reported having experienced them intermittently for 10 years. Her DSM–III–R diagnoses and their clinical severity were Major Depressive Episode (single, moderate) 5 and Anxiety Disorder, Not Otherwise Specified 4.[2]

Case 2

The patient was a man in his mid-30s who had three children (ranging in age from 4 to 12). He worked full time in a semiskilled position. His complaints were "breaking down easy and crying a lot," a "no care attitude," feeling nervous, and feeling like running from his job. When asked about relationships in his life, he said that he and his wife "seemed to be going their own separate ways." However, he then quickly negated the statement by saying that they didn't seem to be growing apart; rather they seemed to be closer but more independent. The diagnosis based on two independent structured diagnostic interviews was co-principal Major Depression Episode (recurrent, moderate) 5 and GAD 5.

Therapists

Two therapists (Karla Moras and Leslie A. Telfer) conducted the treatments. The first is an experienced clinical psychologist; the other was, at the time of the study, a fourth-year graduate student in clinical psychology who had considerable clinical experience.

Instruments

Hamilton Anxiety Rating Scale (HARS)

The HARS (M. Hamilton, 1959) is a clinician-rated 13-item scale that is used in clinical research to assess symptoms conventionally accepted as

---

[2] The case was selected for the study although her anxiety diagnosis was *DSM–III–R* Anxiety Disorder Not Otherwise Specified, rather than GAD. She was accepted because although the diagnostic staff disagreed about whether she met the two spheres of worry criterion required for GAD, evidence for the criterion was presented.

signifiers of anxiety. The possible score range is 0–44. The HARS is included in the ADIS–R interview. HARS ratings were made at each assessment point by a diagnostic interviewer.

Hamilton Rating Scale for Depression (HRSD)

The HRSD (M. Hamilton, 1960) is a clinician-rated instrument that is commonly used to assess symptoms of depression. The 24-item version of the HRSD (Guy, 1976) was used in this study (the possible score range is 0–74). The HRSD is included in the ADIS–R interview. HRSD ratings were made at each assessment point by a diagnostician.

Beck Anxiety Inventory (BAI)

The BAI (Beck, Epstein, & Brown, 1988) is a 21-item self-report measure of somatic and cognitive symptoms of anxiety. The possible score range is 0–63. During treatment, patients completed the BAI weekly, immediately before each treatment session.

Beck Depression Inventory (BDI)

The BDI (Beck, Steer, & Garbin, 1988) is a 21-item, self-report measure of cognitive, mood, and neurovegetative symptoms of depression. The possible score range is 0–63. It was completed according to the same schedule as that used for the BAI.

Weekly Record of Anxiety and Depression (WRAD)

The WRAD (Barlow, 1988) is a self-report instrument that obtains a patient's daily global ratings of depression and average anxiety level, on a scale ranging from *none* (0) to *as much as you can imagine* (8). Patients completed the WRAD every day, starting from the baseline assessment through the posttreatment assessment (i.e., after the first 12 sessions of treatment).

Treatment

The treatment consisted of a modification of Barlow and Craske's (1989) cognitive–behavioral treatment for panic disorder and of Interpersonal Psychotherapy of Depression (IPT) as described by Klerman et al. (1984). The combined treatment included an anxiety control component for GAD and IPT for depression.

Anxiety Control Treatment (ACT) Component

ACT consisted of three modified components of Barlow and Craske's (1989) Panic Control Treatment (PCT), which includes cognitively and behaviorally focused interventions to reduce the frequency and intensity of panic attacks. PCT also is designed to teach skills and strategies for managing generalized anxiety and tension.

When used to treat panic disorder, the components of PCT are information about anxiety and panic attacks, breathing retraining, cognitive restructuring, and interoceptive exposure. Two components, breathing retraining and cognitive restructuring, are anxiety management strategies that can be readily applied to GAD, given that it is defined in the *DSM–III–R* primarily by cognitive (excessive worry and vigilance) and somatic symptoms. The interoceptive exposure component is theoretically more specific to panic disorder and was not used in ACT. We modified the information component of PCT slightly for use in ACT by eliminating sections that specifically explain the physiology of panic attacks.

The breathing retraining component of ACT essentially involved teaching the patient a way to (a) slow his or her breathing when experiencing symptoms of anxiety, and (b) refocus attention away from anxiety-provoking thoughts. Slowing breathing can reduce the intensity of somatic symptoms associated with anxiety, such as lightheadedness. The cognitive restructuring component involved teaching the patient how to identify habitual anxiety-provoking thoughts and then how to evaluate the validity of the negative predictions about future events that characterize anxiety-provoking thoughts.

IPT

A short-term treatment (recommended length is between 12 and 16 sessions) for outpatient depressive disorders such as MD, IPT (Klerman et al., 1984) is based on the premise that symptoms of clinical depression are either caused or maintained by various types of interpersonal problems. It is a very focused and problem-solving–oriented treatment.

The main techniques of IPT are (a) identifying an interpersonal problem area that seems to be most directly involved in a patient's current depressive episode and (b) using therapist interventions for that problem area as described in the IPT manual. The four IPT problem areas are grief, interpersonal role disputes, role transitions, and interpersonal skills deficits.

The problem area that seemed most appropriate for both cases was interpersonal role disputes, with the focal role dispute being within the marriage. In each case, the patient experienced dissatisfaction in the marital role but was unable or unwilling to express that dissatisfaction. Although Case 1 appreciated the opportunity to discuss her disappointments in her marriage with the therapist, she stopped short of actually renegotiating her role vis-à-vis her husband. It is unclear whether she would have eventually responded to encouragement to do so had the therapy gone on longer; however, she declined the offer of additional sessions. Case 2, on the other hand, was able to initiate direct discussions with his wife about his wishes for changes in their relationship. He had some increased satisfaction with the relationship, as well as reduced depression and increased hopefulness about change in their relationship.

Combined Treatment (ACT and IPT)

The standard protocol followed for each case study was six weekly sessions of ACT followed by 1 week with an assessment interview instead of a session, then six weekly sessions of IPT followed by an assessment interview 1 week after the sixth IPT session. Each case also had a follow-up assessment 1 year after the initial evaluation.

At the first treatment session, patients were told that their treatment would consist of two parts; one focused on the anxiety-related problems that they were experiencing, and one focused on depression. They were told that the anxiety-focused treatment would be first, that the depression-focused component would follow, and that the entire treatment was designed to be 12 weekly sessions. At Session 9 or 10, treatment termination was discussed, and patients were asked their opinion of their readiness to terminate. They were told that additional sessions were possible and that the upcoming assessment (after Session 12) could be used to help make a decision. The research plan allowed for 6 to 10 more sessions of IPT, although there was a 12-session "outcome" assessment after the 12th session, regardless of whether the patient wanted additional sessions.[3]

RESULTS

Pattern of Change in Anxiety and Depression Symptoms

Figures 2 and 3 show the weekly BAI and BDI scores of Cases 1 and 2, beginning at baseline and continuing to the post–Session-12 assessment. Figures 4 and 5 show the weekly mean of each patient's daily global ratings of depression and of their "average" level of anxiety. In general, the ratings on both measures show that symptoms of anxiety and depression were not differentially responsive to the anxiety- and the depression-focused components of the treatment; rather, in both cases the symptoms primarily changed in tandem.

---

[3] Up to 10 more sessions of IPT were offered to make the IPT component of the combined treatment comparable to the 12- to 16-session limit specified in the IPT manual and to explore the clinical speculation that more than 6 sessions for depression would be needed.

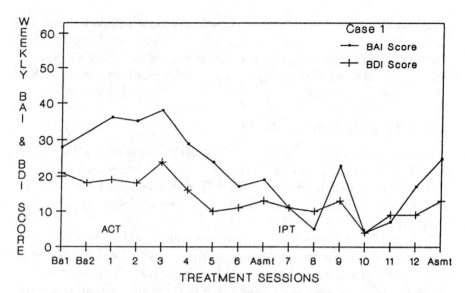

Figure 2. Weekly changes in Beck Anxiety Inventory (BAI; Beck, Epstein, & Brown, 1988) and Beck Depression Inventory (BDI; Beck, Steer, & Garbin, 1988) scores for Case 1. (Ba1 = Baseline Week 1; Ba2 = Baseline Week 2; ACT = anxiety control treatment; Asmt = assessment week; IPT = Interpersonal Psychotherapy of Depression treatment.)

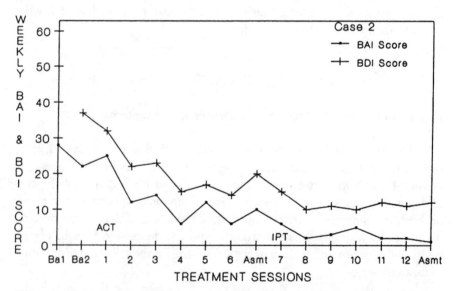

Figure 3. Weekly changes in Beck Anxiety Inventory (BAI; Beck, Epstein, & Brown, 1988) and Beck Depression Inventory (BDI; Beck, Steer, & Garbin, 1988) scores for Case 2. (Ba1 = Baseline Week 1; Ba2 = Baseline Week 2; ACT = anxiety control treatment; Asmt = assessment week; IPT = Interpersonal Psychotherapy of Depression treatment.)

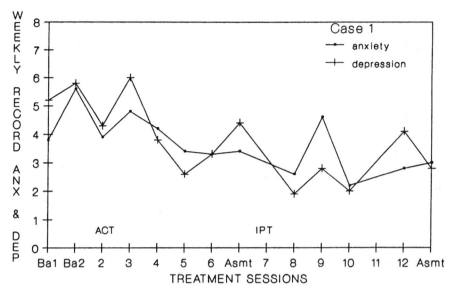

Figure 4. Weekly changes in self-reported anxiety and depression (Weekly Record of Anxiety and Depression; Barlow, 1988) for Case 1. (ANX = anxiety; DEP = depression; Ba1 = Baseline Week 1; Ba2 = Baseline Week 2, which also was the week preceding Session 1; ACT = anxiety control treatment; Asmt = assessment week; IPT = Interpersonal Psychotherapy of Depression treatment.)

Outcome

Efficacy

For the sake of brevity, only two outcome measures are reviewed here, the BDI and BAI scores and the HARS and HRSD scores. The BAI and BDI scores indicated that Case 2 showed remission of anxiety symptoms and mild depression at the end of treatment (see Beck & Steer, 1992a, 1992b, for severity guidelines for BAI and BDI scores) and clinically significant reduction in symptoms from pre- to posttreatment (Figure 3). The BDI and BAI scores for Case 1 were less positive. Although the patient showed remission of both anxiety and depression symptoms at Session 10, the symptoms began to increase again as termination approached. At the posttreatment assessment, anxiety was moderately severe and only slightly lower than at the pretreatment baseline period; depression was mild (Figure 2).

Table 1 shows pre- and posttreatment HARS and HRSD scores for Cases 1 and 2. Both cases showed small but comparable improvement in anxiety. Both showed comparable, slightly greater improvement in depression than in anxiety.

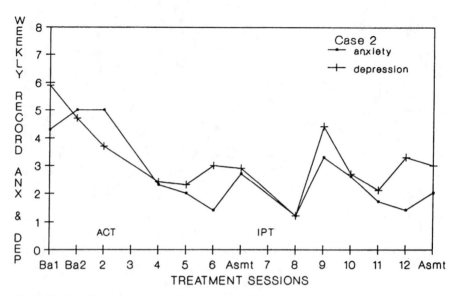

Figure 5. Weekly changes in self-reported anxiety and depression (Weekly Record of Anxiety and Depression; Barlow, 1988) for Case 2. (ANX = anxiety; DEP = depression; Ba1 = Baseline Week 1; Ba2 = Baseline Week 2, which also was the week preceding Session 1; ACT = anxiety control treatment; Asmt = assessment week; IPT = Interpersonal Psychotherapy of Depression treatment.)

Comparative Efficacy

The combined treatment was developed on the basis of the logical premise that if treatments have specific effects on anxiety and depression, then a treatment that combines anxiety-focused and depression-focused components will be associated with greater improvement in patients with comorbid anxiety and depressive disorders, compared with a treatment that focuses on anxiety or depression alone. We examined the premise by comparing the posttreatment HARS and HRSD scores of both cases to two diagnostically and symptomatically similar cases who received up to 15 sessions of an anxiety-focused, cognitive–behavioral treatment for GAD (Barlow et al., 1992). The anxiety treatment consisted of progressive muscle relaxation and cognitive restructuring; thus, it was similar to the ACT treatment used in the case studies that consisted of breathing retraining (which can facilitate relaxation) and cognitive restructuring.

As shown in Table 1, the two case studies, compared with two diagnostically similar cases who received only anxiety-focused treatment, showed small but comparable improvement in anxiety. However, inspection of the HRSD posttreatment scores suggests that the case study patients improved somewhat more in depression than did the comparison patients who were treated only for GAD (and for up to three sessions more than the two case studies). Thus, inspection of the pattern of posttreatment ratings suggests the

TABLE 1
Outcome Comparison of Case Studies and Diagnostically Similar Cases Treated Only for GAD

	Case studies[a]					
	Anxiety Tx only: GAD + MD or D + Marital[b] (n = 2)		Case 1 AnxNos + MD + Marital[b] (n = 1)		Case 2 GAD + MD + Marital[b] (n = 1)	
Measure	Pre-Tx	Post-Tx	Pre-Tx	Post-Tx	Pre-Tx	Post-Tx
Hamilton Anxiety Rating Scale						
M	24.7	21.5	22	19	23	17
Range	22–27.5	19–24				
Hamilton Rating Scale for Depression[c]						
M	24.3	25	25	17	25	18
Range	22–26.5	20–30				

Note. Tx = Treatment; GAD = Generalized Anxiety Disorder as described in the *Diagnostic and Statistical Manual of Mental Disorders* (3rd ed., rev.; *DSM–III–R;* American Psychiatric Association, 1987); MD = *DSM–III–R* Major Depressive Episode; D = *DSM–III–R* Dysthymia; AnxNOS = *DSM–III–R* Anxiety Disorder Not Otherwise Specified (i.e., GAD with one sphere of worry). Cases from Barlow et al. (1992) who received up to 15 sessions of progressive muscle relaxation and cognitive restructuring for GAD.
[a]Patients treated for both GAD and MD.   [b]Marital = marital problems at intake.   [c]24-item version (Guy, 1976).

potential value of the combined treatment for patients with comorbid GAD and MD, at least when an interpersonal problem such as marital distress is also present.

The posttreatment HARS and HRSD scores (see Table 1) also indicate that both case study patients still had clinically significant symptoms of anxiety and depression after 12 sessions of the combined treatment. The same was true of the diagnostically comparable patients from the GAD outcome study. The results suggest that such patients might need longer treatment of the types offered or alternative treatments.[4]

Some data were obtained on the preceding speculation. Case 2 accepted the offer for additional sessions after the posttreatment assessment that followed the depression component of the treatment. He attended 10 more sessions, for a total of 16 sessions of IPT. A termination assessment indicated that he no longer had clinically significant depression (he had an HRSD score of 6), and his HARS score (12) was also lower than his score at the prior 12-session assessment (17). At a follow-up assessment 6 months after treatment was terminated (and 1 year after the intake assessment), the patient's HRSD score was 1 and the HARS score was 6, indicating that

---

[4] Noting evidence such as this that existing cognitive–behavioral treatments for GAD yield less than optimal responses for some GAD patients, another treatment approach for GAD is being developed at the Center for Stress and Anxiety that incorporates several anxiety-focused interventions (Craske, Barlow, & O'Leary, 1992).

clinically significant symptoms were no longer present. Also, he no longer met criteria for any *DSM–III–R* disorder. Thus, for Case 2, the 6-month treatment period (22 weekly sessions) was associated with recovery 6 months later. However, Case 1, who had only 12 sessions (3 months) of treatment, was also recovered at her assessment 1 year after intake. Unfortunately, interpretation of her data in terms of length of treatment required for comorbid GAD and MD is complicated by the fact that she was taking Prozac at the 1-year assessment. However, the fact that she sought additional treatment is consistent with the conclusion that 12 weekly sessions of the treatments offered is not adequate for such patients.

DISCUSSION

We have presented a research strategy based on single-case methodology that can be used to generate preliminary efficacy data on new treatments as well as to examine theory-based hypotheses. The research strategy addresses one of the main impediments to preparing fundable grant applications for studies of the efficacy of promising new psychosocial treatments (i.e., the need for preliminary efficacy data). The problem is a serious one because no reliable source of funds currently is available for conducting needed developmental work on psychosocial treatments.

This report included no statistical tests of outcome differences between anxious and depressed patients who received the new combined treatment for GAD and MD (ACT and IPT) and those who received a cognitive–behavioral treatment focused only on GAD. Also, our case study methodology did not allow us to evaluate the effectiveness of the new treatment using the prevailing scientific standard that requires outcome comparisons between treated cases and diagnostically similar cases who receive no treatment, or a placebo treatment, for the same period of time.

One way to address both of the preceding limitations is to conduct a replication series of cases (i.e., "clinical replication"; see Barlow & Hersen, 1984), pool the data, and do statistical tests on those cases compared with (a) similar cases who were treated in a group outcome study and (b) no-treatment or placebo-treated controls. This approach was partially illustrated by our comparisons of the case study data with data from diagnostically similar patients who participated in a traditional treatment outcome study. Power analysis calculations (Kraemer & Thiemann, 1987) can be used to determine needed sample sizes for such statistical tests.

One strength of case study methodology was illustrated by the failure of the continuous self-report data to show the hypothesized differential impact of the anxiety-focused component of the treatment on anxiety symptoms and of the depression-focused component on symptoms of depression. It has been said that a single case can provide evidence that refutes a hypothesis by documenting a decisive counterexample to a generalization (Edelson, 1988). Although the statement might be arguable (i.e., reasons why a particular case study did not provide a valid test of a hypothesis can usually, perhaps always, be found), failure to support a hypothesis using a case study design that has high internal validity has an inherent persuasiveness that tends to prompt one to revise or refine theory. The foregoing phenomenon illustrates the unique efficiency of single-case methodology for treatment development research and for mechanisms of action studies.

What does the failure of our cases to demonstrate specific symptom effects of two symptom-specific treatments suggest? The finding was not surprising from at least two perspectives: (a) the general failure in the literature to detect hypothesized specific effects of treatments (e.g., Imber et al., 1990; Simons, Garfield, & Murphy, 1984), perhaps particularly with generalized emotional disorders involving negative affect (L. A. Clark & Watson, 1991) such as GAD (Barlow et al., 1992), and (b) evidence that self-reported anxiety and depression ratings are highly correlated (Gotlib & Cane, 1989). The failure to find the predicted specific effects opens the door to numerous speculations on possible reasons for the failure. We offer only two: One is a psychological hypothesis about mechanisms of action of symptom-focused psychotherapeutic interventions; the second posits a relationship between anxiety and depression based on emotion theory.

The psychological hypothesis accepts the premise that anxiety and depression have distinctive aspects, as well as overlapping features (e.g., D. A. Clark, Beck, & Stewart, 1990). The hypothesis also accepts the premise that the distinctive aspects of anxiety and depression can be specifically affected by specifically aimed interventions. The failure to find evidence for specific effects is hypothesized to be due to the impact of a person's psychological context on psychotherapeutic interventions. The construct of psychological context refers to features of psychological functioning that would affect any learning process, features such as verbal intelligence, ability to attend to verbal content, and spontaneous focus of attention (e.g., patients whose attention is predominantly drawn to interpersonal cues rather than to verbal cues and who might, therefore, attend more to how the therapist says something rather than to what the therapist says). The basic premise is that a person's psychological context is a very powerful filter through which our current methods of verbal dyadic intervention must pass. This filter can deflect, diffuse, and recode interventions that, in the therapist's mind, are clearly and precisely aimed at specific symptoms.

Alternatively, from the perspective of emotion theory, our failure to find evidence for specific effects of the anxiety-focused and depression-focused treatment components can be attributed to the underlying nature of depression (Barlow, 1988, 1991a, 1991b). In this theory, both anxiety and depression are characterized fundamentally by the activation of the sense of uncontrollability over negative life events. These negative affective states share similar cognitive and biological features. However, these stages may differ in terms of action tendencies. For example, the psychomotor slowing of depression may reflect "giving up" in the face of an onslaught of negative events, whereas a continuing response set of preparation and coping would be more characteristic of anxiety. Investigators working in the area of depression from a more cognitive perspective have arrived at a very similar formulation (Alloy, Kelly, Mineka, & Clements, 1990).

Inferring from the foregoing emotion theory, specific treatment effects were not found for one of two reasons: (a) the anxiety- and the depression-focused treatment components affected the shared features of anxiety and depression, not their different action tendencies or (b) our self-report measures tapped only the shared features of anxiety and depression (but see D. A. Clark et al., 1990), and measures of the different action tendencies would have shown specific responsiveness to the treatment components.

REFERENCES

Alloy, L. B., Kelly, K. A., Mineka, S., & Clements, C. M. (1990). Comorbidity of anxiety and depressive disorders: A helplessness–hopelessness perspective. In J. D. Maser & C. R. Cloninger (Eds.), *Comorbidity of mood and anxiety disorders* (pp. 499–543). Washington, DC: American Psychiatric Press.

American Psychiatric Association. (1987). *Diagnostic and statistical manual of mental disorders* (3rd ed., rev.). Washington, DC: Author.

Barlow, D. H. (1988). *Anxiety and its disorders.* New York: Guilford Press.

Barlow, D. H. (1991a). Disorders of emotion. *Psychological Inquiry, 2,* 58–71.

Barlow, D. H. (1991b). Disorders of emotion: Clarification, elaboration, and future directions. *Psychological Inquiry, 2,* 97–105.

Barlow, D. H., & Craske, M. G. (1989). *Mastery of your anxiety and panic.* Albany, NY: Graywind.

Barlow, D. H., Hayes, S. C., & Nelson, R. O. (1984). *The scientist practitioner: Research and accountability in clinical settings.* New York: Pergamon Press.

Barlow, D. H., & Hersen, M. (1984). *Single case experimental designs: Strategies for studying behavior change* (2nd ed.). New York: Pergamon Press.

Barlow, D. H., Rapee, R. L., & Brown, T. A. (1992). Behavioral treatment of generalized anxiety disorder. *Behavior Therapy, 23,* 551–570.

Beck, A. T., Epstein, N., & Brown, G. (1988). An inventory for measuring clinical anxiety. *Journal of Consulting and Clinical Psychology, 56,* 893–897.

Beck, A. T., & Steer, R. A. (1992a). *Beck Anxiety Inventory manual.* San Antonio, TX: The Psychological Corporation/Harcourt Brace Jovanovich.

Beck, A. T., & Steer, R. A. (1992b). *Beck Depression Inventory manual.* San Antonio, TX: The Psychological Corporation/Harcourt Brace Jovanovich.

Beck, A. T., Steer, R. A., & Garbin, M. G. (1988). Psychometric properties of the

Beck Depression Inventory: Twenty-five years later. *Clinical Psychology Review*, 8, 77–100.

Clark, D. A., Beck, A. T., & Stewart, B. (1990). Cognitive specificity and positive–negative affectivity: Complementary or contradictory views on anxiety and depression? *Journal of Abnormal Psychology*, 99, 148–155.

Clark, L. A., & Watson, D. (1991). Tripartite model of anxiety and depression: Psychometric evidence and taxonomic implications. *Journal of Abnormal Psychology*, 100, 316–336.

Craske, M. G., Barlow, D. H., & O'Leary, T. (1992). *Mastery of your anxiety and worry*. Albany, NY: Graywind.

Di Nardo, P. A., & Barlow, D. H. (1988). *Anxiety Disorders Interview Schedule–Revised (ADIS-R)*. Albany: Phobia and Anxiety Disorders Clinic, State University of New York.

Edelson, M. (1988). *Psychoanalysis: A theory in crisis*. Chicago: University of Chicago Press.

Gotlib, I. H., & Cane, D. B. (1989). Self-report assessment of depression and anxiety. In P. C. Kendall & D. Watson (Eds.), *Anxiety and depression: Distinctive and overlapping features* (pp. 131–169). San Diego, CA: Academic Press.

Guy, W. (1976). *NCDEU assessment manual for psychopharmacology*. Washington, DC: U.S. Department of Health, Education, and Welfare.

Hamilton, M. (1959). The assessment of anxiety states by rating. *British Journal of Medical Psychology*, 32, 50–55.

Hamilton, M. (1960). A rating scale for depression. *Journal of Neurological and Neurosurgical Psychiatry*, 23, 56–62.

Hersen, M., & Barlow, D. H. (1976). *Single case experimental designs: Strategies for studying behavior change*. New York: Pergamon Press.

Imber, S. D., Pilkonis, P. A., Sotsky, S. M., Elkin, I., Watkins, J. T., Collins, J. F., Shear, M. T., Leber, W. R., & Glass, D. R. (1990). Mode-specific effects among three treatments for depression. *Journal of Consulting and Clinical Psychology*, 58, 352–359.

Kazdin, A. E. (1982). *Single-case research designs: Methods for clinical and applied settings*. New York: Oxford University Press.

Klerman, G. L., Weissman, M. M., Rounsaville, B. J., & Chevron, E. S. (1984). *Interpersonal psychotherapy for depression*. New York: Basic Books.

Kraemer, H. G., & Thiemann, S. (1987). *How many subjects? Statistical power analysis in research*. Beverly Hills, CA: Sage.

Sidman, M. (1960). *Tactics of scientific research*. New York: Basic Books.

Simons, A. D., Garfield, S. L., & Murphy, G. E. (1984). The process of change in cognitive therapy and pharmacotherapy for depression: Changes in mood and cognition. *Archives of General Psychiatry*, 41, 45–51.

Wolpe, J. (1958). *Psychotherapy by reciprocal inhibition*. Stanford, CA: Stanford University Press.

EVALUATING TREATMENT
OR OTHER INTERVENTIONS

23

TESTING THE INTEGRITY OF A PSYCHOTHERAPY PROTOCOL: ASSESSMENT OF ADHERENCE AND COMPETENCE

JENNIFER WALTZ, MICHAEL E. ADDIS, KELLY KOERNER, AND NEIL S. JACOBSON

Many methodological improvements in psychotherapy outcome research have been made in the past 20 years. Perhaps the most important has been the development of treatment manuals that specify interventions used in psychotherapy treatment modalities being investigated (Luborsky & DeRubeis, 1984). In theory, manuals have made the delivery of particular therapies purer; techniques and interventions that make up a given therapy are delivered more consistently, and techniques that are unique to some other treatment are avoided.

The advent of the use of treatment manuals has been accompanied by a related rise in expectations that psychotherapy researchers not only use

Reprinted from the *Journal of Consulting and Clinical Psychology, 61*, 620–630. Copyright 1993 by the American Psychological Association.

Preparation of the manuscript was supported by National Institute of Mental Health Grants MH00868–02, MH43101–03, and MH44063–03 awarded to Neil S. Jacobson.

treatment manuals to improve the purity of their therapy but document that their efforts to achieve purity have been successful. Researchers perform a manipulation check, or an assessment of treatment integrity, to assess whether the independent variable of interest—namely the treatment—has been successfully manipulated. Successful manipulation is achieved to the extent that therapists adhere to the treatment manual during therapy and perform the interventions in a competent manner.

Many procedures for conducting manipulation checks have been used, but no widely accepted methodology exists for this type of inquiry. The methods currently being used have many problems that limit what can be learned from the results produced. For example, they frequently do not allow us to determine whether the therapy was performed competently, and thus deposit adequate adherence, we do not know whether a fair test of the treatment has occurred. The lack of guidelines for documenting therapists, adherence and competence has resulted in many reinventions of the wheel, with little consistency across studies.

In this article, we discuss methodological issues and offer suggestions for improving and perhaps standardizing the assessment of therapist adherence and competence. We also synthesize some of what has been learned thus far from previous efforts.

CURRENT STATUS OF THE ASSESSMENT OF ADHERENCE AND COMPETENCE

Successful tests of treatment integrity include both an assessment of therapist adherence to the treatment protocol and a determination that the interventions are being performed competently. We use the term *adherence* to refer to the extent to which a therapist used interventions and approaches prescribed by the treatment manual and avoided the use of intervention procedures proscribed by the manual.

We use the term *competence* to refer to the level of skill shown by the therapist in delivering the treatment. By skill, we mean the extent to which the therapists conducting the interventions took the relevant aspects of the therapeutic context into account and responded to these contextual variables appropriately. Relevant aspects of the context include, but are by no means limited to, (a) client variables such as degree of impairment; (b) the particular problems manifested by a given client; (c) the client's life situation and life stress; (d) and factors such as stage in therapy, degree of improvement already achieved, and appropriate sensitivity to the timing of interventions within a therapy session. According to this definition, competence presupposes adherence, but adherence does not necessarily imply competence.

Purposes of Treatment Integrity Tests

Manipulation checks are an essential part of good scientific research. If a manipulation check is not performed, it is difficult to draw firm conclusions about treatment effects or their absence. Without a test of treatment integrity, treatment effects could be attributable to differential competence in the implementation of the treatments in question. The absence of treatment effects could similarly disguise differential competence in treatment delivery: Without documentation, relatively incompetent therapists in one treatment condition could disguise what would have emerged as a treatment effect if competence had been higher in that condition. Moreover, null findings could also be due to adherence problems, such as unwanted overlap between treatments. Only a manipulation check that is properly designed and carried out can rule out these alternative explanations.

Tests of treatment integrity are also used to provide information about how treatments are implemented, so that cross-site comparisons can be made. For example, adherence checks that include assessment of the frequency of various therapist behaviors can provide a means of comparing therapists at different sites. This allows us to rule out the possibility that site effects are due to differences in the operationalization of the treatment.

Finally, assessing therapist adherence and competence can inform the training of therapists. If these checks are carried out on training cases, supervisors can get information about the strengths and weaknesses of particular therapists, what types of interventions they are performing competently, and which therapists require additional training and supervisory feedback. This information can be used to improve the quality of training and, ultimately, the treatment.

The process of formulating a treatment, writing a treatment manual, training therapists, and assessing their performance can be viewed as a feedback loop. The information derived from a manipulation check can inform the development and writing of the treatment manual. For example, if some intervention is consistently conducted poorly by therapists, it may not have been adequately described in the manual. Perhaps the developer of the therapy believed that some therapeutic situations should be handled in a particular way but neglected to specify these nuances in the manual. Checks on adherence and competence would also pick this up and provide information that would inform the writing of addenda to the treatment manual.

A Contextual Definition of Competence

With our definition of competence, we move away from a notion of general therapeutic competence and focus instead on competence in performing a certain type of treatment. For example, it may be very important to be warm and empathic in treatment X but not in treatment Y, so a therapist who is rated as being very warm and empathic would receive high competence ratings if conducting treatment X but not if conducting treatment Y. We suggest that the conception of competence be derived from the treatment manual and the theory of change specified in it. We do not assume that any therapist behaviors represent universal expressions of competence across treatments.

State of the Art

Early Efforts to Document Treatment Integrity

Historically, researchers have addressed concerns about treatment integrity by describing the actions they took to establish and maintain adherence and competence, rather than by directly measuring them. Even recent outcome studies do not typically assess adherence and competence. Although use of treatment manuals and supervision of treatment providers undoubtedly increases the probability that treatment will be delivered according to protocol, only about 26% of recently completed outcome studies (Moncher & Prinz, 1991) even used a specific treatment protocol; of these, less than half reported the amount of training (46.7%), fewer reported the nature of training (38%), and fewer still provided documentation of therapist competence (13%). Some have argued that the assessment of competence may appear unnecessary when experienced therapists are used in the study (Snyder & Wills, 1991). However, neither professional training nor amount of therapist experience is correlated with treatment outcome (Berman & Norton, 1985; Durlak, 1979; Hattie, Sharpley, & Rogers, 1984). We cannot infer competence from amount of training or from therapist experience.

The inclusion of treatment integrity checks is not standard practice at this point. Moncher and Prinz's (1991) review found that "despite overall methodological soundness, the majority (55%) of the studies reviewed essentially ignored the issue of treatment fidelity" (p. 257). Less than 6% of the studies ensured that treatment was delivered according to protocol by combining the use of treatment manuals, supervision of treatment providers, and performance of a manipulation check.

Differences Between Measures

Although their use is relatively infrequent, a variety of measures of therapist adherence and competence have been developed. These measures differ in several ways. First, they differ widely in the complexity and specificity of the construct that is rated, and consequently, they differ in the expertise needed to use the measure. Some treatment interventions are easily described, such as developing a desensitization hierarchy or setting a cognitive therapy agenda. Coders who are inexperienced in doing psychotherapy could probably recognize these interventions and code them reliably. Other interventions, such as the establishment of collaboration given client resistance, are less easily described and, therefore, require clinically experienced raters.

Second, current measures use different sources of information, including process notes, transcripts, audiotapes, and videotapes. The type of material that is rated can influence measures of adherence and competence. Chevron and Rounsaville (1983) found low correlations between ratings of videotapes and ratings made using process notes. Because the source material used for ratings may influence the data, source material should retain the most information possible (e.g., videotapes) unless financial constraints or the coding scheme itself necessitate other sources.

Third, various approaches to manipulation checks also differ in the unit of analysis chosen. Some studies have rated segments of individual sessions (e.g., Luborsky, McLellan, Woody, O'Brien, & Auerbach, 1985). An example of such an approach would be randomly choosing a 15-min segment from the fourth session of each case. Alternatively, some studies have involved coding entire single sessions (e.g., O'Malley et al., 1988). For training purposes, others have used entire cases (e.g., Shaw, 1984).

Measures also differ in the criterion with which the therapist's behavior is compared. For example, adherence measures may compare the fit of particular interventions with the treatment manual guidelines. Unfortunately, treatment manuals seldom explicitly state criteria for competence. Competence measures may compare the therapist's performance with an established level of average competence (Shaw, 1984), with an expert's sense of what competence is (Shaw & Dobson, 1988), or with how well the intervention fits the specific client problems or case formulation (Silberschatz, Fretter, & Curtis, 1986).

Occurrence–Nonoccurrence

The simplest method of assessing adherence is using a checklist of techniques and rating the occurrence or nonoccurrence of interventions that are prescribed and proscribed by the treatment protocol. For example, a checklist of techniques for a study comparing individual and marital therapies for depression would include all interventions specific to each type of treatment. The rater might listen to audiotapes of the sessions and check off the interventions that occur (e.g., marital therapy items might include communication training and creating a collaborative set between the partners; individual cognitive therapy items might include identifying automatic thoughts, relating thoughts to feelings, etc.).

Frequency Ratings

A more detailed adherence check is possible with lists of techniques by rating the frequency or extensiveness of interventions during the session rather than merely their presence or absence. For example, Luborsky, Woody, McLellan, O'Brien, and Rosenzweig (1982) measured adherence to three manual-guided therapies (drug counseling, supportive–expressive, and cognitive–behavioral). From each of the three treatments, they randomly sampled 15-min segments taken from the last 20 min of sessions. Using a 5-point scale ranging from *none* (1) to *very much* (5), experienced judges rated these therapy segments on the extent to which core elements specified by the manuals were present in the session. An interesting note here is that, in a related study, Luborsky and his colleagues found that purity (the ratio of prescribed to proscribed techniques) was associated with a favorable outcome (Luborsky et al., 1985).

National Institute of Mental Health (NIMH)
Treatment of Depression Collaborative Research Program

The NIMH Treatment of Depression Collaborative Study generated both adherence and competence measures. The Collaborative Study Psychotherapy Rating Scale (CSPRS: Hollon, Evans, Elkin, & Lowery, 1984) was developed primarily as a measure of adherence to the three conditions in the Collaborative Study. Again, a list of techniques characteristic of each of the three treatments (pharmacotherapy and medical management, cognitive therapy, and interpersonal therapy) was used. However, rather than being a simple checklist of presence versus absence, or rating of frequency, the CSPRS requires the raters' inference about the quality of the intervention in some instances. For example, raters are asked to consider the thoroughness of exploration when rating items such as examining evidence for automatic thoughts. In this case, the adherence and competence constructs are clearly overlapping, although the CSPRS is purported to be merely an adherence measure.

Assessments of competence also vary in terms of complexity of ratings to be made. Another measure developed as part of the NIMH Collaborative Study was the Therapist Strategy Rating Form (TSRF), a 14-item scale designed to measure the quality of therapist intervention in interpersonal therapy (IPT; Klerman, Weissman, Rounsaville, & Chevron, 1984). An experienced rater codes the skillfulness of specific types of therapist interventions on a 7-point scale ranging from *outstanding* (1) to *very poor* (7) while taking into account factors such as the choice of session focus and the sensitivity and timing of intervention. The simplest way to assess competence with this measure is to use a one-shot sample of therapist behavior. For example, O'Malley et al. (1988) asked therapists to rate their own effectiveness immediately after the fourth session and also had supervisors rate therapists after watching a videotape of the same session.

In the NIMH Collaborative Study, the competence of cognitive therapists was measured with the Cognitive Therapy Scale (CTS; Dobson, Shaw, & Vallis, 1985). This 11-item instrument has two subscales; the first measures a combination of general and technical skills in cognitive therapy, and the second measures structuring skills. The scale was designed to detect serious protocol deviations and also subpar performance. The CTS had only moderate interrater reliability; however, the total score discriminated between acceptable and unacceptable cognitive therapy (Shaw & Dobson, 1988). The CTS was used during the training of therapists for the Collaborative Study and included ratings made for each session (Shaw, 1984). CTS ratings from the final training case for each therapist were used to define a "red line," a score on the CTS 1 standard deviation below the mean CTS score. A criterion of competence was developed by generating mean competence ratings across cases and therapists: The ratings were made by experts in cognitive therapy on the basis of how well a given session exemplified cognitive therapy.

Competence Based on Case Formulations

The Mount Zion Psychotherapy Research Group has developed a different criterion for measuring therapist adherence and competence (e.g., Silberschatz, Fretter, & Curtis, 1986). Similar to the TSRF, the Mount Zion group evaluates therapist interventions with respect to their appropriateness given the case formulation. The case formulation is generated by experienced clinicians based on a review of transcripts of several initial interviews. Persons (1989) has discussed a similar case formulation approach.

Therapist Errors

Another aspect of assessing therapist competence involves including a measure of therapist errors in technique. The Vanderbilt Negative Indicators Scale (Suh, O'Malley, & Strupp, 1986) is a 42-item measure used by clinical raters to detect and rate the intensity or frequency of negative indicators, which include items such as failure to make necessary interventions, inflexible use of therapeutic technique, the therapist's critical tendencies, and lack of respect for the client.

Prospective Observation

All of the approaches described thus far have used rating scales applied retrospectively after viewing the session. The segment or session is viewed by the rater, and the instrument is then completed. The primary alternative to such scales is to code the therapist's behavior, the client's behavior, or both on an event-by-event basis. An example of such a scale is the one used by Wills and his colleagues (Wills, Faitler, & Snyder, 1987) to distinguish between insight-oriented marital therapy (IOMT) and behavioral marital therapy (BMT). The coding system had eight categories, two specific to BMT, three specific to IOMT, and the others nonspecific. Each therapist's turn at speech was coded on one of these eight categories, and the proportion of each was used as the indicator of adherence. The investigators found that IOMT interventions were much more prevalent in IOMT, and BMT interventions were much more prevalent in BMT. The disadvantage of these event-by-event coding systems is that they are labor intensive and, therefore, expensive. The advantage is that the basis for the ratings is always clear: The investigators can always identify the exact basis for disagreement among coders; similarly, in the event that there is unwanted convergence between treatments, it is always possible to trace the source of overlap.

Problems With Existing Systems for Assessing Adherence and Competence

Many problems plague the current methodologies. We have alluded to some of them in the previous section.

Some currently used methodologies draw on problematic sources of data. For example, of the studies reviewed by Moncher and Prinz (1991), 23% used therapists or clients themselves as the sources of information about adherence. Therapists are problematic informants, because they are likely to be biased in their perceptions of sessions. Clients are likewise inappropriate, because they do not have the knowledge or training necessary to describe what happened in the session at the level of analysis needed for a manipulation check.

Moncher and Prinz (1991) also reported that only about 32% of the studies included data from more than one treatment session to obtain their ratings. Sampling from only one session is unlikely to be representative.

The tendency to equate adherence to a treatment manual with successful manipulation of the treatment variable has been a consistent unwarranted conceptual leap in psychotherapy research. The leap involves the erroneous assumption that adherence to the treatment manual is tantamount to therapeutic skill or competence. This assumption has led to the widespread exclusive use of adherence measures as a form of manipulation check. Adherence measures often fail to determine if a treatment was actually given a fair test, because therapist competence is not assessed (Schaeffer, 1982; Strupp, 1986).

In light of these inadequacies, some researchers (e.g., Shaw & Dobson, 1988, Weissman, Rounsaville, & Chevron, 1982) have turned to therapist competence ratings as a means of insuring the strength and integrity (Yeaton

& Sechrest, 1981) of a treatment. As a form of manipulation check, therapist competence ratings should guarantee that, in addition to using techniques prescribed by a particular treatment approach, therapists are performing that approach skillfully. For the purposes of quality control, methodologies that force raters to judge the quality of therapy are certainly an improvement over adherence measures that simply tally the frequency of various therapist behaviors. The question remains, however, as to whether available methodologies are suitable for determining whether a particular treatment was administered with sufficient skill to guarantee a fair test of treatments.

One recurring problem with available methodologies has prevented a conclusive answer to this question. The majority of therapist competence scales have fallen prey to the uniformity myth (Kiesler, 1973). In other words, researchers have assumed that the same therapist actions are equally competent across situations, regardless of the context. With few exceptions, competence ratings have been conducted without reference to therapeutic context. Contextual variables may not be as important to consider when assessing adherence, but there are numerous contextual factors that determine whether an intervention is competently delivered. When clinical supervisors attempt to evaluate a student's or trainee's therapeutic competence, they will generally consider such factors as client difficulty, stage of therapy, or other client characteristics such as presence or absence of collateral problems. Each of these factors and many others create a context from which a judgment of therapeutic competence is made. For example, a cognitive therapy supervisor might consider it incompetent for a therapist to explore underlying assumptions or core schemata during the first few sessions of treatment. The same technique might be judged highly competent during later sessions when the therapist has sufficiently explored the client's automatic thoughts and when depressive symptoms have been alleviated. Similarly, at that later point, a therapist's failure to challenge the client's underlying assumptions might be judged incompetent. However, if the client is exceedingly hostile and unwilling to accept what the therapist has to offer, the supervisor would not conclude that the therapist is incompetent. It seems clear that competency within a particular treatment modality is always linked to context.

Despite the importance of contextual variables, researchers conducting competence assessments have failed to incorporate the majority of these factors into their assessment protocols. Stage of therapy is usually excluded from consideration when raters use the same coding scheme and scoring system for all sessions. The CTS, for example, rates the same eleven therapist strategies for each session coded (Young & Beck, 1980). However, as specified in the treatment manual (Beck, Rush, Shaw, & Emery, 1979), cognitive therapy for depression is a treatment in which specific strategies should follow a natural course over time. The skill with which a particular intervention is conducted can only be judged by considering its contribution to the process of therapy over the course of an individual case.

Client difficulty is rarely taken into account in competence ratings. The goal has been to evaluate clinical skill independent of client characteristics. However, an angry, hostile, or otherwise difficult client can prevent even the most competent therapist from successfully using therapeutic strategies prescribed by a treatment manual. Greater client difficulty has been found to predict lower therapist performance ratings by both supervisors and therapists themselves (Foley, O'Malley, Rounsaville, Prusoff, & Weissman, 1987). If client difficulty is not assessed, competence ratings can yield misleading results. As Shaw (1984) noted,

> If the therapist simply performs poorly independent of patient factors the therapy is not getting a fair test . . . if on the other hand, the therapist has difficulty because of factors related to the patient then the therapy is getting a fair test. We would simply find that some patients do not respond to the procedures. (pp. 181–182)

The distinction is impossible to make unless patient difficulty is taken into account by the rating system.

If therapist competence is inseparable from the context of therapy, then why have existing competence measures failed to consider contextual variables? First, it is simply much easier to establish uniform criteria for competent therapy if therapist actions are rated independently of contextual variables. When raters consider only whether the therapist implemented a particular intervention skillfully, without considering the context, they are more likely to achieve high interrater reliability. Moreover, focusing on the same discrete therapist behaviors across sessions reduces the chance of confusing debates over what exactly is competent therapy for a particular case.

Second, by taking therapeutic context into account, the ratings may be more easily confounded with outcome. When clients like their therapist and improve substantially, it is easier for therapists to look competent. If client characteristics and stage of therapy are used as cues for competence ratings, the ratings may become nothing more than a description of the quality of therapeutic interaction or a reflection of progress.

Although confounding therapist competence with therapy outcome is a serious consideration, it is questionable whether it will ever be possible to thoroughly separate the two. Client behaviors are undoubtedly influenced by therapist strategies and techniques. Similarly, variance in therapists' ability to competently use the same strategies and techniques will always overlap with variance in characteristics of the client and the therapy process itself. It is just as misleading to ignore the contribution of client characteristics as it is to assume that client and therapist characteristics are independent.

A final limitation of currently available measures is that they have failed to provide an accepted, standardized methodology. The variability in both sampling procedure and segmentation of therapy sessions has precluded definitive comparisons between studies. Given the difficulties inherent in coding therapy sessions, it is not surprising that researchers have chosen a multitude of methodologies. In all likelihood, approaches are often chosen based on the availability of resources. However, the availability of standardized methodologies would facilitate much needed cross-site comparisons.

RECOMMENDATIONS FOR ASSESSING ADHERENCE AND COMPETENCE

Recommendation 1

Our first recommendation concerns the way in which competence is defined. We suggest that all aspects of therapeutic competence be defined relative to the treatment manual being used. This necessitates the existence of a treatment manual or some form of written documentation explaining how the therapy is to be conducted. We suggest that therapist behaviors that have been regarded traditionally as the nonspecific components also be evaluated relative to the treatment manual. Because different treatment modalities have different recommendations regarding, for example, the role of such nonspecifics as therapist warmth and nurturance, these behaviors should not be lumped together and viewed as therapeutic universals. For example, although Rogerians recommend that therapists be consistently warm, some therapeutic modalities, such as strategic therapy, do not. Therefore, we do not assume any behaviors are universally prescribed but that they rely on therapy manuals to provide the guidelines for all aspects of the therapy. These guidelines should then be used as the basis for determining whether a particular therapist is performing competently.

Recommendation 2

Our second recommendation concerns the process by which researchers formulate the framework for their assessment of adherence and competence. The basic point here is that investigators should carefully fit the manipulation check to the questions being asked. There is a wide range of studies that can usefully be conducted in this area; however, investigators must carefully consider the questions they attempt to answer as they develop the manipulation check. One question could be "Did the therapists performing Treatment A confine themselves to interventions from Treatment A and minimize those from Treatment B?" Another question could be, "Did therapists in Condition A perform that treatment competently?" A study to answer this second question would involve a very different type of measure than one designed to answer the first. In our opinion, many published studies have not tailored their checks to the types of questions to be answered.

When investigators want to determine whether two treatments are distinct, an adherence measure is sufficient. A simple questionnaire requiring raters to make "present-or-absent" distinctions from a list of interventions may provide the necessary information to answer that particular question. Because such a design is both economical and more likely than frequency assessments to produce reliable ratings, it may be the best choice for a simple determination of adherence. Measures of intervention frequency allow for comparisons between treatments; however, greater frequency does not necessarily mean better adherence. Most treatment manuals do not suggest that therapists attempt to do a prescribed intervention as many times as possible during a session. Unfortunately, many tests of treatment integrity have been carried out as if this were the case.

Recommendation 3

To be useful in addressing the assessment of treatment distinctiveness, adherence measures should include four types of items

Therapist Behaviors That Are Unique to That Treatment Modality and Essential to It

Paradoxical directives in strategic therapy exemplify these behaviors. These are therapist behaviors that should be found in the specified treatment, if that treatment is being administered appropriately, and should not be found in any other approach being tested.

Behaviors That Are Essential to the Treatment but Not Unique to It

In a comparison between two treatments, these would be interventions from Treatment A that one would expect to be present if Treatment A was being conducted appropriately, but they may also be present in Treatment B.

Behaviors That Are Compatible With the Specified Modality, and Therefore Not Prohibited, but Neither Necessary nor Unique

An example of this behavior is chatting with the client at the beginning of the sessions. These types of behaviors may reflect a reduced dosage or potency, or they may potentiate the impact of necessary, unique, or both types of interventions.

Behaviors That Are Proscribed

Without noting the occurrence of proscribed behaviors, one cannot determine whether protocol violations are occurring.

TABLE 1
Examples of Four Types of Items for an Adherence Check Comparing Two Treatments

Psychodynamic therapy	Behavioral therapy
Unique and essential	
1. Focus on unconscious determinants of behavior 2. Focus on internalized object relations as historical causes of current problems 3. Focus on defense mechanisms used to ward off pain of early trauma 4. Interpretation of resistance	1. Assigning homework 2. Practicing assertion in the session 3. Forming a contingency contract
Essential but not unique	
1. Establish a therapeutic alliance 2. Setting treatment goals 3. Empathic listening 4. Planning for termination 5. Exploration of childhood	1. Establish a therapeutic alliance 2. Setting treatment goals 3. Empathic listening 4. Planning for termination 5. Providing treatment rationale
Acceptable but not necessary	
1. Paraphrasing 2. Self-disclosure 3. Interpreting dreams 4. Providing treatment rationale	1. Paraphrasing 2. Self-disclosure 3. Exploration of childhood
Proscribed	
1. Prescribing psychotropic medications 2. Assigning homework 3. Practicing assertion in the session 4. Forming contingency contracts 5. Prescribing the symptom	1. Prescribing psychotropic medications 2. Focus on unconscious determinants of behavior 3. Focus on internalized object relations as historical causes of current problems 4. Focus on defense mechanisms used to ward off pain of early trauma 5. Interpretation of resistance

Table 1 presents a hypothetical set of items that may be used to distinguish a behavioral from a psychodynamic treatment. Examples of (a) unique, (b) necessary but not unique, (c) acceptable but not necessary, and (d) proscribed interventions are included. All of the "unique and essential" items for each treatment are "proscribed" interventions for the other. "Essential but not unique items" and "compatible but not necessary" items may be the same across treatments.

Figures 1 through 4 present hypothetical results from adherence scales

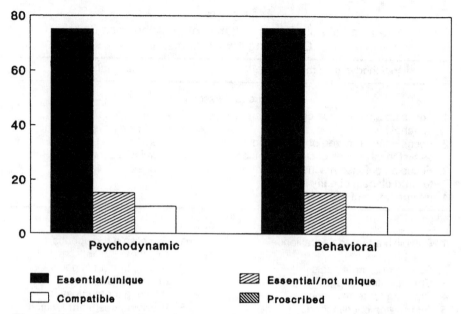

Figure 1. Hypothetical ratings of treatment integrity that are based on maximally discriminable and equally potent therapies.

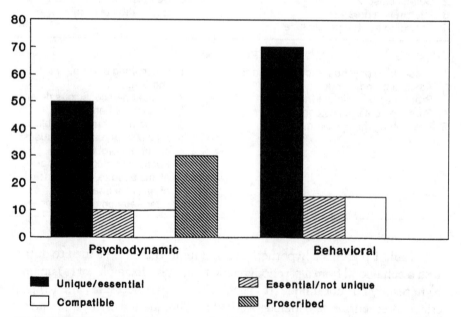

Figure 2. Treatment integrity compromised by presence of proscribed behaviors in one treatment condition.

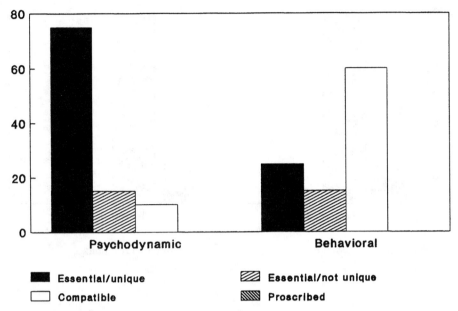

Figure 3. Hypothetical ratings of treatment integrity when therapies are discriminable but one is less potent.

using these four types of items. These figures demonstrate the necessity of including each type. Figure 1 shows an ideal outcome in which two therapies are maximally discriminable and equally potent: Therapists concentrated on essential or unique interventions, with no proscribed interventions and an equal number of low-potency compatible behaviors and essential but not unique behaviors.

Figure 2 depicts a situation in which the therapists performed many of the essential or unique interventions, but in one condition many violations also occurred. Without inclusion of the proscribed items, this information would have been lost, and inaccurate conclusions would have been drawn.

Figure 3 shows an outcome in which although neither group of therapists violated protocol, the psychodynamic treatment appears to have been more potent; that is, therapists in the behavioral treatment condition were engaging in many allowable but inessential behaviors.

Finally, Figure 4 depicts a study in which therapists in both conditions were doing predominantly those interventions that were permitted in *both* treatments. In this case, the two treatments were highly overlapping, and one would not expect differential outcomes. However, if the adherence rating scale had confined itself to essential and unique items from each condition, the treatments would have appeared to be distinct despite this substantial overlap. Items on adherence rating scales should realistically reflect the

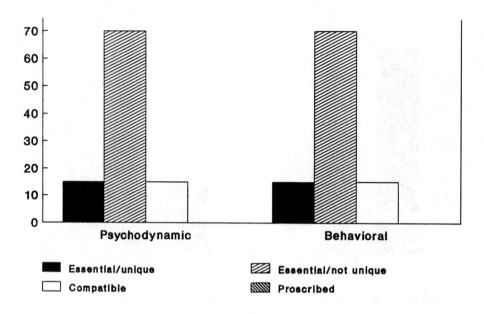

Figure 4. Hypothetical illustration of low treatment integrity caused by lack of unique interventions.

interventions prescribed and proscribed in the treatment manuals, allowing for comparison of treatments on all the relevant treatment dimensions, rather than just on those that are supposed to differ. Studies of adherence should report on how many of the important interventions across the two treatments were the same and how many were different. In Figure 4, the two treatments from different theoretical orientations are actually quite similar. This similarity might help to explain an absence of treatment effects. This issue has been ignored in many adherence scales used until now. It is possible for two treatments to be discriminable but to have significant overlap also. The overlap may be more important in predicting outcome than those aspects that are divergent, yet if the adherence measure focuses only on what is different and does not rate overlapping features, it might create the illusion of treatment distinctiveness when, in fact, the similarities were more important than the differences.

Recommendation 4

To determine whether a treatment has been adequately administered, researchers must assess therapist competence. In addition, they must establish competence through independent measurement and verification, rather than assume that experience level and training are tantamount to competence.

As has been discussed throughout this article, the assessment of therapist competence must be sensitive to relevant aspects of the therapeutic context. In other words, adequate measurement of competence means specifying how sensitively the treatment protocol is applied to individual clients. The most important aspects of the therapeutic context to consider when rating competence are (a) stage of therapy, (b) client difficulty, and (c) client presenting problems.

Stage in Therapy

Stage in therapy must be considered in terms of both number of sessions completed and extent of progress made. To rate therapist competence for a given session, raters must have information about what has been accomplished in previous sessions. For example, in cognitive therapy for depression, if a client is still having difficulty monitoring automatic thoughts, the therapist may still be focusing on automatic thoughts in Session 14. However, for a client who has successfully learned to cope with dysfunctional thinking, the therapist should be focusing on underlying assumptions and core schemata.

The need to consider stage of therapy has implications for session selection and the type of information provided to raters. Instead of randomly selecting tapes to be coded and keeping raters blind to stage in therapy, competence raters must be aware of which session they are rating and what has happened in previous sessions. One way to accomplish this is to have a particular rater code all sessions for a particular client. This approach also allows the rater to evaluate the quality of interventions made within the context of the treatment plan.

It is labor intensive to rate all sessions for a particular client. For competence ratings, researchers may have to randomly select clients to be rated, rather than randomly select sessions. Clients from early, intermediate, and advanced stages of a study need to be sampled to control for drift. Therapists should remain unaware of which sessions are being rated.

Client Difficulty

Assessments of therapist competence should also take client difficulty into account. The appropriateness and skillfulness of interventions are definitely dependent on client behaviors that reflect level of difficulty. For example, depending on the treatment modality, a depressed client who is feeling hopeless may require much more direction and coaching from the therapist than a client who is hopeful and only mildly depressed. The hopeless client may be expected to feel buoyed by such a directive approach, whereas the less hopeless client may find it pushy or intrusive. Similarly, a therapist working with an extremely depressed person might do more of the work than he or she would with a less depressed client. The optimal level of activity and involvement are dependent on the client's level of depression.

Measures of client difficulty will likely have to be multidimensional.

With major depression as an example, the dimensions may include degree of functional impairment, presence of collateral problems, number of previous episodes, or duration of the problem. Ratings may include level of client involvement or collaboration. The means of measuring client difficulty may differ depending on the presenting problem. Client difficulty should be assessed both before therapy begins and early on in treatment. Independent ratings by trained observers may also be used to rate client difficulty. Difficulty ratings could either be used as covariates or as a basis for the selection of cases to be rated. For example, cases varying in degree of difficulty could be selected for each therapist.

Presenting Problems

Presenting complaints and other problems raised by the client should be taken into account when assessing a therapist's competence. Therapists should approach presenting problems in a manner consistent with the treatment manual. Certain client problems may be described by the manual as taking precedence over other problems. Competency would be influenced by whether the therapist dealt with issues in the order of priority presented in the manual. The therapist's competence rating would also be affected by the way in which he or she approaches presenting problems and whether that approach is in accord with the treatment manual. For example, if the manual advises that the therapist set an agenda in a certain way, the therapist should approach presenting issues in that way. Some other treatment modality may require that the therapist react to the material that the client brings into the session, rather than structuring the session for the client.

Competence Raters

The recommendation mentioned earlier requires that raters are sufficiently experienced and sophisticated to understand the implications of the contextual variables described in the manual. It would be impossible for naive raters to make judgments about the appropriateness of interventions taking subtle aspects of the context into account. This necessitates the use of raters who are themselves skilled in the performance and supervision of the given treatment.

A second issue regarding potential raters pertains to their affiliation. Raters who are directly involved in the project have an obvious investment in the demonstration of competence (e.g., principal investigators or clinical supervisors). This affiliation may make it impossible for them to make unbiased ratings. Ideally, raters should be recruited from a different laboratory or site and have no stake in the outcome of the ratings of therapist competence.

Rating therapy session tapes is a labor-intensive enterprise, and hiring expert raters is obviously costly. There are certain factors that determine whether such labor-intensive strategies are necessary. For example, when two different treatment modalities are being compared at a site where the principal investigators are expert in only one of the treatments, it is especially important that competence ratings be made by outside experts. The affiliation of the principal investigator and the site are likely to have a major influence on how the therapy is administered and may make it unlikely that any alternative approach would be administered as competently. However, in other instances, competence can be presumed, such as when expertise in all treatment conditions is equally represented by the investigative or supervisory team. When the study is conducted in a laboratory in which expertise has been established by a previous track record of involvement in the treatment(s) under study, or when the comparisons involve different permutations of the same model of therapy, such as in a dismantling study, competence can be presumed. In short, it is when differential competence could plausibly compete with experimental hypotheses regarding group differences that competence must be assessed. In those instances, the raters must be expert, and they must be disinterested in the outcome of the ratings.

Table 2 shows the two primary treatment integrity questions, with hypothetical examples of measures, sampling techniques, coders, and estimated costs. For purposes of illustration, we presented a hypothetical study with a sample size of 30 subjects per treatment condition, and two treatments represented. Each of three therapists treat 20 clients each, 10 per treatment condition, with each client receiving 20 sessions.

The first question, "To what extent do treatments adhere to manual and differ from each other?" is sufficient when the investigator can either presume competence or when therapist competence is irrelevant to the experimental questions. Adherence rating items would include those representing techniques that are (a) essential and unique to each treatment, (b) essential but not unique, (c) compatible but not essential, and (d) proscribed according to the manual. Trained undergraduate or bachelor's-level raters could rate sessions drawn randomly from the first, middle, and last sessions of therapy. Sessions should be drawn from each phase of therapy, because different therapeutic techniques are likely to be used at different stages of treatment.

Undergraduate or bachelor's-level raters can be used if behaviorally specific rating systems are developed, with clearly identifiable therapist behaviors being coded. The identification of specific techniques is not likely to require a high level of expertise in the raters. Because undergraduate raters can be recruited for course credit in a university setting, the cost of these ratings could be minimal. We base our estimate of $7/hr for trained raters on an informal survey of psychologists from several universities who hire paid coders for similar work.

The second question, "Were the treatments performed competently?" requires an assessment of therapist competence. The approach to this assessment includes ratings of 4 clients for each of the three therapists. The first 10 sessions for each client are rated so that the rater has access to contextual

TABLE 2
Estimating Costs of Manipulation Checks Based on Questions of Adherence and Competence

Question	Measures	Sampling	Number of sessions to be rated	Level of rater training and total cost
To what extent do treatments adhere to manual and differ from one another?	Use manual-based adherence measure, which is behaviorally specific and includes the four types of items described.	Use random sampling of sessions from first, middle, and last third of therapy.	Three sessions/client × 60 clients = 180 sessions to be rated.	1. Raters could be undergraduates working for course credit, ratings requiring 1.5 hr/session. No cost. 2. Raters could be bachelor's-level, paid coders. With each tape requiring 1.5 hr for coding, multiplied by $7/h = $1,890.
Were treatments performed competently?	Use contextual assessment of competence.	Rate first 10 sessions for two difficult and two average cases per therapist on competence measure.	10 sessions × 4 clients × three therapists = 120 sessions.	Expert raters are needed to make competence ratings. Two hours/tape × $75/h = $18,000.

information regarding stage in therapy, progress made, and so forth. Because of the labor-intensive nature of rating many sessions per case, fewer cases are used. Client difficulty ratings can be used to ensure that the cases being rated adequately represent the population of cases from which the samples are taken. In this case, 2 "high difficulty" and 2 "average difficulty" clients could be assessed for each therapist. A discussion of how to assess client difficulty is beyond the scope of this article.

Experienced therapists are needed to assess competence and are particularly necessary given the contextual basis for these ratings. The raters must be sufficiently skilled in the therapy being rated so that they can evaluate the interventions made with important contextual factors in mind. We estimate that expert raters would be paid approximately $75/hr after consulting with several experts who have carried out such ratings.

It is clear from the table that the various factors shown, (i.e., sampling technique, size of sample, who the raters are, etc.) all contribute to the cost of the manipulation check. The importance of each of these factors must be weighed, along with careful consideration of the research question being addressed when designing such a study.

CONCLUSION

We have reviewed different methods for assessing adherence and competence, pointed out some problems with them, and suggested some guidelines for future use of these scales. Treatment integrity is central to the interpretation of results from research on psychotherapy. It is a basic tenet of clinical research methodology that the strength of the manipulation is one of the most important factors in designing interpretable studies. An independent variable involving a form of psychotherapy is about as complex as an independent variable can get. Much progress has been made in the development of potent manipulations and in assessing their strength, but more work needs to be done. We are not there yet.

REFERENCES

Beck, A. T., Rush, A. J., Shaw, B. F., & Emery, G. (1979). *Cognitive therapy of depression*. New York: Guilford Press.

Berman, J. S., & Norton, N. C. (1985). Does professional training make a therapist more effective? *Psychological Bulletin, 89*, 401–407.

Borkovec, T. D., & Mathews, A. M. (1988). Treatment of nonphobic anxiety disorders: A comparison of nondirective, cognitive, and coping desensitization therapy. *Journal of Consulting and Clinical Psychology, 56*, 877–884.

Chevron, E. S., & Rounsaville, B. J. (1983). Evaluating the clinical skills of psychotherapists: A comparison of techniques. *Archives of General Psychiatry, 40*, 1129–1132.

Dobson, K. S., Shaw, B. F., & Vallis, T. M. (1985). Reliability of a measure of the quality of cognitive therapy. *British Journal of Clinical Psychology, 24*, 295–300.

Durlak, J. A. (1979). Obsolescence or lifelong education: A choice for the professional. *American Psychologist, 27*, 486–498.

Foley, S. H., O'Malley, S., Rounsaville, B. J., Prusoff, B. A., & Weissman, M. M. (1987). The relationship of patient difficulty to therapist performance in interpersonal psychotherapy of depression. *Journal of Affective Disorders, 12*, 207–217.

Hattie, J. A., Sharpley, C. F., & Rogers, H. J. (1984). Comparative effectiveness of professional and paraprofessional helpers. *Psychological Bulletin, 95*, 534–541.

Hollon, S. D., Evans, M. D., Elkin, I., & Lowery, H. A. (1984). *System for rating therapies for depression.* Paper presented at the Annual Meeting of the American Psychiatric Association, Los Angeles, CA.

Kiesler, D. J. (1973). *The process of psychotherapy: Empirical foundations and systems of analysis.* Chicago: Aldine.

Klerman, G. L., Weissman, M. M., Rounsaville, B. J., & Chevron, E. S. (1984). *Interpersonal psychotherapy of depression.* New York: Basic Books.

Luborsky, L., & DeRubeis, R. J. (1984). The use of psychotherapy treatment manuals: A small revolution in psychotherapy research style. *Clinical Psychology Review, 4*, 5–14.

Luborsky, L., McLellan, A. T., Woody, G. E., O'Brien, C. P., & Auerbach, A. (1985). Therapist success and its determinants. *Archives of General Psychiatry, 42*, 602–611.

Luborsky, L., Woody, G. E., McLellan, A. T., O'Brien, C. P., & Rosenzweig, J. (1982). Can independent judges recognize different psychotherapies? An experience with manual-guided therapies. *Journal of Consulting and Clinical Psychology, 50*, 49–62.

Mattick, R. P., & Peters, L. (1988). Treatment of severe social phobia: Effects of guided exposure with and without cognitive restructuring. *Journal of Consulting and Clinical Psychology, 56*, 251–260.

Moncher, F. J., & Prinz, R. J. (1991). Treatment fidelity in outcome studies. *Clinical Psychology Review, 11*, 247–266.

O'Malley, S. S., Foley, S. H., Rounsaville, B. J., Watkins, J. T., Sotsky, S. M., Imber, S. D., & Elkin, I. (1988). Therapist competence and patient outcome in interpersonal psychotherapy of depression. *Journal of Consulting and Clinical Psychology, 56*, 496–501.

Persons, J. B. (1989). *Cognitive therapy in practice: A case formulation approach.* New York: Norton.

Schaffer, N. D. (1982). Multidimensional measures of therapist behavior as predictors of outcome. *Psychological Bulletin, 92*, 670–681.

Shaw, B. F. (1984). Specification of the training and evaluation of cognitive therapists for outcome studies. In J. Williams & R. Spitzer (Eds.), *Psychotherapy research: Where are we and where should be go?* (pp. 173–188). New York: Guilford Press.

Shaw, B. F., & Dobson, K. S. (1988). Competency judgments in the training and evaluation of psychotherapists. *Journal of Consulting and Clinical Psychology, 56,* 666–672.

Silberschatz, G., Curtis, J. T., & Nathans, S. (1989). Using the patient's plan to assess progress in psychotherapy. *Psychotherapy, 26,* 40–46.

Silberschatz, G., Fretter, P. B., & Curtis, J. T. (1986). How do interpretations influence the process of psychotherapy? *Journal of Consulting and Clinical Psychology, 54,* 646–652.

Snyder, D. K., & Wills, R. M. (1991). Risks and challenges of long-term psychotherapy outcome research: Reply to Jacobson. *Journal of Consulting and Clinical Psychology, 59,* 146–149.

Strupp, H. H. (1986). Psychotherapy: Research, practice, and public policy (how to avoid dead ends). *American Psychologist, 41,* 120–130.

Suh, C. S., O'Malley, S. S., & Strupp, H. H. (1986). The Vanderbilt process measures: The Psychotherapy Process Scale (VPPS) and the Negative Indicators Scale (VNIS). In L. S. Greenberg & W. M. Pinsof (Eds.), *The psychotherapeutic process: A research handbook* (pp. 285–323). New York: Guilford Press.

Weissman, M. M., Rounsaville, B. J., & Chevron, E. (1982). Training psychotherapists to participate in psychotherapy outcome studies. *American Journal of Psychiatry, 139,* 1442–1446.

Wills, R. M., Faitler, S. L., & Snyder, D. K. (1987). Distinctiveness of behavioral versus insight-oriented marital therapy: An empirical analysis. *Journal of Consulting and Clinical Psychology, 55,* 685–690.

Yeaton, W. H., & Sechrest, L. (1981). Critical dimensions in the choice and maintenance of successful treatments: Strength, integrity, and effectiveness. *Journal of Consulting and Clinical Psychology, 49,* 156–167.

Young, J., & Beck, A. T. (1980). *Cognitive therapy scale rating manual.* Unpublished manuscript.

24

TREATMENT OF APTITUDE × TREATMENT INTERACTIONS

BRADLEY SMITH AND LEE SECHREST

Psychotherapy outcome research is a frustrating business. Experiments are not easy to arrange and control, outcomes are difficult to measure—often even to define—and results are often disappointing. Psychotherapy ought to work better than it appears to. One possible explanation for why it does not is that the effects of psychotherapy depend on specific characteristics of patients and the therapies to which they are exposed (i.e., effects of psychotherapy may depend on Aptitude × Treatment Interactions [ATIs; Cronbach & Snow, 1977]). More specifically, the ATI hypothesis states that appropriate matching of patients with treatment will result in better outcomes. This hypothesis has been optimistically interpreted by many clinical researchers to mean that ATI research can uncover psychotherapy effects that, compared with main effects, are stronger and more reliable. Unfortunately for the optimists, as we will assert and try to account for in this article, compared with main effects, ATIs in psychotherapy research may be

Reprinted from the *Journal of Consulting and Clinical Psychology, 59*, 233–244. Copyright 1991 by the American Psychological Association.

infrequent, undependable, and difficult to detect. The purpose of this article is to take a sober look at the realities and probable impact of ATI research in terms of psychotherapy theory and practice. The ATI approach is not a quick fix to the problem of disappointing results in psychotherapy research. This article outlines a variety of stringent conditions necessary for adequate ATI research. Ironically, if our recommendations are heeded, it is likely that subsequent research will uncover previously "hidden" main effects more frequently than interactions.

WHAT IS AN ATI?

To discuss Aptitude × Treatment interactions, it is necessary to agree on just what is meant by such an interaction. We do not have in mind the purely arithmetic fact that an interaction refers to a multiplicative rather than merely an additive effect of two or more variables, although people without much quantitative training often imagine that when two variables must be taken into account, that implies an interaction. Rather, we are concerned with the fact that an Aptitude × Treatment interaction may be manifest in different ways with entirely different implications. It needs to be noted, however, that demonstration of an interaction requires a minimum of four data points. It is not enough to show that Z therapy is superior to Y therapy with depressed clients in order to infer an interaction. One must show that for some other condition, say clients with anxiety, the difference between Z and Y therapy is either smaller or larger than for depressed patients. An interaction is always specific to particular contrasts. In our example, the contrast is with respect to the problem (psychopathology), but the contrast could be with respect to personal characteristics of patients (e.g., sex), characteristics of therapists (e.g., experience), circumstances of treatment (e.g., voluntary–involuntary), or site of treatment (e.g., inpatient–outpatient). Although Aptitude × Treatment interactions are typically defined as involving contrasts in patient characteristics, that limitation need not apply. The ideas and principles are the same. In essence, however, it is important to understand that the occurrence of an interaction implies a limitation on generalizability of effects of treatments. On the other hand, an interaction also implies a basis for optimism in that the treatment under study works *better* with some persons or under some conditions than under others.

The existence of an interaction does not necessarily mean that circumstances exist under which the two treatments are equal, or that if one is better for one thing, the other must be better for something else. Interactions can be *disordinal* or *ordinal* (Cronbach & Snow, 1977). In the case of disordinal interactions (panel 1 of Figure 1), the lines connecting the like treatment conditions cross. This, for some reason, is often taken as firmer evidence for an interaction than a "mere" ordinal interaction in which the lines do not

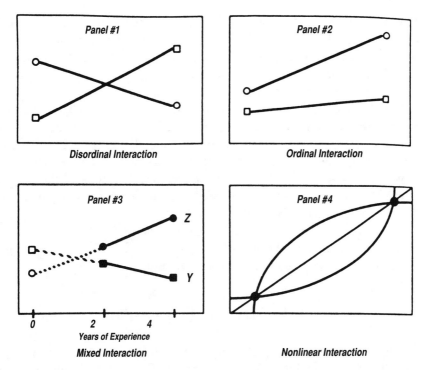

Figure 1. Illustrations of disordinal, ordinal, mixed, and nonlinear Aptitude × Treatment interactions.

cross (at least not within the range of variables studied; see panel 2 of Figure 1). If statistical significance means anything, it surely means that a significant ordinal interaction is just as dependable as a similarly significant disordinal interaction. Some of the mythical superiority of disordinal interactions may be an artifact from the use of statistical models that give priority to main effects. Partialing out main effect variance has differential effects on disordinal and ordinal interactions, and, as a consequence, ordinal interactions may simply not be statistically significant after main effect variance is removed.

Moreover, under some circumstances, apparent ordinality may simply reflect limitations on the representations of independent or dependent variables (Cronbach & Snow, 1977). For example, consider the apparent ordinal interaction depicted in panel 3 of Figure 1. For therapists with 2 years of experience, therapy modalities Y and Z do not differ in effectiveness, but for therapists with 4 years, Z is superior. But consider the dotted lines extending to the level of 0 experience, a level not tested in the experiment.[1] The depiction suggests that the ordinal interaction actually observed would have been disordinal had different levels of the experience variable been included. For inexperienced therapists, Therapy Y would be a better choice. In fact, had only 0 and 2 years of experience been studied, one would have observed quite a different ordinal interaction with Y superior at the lowest level and Y and Z equal at the highest (2-year) level.

The interaction "results" displayed in Figure 1 also permit another observation: the pernicious potential of the inclination to connect two data points by a straight line. The line drawn in panel 4 almost cries out for the interpretation, "With increasing therapist experience, Z is increasingly the intervention to be recommended." That cry should be resisted for reasons portrayed in panel 4, where it is evident that lines of almost any sort may connect two data points. Nevertheless, a straight line is the best guess when only two data points are available. Therefore, anyone who intends to model growth and change should begin with a minimum of three data points. It may be that some ATIs can be measured only by nonlinear models.

VARIED INTERACTION EFFECTS

Interactions may be manifest in treatment effects in different ways with quite different implications. These are worth considering with some care.

First, and most commonly, an Aptitude × Treatment interaction is taken to refer to the greater effect of a treatment in the presence of some characteristics than others. For example, systematic desensitization is relatively more effective for patients with phobias than for patients with obsessive–compulsive disorders; certain forms of behavior modification are more helpful for obsessive–compulsive disorders than for phobias. Underlying such observations is the implicit idea of some absolute effect of therapies, a qualitative difference between them. A medical illustration of this type of interaction would be the use of quinine to treat malaria versus the use of penicillin to treat a bacterial infection.

A second way in which an Aptitude × Treatment interaction might be manifested, however, is in the relative *efficiencies* of two treatments. Whiskey is a "stronger" drink than beer, but that simply reflects the concentration of alcohol per fluid ounce. Beer is just as intoxicating as whiskey if one consumes enough of it. Similarly, two therapies could conceivably differ not in terms of the terminal effect but in the "dose" required to get there. One needs to be cautious in interpreting findings comparing 8 sessions of Therapy Y with 8 of Therapy Z. If Y takes 16 sessions to achieve the same effect of 8 Z sessions, that might make Z a preferable therapy (e.g., in terms of cost-effectiveness; Scott & Sechrest, in press), but that is not an absolute difference between the outcomes of the two therapies. Moreover, psychotherapeutic processes are not necessarily affected by the rate of change. Therefore, some ATIs may reflect differences in the rate of change rather than a qualitative difference in process and outcome.

A third possibility is that Aptitude × Treatment interactions may be specific to the outcome measure(s) chosen. Therapy Z may produce more improvement in self-esteem than Y for female than male patients, but no difference may be observable on any other outcome measure. An obvious implication is that researchers should use multiple outcome measures, and interpreters and users of research should be cautious in inferring the existence of generalized Aptitude × Treatment interactions without considering the possibility of an Aptitude × Treatment × Outcome interaction. It should be noted here, however, that a recent attempt to identify different outcomes for different treatments of depression failed to find any Treatment × Outcome interactions (Imber et al., 1990). This failure may have occurred because, although Imber et al. did enter client aptitudes into their analyses (level of depression), the interaction may not have been significant for a variety of other reasons, such as problems with statistical power, lack of measurement precision, or the simple possibility that there was no interaction effect.

WHO WILL BE AFFECTED BY ATI RESEARCH?

What are the boundaries of what constitutes "treatment" for the purposes of discussing Aptitude × Treatment interactions? If we consider the entire panoply of interventions relevant to the domain of "psychotherapy," then it is manifestly absurd to think that there are no ATIs (e.g., see Lazarus, 1990). It is now widely conceded that behavioral intervention involving exposure to the stimulus is the treatment of choice for phobias; however, such interventions would be irrelevant at best for a wide range of other conditions. For example, it is doubtful that simply exposing depressed patients to depressing stimuli will make them any better. Matching different problems with differentially effective treatments automatically makes for an interaction. Behavioral interventions tend by their very nature to be tailored somewhat to the requirements of different problems so that their use *assumes* an ATI. The recommendation of breathing retraining for hyperventilation is so obvious an instance of an assumed ATI that it is not even interesting; no one would suppose that breathing retraining would be useful in treating bruxism or brutomania.

On the other hand, if psychotherapy has no specific effects, if it is all just a matter of the quality of the relationship, then the search for ATIs is similarly diminished in interest. The search would be reduced to the search for therapist–patient matching variables that would foster the development of a high quality therapeutic relationship. Requirements for matching therapists and patients are not of great practical interest because they are difficult to meet under most conditions of practice. Therapists in agencies are usually under pressure to deliver services and do not often have the luxury of declining to treat a person because of less than optimal matching. Therapists in independent practice are under similar pressures, albeit for somewhat different reasons.

We assume that the interest in ATIs reflects assumptions about strategic and tactical options potentially open to therapists (i.e., that if a therapist knew of ATIs, the therapist could capitalize on them by optimal behavior). Interest in ATIs assumes that therapists are capable of planful flexibility in their decisions about how to approach cases. If the ATI reflects differences in the effectiveness of two or more *modalities* of therapy (e.g., as appears to be the case for treatment of phobias), the ethical therapist has either to master multiple modalities or decline to treat a patient nonoptimally and refer the patient to a therapist competent in the better modality. In actuality, most therapists probably consider themselves generalists and try to treat almost every patient who enters their office. Thus, ATIs may prove to be more interesting in theory development than in actual practice.

A medical analogy can further elucidate the complexity of treatment decisions in the context of ATIs. A cardiologist would not attempt to treat a patient presenting with a sore knee but would refer the patient to an orthopedist (another modality). The orthopedist might conclude that the first challenge would be to reduce swelling and inflammation and might prescribe an anti-inflammatory drug, rather than a painkiller. That tactical decision would involve an ATI. The physician's overall initial strategy might be to rely on natural healing processes on the assumption that the problem was caused by a severe sprain with no critical tissue damage. That strategic approach would involve an assumed ATI. If the problem were caused by tearing of the anterior cruciate ligament, then natural healing processes would produce an unsatisfactory outcome, and surgery would be recommended. The ATI would be a Diagnosis or Problem × Treatment interaction.

The same orthopedist might be faced with another patient who could be considered for a total knee replacement. The doctor might decide that the patient's age and lifestyle would not justify such a radical procedure. With a young but not highly active patient, watchful waiting could be a better treatment choice if a few years of moderate disability were rewarded by improvements in prosthetic technology during the waiting period. That would be a Patient Characteristic × Treatment interaction. If alternative treatments for a damaged knee involved a trade-off between discomfort and reduced mobility, that would be a Treatment × Outcome interaction.

In order to exploit ATIs when they are discovered, it is essential to know exactly how the treatment works and what the mechanisms are. Any ATI is observed in a particular context of therapists, patients, problems, circumstances, and so on. If we are to know how the observed ATI is to be applied to some new set of conditions, then we must know exactly the nature of the interaction in the first place. Our current understanding of most psychotherapies and behavioral interventions is scarcely more sophisticated than would be represented by a description of a medical "treatment" as "some red pills." A pharmacotherapy is not regarded as completely satisfactory until its specific mode of action is understood (i.e., which chemical operating on what structure to produce what response). Acetyl salicylate (aspirin), for example, was a useful therapeutic for centuries, but the medical community was never completely comfortable with it until they began, recently, to understand its various modes of action.

When one considers that a century after the invention of psychotherapy major disagreements still exist about such a fundamental issue as whether there are any specific treatment effects (e.g., Lazarus, 1990; Strupp, 1989), one can believe that we are still at the early aspirin stages in our understanding. Even if ATIs were found, we would not be in a position to interpret them correctly and exploit them in other than the most direct empirical way. In general, as we will elaborate on later, we expect psychotherapy theorists to benefit more from ATI findings than will practicing therapists.

COMPLEXITIES AND DIFFICULTIES IN ATI RESEARCH

Common sense suggests that there *should* be at least some Aptitude × Treatment interactions (ATI) in psychotherapy. The concept of the ATI has received serious attention in the educational psychology literature (see Cronbach & Snow, 1977) and has been proposed as an important, if not essential, strategy for research in all areas of psychology (e.g., Cronbach, 1975). Nonetheless, very little systematic work on ATIs in psychotherapy has been done, and very few replicable ATIs have been reported.

An important reason ATI research has not become a reality is the fact that measuring and interpreting interaction effects is much more difficult than dealing with main effects. ATI research requires greater precision than general effects research. Rather than comparing general packages of treatment delivered to a broad class of patients, in ATI studies one needs to know precisely what it is about the patient that interacts with a precisely defined component of treatment. Interaction effects need to be shown to occur above and beyond the additive influence of main effects, and this requires studies with large sample sizes and at least four treatment cells. Thus, compared with the search for main effects, research on interactions requires better measurement, more subjects, a wider variety of conditions, and specific a priori hypotheses.

To complicate further the problem of ATI research, traditional statistics are relatively insensitive to interaction effects (Wahlsten, 1990). Some of the statistical disadvantage in interaction research arises from the tendency of scientists to consider main effects before interaction effects. This preference is arbitrary, but it supposedly promotes parsimony and has become the accepted rule (actually it may be more parsimonious to propose one interaction instead of two main effects). Some consequences of the "parsimonious approach" are these: (a) Interactions have to be gleaned from the variance left over after main effects are removed, which reduces the likelihood that interactions will be significant; (b) the magnitudes of interaction effects may often be underestimated; and (c) the magnitudes of main effects are often overestimated. We are in general agreement with Dawes's (1988) point that interactions may not be very impressive after main effects are allowed for. But researchers who think interactions are important should understand the handicap they place themselves under in using analytical models that look for interaction effects only in the residuals from main effects predictions. Analyses of variance (ANOVAS) have that unhappy property, and the search for interaction effects might better be carried out by General Linear Models involving regression methods and individual growth curve analyses.

The search for ATIs is also impeded by the inclinations of many investigators to convert continuous measures to categorical measures, thereby sacrificing critical information. That inclination has probably been contributed to by a preference for ANOVA statistics and the custom of graphing interactions by the mean values of individual cells. What Cronbach and Snow (1977) refer to as "ATI regressions" are simply plots of regressions. These have the advantage of showing the shape of the entire function (e.g., revealing nonlinearity if it exists). Interactions will ordinarily be seen as differences in slopes of regression lines, although Cronbach and Snow note that interactions may occasionally affect variances. Not only are regression analyses likely to have greater power for detection of interactions (Cohen & Cohen, 1983) but they are certain to be more sensitive to other features of the phenomena under study.

Few psychotherapy studies are planned to reveal interactions, and most of them have inadequate statistical power to detect interactions, especially given the preference researchers have shown for ANOVAS. Cronbach and Snow (1977) suggest, for example, that an ATI study with subjects assigned randomly to groups should have about 100 subjects *per treatment*, a sample size *much* larger than almost any psychotherapy studies. Blanchard, Appelbaum, Radnitz, Morrill, et al. (1990), in what is a fairly representative example of therapy research, had only 116 cases to allocate to four treatment conditions. It is not surprising that they found no differences among the three active treatments, although two actually had an odds ratio of better than 1.7 for producing improvement when compared with the third. Another study of treatment of a small sample of elderly patients found no differences between treatments (Thompson, Gallagher, & Breckenridge, 1987), although at the end of treatment "major depression still present" was twice as frequent in the cognitive as compared with the behavior therapy group. The possibility in such studies for detecting an interaction indicating that one of the treatments would be better than the others with a particular type of patient is virtually nil.

Unfortunately, power analyses are rarely reported for psychotherapy studies of any kind, an omission that is going to have to be corrected, but that is going to prove painful. Journal editors must begin to insist on properly done power analyses. Power analyses must be done before therapy studies are undertaken if they are to be useful. After the fact analyses permit capitalization on chance to a considerable, although unknown, degree because all the estimates must necessarily be considered biased.

With the exception of the above-mentioned statistical considerations and the minimum requirement that two treatments and two aptitudes must be compared, the difficulties of ATI research are basically similar to those faced in all types of psychotherapy research. Many of these issues are discussed elsewhere in great detail; however, it strengthens the purpose of this article to remind ATI researchers not to perpetuate problems that continue to plague psychotherapy research. As mentioned earlier, simply looking for ATIs will not automatically result in psychotherapy research successes. On the contrary, the ATI approach may exacerbate past problems that, if left uncorrected, could lead to dismal failure. Some of the more troublesome of these research liabilities are discussed later in this article.

DO ATIs REALLY EXIST?

Before discussing possible methodological problems that have made ATIs elusive, it is important to consider the possibility that ATIs do not exist, or at least that they are rare. Virtually every comprehensive analysis of psychotherapy outcomes (e.g., Smith, Glass, & Miller, 1980; Landman & Dawes, 1982; Luborsky, Singer, & Luborsky, 1975) ultimately concluded that type of therapy, experience of the therapist, credentials of the therapist, and so on are unrelated to outcome. If any client variables are consistently related to outcome of therapy, they generally support no more of a conclusion than that clients who are bright, verbal, motivated, and not so bad off in the first place tend to do better in therapy. Those are main effects, rather than interactions, and not very interesting ones. These conclusions have not, however, been much of a deterrent to speculation about ATIs. For example, an ATI reported by Jacobson, Follette, and Pagel (1986) for marital therapy was not only not particularly large in size but it was found only at immediate posttherapy measurement and not at follow-up. Talley, Strupp, and Morey (1990) found an interaction between therapists' tendencies toward affiliative or hostile response and patients' similar tendencies but only for therapist-rated improvement on a single item scale. Other interactions were reported, but they were similarly inconsistent across independent and dependent variables.

Despite the fairly consistent negative outcomes of the search for ATIs, the search is unabated. Why? One answer may lie in what Dawes (1979) calls "arguing from a vacuum." People have a strong tendency to believe and argue that if one desired solution does not work, it must be true that something else will. Psychotherapists would like to believe that therapist experience has a good bit to do with outcome, and when that cannot be shown, the response is to believe that the answer must lie in interactions. If type of therapy does not appear to be related to outcome of therapy, then the effect of type of therapy must lie in an interaction with other variables. All that remains is to ferret out and display the interaction.

In some important ways, the persistence of psychotherapy researchers in searching for ATIs resembles the error in thinking that Dawes (1988) identifies with the commitment to "sunk costs." So much effort has been expended in the attempt to find the "silver bullet" of psychotherapy that it is simply too painful to abandon all that investment, cut losses, and try something else. As the punch line of an old joke has it, "There must be a pony in there somewhere!"

To a metascientist, the movement toward ATI research might be viewed as a symptom of a degenerating program of research. Programs can be said to be degenerating if they (a) fail to yield new predictions or empirical successes and/or (b) deal with empirical anomalies through ad hoc maneuvers that overcomplicate rather than clarify the problem of interest (Gholson & Barker, 1985). Perhaps psychotherapy researchers should be seriously and dispassionately reconsidering the core assumptions of their theories rather than building an elaborate ATI structure on a crumbling theoretical foundation.

The disappointment over empirical outcomes notwithstanding, the case for interactions is, unfortunately, a priori discouraging. Here is why, as Dawes (1991) makes clear. If there is an interaction but no main effect for the treatment variable, then either the interaction must be very small in magnitude in relation to unexplained (error) variance or the interaction must be disordinal (as in panel 1, Figure 1). Now if an interaction involving, for example, therapist experience were disordinal, that would mean that experienced therapists were less helpful, and perhaps harmful, to some clients. Not only would such a conclusion seem unlikely on the face of it, but it would immediately plunge the field into serious ethical difficulties. It would clearly be unethical to assign a client to any form of intervention *known* to be suboptimal. Thus, many ATIs, if they exist at all, may be more confusing and troublesome than past failures to find strong main effects.

TYPE III ERRORS IN PSYCHOTHERAPY RESEARCH

Failures of validity of experiments can lead to three types of erroneous conclusions: (a) The treatment is judged to be effective when it is not (i.e., a Type I error); (b) the treatment is judged to be ineffective when it actually is effective (i.e., a Type II error); or (c) researchers conduct the wrong experiment (i.e., a Type III error). Type III errors occur when faulty measurements, experimental designs, or conceptualization of crucial variables prohibit meaningful interpretation of experimental results. In the case of ATI studies, failures to understand aptitudes or treatments result in Type III errors.

Historically, the possibility of making Type I errors has been more carefully guarded against than the chance of making Type II errors. Meanwhile, the possibility of making Type III errors has been virtually ignored. This oversight is serious because Type III errors override both Type I and Type II errors. Who cares if a hypothesis is erroneously accepted or rejected if the hypothesis is misspecified to begin with? Therefore, to minimize and control for Type I and Type II errors at the expense of Type III errors is a fallacy of misplaced precision (Mitroff & Featheringham, 1974). Most of the issues relevant to controlling and minimizing Type III errors fall under the province of what Mahoney (1978) calls "theoretical validity," which he defines as the extent to which an experiment has some logical bearing on a specific hypothesis or theory. Unfortunately, owing to the proliferation of diverse paradigms for explaining and studying human psychopathology, it is difficult to reach agreement on the minimum standards for theoretical validity. Nevertheless, some aspects of theoretical validity may be less debatable than others. For instance, determining whether a hypothesis is clearly stated a priori is much less problematic than trying to decide whether the hypothesis is theoretically relevant to a certain paradigm. Thus, even though many issues regarding theoretical validity are entrenched in specific schools of psychotherapy, it should be possible to list several methodological issues related to theoretical validity that are ubiquitous across paradigms of psychotherapy.

Concerns over Type III errors pertain to all four of the most widely recognized types of experimental validity: internal, external, construct, and statistical conclusion validity (Cook & Campbell, 1979). Of these four, statistical conclusion validity is probably the least affected by Type III errors. Nevertheless, calculations of statistical power may be dependent on theory-based estimates of treatment effect size (Scott & Sechrest, 1989). When this is the case and the wrong theory is applied or the right theory is misapplied, then a Type III error can result in a problem with estimating statistical power. Thus, statistical conclusion validity might be affected by Type III errors, although threats to statistical conclusion validity do not appear to contribute to Type III errors. Nonetheless, it should be emphasized that statistical conclusion validity issues are, on other grounds, critical to study and interpretation of ATIs.

Proper concern with Type III errors increases as attention shifts to internal validity. The confidence with which one can assert that the outcome of an experiment is attributable to the intervention and to no other variables (i.e., internal validity) is not a purely objective deduction. Formulations of experimental problems, and as a result internal validity, depend to a large extent on the researcher's ability to conceive of and control for rival explanations of treatment effects. Determining whether an effect occurred is a relatively simple endeavor compared with the process of attributing the effect to the independent variable. It is easier to show that a treatment works than to explain how it works, and misattributing a cause to an effect is a Type III error. For example, Jacobson, Follette, and Pagel (1986) may have shown that behavioral marital therapy is more beneficial for egalitarian couples than for others (although only immediately posttherapy), but that finding is not necessarily easily explained; and simply stating that the outcome was some ATI related to the "egalitarian" qualities of the couple would be a mistake. In order to reduce problems with Type III errors, we need to know more about specific and unique qualities of concepts such as "egalitarian" and "behavioral marital therapy."

Problems associated with misunderstanding how a treatment works are especially distressing when one attempts to disseminate findings from an effective study, a shortcoming recognized by Jacobson et al. (1986). The legitimacy of various generalizations of research findings across persons, places, and times (and other dimensions; see Cook, 1990) is the essence of external validity. Even though conclusive evaluation of external validity is based on empirical demonstrations of the replicability of treatment across different settings and subpopulations, most inferences about generalizability are based on theoretical interpretations of treatment. As a result, poor understanding of treatment variables can be expected to result in flawed generalization of treatment.

Out of Cook and Campbell's (1979) list of validities, construct validity is the most closely linked with Type III errors. Construct validity is completely subsumed by the concept of theoretical validity, although a few considerations pertinent to theoretical validity are not traditionally associated with construct validity (e.g., the issue of clinically vs. statistically significant change). We will not attempt to make sharp distinctions between theoretical and construct validity, and these terms may be used interchangeably, as they are in this article. However, we favor the expression "theoretical validity" because it emphasizes the importance of theory in psychotherapy research and promotes the notion that researchers should occasionally look beyond the four types of validity listed by Cook and Campbell (1979).

Theoretical validity refers to the adequacy of our understanding of the experimental variable(s) being studied. If the variables are not operationally defined in a manner that clearly and completely represents the theoretical construct of interest, then the experiment can result in a Type III error. Likewise, if the variables are not accurately described (i.e., poorly reported), there is a risk that subsequent readers and researchers will commit Type III errors. In summary, any severe threat to construct or theoretical validity will almost certainly result in a Type III error, and these errors imply that the worth of the entire experiment is diminished, at least in terms of theoretical or practical meaning. Unfortunately, the psychotherapy literature is replete with instances of poor, and probably inaccurate, description of interventions. Type III errors (i.e., failing to understand what treatment really is) could be the primary reason why main effects research has been disappointing. If these errors are left uncorrected, Type III errors could be an even more formidable barrier to ATI research.

A final note on the theoretical validity of treatment concerns the importance of the timing of formulations of theoretical explanations. Hypotheses that are formulated before the experiment (i.e., a priori hypotheses) are presumably tested by the experiment. Hypotheses generated after inspection of the data (i.e., a posteriori hypotheses) are actually untested and may represent little more than speculation. Thus, accepting a posteriori hypotheses as fact can result in Type III errors. An example is provided by the National Institute of Mental Health (NIMH) Depression Collaborative Research Program, for which a recent analysis (Elkin et al., 1989) appeared to show a reasonable, but unanticipated, ATI. More severely depressed patients got greater benefit from drug treatment than from other treatments, although no greater benefit from drugs existed for less severely depressed patients. This ordinal ATI would have been considerably more persuasive had it been predicted in advance, because compared with hindsight, a priori prediction suggests a greater understanding of the topic of interest.

SURMOUNTING THE BARRIERS
TO ADEQUATE ATI RESEARCH

This article has described four major barriers to measuring ATI effects: (a) the need for relatively more complex designs and the ensuing practical and economic difficulties; (b) conditions that promote Type II errors, including small sample size and inappropriate statistical techniques for detecting interactions; (c) Type III errors, especially failing to understand the exact nature of treatments; and (d) the very real possibility that ATIs are infrequent and undependable. These barriers are formidable but not entirely insurmountable. The following section offers suggestions for overcoming adversity in ATI research.

Collaboration and More Appropriate Statistical Models

The requirement that experiments have sufficient designs and degrees of freedom to detect interaction is, obviously, not easy to meet, but ignoring that requirement has not gotten us, and will not get us, anywhere either. It will not do the field of psychotherapy any good simply to bemoan the fact that large sample sizes and elaborate designs are required for ATI research and then to ignore that fact in practice.

One possibility is that more studies can be carried out collaboratively. Successful completion of collaborative studies is not easy, but it is wasteful of money and effort to do studies that will not accomplish their aims. It should be recognized, however, that power to detect effects is not solely a matter of sample size (see also Higgenbotham, West, & Forsyth, 1988). It may be that for some effects the reduction of alpha from .05 to .10 would be justified; too much emphasis is placed on statistical significance in any case (Cohen, 1990). A second determinant of statistical power is the effect size anticipated, which may depend heavily on the strength of the intervention. Strength of intervention is often under the control of the investigative team, and treatment should be planned to be strong to begin with, and lapses in integrity of treatment should be protected against (Sechrest & Redner, 1979). Investigators should also, if they value and predict interactions, think of giving them priority over main effects in their statistical models. Finally, statistical power is a function in part of the size of the error term. The magnitude of experimental error is also very often under control of the investigative team. Experimental error can be reduced by decreasing heterogeneity in the sample, by better measurement procedures, by greater precision in conducting the experiment, and other maneuvers (Sechrest & Yeaton, 1981b).

Theory Driven Research

We believe strongly that if psychotherapeutic interventions are going to be improved substantially, and particularly if that improvement is to be derived from ATIs, better theory is going to be required, and that theory will have to have its basis in fundamental psychological research. Twenty-five years ago, Goldstein, Heller, and Sechrest (1966) proposed that psychotherapy should be, first, and foremost, *psychological*, and that meant grounding theory and practice in the basic concepts and findings of the field. They did not believe that much progress could be made by trying to develop what would be a separate, isolated discipline of psychotherapy. Moreover, the three authors demonstrated by systematic reviews of research literature that hypotheses important to the psychotherapeutic enterprise could be derived from more basic research in the field. Despite a good bit of assent from others at the time, even some acclaim, the main thesis of Goldstein, Heller, and Sechrest has been, we think, largely ignored. Some of their ideas have been realized to some extent (e.g., the importance of generalization as an aspect of psychotherapy), but for the most part current literature on psychotherapy appears to pay scant attention to research on basic behavioral and conceptual processes. One cannot determine that, for example, cognitive therapy owes any more than the most general debts to cognitive psychology. If cognitive therapy is to develop and improve, one would think that it ought to take account of what cognitive psychologists are learning about cognition. A recent volume, *Psychotherapy and Behavior Change* (Higgenbotham et al., 1988), which is a descendent of Goldstein, Heller, and Sechrest, provides contemporary instances of the need to apply more basic research in developing thinking and research about psychotherapy. We would observe, however, that the material reviewed and the hypotheses developed tend strongly to suggest that any major improvements in psychotherapy are more likely to be in the form of main effects than ATIs.

Multitrait–Multimethod Experimental Designs

When testing psychological theories, researchers need to determine if their operationalization of the theory is accurate and representative of the problem of interest. Theoretical validity problems need to be subjected to the rigorous methodology of the multitrait–multimethod approach (Campbell & Fiske, 1959), which has been largely ignored in psychotherapy research. This approach attempts to get at the true meaning of a measure (the construct "true score") and, at the same time, to identify and attempt to neutralize the effect of any systematic bias introduced by measurement and analytic strategies. Thanks to modern statistical procedures such as structural modeling researchers are now in the position to undertake theory-driven determinations of convergent and divergent validity of experimental measures.

Manipulation Checks

Once the underlying traits of experimental measures are determined, dependent variables (DVs) can be chosen that should reveal the operation of the theorized mechanisms of change. For example, if a treatment for drug users focuses on self-concept because improved self-esteem is thought to result in better recovery, then treatment evaluation should use measures of self-esteem. Assuming that the DVs are perfectly psychometrically sound (which is rarely the case), if no reliable differences are recorded for these DVs, then the construct validity of the treatment should be questioned. In the drug abuser self-esteem example, failure to observe changes in self-esteem threatens the construct validity of treatment, at least to the extent that self-esteem is critical to the overall treatment theory. The methodology of recording changes in hypothesized mediating variables has been called "manipulation checks" (Aronson & Carlsmith, 1968). In our opinion, if the psychotherapy research paper does not report manipulation checks, then the reader should be skeptical about the construct validity of treatment.

Manipulation checks have also been shown to be useful in studying the believability of alternative treatments, especially those intended as placebos (Dush, 1987). If, as is usually assumed, placebos have their effect through arousal of expectancies for change, if they do not arouse those expectancies, they are not good placebos. Manipulation checks can be used to determine whether alternative treatments arouse similar expectancies, are equally believable, and so on. Alternatively, manipulation checks may reveal that alternative, nonspecific treatments were more "active" than they were intended to be. An example is provided by Blanchard, Appelbaum, Radnitz, Michultka, et al. (1990), who found that the placebo condition probably functioned much like a relaxation treatment. Elkin et al. (1989) also noted that the placebo condition in the National Depression Collaborative Research Program was not inactive.

We also think that manipulation checks should be more generally used to assess the nature of therapy *as perceived* by patients. For example, the National Depression Collaborative Research Program intended to compare the effects of interpersonal and cognitive behavioral therapies, for which extensive manuals were prepared in order to achieve uniformity in implementation of treatment. We are not, however, aware of any attempts to determine whether patients experienced the two therapies in any different ways (e.g., whether patients in cognitive behavior therapy viewed their therapists or therapy in any way different from the views of interpersonal therapy patients). This type of information is crucial to ATI research because patient aptitudes may have a major effect on perception of treatment and subsequent outcome. Unfortunately, with the exception of detailed process analyses on the role of patient expectancy in psychotherapy (e.g., Elliott, 1986), there appears to be very little information about the phenomenology of patienthood.

Dawes (1991) also makes the point that the fallback position of asserting that it is the importance of "the relationship" or the "therapeutic alliance" is weak unless we have measures of the relationship or alliance that predict outcome. Even then, the causal connection of the quality of the therapeutic alliance to outcome may be uncertain. The therapeutic alliance is likely to grow stronger when things are going well, and the perception of improvement (e.g., in symptoms) might well lag behind the perception of the quality of the alliance without any necessary inference of a causal relationship. In recovering from medical illnesses, people often report feeling much better or even "well" long before their relevant biomedical parameters have shown much change.

Strength of Treatment

A critical parameter in the understanding of an intervention, including psychotherapy, is the strength of the treatment. Strength is viewed here as a close analog to the strength of a drug treatment. A strong treatment of aspirin would be 10 mg; a weak treatment would be 2 mg. What would "strong" psychotherapy look like? We do not know. We can, however, conjecture as follows, allowing our description to reflect rather more common sense and consensus than actual empirical evidence. Strong psychotherapy might include

- Doctoral trained therapist;
- Therapist with at least 10 years experience;
- Therapist specialized in type of problem involved;
- Therapist well-versed in empirical and theoretical literature;
- Therapist highly regarded by peers for professional expertise;
- Well-developed therapy protocol (manual) for specific problem;
- Two sessions per week in the beginning, one per week thereafter;
- Intense sessions with minimum wasted time;
- Specific recommendations for intersession "practice" activities;
- Therapy of at least one year duration if required;
- Therapist is accountable for integrity of treatment and for its outcome.

Obviously, the characteristics listed are not likely to be orthogonal in real life (e.g., a therapist who is highly regarded is likely to have a doctorate and to have a good bit of experience). If all these characteristics were, however, descriptive of the therapy being provided to a client, we could probably all agree that the treatment should be regarded as strong. Conversely, a minimally trained, inexperienced therapist doing short-term, unfocused treatment not guided by protocol and at a low level of intensity for only a few weeks would be regarded as providing weak treatment or, at the very least, poorly understood treatment. The major problem is to understand just how strong and weak the two implementations would be and just where in between the two any other real-life instance of therapy might lie. For example, what about a new doctoral-level therapist a few months out of internship but very well-read, following a protocol, one session per week for 12 weeks? We are not even close to being able to estimate strengths of various psychotherapeutic interventions, but that is not because the task is impossibly difficult.

Treatment strength can be quantified. One could, for example, assemble panels of experts and ask them to assign weights to different aspects of therapeutic interventions. In a study of rehabilitative efforts directed at criminal offenders, for example, Sechrest and West (1983) found that professional training beyond the master's level was not accorded any additional weight. On the other hand, time in treatment was weighted in a virtually linear fashion. Alternatively, one could, perhaps by means of magnitude estimation techniques, ask experts to imagine "ideal" treatment and no treatment and then to assign a globally descriptive number to a description such as one of the above. We have regularly used a class exercise involving such judgments of smoking cessation interventions and have found graduate students quite sensitive to the methods and in generally good agreement in their judgments.

Knowing the strength of treatments is crucial in ATI research because comparing weak with strong treatments is not likely to produce a very meaningful interaction effect (unless, of course, the "real-life" strengths of treatments are represented, and this also requires understanding the strength of treatment).

Manualized Treatment

A move toward "manualized" treatment appears to be developing, fostered by the examples used in the National Depression Collaborative Research Program (Elkin, Parloff, Hadley, & Autry, 1985). Brief focused treatment used for high utilizers of health services is another example (Cummings, Dorken, Pallak, & Henke, 1989). Manualized treatments (i.e., those with formal protocols) may well turn out to be stronger treatments. A study of chemotherapy for cancer patients done in Finland (Karjalainen & Palva, 1989), for example, showed that patients treated by a protocol had better outcomes than patients treated according to the clinical judgments of their physicians. Holding therapists accountable (e.g., by close supervision) may also strengthen treatment. Noting that their analyses suggested weaker treatment effects than in another similar study, Elkin et al. (1989) suggest that the results may be attributable to the fact that therapists in the other study (Rush, Beck, Kovacs, & Hollon, 1977) were more closely supervised.

Study a Broader Range of Variability

The size of any effect, whether measured in terms of mean differences produced or variance accounted for, depends in part on the strength of the intervention. In the case of psychotherapy, strength would be adjusted in terms of the "amount" or size of the "dose" of therapy. In the case of variables not directly manipulated, the strength of the intervention would be realized by the range of values over which the variables were studied. Thus, for example, if one wanted to determine the effect of therapist experience on outcome, one could include values of therapist experience ranging from no experience, to, say, 30 years. In fact, the first Vanderbilt Psychotherapy Research project (Strupp & Hadley, 1979) included untrained (no experience) therapists and others with an average of 23 years of experience. If one wanted to determine the relationship between initial level of depression and outcome of treatment, one could include clients ranging from those with very mild depression (or maybe no depression) to those with depression so severe that they require round-the-clock care. Amount of therapy could range from zero to at least hundreds of sessions. A type of therapy could be varied from just barely adherent to principles of a certain treatment approach to extraordinarily adherent to those principles.

Our impression is that, over the large body of studies that exist, many variables have been tested at fairly extreme values, but most individual studies have included only a fairly narrow range of values. Moreover, few studies have used extreme values of more than one variable, so that sensitivity to interactions has probably been limited. To wit, Wahlsten (1990) argues that reliable Heredity × Environment interactions have not been found in humans because only a narrow range of human environments have been studied. Although one may argue that studies should have representative designs, which might limit values of most variables to medium ranges, that argument may not be so strong if one believes that the main advantage of the search for interactions is the light it sheds on theoretical processes (see Shoham-Salomon & Hannah, 1991).

Using Strong Inference and Testing Alternative Models

For many years, research in psychotherapy was dominated by a strategy of opposing one therapy against one or more control groups chosen—or designed—to weaken or rule out some artifactual explanation for any therapeutic effect that might be found. Those artifacts to be ruled out often included, of course, nonspecific "ingredients" of treatment. If a therapeutic intervention proved no more effective than, for example, an intervention thought to do no more than arouse expectancies for improvement, then any appeal to a specific therapeutic effect was superfluous. That research strategy was quite consistent with the Popperian (Popper, 1959) epistemology emphasizing falsification of plausible rival hypotheses. However, more contemporary metascientists, especially Lakatos and Laudan, convincingly argue that different research traditions are not incommensurable and can be tested within the same experiment (Gholson & Barker, 1985).

At about the time psychotherapy had its beginnings, Chamberlin (1895/1965), a geologist, was urging the "method of multiple working hypotheses," insisting that progress in science would be faster if experimentation involved pitting alternative explanations against each other. Testing the effects of one variable against nothing is not at all efficient, nor is it very interesting. Many more ways exist for an idea to be wrong than right (Dawes, 1988), and showing that a hypothesis is not wrong (i.e., it is better than nothing) does not mean that the hypothesis is correct. Perhaps it is not even strengthened much by being found not wrong. On the other hand, if two rival explanations are pitted against each other, differing in some crucial respects, a result favoring one over the other is highly satisfying, even if not to be taken as proof. Cronbach and Snow (1977) point to the importance of selecting theoretically important variables from among the panoply imaginable and putting them to competitive tests, a process closely akin to what Platt (1964) called "strong inference."

Perhaps the time has come to abandon groups included in psychotherapy studies solely for the purpose of testing for nonspecific treatment effects. In fact, it has been suggested that strategies involving pitting of alternative therapies against each other should be adopted (Dance & Neufeld, 1988; Garfield, 1990). The need for "no treatment" controls may have diminished, or disappeared altogether, with the introduction of "norms" that can now be derived from the work of meta-analysts (Sechrest & Yeaton, 1981a). If, on the average, therapeutic interventions can be estimated to have an effect amounting to 0.6 standard deviations improvement on a relevant dependent measure, then one does not need a no-treatment group to determine whether that effect is achieved by a therapy being tested. If a standard therapy against which a new therapy is to be tested is known to have generally larger effects than those produced by nonspecific treatment groups, then one does not need to introduce such groups into every therapy study. Control groups do consume resources that might better be spent on improvements in comparisons between studies. A strong conceptual feature of the NIMH Treatment of Depression Collaborative Research Program (Elkin et al., 1985) was the use of imipramine plus clinical management as a "standard referent treatment."

The purposes of pitting therapies against each other would be broader than simply determining which might be most effective. Ideally, therapies should be pitted against each other because they involved different assumptions about mechanisms of action, likely outcomes, and so on.

Make Sure the ATI Is Meaningful

Last, but not least, if researchers are going to test ATI hypotheses, they need to justify the expense of the ATI research effort in terms of the meaningfulness of the interaction effect. If an interaction is ordinal (panel 2, Figure 1), the mean of clients in one condition would be higher overall than the mean of clients in the other condition. That is, there should be a main effect for that condition, although the main effect might be altogether spurious in the sense of being solely attributable to the interaction. If the interaction were strong, both the main effect and the interaction should be apparent. In any case, in a meta-analysis across a population of studies, one would think that an important interaction would be manifest in a consistent tendency for one condition, say experienced therapist, to have better outcomes than another (e.g., inexperienced therapist). Dawes (1988) also shows that ordinal interactions are usually very well estimated by separate linear effects so that even when they occur, they provide little improvement over estimates made by additive combinations of the variables involved (see Figure 2). This point is illustrated by the results of Kadden, Cooney, Getter, & Litt (1989) in which matching alcoholics with treatments improved R^2 from .10 to .16. Even though this ATI improved prediction *by* 60%, overall it resulted in an improvement *of* only 6% (see Pickering, 1983). A 6% gain is probably not

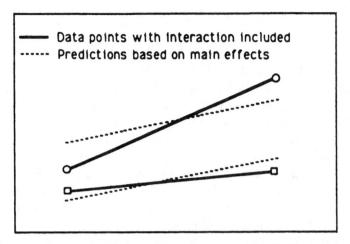

Figure 2. Illustration of the relative predictive value of main effects versus ordinal interactions.

enough to justify the considerable amount of effort required to effect differential assignment. Even from a purely theoretical perspective, it is questionable that such a small increase in explanatory power should be viewed as a particularly important finding.

Dawes's conclusions about the extent to which ordinal interactions may be approximated by additive linear effects are often obscured by the ways in which effects are graphed. Slopes can be made to appear flat or steep depending on the scales chosen for the ordinates and abscissae. One needs to determine the goodness of fit of the additive model by statistical, not visual, analyses.

An additional problem of interpretation is created by the fact that the metrics in which outcome measures are expressed often lack direct meaning (Cronbach & Snow, 1977; Sechrest & Yeaton, 1981c). What exactly does it mean when, according to their therapists, some clients are $-.5$ and others $.3$ on a standardized residual of global outcome rating (Talley, Strupp, & Morey, 1990)? (We do not mean to devalue this or any other studies cited but use them only as examples; the problem is ubiquitous.) The problem of difficult-to-interpret metrics is, of course, not peculiar to analyzing interactions, but it is more troublesome in ATI than in main effect research. A main effect of $.6$ merely suggests that all cases should be treated in a uniform way, which, unless the costs of doing so are large, poses no problem. An interaction requires, however, that treatment be differential, which means that differential classification must be carried out, that two or more forms of treatment be available, and so on. Consequently, the question of whether an effect size is large enough in some absolute and practically meaningful sense to justify accepting the implications of an interaction is potentially the most important question in ATI research.

CONCLUSIONS

We do not believe that it is fruitful to continue to try to "discover" ATIs in psychotherapy. In this discovery mode of research, therapeutic interventions are studied and, incidentally, a long list of other variables are measured. Then, especially in the context of failure to find anticipated main effects, a search for interactions is doomed to failure. Few ATIs are ever found, and those that are found prove to be trivial, ephemeral, or both.

We believe that if important ATIs are to be identified, it will be through deliberate tests of theoretically driven a priori hypotheses. First, ATI hypotheses must be justified in advance, just as main effects must be. No one would advocate trying interventions at random to see whether it might be possible to find one that works. Similarly, we do not think it worth looking randomly for ATIs. Second, we believe that a priori analysis of the practical or theoretical import of ATIs should be considered. If one has a notion that an ATI might have some practical value, then it ought to be possible to specify in advance just how and under what circumstances it might have value. One should also be able to say in advance just how the verification of an ATI intended to advance theory would actually advance it. Third, the treatment, or intervention, should be developed in such a way as to have a high likelihood of inducing the interaction and at sufficient strength to make it likely that the interaction could be detected if it is operative. Fourth, experiments must be of sufficient size to permit study of interactions. This means that power calculations need to be done for interactions rather than merely for main effects. Most therapy studies are not large enough to have reasonable power to detect interactions. But power calculations are not often done in any case. They must be done, and they must be done before the fact. Finally, statistical analyses should be appropriate to the problem posed and the data collected. The inclination to convert continuous variables into categorical variables must be abandoned (e.g., see Cronbach & Snow, 1977), and journal editors should begin enforcing that ban immediately. Much more attention needs to be paid to the possibility, indeed probability, that a large proportion of the relationships we are interested in are not linear, and some may not even be close to linear. We need not worry overly much about modest curvilinearity, but some variables are probably sharply curvilinear (e.g., asymptotic), and some may even be nonmonotonic. It is *possible*, as an instance, that the relationship between the amount of training for therapy and treatment outcome could be asymptotic or parabolic (i.e., an inverted U-shaped function). It is quite plausible that a moderate amount of training could produce maximum effects and, as a result, experience is not expected to be linearly related to therapeutic success.

The above discussion of therapist experience offers an example of how inaccuracy in measurement can lead to Type III errors. Therapist experience is a relatively easy-to-collect pseudomeasure of something researchers are truly interested in, that is, therapist competence. The lacunae in psychotherapy outcome research concerning the role of therapist competence is rather peculiar (see also Schaffer, 1982). To the best of our knowledge, therapist competence has never been directly assessed and studied in relation to therapy process or outcome. Inadequate proxies such as therapist training and years of experience have been used, and their observed effect seems to be nil. Competence needs to be assessed in some other, more meaningful way. Indeed, most constructs of interest to psychotherapists are measured very inaccurately. Until we set higher standards for the reliability and validity of our measures of aptitudes and treatments (As and Ts) it is very unlikely that we will find any ATIs.

We want to end by noting that, as in all scientific enterprises, knowledge about psychotherapy must advance by increments, usually small ones. Neither for main effects nor for ATIs are answers going to come from single studies. The task of generalizing from extant research is one whose difficulty has been greatly underestimated, as a reading of Cook (1990) will make clear. If we are to advance in our understanding it will have to be on the basis of extensive research and broad wisdom and intelligence about it. "Extrapolation and broad interpretation are guided by theoretical understanding, based on intelligent consideration of findings from the whole corpus of research" (Cronbach & Snow, 1977, p. 22). We agree.

REFERENCES

Aronson, E., & Carlsmith, J. M. (1968). Experimentation in social psychology. In G. Lindzey & E. Carlsmith (Eds.), *Handbook of social psychology* (Vol. 2, 2nd ed., pp. 1–79). Reading, MA: Addison-Wesley.

Blanchard, E. B., Appelbaum, K. A., Radnitz, C. L., Michultka, D., Morrill, B., Kirsch, C., Hillhouse, J., Evans, D. D., Guarnieri, P., Attanasio, V., Andrasik, F., Jaccard, J., & Dentinger, M. P. (1990). Placebo-controlled evaluation of abbreviated progressive muscle relaxation and relaxation combined with cognitive therapy in the treatment of tension headache. *Journal of Consulting and Clinical Psychology, 58*, 210–215.

Blanchard, E. B., Appelbaum, K. A., Radnitz, C. L., Morrill, B., Michultka, D., Kirsch, C., Guarnieri, P., Hillhouse, J., Evans, D. D., Jaccard, J., & Barron, K. D. (1990). A controlled evaluation of thermal biofeedback and thermal biofeedback combined with cognitive therapy in treatment of vascular headache. *Journal of Consulting and Clinical Psychology, 58*, 216–224.

Campbell, D. T., & Fiske, D. W. (1959). Convergent and discriminant validation by the multitrait–multimethod matrix. *Psychological Bulletin, 56*, 81–105.

Chamberlin, T. (1965). The method of multiple working hypotheses. *Science, 148*, 754–759. (Originally published 1895)

Cohen, J. (1990). Some things I have learned. *American Psychologist.*, *45*, 1304–1312.

Cohen, J., & Cohen, P. (1983). *Applied multiple regression-correlation: Analysis for the behavioral sciences*. Hillsdale, NJ: Erlbaum.

Cook, T. D. (1990). The generalization of causal connections: Multiple theories in search of clear practice. In L. Sechrest, E. Perrin, & J. Bunker (Eds.), *Research methodology: Strengthening causal interpretations of nonexperimental data* (pp. 9–31). Rockville, MD: Agency for Health Care Policy and Research.

Cook, T. D., & Campbell, D. T. (1979). *Quasi-experimentation: Design and analysis for field settings*. Boston: Houghton Mifflin.

Cronbach, L. J. (1975). Beyond the two disciplines of scientific psychology. *American Psychologist, 30*, 116–126.

Cronbach, L. J., & Snow, R. E. (1977). *Aptitudes and instructional methods: A handbook for research on interactions*. New York: Irvington.

Cummings, N. A., Dorken, H., Pallak, M. S., & Henke, C. (1989). *The impact of psychological intervention on health care utilization and costs: The Hawaii Medicaid Project*. Unpublished Final Project Report No. 11-C-98344/9.

Dance, K. A., & Neufeld, R. W. (1988). Aptitude-treatment interaction research in clinical settings: A review of attempts to dispel the "patient uniformity" myth. *Psychological Bulletin, 104*, 192–213.

Dawes, R. M. (1979). The robust beauty of improper linear models in decision making. *American Psychologist, 34*, 571–582.

Dawes, R. M. (1988). *Rational choice in an uncertain world*. New York: Harcourt Brace Jovanovich.

Dawes, R. M. (1991). *Professional practice versus knowledge in psychology*. Manuscript in preparation.

Dush, D. M. (1987). The placebo in psychosocial outcome evaluations. *Evaluation and the Health Professions, 9*, 421–438.

Elkin, I., Parloff, M., Hadley, S., & Autry, J. (1985). NIMH Treatment of Depression Collaborative Research Program: Background and research plan. *Archives of General Psychiatry, 42*, 305–316.

Elkin, I., Shea, M. T., Watkins, J. T., Imber, S. D., Sotsky, S. M., Collins, J. F., Glass, D. R., Pilkonis, P. A., Leber, W. R., Docherty, J. P., Fiester, S. J., & Parloff, M. B. (1989). National Institute of Mental Health Treatment of Depression Collaborative Research Program: General effectiveness of treatments. *Archives of General Psychiatry, 46*, 971–982.

Elliot, R. (1986). Interpersonal process recall as a psychotherapy process research method. In L. S. Greenberg & W. M. Pinsoff (Eds.), *The psychotherapeutic process: A research handbook*. New York: Guilford Press.

Garfield, S. L. (1990). Issues and methods in psychotherapy process research. *Journal of Consulting and Clinical Psychology, 58*, 273–280.

Gholson, B., & Barker, P. (1985). Kuhn, Lakatos, and Laudan: Applications in the history of physics and psychology. *American Psychologist, 40*, 755–769.

Goldstein, A. P., Heller, K. H., & Sechrest, L. B. (1966). *Psychotherapy and the psychology of behavior change*. New York: Wiley.

Higgenbotham, H. N., West, S. G., & Forsyth, D. R. (1988). *Psychotherapy and behavior change*. New York: Pergamon Press.

Imber, S. D., Pilkonis, P. A., Stotsky, S. M., Elkin, I., Watkins, J. T., Collins, J. F., Shea, M. T., Leber, W. R., & Glass, D. R. (1990). Mode-specific effects among three treatments for depression. *Journal of Consulting and Clinical Psychology, 58*, 352–359.

Jacobson, N. S., Follette, W. C., & Pagel, M. (1986). Predicting who will benefit from behavioral marital therapy. *Journal of Consulting and Clinical Psychology, 54*, 518–522.

Kadden, R. M., Cooney, N. L., Getter, H., & Litt, M. D. (1989). Matching alcoholics to coping skills or intractional therapies: Posttreatment results. *Journal of Consulting and Clinical Psychology, 57*, 698–704.

Karjalainen, S., & Palva, I. (1989). Do treatment protocols improve end results? A study of survival of patients with multiple myeloma in Finland. *British Medical Journal, 299*, 1069–1072.

Landman, T. J., & Dawes, R. M. (1982). Psychotherapy outcome: Smith and Glass's conclusions stand up. *American Psychologist, 37*, 504–516.

Lazarus, A. A. (1990). If this be research. . . . *American Psychologist, 44*, 670–671.

Luborsky, L., Singer, B., & Luborsky, L. (1975). Comparative studies of psychotherapy: Is it true that "everyone has won and all must have prizes?" *Archives of General Psychiatry, 32*, 995–1008.

Mahoney, M. J. (1978). Experimental methods and outcome evaluation. *Journal of Consulting and Clinical Psychology, 46*, 660–672.

Mitroff, I. A., & Featheringham, T. R. (1974). On systemic problem solving and the error of the third kind. *Behavioral Science, 19*, 383–393.

Pickering, T. G. (1983). Treatment of mild hypertension and the reduction of cardiovascular mortality: The "of or by" dilemma. *Journal of the American Medical Association, 249*, 399–400.

Platt, J. R. (1964). Strong inference. *Science, 146*, 347–353.

Popper, K. R. (1959). *The logic of scientific discovery*. New York: Basic Books.

Rush, A. J., Beck, A. T., Kovacs, M., & Hollon, S. (1977). Comparative efficacy of cognitive therapy and pharmacotherapy in the treatment of depressed patients. *Cognitive Therapy Research, 1*, 17–37.

Schaffer, N. D. (1982). Multidimensional measures of therapist behavior as predictors of outcome. *Psychological Bulletin, 92*, 670–681.

Scott, A. G., & Sechrest, L. (1989). Strength of theory and theory of strength. *Evaluation and Program Planning, 12*, 329–336.

Scott, A. G., & Sechrest, L. (in press). Theory driven approach to cost-benefit analysis: Implications of program theory. In H. Chen & P. Rossi (Eds.), *Policy studies organization*. Westport, CT: Greenwood Press.

Sechrest, L., & Redner, R. (1979). Strength and integrity of treatments in evaluation studies. In *How well does it work? Review of criminal justice evaluation, 1978: 2. Review of evaluation results, corrections* (pp. 19–62). Washington, DC: National Criminal Justice Reference Service.

Sechrest, L., & West, S. G. (1983). Measuring the intervention in rehabilitation experiments. *International Annals of Criminology, 21*(1), 11–19.

Sechrest, L., & Yeaton, W. H. (1981a). Empirical bases for estimating effect size. In R. F. Boruch, P. M. Wortman, D. S. Cordray, & Associates (Eds.), *Reanalyzing program valuations: Policies and practices for secondary analysis of social and educational programs* (pp. 212–224). San Francisco: Jossey-Bass.

Sechrest, L., & Yeaton, W. H. (1981b). Estimating magnitudes of experimental effects. (*Journal Supplements Abstract Service: Catalog of Selected Documents in Psychology, 11*, Ms. No. 2355, 39 pp.)

Sechrest, L., & Yeaton, W. H. (1981c). Meaningful measures of effect. *Journal of Consulting and Clinical Psychology, 49*, 766–767.

Shoham-Salomon, V., & Hannah, M. T. (1991). Client–treatment interactions in the study of differential change processes. *Journal of Consulting and Clinical Psychology, 59*, 217–225.

Smith, M. L., Glass, G. V., & Miller, T. I. (1980). *The benefits of psychotherapy.* Baltimore: Johns Hopkins University Press.

Strupp, H. H. (1989). Psychotherapy: Can the practitioner learn from the researcher? *American Psychologist, 44*, 717–724.

Strupp, H. H., & Hadley, S. W. (1979). Specific vs. nonspecific factors in psychotherapy. *Archives of General Psychiatry, 36*, 1125–1136.

Talley, P. F., Strupp, H. H., & Morey, L. C. (1990). Matchmaking in psychotherapy: Patient–therapist dimensions and their impact on outcome. *Journal of Consulting and Clinical Psychology, 58*, 182–188.

Thompson, L. W., Gallagher, D., & Breckenridge, J. S. (1987). Comparative effectiveness of psychotherapies for depressed elders. *Journal of Consulting and Clinical Psychology, 55*, 385–390.

Wahlsten, D. (1990). Insensitivity of the analysis of variance to heredity-environment interaction. *Behavioral and Brain Sciences, 13*, 109–120.

25

CLINICAL SIGNIFICANCE: A STATISTICAL APPROACH TO DEFINING MEANINGFUL CHANGE IN PSYCHOTHERAPY RESEARCH

NEIL S. JACOBSON AND PAULA TRUAX

There has been growing recognition that traditional methods used to evaluate treatment efficacy are problematic (Barlow, 1981; Garfield, 1981; Jacobson, Follette, & Revenstorf, 1984; Kazdin, 1977; Kendall & Norton-Ford, 1982; Smith, Glass, & Miller, 1980; Yeaton & Sechrest, 1981). Treatment effects are typically inferred on the basis of statistical comparisons between mean changes resulting from the treatments under study. This use of statistical significance tests to evaluate treatment efficacy is limited in at least two respects. First, the tests provide no information on the variability of response to treatment within the sample; yet information regarding within-treatment variability of outcome is of the utmost importance to clinicians.

Reprinted from the *Journal of Consulting and Clinical Psychology*, 59, 12–19. Copyright 1991 by the American Psychological Association.

Preparation of this article was supported by Grants MH 33838-10 and MH-44063 from the National Institute of Mental Health, awarded to Neil S. Jacobson.

Second, whether a treatment effect exists in the statistical sense has little to do with the clinical significance of the effect. Statistical effects refer to real differences as opposed to ones that are illusory, questionable, or unreliable. To the extent that a treatment effect exists, we can be confident that the obtained differences in the performance of the treatments are not simply chance findings. However, the existence of a treatment effect has no bearing on its size, importance, or clinical significance. Questions regarding the *efficacy* of psychotherapy refer to the benefits derived from it, its potency, its impact on clients, or its ability to make a difference in peoples' lives. Conventional statistical comparisons between groups tell us very little about the efficacy of psychotherapy.

The effect size statistic used in meta-analysis seems at first glance to be an improvement over standard inferential statistics, inasmuch as, unlike standard significance tests, the effect size statistic does reflect the size of the effect. Unfortunately, the effect size statistic is subject to the same limitations as those outlined above and has been even more widely misinterpreted than standard statistical significance tests. The size of an effect is relatively independent of its clinical significance. For example, if a treatment for obesity results in a mean weight loss of 2 lb and if subjects in a control group average zero weight loss, the effect size could be quite large if variability within the groups were low. Yet the large effect size would not render the results any less trivial from a clinical standpoint. Although large effect sizes are more likely to be clinically significant than small ones, even large effect sizes are not necessarily clinically significant.

The confusion between statistical effect or effect size and efficacy is reflected in the conclusions drawn by Smith et al. (1980) on the basis of their meta-analysis of the psychotherapy outcome literature. In their meta-analysis, they found moderate effect sizes when comparing psychotherapy with no or minimal treatment; moreover, the direction of their effect sizes clearly indicated that psychotherapy outperformed minimal or no treatment. On the basis of the moderate effect sizes, the authors concluded that "Psychotherapy is *beneficial,* [italics added] consistently so and in many different ways. . . . The evidence overwhelmingly supports the *efficacy* [italics added] of psychotherapy" (p. 184).

Such conclusions are simply not warranted on the basis of either the existence or the size of statistical effects. In contrast to criteria based on statistical significance, judgments regarding clinical significance are based on external standards provided by interested parties in the community. Consumers, clinicians, and researchers all expect psychotherapy to accomplish particular goals, and it is the extent to which psychotherapy succeeds in accomplishing these goals that determines whether or not it is effective or beneficial. The clinical significance of a treatment refers to its ability to meet standards of efficacy set by consumers, clinicians, and researchers. While there is little consensus in the field regarding what these standards should be, various criteria have been suggested: a high percentage of clients improving; a level of change that is recognizable by peers and significant others (Kazdin, 1977; Wolf, 1978); an elimination of the presenting problem (Kazdin & Wilson, 1978); normative levels of functioning by the end of therapy (Kendall & Norton-Ford, 1982; Nietzel & Trull, 1988); high end-state functioning by the end of therapy (Mavissakalian, 1986); or changes that significantly reduce one's risk for various health problems.

Elsewhere we have proposed some methods for defining clinically significant change in psychotherapy research (Jacobson, Follette, & Revenstorf, 1984, 1986; Jacobson & Revenstorf, 1988). These methods had three purposes: to establish a convention for defining clinically significant change that could be applied, at least in theory, to any clinical disorder; to define clinical significance in a way that was consistent with both lay and professional expectations regarding psychotherapy outcome; and to provide a precise method for classifying clients as "changed" or "unchanged" on the basis of clinical significance criteria. The remainder of this article describes the classification procedures, illustrates their use with a sample of data from a previous clinical trial (Jacobson et al., 1989), discusses and provides tentative resolutions to some dilemmas inherent in the use of these procedures, and concludes by placing our method within a broader context.

A STATISTICAL APPROACH TO CLINICAL SIGNIFICANCE

Explanation of the Approach

Jacobson, Follette, and Revenstorf (1984) began with the assumption that clinically significant change had something to do with the return to normal functioning. That is, consumers, clinicians, and researchers often expect psychotherapy to do away with the problem that clients bring into therapy. One way of conceptualizing this process is to view clients entering therapy as part of a dysfunctional population and those departing from therapy as no longer belonging to that population. There are three ways that this process might be operationalized.

(a) The level of functioning subsequent to therapy should fall outside the range of the dysfunctional population, where range is defined as extending to two standard deviations beyond (in the direction of functionality) the mean for that population.

(b) The level of functioning subsequent to therapy should fall within the range of the functional or normal population, where range is defined as within two standard deviations of the mean of that population.

(c) The level of functioning subsequent to therapy places that client closer to the mean of the functional population than it does to the mean of the dysfunctional population.

This third definition of clinically significant change is the least arbitrary. It is based on the relative likelihood of a particular score ending up in dysfunctional versus functional population distributions. Clinically significant change would be inferred in the event that a posttreatment score falls within (closer to the mean of) the functional population on the variable of interest. When the score satisfies this criterion, it is statistically more likely to be drawn from the functional than from the dysfunctional population.

Let us first consider some hypothetical data to illustrate the use of these definitions. Table 1 presents means and standard deviations for hypothetical functional and dysfunctional populations. The variances of the two populations are equal in this data set. Assuming normal distributions, the point that lies half-way between the two means would simply be

$$c = (60 + 40)/2 = 50$$

where c is the cutoff point for clinically significant change. The cutoff point is the point that the subject has to cross at the time of the posttreatment assessment in order to be classified as changed to a clinically significant degree. The relationship between cutoff point c and the two distributions is depicted in Figure 1. If the variances of the functional and dysfunctional populations are unequal, it is possible to solve for c, because

$$(c - M_1)/s_1 = (M_0 - c)/s_0;$$

or

$$c = \frac{s_0 M_1 + s_1 M_0}{s_0 + s_1}.$$

Because the cutoff point is based on information from both functional

TABLE 1
Hypothetical Data From an Imaginary Measure Used to Assess Change in a Psychotherapy Outcome Study

Symbol	Definition	Value
M_1	Mean of pretest experimental and pretest control groups	40
M_2	Mean of experimental treatment group at posttest	50
M_0	Mean of well functioning normal population	60
s_1, s_0	Standard deviation of control group, normal population, and pretreatment experimental group	7.5
s_2	Standard deviation of experimental group at posttest	10
r_{xx}	Test–retest reliability of this measure	.80
x_1	Pretest score of hypothetical subject	32.5
x_2	Posttest score of hypothetical subject	47.5

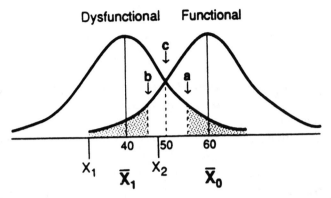

Figure 1. Pretest and posttest scores for a hypothetical subject (x) with reference to three suggested cutoff points for clinically significant change (a, b, c).

and dysfunctional populations and because it allows precise determination of which population a subject's score belongs in, it is often preferable to compute a cutoff point based only on one distribution or the other.

Unfortunately, in order to solve for c, data from a normative sample are required on the variable of interest, and such norms are lacking for many measures used in psychotherapy research. When normative data on the variable of interest are unavailable, the cutoff point can be estimated using the two standard deviation solution (a) suggested above as an alternative option. But because the two standard deviation solution does not take well-functioning people into account, it will not provide as accurate an estimate of how close subjects are to their well-functioning peers as would a cutoff point that takes into account both distributions. When the two distributions are overlapping as in the hypothetical data set, the two standard deviation solution will be quite conservative. As Figure 1 indicates, the cutoff point established by the two standard deviation solution is more stringent than c:

$$a = M_1 + 2s_1 = 40 + 15 = 55.$$

When functional and dysfunctional solutions are nonoverlapping, a will not be conservative enough. Not only are norms on functional populations desirable, but ideally norms would also be available for the dysfunctional population. As others have noted (Hollon & Flick, 1988; Wampold & Jensen, 1986), if each study uses its own dysfunctional sample to calculate a or c, then each study will have different cutoff points. The results would then not be comparable across studies. For example, the more severely dysfunctional the sample relative to the dysfunctional population as a whole, the easier it will be to "recover" when the cutoff point is study specific.

A third possible method for calculating the cutoff point is to adopt the second method mentioned above, and use cutoff point b, which indicates two standard deviations from the mean of the functional population. As Figure 1 shows, with our hypothetical data set the cutoff point would then be

$$b = M_0 - 2s_1 = 60 - 15 = 45.$$

When functional and dysfunctional distributions are highly overlapping, as in our hypothetical data set, b is a relatively lenient cutoff point relative to a and c (see Figure 1). On the other hand, if distributions are nonoverlapping, b could turn out to be quite stringent. Indeed, in the case of nonoverlapping distributions, only b would ensure that crossing the cutoff point could be translated as "entering the functional population." Another potential virtue of b is that the cutoff point would not vary depending on the nature of a particular dysfunctional sample: Once norms were available, they could be applied to any and all clinical trials, thus ensuring standard criteria for clinically significant change.

Which criteria are the best? That depends on one's standards. On the basis of our current experience using these methods, we have come to some tentative conclusions. First, when norms are available, either b or c is often preferable to a as a cutoff point: In choosing between b and c, when functional and dysfunctional populations overlap, c is preferable to b; but when the distributions are nonoverlapping, b is the cutoff point of choice. When norms are not available, a is the only cutoff point available: To avoid the problem of different cutoff points from study to study, a should be standardized by aggregating samples from study to study so that dysfunctional norms can be established. An example is provided by Jacobson, Wilson, and Tupper (1988), who reanalyzed outcome data from agoraphobia clinical trials and aggregated data across studies using the Fear Questionnaire to arrive at a common cutoff point that could be applied to any study using this questionnaire.

A Reliable Change Index

Thus far we have confirmed our discussion of clinically significant change to the question of where the subject ends up following a regimen of therapy. In addition to defining clinically significant change according to the status of the subject subsequent to therapy, it is important to know *how much* change has occurred during the course of therapy. When functional and dysfunctional distributions are nonoverlapping, this additional information is superfluous, because by definition anyone who has crossed the cutoff point would have changed a great deal during the course of therapy. But when distributions do overlap, it is possible for posttest scores to cross the cutoff point yet not be statistically reliable. To guard against these possibilities, Jacobson et al. (1984) proposed a reliable change index (RC), which was later amended by Christensen and Mendoza (1986):

$$RC = \frac{x_2 - x_1}{S_{diff}}$$

where x_1 represents a subject's pretest score, x_2 represents that same subject's posttest score, and S_{diff} is the standard error of difference between the two test scores. S_{diff} can be computed directly from the standard error of measurement S_E according to this:

$$S_{diff} = \sqrt{2(S_E)^2}$$

S_{diff} describes the spread of the distribution of change scores that would be expected if no actual change had occurred. An RC larger than 1.96 would be unlikely to occur ($p < .05$) without actual change. On the basis of data from Table 1,

$$S_E = s_1\sqrt{1 - r_{xx}} = 7.5\sqrt{1 - .80} = 3.35$$

$$S_{diff} = \sqrt{2(3.35)^2} = 4.74$$

$$RC = 47.5 - 32.5/4.74 = 3.16.$$

Thus, our hypothetical subject has changed. RC has a clearer criterion for improvement that is psychometrically sound. When RC is greater than 1.96, it is unlikely that the posttest score is not reflecting real change. RC tells us whether change reflects more than the fluctuations of an imprecise measuring instrument.

AN EXAMPLE USING A REAL DATA SET

To illustrate the use of our methods with an actual data set, we have chosen a study in which two versions of behavioral marital therapy were compared to a research-based structured version and a clinically flexible version (Jacobson et al., 1989). The purpose of this study was to examine the generalizability of the marital therapy treatment used in our research to a situation that better approximated an actual clinical setting. However, for illustrative purposes, we have combined that data from the two treatment conditions into one data set. Table 2 shows the pretest and posttest scores of all couples on two primary outcome measures, the Dyadic Adjustment Scale (DAS; Spanier, 1976) and the global distress scale of the Marital Satisfaction Inventory (GDS; Snyder, 1979), and a composite measure, which will be explained below. Data from the DAS only are also depicted in Figure 2. Points falling above the diagonal represent improvement, points right on the diagonal indicate no change, and points below the line indicate deterioration.

TABLE 2
Individual Couple Scores and Change Status
on Dyadic Adjustment Scale, Global Distress Scale,
and Composite Measures

Subject	Pretest	Posttest	Improved but not recovered	Re- covered
		Dyadic Adjustment Scale		
1	90.5	97.0	N	N
2	74.0	124.0	N	Y
3	97.0	97.5	N	N
4	73.5	88.0	Y	N
5	61.0	96.5	Y	N
6	66.5	62.5	N	N
7	68.5	112.5	N	Y
8	86.5	103.5	Y	N
9	88.5	90.0	N	N
10	68.5	82.5	Y	N
11	98.0	105.0	N	N
12	80.5	99.5	Y	N
13	89.5	112.5	N	Y
14	91.5	101.0	N	N
15	83.5	99.5	Y	N
16	60.5	79.5	Y	N
17	83.0	88.0	N	N
18	88.0	100.5	Y	N
19	98.5	119.0	N	Y
20	78.5	116.0	N	Y
21	99.5	116.0	N	Y
22	79.5	129.0	N	Y
23	84.5	113.0	N	Y
24	92.5	118.0	N	Y
25	93.0	92.0	N	N
26	85.0	114.0	N	Y
27	64.0	68.0	N	N
28	61.0	52.0	N	N
29	80.0	60.5	N	N
30	82.5	104.5	Y	N
		Global Distress Scale		
1	68.0	62.5	N	N
2	74.5	56.0	N	Y
3	58.5	58.0	N	N
4	73.5	71.0	N	N
5	78.5	60.5	Y	N
6	76.0	77.0	N	N
7	76.5	58.5	N	Y
8	63.0	52.0	N	Y
9	70.0	65.5	N	N
10	75.0	73.0	N	N
11	63.5	64.0	N	N
12	73.5	55.5	N	Y
13	71.5	53.0	N	Y
14	63.5	55.0	N	Y
15	57.0	50.0	N	N

TABLE 2 (*continued*)

Subject	Pretest	Posttest	Improved but not recovered	Re-covered
Global Distress Scale (*continued*)				
16	75.0	78.0	N	N
17	63.0	65.5	N	N
18	75.0	62.0	Y	N
19	71.5	60.5	Y	N
20	68.0	51.0	N	Y
21	75.5	50.0	N	Y
22	67.5	44.0	N	Y
23	62.5	55.5	N	N
24	69.5	56.0	N	Y
25	61.0	60.5	N	N
26	67.0	47.5	N	Y
27	75.5	—	—	—
28	75.5	—	—	—
29	69.5	—	—	—
30	66.5	—	—	—
Composite				
1	64.8	57.9	N	N
2	75.9	43.0	N	Y
3	58.5	55.9	N	N
4	74.7	65.4	Y	N
5	82.4	57.3	N	Y
6	78.9	79.4	N	N
7	78.2	49.2	N	Y
8	64.6	50.7	Y	N
9	66.5	62.3	N	N
10	77.6	68.7	Y	N
11	59.6	54.8	N	N
12	71.6	53.9	N	Y
13	66.7	47.0	N	Y
14	62.6	53.0	Y	N
15	63.6	51.7	Y	N
16	81.3	72.0	Y	N
17	66.2	63.2	N	N
18	68.7	56.1	Y	N
19	62.6	47.1	N	Y
20	70.3	44.6	N	Y
21	63.7	44.2	N	Y
22	69.6	35.7	N	Y
23	65.3	47.8	N	Y
24	65.5	45.7	N	Y
25	60.9	59.4	N	N
26	66.9	43.9	N	Y
27	—	—	—	—
28	—	—	—	—
29	—	—	—	—
30	—	—	—	—

Note. Composite = Average of Dyadic Adjustment Scale and Global Distress Scale estimated true scores. Y = yes; N = no. Dash = information not available.

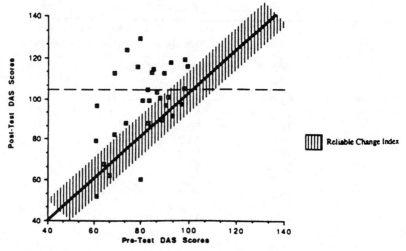

Figure 2. Scatter plot of pretest and posttest scores on the Dyadic Adjustment Scale with jagged band showing reliable change index.

Points falling outside the shaded area around the diagonal represent changes that are statistically reliable on the basis of RC ($> 1.96S_{diff}$); above the shaded area is "improvement" and below is "deterioration." One can see those subjects, falling within the shaded area, who showed improvement that was not reliable and could have constituted false positives or false negatives were it not for RC. Finally, the broken line shows the cutoff point separating distressed (D) from nondistressed (ND) couples. Points above the dotted line represent couples who were within the functional range of marital satisfaction subsequent to therapy. Subjects whose scores fall above the dotted line and outside the shaded area represent those who recovered during the course of therapy.

To understand how individual couples were classified, let us first consider Figure 3. Figure 3 depicts approximations of the distributions of dysfunctional (on the basis of this sample) and functional (on the basis of Spanier's norms) populations for the DAS. Using cutoff point criterion c, the point halfway between dysfunctional and functional means is 96.5. This is almost exactly the cutoff point that is found using Spanier's norms for functional (married) and dysfunctional (divorced) populations (cf. Jacobson, Follette, Revenstorf, Baucom, Hahlweg, & Margolin, 1984). If norms had not been available and we had to calculate a cutoff point based on the dysfunctional sample alone using the two standard deviation solution, the cutoff point would be 105.2. Finally, b, the cutoff point that signifies entry into the functional population, is equal to 79.4.

Given that the dysfunctional and functional distributions overlap, we have already argued that c is the preferred criterion. Indeed, a convention has developed within the marital therapy field to use 97 as a cutoff point, which is virtually equivalent to *c*. However, there is a complication with this particular measure, which has led us to rethink our recommendations. The norms of the DAS consist of a representative sample of married people, without regard to level of martial satisfaction. This means that a certain percentage of the sample is clinically distressed. The inclusion of such subjects in the normative sample shifts the distribution in the direction of dysfunctionality and creates an insufficiently stringent *c*. If all dysfunctional people had been removed from this married sample, the distribution would have been harder to enter, and a smaller percentage of couples would be classified as recovered. An ideal normative sample would exclude members of a clinical population. Such subjects are more properly viewed as members of the dysfunctional population and therefore distort the nature of the normative sample. Given the problems with this normative sample, it seemed to us that *a* was the best cutoff point for clinically significant change. At least when *a* is crossed we can be confident that subjects are no longer part of the maritally distressed population, whereas the same cannot be said of *c*, given the failure to exclude dysfunctional couples in the normative sample.

Table 2 also shows how subjects were classified on the basis of RC. Some couples showed improvement but not enough to be classified as recovered, whereas others met criteria for both improvement and recovery. In point of contrast, Table 2 depicts pretest and posttest data for a second measure of marital satisfaction, the Global Distress Scale (GDS) of the Marital Satisfaction Inventory (Snyder, 1979). Subjects were also classified as improved (on the basis of RC) or recovered (on the basis of a cutoff point) on this measure. Figure 4 shows approximations of the dysfunctional and functional populations. If we consider the three possible cutoff points for clinically significant change, criterion *c* seems preferable given the rationale

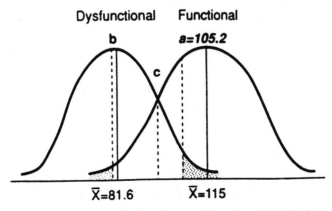

Figure 3. Approximations to the dysfunctional and functional distributions on the Dyadic Adjustment Scale with reference to three suggested cutoff points for clinically significant change (a, b, c).

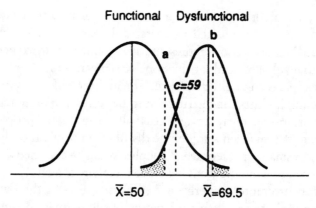

Functional   Dysfunctional

c=59

X̄=50   X̄=69.5

Figure 4. The same approximation of dysfunctional and functional distributions for Global Distress Scale of the Marital Satisfaction Inventory with reference to three suggested cutoff points for clinically significant change (a, b, c).

stated earlier for choosing among the three. The distributions do overlap, and if c is crossed, a subject is more likely to be a member of the functional than the dysfunctional distribution of couples. The criteria for recovery of the GDS listed in Table 2 are based on the use of c as a cutoff point.

Table 3 summarizes the data from both the DAS and the GDS, indicating the percentage of couples who improved and recovered according to each measure. Not surprisingly, there was less than perfect correspondence between the two measures. It is unclear how to assimilate these discrepancies. Moreover, some subjects were recovered on one measure but not on the other, thus creating interpretive problems regarding the status of individual subjects.

Given that both the DAS and GDS measure the same construct, one solution to integrating the findings would be to derive a composite score. These two measures of global marital satisfaction can each be theoretically divided into components of true score and error variance. However, it is unlikely that either duplicates the true score component of the construct "marital satisfaction." To preserve the true score component of each measure, a composite could be constructed that retained the true score component. Jacobson and Revenstorf (1988) have suggested estimating the true score for any given subject (j), using test theory, by adopting the formula

$$T_j = Rel(X_j) + (1 - Rel)M$$

where T represents true score, *Rel* equals reliability (e.g., test–retest), and X is the observed score (Lord & Novick, 1968). The standardized true score estimates can then be averaged to derive a multivariate composite. Cutoff points can then be established.

Tables 2 and 3 depict results derived from this composite. Because no

TABLE 3
Percentages of Improved and Recovered Couples
on DAS, GDS, and Composite Scores

Measure	N	% improved	% recovered	% unimproved or deteriorated
DAS	30	30	33	37
GDS	26	12	42	46
Composite	26	27	46	27

Note. DAS = Dyadic Adjustment Scale, GDS = Global Distress Scale of the Marital Satisfaction Inventory, and composite-average of DAS and GDS estimate true scores.

norms are available on the composite, the cutoff point was established using the two standard deviation solution.[1]

Finally, let us use this data set to illustrate one additional problem with these statistical definitions of clinically significant change. We have been using a discrete cutoff point to separate dysfunctional from functional distributions, without taking into account the measurement error inherent in the use of such cutoff points. Depending on the reliability of the measure, all posttest scores will be somewhat imprecise due to the limitations of the measuring instrument. Thus, some subjects are going to be misclassified simply due to measurement error.

One solution to the problem involves forming confidence intervals around the cutoff point, using RC to derive the boundaries of the confidence intervals. RC defines the range in which an individual score is likely to fluctuate because of the imprecision of a measuring instrument. Figure 5 illustrates the use of RC to form confidence intervals. The confidence intervals form a band of uncertainty around the cutoff point depicted in Figure 5. On the basis of this data set, for the DAS a score can vary by as much as 9.83 points and still reasonably ($p > .05$) be considered within the bounds of measurement error. Variations of 10 points or more are unlikely to be explainable by measurement error alone. We then formed confidence intervals around the cutoff point, with the cutoff point serving as the midpoint of the interval. Approximately 10 points on either side of the interval are within the band of uncertainty, but beyond this band we felt confident that the cutoff point had truly been crossed.[2]

As Figure 5 shows, 14 subjects fell within the band of uncertainty created

---

[1] The proportion of recovered couples is greater in the composite than it is for the component measures for several reasons. First, there are four couples for whom GDS data are missing. In all four instances, the couples failed to recover. Composites could be computed only on the 26 cases for whom he had complete data. Second, in several instances couples were subthreshold on one or both component measures but reached criteria for recovery on the composite measure. It is of interest that in this important sense the composite measure was more sensitive to treatment effects than either component was.

[2] As Jacobson and Revenstorf (1988) noted, the use of confidence intervals in this manner is a convenience. The cutoff point is merely a theoretical point, and the actual measurement error logically pertains to the individual subject's score.

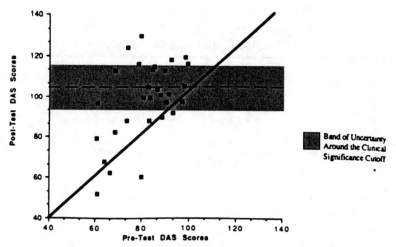

Figure 5. Scatter plot of pretest and posttest scores on the Dyadic Adjustment Scale including band of uncertainty around cutoff point for clinically significant

by these confidence intervals. Should these couples be classified as improved, recovered, deteriorated, or uncertain? One possibility would be to add a new category to the classification system: the proportion of subjects who fell within this band of uncertainty. These were couples about whose status we were unsure. If we added this category to our classification system, the revised percentages would be 20% recovered, 47% unclassifiable, and 33% unchanged or deteriorated. Having identified the proportion of subjects about whom we were uncertain, we could use the remainder of the sample and exclude the uncertain subjects in our calculations of proportions of recovered and unrecovered couples. This exclusion would lead to figures of 38% recovered, 19% improved but not recovered, and 44% unchanged or deteriorated. These proportions are probably a more accurate reflection of the true proportion of recovered subjects, inasmuch as subjects within the band of uncertainty are, on the average, going to be equally likely to fall into both categories. In fact, as Jacobson and Revenstorf (1988) noted, this latter suggestion is almost like splitting the difference (i.e., dividing the uncertain subjects equally between recovered and improved but not recovered groups). Although splitting the difference would not reduce ambiguity regarding the status of individual subjects who fall within the band of uncertainty, it would lead to a summary statistic that would include the entire sample. Essentially, such a solution amounts to redistributing subjects within the band rather than ignoring it entirely. When equal numbers of subjects fall on either side of the cutoff point within the band, the proportion of recovered subjects will be identical to that calculated without consideration of measurement error at all. Splitting the difference with our sample data set would have resulted in 43% recovered, 23% improved but not recovered, and 34% unchanged or deteriorated.

CONCLUSION

In the past decade, the discussion of clinical significance has taken center stage in psychotherapy research. In a recent review appearing in the *Annual Review of Psychology*, Goldfried, Greenberg, and Marmar (1990) referred to it as one of the major methodological advances. There is no doubt that discussion has moved from occasional mention by a group of prescient observers (e.g., Barlow, 1981; Kazdin, 1977) to a lively topic for discussion and debate, as evidenced by the recent special issue of *Behavioral Assessment* devoted to the topic (Jacobson, 1988).

The editors of this special section have asked us to compare the results of using our system with what would have been obtained using standard inferential statistics or other criteria of improvement. When our statistics have been used, the impact has generally been to add additional information rather than to contradict the results of other data analytic strategies. However, the information from these additional analyses has generally led to more modest conclusions regarding the efficacy of the treatment in question. For example, Jacobson and colleagues (Jacobson, Follette, Revenstorf, Baucom, et al., 1984) reanalyzed data from previously published marital therapy outcome studies. Standard inferential statistical analyses yielded results that supported the effects of the marital therapies, in that treatments outperformed various control groups. The reanalyses reported by Jacobson and colleagues addressed the issue of clinical significance, and the results were somewhat disappointing: Fewer than half of the treated couples ended up in the happily married range after therapy on measures of marital satisfaction. Similar reanalyses based on studies looking at exposure treatments for agoraphobia led to similar results (i.e., treatments outperformed control groups but yielded a relatively small proportion of truly recovered clients; Jacobson, Wilson, & Tupper, 1988).

Experimenters who have used different statistical procedures based on similar principles have often found that clinical significance data make the treatments look less effective than standard statistical comparisons would imply. For example, Kazdin, Bass, Siegel, and Thomas (1989) recently reported on an apparently highly effective behavioral treatment for conduct-disordered children, but a clinical significance analysis suggested that celebration was perhaps premature. Whereas behavioral treatments outperformed a client-centered relationship therapy, comparisons with nonclinic samples revealed that the majority of subjects remained in the dysfunctional range on primary measures of conduct disorder. Similarly, Robinson, Berman, and Neimeyer (1990) recently reported a meta-analysis of studies investigating psychotherapy for depression. Whereas they reported substantial effect sizes for comparisons between psychotherapy and control groups, comparisons with normative samples suggested that subjects remained outside the normal range even after psychotherapeutic intervention.

The approach we have outlined is only one of many possible ways of reporting on clinical significance. On the one hand, our approach has a number of features that we believe should be part of any method for highlighting clinical significance: It operationalizes recovery in a relatively objective, unbiased way; its definition is not tied to a specific disorder, which means that it has potentially broad applicability; because of its general applicability, it could evolve into a convention within psychotherapy research, which in turn would facilitate comparison between studies; and it provides information on variability in outcome as well as clinical significance.

On the other hand, there are a number of unsolved problems that currently limit the generalizability of the method. First, it is unclear at present how robust the method will be to violations of the assumption that dysfunctional and functional distributions are normal. The concept that we have proposed for defining clinical significance does not depend on any formula. The formula is simply one way of determining the midpoint between functional and dysfunctional populations. Even when the formulas for RC and the cutoff points are not applicable, the concept can be applied by determining the cutoff point empirically. However, the formulas discussed in this and other articles assume normal distributions. Second, operationalizing clinical significance in terms of recovery or return to normal functioning may not be appropriate for all disorders treated by psychotherapy. For example, schizophrenia and autism are two disorders in which a standard of recovery would exceed the expectations of most who work in the field. Third, without psychometrically sound measures of psychotherapy outcomes, there are practical constraints that prevent optimal use of our methods, no matter how valuable they might be in theory. In particular, the absence of normative data for functional and dysfunctional populations on many commonly used outcome measures deters the development of standardized cutoff points.

In addition to these and other current problems, there are still a number of subjective decisions to be made regarding optimal use of these statistical methods. These were illustrated in our examples. Only by testing theoretical propositions with real data sets will these ambiguities be resolved. Thus, while it is not premature to expect psychotherapy investigators to report on the clinical significance of their treatment effects, it is far too early to advocate any particular method or set of conventions. Clinical significance has clearly arrived, but the optimal methods for deriving it remain to be determined.

REFERENCES

Barlow, D. H. (1981). On the relation of clinical research to clinical practice: Current issues, new directions. *Journal of Consulting and Clinical Psychology, 49*, 147–155.

Christensen, L., & Mendoza, J. L. (1986). A method of assessing change in a single subject: An alteration of the RC index. *Behavior Therapy, 17,* 305–308.

Garfield, S. L. (1981). Evaluating the psychotherapies. *Behavior Therapy, 12,* 295–307.

Goldfried, M. R., Greenberg, L. S., & Marmar, C. (1990). Individual psychotherapy: Process and outcome: *Annual Review of Psychology, 41,* 659–688.

Hollon, S. D., & Flick, S. N. (1988). On the meaning and methods of clinical significance. *Behavioral Assessment, 10,* 197–206.

Jacobson, N. S. (1988). Defining clinically significant change: An introduction. *Behavioral Assessment, 10,* 131–132.

Jacobson, N. S., Follette, W. C., & Revenstorf, D. (1984). Psychotherapy outcome research: Methods for reporting variability and evaluating clinical significance. *Behavior Therapy, 15,* 336–352.

Jacobson, N. S., Follette, W. C., & Revenstorf, D. (1986). Toward a standard definition of clinically significant change. *Behavior Therapy, 17,* 308–311.

Jacobson, N. S., Follette, W. C., Revenstorf, D., Baucom, D. H., Hahlweg, K., & Margolin, G. (1984). Variability in outcome and clinical significance of behavioral marital therapy: A reanalysis of outcome data. *Journal of Consulting and Clinical Psychology, 52,* 497–504.

Jacobson, N. S., & Revenstorf, D. (1988). Statistics for assessing the clinical significance of psychotherapy techniques: Issues, problems, and new developments. *Behavioral Assessment, 10,* 133–145.

Jacobson, N. S., Schmaling, K. B., Holtzworth-Munroe, A., Katt, J. L., Wood, L. F., & Follette, V. M. (1989). Research-structured versus clinically flexible versions of social learning-based marital therapy. *Behaviour Research and Therapy, 27,* 173–180.

Jacobson, N. S., Wilson, L., & Tupper, C. (1988). The clinical significance of treatment gains resulting from exposure-based interventions for agoraphobia: A reanalysis of outcome data. *Behavior Therapy, 19,* 539–552.

Kazdin, A. E. (1977). Assessing the clinical or applied importance of behavior change through social validation. *Behavior Modification, 1,* 427–452.

Kazdin, A. E., Bass, D., Siegel, T., & Thomas, C. (1989). Cognitive-behavioral therapy and relationship therapy in the treatment of children referred for antisocial behavior. *Journal of Consulting and Clinical Psychology, 57,* 522–535.

Kazdin, A. E., & Wilson, G. T. (1978). *Evaluation of behavior therapy: Issues, evidence, and research strategies.* Cambridge, MA: Ballinger.

Kendall, P. C., & Norton-Ford, J. D. (1982). Therapy outcome research methods. In P. C. Kendall & J. N. Butcher (Eds.), *Handbook of research methods in clinical psychology* (pp. 429–460). New York: Wiley.

Lord, F. M., & Novick, M. R. (1968). *Statistical theories of mental test scores.* Reading, MA: Addison-Wesley.

Mavissakalian, M. (1986). Clinically significant improvement in agoraphobia research. *Behaviour Research and Therapy, 24,* 369–370.

Nietzel, M. T., & Trull, T. J. (1988). Meta-analytic approaches to social comparisons: A method for measuring clinical significance. *Behavioral Assessment, 10*, 146–159.

Robinson, L. A., Berman, J. S., & Neimeyer, R. A. (1990). Psychotherapy for the treatment of depression: A comprehensive review of controlled outcome research. *Psychological Bulletin, 108*, 30–49.

Smith, M. L., Glass, G. V., & Miller, T. I. (1980). *The benefits of psychotherapy.* Baltimore: Johns Hopkins University Press.

Snyder, D. K. (1979). Multidimensional assessment of marital satisfaction. *Journal of Marriage and the Family, 41*, 813–823.

Spanier, G. B. (1976). Measuring dyadic adjustment: New scales for assessing the quality of marriage and similar dyads. *Journal of Marriage and the Family, 38*, 15–28.

Wampold, B. E., & Jensen, W. R. (1986). Clinical significance revisited. *Behavior Therapy, 17*, 302–305.

Wolf, M. M. (1978). Social validity: The case for subjective measurement or how applied behavior analysis is finding its heart. *Journal of Applied Behavior Analysis, 11*, 203–214.

Yeaton, W. H., & Sechrest, L. (1981). Critical dimensions in the choice and maintenance of successful treatments: Strength, integrity, and effectiveness. *Journal of Consulting and Clinical Psychology, 49*, 156–167.

DESIGNING RESEARCH TO BE RELEVANT FOR PRACTICE AND POLICY

26

IMPROVING THE TRANSITION FROM BASIC EFFICACY RESEARCH TO EFFECTIVENESS STUDIES: METHODOLOGICAL ISSUES AND PROCEDURES

GREGORY N. CLARKE

Recent proposed changes in the financing and organization of health service systems provide a compelling background for discussion of the relevance and applicability of findings from controlled laboratory studies (efficacy investigations) to broader mental health services systems (effectiveness research). If certain interventions prove effective in both laboratories and clinics, this may result in meaningful health care reforms with potentially improved services for consumers. Brook and Lohr (1985) advocate this perspective, noting that health care systems are improved not just by data from a single perspective but from an integration of data from efficacy, effectiveness, and quality-of-care perspectives.

Reprinted from the *Journal of Consulting and Clinical Psychology, 63*, 718–725. Copyright 1995 by the American Psychological Association.

However, several barriers limit consensus on the effectiveness and usefulness of mental health treatments in service system settings. First, empirical treatment outcome information is often incomplete and, for many disorders, all but unavailable. This lack of advanced treatment efficacy data is particularly true in child and adolescent mental health. Lacking controlled outcome research for a given disorder or problem area, it is difficult to resolve whether a given intervention will work as well in the clinical setting as it may in the laboratory. This should not be seen as a call to exhaust all avenues of efficacy research before initiating treatment effectiveness trials. Instead, the goal of this article is to encourage concurrent advances in both efficacy and effectiveness research, even to the point of addressing both perspectives within the same investigation.

Moving beyond the availability of research, however, there are several design and methodological shortcomings in the existing literature that limit the integration of efficacy methods within effectiveness trials. These shortcomings exist, in large part, because mental health outcome research is often designed to answer efficacy or theoretical questions. Scant attention is generally paid to generalization beyond the research paradigm (e.g., how well could this intervention be carried out in a clinical setting?).

This article attempts to address this issue by proposing methodological strategies that, if used in treatment outcome research, may help shift efficacy research findings and methods into effectiveness trials conducted in clinical and service delivery settings. Whenever possible, these issues are examined in the context of our own research in school- and clinic-based interventions for adolescent depression (Clarke, Hawkins, Murphy, Sheeber, Lewinsohn, & Seeley, 1995; Lewinsohn, Clarke, Hops, & Andrews, 1990), with examples of how the generalization of these studies may be improved.

Periodic reviews of methodological design and strategy in psychotherapy outcome research are nothing new (e.g., Kazdin, 1986). However, most previous discussions have been in the efficacy research literature, often weighted in favor of greater experimental control at the expense of generalization to real-world settings. This article revisits these same issues, but with the perspective of stretching research designs to encompass effectiveness issues. Bear in mind that this is not meant to preclude scientific rigor. Instead, I advocate retaining as much experimental control as possible while using greater creativity in the methodology and issues studied in treatment outcome research.

This article was inspired by Weisz, Weiss, and Donenberg's (1992) examination of the positive child psychotherapy effects in research studies, compared with the general absence of such effects in clinic-based studies. In their conclusion, Weisz et al. suggested that "a key task for researchers [is] . . . identifying those proper conditions under which effects of child therapy may be optimized." The present article responds to this issue by considering how study design features might help identify these optimizing conditions.

TABLE 1
Potential Mediating Factors

Factor	Description
1	Therapist training; degree of treatment structure; monitoring, protocol compliance
2	Combined or multiple treatments (e.g., pharmacotherapy and psycho-therapy)
3	Multiple roles vs. single role for therapist
4	Participant selection (homogeneity vs. heterogeneity; comorbidity)
5	Control group (no treatment vs. attention placebo vs. usual care)
6	Treatment parameters (duration, dose, modality, location)

METHODOLOGICAL ISSUES

Weisz and Weiss (1989) provide a detailed review of aspects of controlled experimental methodology that differ enough between research and clinical settings to limit the generalization of positive findings from the former to the latter. A circumscribed set of these issues is summarized in Table 1. Each of these is briefly reviewed in turn, followed by suggestions for methodological changes to enhance generalizability.

Other issues identified by these and other authors (Kazdin, 1978), but not addressed here, include participant recruitment methods; professional versus nonprofessional therapists; measurement technology; participant, therapist, and assessor masking to therapy condition; service setting; and participant assignment. This article does not attempt to exhaustively catalog method variants to address each of these parameters. Instead, a sampler of design features is proposed to motivate investigators to broaden the scope of treatment outcome paradigms under consideration or in the planning stages.

DEGREE OF THERAPY STRUCTURE

Increasingly, controlled outcome trials of psychotherapy treatments provide intensive, specialized training in the specific research intervention protocol (Luborsky & DeRubeis, 1984). To simplify replication of the intervention across studies, researchers often "manualize" treatments by providing scripted therapist guidebooks (e.g., Clarke, Lewinsohn, & Hops, 1990; Moreau, Mufson, Weissman, & Klerman, 1991; see also Lambert & Ogles, 1988). Close compliance with these treatment manuals is often encouraged by audio or videotaping therapy sessions for later compliance review by research staff (Clarke et al., 1995; Lewinsohn et al., 1990; Hollon, 1988).

These training and implementation methods result in interventions that are highly regimented and very reproducible, with high adherence to a predefined protocol. From a pure efficacy perspective, these are desirable features because they control for extraneous contributors to treatment outcome. However, these controls are unlikely to be used in nonresearch settings because of the increased effort and burden they require, as well as a lack of interest in enforcing a reproducible treatment regime in many clinical or service settings.

These therapy structure methodologies impede effectiveness trials of research treatments because, in my experience, real-world therapists often resist following rigid or uni-modality interventions. Many clinicians prefer to be responsive to client session-by-session presentations with a blended or "eclectic" therapy model, borrowing pieces of interventions as they seem relevant rather than using a scripted but potentially more cohesive protocol. Research interventions are often viewed as too regimented, leading clinicians (the interventionists in effectiveness trials) to resist using them out of concern that they may reduce psychotherapy to an automated "cookbook" approach, lacking responsiveness to individual client presentation.

How might outcome researchers design their studies differently to address this issue? One approach, which elaborates on a suggestion by Kendall and Lipman (1991), is to conduct treatment efficacy studies with several levels of experimental control over the implementation of therapy protocols to examine the effect on treatment outcome. Experimental conditions with less structured therapy content and implementation would resemble real-life clinical settings, although in a limited fashion. Of course, this does not mean that therapists would be allowed to deliver interventions completely unobserved or without limits. It is important to measure how much and in what way therapists deviate from a planned intervention (e.g., by using expert raters, a therapy content coding system, and videotaped intervention sessions).

An illustration of this proposal may examine the hypothetical effects of several potential mediators in the research on adolescent depression prevention. In a previous investigation (Clarke et al., 1995), my colleagues and I provided high school counselors with 40 hr of supervised training in the use of a scripted manual of cognitive intervention to prevent depression in at-risk youths. These counselors were strongly discouraged from deviating from the intervention protocol. Audiotaped reliability checks revealed that they were very compliant (94%) with the scripted protocol. Although satisfactory effects were obtained with the manual-specified intervention, it would be interesting to conduct this study again with the intent of exploring "therapy structure" issues. For example, a semi-factorial design may be used to examine the extent to which planned and measured variations in (a) therapist deviation from a regimented treatment protocol and (b) the use of structured intervention manuals and specialized training had an effect on outcome.

Three different implementation versions of the same cognitive therapy intervention could be used:[1]

1. Rigorous therapist training with a structured manual and minimal protocol deviation (enforced by means of video-taped monitoring). This is essentially the study as it was originally conducted, and it represents typical efficacy research design.
2. Similar therapist training with a structured manual but with minor to moderate protocol deviation permitted on the basis of therapists' clinical judgment. For example, anger management, although not part of the original protocol, might be offered to a depressed adolescent with comorbid conduct disorder. Therapists would be monitored by means of videotaped sessions, and deviations would be assessed and coded, but not corrected through supervision.
3. General therapist training in the same theoretical approach as espoused in the manual, but with no structured manual provided. Treatment course and planning would be based on the therapists' best clinical judgment. Similar to the second condition, therapist deviations would be assessed but not corrected.

Measuring how experienced clinicians elect to deviate from protocols is a difficult task but necessary in this design. If certain so-called deviations from protocol are associated with good client outcome, structured research interventions may be improved by the incorporation of these techniques or activities in the protocol. In this way, unstructured clinical practices might more systematically influence the development of effective structured research interventions, contributing to a two-way exchange of information between researchers and clinicians. At the very least, researchers may better understand which components of psychotherapy approaches are fairly robust and tolerant of individual therapist deviations, and which aspects are relatively fragile and should be carried out in a fairly uniform manner.

One may argue that this design introduces too many opportunities for unexplained results. For example, what if the least structured condition was associated with the best outcome? How would one know what aspects of the treatment accounted for this finding? Furthermore, can these positive findings be replicated, or were they just a function of unique therapist characteristics? Certainly therapy content data (from coded videotaped sessions)

---

[1] Note that the remaining cell in this design (no manual, but no deviation permitted) cannot be implemented, because where a manual is not provided it is not possible to ascertain whether protocol has been followed.

must be examined to determine whether systematic therapist deviations from established protocol were associated with better outcome. If so, subsequent studies could be conducted with controlled variations of these deviations to further test their impact on outcome. Regarding replication, a single study of this type is not meant to answer all questions. Replication is still as important to this type of design as it is in efficacy research, and failure to replicate would indeed raise questions as to whether uncontrolled therapy implementation is best.

Too few controlled psychotherapy studies have specifically tested these issues to predict what results would be obtained. However, Weiss and Weisz's (1990) meta-analysis of methodological factor effects on child psychotherapy outcome research suggests that increased methodological rigor is generally (although not uniformly) associated with more beneficial treatment outcome across unrelated studies. Although Weiss and Weisz (1990) did not specifically examine the mediating effects of intervention implementation rigor, extrapolating from their data suggests that more positive results may be obtained when treatment protocol is carefully carried out.

Although studies examining treatment implementation issues in a controlled paradigm are virtually unavailable in psychotherapy outcome research, these issues are an increasing focus of school-based prevention and health promotion research (Felner, Phillips, DuBois, & Lease, 1991). For example, Rohrbach, Graham, and Hansen (1993) examined the relationship between integrity of program delivery and outcomes of a school-based, psychosocial substance abuse prevention program. School districts were randomly assigned to either intensive or brief teacher training in the program: schools within districts were randomly assigned to have the principal involved or not involved in the intervention. Not only was program implementation highly variable but it also faded from the first to the second year. Delivery of the program in a rigorous manner was predictive of positive student outcomes. These results are similar to those reported in other studies of school-based substance abuse prevention programs (e.g., Botvin et al., 1989; Pentz et al., 1990). Although these findings are not directly applicable to traditional psychotherapy, many design and hypothesis issues examined by Rohrbach et al. (1993) are relevant to effectiveness studies that examine the implementation and real-life usefulness of psychotherapy services.

If future studies find that greater adherence to psychotherapy protocols predicts better client outcome, what implications would this have? Such a conclusion might be unpopular with clinicians, especially those who favor therapist autonomy. This likely fallout is an effect that researchers should acknowledge, because concerns regarding this use of effectiveness data is a major contributor to clinician resistance to the adoption of research interventions.

INTEGRATED VERSUS ISOLATED SERVICES

Efficacy studies typically offer their treatments in isolation, often to focus on the disorder of interest or to remove or control extraneous mediating factors (e.g., other treatments). This isolation is often twofold; first, research treatments often target only one disorder, diagnosis, or problem domain, without addressing psychiatric or general medical comorbidity in individuals. A second and related form of treatment isolation arises when efficacy studies provide only the research intervention, without the frequent clinical requirement to offer an integrated array of multiple different assessment, intervention, referral, and advocacy services in addition to the single research focus. This insularity means that research projects have a generally greater capacity to devote more time, resources, and follow-up to their limited number of participants. In contrast, effectiveness trials conducted at sites such as schools and community mental health programs can typically provide only a limited number of visits and contact hours to each client.

Although for theory testing it is often desirable to pare interventions down to a single, internally cohesive treatment component, this may not reflect mental health services as often provided in the community. For at least some populations and settings, services are often provided in an integrated intervention "package," consisting of several interconnected parts. For example, community-based services for individuals with chronic mental illnesses such as schizophrenia often include a physical examination, psychotropic medications, psychological services, case management, housing support, and social welfare services, with other components added as required (e.g., Solomon, 1992). Researchers must acknowledge that mental health interventions are often embedded in a larger context of general health and social services, and intervention trials of "atomized" psychotherapy components may have little external validity. Initial outcome studies of psychotherapy services may be geared toward testing the larger, integrated intervention package, with subsequent "component analyses" conducted only after the composite intervention is associated with beneficial outcome.

How could methodological variations in outcome research address this issue? Although daunting, one obvious solution is to develop an integrated intervention regime that offers research-based intervention tracks for a variety of common disorders, with clear triage rules regarding assignment to intervention (or interventions) on the basis of assessment findings. Furthermore, interventions must be integrated to address those instances in which participants have more than one disorder, and thus, they must enroll in more than one intervention track. The control condition for this design may be the locally evolved intervention standards for addressing the heterogeneous clinical presentation seen in the community. Defining these local standards for the purposes of an effectiveness trial requires substantial preliminary meetings with representative local providers to clarify and codify the usual and customary services provided for a given client population.

Such a protocol might also introduce realistic personnel and fiscal budgets to both research and control conditions, within which both conditions must provide all services required by the client sample. Budgetary caps of this sort simulate service system limits and may address the perception that research interventions are overly enriched. Caseloads and service burden would be comparable, increasing confidence in the generalizability of outcome findings.

Examples of research-based treatment parameters for psychiatric disorders are rare, but becoming less so. For example, the *Journal of the American Academy of Child and Adolescent Psychiatry* recently published practice parameters for several common child mental health disorders, including anxiety disorders (Bernstein & Shaw, 1993), attention-deficit hyperactivity disorders (Jaffe, 1991), schizophrenia (McClellan & Werry, 1994), and conduct disorder (Jaffe, 1992). Similarly, this journal has recently published several articles on the treatment of common combinations of comorbid disorders (e.g., Mueser, Bellack, & Blanchard, 1992; Shea, Widiger, & Klein, 1992). Parameters such as these may form the basis for developing the "integrated intervention regime" advocated earlier.

Of course, mounting a comprehensive study of this type might prove so costly that it would quickly exceed traditional research budget limits. Although easier said than done, the only realistic solution is to forge an alliance between traditional research funding bodies such as the National Institute of Mental Health and the public and private agencies that already provide some version of these services to the general population. This cooperation is the essence of successful services research, and readers interested in developing these unlikely yet necessary alliances will find that much has already been written about the process (e.g., Attkisson et al., 1992).

A less ambitious option would be to select participants with predefined comorbidity combinations (e.g., depression and substance abuse) and require research therapists to address the treatment and associated clinical issues important to both problem areas. Developing an assessment, triage, and intervention protocol for this circumscribed sample would be considerably easier. Although less realistic and less integrated than the totally comprehensive approach described first, this nonetheless represents a significant advance over existing efficacy studies.

Despite the difficulty of mounting an integrated research protocol, some investigators have made initial inroads toward developing such a model. For instance, the FAST (Families and Schools Together) Track Program (Conduct Problems Prevention Research Group, 1992) provides a research-based intervention model for the prevention of conduct disorder in youths by integrating family, school, peer group, and child intervention components. However, even this model is limited in terms of encompassing other disorders that may be comorbid with conduct disorder (e.g., depression).

Historically, my own investigations of adolescent depression treatment and prevention (see Clarke et al., 1995) have similarly taken a relatively narrow focus. However, future investigations could broaden both the sample and the intervention to address common comorbid diagnosis combinations, following the less ambitious of the two paradigms suggested earlier. Because alcohol and drug abuse–dependence is the most common comorbid *DSM–III–R* (*Diagnostic and Statistical Manual of Mental Disorders* [3rd ed., rev.; American Psychiatric Association, 1987]) diagnosis for adolescent depression (Rohde, Lewinsohn, & Seeley, 1991), focusing on this combination is a reasonable starting point. An omnibus, school-based, adolescent depression and substance abuse preventive intervention might combine the best features of the depression prevention program (Clarke et al., 1995) with aspects of successful substance abuse prevention programs such as the Midwestern Prevention Project (Pentz et al., 1990). One interesting study design among many possibilities is the implementation of both the separate and the combined prevention programs in the high school setting, with at-risk youths randomly assigned to depression-only, substance abuse-only, or the combined program. This design could be crossed with an "implementation" independent variable, with the programs administered either by school counselors (who would be obliged to provide all other services required by these youths) or by "single-purpose" research therapists (with no obligation to provide associated services). This design would contribute to the theoretical question of shared versus separate etiologies and treatments of depression and substance abuse, as well as address pragmatic issues of outcome as a function of therapist treatment obligations and their degree of integration in the service setting.

As stated earlier, this design example is not meant to capture all elements related to the issue of integrated versus isolated interventions but provides just one concrete example of how efficacy trials could extend their methodology to address effectiveness issues. Rather than representing a relaxing of research standards, this design is meant to be an example of extending efficacy research rigor to topics that previously have been studied (if at all) with less careful and controlled methods.

USUAL CARE VERSUS NO-TREATMENT OR PLACEBO-ATTENTION CONTROLS

The sine qua non (Parloff, 1986) of psychotherapy efficacy research is the randomly assigned control condition. Several variations exist, but the most common are the enforced no-treatment control, the waiting-list control, and the placebo-attention control. In the no-treatment and waiting-list control conditions, participants are prohibited from obtaining an active intervention altogether or for some predefined period, respectively. Participants enrolled in a placebo-attention control condition are provided with some structured activity believed to be therapeutically neutral (at least with respect to the theoretical model underlying the experimental treatment), in an attempt to control for the nonspecific aspects of interpersonal contact and the number of service hours provided in the experimental condition.

Although these control conditions help resolve theoretical issues and control threats to internal validity, they are usually untenable in clinical settings appropriate for effectiveness trials (Weisz, Weiss, & Donenberg, 1992). Furthermore, they do not provide outcome information specifically applicable to the extension of the treatment to a clinical care setting; that is, none of these control conditions represent what typically happens to clients who seek treatment but are not provided with it. If the problem is severe and chronic enough, these individuals often go elsewhere to obtain meaningful treatment.

These control conditions generate other problems. Participant dropout from enforced no-treatment and waiting-list control conditions can often be more pronounced than dropout from the active intervention, contributing to potential bias in comparisons of the retained control sample and the experimental condition. The placebo-attention control condition is also problematic in that it may not be as therapeutically neutral as advertised. Elkin et al. (Elkin, Parloff, Hadley, & Autry, 1985), Strupp (1977), and Parloff (1986) argued that most placebo-attention conditions include elements (e.g., a feeling of being understood, an opportunity for social contacts) which would be considered therapeutically active by at least some intervention modalities (e.g., client-centered therapies).

In our recent outcome studies (Clarke et al., 1995; Clarke & Hornbrook, 1994) we have shifted away from these traditional control conditions to a randomized usual-care control condition, identified as a "minimal-treatment" control by Weiss and Weisz (1990). In this condition, subjects are provided with mental health services typically offered in the service setting.[2] A similar control condition, the "best alternative treatment," compares the experimental therapy against the best available treatment, if such exists (O'Leary & Borkovec, 1978). These designs are all subsumed under the comparative outcome study design, the relative advantages and disadvantages of which are discussed by Basham (1986) and Kazdin (1986).

---

[2] This differs somewhat in our prevention trials (Clarke et al., 1995), where participants not yet meeting a clinical diagnosis are less likely to seek enrollment in treatment. Under these circumstances, usual-care participants are free to continue with any preexisting intervention or to seek any new assistance during the study period if they so desire. To equate the base level of nonexperimental intervention across both conditions, participants enrolled in the active prevention program are also permitted to continue any preexisting treatment and to seek out any additional treatment.

What impact would the use of this control condition have on outcome research? Weiss and Weisz (1990) reported in their meta-analysis of child psychotherapy studies that the outcome effect sizes associated with the minimal-treatment control group is indistinguishable from that associated with other, more traditional control conditions. From this data at least, using this type of control condition appears to neither endanger the internal validity of controlled outcome studies nor alter estimates of beneficial effect associated with the experimental intervention.

Given these cautions, what (if any) benefits are associated with a usual-care control condition that make it superior to traditional controls in effectiveness trials? I believe that the most important benefit of a usual-care control condition is that it represents a more generalizable test of the intervention. It has the greatest ecological validity of all common control conditions, with the greatest likelihood of corresponding to a real-world counterpart. Although a waiting-list control seems realistic, in my experience substantial numbers of these participants may surreptitiously seek other treatment and eventually drop out of the study. Enforced no-treatment and attention-placebo controls also have limited real-life counterparts.

More pragmatically, I agree with Weisz et al. (1992) that a comparative treatment design is more likely to be tolerated in clinical settings and, thus, overcome clinic staff resistance to effectiveness studies on their premises. Providentially, a usual-care control provides a more conservative test of the experimental intervention, as the new intervention must exceed the benefits associated with usual mental health care to emerge as successful, with the presumption, of course, that usual care imparts at least a minimum benefit. However, a control or comparison condition of this type should not be used uncritically. For example, the usual-care condition makes it much more difficult to characterize the services received by control participants, and in many situations this is important to assess. Kazdin (1986) provides a thorough review of the advantages and disadvantages of each type of control condition, and investigators should carefully examine these issues during planning for any outcome trial.

SAMPLE REPRESENTATIVENESS, HETEROGENEITY VERSUS HOMOGENEITY

As noted by Weisz and Weiss (1989), controlled outcome research studies typically use very strict participant inclusion criteria, resulting in a sample that may have only a limited resemblance to the usual cases of that disorder served in the community. For example, in previous adolescent depression treatment research (Lewinsohn et al., 1990) my colleagues and I limited the sample by restricting (but not eliminating) psychiatric comorbidity, requiring minimum reading levels, placing a moratorium on all other mental health treatment (or treatments), and placing other restrictions on sample characteristics.

Although there are compelling conceptual reasons to select a highly homogeneous patient sample (see Kendall & Lipman, 1991), the downside of homogeneity is that it yields patients that may be very different from their nonresearch counterparts, making generalization of results suspect. Pragmatically, overselection may also make participant recruitment more difficult. For example, local referral sources reported having many depressed adolescents to send to depression treatment studies, but only a few that met the stringent selection criteria.

In contrast, effectiveness studies must deal with the viscidities of the clinical world, where comorbidity is common, connection with multiple providers of therapy or social services (or both) is the norm among certain populations (e.g., children; severely mentally ill individuals), placing limits on other treatments is usually neither possible nor ethical, and participant characteristics are generally much more heterogeneous.

How might researchers design different studies to satisfy the goal of a homogeneous sample and also examine the intervention for effects among a more realistic and heterogeneous population? Although it is hardly the only approach, I recommend broadening recruitment for most all intervention outcome studies with a two-tiered participant recruitment strategy; I call this the "donut" model. A highly selected, homogeneous core sample (the "donut hole") could be recruited for testing basic theoretical issues regarding outcome, not dissimilar from efficacy study recruitment as presently practiced. However, to this I recommend adding a relatively unselected, comorbid, and heterogeneous sample (the donut ring) that would be recruited to examine generalizability and real-world effectiveness. Participant heterogeneity or homogeneity could be used as a dichotomous blocking variable in a factorial design, crossed with experimental condition, or it could be examined in the full sample by means of post hoc multivariate analyses of the mediating effects of several client and environment variables that differ across the two subsamples.

Increasing the heterogeneity of samples may be justified by the increased generalizability of the results; it also rests on the acknowledgment that many psychotherapies are potentially applicable with more than just one diagnosis. For example, cognitive therapy has been successfully used with depression (Beck, 1991), anxiety disorders (Butler, Fennell, Robson, & Gelder, 1991; Chambless & Gillis, 1993), and eating disorders (Fairburn et al., 1991; Wilson & Fairburn, 1993). Effectiveness studies of cognitive therapy may justifiably recruit more broadly within the broadband categorizations of overcontrolled or internalizing diagnoses, such as those listed earlier, and still hypothesize successful outcomes. The same approach could be used with the undercontrolled or externalizing disorders.[3] This strategy not only eases recruitment, a stumbling block to developing the large samples required in outcome studies, but simultaneously broadens sample heterogeneity. As long as diagnostic and other participant characteristic data is carefully assessed and recorded, post hoc regression analyses can be used to examine the effects of these characteristics on outcome.

Sample heterogeneity may also be increased by including different severity levels within the same problem area or symptom constellation, including individuals who may not meet a DSM–III–R diagnostic category but who have some subdiagnostic syndrome consisting of a reduced set of symptoms within the same category. Expanding samples in this manner may be important, as many individuals seeking service for mental health problems do not appear to qualify for a full DSM–III–R diagnosis yet may still be clearly impaired. For instance, Johnson, Weissman, and Klerman (1992) reported that in the general adult population, as much service burden and health impairment (or more) was associated with subdiagnostic depressive symptoms as with the clinical diagnoses of major depression or dysthymia. These data suggest that it is important to collect outcome data for these individuals as well as those who qualify for the full diagnostic categories.

Mark Hornbrook and I (Clarke & Hornbrook, 1994) are currently conducting just such a study. Adolescents at risk for depression by virtue of having a parent being treated for depression (see review by Downey & Coyne, 1990) are carefully assessed and then triaged to one of three severity levels: (a) clinically depressed adolescents (major depression, dysthymia, or both); (b) at-risk adolescents (elevated but subdiagnostic depressive symptom levels, past depressive episodes, or both); and (c) resilient adolescents (no current depressive symptoms or history). Randomized outcome trials are conducted at each severity level, with increasingly more intensive psychotherapeutic interventions (corresponding to clinical severity) contrasted against a usual-care control condition. Because this study is conducted within a large health maintenance organization (HMO), the costs of delivering experimental interventions are relatively easily measured and compared with the costs of all health care services consumed by the control group. Although the aims of the study go beyond the issues raised in the present article, the participant recruitment and triage methodology has been influenced by a broadened perspective of whom might benefit from psychotherapeutic interventions.

My experience working with schools and public agencies in psychotherapy outcome trials suggests that a broadening of the eligible pool of participants would simplify and enhance recruitment rather than complicate it.

---

[3] Child and adolescent examples of overcontrolled disorders include depression, anxiety, and eating disorders; examples of undercontrolled conditions include attention-deficit hyperactivity disorder, conduct disorder, and oppositional defiant disorders.

Because referring agencies do not have to cull out just the "pure" cases, the referral process is a less time-consuming and frustrating task. Another advantage of extending the sample in this way is that client and psychopathological characteristics, process variables, and other potential outcome mediators may have greater variability than is typically the case with a more homogeneous sample. Up to a point, this increased variability may potentiate multivariate analyses examining the effect of these mediators on treatment outcome across the combined sample, an often desirable post hoc analytical strategy to help identify important therapy issues and directions for future research.

TREATMENT PARAMETERS: DOSAGE, MODALITY, LOCATION, IMPLEMENTATION

This may be the most neglected yet potentially most important area of effectiveness research. After posing the general question "Does psychotherapy work?" most legislators and policy makers in the current national health care debate focus on the effectiveness of multiple variations in the delivery of efficacious intervention. For example, are patients with severe major depression better treated in inpatient or outpatient facilities, and at what costs? For how long? In groups or individual therapy, or both? Delivered by professionals or paraprofessionals? At present, there are few clear answers to these questions.

These are not just pragmatic (read "nonscientific") issues; they represent exciting questions that can have important and fundamental theoretical implications. For example, the relative benefit of group versus individual psychotherapy is obviously relevant from an effectiveness perspective; in service systems such as HMOs such a finding could have major implications for mental health service delivery (see Budman, 1992). However, studies examining this seemingly pragmatic issue can also address numerous theoretical issues related to therapeutic change. For instance, in several models of therapeutic process and change (Orlinsky & Howard, 1986) it is hypothesized that working through the dynamics of a developing therapist–client relationship is a significant contributor to positive treatment outcome. This relationship is presumably optimized in individual therapy and could be argued to be proportionally much weaker in group therapy, in which the therapist's attention is divided across many group participants.

However, suppose that future research were to find that individual and group versions of the same treatment approach produce roughly equivalent beneficial outcome (Tillitski [1990] and Weisz, Weiss, Alicke, & Klotz [1987] review these issues in child and adolescent psychotherapy). This hypothetical finding might suggest that a combination of client-to-client relationships in combination with a weaker therapist–client relationship is equivalent to an intensive therapist–client relationship, at least as far as psychotherapeutic benefit is concerned.

The key issue here is not whether this is a correct interpretation (this is, after all, only an example based on hypothetical findings), but that investigations of these more pragmatic implementation issues may also lead to a more thorough understanding of theoretical treatment models. In short, studies need not address only basic research or pragmatic issues; they may be designed to address both.

CONCLUSION

In summary, this article calls for the inclusion of methodological features to transfer desirable aspects of efficacy research (e.g., greater independent variable control) into combined efficacy–effectiveness trials. This message parallels several earlier calls for accelerated study of psychotherapy process variables (summarized by Marmar, 1990). However, the articles in this special section are proposing a different set of variables than those that have been the major focus of process researchers such as Orlinsky and Howard (1986). Traditionally, psychotherapy process research has focused on client and therapist characteristics and interactions, which is reasonable given the focus on how psychotherapy works. In contrast, the blending of psychotherapy efficacy and effectiveness approaches is better served by detailed study of the mediating effects of variables such as the setting in which services are delivered (e.g., school vs. clinic vs. home), the type of clinician who delivers these services, and other issues addressed earlier.

Marmar (1990), in a review of psychotherapy process research, argued for the value of embedding substudies of process variables within larger clinical (efficacy) trials. I agree with this position, but I argue that investigators must look beyond traditional therapeutic relationship variables and include what Kazdin (1986) calls treatment parameter variables, such as the frequency and duration of sessions, the setting in which the treatment is offered, therapist training and profession, and other parameters discussed in this article.

Such studies may manipulate these factors as independent variables or allow them to vary naturally and examine their effect on outcome with post hoc multivariate analyses. The first, more controlled approach is more likely to appeal to efficacy researchers, whereas the latter approach may be more acceptable to confirmed effectiveness investigators. Regardless, both groups (if researchers do self-identify into one or the other group) should be encouraged to generate hybrid studies, broadening the sample and issues under study to address effectiveness concerns while still maintaining as much rigor and experimental control as possible to eliminate or minimize competing explanatory hypotheses. In short, efficacy versus effectiveness is a somewhat artificial distinction, an unnatural dichotomy that a new generation of hybrid studies may help to break down.

REFERENCES

American Psychiatric Association. (1987). *Diagnostic and statistical manual of mental disorders* (3rd ed., rev.). Washington, DC: Author.

Attkisson, C., Cook, J., Karno, M., Lehman, A., McGlashan, T. H., Meltzer, H. Y., O'Connor, M., Richardson, D., Rosenblatt, A., Wells, K., et al. (1992). Clinical services research. *Schizophrenia Bulletin, 18,* 561–626.

Basham, R. B. (1986). Scientific and practical advantages of comparative design in psychotherapy outcome research. *Journal of Consulting and Clinical Psychology, 54,* 88–94.

Beck, A. T. (1991). Cognitive therapy: A 30-year retrospective. *American Psychologist, 46,* 368–375.

Bernstein, G. A., & Shaw, K. (1993). Practice parameters for the assessment and treatment of anxiety disorders. *Journal of the American Academy of Child and Adolescent Psychiatry, 32,* 1089–1098.

Botvin, G. J., Batson, H. W., Witts-Vitale, S., Bess, V., Baker, E., & Dusenbury, L. (1989). A psychosocial approach for smoking prevention for urban black youth. *Public Health Report, 104,* 573–582.

Brook, R. H., & Lohr, K. N. (1985). Efficacy, effectiveness, variations, and quality. *Medical Care, 23,* 710–722.

Budman, S. H. (1992). Models of brief individual and group psychotherapy. In J. L. Feldman & R. J. Fitzpatrick (Eds.), *Managed mental health care: Administrative and clinical issues* (pp. 231–248). Washington, DC: American Psychiatric Press.

Butler, G., Fennell, M., Robson, P., & Gelder, M. (1991). Comparison of behavior therapy and cognitive behavior therapy in the treatment of generalized anxiety disorder. *Journal of Consulting and Clinical Psychology, 59,* 167–175.

Chambless, D. L., & Gillis, M. M. (1993). Cognitive therapy of anxiety disorders. *Journal of Consulting and Clinical Psychology, 61,* 248–260.

Clarke, G. N., Hawkins, W., Murphy, M., Sheeber, L., Lewinsohn, P. M., & Seeley, J. R. (1995). Targeted prevention of unipolar depressive disorder in an at-risk sample of high school adolescents: A randomized trial of a group cognitive intervention. *Journal of the American Academy of Child and Adolescent Psychiatry, 34,* 312–321.

Clarke, G. N., & Hornbrook, M. (1994). *Prevention of depression in adolescent offspring of parents enrolled in a HMO.* (Grant application funded by the Services Research Branch of the National Institute of Mental Health [R01-MH51318-01A1])

Clarke, G. N., Lewinsohn, P. M., & Hops, H. (1990). *Instructor's manual for the Adolescent Coping with Depression Course.* Eugene, OR: Castalia Press.

Conduct Problems Prevention Research Group. (1992). A developmental and clinical model for the prevention of conduct disorder: The FAST Track Program. *Development and Psychopathology, 4*, 509–527.

Downey, G., & Coyne, J. C. (1990). Children of depressed parents: An integrative review. *Psychological Bulletin, 108*, 50–76.

Elkin, I., Parloff, M. B., Hadley, S. W., & Autry, J. H. (1985). NIMH Treatment of Depression Collaborative Research Program: Background and research plan. *Archives of General Psychiatry, 42*, 305–316.

Fairburn, C. G., Jones, R., Peveler, R. C., Carr, S. J., Solomon, R. A., O'Connor, M. E., Burton, J., & Hope, R. A. (1991). Three psychological treatments for bulimia nervosa: A comparative trial. *Archives of General Psychiatry, 48*, 463–469.

Felner, R. D., Phillips, R. S., DuBois, D., & Lease, A. M. (1991). Ecological interventions and the process of change for prevention: Wedding theory and research to implementation in real world settings. *American Journal of Community Psychology, 19*, 379–387.

Hollon, S. D. (1988, June). *Rating therapies for depression: Final report on the CSPRS.* Paper presented at the annual meeting of the Society for Psychotherapy Research, Santa Fe, NM.

Hopkins, K. D. (1982). The unit of analysis: Group means versus individual observation. *American Educational Research Journal, 19*, 5–18.

Jaffe, S. (1991). Practice parameters for the assessment and treatment of attention deficit hyperactivity disorder. Work Group on Quality Issues. *Journal of the American Academy of Child and Adolescent Psychiatry, 30*, i–iii.

Jaffe, S. (1992). Practice parameters for the assessment and treatment of conduct disorders. Work Group on Quality Issues. *Journal of the American Academy of Child and Adolescent Psychiatry, 31*, iv–vii.

Johnson, J., Weissman, M. M., & Klerman, G. L. (1992). Service utilization and social morbidity associated with depressive symptoms in the community. *Journal of the American Medical Association, 267*, 1478–1483.

Kazdin, A. E. (1978). Evaluating the generality of findings in analogue therapy research. *Journal of Consulting and Clinical Psychology, 46*, 673–686.

Kazdin, A. E. (1986). Comparative outcome studies of psychotherapy: Methodological issues and strategies. *Journal of Consulting and Clinical Psychology, 54*, 95–105.

Kendall, P. C., & Lipman, A. J. (1991). Psychological and pharmacological therapy: Methods and modes for comparative outcome research. *Journal of Consulting and Clinical Psychology, 59*, 78–87.

Lambert, M. J., & Ogles, B. M. (1988). Treatment manuals: Problems and promise. *Journal of Integrative and Eclectic Psychotherapy, 7*, 187–204.

Lewinsohn, P. M., Clarke, G. N., Hops, H., & Andrews, J. (1990). Cognitive-behavioral group treatment of depression in adolescents. *Behavior Therapy, 21*, 385–401.

Luborsky, L., & DeRubeis, R. J. (1984). The use of psychotherapy treatment manuals: A small revolution in psychotherapy research studies. *Clinical Psychology Review, 4*, 5–14.

Marmar, C. R. (1990). Psychotherapy process research: Progress, dilemmas, and future directions. *Journal of Consulting and Clinical Psychology, 58*, 265–272.

McClellan, J., & Werry, J. (1994). Practice parameters for the assessment and treatment of children and adolescents with schizophrenia. Work Group on Quality Issues. *Journal of the American Academy of Child and Adolescent Psychiatry, 33*, 616–635.

Moreau, D., Mufson, L., Weissman, M. M., & Klerman, G. L. (1991). Interpersonal psychotherapy for adolescent depression: Description of modification and preliminary application. *Journal of the American Academy of Child and Adolescent Psychiatry, 30*, 642–651.

Mueser, K. T., Bellack, A. S., & Blanchard, J. J. (1992). Comorbidity of schizophrenia and substance abuse: Implications for treatment. *Journal of Consulting and Clinical Psychology, 60*, 845–856.

O'Leary, K. D., & Borkovec, T. D. (1978). Conceptual, methodological, and ethical problems of placebo groups in psychotherapy research. *American Psychologist, 33*, 821–830.

Orlinsky, D. E., & Howard, K. I. (1986). Process and outcome in psychotherapy. In S. L. Garfield & A. E. Bergin (Eds.), *Handbook of psychotherapy and behavior change* (3rd ed., pp. 311–384). New York: Wiley.

Parloff, M. B. (1986). Placebo controls in psychotherapy research: A sine qua non or a placebo for research problems? *Journal of Consulting and Clinical Psychology, 54*, 79–87.

Pentz, M. A., Trebow, E. A., Hansen, W. B., MacKinnon, D. P., Dwyer, J. H., Johnson, C. A., Flay, B., Daniels, S., & Cormack, C. (1990). Effects of program implementation on adolescent drug use behavior: The Midwestern Prevention Project (MPP). *Evaluation Research, 14*, 264–289.

Rohde, P., Lewinsohn, P. M., & Seeley, J. R. (1991). Comorbidity with unipolar depression: II. Comorbidity with other mental disorders in adolescents and adults. *Journal of Abnormal Psychology, 100*, 214–222.

Rohrbach, L. A., Graham, J. W., & Hansen, W. B. (1993). Diffusion of a school-based substance abuse prevention program: Predictors of program implementation. *Preventive Medicine, 22*, 237–260.

Shea, M. T., Widiger, T. A., & Klein, M. H. (1992). Comorbidity of personality disorders and depression: Implications for treatment. *Journal of Consulting and Clinical Psychology, 60*, 857–868.

Solomon, P. (1992). The efficacy of case management services for severely mentally disabled adults. *Community Mental Health Journal, 28*, 163–180.

Strupp, H. (1977). A reformulation of the dynamics of the therapist's contribution. In A. S. Gurman & A. M. Razin (Eds.), *Effective psychotherapy: A handbook of research* (pp. 3–22). New York: Pergamon.

Tillitski, C. J. (1990). A meta-analysis of estimated effect sizes for group versus individual versus control treatments. *International Journal of Group Psychotherapy*, 40, 215–224.

Weiss, B., & Weisz, J. R. (1990). The impact of methodological factors on child psychotherapy outcome research: A meta-analysis for researchers. *Journal of Abnormal Child Psychology*, 18, 639–670.

Weisz, J. R., & Weiss, B. (1989). Assessing the effects of clinic-based psychotherapy with children. *Journal of Consulting and Clinical Psychology*, 57, 741–746.

Weisz, J. R., Weiss, B., Alicke, M. D., & Klotz, M. L. (1987). Effectiveness of psychotherapy with children and adolescents: A meta-analysis for clinicians. *Journal of Consulting and Clinical Psychology*, 55, 542–549.

Weisz, J. R., Weiss, B., & Donenberg, G. R. (1992). The lab versus the clinic: Effects of child and adolescent psychotherapy. *American Psychologist*, 47, 1578–1585.

Wilson, G. T., & Fairburn, C. G. (1993). Cognitive treatments for eating disorders. *Journal of Consulting and Clinical Psychology*, 61, 261–269.

27

THERAPY OUTCOME RESEARCH, HEALTH CARE POLICY, AND THE CONTINUING LACK OF ACCUMULATED KNOWLEDGE

WOLFGANG LINDEN AND FRANCES K. WEN

A vast amount of published research attests to the increasing professionalism of clinical psychologists and has contributed to the certification of psychologists in many countries; certification is generally considered the first step in the inclusion of psychotherapy in national health care systems (Fichter & Wittchen, 1980). It is safe to argue that governments and health insurance agencies in the United States, Canada, and many European countries are more aware of and insightful regarding the necessity of financing effective psychotherapy interventions than ever before, and accordingly, legislation for financing psychotherapy exists or is under way (Fichter & Wittchen, 1980). Therefore, researchers and clinicians are called on to clearly demonstrate the effectiveness of their interventions to secure appropriate legislation and long-term financing of clinical services, research, and

Reprinted from *Professional Psychology: Research and Practice, 21*, 482–488. Copyright 1990 by the American Psychological Association.

training. The key question is whether psychotherapy works (i.e., effectiveness) and whether it is cost efficient (i.e., cost–benefit).

There is convincing evidence from meta-analyses that therapy is better than no therapy, placebo, or minimal therapy (Bowers & Clum, 1988; Shapiro & Shapiro, 1982); however, despite enormous research efforts there remains little consensus among researchers and clinicians as to which therapy best suits which kind of problem and patient (cf. Beutler, 1979; Shapiro & Shapiro, 1982). Therefore, it should not come as a surprise that clinicians', consumers', and policymakers' questions concerning psychotherapy have not been satisfactorily answered (Parloff, 1979). Continuing inability to respond to those questions, however, jeopardizes further progress in needed legislation. The lack of certainty regarding therapy outcome is typically reflected in the discussion sections of research reports in which the speculative or preliminary nature of findings is underlined. The result of such inconclusiveness is that clinical practitioners rate research articles and books as being on the bottom of the scale when they evaluate the usefulness of information sources (Cohen, Sargent, & Sechrest, 1986; Morrow-Bradley & Elliot, 1986). Although therapy-outcome studies published in scientific journals are not designed for primary digestion by policymakers or the patients themselves, researchers and clinicians are expected to translate the findings into clinical practice or use them for input into critical decision making within health care delivery systems. Cohen et al. and Morrow-Bradley and Elliot suggested that consumers and policymakers are never reached because even the practitioners who could serve as agents of change and as translators of scientific findings are not impressed with the evidence. When addressing the reasons for such a lack of conclusive evidence, it has been argued that the outcome literature is essentially noncumulative (Parloff, 1979) and not informative enough for clinicians (Jacobson, Follette, & Revenstorf, 1984), that studies lack the power to detect effects (Sedlmeier & Gigerenzer, 1989), and that the current review and publication process is more a hindrance than a help for accumulating a solid data base on therapy outcome (Kupfersmid, 1988). The lack of accumulated knowledge has been attributed to a tendency among researchers to conduct mostly analogue studies (Shapiro & Shapiro, 1982) and typically small scale, independently initiated, and uncoordinated studies (Parloff, 1979).

The present article outlines how clinicians', consumers', and policymakers' questions have been or may be addressed in therapy research. To this end, frequent design characteristics are evaluated with regard to their inherent potential in responding to practitioners' and to the public's interest. Publication trends are investigated, and it is demonstrated whether and how outcome studies answer these questions. Research guidelines that facilitate the communication of results to the consumer (i.e., clinicians, patients, and policymakers) and that enhance the accumulation of knowledge are then derived from the review of publication trends.

Three issues in outcome research are considered to be of particular interest to consumers: (a) the generalizability of findings, (b) the clinical benefits of therapy, and (c) the costs involved. The generalizability of a result is essentially determined by the size and representativeness of the samples investigated and the consistency in replicating the same finding in different settings, with varying patient samples and therapists. Benefits of therapy are usually assessed by self- and therapist ratings, physiological indices, questionnaires, and behavioral measures. The assessment of outcome often relies on the quantification of psychological constructs such as anxiety, ego strength, or neuroticism. Measures of this kind are typically theory based and necessitate external validation (e.g., criterion or predictive validity) before becoming meaningful indicators of change comprehensible to policymakers and the lay public. Unfortunately, such validation data are missing for many—if not most—psychological measures in frequent usage (Nelson, 1981). On these grounds, indices of change such as return-to-work rates, length of hospitalization, changes in drug-taking patterns and so forth appear more valuable in demonstrating therapy effectiveness and cost–benefit to the consumer and policymaker. Throughout this article, we refer to such measures as "hard" criterion measures. There is no intention on our part to call these inherently better research measures; however, we feel strongly that they are easier to explain and more persuasive to professional and lay consumers. Given that such measures based on hard criteria may not always be available or may be difficult to apply, a simple percentage-improvement rating (separating the number of patients in worsened, no change, improved, and total remission categories) would easily be understood by professionals and the lay public.

An even better, two-pronged strategy for demonstrating the clinical meaning of findings has been proposed by Jacobson et al. (1984). These writers suggested using a statistical criterion for reliability of effect ($S_E > 1.96$), as well as norms or cutoffs for levels of functionality on such dimensions as, for example, depression, anxiety, or marital adjustment. Jacobson et al. emphasized the importance of studying within-sample variability, especially for follow-up evaluations in which within-group variability in treatment response typically exceeds that observed during active-intervention periods.

The issue of cost–benefit interacts with the effectiveness of a treatment. The central question is how much effect can be "bought" for how much therapy. This question is most comprehensively answered by cost–benefit analyses in which the cost–benefit is pragmatically defined as cost of therapy relative to the savings associated with shorter hospitalization periods or early rehabilitation of work ability. Cost is indirectly addressed when comparing varying forms of demonstratedly effective therapy that imply less therapist time per patient for possibly the same effect (e.g., short- vs. long-term treatment, groups vs. individual therapy, and therapist-contact vs. self-control conditions).

We reviewed publication trends in outcome research to identify how often these issues are addressed in experimental designs. Data had initially been collected in 1980 covering publication samples of the years 1978 and 1979; for the purposes of this article, the equivalent data were also collected for the years 1986 and 1987. The 8 years separating these data sets permitted an evaluation of patterns in therapy-research design at a given time as well as change in such patterns over time. The idea to study trends was partially inspired by Sedlmeier and Gigerenzer's (1989) disturbing finding of decreasing power of studies to actually detect effects.

METHOD

The present sample consisted of all outcome studies published in 1978/1979 and 1986/1987 in the *Journal of Consulting and Clinical Psychology* (JCCP), the *Journal of Clinical Psychology* (JCP), and *Behavior Therapy* (BT). These journals were selected because they frequently publish therapy studies generally considered of high design quality as documented in citation counts and citation-impact evaluations. We chose three different journals to reduce the possibility that trends that occurred in only one journal would be mistaken for trends in the field as a whole.

Outcome studies were defined as psychological interventions evaluated before and after, with either a psychological construct or a problematic overt behavior as the target. Studies were analyzed with respect to generalizability, clinical effectiveness, and cost. More specifically, we investigated which proportion of studies could be categorized as case ($n = 1-4$), small-sample ($n = 5-20$), or large-sample ($n > 20$) studies (sample size being defined as the n of the smallest treatment condition); how many of the studies were replications; and what proportion was based on dissertations (which by tradition implies independently conducted, original contributions). Furthermore, we determined the frequency and type of hard, externally valid measures used to evaluate effectiveness. We also determined how often the results included ratings of the "percentage of patients clinically improved" or any other indication of individual patient's clinical improvement. We noted whether the issue of therapy cost had been addressed by including a cost–benefit analysis or study of cost-related factors like short- versus long-term therapy. Finally, we investigated whether studies addressed the question of power to detect differences between treatment conditions or baseline to posttreatment change.

RESULTS

Results from our analysis of design features are displayed in Table 1 to permit easy comparison across journals and over time. The 1978/1979

TABLE 1
Frequency of Selected Design Features in Therapy Outcome Studies Published in Three Journals During 1978/1979 and 1986/1987

Design Features	Journal of Consulting and Clinical Psychology				Journal of Clinical Psychology				Behavior Therapy			
	1978/1979 (89 studies)		1986/1987 (63 studies)		1978/1979 (37 studies)		1986/1987 (11 studies)		1978/1979 (65 studies)		1986/1987 (37 studies)	
	No. of studies	% of total	No. of studies	% of total	No. of studies	% of total	No. of studies	% of total	No. of studies	% of total	No. of studies	% of total
Sample size												
<5	3	3	1	2	2	5	0	0	26	40	8	22
5–20	65	73	44	70	21	57	2	18	35	54	22	59
>20	21	24	18	28	14	38	9	82	4	6	7	19
Power of treatment calculated	0	0	0	0	0	0	0	0	0	0	1	3
Identified replications	3	3	1	2	1	3	0	0	1	2	4	11
Dissertations	33	38	9	14	1	3	1	9	8	12	8	22
"Hard" measures incorporated	43	48	47	75	27	73	8	73	58	89	28	76
Clinical improvement ratings	19	21	23	36	11	30	5	45	42	65	25	68
Cost issues addressed	10	11	18	29	9	24	7	64	4	6	9	24

articles are referred to as the "early sample." The 1986/1987 articles are referred to as the "later sample." We split the task of reviewing journals, but one volume (Volume 54 of JCCP) was read by both of us to permit an interrater reliability check on the sometimes difficult distinction of psychological versus hard criterion measures. Only one disagreement was noted, and we were satisfied with the 97% agreement score. The presentation of the findings is grouped according to number of studies published, generalizability, effectiveness, and cost–benefit. Within each of these sections, comparisons of journals are made, early and late sample findings are contrasted, and emerging trends are discussed.

Number of Studies

A rather striking first observation is that of a decreased total number of published outcome studies in all three journals over time (191 studies in 1978/1979 vs. 111 in 1986/1987, a decline of 42%). Because of the large total number and parallel findings for all three journals, this suggests a strong, general trend in the field. The decline was particularly evident for the case-study category (from 31 to 9) and for the small-sample studies (from 121 to 68) and was less evident for the large-sample studies (from 39 to 34).

Generalizability

One aspect of the generalization question is sample size (the relationship of sample size to statistical power is highlighted later). Considerable differences among journals were apparent, with BT having a particularly great proportion of its outcome studies falling into the case-study category (40% in the early sample, and 22% in the later sample). Three fourths of the outcome studies in JCCP fell into the small-sample category, and this was true of the early and later samples alike. Both JCCP and JCP had more large-sample studies than did BT. The relative frequencies of case-, small-group, and large-group studies were unchanged in JCCP over time, whereas in JCP and BT there was a shift away from the case-studies toward large-sample studies. When findings were summed across journals, there appeared a corresponding overall trend toward fewer case-studies and more large samples (from 16% to 8% for case studies, from 63% to 49% for small-sample studies, and from 23% to 43% for large-sample studies). The averaged percentage figures need to be interpreted cautiously because of the relatively small total number of outcome studies found in JCP.

Although findings of large-sample studies are likely to appear convincing to consumers without statistical training, critical evaluations of outcome research also have to deal with the issue of power to detect effects in addition to sample size (Muenz, 1989). Sedlmeier and Gigerenzer (1989) convincingly showed that studies in psychology have lost rather than gained in power during the past 20 years and that approximately two thirds of the studies published in a prestigious clinical journal did not have the power to detect a medium-sized effect. With the exception of one recent study in *BT*, there was no attention given to the question of statistical power to detect treatment effects (relative to baseline or control-treatment conditions). To us this was a striking finding, especially because Wolfgang Linden has been a member of a grant-review committee in which proposals for therapy-outcome research are required to have a power estimate for justifying the proposed sample size. Without knowing anything about the power of given treatments to produce meaningful clinical changes, however, even professional readers cannot truly judge the importance of given findings. Implications of the power issue are also addressed in the discussion and suggestion section.

In the early sample, only five (3%) of the studies were identified as a replication of a previously published intervention study. In the later sample, another five (5%) were replications. Given the small numbers, we could not compare journals in a meaningful way. After careful reading of the procedural descriptions, however, we speculate that approximately 30% of the studies were conceptual replications (i.e., the therapy components were similar or equivalent to research described earlier).

Despite the nearly standard comment in discussion sections of outcome studies that "the present findings remain speculative until replicated," such replication is rarely executed (3% and 5% in the early and later samples, respectively) or, if such studies are executed, at least they tend not to reach publication (see also Kupfersmid, 1988). Even worse, some articles seem to have many components in common with previous research but tend to underline the originality of the new approach rather than explicitly identify the common ground. Editorial policy and practice of *BT* permits a particularly intriguing observation on this issue. In the 1987 volume of *BT*, the editors implemented a special section for case and replication studies. Although this is unique and most laudable, only two replications were found in this category. Two other studies, however, that were explicit replications (as indicated in their titles) were published in the same journal but outside of the replication section.

Whereas the tendency to de-emphasize replications is understandable given that novelty and originality of publications are associated with high academic and professional reputation (Kendall & Ford, 1979), it is at the same time highly detrimental to the accumulation of knowledge. One is tempted to raise the question of whether editors an reviewers confronted with floods of manuscripts can free themselves from giving preference to an original study rather than a replication. Also, knowing that originality is more prestigious and more likely to result in publication and citation, there appears to be little reason for an author to stress that a replication was in fact executed.

Undoubtedly, many student theses reflect high quality research and have generated exciting ideas in the past. All of that, however, also enhances the conflict of choice for the student researcher between widening a provisionally established basis of knowledge or adding a new, original finding. The change from 18% to 15% of studies being student theses suggests only a minor shift in publication pattern, but it must be emphasized that in BT and in JCP the proportion of theses has gone up (from 12% to 22% and from 3% to 9%, respectively), whereas it has strongly decreased in JCCP (from 38% to 14%).

Effectiveness

In the early sample, 70% of the studies incorporated outcome measures that were hard measures by our definition. These included, for example, days out of the hospital, discharge and recidivism counts, employment statistics, blood pressure, weight, incontinence records in a geriatric population, and behavioral approach–avoidance tests. In the later sample, a slightly improved picture emerged, with 75% of the studies including at least one such measure. Next, we investigated trends across different journals. Interestingly, the percentage of studies with hard measures tended to be high for all three journals, but only for JCP did the trend remain unchanged. BT and JCCP showed trends in opposing directions: In BT the percentage dropped from 89% to 76%, whereas in JCCP it increased from 48% to 75%.

Clinical-improvement ratings (rather than indices of group means only) were included in 39% of the studies in the early sample and 50% of those in the later sample. Again, differences between journals emerged. In BT, the descriptions of clinical improvement were consistently frequent in the early and later samples (65% and 68%, respectively), whereas in JCP and JCCP the frequency of inclusion clearly increased over time. But even in the later sample the frequency of indices of clinical change in JCP and JCCP remained substantially below the rate found in BT. Much of this discrepancy is of course related to the fact that BT also published more case studies in which individual descriptions of clinical improvement are the primary means of reporting change and, given this design feature, group comparisons of outcome are impossible. Although of major interest to clinicians (whose patients want to know how likely they are, as individual patients, to get better) and easily comprehended by nonprofessionals, the data indicate that such ratings are incorporated in only half of all studies, albeit the trend suggests an improvement. No logical or technical reason appears to justify the absence of such clinical criteria when inclusion would greatly enhance the apparent clinical significance of findings. Preference for more sophisticated (and more difficult to interpret [Kupfersmid, 1988]) statistics involving group means override the clinically relevant reports of individual progress or failure in most studies.

Cost

A cost–benefit analysis was part of only one outcome study in the early sample and one in the later sample. In one instance (early sample) the direct cost of treatment was mentioned. Research issues related to cost were investigated in 23 studies (8%) in the early sample and 18 studies (31%) in the later sample. Studies compared individual with group treatment, evaluated therapist- and self-controlled treatment approaches, and contrasted inpatient with outpatient therapy and professional with lay therapists. The lack of more cost–benefit analyses may be partially attributed to the unresolved controversy over the definition of benefit and the administrative problem of identifying the direct (therapist hours, days in hospital, etc.) and indirect costs (impact on work, home, and social environment) involved. Also, the cost of such an analysis may not warrant its application in small-sample studies. However, on the basis of those studies that included indirect-cost comparisons (e.g., therapist involvement and treatment-length comparisons), global evaluations of differential costs may be executed even in a post hoc manner. The value of such cost comparisons for the public and policy-makers need not be underlined further. Nevertheless, over time the interest in cost-related issues has grown and is equally reflected in all three journals.

DISCUSSION

The results from this descriptive analysis clearly underline that the clinicians' questions and the public's questions still remain unanswered far too often. They also support Parloff's (1979) tenet that typically small scale, independent and uncoordinated studies may account for this phenomenon. However, comparison of relevant data from the same journals for the years 1978/1979 with those from 1986/1987 indicate that some positive change (provided the reader agrees with our value judgment of "positive") has occurred over time. The trends for sample size show a shift toward larger samples, the prevalence of replications continues to be disappointingly low, and the inclusion of hard measures has improved, but only for JCCP. Frequency of cost–benefit calculations are unchanged and very rare. The ratings of clinical improvement have increased for JCCP and JCP but still remain unnecessarily low overall. The absence of replication studies and the absence of power calculations is worrisome. To us, the building of a broad knowledge base is not evident in these data and requires much more concerted effort.

Two observations on the differences between early- and later-sample data invite further notice and interpretation. The total number of published therapy-outcome studies in the three journals has dropped by more than 40%, although the journals published a similar total number of articles during the two periods of sampling. Also, the percentage of therapy studies that are dissertations has decreased in JCCP but increased in BT. We offer two speculative interpretations of the overall trends. First, we think that fewer outcome studies are conducted now because of an enhanced awareness of the difficulty (conceptually and economically, as well as logistically) of conducting a good therapy-outcome study. Along these lines, one can argue that fewer published outcome studies may actually be symptomatic of a positive trend, that is, only the best, presumably the most clinically meaningful, therapy studies get published.

A second explanation is a shift in values. Researchers, clinicians, and granting agencies may simply see increasingly less value in "horse-race" comparisons of therapy techniques. Support for this argument can be seen in the growing trend to investigate qualitative features of psychotherapy, including the study of patient and therapist characteristics and the therapy process itself. Our personal view is that both interpretations are valid.

In summary, the data as reported here indicate that the therapy-outcome literature still does not maximize the possibilities for accumulation of a broad data base and provide at least a partial explanation for why neither clinicians nor the public can easily be convinced of the usefulness of therapy-outcome research (Cohen et al., 1986; Morrow-Bradley & Elliott, 1986). The next logical question is how this unsatisfactory state of affairs can be improved. Below, we provide a number of suggestions that we hope can contribute to a critical discussion of the issues.

We would like to stress at this point that the suggestions made below are not entirely novel, do not deal with every aspect of a very complex phenomenon, and are not held up to be a panacea. The current data on publication trends, however, do indicate that previous suggestions (like the one on replications; Smith, 1970) have not been acted on. Therefore, the repetition and extension of such suggestions is not redundant.

SUGGESTIONS FOR INCREASED
KNOWLEDGE ACCUMULATION

Numerous propositions on research issues (e.g., evaluation of placebo effects, therapist effects, and measurement of change) have been made earlier (Frank, 1979; Mahoney, 1978) and are not repeated here. The suggestions made below are directed mostly at providing responses to the public and acknowledge the premise that (a) available research funds are limited and higher expenses per se do not guarantee more accumulation of established conclusions and (b) despite their limitations, small-scale studies will probably continue to prevail because of the practical, organizational, and educational advantages mentioned. Given these premises, the suggested changes should neither require a scientific revolution nor make increases in spending necessary. A critical evaluation of some traditions and policies as well as some modifications in approaching and designing outcome studies, however, would be most important. Some of the suggestions below were inspired by Kupfersmid's (1988) persuasive criticisms of the current review process for journal manuscripts.

Suggestion 1: Replication Studies

The need for replication studies was noted earlier (Smith, 1970), however, given the above-noted absence of published replications, the necessity of these cannot be stressed enough. However, if change in the direction of more published replications is to come, one must first address the reasons why replications have not been executed more often in the past. A major obstacle appears to be the differential value placed on original versus replication research. Graduate (and sometimes even honors) students are required to present original work as dissertations, and academic psychologists publish as evidence of their professional competence ("publish or perish"). Novel ideas and findings carry more reputational weight, but this attitude is usually not explicit. Change in these attitudes necessitates relabeling of value etiquettes and requires some discussion of traditions. Universities may contribute to that responsibility by opening the discussion as to whether honors and master's theses requirements could not be met by a replication study (either through a straightforward replication or through a design that improves a potential shortcoming of an earlier study). An enriching learning experience will certainly be the result for the student researcher. Publishing replications could be facilitated through editorial policy (i.e., identifying and *reserving* a subsection of each journal issue for replications; the efforts of the *BT* editors are to be commended here. Original research and replications ought not compete with each other for journal space because they serve different, but complementary, functions. Replications can be planned ahead: Two research teams may, after completion of the first study, collaborate by replicating each other's study (Team A provides its method and materials, but not the results, to team B and vice versa). Sample sizes would thus be doubled, generalizability would clearly be enhanced (because of increased randomization of location, therapists, and time), and costs for planning and evaluating could be minimized. A change in attitude might then follow the suggested structural changes.

Suggestion 2: Enhance Comparability

We present three ideas as to how comparability across studies can be enhanced and how data bases may thus become more cumulative.

An expert committee could determine one or two psychological measures (or a criterion) to be incorporated in *every* study with a particular target.

An example of this can be seen in recent standardization efforts by the National Institute for Mental Health (Elkin, Parloff, Hadley, & Autry, 1985).

Wherever possible, detailed therapy manuals should be made available to facilitate replications of a procedure (Dobson & Shaw, 1988). Examples of already existing manuals are the Self Control and Assertion Skills Manual (Rehm, Fuchs, Roth, Kornblith, & Romano, 1979), Sank and Shaffer's (1984) manual on cognitive therapy in groups, and Luborsky's (1984) manual on supportive–expressive treatment.

When a novel treatment approach is tested, a treatment-control group that is a straightforward replication of an earlier study on the same target could be included; the replicated outcome then needs to be highlighted in resulting publications. In this manner, originality, comparability, and consolidation of an earlier finding can be achieved.

Reports of data could contain group means as well as percentage-improvement ratings and evaluations of change on functional norms (Jacobson et al., 1984). Given that at least one standard measure will be used in every study on a particular target, the issue of defining worsened, no change, improved, or total-remission conditions becomes more easily solvable.

Suggestion 3: Enhance Clinical Relevance

A major portion of outcome studies are planned and executed by academic researchers (professors and graduate students; Kendall & Ford, 1979), and two thirds were found to be analogue in nature (Shapiro & Shapiro, 1982). The academic approach typically begins with a literature review and the formulation of an experimental hypothesis; the development of a test design and the search for the appropriate subject population follow.

For this group of researchers, one may suggest to partially reverse this order. First, contact with clinical service facility (hospital, outpatient clinic, etc.) could be established. In collaboration with clinicians, the most important questions for therapy research may be selected, and many procedural aspects (such as subject solicitation, population characteristics, critical outcome criteria, and appropriate follow-up procedures) can be attended to when reviewing the literature and in the design of the study. Also, at this time power estimates are needed and the effect of power on sample size needs to be determined (Sedlmeier & Gigerenzer, 1989). It is entirely possible that some projects will justifiably be scrapped at this stage because a given treatment effect is too weak or the sample sizes necessary to show the effect are unattainable. It is a terrible waste of funds to complete, at typically high cost, studies that never had sufficient power to detect effects in the first place.

A potential drawback to the clinical approach proposed here is that independent clinicians may not want to collaborate because of work overload, competitiveness, defensiveness, or a combination thereof. Notwithstanding this important limitation, it is much better to recognize the obstacles to satisfactory study completion in the design stage rather than finding out later that nobody will refer the necessary patients. We furthermore posit that a clinician who shows no interest in a study when asked to participate in the planning is even less interested in the referring process after the design is complete; in contrast, a clinician who was involved in the planning is likely to be interested in referring patients.

The proposed clinical approach has multiple advantages that we believe are worth the drawbacks:

1. Clinical relevance and realistic measures may be incorporated more easily and the necessity to resort to questionable analogue studies may decrease. In the past, many studies were so intellectually and logistically demanding that only analogue populations could be expected to fit the requirements, agree to participate, and follow through with the study.

2. Academic researchers would not have to rely on subject solicitation through public media and inherent sampling biases would be minimized (Little, Curran, & Gilbert, 1977; Schact, 1983).

3. Because of the existence of systematic data collections (i.e., medical files) and the continuing presence of the institution, long-term clinical evaluations are facilitated. Follow-up with theory-independent measures (i.e., rehospitalizations and frequency of outpatient service use) may be executed even if the principal investigator has left the institution. Researchers in clinical settings should be encouraged to use the full potential of available theory-independent measures.

Suggestion 4: Address Cost Issues

Complex cost–benefit analyses have been incorporated in some large-scale studies (cf. Paul & Lentz, 1977) but cannot reasonably be executed in all sizes of studies. Important questions like "What is the dollar value of a high quality of life?" remain difficult to answer. However, some low-cost approaches have been demonstrated to produce equal impact (e.g., group vs. individual exposure for agoraphobia; Linden, 1981), and research on these issues warrants full support and increased attention (Shapiro & Shapiro, 1982). It was rather surprising to note that a good number of researchers were interested in cost-related issues but failed to *explicitly* state observed cost advantages. It is not difficult for most readers to see the cost–benefit of Therapy A, which produces comparable outcome to Therapy B but with less therapist time. But it is certainly more effective to explicitly point out such cost advantages in the Discussion section by saying something like "Therapy A costs 66% less" or "Therapy A reduced number of days in hospital over a

12-month follow-up from an average of 18 to 11 days. At a cost of $500 per day, this amounts to a $3,500 saving per patient." As little as necessary should be left for the reader to extract and compute. "How can cost–benefit be demonstrated?" should be a routine question in the planning stages of any given study, and journal editors may want to routinely challenge authors to be explicit about cost factors wherever possible.

CONCLUSION

These suggestions for improvement reflect our personal opinions, and some readers may not agree with them. However, we do hope that even those in disagreement with the recommendations are as concerned as we are about the findings on publication trends per se. If the field of psychotherapy research is to have some real impact on clinical practice and health care policy, much more attention needs to be given to replication, to cost issues, to descriptions of clinical outcome, and to the question of power to detect effects. Many tools for improvement already exist; they are just not used often and consistently enough. Also, it is not exclusively a lack of funds that stands in the way of building a more solid data base. Habits in research design and reporting and researchers and editors' underlying attitudes and values, however, need closer scrutiny.

REFERENCES

Beutler, L. E. (1979). Toward specific psychological therapies for specific conditions. *Journal of Consulting and Clinical Psychology, 47,* 882–887.

Bowers, T. G., & Clum, G. A. (1988). Relative contribution of specific and non-specific treatment effects: Meta-analysis of placebo-controlled behavior therapy research. *Psychological Bulletin, 103,* 315–323.

Cohen, L., Sargent, M., & Sechrest, L. (1986). Use of psychotherapy research by professional psychologists. *American Psychologist, 41,* 198–206.

Dobson, K. S., & Shaw, B. F. (1988). The use of treatment manuals in cognitive therapy: Experience and issues. *Journal of Consulting and Clinical Psychology, 56,* 673–680.

Elkin, I., Parloff, M., Hadley, S., & Autry, I. (1985). The NIMH treatment of depression collaborative research program: Background and research plan. *Archives of General Psychiatry, 42,* 305–316.

Fichter, M. M., & Wittchen, H. U. (1980). Clinical psychology and psychotherapy: A survey of the present state of professionalization in 23 countries. *American Psychologist, 35,* 16–25.

Frank, J. D. (1979). The present status of outcome studies. *Journal of Consulting and Clinical Psychology, 47,* 310–316.

Jacobson, N. S., Follette, W. L., & Revenstorf, D. (1984). Psychotherapy outcome research: Methods of reporting variability and evaluating clinical significance. *Behavior Therapy, 15,* 336–352.

Kendall, P. C., & Ford, J. D. (1979). Reasons for clinical research: Characteristics of contributors and their contributions to the *Journal of Consulting and Clinical Psychology. Journal of Consulting and Clinical Psychology, 47,* 99–105.

Kupfersmid, J. (1988). Improving what is published: A model in search of an editor. *American Psychologist, 43,* 635–642.

Linden, W. (1981). Exposure treatments for focal phobias. *Archives of General Psychiatry, 38,* 769–775.

Little, M., Curran, J. P., & Gilbert, F. S. (1977). The importance of subject recruitment procedures in therapy analogue studies on heterosexual–social anxiety. *Behavior Therapy, 8,* 24–29.

Luborsky, L. (1984). *Principles of psychoanalytic psychotherapy: A manual for supportive–expressive psychotherapy.* New York: Basic Books.

Mahoney, M. J. (1978). Experimental methods and outcome evaluation. *Journal of Consulting and Clinical Psychology, 46,* 660–672.

Morrow-Bradley, C., & Elliot, R. (1986). Utilization of psychotherapy research by practicing psychotherapists. *American Psychologist, 41,* 188–197.

Muenz, L. R. (1989). Power calculations for statistical design. In N. Schneiderman, S. M. Weiss, & P. G. Kaufmann (Eds.), *Handbook of research methods in cardiovascular behavior medicine* (pp. 615–634). New York: Plenum Press.

Nelson, R. O. (1981). Realistic dependent measures for clinical use. *Journal of Consulting and Clinical Psychology, 49,* 168–182.

Parloff, M. B. (1979). Can psychotherapy research guide the policymaker? A little knowledge may be a dangerous thing. *American Psychologist, 34,* 296–306.

Paul, G. L., & Lentz, R. J. (1977). *Psychosocial treatment of chronic mental patients: Milieu versus social learning programs.* Cambridge, MA: Harvard University Press.

Rehm, L. P., Fuchs, C. Z., Roth, D. M., Kornblith, S. J., & Romano, J. M. (1979). A comparison of self-control and assertion skills treatments of depression. *Behavior Therapy, 10,* 429–442.

Sank, L., & Shaffer, C. (1984). *A therapist's manual for cognitive behavior therapy in groups.* New York: Plenum Press.

Schact, T. E. (1983). Is subject selection a source of subtle artifact in psychotherapy research? *Psychotherapy: Theory, Research, and Practice, 20,* 359–367.

Sedlmeier, P., & Gigerenzer, G. (1989). Do studies of statistical power have an effect of the power of studies? *Psychological Bulletin, 105,* 309–316.

Shapiro, D. A., & Shapiro, D. (1982). Meta-analysis of comparative therapy outcome studies: A replication and refinement. *Psychological Bulletin, 92,* 581–604.

Smith, N. C., Jr. (1970). Replication studies: A neglected aspect of psychological research. *American Psychologist, 25,* 970–975.

28

TOWARD THE INCORPORATION OF COSTS, COST-EFFECTIVENESS ANALYSIS, AND COST–BENEFIT ANALYSIS INTO CLINICAL RESEARCH

BRIAN T. YATES

I believe that we can understand, in a scientific manner, not only the techniques of treatment and their potential outcomes but also how treatment systems can deliver those techniques in ways that better realize their full potential effectiveness and that cost less. In clinical research, we devote most of our resources to the development and testing of new psychological techniques. The effectiveness of these technologies is our paramount concern in grant proposals, experimental designs, instrumentation, procedures, statistical analyses, and discussions of findings. The costs of psychological technologies can be measured too, but they seldom are. These costs may include the value of temporal and other personnel resources; spatial resources such as offices, supplies, and transportation; and particularly the time spent

Reprinted from the *Journal of Consulting and Clinical Psychology, 62*, 729–736. Copyright 1994 by the American Psychological Association.

by clients and others in treatment. I hope to show that the costs of clinical efforts are not mundane, unimportant, irrelevant, or too predictable to be of interest. Furthermore, once costs have been accurately and comprehensively assessed, we can empirically explore the entire system of linkages among the specific resources consumed in treatment, the therapeutic procedures that those resources make possible, the psychological and other processes produced by those procedures, and the outcomes achieved.

OUR INCOMPLETE RESEARCH AGENDA

By focusing scientific scrutiny on only the outcomes of treatment, investigators may be making mistakes that could become serious as budgets dwindle and clients become more sophisticated consumers of health services. The research methods that have been used for decades have generated a literature that now allows researchers to say much about which treatments are effective and why but little about how much treatments cost and hardly anything about which treatments deliver the best outcomes for the least money. Methods for assessing costs and for contrasting costs to effectiveness and benefits have been available for a decade or two, but they have not been used (e.g., Carter & Newman, 1976; Fishman, 1975; Levin, 1975; Newman & Sorensen, 1985; Rufener, Rachal, & Cruze, 1977; Weisbrod, 1983; Yates, 1980, 1985; cf. Yates & Newman, 1980a, 1980b). As pressure for cost containment evolves into pressure for cost cuts, investigators risk being unable to provide scientific answers to the questions that potential clients or funders may ask even before they inquire as to effectiveness (i.e., "What does it cost?" and "Is it really worth it?"; cf. McGuire, 1989). Essentially, I am saying our current approach to research in clinical psychology is incomplete. Assessing costs as well as outcomes also would allow researchers to construct a more complete theoretical and empirical model of psychological treatment. To these ends, I propose that we pay as much attention to the resources consumed in treatment as we do to the outcomes made possible by expenditure of those resources.

Furthermore, investigators need to focus beyond the comparison of treatments in terms of their outcomes and their costs, to analyze and really understand their cost-effectiveness and cost–benefit. Simple ratios of cost to effectiveness or monetary benefit only provide a limited and possibly mistaken understanding of how to squeeze the most effectiveness out of mental health technologies at the lowest possible costs. What researchers need to do is to go beyond a tabular comparison of costs and outcomes to the point where it is possible not only to measure costs, processes, and outcomes but also to discover and quantify the strength of the relationships among (a) resources consumed, (b) treatment procedures funded, (c) psychological and biological processes engendered by those procedures, and (d) interim and long-term outcomes produced.

This article considers several beliefs that may have impeded the measurement and analysis of relationships among the resources that make treatment possible, the procedures conducted in treatment, and the changes that therapists hope to make in clients' lives. Discussed briefly here are several of the more important beliefs regarding (a) the assessment of costs, (b) the degree to which psychological techniques, as opposed to treatment delivery systems, determine the outcome of services, and (c) what cost-effectiveness analysis and cost–benefit analysis are and can do for psychological treatment.

BELIEFS ABOUT COSTS AND COST-OUTCOME RELATIONSHIPS

"Cost is Directly Related to Outcome (or You Get What You Pay For)"

Howard, Kopta, Krause, and Orlinsky (1986) and Newman and Howard (1986) have shown with meta-analysis that there often is a direct relationship between the "dose" of a specific therapy procedure (e.g., number of sessions) and its effectiveness. This important, familiar relationship may be different from the relationship between the expense of a therapy session and the benefits one obtains from it. More expensive therapy is not necessarily better therapy, although spending more money for more sessions of an effective form of therapy may increase the likelihood of positive outcomes. When this is suggested, most people acknowledge the possibility of an indirect relationship between the resources expended in therapy and the outcomes attained. Most, however, maintain the position that more expensive therapy must be better therapy because, if it were not, then why would people pay so much for it? The laws of supply and demand may not, however, be operating in the mental health marketplace. The adjustment of price to reflect quality would likely occur if mental health services were provided in an open market with widely advertised prices and well-informed, rational consumers, but this is seldom the case in the mental health sector (McGuire, 1980, 1989).

Many studies could be cited to describe the position that more costly treatment is not necessarily more effective treatment (cf. Yates & Newman, 1980b). Karon and VandenBos (1976), for example, found that psychologists were as effective as psychiatrists in treating schizophrenics but were less expensive. Weisbrod (1983), among others, showed that inpatient treatment of schizophrenics is more expensive, but not more effective, than community care. Siegert and Yates (1980) found that therapy delivered by the most expensive delivery system for child management training was not more effective than therapy delivered by their least expensive delivery system. Hayashida et al. (1989) found that a drug abuse treatment that required more

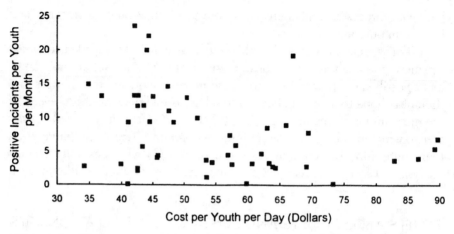

Figure 1. Desired outcomes may be inversely related to costs: Positive incidents in youth residential programs as a function of cost per youth ($r = -.33$, $N = 48$, $p < .05$).

time of clients, as well as more funds, was not more effective than another treatment that was considerably less expensive for clients and funders.

It even appears that outcomes can be inversely related to costs. I found that positive incidents reported in four residential treatment facilities for dependent and neglected urban youths were negatively correlated with monthly expenditures. As shown in Figure 1, the average number of positive incidents per youth per month had a correlation of $-.33$ with the average cost per youth per day ($p < .05$, two-tailed). the N for this Pearson r was 48, corresponding to one data point per month per home for 1 year.

The possibility of an occasional negative relationship between outcome and cost has been demonstrated in other areas of treatment as well. For example, in a study of clients with a phobia for snakes, Bandura, Blanchard, and Ritter (1969) not only contrasted the increase in clients' approaching a snake produced by (a) participant modeling, (b) symbolic modeling, and (c) systematic desensitization but also measured the minutes spent by therapists and clients in sessions. (Similar delivery systems were used in all treatment conditions [i.e., individual sessions in a clinic].) An analysis of variance showed that participant modeling was the most effective treatment procedure. Ninety-two percent of clients receiving the participant modeling procedure attained the terminal step in a "snake-approach" continuum of being able to sit with a 3-foot snake in their lap for 2 min. Systematic desensitization allowed only 25% of clients to reach the same terminal step. Bandura et al. also reported that participant modeling required the least time of clients: only 2 hr, 10 min on the average. Systematic desensitization required a significantly greater mean of 4 hr, 33 min. The amount of time required by the film modeling was an average 2 hr, 46 min. Film modeling was conducted by the client after the therapist had a brief discussion of the procedure with the client and after the client was shown how to operate the film projector.

For snake phobias, it seems possible that effectiveness may be maximized and costs minimized with the use of the participant modeling procedure. (This statement could not, of course, be made for any other simple phobia or any more general avoidance problem without careful replication of the Bandura et al. [1969] procedure with clients who have these different disorders.) These findings run contrary to the commonly encountered wisdom that "you get what you pay for." That adage most likely applies in economic situations in which outcomes and costs are accurately measured and widely known, so that supply and demand forces a positive price–outcome relationship.

"Money Spent Reflects Resources Used"

A primary reason for the dearth of cost data in clinical research may be the supposition that costs are trivial to measure (i.e., that they are simply the money spent on treatment). However, when costs are assessed carefully and thoroughly, as the value of resources consumed in treatment, it becomes evident that the crucial resource expenditures may be measured best in units not commonly associated with costs. For example, Yates, Haven, and Thoresen (1979) found that the assessment of staff resources expended in a residential treatment for predelinquent youths was most complete when the units of measurement were not dollars of salary paid to staff but minutes of time spent by staff in treatment-related activities. As shown in Table 1, valuation of the time actually spent by staff in treatment-related activities resulted in cost figures that varied considerably from the salary paid.

Generally, Yates et al. found that, during the month in which costs were assessed, individuals who received the highest rates of pay expended the exact amount of time for which they received payment: the doctoral staff, however, actually worked fewer hours than they should have to justify their salary. The majority of staff, who held lower degrees, expended far more resources than they were paid for. For instance, individuals with undergraduate degrees worked enough hours to have received a total of $13,675 if they had been paid for the hours they worked. They were paid only $2,972, however. This difference between resources expended and resources reimbursed was justified as being reimbursed by a barter of services (i.e., by the extensive training opportunities and supervision received by the BA-level staff). Nevertheless, the finding that the salaries of BA-level staff reflected only 21.7% of the time that the staff devoted to treatment suggests that relying on accounting records may underestimate treatment costs. This finding may not be limited to the settings that use volunteers and trainees to deliver much of the direct services.

TABLE 1
Differences Between Dollars Paid and the Value of Time Spent in Treatment-Related Activities for Different Staff Groupings

Personnel Category	Salary Paid ($)	Hourly pay rate ($) (from local mental health pay scales)	Hours spent in treatment-related activities per month	Value of staff time (Hourly Pay Rate × Hours Spent)
MD, JD, CPA	1,462	45.00	32.5	1,462
PhD	849	15.67	50.9	798
MA	2,706	7.78	829.3	6,452
BA	2,972	7.66	1,785.2	13,675
Paraprofessional	0	5.53	532.3	2,943
Undergraduate	0	1.70	699.4	1,189
Other (includes clients' parents)	0	2.00	297.0	594
Total	7,988			27,112

Note. From *Improving Effectiveness and Reducing Costs in Mental Health* (p. 52) by B. T. Yates. 1980. Springfield, IL: Charles C Thomas. Copyright 1980 by Charles C Thomas. Reprinted by permission. MD = doctor of medicine (medical degree); JD = doctor of law (law degree); CPA = certified public accountant; PhD = doctor of philosophy; MA = master of arts; BA = bachelor of arts.

BELIEFS ABOUT TREATMENT TECHNIQUES VERSUS TREATMENT DELIVERY SYSTEMS

"It's Not the Medium; It's the Message"

We all too often hope that the innovative psychological techniques that are developed and, it is hoped, that others adopt will be so powerful that they can overcome barriers to the delivery of the techniques. Little research has been conducted on either (a) the way in which the procedures for applying those techniques to specific individuals transmit the full impact of these well-investigated techniques or (b) how much these different delivery systems cost. Research on how different delivery media may affect the costs and effectiveness of therapeutic "messages" can be revealing. For example, Yates (1978) contrasted a rigorously structured treatment program that used state-of-the-art techniques for obesity reduction to an eclectic commercial weight loss program. Both programs generated approximately the same outcomes: an average 30% reduction in excess adipose tissue. The average cost per percent reduction in obesity was $44.60 in the state-of-the-art program and $3 in the commercial program.

It can be argued that the state-of-the-art program spared no expense in implementing what had been hoped to be techniques of superior effectiveness and that this is justified when trying to translate basic research and theory into clinical practice. Certainly, more highly paid personnel were involved in the more expensive program. Also, the incentives under which the commercial program functioned were different from those governing the state-of-the-art program: Cost was something to be minimized in the commercial program, whereas superior effectiveness was the goal in the other program. Nonetheless, this study points out the impact that delivery systems can have on treatment effectiveness and costs. It illustrates what may be the case in much of psychology: There may be little or no substantial difference in effectiveness when different treatment technologies are delivered in clinical settings, but the systems used to deliver the new or old technology certainly can make a difference in the costs of treatment.

"More is Better"

A major assumption about the delivery of treatment services that probably creates unnecessary expenditures of time and energy by therapists and clients alike is that adding another technique to the treatment "stew" will improve outcome. It is understood, of course, that those techniques must be compatible with others used in treatment and that they have to be part of a coherent program of treatment. However, enthusiasm to provide the best treatment to the client may not only lead to unnecessary expense but also evoke psychology processes that actually diminish treatment outcomes.

For example, in a nine-condition treatment outcome study on a program developed by Yates (1987), it was found that adding a cognitive component or an exercise component to a diet component produced no more weight loss than the diet component alone. Exercise and cognitive components alone and in combination produced no significant weight loss. If these findings are considered generalizable, the common inclusion of cognitive and exercise components in weight loss programs seems unjustified. In fact, Yates' clients in the (a) diet + cognitive, (b) diet + exercise, and (c) diet + cognitive + exercise conditions spent substantially more time in program-related activities than did diet-only clients (see Table 2) to no apparent effect. A bibliotherapy condition, which involved no therapist contact, produced weight loss that was slightly but not significantly greater than the weight loss produced by the diet condition.

"Clients Have to Pay for Therapy for It to Work"

It is commonly believed that the more clients pay for treatment, the more benefit they will gain from it, although empirical investigations provide little support for this assumption (e.g., DeMuth & Kamis, 1980). It still can be maintained, however, that the outcomes of therapy may be better if clients struggle with treatment or if they devote more time or other personal resources to it. This also does not seem to be the case always.

Returning to the Yates (1987) study, an analysis of client perceptions of

TABLE 2
Cost and Effectiveness of Alternative Combinations
of Obesity Treatments

Treatment Component Combination	n	Median Weight Reduction Index (essentially % excess weight lost)[a]	Median no. of minutes spent by clients per day in treatment-related activities
Cognitive therapy	10	1.7	40
Diet	12	15.9[b]	13
Exercise	11	0.0	104
Cognitive therapy + diet	13	17.1[b]	36
Cognitive therapy + exercise	14	2.6	93
Diet + exercise	14	2.7	73
Cognitive therapy + diet + exercise	12	10.2[b]	128
Bibliotherapy + self-monitoring only[c]	12	4.5	51
Bibliotherapy only[d]	10	20.0[b]	70

Note. Adapted from "Cognitive vs. Diet vs. Exercise Components in Obesity Bibliotherapy: Effectiveness as a Function of Psychological Benefits Versus Psychological Costs" by B. T. Yates, 1987, *The Southern Psychologist, 3,* p. 38. Clients in all but the bibliotherapy + self-monitoring only condition and bibliotherapy only condition were reinforced by deposit return for the attainment of (a) self-monitoring goals and (b) change goals for the component or combination listed.
[a] Compare with the findings of Wilson (1978). [b] Percentages from weight-loss-producing conditions that Mann-Whitney *U* tests showed to differ significantly as a group from all other conditions. However, these conditions did not differ significantly among themselves. Dropouts were included in analyses and were given the last weight reported. [c] Clients in this condition were not reinforced by deposit return to achieving goals for completion of changes in diet, exercise, and analyses of cognitive self-statements. Only attainment of self-monitoring goals and attendance at mid- and posttreatment weighings were required for deposit return. [d] Clients in this condition were reinforced by deposit return solely for attending mid-and posttreatment weighings.

the costs of treatment to clients showed that the treatment for which clients reported spending the least amount of time (diet, with an average of 13 min/ week) was not significantly different in outcome from conditions that inspired clients to devote significantly more time to treatment (see Table 2). Additional analyses showed that outcomes were highest in conditions that clients perceived to be cost beneficial (i.e., for which psychological benefits exceeded psychological costs).

Throughout the 10-week program, clients reported two costs (ratings of treatment difficulty on 10-point Likert scales and minutes spent in treatment-related activities) and two benefits (usefulness of and satisfaction with treatment, each rated on 10-point scales). Subjects seemed to carry out the suggested activities more in treatment conditions that seemed to offer more value, in terms of outcomes, than they required in terms of resources from the client.

Subject compliance with the treatment regimen may be related to subjects' perceptions of the benefits of treatment *relative* to the "hassle" and time costs required. Ratios were calculated for each subject to contrast psychological benefits to psychological costs. *Each* of the four possible benefit/cost ratios were significantly higher for the weight loss producing conditions . . . for ratios of satisfaction/difficulty, usefulness/difficulty, satisfaction/time, and usefulness/time. (Yates, 1987, p. 39)

Conditions that did not produce weight loss were viewed as having psychological costs that were not exceeded by psychological benefits: "The median benefit/cost ratios for all other [non-weight-loss producing] conditions were 1.0 for both satisfaction and usefulness versus difficulty . . ." (Yates, 1987, p. 39).

These findings suggest another observation about the importance of considering costs as well as outcomes in treatment. It is possible that most psychological treatments would achieve respectable outcomes if clients complied with the suggested regimen. Compliance is, however, a function of many variables. Among these may be the cost–benefit of the treatment as perceived by the client. Evaluations of psychological treatments may find that substantial amounts of previously unexplained variance in treatment outcomes can be explained by treatment costs and benefits, as they were seen by treatment recipients.

BELIEFS AND CONCERNS ABOUT COST-EFFECTIVENESS ANALYSIS AND COST–BENEFIT ANALYSIS

The study discussed earlier illustrates a simple, even simplistic, method of analyzing the relationships between outcomes achieved (benefits, as perceived by the client, in this case) and resources consumed (costs, again as perceived by the client). Just dividing outcome by cost does not a cost–benefit or cost-effectiveness analysis make, however. The methodologies of cost-effectiveness analysis and cost–benefit analysis are complex (cf. Apsler & Harding, 1991). A description of these methods is beyond the scope of this article, and a variety of sources exist for more information (e.g., Levin, 1975, 1980; Newman & Sorensen, 1985; Rufener et al., 1977; Thompson, 1980; Warner, Luce, & Hellinger, 1983; Yates, 1980, 1985). There is, or at least can be, more to cost-effectiveness analysis and cost–benefit analysis than a few ratios or net benefit figures, also.

"Cost–Benefit Analysis Reduces Everything to the Lowest Common Denominator: Money"

Cost–benefit analysis does not require the use of any monetary figures. All that it requires is that the outcomes of services provided and the resources consumed to make those services possible be measured in the same units. The benefit/cost ratios computed earlier for client ratings of the usefulness of treatment versus its difficulty used no monetary units. Monetary units are simply the most common units in which resource data are available in most psychological service systems, and they allow resource expenditure information about staff, space, supplies, and equipment to be pooled for more global analyses.

"Cost–Benefit Analysis of Psychological Services Ignores the Most Important Outcomes"

Benefit is often interpreted as implying that one must show a profit or some other type of positive income flow. Although many psychologists seem adverse to placing a dollar sign on the results of their services, substantial increases in client income and corporate earnings have been shown to result from many types of psychological service (Jones & Vischi, 1979; Manuso, 1978; Silkman, Kelley, & Wolf, 1983). Furthermore, some of the most powerful arguments in favor of including psychological treatments in corporate health care packages have been the savings produced in health care costs. Cummings (1977) showed that one to four sessions of therapy returned $2.59, on the average, for every dollar spent on therapy. In general, many outcomes of psychological services are indeed nonmonetary, but those that are can be shown to often exceed the monetary value of resources consumed at levels of profit attractive to government agencies and most businesses (cf. Cummings & Follette, 1968; Jones & Vischi, 1979; Rufener et al., 1977; Yates, 1984). These findings also may allay the fears of those who were opposed to cost–benefit analysis largely because they feared that psychological therapies would not be cost beneficial according to quantitative analyses.

"To Be Meaningful, Cost-Effectiveness Analysis Requires Comparisons to Other Treatments"

Treatments that produce outcomes that are difficult to measure in the same units as those used to value resources (e.g., money) still can be assessed for the amount of resources consumed in cost-effectiveness analysis. In cost-effectiveness analysis, the outcomes of treatment are measured in whatever units are appropriate, whereas the value of resources consumed can be measured in different (e.g., monetary) units. Although a single cost-effectiveness ratio does not provide quite as much information about the potential return on investment as that yielded by a ratio of benefits to costs, the cost per outcome can be compared between treatments. Moreover, some people perceive some value in single ratios of cost to effectiveness with no explicit comparison (e.g., the cost per pound lost or average cost per former drug abuser not receded for 10 years).

"Cost–Benefit Analysis and Cost-Effectiveness Analysis Are Just Rationalizations for Funding Cuts"

In general, program evaluation can be either summative or formative (Scriven, 1967). *Summative* evaluations are designed to yield judgments about the worth of programs, and any evaluation—including cost–benefit analysis and cost-effectiveness analysis—can be summative. Inclusion of cost data in an evaluation may indeed increase the attention that a summative evaluation receives. *Formative* evaluations are attempts to understand the program as it currently operates, so that it can be improved. Formative cost-effectiveness analysis and cost–benefit analysis are just as possible as other forms of program evaluation that ignore costs. They may contribute more to program development than other forms of program evaluation because they consider financial and other resource-oriented aspects of the context in which the program functions.

I and other researchers have attempted to conduct cost-effectiveness and cost–benefit analyses that go beyond descriptions of cost/effectiveness ratios to more complex descriptions of relationships between costs and outcomes. Even simple graphs of the outcomes of one or more programs against costs can describe some of the complexity of cost–outcome relationships (cf. Siegert & Yates, 1980; Yates, 1978, 1985). More complex, mathematical models can be constructed to depict relationships between costs and outcomes and among resources spent, treatment procedures implemented, psychological changes achieved, and significant behavioral and lifestyle goals attained (cf. Yates, 1980). By incorporating information on budgets and other resource constraints into these models, researchers may be able to systematically determine how to maximize treatment outcomes while keeping within budgets. The more complete treatment models that are possible when cost data are combined with process and outcome data may increase the ability to deliver the best services to the most clients within the limits imposed by society and economy.

POSSIBLE IMPEDIMENTS TO COST-EFFECTIVENESS ANALYSIS AND COST–BENEFIT ANALYSIS

Assessing, analyzing, reporting, and using data on costs, cost-effectiveness, and cost–benefit can be seen as four stages of incorporating information about the resources consumed in clinical efforts into research on those efforts. Some studies already report or discuss costs along with effectiveness or benefits, but growth of this literature seems to have stalled. A search was conducted of the American Psychological Association's Psychological Abstracts Information Services (PsycINFO) database from 1967 through 1991 (the last full year accessible at the time this article was written). The search

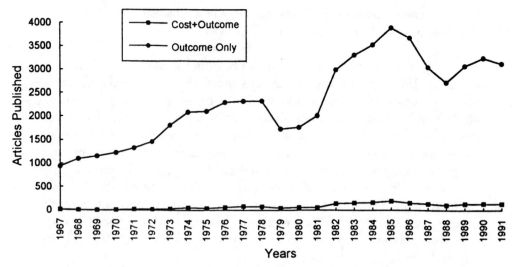

Figure 2. Change over a quarter of a century in articles in the *PsycINFO* database that include data on or discussion of cost, as well as effectiveness or benefit.

terms used were "((cost and effective\$) or (cost and benefi\$)) and 19__.yr.," where "\$" was the wildcard used by the database service for one or more characters. The search for "effectiveness" or "benefits" articles simply omitted the "cost and" phrases. The terms *cost-effectiveness* and *cost–benefit analysis* could not be used directly, as these do not seem to be recognized search terms in PsycINFO. Figure 2 shows how few even these increased publications are, in relation to publications concerned with treatment effectiveness or benefits. Following a marked increase in both outcome-only publications and cost-plus-outcome publications in the mid-1980s, there has been a decline and subsequent plateauing of the number of both types. Figure 3 shows that this percentage has grown slowly but steadily over a quarter of a century from less than 1% in the late 1960s to slightly over 5% in the mid-1980s, settling in at about 4.5% for the past few years.

Of course, a variety of topics other than the outcome and cost outcome of therapy are addressed in some of the articles entered into these counts. Also, the introduction of keywords related to cost, cost-effectiveness, and cost–benefit in the abstracting process also may affect the number of citations retrieved in literature searches such as this. Nevertheless, the proportion of such articles is likely to be constant across years. These data suggest that interest in cost, cost-effectiveness analysis, and cost–benefit analysis continues, but that only a small portion of the research and discussion on treatment outcome includes any mention of treatment cost or the relationship between outcome and cost. The inclusion of cost and related information in research and discussion articles occurs in a small and no longer growing percent of those articles.

Why? Perhaps a cost-outcome analysis of these findings about cost- and outcome-oriented publications would be illuminating. Any effort requires the expenditure of resources: Research and article preparation certainly consume time and money. Adding to therapy outcome studies another class of variables to assess (i.e., costs and several more stages of analysis such as cost-effectiveness and cost–benefit analyses) requires additional time from researchers and support staff. In addition, many researchers would need to be familiar with the nuances of cost assessment, cost-effectiveness analysis, and cost–benefit analysis to routinely use these in addition to standard analyses. The costs of these new endeavors are considerable, at least relative to a lack of increment in understanding or increased possibility of publication or funding that many researchers perceive. In this article, I have tried to change these perceptions; it is not enough.

One way in which cost-effectiveness and cost–benefit analyses could be encouraged is for reviewers and editors to make some reporting of costs and of these analyses a recommended part of articles to be submitted to journals. Government funders use similar or more absolute contingencies to promote research into specific topics, on certain subject populations, or using particular methods, when announcing grant or contract programs. A similar call for inclusion of cost–benefit analysis was made in the public health arena several decades ago by Deniston, Rosenstock, and Getting (1968). Another important strategy for encouraging these analyses is to include these topics in training programs in clinical research and texts (e.g., see Kazdin, 1980, 1992).

Finally, economic and political disincentives for cost-effectiveness analysis, cost–benefit analysis, and program evaluation in general need to be

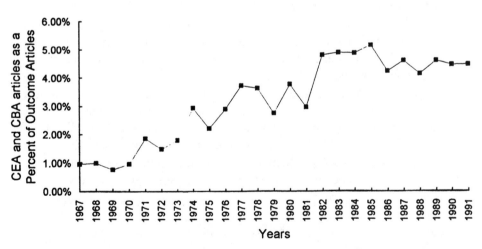

Figure 3. Articles in the PsycINFO database that include data on or discussion of cost as well as effectiveness of benefit. CEA = cost-effectiveness analysis. CBA = cost-benefit analysis.

eliminated from the arena of funding policy and decision making. Mental health administrators who may otherwise conduct or support cost-effectiveness analysis and cost–benefit analysis may not do so because they believe, based on previous personal or vicarious experience, that (a) data collected on program costs, procedures, and outcomes will be used against the program; (b) devoting resources to data collection, analysis, and feedback will result in funding cuts because "if your program can afford to do research, we can trim it and not hurt treatment"; and (c) programs that reduce their cost per client will have their funding reduced in proportion to their efficiency. To researchers, these beliefs may seem outlandish, but for many administrators and evaluators, these statements are all too real too often.

TOWARD DISCUSSIONS, DEBATES, AND DEVELOPMENT OF A NEW MODEL OF CLINICAL RESEARCH

There are many more misconceptions of research that considers costs as well as outcomes. I am certain that I still have much to learn about the possible negative consequences of examining costs as closely as outcomes (cf. Book, 1991). I hope that this article fosters an active dialogue among scientists, managers, and practitioners regarding how information about resources consumed, as well as outcomes produced, is used in formulating policy and making administrative and therapeutic decisions. The tensions that occasionally have pushed such discussions into the foreground in the past have not dissipated. Financial crises and limits on (and decrements in) public spending are, if anything, more common now. Competition among the mental health professions is considerable and will grow as funding diminishes. Divisions between scientists and practitioners may be widening further. My personal hope is that out of the vigorous discussions that usually occur when costs as well as outcomes are evaluated will come a revision of the scientist–practitioner model of practice and training. This much-debated model may fail too often because there is too strained and meager a connection between scientific research and clinical practice. Perhaps what's missing is a third component: the research-oriented as well as clinically sensitive management of the provision of psychological services (DeMuth, Yates, & Coates, 1984). By examining, discussing, and better understanding costs, cost-effectiveness, and cost–benefit in addition to effectiveness, perhaps we will find it easier to become better scientist–manager–practitioners.

REFERENCES

Apsler, R., & Harding, W. M. (1991). Cost-effectiveness analysis of drug abuse treatment: Current status and recommendations for future research. *NIDA Drug*

Abuse Services Research Series No. 1, 58–81 (DHHS Publication No. ADM 91-17777). Washington, DC: National Institute on Drug Abuse.

Bandura, A., Blanchard, E. B., & Ritter, B. (1969). Relative efficacy of desensitization and modeling approaches for inducing behavioral, affective, and attitudinal changes. *Journal of Personality and Social Psychology, 13,* 173–199.

Book, H. E. (1991). Is empathy cost efficient? *American Journal of Psychotherapy, 45,* 21–30.

Carter, D. E., & Newman, F. L. (1976). *A client-oriented system of mental health service delivery and program management: A workbook and guide* (DHEW Publication No. ADM 76-307). Rockville, MD: National Institute of Mental Health.

Cummings, N. A. (1977). Prolonged (ideal) versus short-term (realistic) psychotherapy. *Professional Psychology: Research and Practice, 8,* 491–501.

Cummings, N. A., & Follette, W. T. (1968). Psychiatric services and medical utilization in a prepaid health plan setting. *Medical Care, 5,* 31–41.

DeMuth, N. M., & Kamis, E. (1980). Fees and therapy: Clarification of the relationship of payment source to service utilization. *Journal of Consulting and Clinical Psychology, 48,* 793–795.

DeMuth, N. M., Yates, B. T., & Coates, T. C. (1984). Psychologists as managers: Overcoming old guilts and accessing innovative pathways for enhanced skills. *Professional Psychology: Research and Practice, 15,* 758–768.

Deniston, O. L., Rosenstock, I. M., & Getting, V. A. (1968). Evaluation of program effectiveness. *Public Health Reports, 83,* 323–335.

Fishman, D. B. (1975). Development of a generic cost-effectiveness methodology for evaluating patient services of a community mental health center. In J. Zusman & C. R. Wurster (Eds.), *Evaluation in alcohol, drug abuse, and mental health service programs* (pp. 139–159). Lexington, MA: Heath.

Hayashida, M., Alterman, A. I., McLellan, A. T., O'Brien, C. P., Purtill, J. J., Volricelli, J. R., Raphaelson, A. H., & Hall, C. P. (1989). Comparative effectiveness and costs of inpatient and outpatient detoxification of patients with mild-to-moderate alcohol withdrawal syndrome. *New England Journal of Medicine, 320,* 358–365.

Howard, K. I., Kopta, S. M., Krause, M. S., & Orlinsky, D. E. (1986). The dose–effect relationship in psychotherapy. *American Psychologist, 41,* 159–164.

Jones, K. R., & Vischi, T. R. (1979). Impact of alcohol, drug abuse, and mental health treatment on medical care utilization: A review of the research literature. *Medical Care, 17,* (Suppl.).

Karon, B. P., & VandenBos, G. R. (1976). Cost/benefit analysis: Psychologist versus psychiatrist for schizophrenics. *Professional Psychology: Research and Practice, 7,* 107–111.

Kazdin, A. E. (1980). *Research design in clinical psychology.* New York: Harper & Row.

Kazdin, A. E. (1992). *Research design in clinical psychology.* (2nd ed.). New York: Macmillan.

Levin, H. M. (1975). Cost-effectiveness analysis in evaluation research. In M. Guttentag & E. L. Struening (Eds.), *Handbook of evaluation research* (Vol. 2, pp. 89–122). Beverly Hills, CA: Sage.

Levin, H. M. (1980). *Cost-effectiveness: A primer*. Beverly Hills, CA: Sage.

Manuso, J. (1978). Testimony to the President's Commission on Mental Health, Panel on Cost and Financing. *Report of the President's Commission on Mental Health: Appendix* (Vol. 2, p. 512). Washington, DC: U.S. Government Printing Office.

McGuire, T. G. (1980). Markets for psychotherapy. In G. VandenBos (Ed.), *Psychotherapy: Practice, research, and policy* (pp. 187–245). Beverly Hills, CA: Sage.

McGuire, T. (1989). Outpatient benefits for mental health services in Medicare: Alignment with the private sector? *American Psychologist, 44*, 818–824.

Newman, F. L., & Howard, K. I. (1986). Therapeutic effort, treatment outcome, and national health policy. *American Psychologist, 41*, 181–187.

Newman, F. L., & Sorensen, J. E. (1985). *Integrated clinical and fiscal management in mental health: A guidebook*. Norwood, NJ: Ablex.

Rufener, B. L., Rachal, J. V., & Cruze, A. M. (1977). *Management effectiveness measures for NIDA drug abuse treatment programs* (GPO Stock No. 017-024-00577-1). Washington, DC: U.S. Government Printing Office.

Scriven, M. (1967). The methodology of evaluation. In R. W. Tyler, R. M. Gagne, & M. Scriven (Eds.), *Perspectives of curriculum evaluation* (pp. 39–83). Chicago: Rand-McNally.

Siegert, F. E., & Yates, B. T. (1980). Behavioral child-management cost-effectiveness: A comparison of individual in-office, individual in-home, and group delivery systems. *Evaluation & the Health Professions, 3*, 123–152.

Silkman, R., Kelley, J. M., & Wolf, W. C. (1983). An evaluation of two preemployment services: Impact on employment and earnings of disadvantaged youths. *Evaluation Review, 7*, 467–496.

Thompson, M. S. (1980). *Benefit–cost analysis for program evaluation*. Beverly Hills, CA: Sage.

Warner, K. E., Luce, B. R., & Hellinger, F. J. (1983). Cost–benefit and cost-effectiveness analysis in health care. *Inquiry, 20*, 193.

Weisbrod, B. A. (1983). A guide to benefit–cost analysis, as seen through a controlled experiment in treating the mentally ill. *Journal of Health Politics, Policy and Law, 6*, 808–845.

Wilson, G. T. (1978). Methodological considerations in treatment outcome research on obesity. *Journal of Consulting and Clinical Psychology, 46*, 687–702.

Yates, B. T. (1978). Improving the cost-effectiveness of obesity programs: Reducing the cost per pound. *International Journal of Obesity, 2*, 377–387.

Yates, B. T. (1980). *Improving effectiveness and reducing costs in mental health*. Springfield, IL: Charles C. Thomas.

Yates, B. T. (1984). How psychology can improve the effectiveness and reduce the costs of health services. *Psychotherapy, 21*, 439–451.

Yates, B. T. (1985). Cost-effectiveness analysis and cost–benefit analysis: An introduction. *Behavioral Assessment, 7,* 207–234.

Yates, B. T. (1987). Cognitive vs. diet vs. exercise components in obesity bibliotherapy: Effectiveness as a function of psychological benefits versus psychological costs. *The Southern Psychologist, 3,* 35–40.

Yates, B. T., Haven, W. G., & Thoresen, C. E. (1979). Cost-effectiveness analysis at Learning House: How much change for how much money? In J. S. Stumphauzer (Ed.), *Progress in behavior therapy with delinquents* (pp. 186–222). Springfield, IL: Charles C. Thomas.

Yates, B. T., & Newman, F. L. (1980a). Approaches to cost-effectiveness and cost–benefit analysis of psychotherapy. In G. VandenBos (Ed.), *Psychotherapy: Practice, research, and policy* (p. 103–162). Beverly Hills, CA: Sage.

Yates, B. T., & Newman, F. L. (1980b). Findings of cost-effectiveness and cost–benefit analysis of psychotherapy. In G. VandenBos (Ed.), *Psychotherapy: Practice, research, and policy* (pp. 163–185). Beverly Hills, CA: Sage.

VI

ETHICS IN RESEARCH

Psychological research raises a number of ethical issues and dilemmas. Two broad domains capture the range of issues and responsibilities of the investigator. First, the investigator has multiple responsibilities to the research participants. Key among these are the protection of participant rights and confidentiality. Conditions to which the participant is exposed (e.g., measures, interventions, experimental manipulations), information that may be presented or withheld, and use of the results all reflect domains in which a research participant is in some way vulnerable. Apart from the procedures of the investigation, how the information is used also can have adverse consequences for groups of subjects. Scientific findings, particularly those that study human functioning in context (e.g., different cultural groups), are not ethically neutral, and many studies may have adverse consequences if they are considered to reflect deficiencies or untoward characteristics of groups of individuals (e.g., as a function of age, gender, ethnicity). These are some of the salient ethical issues raised in relation to subjects, their treatment, and use of the information that they provide. Second, the investigator has multiple responsibilities to the profession, science, and society at large. These pertain to obligations about maintaining the integrity of the research, reporting information accurately and honestly, sharing information, and ensuring that one's work is open to scrutiny. Violations of these obligations have been evident in cases of fraud, fabrication of data, and plagiarism that undermine the integrity of scientific research and public confidence (see

Miller & Hersen, 1992). Addressing these matters explicitly in the training of researchers is an important priority (National Academy of Sciences, 1989).

Psychologists assume many roles in performing their professional activities (e.g., consultant to the courts, psychotherapist, academic), and these roles raise diverse ethical issues and responsibilities. The articles in this section pertain primarily to those ethical issues and considerations that arise in the context of research with human participants. Ethical issues in other contexts (e.g., animal research, clinical practice, consultation with the courts) are no less significant in terms of professional responsibilities, but they are beyond the purview of this section.

GUIDELINES AND CODES

The first article in this section consists of the Ethical Principles of Psychologists and Code of Conduct, a set of professional standards, principles, and recommendations to guide research, practice, consultation, and other activities related to execution of the profession. The guidelines are revised periodically to make refinements, to address emergent issues, and to handle the expanding roles of psychologists in daily life (e.g., litigation, consultation). The way the guidelines are formulated emphasizes the investigator's responsibilities toward individuals who participate in research and toward the scientific enterprise. The full set of professional guidelines rather than those specific to research are provided here because they are critically important in defining what it means to be a psychologist and the types of activities that are required. Although issues that tend to be specific to research can be identified (e.g., informed consent, use of deception; see Section 6.06 to 6.26), the ethical responsibilities associated with research cannot be divorced from more general principles and practices having to do with integrity and responsibility of the investigator and concern for the welfare of others (see the Introduction to Section 2.10). Thus, mastery of the letter and spirit of the ethical principles and codes is important.

General principles to guide behavior are presented at the beginning of the ethical code and serve as an overarching context to address a broad set of circumstances that may not be easily anticipated. Critical to the ethical codes is attention to the decision-making process. Investigators cannot be expected to be the arbiters of critical issues in which they may have a vested interest. Thus, they are encouraged to seek the input of colleagues to address ethically sensitive issues. In addition, more formal procedures for evaluating one's research are used to supplement ethical codes. Review committees in universities and research institutions are intended to evaluate research from the perspective of ethical issues and subject rights.

In the second article, Joan Sieber raises questions about the limits of the APA ethical codes, that is, the extent to which they provide useful guidelines for the researcher. Asking researchers to be ethical and to follow general principles may not be sufficient to guide researchers, to protect subject rights, and to ensure that standards of scientific competence and integrity are met on a day-to-day basis. Sieber discusses the ethical codes in the context of different objectives, namely, to educate the researcher, to guide practices in research, and to provide standards to evaluate and censure unacceptable behavior. Research that focuses on value-complex and sensitive topics (e.g., marital rape, AIDS screening) or that focuses on special populations (e.g., infants, children, the elderly, mentally ill individuals) requires additional sensitivities and provisions. For example, many populations cannot provide consent on their own behalf, and obtaining consent from others raises unique obstacles. Special issues pertinent to clinical research are highlighted in the article along with recommendations for improving the existing codes.

The next article, from the American Psychological Association Committee on Standards in Research, was prepared by Peter David Blanck, Alan Bellack, Ralph Rosnow, Mary Jane Rotheram-Borus, and Nina Schooler. The committee advises APA on policy and ethical issues. Three issues are addressed: confidentiality, debriefing, and the use of volunteer subjects. The article is included here because it raises ethical issues in two contexts, protection of participant rights and the implications of these protections for the design of studies and the findings that they yield. For example, selecting volunteers to participate is critically important to ensure that there has been no coercion of the participants and to protect their individual rights. Yet, what are the implications of selecting volunteers for the conclusions that are reached about substantive questions that guide research? For each issue, the authors discuss the balance of ethical, moral, and scientific values and how studies can be designed to protect the subjects and achieve the goals of the researcher. Several examples are drawn from clinical research.

SPECIAL TOPICS AND ISSUES

In addition to ethical codes, the advice of colleagues, and (one hopes) sound judgment, the ethical and scientific standards of research are also guided and evaluated by Institutional Review Boards (IRBs). An IRB is a group or committee within a university or institution that is formed to evaluate research proposals and their ethical merit. Although emphasis is placed on procedures and assurances to protect the subjects, IRBs also evaluate the design of studies to the extent that members (researchers drawn from many disciplines) can do so. The technical merit of the research proposal is relevant to ethical concerns. The rationale for evaluating the study is that if the investigation is not designed well, there is no point to subjecting the participant to any risk or inconvenience or to use governmental, institutional, or other resources.

IRBs consider many different types of research (e.g., organ transplant, fertilization, cloning, psychotherapy, eyelid conditioning). Consequently, within a university, different committees may be constituted to evaluate different types of research on the basis of the level of risk to which subjects will be exposed. It is important to be familiar with the IRB, its functions, and challenges. The investigator is required to comply with practices that govern research and to understand how these practices are designed to protect subjects. The next article, like the previous article, was prepared by the Committee on Standards in Research; the authors are Ralph Rosnow, Mary Jane Rotheram-Borus, Stephen Ceci, Peter David Blanck, and Gerald Koocher. The article discusses the development of the IRB, the responsibilities in protecting subject rights, and ethical dilemmas that emerge in evaluating risks and benefits.

Ethical issues in research extend beyond those related to the protection of participants. Several ethical issues pertain to responsibilities of the investigator to one's colleagues, the profession, and science more generally. Included are issues such as fraud, deception, allocation of credit for ideas and research efforts of one's collaborators, sharing of materials, and others (National Academy of Sciences, 1989). Fraud in science, including the fabrication and misreporting of data, is the most flagrant abridgment of ethical responsibilities of the investigator. Fraud can have multiple consequences by misrepresenting the findings in a particular area, jeopardizing public safety, and undermining confidence in research. Public safety is potentially jeopardized when the results of studies of the cause or treatment of disease (e.g., leukemia, heart disease) are fabricated and decisions may follow that affect the care of individuals. It is no consolation that fraud is considered to be quite rare in relation to the number of studies that are completed.

Professional guidelines convey explicitly that misconduct in its many forms violate professional codes of conduct. In addition, misconduct can involve criminal activity (e.g., misappropriation of federal funds, damage or harm to others). Sanctions and methods of evaluating misconduct have emerged to provide due process for both the accused and the accuser. The National Institutes of Health (NIH), which funds a great deal of research, have developed guidelines and procedures to handle allegations of misconduct to address both ethical and legal issues (e.g., misappropriation of funds) that such allegations may reflect. The article by Mary Miers highlights a range of concerns that emerge in relation to misconduct and how the NIH has dealt with allegations of fraud. Since this article was written, policies and procedures have continued to evolve to address competing interests. On the one hand, procedures are needed to investigate allegations of misconduct and to pursue appropriate sanctions and sources of punishment. On the other hand, safeguards are needed to protect investigators who are falsely accused or who have made the accusations (e.g., frivolous or malicious allegations). The article conveys several considerations involved in achieving balance in investigating misconduct.

Allocation of credit in research is one area of scientific misconduct and raises significant ethical issues and often serves as a source of misery among investigators. Allocation of credit includes two major issues: (a) the failure to acknowledge one's sources or the direct use and copying of someone else's material without providing credit or acknowledgment (plagiarism) and (b) the division of credit among collaborators in research and published reports of that research. The misconduct that plagiarism represents is generally brought to the attention of students early in their education; the lesson is clear, namely, one is to acknowledge all sources of information and as a general guideline, when in doubt, recognize the sources of one's ideas and prior work. In general, few cases of plagiarism emerge, and sanctions can be severe.

There is another issue related to allocation of credit where guidelines are less clear and where sanctions are rarely invoked. Research projects are often collaborative; they involve multiple investigators and a team of persons who have responsibility of varying types and in varying degrees for the completion of the study. The different components of research and responsibilities from idea to the final published report are numerous. Allocation of credit emerges in deciding whom to list as authors on a research article, the order in which they are to appear, the relation between junior and senior scientists or faculty and students, and the different roles and contributions that affect authorship. The problems of allocation of credit are exacerbated by differences in status and power among the collaborators. There are no clear guidelines regarding authorship, and the topic remains undiscussed in most training programs.

In the article by Mark Fine and Lawrence Kurdek, the issues related to allocation of authorship credit and order are elaborated. The context is in collaborations between faculty and student, which is special in the sense that students can be involved in all facets of the study and indeed graduate students are often full collaborators, colleagues, or the primary investigators for a given project in their advisor's laboratory. In this article, the authors convey how allocation of credit and authorship relate specifically to the Ethical Principles of Psychologists and Code of Conduct. Hypothetical cases are provided to convey different scenarios in which allocation of credit and authorship raise problems. A very special feature of the article are the recommendations for determining authorship and order of authorship. The article discusses authorship in the context of ethical issues. The topic of publishing and communication of research findings is taken up in the next section.

GUIDELINES AND CODES

29

ETHICAL PRINCIPLES OF PSYCHOLOGISTS AND CODE OF CONDUCT

AMERICAN PSYCHOLOGICAL ASSOCIATION

CONTENTS

Reprinted from the *American Psychologist, 47,* 1597–1611. Copyright 1992 by the American Psychological Association.

ETHICAL STANDARDS

1. General Standards

2. Evaluation, Assessment, or Intervention

3. Advertising and Other Public Statements

3.01 Definition of Public Statements
3.02 Statements by Others
3.03 Avoidance of False or Deceptive Statements
3.04 Media Presentations
3.05 Testimonials
3.06 In-Person Solicitation

4. Therapy

4.01 Structuring the Relationship
4.02 Informed Consent to Therapy
4.03 Couple and Family Relationships
4.04 Providing Mental Health Services to Those Served by Others
4.05 Sexual Intimacies With Current Patients or Clients
4.06 Therapy With Former Sexual Partners
4.07 Sexual Intimacies With Former Therapy Patients
4.08 Interruption of Services
4.09 Terminating the Professional Relationship

5. Privacy and Confidentiality

5.01 Discussing the Limits of Confidentiality
5.02 Maintaining Confidentiality
5.03 Minimizing Intrusions on Privacy
5.04 Maintenance of Records
5.05 Disclosures
5.06 Consultations
5.07 Confidential Information in Databases
5.08 Use of Confidential Information for Didactic or Other Purposes
5.09 Preserving Records and Data
5.10 Ownership of Records and Data
5.11 Withholding Records for Nonpayment

6. Teaching, Training Supervision, Research, and Publishing

6.01 Design of Education and Training Programs
6.02 Descriptions of Education and Training Programs
6.03 Accuracy and Objectivity in Teaching
6.04 Limitation on Teaching
6.05 Assessing Student and Supervisee Performance
6.06 Planning Research
6.07 Responsibility
6.08 Compliance With Law and Standards
6.09 Institutional Approval

INTRODUCTION

The American Psychological Association's (APA's) Ethical Principles of Psychologists and Code of Conduct (hereinafter referred to as the Ethics Code) consists of an Introduction, a Preamble, six General Principles (A–F), and specific Ethical Standards. The Introduction discusses the intent, organization, procedural considerations, and scope of application of the Ethics

Code. The Preamble and General Principles are *aspirational* goals to guide psychologists toward the highest ideals of psychology. Although the Preamble and General Principles are not themselves enforceable rules, they should be considered by psychologists in arriving at an ethical course of action and may be considered by ethics bodies in interpreting the Ethical Standards. The Ethical Standards set forth *enforceable* rules for conduct as psychologists. Most of the Ethical Standards are written broadly, in order to apply to psychologists in varied roles, although the application of an Ethical Standard may vary depending on the context. The Ethical Standards are not exhaustive. The fact that a given conduct is not specifically addressed by the Ethics Code does not mean that it is necessarily either ethical or unethical.

Membership in the APA commits members to adhere to the APA Ethics Code and to the rules and procedures used to implement it. Psychologists and students, whether or not they are APA members, should be aware that the Ethics Code may be applied to them by state psychology boards, courts, or other public bodies.

This Ethics Code applies only to psychologists' work-related activities, that is, activities that are part of the psychologists' scientific and professional functions or that are psychological in nature. It includes the clinical or counseling practice of psychology, research, teaching, supervision of trainees, development of assessment instruments, conducting assessments, educational

This version of the APA Ethics Code was adopted by the American Psychological Association's Council of Representatives during its meeting, August 13 and 16, 1992, and is effective beginning December 1, 1992. Inquiries concerning the substance or interpretation of the APA Ethics Code should be addressed to the Director, Office of Ethics, American Psychological Association, 750 First Street, NE, Washington, DC 20002-4242.

This Code will be used to adjudicate complaints brought concerning alleged conduct occurring on or after the effective date. Complaints regarding conduct occurring prior to the effective date will be adjudicated on the basis of the version of the Code that was in effect at the time the conduct occurred, except that no provisions repealed in June 1989, will be enforced even if an earlier version contains the provision. The Ethics Code will undergo continuing review and study for future revisions; comments on the Code may be sent to the above address.

The APA has previously published its Ethical Standards as follows:

American Psychological Association. (1953). *Ethical standards of psychologists.* Washington, DC: Author.

American Psychological Association. (1958). Standards of ethical behavior for psychologists. *American Psychologist, 13,* 268–271.

American Psychological Association. (1963). Ethical standards of psychologists. *American Psychologist, 18,* 56–60.

American Psychological Association. (1968). Ethical standards of psychologists. *American Psychologist, 23,* 357–361.

American Psychological Association. (1977, March). Ethical standards of psychologists. *APA Monitor,* pp. 22–23.

American Psychological Association. (1979). *Ethical standards of psychologists.* Washington, DC: Author.

American Psychological Association. (1981). Ethical principles of psychologists. *American Psychologist, 36,* 633–638.

American Psychological Association. (1990). Ethical principles of psychologists (Amended June 2, 1989). *American Psychologist, 45,* 390–395.

Request copies of the APA's Ethical Principles of Psychologists and Code of Conduct from the APA Order Department, 750 First Street, NE, Washington, DC 20002-4242, or phone (202) 336-5510.

counseling, organizational consulting, social intervention, administration, and other activities as well. These work-related activities can be distinguished from the purely private conduct of a psychologist, which ordinarily is not within the purview of the Ethics Code.

The Ethics Code is intended to provide standards of professional conduct that can be applied by the APA and by other bodies that choose to adopt them. Whether or not a psychologist has violated the Ethics Code does not by itself determine whether he or she is legally liable in a court action, whether a contract is enforceable, or whether other legal consequences occur. These results are based on legal rather than ethical rules. However, compliance with or violation of the Ethics Code may be admissible as evidence in some legal proceedings, depending on the circumstances.

In the process of making decisions regarding their professional behavior, psychologists must consider this Ethics Code, in addition to applicable laws and psychology board regulations. If the Ethics Code establishes a higher standard of conduct than is required by law, psychologists must meet the higher ethical standard. If the Ethics Code standard appears to conflict with the requirements of law, then psychologists make known their commitment to the Ethics Code and take steps to resolve the conflict in a responsible manner. If neither law nor the Ethics Code resolves an issue, psychologists should consider other professional materials[1] and the dictates of their own conscience, as well as seek consultation with others within the field when this is practical.

The procedures for filing, investigating, and resolving complaints of unethical conduct are described in the current Rules and Procedures of the APA Ethics Committee. The actions that APA may take for violations of the Ethics Code include actions such as reprimand, censure, termination of APA membership, and referral of the matter to other bodies. Complainants who seek remedies such as monetary damages in alleging ethical violations by a psychologist must resort to private negotiation, administrative bodies, or the courts. Actions that violate the Ethics Code may lead to the imposition of sanctions on a psychologist by bodies other than APA, including state psychological associations, other professional groups, psychology boards, other

---

[1] Professional materials that are most helpful in this regard are guidelines and standards that have been adopted or endorsed by professional psychological organizations. Such guidelines and standards, whether adopted by the American Psychological Association (APA) or its Divisions, are not enforceable as such by this Ethics Code, but are of educative value to psychologists, courts, and professional bodies. Such materials include, but are not limited to, the APA's *General Guidelines for Providers of Psychological Services* (1987), *Specialty Guidelines for the Delivery of Services by Clinical Psychologists, Counseling Psychologists, Industrial/Organizational Psychologists, and School Psychologists* (1981), *Guidelines for Computer Based Tests and Interpretations* (1987), *Standards for Educational and Psychological Testing* (1985), *Ethical Principles in the Conduct of Research With Human Participants* (1982), *Guidelines for Ethical Conduct in the Care and Use of Animals* (1986), *Guidelines for Providers of Psychological Services to Ethnic, Linguistic, and Culturally Diverse Populations* (1990), and *Publication Manual of the American Psychological Association* (3rd ed., 1983). Materials not adopted by APA as a whole include the APA Division 41 (Forensic Psychology)/American Psychology–Law Society's *Specialty Guidelines for Forensic Psychologists* (1991).

state or federal agencies, and payors for health services. In addition to actions for violation of the Ethics Code, the APA Bylaws provide that APA may take action against a member after his or her conviction of a felony, expulsion or suspension from an affiliated state psychological association, or suspension or loss of licensure.

PREAMBLE

Psychologists work to develop a valid and reliable body of scientific knowledge based on research. They may apply that knowledge to human behavior in a variety of contexts. In doing so, they perform many roles, such as researcher, educator, diagnostician, therapist, supervisor, consultant, administrator, social interventionist, and expert witness. Their goal is to broaden knowledge of behavior and, where appropriate, to apply it pragmatically to improve the condition of both the individual and society. Psychologists respect the central importance of freedom of inquiry and expression in research, teaching, and publication. They also strive to help the public in developing informed judgments and choices concerning human behavior. This Ethics Code provides a common set of values upon which psychologists build their professional and scientific work.

This Code is intended to provide both the general principles and the decision rules to cover most situations encountered by psychologists. It has as its primary goal the welfare and protection of the individuals and groups with whom psychologists work. It is the individual responsibility of each psychologist to aspire to the highest possible standards of conduct. Psychologists respect and protect human and civil rights, and do not knowingly participate in or condone unfair discriminatory practices.

The development of a dynamic set of ethical standards for a psychologist's work-related conduct requires a personal commitment to a lifelong effort to act ethically; to encourage ethical behavior by students, supervisees, employees, and colleagues, as appropriate; and to consult with others, as needed, concerning ethical problems. Each psychologist supplements, but does not violate, the Ethics Code's values and rules on the basis of guidance drawn from personal values, culture, and experience.

GENERAL PRINCIPLES

Principal A: Competence

Psychologists strive to maintain high standards of competence in their work. They recognize the boundaries of their particular competencies and the limitations of their expertise. They provide only those services and use only those techniques for which they are qualified by education, training, or experience. Psychologists are cognizant of the fact that the competencies required in serving, teaching, and/or studying groups of people vary with the distinctive characteristics of those groups. In those areas in which recognized professional standards do not yet exist, psychologists exercise careful judgment and take appropriate precautions to protect the welfare of those with whom they work. They maintain knowledge of relevant scientific and professional information related to the services they render, and they recognize the need for ongoing education. Psychologists make appropriate use of scientific, professional, technical, and administrative resources.

Principle B: Integrity

Psychologists seek to promote integrity in the science, teaching, and practice of psychology. In these activities psychologists are honest, fair, and respectful of others. In describing or reporting their qualifications, services, products, fees, research, or teaching, they do not make statements that are false, misleading, or deceptive. Psychologists strive to be aware of their own belief systems, values, needs, and limitations and the effect of these on their work. To the extent feasible, they attempt to clarify for relevant parties the roles they are performing and to function appropriately in accordance with those roles. Psychologists avoid improper and potentially harmful dual relationships.

Principle C: Professional and Scientific Responsibility

Psychologists uphold professional standards of conduct, clarify their professional roles and obligations, accept appropriate responsibility for their behavior, and adapt their methods to the needs of different populations. Psychologists consult with, refer to, or cooperate with other professionals and institutions to the extent needed to serve the best interests of their patients, clients, or other recipients of their services. Psychologists' moral standards and conduct are personal matters to the same degree as is true for any other person, except as psychologists' conduct may compromise their professional responsibilities or reduce the public's trust in psychology and psychologists. Psychologists are concerned about the ethical compliance of their colleagues' scientific and professional conduct. When appropriate, they consult with colleagues in order to prevent or avoid unethical conduct.

Principle D: Respect for People's Rights and Dignity

Psychologists accord appropriate respect to the fundamental rights, dignity, and worth of all people. They respect the rights of individuals to privacy, confidentiality, self-determination, and autonomy, mindful that legal and other obligations may lead to inconsistency and conflict with the exercise of these rights. Psychologists are aware of cultural, individual, and role differences, including those due to age, gender, race, ethnicity, national origin, religion, sexual orientation, disability, language, and socioeconomic status. Psychologists try to eliminate the effect on their work of biases based on those factors, and they do not knowingly participate in or condone unfair discriminatory practices.

Principle E: Concern for Others' Welfare

Psychologists seek to contribute to the welfare of those with whom they interact professionally. In their professional actions, psychologists weigh the welfare and rights of their patients or clients, students, supervisees, human research participants, and other affected persons, and the welfare of animal subjects of research. When conflicts occur among psychologists' obligations or concerns, they attempt to resolve these conflicts and to perform their roles in a responsible fashion that avoids or minimizes harm. Psychologists are sensitive to real and ascribed differences in power between themselves and others, and they do not exploit or mislead other people during or after professional relationships.

Principle F: Social Responsibility

Psychologists are aware of their professional and scientific responsibilities to the community and the society in which they work and live. They apply and make public their knowledge of psychology in order to contribute to human welfare. Psychologists are concerned about and work to mitigate the causes of human suffering. When undertaking research, they strive to advance human welfare and the science of psychology. Psychologists try to avoid misuse of their work. Psychologists comply with the law and encourage the development of law and social policy that serve the interests of their patients and clients and the public. They are encouraged to contribute a portion of their professional time for little or no personal advantage.

ETHICAL STANDARDS

1. General Standards

These General Standards are potentially applicable to the professional and scientific activities of all psychologists.

1.01 Applicability of the Ethics Code

The activity of a psychologist subject to the Ethics Code may be reviewed under these Ethical Standards only if the activity is part of his or her work-related functions or the activity is psychological in nature. Personal activities having no connection to or effect on psychological roles are not subject to the Ethics Code.

1.02 Relationship of Ethics and Law

If psychologists' ethical responsibilities conflict with law, psychologists make known their commitment to the Ethics Code and take steps to resolve the conflict in a responsible manner.

1.03 Professional and Scientific Relationship

Psychologists provide diagnostic, therapeutic, teaching, research, supervisory, consultative, or other psychological services only in the context of a defined professional or scientific relationship or role. (See also Standards 2.01, Evaluation, Diagnosis, and Interventions in Professional Context, and 7.02, Forensic Assessments.)

1.04 Boundaries of Competence

(a) Psychologists provide services, teach, and conduct research only within the boundaries of their competence, based on their education, training, supervised experience, or appropriate professional experience.

(b) Psychologists provide services, teach, or conduct research in new areas or involving new techniques only after first undertaking appropriate study, training, supervision, and/or consultation from persons who are competent in those areas or techniques.

(c) In those emerging areas in which generally recognized standards for preparatory training do not yet exist, psychologists nevertheless take reasonable steps to ensure the competence of their work and to protect patients, clients, students, research participants, and others from harm.

1.05 Maintaining Expertise

Psychologists who engage in assessment, therapy, teaching, research, organizational consulting, or other professional activities maintain a reasonable level of awareness of current scientific and professional information in their fields of activity, and undertake ongoing efforts to maintain competence in the skills they use.

1.06 Basis for Scientific and Professional Judgments

Psychologists rely on scientifically and professionally derived knowledge when making scientific or professional judgments or when engaging in scholarly or professional endeavors.

1.07 Describing the Nature and Results of Psychological Services

(a) When psychologists provide assessment, evaluation, treatment, counseling, supervision, teaching, consultation, research, or other psychological services to an individual, a group, or an organization, they provide, using language that is reasonably understandable to the recipient of those services, appropriate information beforehand about the nature of such services and appropriate information later about results and conclusions. (See also Standard 2.09, Explaining Assessment Results.)

(b) If psychologists will be precluded by law or by organizational roles from providing such information to particular individuals or groups, they so inform those individuals or groups at the outset of the service.

1.08 Human Differences

Where differences of age, gender, race, ethnicity, national origin, religion, sexual orientation, disability, language, or socioeconomic status significantly affect psychologists' work concerning particular individuals or groups, psychologists obtain the training, experience, consultation, or supervision necessary to ensure the competence of their services, or they make appropriate referrals.

1.09 Respecting Others

In their work-related activities, psychologists respect the rights of others to hold values, attitudes, and opinions that differ from their own.

1.10 Nondiscrimination

In their work-related activities, psychologists do not engage in unfair discrimination based on age, gender, race, ethnicity, national origin, religion, sexual orientation, disability, socioeconomic status, or any basis proscribed by law.

1.11 Sexual Harassment

(a) Psychologists do not engage in sexual harassment. Sexual harassment is sexual solicitation, physical advances, or verbal or nonverbal conduct that is sexual in nature, that occurs in connection with the psychologist's activities or roles as a psychologist, and that either: (1) is unwelcome, is offensive, or creates a hostile workplace environment, and the psychologist knows or is told this; or (2) is sufficiently severe or intense to be abusive to a reasonable person in the context. Sexual harassment can consist of a single intense or severe act or of multiple persistent or pervasive acts.

(b) Psychologists accord sexual-harassment complainants and respondents dignity and respect. Psychologists do not participate in denying a person academic admittance or advancement, employment, tenure, or promotion, based solely upon their having made, or their being the subject of, sexual-harassment charges. This does not preclude taking action based upon the outcome of such proceedings or consideration of other appropriate information.

1.12 Other Harassment

Psychologists do not knowingly engage in behavior that is harassing or demeaning to persons with whom they interact in their work based on factors such as those persons' age, gender, race, ethnicity, national origin, religion, sexual orientation, disability, language, or socioeconomic status.

1.13 Personal Problems and Conflicts

(a) Psychologists recognize that their personal problems and conflicts may interfere with their effectiveness. Accordingly, they refrain from undertaking an activity when they know or should know that their personal problems are likely to lead to harm to a patient, client, colleague, student, research participant, or other person to whom they may owe a professional or scientific obligation.

(b) In addition, psychologists have an obligation to be alert to signs of, and to obtain assistance for, their personal problems at an early stage, in order to prevent significantly impaired performance.

(c) When psychologists become aware of personal problems that may interfere with their performing work-related duties adequately, they take appropriate measures, such as obtaining professional consultation or assistance, and determine whether they should limit, suspend, or terminate their work-related duties.

1.14 Avoiding Harm

Psychologists take reasonable steps to avoid harming their patients or clients, research participants, students, and others with whom they work, and to minimize harm where it is foreseeable and unavoidable.

1.15 Misuse of Psychologists' Influence

Because psychologists' scientific and professional judgments and actions may affect the lives of others, they are alert to and guard against personal, financial, social, organizational, or political factors that might lead to misuse of their influence.

1.16 Misuse of Psychologists' Work

(a) Psychologists do not participate in activities in which it appears likely that their skills or data will be misused by others, unless corrective mechanisms are available. (See also Standard 7.04, Truthfulness and Candor.)

(b) If psychologists learn of misuse or misrepresentation of their work, they take reasonable steps to correct or minimize the misuse or misrepresentation.

1.17 Multiple Relationships

(a) In many communities and situations, it may not be feasible or reasonable for psychologists to avoid social or other nonprofessional contacts with persons such as patients, clients, students, supervisees, or research participants. Psychologists must always be sensitive to the potential harmful effects of other contacts on their work and on those persons with whom they deal. A psychologist refrains from entering into or promising another personal, scientific, professional, financial, or other relationship with such persons if it appears likely that such a relationship reasonably might impair the psychologist's objectivity or otherwise interfere with the psychologist's effectively performing his or her functions as a psychologist, or might harm or exploit the other party.

(b) Likewise, whenever feasible, a psychologist refrains from taking on professional or scientific obligations when preexisting relationships would create a risk of such harm.

(c) If a psychologist finds that, due to unforeseen factors, a potentially harmful multiple relationship has arisen, the psychologist attempts to resolve it with due regard for the best interests of the affected person and maximal compliance with the Ethics Code.

1.18 Barter (With Patients or Clients)

Psychologists ordinarily refrain from accepting goods, services, or other nonmonetary remuneration from patients or clients in return for psychological services because such arrangements create inherent potential for conflicts, exploitation, and distortion of the professional relationship. A psychologist may participate in bartering *only* if (1) it is not clinically contraindicated, *and* (2) the relationship is not exploitative. (See also Standards 1.17, Multiple Relationships, and 1.25, Fees and Financial Arrangements.)

1.19 Exploitative Relationships

(a) Psychologists do not exploit persons over whom they have supervisory, evaluative, or other authority such as students, supervisees, employees, research participants, and clients or patients. (See also Standards 4.05–4.07 regarding sexual involvement with clients or patients.)

(b) Psychologists do not engage in sexual relationships with students or supervisees in training over whom the psychologist has evaluative or direct authority, because such relationships are so likely to impair judgment or be exploitative.

1.20 Consultations and Referrals

(a) Psychologists arrange for appropriate consultations and referrals based principally on the best interests of their patients or clients, with appropriate consent, and subject to other relevant considerations, including applicable law and contractual obligations. (See also Standards 5.01, Discussing the Limits of Confidentiality, and 5.06, Consultations.)

(b) When indicated and professionally appropriate, psychologists cooperate with other professionals in order to serve their patients or clients effectively and appropriately.

(c) Psychologists' referral practices are consistent with law.

1.21 Third-Party Requests for Services

(a) When a psychologist agrees to provide services to a person or entity at the request of a third party, the psychologist clarifies to the extent feasible, at the outset of the service, the nature of the relationship with each party. This clarification includes the role of the psychologist (such as therapist, organizational consultant, diagnostician, or expert witness), the probable uses of the services provided or the information obtained, and the fact that there may be limits to confidentiality.

(b) If there is a foreseeable risk of the psychologist's being called upon to perform conflicting roles because of the involvement of a third party, the psychologist clarifies the nature and direction of his or her responsibilities, keeps all parties appropriately informed as matters develop, and resolves the situation in accordance with this Ethics Code.

1.22 Delegation to and Supervision of Subordinates

(a) Psychologists delegate to their employees, supervisees, and research assistants only those responsibilities that such persons can reasonably be expected to perform competently, on the basis of their education, training, or experience, either independently or with the level of supervision being provided.

(b) Psychologists provide proper training and supervision to their employees or supervisees and take reasonable steps to see that such persons perform services responsibly, competently, and ethically.

(c) If institutional policies, procedures, or practices prevent fulfillment of this obligation, psychologists attempt to modify their role or to correct the situation to the extent feasible.

1.23 Documentation of Professional and Scientific Work

(a) Psychologists appropriately document their professional and scientific work in order to facilitate provision of services later by them or by other professionals, to ensure accountability, and to meet other requirements of institutions or the law.

(b) When psychologists have reason to believe that records of their professional services will be used in legal proceedings involving recipients of or participants in their work, they have a responsibility to create and maintain documentation in the kind of detail and quality that would be consistent with reasonable scrutiny in an adjudicative forum. (See also Standard 7.01, Professionalism, under Forensic Activities.)

1.24 Records and Data

Psychologists create, maintain, disseminate, store, retain, and dispose of records and data relating to their research, practice, and other work in accordance with law and in a manner that permits compliance with the requirements of this Ethics Code. (See also Standard 5.04, Maintenance of Records.)

1.25 Fees and Financial Arrangements

(a) As early as is feasible in a professional or scientific relationship, the psychologist and the patient, client, or other appropriate recipient of psychological services reach an agreement specifying the compensation and the billing arrangements.

(b) Psychologists do not exploit recipients of services or payors with respect to fees.

(c) Psychologists' fee practices are consistent with law.

(d) Psychologists do not misrepresent their fees.

(e) If limitations to service can be anticipated because of limitations in financing, this is discussed with the patient, client, or other appropriate recipient of services as early as is feasible. (See also Standard 4.08, Interruption of Services.)

(f) If the patient, client, or other recipient of services does not pay for services as agreed, and if the psychologist wishes to use collection agencies or legal measures to collect the fees, the psychologist first informs the person that such measures will be taken and provides that person an opportunity to make prompt payment. (See also Standard 5.11, Withholding Records for Nonpayment.)

1.26 Accuracy in Reports to Payors and Funding Sources

In their reports to payors for services or sources of research funding, psychologists accurately state the nature of the research or service provided, the fees or charges, and where applicable, the identity of the provider, the findings, and the diagnosis. (See also Standard 5.05, Disclosures.)

1.27 Referrals and Fees

When a psychologist pays, receives payment from, or divides fees with another professional other than in an employer–employee relationship, the payment to each is based on the services (clinical, consultative, administrative, or other) provided and is not based on the referral itself.

2.   Evaluation, Assessment, or Intervention

2.01 Evaluation, Diagnosis, and Interventions in Professional Context

(a) Psychologists perform evaluations, diagnostic services, or interventions only within the context of a defined professional relationship. (See also Standard 1.03, Professional and Scientific Relationship.)

(b) Psychologists' assessments, recommendations, reports, and psychological diagnostic or evaluative statements are based on information and techniques (including personal interviews of the individual when appropriate) sufficient to provide appropriate substantiation for their findings. (See also Standard 7.02, Forensic Assessments.)

2.02 Competence and Appropriate Use of Assessments and Interventions

(a) Psychologists who develop, administer, score, interpret, or use psychological assessment techniques, interviews, tests, or instruments do so in a manner and for purposes that are appropriate in light of the research on or evidence of the usefulness and proper application of the techniques.

(b) Psychologists refrain from misuse of assessment techniques, interventions, results, and interpretations and take reasonable steps to prevent others from misusing the information these techniques provide. This includes refraining from releasing raw test results or raw data to persons, other than to patients or clients as appropriate, who are not qualified to use such information. (See also Standards 1.02, Relationship of Ethics and Law, and 1.04, Boundaries of Competence.)

2.03 Test Construction

Psychologists who develop and conduct research with tests and other assessment techniques use scientific procedures and current professional knowledge for test design, standardization, validation, reduction or elimination of bias, and recommendations for use.

2.04 Use of Assessment in General and With Special Populations

(a) Psychologists who perform interventions or administer, score, interpret, or use assessment techniques are familiar with the reliability, validation, and related standardization or outcome studies of, and proper applications and uses of, the techniques they use.

(b) Psychologists recognize limits to the certainty with which diagnoses, judgments, or predictions can be made about individuals.

(c) Psychologists attempt to identify situations in which particular interventions or assessment techniques or norms may not be applicable or may require adjustment in administration or interpretation because of factors such as individuals' gender, age, race, ethnicity, national origin, religion, sexual orientation, disability, language, or socioeconomic status.

2.05 Interpreting Assessment Results

When interpreting assessment results, including automated interpretations, psychologists take into account the various test factors and characteristics of the person being assessed that might affect psychologists' judgments or reduce the accuracy of their interpretations. They indicate any significant reservations they have about the accuracy or limitations of their interpretations.

2.06 Unqualified Persons

Psychologists do not promote the use of psychological assessment techniques by unqualified persons. (See also Standard 1.22, Delegation to and Supervision of Subordinates.)

2.07 Obsolete Tests and Outdated Test Results

(a) Psychologists do not base their assessment or intervention decisions or recommendations on data or test results that are outdated for the current purpose.

(b) Similarly, psychologists do not base such decisions or recommendations on tests and measures that are obsolete and not useful for the current purpose.

2.08 Test Scoring and Interpretation Services

(a) Psychologists who offer assessment or scoring procedures to other professionals accurately describe the purpose, norms, validity, reliability, and applications of the procedures and any special qualifications applicable to their use.

(b) Psychologists select scoring and interpretation services (including automated services) on the basis of evidence of the validity of the program and procedures as well as on other appropriate considerations.

(c) Psychologists retain appropriate responsibility for the appropriate application, interpretation, and use of assessment instruments, whether they score and interpret such tests themselves or use automated or other services.

2.09 Explaining Assessment Results

Unless the nature of the relationship is clearly explained to the person being assessed in advance and precludes provision of an explanation of results (such as in some organizational consulting, preemployment or security screenings, and forensic evaluations), psychologists ensure that an explanation of the results is provided using language that is reasonably understandable to the person assessed or to another legally authorized person on behalf of the client. Regardless of whether the scoring and interpretation are done by the psychologist, by assistants, or by automated or other outside services, psychologists take reasonable steps to ensure that appropriate explanations of results are given.

2.10 Maintaining Test Security

Psychologists make reasonable efforts to maintain the integrity and security of tests and other assessment techniques consistent with law, contractual obligations, and in a manner that permits compliance with the requirements of this Ethics Code. (See also Standard 1.02, Relationship of Ethics and Law.)

3. *Advertising and Other Public Statements*

3.01 Definition of Public Statements

Psychologists comply with this Ethics Code in public statements relating to their professional services, products, or publications or to the field of psychology. Public statements include but are not limited to paid or unpaid advertising, brochures, printed matter, directory listings, personal resumes or curricula vitae, interviews or comments for use in media, statements in legal proceedings, lectures and public oral presentations, and published materials.

3.02 Statements by Others

(a) Psychologists who engage others to create or place public statements that promote their professional practice, products, or activities retain professional responsibility for such statements.

(b) In addition, psychologists make reasonable efforts to prevent others whom they do not control (such as employers, publishers, sponsors, organizational clients, and representatives of the print or broadcast media) from making deceptive statements concerning psychologists' practice or professional or scientific activities.

(c) If psychologists learn of deceptive statements about their work made by others, psychologists make reasonable efforts to correct such statements.

(d) Psychologists do not compensate employees of press, radio, television, or other communication media in return for publicity in a news item.

(e) A paid advertisement relating to the psychologist's activities must be identified as such, unless it is already apparent from the context.

3.03 Avoidance of False or Deceptive Statements

(a) Psychologists do not make public statements that are false, deceptive, misleading, or fraudulent, either because of what they state, convey, or suggest or because of what they omit, concerning their research, practice, or other work activities or those of persons or organizations with which they are affiliated. As examples (and not in limitation) of this standard, psychologists do not make false or deceptive statements concerning (1) their training, experience, or competence; (2) their academic degrees; (3) their credentials; (4) their institutional or association affiliations; (5) their services; (6) the scientific or clinical basis for, or results or degree of success of, their services; (7) their fees; or (8) their publications or research findings. (See also Standards 6.15, Deception in Research, and 6.18, Providing Participants With Information About the Study.)

(b) Psychologists claim as credentials for their psychological work, only degrees that (1) were earned from a regionally accredited educational institution or (2) were the basis for psychology licensure by the state in which they practice.

3.04 Media Presentations

When psychologists provide advice or comment by means of public lectures, demonstrations, radio or television programs, prerecorded tapes, printed articles, mailed material, or other media, they take reasonable precautions to ensure that (1) the statements are based on appropriate psychological literature and practice, (2) the statements are otherwise consistent with this Ethics Code, and (3) the recipients of the information are not encouraged to infer that a relationship has been established with them personally.

3.05 Testimonials

Psychologists do not solicit testimonials from current psychotherapy clients or patients or other persons who because of their particular circumstances are vulnerable to undue influence.

3.06 In-Person Solicitation

Psychologists do not engage, directly or through agents, in uninvited in-person solicitation of business from actual or potential psychotherapy patients or clients or other persons who because of their particular circumstances are vulnerable to undue influence. However, this does not preclude attempting to implement appropriate collateral contacts with significant others for the purpose of benefiting an already engaged therapy patient.

4. *Therapy*

4.01 Structuring the Relationship

(a) Psychologists discuss with clients or patients as early as is feasible in the therapeutic relationship appropriate issues, such as the nature and anticipated course of therapy, fees, and confidentiality. (See also Standards 1.25, Fees and Financial Arrangements, and 5.01, Discussing the Limits of Confidentiality.)

(b) When the psychologist's work with clients or patients will be supervised, the above discussion includes that fact, and the name of the supervisor, when the supervisor has legal responsibility for the case.

(c) When the therapist is a student intern, the client or patient is informed of that fact.

(d) Psychologists make reasonable efforts to answer patients' questions and to avoid apparent misunderstandings about therapy. Whenever possible, psychologists provide oral and/or written information, using language that is reasonably understandable to the patient or client.

4.02 Informed Consent to Therapy

(a) Psychologists obtain appropriate informed consent to therapy or related procedures, using language that is reasonably understandable to participants. The content of informed consent will vary depending on many circumstances; however, informed consent generally implies that the person (1) has the capacity to consent, (2) has been informed of significant information concerning the procedure, (3) has freely and without undue influence expressed consent, and (4) consent has been appropriately documented.

(b) When persons are legally incapable of giving informed consent, psychologists obtain informed permission from a legally authorized person, if such substitute consent is permitted by law.

(c) In addition, psychologists (1) inform those persons who are legally incapable of giving informed consent about the proposed interventions in a manner commensurate with the persons' psychological capacities, (2) seek their assent to those interventions, and (3) consider such persons' preferences and best interests.

4.03 Couple and Family Relationships

(a) When a psychologist agrees to provide services to several persons who have a relationship (such as husband and wife or parents and children), the psychologist attempts to clarify at the outset (1) which of the individuals are patients or clients and (2) the relationship the psychologist will have with each person. This clarification includes the role of the psychologist and the probable uses of the services provided or the information obtained. (See also Standard 5.01, Discussing the Limits of Confidentiality.)

(b) As soon as it becomes apparent that the psychologist may be called on to perform potentially conflicting roles (such as marital counselor to husband and wife, and then witness for one party in a divorce proceeding), the psychologist attempts to clarify and adjust, or withdraw from, roles appropriately. (See also Standard 7.03, Clarification of Role, under Forensic Activities.)

4.04 Providing Mental Health Services to Those Served by Others

In deciding whether to offer or provide services to those already receiving mental health services elsewhere, psychologists carefully consider the treatment issues and the potential patient's or client's welfare. The psychologist discusses these issues with the patient or client, or another legally authorized person on behalf of the client, in order to minimize the risk of confusion and conflict, consults with the other service providers when appropriate, and proceeds with caution and sensitivity to the therapeutic issues.

4.05 Sexual Intimacies With Current Patients or Clients

Psychologists do not engage in sexual intimacies with current patients or clients.

4.06 Therapy With Former Sexual Partners

Psychologists do not accept as therapy patients or clients persons with whom they have engaged in sexual intimacies.

4.07 Sexual Intimacies With Former Therapy Patients

(a) Psychologists do not engage in sexual intimacies with a former therapy patient or client for at least two years after cessation or termination of professional services.

(b) Because sexual intimacies with a former therapy patient or client are so frequently harmful to the patient or client, and because such intimacies undermine public confidence in the psychology profession and thereby deter the public's use of needed services, psychologists do not engage in sexual intimacies with former therapy patients and clients even after a two-year interval except in the most unusual circumstances. The psychologist who engages in such activity after the two years following cessation or termination of treatment bears the burden of demonstrating that there has been no exploitation, in light of all relevant factors, including (1) the amount of time that has passed since therapy terminated, (2) the nature and duration of the therapy, (3) the circumstances of termination, (4) the patient's or client's personal history, (5) the patient's or client's current mental status, (6) the likelihood of adverse impact on the patient or client and others, and (7) any statements or actions made by the therapist during the course of therapy suggesting or inviting the possibility of a posttermination sexual or romantic relationship with the patient or client. (See also Standard 1.17, Multiple Relationships.)

4.08 Interruption of Services

(a) Psychologists make reasonable efforts to plan for facilitating care in the event that psychological services are interrupted by factors such as the psychologist's illness, death, unavailability, or relocation or by the client's relocation or financial limitations. (See also Standard 5.09, Preserving Records and Data.)

(b) When entering into employment or contractual relationships, psychologists provide for orderly and appropriate resolution of responsibility for patient or client care in the event that the employment or contractual relationship ends, with paramount consideration given to the welfare of the patient or client.

4.09 Terminating the Professional Relationship

(a) Psychologists do not abandon patients or clients. (See also Standard 1.25e, under Fees and Financial Arrangements.)

(b) Psychologists terminate a professional relationship when it becomes reasonably clear that the patient or client no longer needs the service, is not benefiting, or is being harmed by continued service.

(c) Prior to termination for whatever reason, except where precluded by the patient's or client's conduct, the psychologist discusses the patient's or client's views and needs, provides appropriate pretermination counseling, suggests alternative service providers as appropriate, and takes other reasonable steps to facilitate transfer of responsibility to another provider if the patient or client needs one immediately.

5.   *Privacy and Confidentiality*

These Standards are potentially applicable to the professional and scientific activities of all psychologists.

5.01 Discussing the Limits of Confidentiality

(a) Psychologists discuss with persons and organizations with whom they establish a scientific or professional relationship (including, to the extent feasible, minors and their legal representatives) (1) the relevant limitations on confidentiality, including limitations where applicable in group, marital, and family therapy or in organizational consulting, and (2) the foreseeable uses of the information generated through their services.

(b) Unless it is not feasible or is contraindicated, the discussion of confidentiality occurs at the outset of the relationship and thereafter as new circumstances may warrant.

(c) Permission for electronic recording of interviews is secured from clients and patients.

5.02 Maintaining Confidentiality

Psychologists have a primary obligation and take reasonable precautions to respect the confidentiality rights of those with whom they work or consult, recognizing that confidentiality may be established by law, institutional rules, or professional or scientific relationships. (See also Standard 6.26, Professional Reviewers.)

5.03 Minimizing Intrusions on Privacy

(a) In order to minimize intrusions on privacy, psychologists include in written and oral reports, consultations, and the like, only information germane to the purpose for which the communication is made.

(b) Psychologists discuss confidential information obtained in clinical or consulting relationships, or evaluative data concerning patients, individual or organizational clients, students, research participants, supervisees, and employees, only for appropriate scientific or professional purposes and only with persons clearly concerned with such matters.

5.04 Maintenance of Records

Psychologists maintain appropriate confidentiality in creating, storing, accessing, transferring, and disposing of records under their control, whether these are written, automated, or in any other medium. Psychologists maintain and dispose of records in accordance with law and in a manner that permits compliance with the requirements of this Ethics Code.

5.05 Disclosures

(a) Psychologists disclose confidential information without the consent of the individual only as mandated by law, or where permitted by law for a valid purpose, such as (1) to provide needed professional services to the patient or the individual or organizational client, (2) to obtain appropriate professional consultations, (3) to protect the patient or client or others from harm, or (4) to obtain payment for services, in which instance disclosure is limited to the minimum that is necessary to achieve the purpose.

(b) Psychologists also may disclose confidential information with the appropriate consent of the patient or the individual or organizational client (or of another legally authorized person on behalf of the patient or client), unless prohibited by law.

5.06 Consultations

When consulting with colleagues, (1) psychologists do not share confidential information that reasonably could lead to the identification of a patient, client, research participant, or other person or organization with whom they have a confidential relationship unless they have obtained the prior consent of the person or organization or the disclosure cannot be avoided, and (2) they share information only to the extent necessary to achieve the purposes of the consultation. (See also Standard 5.02, Maintaining Confidentiality.)

5.07 Confidential Information in Databases

(a) If confidential information concerning recipients of psychological services is to be entered into databases or systems of records available to persons whose access has not been consented to by the recipient, then psychologists use coding or other techniques to avoid the inclusion of personal identifiers.

(b) If a research protocol approved by an institutional review board or similar body requires the inclusion of personal identifiers, such identifiers are deleted before the information is made accessible to persons other than those of whom the subject was advised.

(c) If such deletion is not feasible, then before psychologists transfer such data to others or review such data collected by others, they take reasonable steps to determine that appropriate consent of personally identifiable individuals has been obtained.

5.08 Use of Confidential Information for Didactic or Other Purposes

(a) Psychologists do not disclose in their writings, lectures, or other public media, confidential, personally identifiable information concerning their patients, individual or organizational clients, students, research participants, or other recipients of their services that they obtained during the course of their work, unless the person or organization has consented in writing or unless there is other ethical or legal authorization for doing so.

(b) Ordinarily, in such scientific and professional presentations, psychologists disguise confidential information concerning such persons or organizations so that they are not individually identifiable to others and so that discussions do not cause harm to subjects who might identify themselves.

5.09 Preserving Records and Data

A psychologists makes plans in advance so that confidentiality of records and data is protected in the event of the psychologist's death, incapacity, or withdrawal from the position or practice.

5.10 Ownership of Records and Data

Recognizing that ownership of records and data is governed by legal principles, psychologists take reasonable and lawful steps so that records and data remain available to the extent needed to serve the best interests of patients, individual or organizational clients, research participants, or appropriate others.

5.11 Withholding Records for Nonpayment

Psychologists may not withhold records under their control that are requested and imminently needed for a patient's or client's treatment solely because payment has not been received, except as otherwise provided by law.

6. Teaching, Training Supervision, Research, and Publishing

6.01 Design of Education and Training Programs

Psychologists who are responsible for education and training programs seek to ensure that the programs are competently designed, provide the proper experiences, and meet the requirements for licensure, certification, or other goals for which claims are made by the program.

6.02 Descriptions of Education and Training Programs

(a) Psychologists responsible for education and training programs seek to ensure that there is a current and accurate description of the program content, training goals and objectives, and requirements that must be met for satisfactory completion of the program. This information must be made readily available to all interested parties.

(b) Psychologists seek to ensure that statements concerning their course outlines are accurate and not misleading, particularly regarding the subject matter to be covered, bases for evaluating progress, and the nature of course experiences. (See also Standard 3.03, Avoidance of False or Deceptive Statements.)

(c) To the degree to which they exercise control, psychologists responsible for announcements, catalogs, brochures, or advertisements describing workshops, seminars, or other non-degree-granting educational programs ensure that they accurately describe the audience for which the program is intended, the educational objectives, the presenter, and the fees involved.

6.03 Accuracy and Objectivity in Teaching

(a) When engaged in teaching or training, psychologists present psychological information accurately and with a reasonable degree of objectivity.

(b) When engaged in teaching or training, psychologists recognize the power they hold over students or supervisees and therefore make reasonable efforts to avoid engaging in conduct that is personally demeaning to students or supervisees. (See also Standards 1.09, Respecting Others, and 1.12, Other Harassment.)

6.04 Limitation on Teaching

Psychologists do not teach the use of techniques or procedures that require specialized training, licensure, or expertise, including but not limited to hypnosis, biofeedback, and projective techniques, to individuals who lack the prerequisite training, legal scope of practice, or expertise.

6.05 Assessing Student and Supervisee Performance

(a) In academic and supervisory relationships, psychologists establish an appropriate process for providing feedback to students and supervisees.

(b) Psychologists evaluate students and supervisees on the basis of their actual performance on relevant and established program requirements.

6.06 Planning Research

(a) Psychologists design, conduct, and report research in accordance with recognized standards of scientific competence and ethical research.

(b) Psychologists plan their research so as to minimize the possibility that results will be misleading.

(c) In planning research, psychologists consider its ethical acceptability under the Ethics Code. If an ethical issue is unclear, psychologists seek to resolve the issue through consultation with institutional review boards, animal care and use committees, peer consultations, or other proper mechanisms.

(d) Psychologists take reasonable steps to implement appropriate protections for the rights and welfare of human participants, other persons affected by the research, and the welfare of animal subjects.

6.07 Responsibility

(a) Psychologists conduct research competently and with due concern for the dignity and welfare of the participants.

(b) Psychologists are responsible for the ethical conduct of research conducted by them or by others under their supervision or control.

(c) Researchers and assistants are permitted to perform only those tasks for which they are appropriately trained and prepared.

(d) As part of the process of development and implementation of research projects, psychologists consult those with expertise concerning any special population under investigation or most likely to be affected.

6.08 Compliance With Law and Standards

Psychologists plan and conduct research in a manner consistent with federal and state law and regulations, as well as professional standards governing the conduct of research, and particularly those standards governing research with human participants and animal subjects.

6.09 Institutional Approval

Psychologists obtain from host institutions or organizations appropriate approval prior to conducting research, and they provide accurate information about their research proposals. They conduct the research in accordance with the approved research protocol.

6.10 Research Responsibilities

Prior to conducting research (except research involving only anonymous surveys, naturalistic observations, or similar research), psychologists enter into an agreement with participants that clarifies the nature of the research and the responsibilities of each party.

6.11 Informed Consent to Research

(a) Psychologists use language that is reasonably understandable to research participants in obtaining their appropriate informed consent (except as provided in Standard 6.12, Dispensing With Informed Consent). Such informed consent is appropriately documented.

(b) Using language that is reasonably understandable to participants, psychologists inform participants of the nature of the research; they inform participants that they are free to participate or to decline to participate or to withdraw from the research; they explain the foreseeable consequences of declining or withdrawing; they inform participants of significant factors that may be expected to influence their willingness to participate (such as risks, discomfort, adverse effects, or limitations on confidentiality, except as provided in Standard 6.15, Deception in Research); and they explain other aspects about which the prospective participants inquire.

(c) When psychologists conduct research with individuals such as students or subordinates, psychologists take special care to protect the prospective participants from adverse consequences of declining or withdrawing from participation.

(d) When research participation is a course requirement or opportunity for extra credit, the prospective participant is given the choice of equitable alternative activities.

(e) For persons who are legally incapable of giving informed consent, psychologists nevertheless (1) provide an appropriate explanation, (2) obtain the participant's assent, and (3) obtain appropriate permission from a legally authorized person, if such substitute consent is permitted by law.

6.12 Dispensing With Informed Consent

Before determining that planned research (such as research involving only anonymous questionnaires, naturalistic observations, or certain kinds of archival research) does not require the informed consent of research participants, psychologists consider applicable regulations and institutional review board requirements, and they consult with colleagues as appropriate.

6.13 Informed Consent in Research Filming or Recording

Psychologists obtain informed consent from research participants prior to filming or recording them in any form, unless the research involves simply naturalistic observations in public places and it is not anticipated that the recording will be used in a manner that could cause personal identification or harm.

6.14 Offering Inducements for Research Participants

(a) In offering professional services as an inducement to obtain research participants, psychologists make clear the nature of the services, as well as the risk, obligations, and limitations. (See also Standard 1.18, Barter [With Patients or Clients].)

(b) Psychologists do not offer excessive or inappropriate financial or other inducements to obtain research participants, particularly when it might tend to coerce participation.

6.15 Deception in Research

(a) Psychologists do not conduct a study involving deception unless they have determined that the use of deceptive techniques is justified by the study's prospective scientific, educational, or applied value and that equally effective alternative procedures that do not use deception are not feasible.

(b) Psychologists never deceive research participants about significant aspects that would affect their willingness to participate, such as physical risks, discomfort, or unpleasant emotional experiences.

(c) Any other deception that is an integral feature of the design and conduct of an experiment must be explained to participants as early as is feasible, preferably at the conclusion of their participation, but no later than at the conclusion of the research. (See also Standard 6.18, Providing Participants With Information About the Study.)

6.16 Sharing and Utilizing Data

Psychologists inform research participants of their anticipated sharing or further use of personally identifiable research data and of the possibility of unanticipated future uses.

6.17 Minimizing Invasiveness

In conducting research, psychologists interfere with the participants or milieu from which data are collected only in a manner that is warranted by an appropriate research design and that is consistent with psychologists' roles as scientific investigators.

6.18 Providing Participants With Information About the Study

(a) Psychologists provide a prompt opportunity for participants to obtain appropriate information about the nature, results, and conclusions of the research, and psychologists attempt to correct any misconceptions that participants may have.

(b) If scientific or humane values justify delaying or withholding this information, psychologists take reasonable measures to reduce the risk of harm.

6.19 Honoring Commitments

Psychologists take reasonable measures to honor all commitments they have made to research participants.

6.20 Care and Use of Animals in Research

(a) Psychologists who conduct research involving animals treat them humanely.

(b) Psychologists acquire, care for, use, and dispose of animals in compliance with current federal, state, and local laws and regulations, and with professional standards.

(c) Psychologists trained in research methods and experienced in the care of laboratory animals supervise all procedures involving animals and are responsible for ensuring appropriate consideration of their comfort, health, and humane treatment.

(d) Psychologists ensure that all individuals using animals under their supervision have received instruction in research methods and in the care, maintenance, and handling of the species being used, to the extent appropriate to their role.

(e) Responsibilities and activities of individuals assisting in a research project are consistent with their respective competencies.

(f) Psychologists make reasonable efforts to minimize the discomfort, infection, illness, and pain of animal subjects.

(g) A procedure subjecting animals to pain, stress, or privation is used only when an alternative procedure is unavailable and the goal is justified by its prospective scientific, educational, or applied value.

(h) Surgical procedures are preformed under appropriate anesthesia; techniques to avoid infection and minimize pain are followed during and after surgery.

(i) When it is appropriate that the animal's life be terminated, it is done rapidly, with an effort to minimize pain, and in accordance with accepted procedures.

6.21 Reporting of Results

(a) Psychologists do not fabricate data or falsify results in their publications.

(b) If psychologists discover significant errors in their published data, they take reasonable steps to correct such errors in a correction, retraction, erratum, or other appropriate publication means.

6.22 Plagiarism

Psychologists do not present substantial portions or elements of another's work or data as their own, even if the other work or data source is cited occasionally.

6.23 Publication Credit

(a) Psychologists take responsibility and credit, including authorship credit, only for work they have actually performed or to which they have contributed.

(b) Principal authorship and other publication credits accurately reflect the relative scientific or professional contributions of the individuals involved, regardless of their relative status. Mere possession of an institutional position, such as Department Chair, does not justify authorship credit. Minor contributions to the research or to the writing for publications are appropriately acknowledged, such as in footnotes or in an introductory statement.

(c) A student is usually listed as principal author on any multiple-authored article that is substantially based on the student's dissertation or thesis.

6.24 Duplicate Publication of Data

Psychologists do not publish, as original data, data that have been previously published. This does not preclude republishing data when they are accompanied by proper acknowledgment.

6.25 Sharing Data

After research results are published, psychologists do not withhold the data on which their conclusions are based from other competent professionals who seek to verify the substantive claims through reanalysis and who intend to use such data only for that purpose, provided that the confidentiality of the participants can be protected and unless legal rights concerning proprietary data preclude their release.

6.26 Professional Reviewers

Psychologists who review material submitted for publication, grant, or other research proposal review respect the confidentiality of and the proprietary rights in such information of those who submitted it.

7. *Forensic Activities*

7.01 Professionalism

Psychologists who perform forensic functions, such as assessments, interviews, consultations, reports, or expert testimony, must comply with all other provisions of this Ethics Code to the extent that they apply to such activities. In addition, psychologists base their forensic work on appropriate knowledge of and competence in the areas underlying such work, including specialized knowledge concerning special populations. (See also Standards 1.06, Basis for Scientific and Professional Judgments; 1.08, Human Differences; 1.15, Misuse of Psychologists' Influence; and 1.23, Documentation of Professional and Scientific Work.)

7.02 Forensic Assessments

(a) Psychologists' forensic assessments, recommendations, and reports are based on information and techniques (including personal interviews of the individual, when appropriate) sufficient to provide appropriate substantiation for their findings. (See also Standards 1.03, Professional and Scientific Relationship; 1.23, Documentation of Professional and Scientific Work; 2.01, Evaluation, Diagnosis, and Interventions in Professional Context; and 2.05, Interpreting Assessment Results.)

(b) Except as noted in (c), below, psychologists provide written or oral forensic reports or testimony of the psychological characteristics of an individual only after they have conducted an examination of the individual adequate to support their statements or conclusions.

(c) When, despite reasonable efforts, such an examination is not feasible, psychologists clarify the impact of their limited information on the reliability and validity of their reports and testimony, and they appropriately limit the nature and extent of their conclusions or recommendations.

7.03 Clarification of Role

In most circumstances, psychologists avoid performing multiple and potentially conflicting roles in forensic matters. When psychologists may be called on to serve in more than one role in a legal proceeding—for example, as consultant or expert for one party or for the court and as a fact witness—they clarify role expectations and the extent of confidentiality in advance to the extent feasible, and thereafter as changes occur, in order to avoid compromising their professional judgment and objectivity and in order to avoid misleading others regarding their role.

7.04 Truthfulness and Candor

(a) In forensic testimony and reports, psychologists testify truthfully, honestly, and candidly and, consistent with applicable legal procedures, describe fairly the basis for their testimony and conclusions.

(b) Whenever necessary to avoid misleading, psychologists acknowledge the limits of their data or conclusions.

7.05 Prior Relationships

A prior professional relationship with a party does not preclude psychologists from testifying as fact witnesses or from testifying to their services to the extent permitted by applicable law. Psychologists appropriately take into account ways in which the prior relationship might affect their professional objectivity or opinions and disclose the potential conflict to the relevant parties.

7.06 Compliance With Law and Rules

In performing forensic roles, psychologists are reasonably familiar with the rules governing their roles. Psychologists are aware of the occasionally competing demands placed upon them by these principles and the requirements of the court system, and attempt to resolve these conflicts by making known their commitment to this Ethics Code and taking steps to resolve the conflict in a responsible manner. (See also Standard 1.02, Relationship of Ethics and Law.)

8. *Resolving Ethical Issues*

8.01 Familiarity With Ethics Code

Psychologists have an obligation to be familiar with this Ethics Code, other applicable ethics codes, and their application to psychologists' work. Lack of awareness or misunderstanding of an ethical standard is not itself a defense to a charge of unethical conduct.

8.02 Confronting Ethical Issues

When a psychologist is uncertain whether a particular situation or course of action would violate this Ethics Code, the psychologist ordinarily consults with other psychologists knowledgeable about ethical issues, with state or national psychology ethics committees, or with other appropriate authorities in order to choose a proper response.

8.03 Conflicts Between Ethics and Organizational Demands

If the demands of an organization with which psychologists are affiliated conflict with this Ethics Code, psychologists clarify the nature of the conflict, make known their commitment to the Ethics Code, and to the extent feasible, seek to resolve the conflict in a way that permits the fullest adherence to the Ethics Code.

8.04 Informal Resolution of Ethical Violations

When psychologists believe that there may have been an ethical violation by another psychologist, they attempt to resolve the issue by bringing it to the attention of that individual if an informal resolution appears appropriate and the intervention does not violate any confidentiality rights that may be involved.

8.05 Reporting Ethical Violations

If an apparent ethical violation is not appropriate for informal resolution under Standard 8.04 or is not resolved properly in that fashion, psychologists take further action appropriate to the situation, unless such action conflicts with confidentiality rights in ways that cannot be resolved. Such action might include referral to state or national committees on professional ethics or to state licensing boards.

8.06 Cooperating With Ethics Committees

Psychologists cooperate in ethics investigations, proceedings, and resulting requirements of the APA or any affiliated state psychological association to which they belong. In doing so, they make reasonable efforts to resolve any issues as to confidentiality. Failure to cooperate is itself an ethics violation.

8.07 Improper Complaints

Psychologists do not file or encourage the filing of ethics complaints that are frivolous and are intended to harm the respondent rather than to protect the public.

30

WILL THE NEW CODE HELP RESEARCHERS TO BE MORE ETHICAL?

JOAN E. SIEBER

The new American Psychological Association (APA) code of ethics (APA, 1992) devotes 21 paragraphs to research ethics, covering such diverse topics as research planning, consulting with one's institutional review board, compliance with laws, informed consent, data sharing, and serving as a reviewer. The overarching APA code includes additional material relevant to research: an Introduction, a Preamble, a set of six general principles that pertain to all psychological endeavors, and, in a footnote to the Introduction, encouragement for the reader to consult *Ethical Principles in the Conduct of Research With Human Participants* (APA, Board of Professional Affairs, Committee on Professional Standards, 1982), an excellent book that goes far beyond the code in providing ethical socialization to the student or researcher. To the naive reader, however, this complete-looking package is very confusing.

Reprinted from the *Professional Psychology: Research and Practice, 25*, 369–375. Copyright 1994 by the American Psychological Association.

JUST BE ETHICAL

The code seems to assume that researchers already possess the knowledge and judgment to behave ethically, for in many instances it simply exhorts the reader to exercise such judgment. It fails to address the problem that many who will undertake research lack the required knowledge or judgment to behave ethically. For example, the code states, in Standard 6.06 (d), that "psychologists take reasonable steps to implement appropriate protections" (APA, 1992, p. 1608). What is reasonable? This requirement is neither enforceable nor educational. If the code seeks to educate, it should tell the reader where to find information on assessing and minimizing risk in given kinds of research. Similarly, the code exhorts the reader, in Standard 6.07 (a), to have "due concern" (p. 1608) for the dignity and welfare of participants and, in Standard 6.19, to take "reasonable measures" (p. 1609) to honor commitments to participants. This is analogous to an etiquette book that simply advises readers to be considerate. Etiquette books are useful when they tell readers exactly how to be considerate in situations in which social disasters readily occur. Analogously, the APA ethics code must either tell its readers how to be ethical in those contexts in which researchers are likely to go astray or direct them to the appropriate sources.

A code of ethics tries to lay out a general framework of limits for decision making, in much the same way that road signs serve to guide us to a destination. Many motorists who are new to a particular area, however, have been thoroughly confused by the road signs they encounter. Which signs pertain to them, and which can be safely ignored? What, exactly, do some signs mean? Some signs come into view only after it is too late to do anything about them; planning ahead is not always possible. Some road signs make sense only to those who are already familiar with the territory and scarcely need signs.

The sections of the new code dealing with research ethics raise analogous problems for those not already deeply immersed in the analysis and resolution of ethical issues in psychological research. These problems arise because it is virtually impossible to write clear ethical guidelines that teach or invoke ethical conduct in those who have not already received the necessary ethical socialization, and, in the same document, to set forth enforceable minimal standards so that violators may be identified and punished.

Ethical issues are framed differently depending on which of these two functions one seeks to fulfill. Understandably, those who framed the new code for researchers were guided by the necessity of creating an enforceable code. APA needs an instrument that enables it to censure those whose conduct is outside the bounds of acceptable behavior. Thus, for example, we find under Planning Research, Standard 6.06, that "psychologists design, conduct, and report research in accordance with recognized standards of scientific competence and ethical research" (APA, 1992, p. 1608). This is a requirement that an APA ethics committee could, after some discussion, apply to a case of alleged violation of research ethics. There would be little consensus among students or psychologists at large, however, about what comprised "recognized standards of scientific competence and ethical research," nor would they learn anything about standards from the code.

STANDARDS OF SCIENTIFIC COMPETENCE AND ETHICAL RESEARCH

Actual standards, as they would be conceived and applied by a competent ethics committee, must, of necessity, bend and change with the scientific, social, and political contexts of the particular research to which they were applied (Renzetti & Lee, 1992). Yet how may the standards be "bent" in each particular case? Because the contexts of psychological research are extremely diverse, the many resulting idiosyncrasies in standards cannot possibly be reflected in a code of ethics. The diversity of scientific, social, and political contexts of research currently considered important was aptly illustrated by the contents of two recent issues of *American Psychologist* (October 1993 and November 1993) that included articles on the following topics: the illusion of mental health, psychology's problems with race, determination of authorship credit and authorship order on faculty–student collaborations, the science of prevention, psychological interventions to prevent HIV infection, psychology and the ethics of social policy, male violence against women, rape, sexual harassment, and violence against women by male partners.

Indeed, these are the kinds of value-laden, socially relevant, ethically complex research topics that interest many of today's researchers, but neither the code nor many senior researchers can offer relevant guidance on how to "design, conduct, and report [this kind of] research in accordance with recognized standards of scientific competence and ethical research" (APA, 1992, p. 1608). Yet it is this kind of socially sensitive research that raises the most difficult ethical questions, as the following examples illustrate.

Case 1: Marital Rape Research
The study of survivors of marital rape typically occurs through interviews conducted by women psychologists with women who are divorcing or have divorced their husbands and who have been sexually assaulted after leaving or announcing their intention to leave. Bergen (1992) wrote that such research is sensitive in various ways: (a) Speaking of their experiences is potentially life-threatening for the women involved in the research process (Russell, 1990), (b) being found in the interview context by the ex-husband is threatening for the researcher, (c) conducting such research poses a threat to the sacred institution of marriage—the private sexual relationship between spouses and the

ideology of the family, and (d) conducting such research threatens the notion still held by some that marriage is a license to rape. Because of the privacy and sensitivity of this topic, some ethicists might even consider it too private for study; for example, MacIntyre (1982) indicated that "certain areas of personal and social life should be especially protected. Intimacy cannot exist where everything is disclosed" (p. 188). However, many psychologists would argue that sensitive topics should be explored to uncover facts that would otherwise be hidden, distorted, or misunderstood. But how should this be done? Feminist researcher Mies (1983) advocated "conscious partiality" (p. 123), which involves partial identification with the participants on the basis of personal interaction, in which the researcher is an empathic listener who neither exploits nor manipulates the participant. Duelli Klein (1983) recommended co-authorship and collective consciousness raising between researcher and participant. She argued that this interactive process empowers by enabling participants to recognize that their personal experiences are no longer simply raw data—that they are actively involved with others and are evoking change.

What ethical dilemmas await the women (or men) who enter this field of research? Who will guide them?

Case 2: Understanding How AIDS Is Spread by Crack Users
The AIDS epidemic could become the major catastrophe of our time. Should researchers operate within traditional scientific standards that produce academic tenure, or should they experiment with new standards that are more likely to help prevent AIDS? Traditional descriptive methods have provided crucial information about the lifestyles of various HIV high-risk groups (Fullilove, Fullilove, Bowser, & Gross, 1990); now interventions that reduce risky behavior need to be developed, evaluated, and refined (Bowser & Sieber, 1992). Successful intervention across social classes, racial groups, and subcultures would require sound theory about causes of high-risk behavior. Such theory is lacking, and the inductive method that has been the "gold standard" of the physical and social sciences is self-limiting and inadequate when applied to a problem such as AIDS prevention (Popper, 1968). Bowser and Sieber (1992) have shown how to balance and strengthen inductive research methods in their research on young Black inner-city drug dealers, by a combination of ethnographic, focus group, and peer interviewing methods, which draw on the researchers' and their subjects' subjectivity; the theories and interventions built out of this process are then empirically tested. Because recognized empirical standards such as random sampling cannot be used for groups that cannot be enumerated (e.g., drug dealers), recruitment is done from diverse sources and by personal referral of those already sampled (see also Martin & Dean, 1992). Are these approaches rigorous and ethical? What are the alternatives? How can the newcomer to this important area of research gain the needed ethical socialization?

Indeed, theory development and sampling for many kinds of problems and populations (not just sensitive and marginal populations) requires non-traditional standards like those Bowser and Sieber have proposed. For example, the following advertisement appeared in the December 5, 1993 issue of the *San Francisco Examiner* (p. B-6):

> Case 3: Lost Love Experience?
> Did you part from someone you loved, then 5 or more years later try another relationship with that person? If so, please contact CSU researcher for anonymous questionnaire. Send your address to: Lost Love Project, P.O. Box 19692, Sacto, CA 95819.

Are not some of the methodological issues raised by this innocuous study similar to those addressed by Bowser and Sieber? They are simpler in that the research will be less costly and less noticed by grant reviewers, institutional review boards, journalists, religious leaders, and other gatekeepers, and they will be of less political concern; hence, they will be less likely to be scrutinized with respect to traditional standards and ethics.

In contrast to others to whom the APA directs a specific code of ethics (e.g., clinicians, forensic psychologists, psychology teachers, and testing specialists), those who conduct psychological research are an extraordinary diverse lot. They range from undergraduate students with GPAs that are below average to brilliant senior scientists; from physiological psychologists working in laboratories to community psychologists working with the homeless or social psychologists studying the lovelorn; from academicians in almost every conceivable university department to employees in industry, government, and a range of social agencies. The task of formulating ethical requirements general enough to enable the APA Ethics Committee to govern researchers is daunting.

Codes as Useful Educational Tools

Making a code useful or educational to the unsophisticated as well as to the experienced researcher is virtually impossible. Where does one begin, and in what depth does one discuss issues? As exemplified in the cases described above, ethical issues vary with context, and psychological research occurs in diverse contexts. Ethical issues also vary with the times, and the past decade has brought many new issues to the fore. For example, in community-based AIDS research on gay populations, researchers accustomed to unilaterally designing research were forced by the gay community to involve members of their well-educated research population in the research planning process (e.g., Melton, Levine, Koocher, Rosenthal, & Thompson, 1988). Such idiosyncratic problems and solutions comprise the content of contemporary discussions of the ethics of research on humans, yet they are not mentioned specifically in the APA code.

The framers of the code were not oblivious to these idiosyncratic problems. Indeed, Standard 6.07 (d) states that, "as part of the process of development and implementation of research projects, psychologists consult those with expertise concerning any special population under investigation or most likely to be affected" (APA, 1992, p. 1608). In addition, Principle C: Professional and Scientific Responsibility (in the General Principles), states that psychologists adapt their methods to the needs of different populations. Yet how does the inexperienced researcher get from Principle C, or even from consultation with a mentor, to a sophisticated understanding of the needs of the population to be studied, and from there to effective research practice? Few students or researchers are fortunate enough to be able to learn such ethnographic sophistication under the personal tutelage of an expert. Most do not even recognize what it is that they need to know. What do researchers need to know, and how can they acquire the needed knowledge? They cannot acquire these things from the code. In addition, in most cases, they cannot acquire these things from their institutional review board either.

Basic ethical principles, however, such as respecting the needs and feelings of one's research population and achieving good ends at minimal risk, are universally applicable. Accomplishment of these varies by situation. The researcher must understand the specific needs, politics, and social norms of the setting. This includes the subjects, the gatekeepers, and other legitimate and self-appointed stakeholders who have the power to make or break the research and to exploit or respect the subjects, as the following exemplify.

Organizational Gatekeepers

Those studying school-based learning must be highly sensitive to the rights and feelings of parents and teachers and to the political context in which the school operates. There may be self-appointed gatekeepers, such as the teacher's union, the local newspaper, the clergy, and talk-show hosts. The researcher must be continually available and hospitable, maintaining open lines of communication with all of these stakeholders in the research enterprise. Providing benefits such as new curriculum materials, training for teachers, praise and acknowledgment of all who participate in the program, and good publicity may be vital to the continuation of the research program. The signed assent of students and parental permission are essential.

"Street" Gatekeepers

In contrast, street-based research on prostitutes might be possible only through a cooperative alliance with a prostitute health organization, the provision of food and other material assistance to all prostitutes who participate, and active political participation in efforts to prevent police interference with prostitute health programs. For example, one researcher learned that the police were confiscating prostitutes' condom supplies, photocopying them as "evidence" of prostitution, and punching pinholes in them before returning them. A trip to the mayor's office was required to stop this practice (Lockett, 1990). A certificate of confidentiality should be sought from the National Institutes of Health Office for Protection From Research Risk to prevent having data subpoenaed. Signed consent forms would be unacceptable to and risky for participants (Melton, 1990).

Respect, Rapport, and Food

Various examples of field research presented so far have mentioned food. As most field researchers know, to create effective communication in long-term field research, the investigator needs to serve food. People relax, develop rapport, communicate, and make decisions best over food. However, most funders do not allow food as a budget item. Hence, the researcher must provide, by other means, pizza, donuts, salads, hors d'oeuvres, hot dogs, cookies, health food, power breakfasts, or whatever one's particular participants and gatekeepers like to eat. Would any dignified code of ethics suggest such a thing? No. And it should not.

REDUCING THE CONFUSION BY PROVIDING PERTINENT BIBLIOGRAPHIES

Psychologists need to be informed, specifically, that the code is not an adequate guide to the ethical conduct of research but only a set of very general rules that must be supplemented with ethical and methodological guidelines appropriate to one's specific area of research. This disclaimer should be prominently located in the code, just before Standard 6.06. It should mention issues that the researcher should know about, and it should direct the reader to a pertinent annotated bibliography.

The following four broad ethical issues are exceedingly complex and idiosyncratic to the context, and they receive virtually no attention in the code: lack of autonomy, research in organizations or institutions, research on marginal populations, and issues of privacy and confidentiality. The nature and importance of these issues should be addressed in the code, and the reader should be directed to pertinent information.

Lack of Autonomy

Some traditional areas of psychological research in which special problems arise include research on infants, children, frail elderly, mentally ill people, and developmentally disabled people. These research participants lack autonomy and typically cannot give legal or meaningful consent to participate in research. Special provisions are needed if they are to be included and safeguarded in research. A large literature has, by now, been amassed to describe these issues and ways of resolving them.

Institutions or Organizations

If the context of research is the workplace, school, university, medical facility, prison, family, or military facility, for example, a powerful third party typically serves as a gatekeeper and may prevent or manipulate participation, may seek access to confidential data on their charges, and may seek to use such information for coercive purposes. Alternatively, participants may suspect that these coercive forces will be at work and respond accordingly. Consider, for example, the case in which a youngster in a reformatory is asked to participate in research; what probably goes through his or her mind is whether the length of his or her sentence will be affected by his or her participation and whether the results will be known to the authorities or to his or her parents. In arranging to conduct research within such settings, one must be mindful of the rights and vulnerabilities of all concerned, do no harm to the institution within which the research occurs, prevent harm to participants arising from their participation, and communicate to participants the ways in which their rights and interests are protected. Additionally, one can reasonably expect intrusion from self-appointed stakeholders, such as unions and concerned community organizations. Indeed, the ethical problems that may arise in institutional or organizational settings are so complex and arcane that a researcher should fully immerse himself or herself in the literature on these problems before making any research efforts in such settings.

Marginal Populations

People such as the homeless, runaways, unassimilated ethnic minorities, prostitutes, intravenous drug and crack users, dual-diagnosis mentally ill persons, and persons with alcoholism are involved in many problems that require research. Many researchers are attracted to these research problems by a social conscience or by offers of funding but typically lack the cultural sensitivity required to adapt methodological and ethical principles to these settings. There is a rapidly emerging literature on such community-based research and its associated ethical problems (e.g., Renzetti & Lee, 1992).

Privacy and Confidentiality

The concepts of privacy and confidentiality are poorly understood by most researchers and institutional review board members. Most fail to realize that what is private to an individual is largely determined by their developmental stage, their culture, and their relative power and autonomy (Laufer & Wolfe, 1977). The researcher or institutional review board member's notion of privacy may differ from that of the research participant. Privacy does not mean being left alone. Privacy means being able to control the access others have to oneself. Indeed, many lonely people do not want the polite survey researcher to leave.

Confidentiality is widely misunderstood by some researchers and institutional review boards to mean not revealing (or publishing) names (or unique identifiers). In fact, confidentiality should take into account any form of disclosure (e.g., the subpoena of records and the inappropriate reading of files by research assistants and of data files by hackers), including unrealistic fears of participants that need to be allayed. Confidentiality refers to whatever communication or agreement the researcher makes with participants regarding revelation of information about them. There is now a large literature on privacy and confidentiality and on procedural, statistical, legal, and other means of assuring confidentiality (e.g., Boruch & Cecil, 1979). This literature, unfortunately, remains unknown to most researchers.

Much research with high-risk populations incorporates more than one of these problems. For example, research on hospitalized young, gay runaways with HIV infection incorporates all four of these special problems.

Psychologists should be directed by the ethics code to the literatures on ethical issues in these particularly problematic research contexts as well as to ethical issues in research in general. The APA should develop and continually update an annotated bibliography of books and articles dealing with ethical issues in each relevant area of research. Such a bibliography could be developed largely out of existing bibliographic material and should include materials in addition to those that have been adopted or endorsed by professional psychological organizations. The initial bibliography and annual updates should be published in *American Psychologist* and should be available on-line so that they can be accessed by modem by any individual or library. Full-text retrieval of at least some of the on-line material would be highly desirable. Some of the key terms around which the bibliography should be organized include the terms found in the name of each subsection of the research code and in the body of this code. Included among the key terms would be (a) research methods or procedures, (b) populations studied, and (c) ethical issues. Thus, searches could be performed to yield specifically defined literatures, such as approaches to debriefing in deception research on children and adolescents or methods of assuring confidentiality in observational research on dysfunctional families. It should be possible to extend searches to include reports of empirical research exemplifying the ethical issue, even if the report does not address the ethical issue as such.

The availability of such an on-line bibliography with full-text retrieval capabilities would encourage the responsible researcher to peruse the ethical literature in his or her field. It would encourage enterprising scholars to contribute periodic reviews of selected parts of this literature. In addition, it would provide an important resource for scholarship and empirical study of ethical issues that arise in psychological research. This, in turn, would enhance the effectiveness of the ethical code and simplify the role of those who develop successive revisions of it.

IMPROVING THE CODE

As the preceding remarks suggest, I find the 1992 code for researchers to be adequate if regarded as a minimal, enforceable code and not as a tool for educating psychologists about the ethical conduct of research. However, it may be seriously misleading to the naive researcher in several respects.

Some statements in the code invite the naive reader to assume that there are no issues where, in fact, serious issues may arise. Other statements suggest that there are no solutions to complex problems (e.g., problems of confidentiality), although precise solutions exist. Some statements, in the hands of an unsophisticated review board, could cause undue restriction of research activities. And the advice to researchers to rely on the institutional review board misplaces responsibility for ethical conduct of research. In many cases, the researcher must supply the review board with appropriate literature on ethical standards in a particular kind of research before the board can wisely govern the researcher. The code should facilitate this two-way process rather than imply that the process is one-way.

The following are specific areas in which the code needs to be improved:

Compliance With Federal Law and Regulations (Standard 6.08)

Many inexperienced researchers are unaware of the extent to which psychological research is governed by the Federal Regulations of Human Research. Somehow the code should make researchers aware of the existence of those regulations and of the National Institutes of Health Office for Protection From Research Risk and their relationship to institutional review boards. In some context, perhaps in conjunction with the annotated bibliography suggested herein, the reader should also be made aware of the many regional workshops on research ethics that are partially sponsored by the Office for Protection From Research Risk.

Research Ethics Review Boards

Standard 6.06 (c) implies that institutional review boards and animal care committees are wise and well-informed bodies. Some are not. Worse, some members may have been pressured into service, and some may have sought membership because they had axes to grind. The code should emphasize the importance of seeking understanding and resolution of issues from the literature, as well as from available experts and review boards. For example, back issues of the journal *IRB: A Review of Human Subjects Research* are a far richer source of assistance than are most institutional review board members. Moreover, when a source, such as an article in *IRB*, offers a discussion that is pertinent to one's chosen research method, and when one suspects that one's review board may question the method, this discussion (with references) should be included in the protocol submitted to the review board.

Animal researchers, especially those who study species rarely found in animal laboratories, should be advised to become scholars of the literature on the care and ecology of those species in the research environment. Standards for laboratory animal care often overlook the special needs of some species. To illustrate, the National Science Foundation has sponsored inquiry into the humane care of diverse animal species and found that some wild species do not thrive under conditions generally specified for animal care. For example, birds suffer less if not anesthetized for surgery; mice will mark their litter each time it is changed; and reptiles that are cooled prior to death suffer because of the slowing of the death process (Orlans, 1990).

Children

Although much psychological research is done with children, the code is curiously silent on this topic. Parents, institutions, and society at large are sensitive to what is done with children in research. Developmental psychologists recognize many kinds of risks inherent in research on children and adolescents; moreover, these risks vary with each developmental stage. For example, in middle childhood, excessive concerns about physical privacy arise and are replaced by informational privacy concerns in adolescence (Melton, 1991). In fact, type of risk and maturity interact in a variety of ways; see Sieber (1992a) for discussion of risk from a developmental perspective.

The Federal Regulations devote considerable attention to the ethics of research on children, and much has been written by psychologists, ethicists, and legal scholars on this topic. Standard 6.10, however, would seem to imply that one could conduct anonymous surveys with children on any topic or station oneself on the school playground and systematically observe children without permission from parents or the school or the assent of the children. Perhaps the framers of the code consider this issue to be covered under Standard 6.08, which addresses requiring compliance with laws; Standard 6.09, which addresses obtaining institutional approval; or Standard 6.12, which addresses dispensing with informed consent. Others might not get that impression, however. As a former chair of an institutional review board, I can think of many such cases. The code should also point to the emerging literatures on conditions under which parental permission is required and under which a court or other appropriate guardian may act *in loco parentis.*

Inducements to Participants

Standard 6.14 (b) states that "psychologists do not offer excessive or inappropriate financial or other inducements to obtain research participants, particularly when it might tend to coerce participation" (APA, 1992, p. 1609). This section will cause problems for those who study marginal populations such as drug addicts if it is taken literally by their institutional review board. Drug addicts may have no intrinsic interest in participating in research and will participate only if induced by enough money to buy more drugs. Most homeless persons will participate only if offered money or food in return. In short, most marginal populations will only participate if given money, and many advocates for poor and marginal populations argue that they should receive significant financial incentives if their participation is desired by scientists. Arguably such inducements are coercive, but they can cause no risk greater than the risk that exists in the daily lives of those individuals, and, on balance, they can bring about more good than harm to the participants and to society at large. This risk–benefit argument needs to be stated in Standard 6.14 (b).

Deception

Although I agree, generally, with the spirit of Standard 6.15, I am troubled by several aspects of it. First, the term *deception* implies many kinds of activities, some innocent and harmless and others wrongful or harmful; it could mean that the investigator lies, uses mental reservations, lets people deceive themselves, uses deceptive equipment in the research setting, plays a false role, conceals, observes a third party deceiving someone in naturalistic observation, or simply fails to tell the whole story. Deception research might proceed without the consent of subjects, with false informing, with the consent of subjects to be deceived, or with the consent of subjects to participate in a study whose purpose can be revealed or explained only later. Deception research can involve something as innocent as offering people a cookie and seeing whether they will help someone who has just dropped a book, or as nasty as leaving some money on a table and seeing whether people will steal it. Moreover, the induction to do good or harm can vary from being minimal to being very powerful. In short, the term *deception* is a red herring (see Sieber, 1983a, 1983b, for a taxonomy of deception and its risks). It tempts institutional review boards and others to think very simplistically about the ethics of psychological research. Yet there are important phenomena such as conformity behavior that cannot be studied without using some form of deception.

Second, debriefing, although generally very desirable, can be unnecessary and even harmful, as explained by Holmes (1976). It must be done in such a way that subjects are left in good emotional condition. If this is impossible, perhaps the research should not be done, or perhaps debriefing should not be done. What of children or adults who are mildly tempted to take something that is not theirs, or to tell a white lie? Should they be debriefed? Is this not a case in which the research is harmless, but the debriefing is harmful? These issues are examined in *Ethical Principles in the Conduct of Research With Human Participants* (APA, Board of Professional Affairs, Committee on Professional Standards, 1982) and in Sieber (1983b).

Third, there are many ways to do research, including deception research. One needs to examine the kinds of deception research and their consequences and decide which is the most ethical, if indeed the deception is scientifically necessary. (See Sieber, 1982, 1983a, 1983b, for a full discussion of these issues.)

Providing Participants With Information About the Study

The code, in Standard 6.18, requires that

(a) Psychologists provide a prompt opportunity for participants to obtain appropriate information about the nature, results, and conclusions of the research, and psychologists attempt to correct any misconceptions that participants may have. (b) If scientific or humane values justify delaying or withholding this information, psychologists take reasonable measures to reduce the risk of harm. (APA, 1992, p. 1609)

Providing results and conclusions is generally a great idea, and indeed some research is important enough to be of interest to the participants and is completed quickly enough that they still remember having participated by the time results are available. This is rarely the case, however. Moreover, locating the participants and transmitting this information is often impossible. A more timely and informative piece of information might be a brief, appropriately worded summary of the literature and the rationale on which the research is based. Rarely are the results of a single study more meaty or useful than what was already known about the topic. Also, this information can be handed out to participants at the time of their participation, when it would be most relevant to satisfying their curiosity and needs.

Sharing Data

The code, in Standard 6.25, requires that

after research results are published, psychologists do not withhold the data on which their conclusions are based from other competent professionals who seek to verify the substantive claims through reanalysis *and who intend to use such data only for that purpose, provided that the confidentiality of the participants can be protected and unless legal rights concerning proprietary data preclude their release* [italics added]. (APA, 1992, p. 1610)

The National Academy of Sciences, in *Sharing Research Data* (Fienberg, Martin, & Straf, 1985), and Sieber (1992b), in *Sharing Social Research Data*, list many purposes for which data can and should be shared, for example, verifying data, conducting methodological research, teaching, reanalyzing by other methods, testing of other hypotheses, building on with additional data sets, extending with newly gathered data, and so on. Moreover, the National Science Foundation and the National Institute of Justice now require grantees to document and share their data and not to restrict the scientific uses to which others might apply those data.

The meaning of Standard 6.25, however, is unclear. It is probably intended to mean that the APA would censure only those who withhold their data from those who seek to verify the findings. However, given the general unwillingness of psychologists to provide their data for any purpose (see, e.g., Sieber, 1992b, Chapters 1 and 8), Standard 6.25 is likely to be used as an excuse for prohibiting other uses of shared data and for refusing to share data with persons who wish to use it for legitimate purposes such as testing new hypotheses, teaching data analysis, or building on it with related new data.

Privacy and Confidentiality

Perhaps the most glaring omission from the code is discussion of issues of privacy and confidentiality as they pertain to research. As research topics become ever more sensitive, it is even more important that psychologists have a correct understanding of issues of privacy and confidentiality. The nature of privacy (Laufer & Wolfe, 1977), especially in social research (Sieber, 1992a, Chapter 5), and solutions to problems of privacy and confidentiality have been discussed extensively. Some clear and specific discussion of these problems and solutions should appear in the code, and an annotated bibliography of this literature should be made available by APA on-line and in hard copy.

SUMMARY

The APA Ethics Committee has undertaken a Herculean task and performed as well as could be expected. More is needed, however, especially with respect to issues of limited autonomy, privacy and confidentiality, research on marginal populations, and research conducted in organizations or institutions. The book, *Ethical Principles in the Conduct of Research With Human Participants* (APA, Board of Professional Affairs, Committee on Professional Standards, 1982), is helpful but somewhat out-of-date and contains little that would guide those engaged in research that is politically or socially sensitive. Rather than commissioning a new book, APA might better use its resources to further the ethics of research by providing a bibliographic resource that would stimulate independent interest, scholarship, and research in this area.

REFERENCES

American Psychological Association, Board of Professional Affairs, Committee on Professional Standards. (1982). *Ethical principles in the conduct of research with human participants*. Washington, DC: Author.

American Psychological Association. (1992). Ethical principles of psychologists and code of conduct. *American Psychologist, 47*, 1597–1611.

Bergen, R. K. (1992). Interviewing survivors of marital rape: Doing feminist research on sensitive topics. In C. M. Renzetti & R. Lee (Eds.), *Researching sensitive topics* (pp. 197–211). Newbury Park, CA: Sage.

Boruch, R. F., & Cecil, J. S. (1979). *Assuring the confidentiality of social research data*. Philadelphia: University of Pennsylvania.

Bowser, B. P., & Sieber, J. E. (1992). AIDS prevention research: Old problems and new solutions. In C. M. Renzetti & R. Lee (Eds.), *Researching sensitive topics* (pp. 160–176). Newbury Park, CA: Sage.

Duelli Klein, R. (1983). How to do what we want to do: Thoughts about feminist methodology. In G. Bowles & R. Duelli Klein (Eds.), *Theories of women's studies* (pp. 81–97). London: Routledge & Kegan Paul.

Fienberg, S., Martin, M., & Straf, M. (1985). *Sharing research data*. Washington, DC: National Academy Press.

Fullilove, R. E., Fullilove, M. T., Bowser, B. P., & Gross, S. A. (1990). Risk of sexually transmitted disease among Black adolescent crack users in Oakland and San Francisco, California. *Journal of the American Medical Association, 263*, 851–855.

Holmes, D. (1976). Debriefing after psychological experiments: Effectiveness of post experimental desensitizing. *American Psychologist, 32*, 868–875.

Laufer, R., & Wolfe, M. (1977). Privacy as a concept and a social issue: A multi-dimensional developmental theory. *Journal of Social Issues, 33*, 44–87.

Lockett, G. (1990). AIDS prevention with Cal-PEP, COYOTE, and Project Aware. In J. E. Sieber, Y. Song-Kim, & P. Kelzer (Eds.), *Vulnerable populations and AIDS: Ethical and procedural requirements for social and behavioral research and interventions* (pp. 47–59). Hayward, CA: Pioneer Bookstore.

MacIntyre, A. (1982). Risk, harm and benefit assessments as instruments of moral evaluation. In T. L. Beauchamp, R. R. Faden, R. J. Wallace, Jr., & L. Walters (Eds.), *Ethical issues in social science research* (pp. 181–198). Baltimore: Johns Hopkins University Press.

Martin, J. L., & Dean, L. (1992). Developing a community sample of gay men for an epidemiological study of AIDS. In C. M. Renzetti & R. Lee (Eds.), *Researching sensitive topics* (pp. 82–100). Newbury Park, CA: Sage.

Melton, G. (1990). Brief research report: Certificate of confidentiality under the Public Health Service Act: Strong protection but not enough. *Violence and Victims, 5*(1), 67–70.

Melton, G. (1991). Respecting boundaries: Minors, privacy and behavioral research. In B. Stanley & J. E. Sieber (Eds.), *The ethics of research on children and adolescents*. Newbury Park, CA: Sage.

Melton, G. B., Levine, R. J., Koocher, G. P., Rosenthal, R., & Thompson, W. C. (1988). Community consultation in socially sensitive research: Lessons from clinical trials on treatment for AIDS. *American Psychologist, 43*, 573–581.

Mies, M. (1983). Toward a methodology for feminist research. In G. Bowles & R. Duelli Klein (Eds.), *Theories of women's studies* (pp. 118–131). London: Routledge & Kegan Paul.

Orlans, F. B. (1990). Fundamental differences between field and laboratory investigations. *Laboratory Animal, 19*(3), 43–44.

Popper, K. (1968). *The logic of scientific discovery*. New York: Harper & Row.

Renzetti, C. M., & Lee, R. (1992). *Researching sensitive topics*. Newbury Park, CA: Sage.

Russell, D. (1990). *Rape in marriage*. New York: Macmillan.

Sieber, J. E. (1982). Deception in social research: I. Kinds of deception and the wrongs they may involve. *IRB: A Review of Human Subjects Research, 4*, 1–2, 12.

Sieber, J. E. (1983a). Deception in social research: II. Factors influencing the magnitude of potential for harm or wrong. *IRB: A Review of Human Subjects Research, 5*, 1–3, 12.

Sieber, J. E. (1983b). Deception in social research: III. The nature and limits of debriefing. *IRB: A Review of Human Subjects Research, 5*, 1–2, 4.

Sieber, J. E. (1992a). *Planning ethically responsible research: A guide for students and internal review boards*. Applied Social Research Methods Series. Newbury Park, CA: Sage.

Sieber, J. (1992b). *Sharing social research data*. Newbury Park, CA: Sage.

31

SCIENTIFIC REWARDS AND CONFLICTS OF ETHICAL CHOICES IN HUMAN SUBJECTS RESEARCH

PETER DAVID BLANCK, ALAN S. BELLACK, RALPH L. ROSNOW,
MARY JANE ROTHERAM-BORUS, AND NINA R. SCHOOLER

The main purpose of the Committee on Standards in Research (CSR) has been to advise the American Psychological Association (APA) on issues and standards related to the protection of human participants in psychological research. In recognition of the increased variety of ethical concerns facing the field, the scope of CSR has broadened considerably. Recent efforts have addressed such topics as informed consent, confidentiality of human participants at risk, and scientific misconduct (Grisso et al., 1991).

CSR operates as an advisory committee, not a standard-setting or sanctioning body. The committee has four general functions: (a) to review proposed APA policies, (b) to be a point of inquiry for researchers, (c) to identify and analyze emerging ethical issues, and (d) to disseminate information that helps to clarify standards and ethical obligations of research psychologists toward their human participants (Grisso et al., 1991). In this article, we

Reprinted from the American Psychologist, 47, 959–965. Copyright 1992 by the American Psychological Association.

offer a number of suggestions designed to increase the rewards and identify potential conflicts of research with human participants. The suggestions emanate from the different backgrounds and perspectives of the CSR members—laboratory and clinical researchers, social and clinical psychologists, and an attorney.

In the 1970s, in the wake of growing concern over what were seen as moral issues, the APA set out to formulate a code of ethical practices to govern research involving human participants. An ad hoc committee developed a document that was adopted by the Council of Representatives in 1972 and issued as an informative booklet the following year (APA, 1973). The document was revised a decade later by the Committee for the Protection of Human Participants in Research (APA, 1982), and a further revision is currently under way by the CSR. At the core of this document is a set of principles representing ethical practice and linked to the use of stringent safeguards to protect the rights of research participants. In the past 10 years there has also been a proliferation of governmental and institutional regulations that give voice and meaning to participants' rights in human research. Last year, for example, the United States Office of Science and Technology issued regulations that set forth a comprehensive federal policy for the protection of human subjects (Federal Register, 1991, p. 28003). As a consequence of these efforts, psychological researchers have become accustomed to the close scrutiny of institutional and professional review boards as proposals are evaluated in regard to ethical practices. Recent research also suggests that individual researchers differ systematically in the ways they formulate and evaluate ethical principles (Kimmel, 1991).

Since the 1970s, the APA code has underscored the idea that sound research often calls for a delicate balance between humane, moral, and scientific values. For example, it is considered essential that people have freedom of choice in deciding whether or not to participate in psychological research (Sieber & Sorensen, 1991). However, the nature of freedom in choosing to participate is often hazy, and may have a significant effect on the nature of the sample. We will return to this point, but it is recognized generally that, in the absence of a special effort to stimulate participation, the characteristics of persons who volunteer for laboratory and community-based research differ in important ways from those participants with relatively less freedom of choice to participate. This tension is particularly apparent, for example, in research in which persons of lower income levels are induced to participate (Blanck, in press-b; Rosenthal & Rosnow, 1975).

Given the strong relations among methodology, ethics, and research artifacts, the APA code encourages researchers to invest their ingenuity in discovering ways of conducting studies that avoid ethical violations. In this article, we suggest ways in which the APA code can serve also as a window onto opportunities to increase the rewards of ethical choices to researchers who are able to adopt such practices.

We discuss three ethical practices that may engender scientific rewards: (a) the use of confidentiality to protect the privacy of disclosures, (b) the use of debriefing to clarify the nature of the study, and (c) the use of volunteers to assure freedom from coercion to participate. We realize that these practices are not always feasible, such as when the obligation to advance knowledge appropriately overrides privacy (Blanck, 1987; Blanck & Turner, 1987; Pattullo, 1982; Sieber & Sorenson, 1991; Veatch, 1982) or when providing complete information about significant research compromises the validity of the data. Given the "double-edged potentiality" of ethical issues (APA, 1973, p. 8), we suggest some limiting conditions (or potential conflicts) so as not to present an overly optimistic view of what is possible. But the primary objective of this article is to make a number of suggestions designed to foster a view of research ethics not as a hinderance to the integrity of sound research, but as an opportunity for scientific rewards in psychological research with human participants.

USE OF CONFIDENTIALITY

Three basic principles appear in all European and American ethical codes for psychological research: (a) avoid physical harm, (b) avoid psychological harm, and (c) keep the data confidential (Schuler, 1982). The first two principles emanate from the Nuremberg code of 1946–1949, developed in conjunction with expert testimony against Nazi doctors at the Nuremberg Military Tribunal after World War II (Beecher, 1970). Confidentiality, the third principle, evolved to safeguard information divulged by research participants and clients. Confidentiality is commonly justified on the basis of three claims: (a) that researchers have a professional right to keep subjects' disclosures secret, (b) that fairness requires respect for privacy, and (c) that enhanced credibility or validity should result when the researcher has promised to keep disclosures confidential (Bok, 1978).

The protection of confidentiality can sometimes present legal, methodological, and ethical dilemmas for researchers (Appelbaum & Rosenbaum, 1989). Special problems are apparent and have been documented in detail elsewhere with respect to confidentiality in community-based research projects (e.g., Blanck, in press-b; Sieber & Sorensen, 1991). For example, certain research data (e.g., field studies of child abuse or venereal disease) are ordinarily not immune to subpoena (Knerr & Carroll, 1978; Melton & Gray, 1988; Rozovsky, 1990; Sieber, 1982). Likewise, routine partner notification (as a breach of confidentiality) could limit in certain circumstances the validity of community-based research findings, such as those involving human immunodeficiency virus (HIV) testing (Melton & Gray, 1988; Sieber & Sorensen, 1991). However, in certain sensitive research situations, it is possible to obtain a "certificate of confidentiality" from the Public Health

Service (for a review, see Melton & Gray, 1988; Sieber, 1992). These certificates protect participants' names and other identifying information from being subject to a court's subpoena power. However, prior research suggests that most ethically sensitive studies involving human participants are not typically covered by certificates of confidentiality (Melton & Gray, 1988).

Most institutions require that consent forms specify that the data will be confidential, but this pledge can be highlighted to different degrees. Assuring participants of the confidentiality of their responses is not simply for their benefit, but may increase the likelihood that they will be honest and open in their responses (Boruch & Cecil, 1979). An experiment by Esposito, Agard, and Rosnow (1984) tested the hypothesis that a written assurance of confidentiality would improve self-disclosures by college-age research participants. The participants were administered Spielberger's (1979) Trait–State Personality Inventory and Crowne and Marlowe's (1964) Social Desirability Scale under one of two conditions. In the experimental condition, the instruction page asked for the respondent's name and contained the statement "Your responses on these measures will be kept strictly confidential." In the control condition, the instructions asked for the respondent's name but contained no mention of confidentiality. Participants' self-ratings of anxiety, curiosity, and anger showed lower correlations with social desirability in the confidentiality than in the control condition. This finding suggests that confidentiality can attenuate evasive answer bias.

Circumstantial support for the view that a written or verbal assurance of confidentiality promotes more honest disclosures comes from a number of other areas, although the pattern of results is not unequivocal. Ceci and Peters (1984) observed that letters of recommendation written by faculty advisors were more critical when the form indicated that the student had waived his or her right to inspect the letter. Likewise, Merluzzi and Brischetto (1983) reported that male undergraduate students evaluated counselors as less trustworthy when the counselors had breached confidentiality. A survey study by Singer (1984) found that the great majority of respondents believed that assurances of confidentiality foster cooperativeness in answering questions. On the other hand, Reamer (1979) reported no effect of confidentiality in an interview study of youths previously arrested for status offenses.

This topic requires a more detailed analysis because little is known about the general magnitude of the relationship between verbal and written assurances of confidentiality and the subsequent quality of data in human participant research (cf. Committee on Federal Statistics, 1979). The size of the relationship obtained by Esposito et al. (1984) is modest by conventional standards of psychological research, but is not unimpressive when recast in terms of its practical significance (e.g., Rosenthal, 1990). The effect sizes in Ceci and Peters's (1984) study seemingly ranged from moderate to substantial, corresponding to different questions that were asked of the faculty advisors. It is still unclear what might be expected of research participants in diverse situations.[1] For example, volunteers for studies of a new medication for acquired immunodeficiency syndrome (AIDS), marital conflict, or sexual practices would likely value confidentiality much more than college students in a study on perceptual acuity. Conversely, parents of child participants in a clinical trial generally demand information about their children, a potential breach of the child's confidentiality. It would be important to study the effects of verbal and written assurances of confidentiality in such highly sensitive research studies, such as those involving persons at risk or children (Grisso et al., 1991). It is also worth noting situations in which clear guarantees of confidentiality are essential for recruiting representative samples. Research on AIDS is a case in point. In such cases the usual pro forma statement will not be sufficient to allay the concerns of potential participants who are terrified by the possibility of public disclosure.

Thus, researchers face a difficult task to ensure confidentiality in a climate of shifting ethical standards (Bayer, 1985). As suggested above, the AIDS pandemic presents researchers with such challenging ethical dilemmas. Researchers must ensure confidentiality knowing that the rationale guiding the procedures established to protect participants' disclosures may shift over time (Bayer, 1985; Bayer, Levine, & Murray, 1984; Bayer & Toomey, in press). For example, several large longitudinal research studies examining HIV risk acts (e.g., the Multi-Site AIDS Cohort Study, the New York City Gay Men Study) were ongoing when HIV testing procedures were developed. Because of the particular data collection procedures, it was possible for researchers to know the HIV serostatus of the participants and for participants to choose to know their status or not. Researchers had the opportunity to examine the effect that knowledge of one's HIV serostatus had on behavior change and on participants' reported quality of life (Ostrow, 1991; Martin, 1987). Participants who were tested for HIV could choose not to be informed of their serostatus. Later, the National Institutes of Health adopted a policy that it was unethical to conduct research in which the participants were tested for HIV and not informed of their serostatus. Participants who chose to get tested for HIV and declined to be informed of their serostatus under earlier guidelines no longer had the option to remain uninformed. The circumstances existing at the time of choosing to participate shifted during the duration of the study. The AIDS pandemic has required

---

[1] One statistical procedure worth mentioning that has been used to protect participant confidentiality is the *randomized response technique* (RRT), pioneered by Warner (1965, 1971) for use in large-scale survey research. The participant uses a randomizing device (such as flipping a coin) to select how to respond to a sensitive question (Fidler & Kleinknecht, 1977; Krotki & Fox, 1974). Suppose the question asks, "Have you ever used cocaine?" The subject is instructed to flip the coin, out of the researcher's sight, and to respond "yes" if it lands heads and to respond truthfully either "yes" or "no" if it lands tails. Knowing that 50 percent of the participants are expected to get heads to respond "yes," it is then possible to estimate the proportion of participants that actually responded that they had sampled cocaine. Although RRT calls for a larger number of participants to produce reliable estimates than may be feasible in most psychological research, the results of RRT might serve as a yardstick for appraising the general effect sizes of simple written and verbal assurances of confidentiality on the quality of research findings.

many ethical decisions to be made with insufficient and shifting community standards (Dickens, 1988). Similar concerns exist around the issues of confidential versus anonymous testing (Annas, 1988; Curran, Gostin, & Clark, 1988), partner notification (Bayer & Toomey, in press), recruitment of pregnant users of intravenous drugs whose children may be born addicted (Macklin, 1990), and HIV testing of adolescents (Rotheram-Borus, 1991b).

USE OF DEBRIEFING

The word *debriefing* has its roots in military jargon; it was first used during World War II to refer to the process of interrogating pilots who had returned from bombing missions. In its current usage in psychological research, the term emphasizes a kind of catharsis after treatment. The purpose of debriefing is to remove any misconceptions and anxieties that the participants have about the research and to leave them with a sense of dignity, knowledge, and a perception of time not wasted (Harris, 1988). Jones and Gerard (1967) suggested that debriefing should regularly include discovering what each participant thought of the research situation, thereby providing a more personal context in which to interpret the nature of the results.

In cases in which deception or misdirection is used as part of an experimental design, debriefing is also meant to remove any "detrimental impact on the participant's feeling of trust in interpersonal relationships" (APA, 1973, p. 77). It might be hypothesized that the revelation that a deception was part of the study could spawn skepticism and suspicion, which in turn could influence future behavior (either as part of this or another study or in other life activities). However, there is little evidence of any changes in behavior when debriefed participants, even those previously suspicious, participate in subsequent tests or experiments (e.g., Brock & Becker, 1966; Fillenbaum, 1966; McGuire, 1969).

Clinical subjects often participate in research to learn something about themselves, and debriefing is an opportunity to receive feedback regarding performance or response (Sieber, 1992). Participation in clinical research provides a chance to be altruistic by contributing to science and improving clinical services, helping others through participation. Thus, information about one's own performance or the findings of the study enhances the personal sense of participating and contributing to an important program (Jones & Gerard, 1967).

Debriefing also offers the researcher the opportunity to discover the personal meaning of the study for the participants—whether the experimental procedure was actually perceived or experienced by the participants as the researcher intended. Such information is essential for accurate interpretation of findings. For example, if participants in a pseudo-treatment group guess that their treatment was not real, the value of this condition as a control for positive treatment expectancies is compromised. Similarly, investigators who compare clinical and nonclinical populations may be particularly rewarded by appropriate debriefing strategies, as the meaning of an experimental manipulation or the value of participant payment often differs between groups.

Debriefing has been critical to examining the efficacy of clinical trials for drugs aimed at slowing disease progression for persons infected with HIV. Middle-class gay men in AIDS epicenters (e.g., San Francisco, Chicago, and New York) are well informed about drugs being used to treat symptomatic persons (Gorman et al., 1991). It has been a common practice for participants in clinical trials to share medication with each other, gain access to drugs or treatments available outside of the United States, and take multiple drugs simultaneously. In the supportive, cohesive community climate, it is almost impossible to conduct an evaluation of a single drug uncontaminated by auxiliary treatments. Rather than force research participants to be duplicitous about their multiple treatments and contaminate the protocol in unknown ways, debriefing is a central tool to monitor the degree and type of multiple drug use among gay men in research trials.

Debriefing often can provide researchers with leads for future research and help identify problems in their current protocols. Rotheram-Borus, Koopman, and Bradley (1989) found that adolescents who had received an AIDS prevention program reported during debriefing that they frequently engaged in group sex (i.e., sexual intercourse with multiple partners during a single encounter). Despite substantial pilot work, including focus groups with youths and their counselors, extensive interviews and self-reports of sexual activities, and participation in 10 intervention sessions, these adolescents had not reported their group encounters until the debriefing. When the protocol was subsequently revised to include assessment of sexual encounters with multiple partners, many adolescents conveyed their participation in such activities.

In long-term clinical studies, debriefing is sometimes so much delayed for practical and methodological reasons that when it does take place it is irrelevant to the investigator and the participants may no longer be accessible or interested. Delay may result from the investigator's need not to compromise the short-term conduct of the study or to sacrifice statistical power by interim analysis of an experiment. However, it is usually possible to conduct ongoing post-study interviews with individual participants that allow them to describe their perceptions of the study, even if the debriefing cannot provide complete information about the outcome of the research. More study is needed of the use of post-study debriefing as a source of data in clinical studies. CSR is not aware of a clinical study that has investigated participant satisfaction by comparing a group that was debriefed with one that was not.

USE OF VOLUNTEERS

We mentioned previously that participant selection bias can upset the balance between methodological requirements and ethics, producing artifacts in the data (Rosnow, in press; Suls & Rosnow, 1981). *Artifact* refers generally to research findings resulting from factors other than those intended by the investigator (Rosnow, in press). The term does not refer simply to serendipitous findings, but to scientific observations resulting from unrecognized factors that might jeopardize the validity of the investigator's conclusions (Rosnow, in press). For example, to reduce a threat to the external validity of research findings resulting from limited participant samples (e.g., only volunteer subjects), methods for enhancing the diversity of participants are often warranted. The associated ethical issue concerns the point at which the researcher threatens the individual's right and freedom not to participate, such as by offering inducements to participate that are coercive (Blanck, in press-a, in press-c).

In one representative example, Strohmetz, Alterman, and Walter (1990) examined baseline differences in problem severity among alcoholics who did and did not volunteer to participate in a treatment outcome study. The level of the patient's volunteer status (i.e., willingness to participate in the treatment intervention) was positively related to the severity of alcoholism problems reported during the pretreatment period. Although the results can be interpreted in different ways, one plausible implication raised by Strohmetz et al. is that patients who agree to randomization in intervention experiments may somehow be different from the population of interest. King and King (1991) have noted a similar concern regarding intervention research on the adjustment of Vietnam veterans.

As suggested above, ethical practice requires researchers to respect individuals' freedom to decline to participate. However, a number of research strategies have been described to deal with the potential costs of subject selection bias. Rosenthal and Rosnow (1975, 1991) described how, in certain psychological studies in which the population can be stratified into respondents and nonrespondents, it is possible to assess the direction of subject selection bias (cf. Saks & Blanck, 1992). They also noted a number of empirically derived strategies for improving the representativeness of subject samples by inducing more nonvolunteers to enter the sampling pool. For example, volunteering rates are likely to increase the greater the material incentive to participate and the less aversive, more interesting, and more important the task.

The scientific rewards that accrue from the idea that the implementation of such strategies should make researchers more careful and thoughtful not only in how appeals for volunteers are made, but in planning the research. For instance, if researchers tell participants as much as possible about the significance of the research, as though they were another granting agency—which in fact they are, granting researchers time instead of money—the emphasis is placed more heavily on the scientific rewards of doing important rather than trivial research.

Researchers who study clinical populations are bound generally to restrict participation to those who agree to participate. Rarely, an exception is made when the question to be studied is one that effectively precludes consent but is of such major public health concern that an institutional review board (IRB) will waive the requirement for consent. Salzman et al. (1991) compared two pharmacologic agents for management of disruptive psychotic behavior in a psychiatric intensive care ware. Patients whose behavior was self-destructive or dangerous to others routinely received one of these medications. The question posed was whether the drugs differed in terms of efficacy or side effects. The requirement of written informed consent would have precluded the research. A dual level of review by the local IRB and the state Department of Mental Health waived the requirement for prior informed consent. The study met two perceived criteria for waiver of individual informed consent: (a) the research question had high public health significance, and (b) the conduct of the research did not increase the level of risk to participants, because patients would have received one of the two medications studied. Studies such as that conducted by Salzman et al. are extremely rare. Virtually all research with clinical populations is conducted within the framework of individual informed consent to ensure the voluntary nature of participation. As is true in other research contexts, the voluntary nature of participation ranges from general announcements of the availability of participation to screening of all potential subjects followed by direct, and sometimes intense, efforts to encourage or urge participation by those who meet criteria.

In clinical research, the identification of a potential subject pool creates a sampling frame that allows comparison of the included volunteers with those who are not included in a study. Such comparisons are valuable to investigators, who are often able to compare systematically the included and excluded participants on a wide range of demographic or other characteristics.

There is one essential characteristic that distinguishes volunteers from nonvolunteers, and that is participation itself. Access to potential participants in clinical settings is often gained through the clinicians responsible for treatment. This poses a potential bias in recruiting. Many clinical researchers report informally, for example, that although patients are recruited from large numbers of wards, a disproportionate number of participants come from only one or two of them. Spohn and Fitzpatrick (1980) compared participating and nonparticipating subjects representing successive screening and self-selection in a population of schizophrenic patients being considered for a study of medication withdrawal. Patients who were research eligible were divided into those whose treating teams allowed them to be approached and those whose teams did not believe they should be approached. Furthermore, individuals asked to participate were divided into two groups—those who ultimately agreed and those who did not. Subsequent comparisons among groups revealed substantial differences between the original reference sample and the final consenting sample that, the researchers concluded, limit interpretation of data from the actual study.

In another example, Schooler (1980) identified a population of schizophrenic patients and compared participants in a clinical trial of injected versus oral medication with those who refused to participate because it was an experiment. There were no differences between the groups in relevant background characteristics. The hypothesis tested was that patients who had to take medication daily would relapse sooner than those who received medication by injection every few weeks, because the oral medication group would forget and stop taking their pills. The null hypothesis could not be rejected.

But, if the potential subjects in Schooler's (1980) study who refused to participate in experiments tended to be those who are not compliant medication takers, the experiment could have been seriously flawed. Schooler tested this possibility by assuming that all who refused to participate were included in the study. If randomized to oral medication, they would have stopped taking it and relapsed. If randomized to injectable medication, they would not have relapsed. A comparison of relapse rates based on this hypothetical subject pool, not biased by exclusion of refusers, showed no significant differences between the groups. Thus, detailed descriptions of individuals who are excluded from clinical studies may provide valuable research rewards that increase knowledge and allow the test of focused hypotheses about potential effects in nonvolunteers. Such detailed comparisons are too rare in the clinical literature and are another example of investigations that warrant further study.

In summary, the psychology of recruiting participants for a research protocol is not dissimilar from other social marketing situations. There is a gray line between applying pressure to participate and being a competent recruiter and researcher. The gray area creates the opportunity for many ethical dilemmas. For example, is it ethical to employ young, attractive, verbal, and intelligent assistants of ethnic backgrounds similar to the target population in order to recruit participants? Participants may be trying to please the recruiter. Participants are also more likely to participate if they are familiar with the research assistants. Is it ethical to have research assistants spend time in the recruitment site, building a positive reputation, so that the potential participants are familiar with the researchers? Such a strategy is likely to increase the recruitment rate, but is that undue pressure? May a researcher ethically reward children with a classroom party for returning parental consent forms for a research project, the reward contingent on return of the consent form whether or not the parent granted approval? Is it ethical for a researcher to convince a school district to adopt a proposed intervention as a schoolwide curriculum? Evaluation of a schoolwide program in collaboration with the district does not generally require parental consent. However, a researcher initiating and evaluating a similar program does require parental consent and extensive review by an IRB. The extent to which researchers must divorce themselves from the recruitment setting and restrain from creating an environment that enhances recruitment is unclear ethical territory.

CONCLUSION

This article is meant to raise more questions that it answers. As in the committee's previous article (Grisso et al., 1991), we have highlighted a number of issues because they reflect the special interests and backgrounds of those serving on the CSR, not because they are any more pressing than the many other questions about ethical standards facing research psychologists (cf. Pope & Vetter, 1992). The primary objective of this article is to continue the discussion and view of ethics as presenting opportunities for scientific rewards in psychological research with human participants.

In future articles, the CSR hopes to explore criticisms of review boards as overly zealous in exercising their gatekeeping function at the expense of scientists, who also have the ethical imperative to do sound research (e.g., Ceci, Peters, & Plotkin, 1985; Rosenthal & Rosnow, 1984). As Darley (1980) stated, there is an ethical imperative in doing sound research, for otherwise "we leave those who are attempting social change the prey of hucksters who are willing to put forth undocumented claims based on inadequate evidence" (p. 15). The study of this issue is meant to shed light on the difficulties currently faced by review boards (institutional or governmental) in assessing the rewards and potential conflicts of ethical choices in human subjects research.

REFERENCES

American Psychological Association. (1973). *Ethical principles in the conduct of research with human participants.* Washington, DC: Author.

American Psychological Association. (1982). *Ethical principles in the conduct of research with human participants.* Washington, DC: Author.

Annas, G. J. (1988). Not saints but healers: The legal duties of health care professionals in the AIDS epidemic. *American Journal of Public Health, 8,* 844–849.

Appelbaum, P. S., & Rosenbaum, A. (1989). *Tarasoff* and the researcher: Does the duty to protect apply in the research setting? *American Psychologist, 44,* 885–894.

Bayer, R. (1985). AIDS and the gay community: Between the specter and the promise of medicine. *Social Research, 52,* 581–606.

Bayer, R., Levine, C., & Murray, T. (1984). Guidelines for confidentiality in research on AIDS. *IRB: A review of human subjects research, 6*(6), 1–12.

Bayer, R., & Toomey, K. E. (in press). HIV prevention and the two faces of partner notification: Policy, politics and ethics. *American Journal of Public Health.*

Beecher, H. K. (1970). *Research and the individual: Human studies.* Boston: Little, Brown.

Blanck, P. D. (1987). The process of field research in the courtroom. *Law and Human Behavior, 11,* 337–358.

Blanck, P. D. (in press-a). The emerging work force: Empirical study of the Americans with Disabilities Act. *Journal of Corporate Law.*

Blanck, P. D. (in press-b). Empirical study of the employment provisions of the Americans with Disabilities Act: Methods, preliminary findings and implications. *New Mexico Law Review.*

Blanck, P. D. (in press-c). On integrating persons with mental retardation: The ADA and ADR. *New Mexico Law Review.*

Blanck, P. D., & Turner, A. (1987). Gestalt research: Clinical–field research approaches to studying organizations. In J. Lorsch (Ed.), *Handbook of organizational behavior* (pp. 109–125). Englewood Cliffs, NJ: Prentice-Hall.

Bok, S. (1978). *Lying: Moral choice in public and private life.* New York: Pantheon Books.

Boruch, R. F., & Cecil, J. S. (1979). *Assuring the confidentiality of research data.* Philadelphia, PA: University of Pennsylvania Press.

Brock, T. C., & Becker, L. A. (1966). "Debriefing" and susceptibility to subsequent experimental manipulation. *Journal of Experimental Social Psychology, 2,* 314–323.

Ceci, S. J., & Peters, D. (1984). Letters of reference: A naturalistic study of the effects of confidentiality. *American Psychologist, 39,* 29–31.

Ceci, S. J., Peters, D., & Plotkin, J. (1985). Human subjects review, personal values, and the regulation of social science research. *American Psychologist, 40,* 994–1002.

Committee on Federal Statistics. (1979). *Privacy and confidentiality as factors in survey response.* Washington, DC: National Academy of Science.

Crowne, D. P., & Marlowe, D. (1964). *The approval motive: Studies in evaluative dependence.* New York: Wiley.

Curran, W. J., Gostin, L., & Clark, M. (1988). *Acquired immunodeficiency syndrome: Legal and regulatory policy analysis.* Washington, DC: U.S. Department of Commerce.

Darley, J. M. (1980). The importance of being earnest—and ethical. *Contemporary Psychology, 25,* 14–15.

Dickens, B. (1988). Legal limits of AIDS confidentiality. *Journal of the American Medical Association, 259,* 3449–3451.

Esposito, J. L., Agard, E., & Rosnow, R. L. (1984). Can confidentiality of data pay off? *Personality and Individual Differences, 5,* 477–480.

Federal Register. (1991, June 18). Vol. 56, pp. 28003–28032.

Fidler, D. S., & Kleinknecht, R. E. (1977). Randomized response versus direct questioning: Two data-collection methods for sensitive information. *Psychological Bulletin, 84*, 1045–1049.

Fillenbaum, S. (1966). Prior deception and subsequent experimental performance: The "faithful" subject. *Journal of Personality and Social Psychology, 4*, 537.

Gorman, J., Kertzner, R., Todak, G., Goetz, R., Williams, J., Rabkin, J., Meuer-Bahlberg, H., Mayeux, R., Stern, Y., Lange, M., Dobkin, J., Spitzer, R., & Ehrhardt, A. (1991). Multidisciplinary baseline assessment of homosexual men with and without HIV infection: 1. Overview of study design. *Archives of General Psychiatry, 48*, 120–123.

Grisso, T., Baldwin, E., Blanck, P. D., Rotheram-Borus, M. J., Schooler, N., & Thompson, T. (1991). Standards in research: APA's mechanism for monitoring the challenges. *American Psychologist, 46*, 758–766.

Harris, B. (1988). Key words: A history of debriefing in social psychology. In J. Morawski (Ed.), *The rise of experimentation in American psychology* (pp. 188–212). New Haven, CT: Yale University Press.

Jones, E. E., & Gerard, H. B. (1967). *Foundations of social psychology.* New York: Wiley.

Kimmel, A. J. (1991). Predictable biases in the ethical decision making of American psychologists. *American Psychologist, 46*, 786–788.

King, D. W., & King, L. A. (1991). Validity issues in research on Vietnam veteran adjustment. *Psychological Bulletin, 109*, 107–124.

Knerr, C. R., & Carroll, J. D. (1978). Confidentiality and criminological research: The evolving body of law. *Journal of Criminal Law and Criminology, 69*, 311–321.

Krotki, K. J., & Fox, B. (1974). The randomized response technique, the interview, and the self-administered questionnaire: An empirical investigation of fertility reports. *Proceedings of the Social Statistics Section: American Statistical Association* (pp. 367–371). Washington, DC: American Statistical Association.

Macklin, R. (1990, September). *Ethical dilemmas.* Presentation to the Policy Division, HIV Center for Clinical and Behavioral Studies, Columbia University, New York.

Martin, J. (1987). The impact of AIDS on gay male sexual behavior patterns in New York City. *American Journal of Public Health, 77*, 578–581.

McGuire, W. J. (1969). Suspiciousness of experimenter's intent. In R. Rosenthal & R. L. Rosnow (Eds.), *Artifact in behavioral research* (pp. 13–57). San Diego, CA: Academic Press.

Melton, G. B., & Gray, J. W. (1988). Ethical dilemmas in AIDS research. *American Psychologist, 43*, 60–64.

Merluzzi, T. V., & Brischetto, C. S. (1983). Breach of confidentiality and perceived trustworthiness of counselors. *Journal of Counseling Psychology, 30*, 245–251.

Ostrow, D. (1991, May). *Research on longitudinal patterns on sex and drug use behav-*

iors. Paper presented at the HIV Center for Clinical and Behavioral Studies, Columbia University, New York.

Pattullo, E. L. (1982). The limits of the "right" of privacy. *IRB: A Review of Human Subjects Research, 4*, 3–5.

Pope, K. S., & Vetter, V. A. (1992). Ethical dilemmas encountered by members of the American Psychological Association: A national survey. *American Psychologist, 47*, 397–411.

Reamer, F. G. (1979). Protecting research subjects and unintended consequences: The effects of guarantees of confidentiality. *Public Opinion Quarterly, 43*, 497–506.

Rosenthal, R. (1990). How are we doing in soft psychology? *American Psychologist, 45*, 775–777.

Rosenthal, R., & Rosnow, R. L. (1975). *The volunteer subject*. New York: Wiley.

Rosenthal, R., & Rosnow, R. L. (1984). Applying Hamlet's question to the ethical conduct of research. *American Psychologist, 39*, 561–563.

Rosenthal, R., & Rosnow, R. L. (1991). *Essentials of behavioral research: Methods and data analysis* (2nd ed.). New York: McGraw-Hill.

Rosnow, R. L. (in press). The volunteer problem revisited. In P. D. Blanck (Ed.), *Interpersonal expectations: Theory, research, applications*. New York: Cambridge University Press.

Rotheram-Borus, M. (1991a, June). *AIDS and adolescents*. Presentation of evidence to Congressional Task force on Women and Children, Washington, DC.

Rotheram-Borus, M. (1991b). *HIV interventions for adolescents*. Washington, DC: Surgeon General's Panel on HIV.

Rotheram-Borus, M., Koopman, C., & Bradley, J. (1989). Barriers to successful AIDS prevention programs with runaway youth. In J. O. Woodruff, D. Doherty, & J. G. Athey (Eds.). *Troubled adolescents and HIV infection: Issues in prevention and treatment* (pp. 37–55). Washington, DC: Janis Press.

Rozovsky, F. A. (1990). *Consent to treatment: A practical guide* (2nd ed.). Boston: Little, Brown.

Saks, M. J., & Blanck, P. D. (1992). Justice improved: The unrecognized benefits of aggregation and sampling in the trial of mass torts. *Stanford Law Review, 44*, 815–851.

Salzman, C., Solomon, D., Miyawaki, E., Glassman, R., Rood, L., Flowers, E., & Thayer, S. (1991). Parenteral lorazepam v. parenteral haloperidol for the control of psychotic disruptive behavior. *Journal of Clinical Psychiatry, 52*, 177–180.

Schooler, N. R. (1980). How generalizable are the results of clinical trials? *Psychopharmacology Bulletin, 16*, 29–31.

Schuler, H. (1982). *Ethical principles in psychological research*. San Diego, CA: Academic Press.

Sieber, J. E. (Ed.). (1982). *The ethics of social research: Fieldwork, regulation, and publication*. New York: Springer-Verlag.

Sieber, J. E. (1992). *Planning ethically responsible research*. Newbury Park, CA: Sage.

Sieber, J. E., & Sorensen, J. L. (1991). Ethical issues in community-based research and intervention. In J. Edwards, R. S. Tindale, L. Heath, & E. J. Posavac (Eds.), *Social psychological applications to social issues: Vol. 2. Methodological issues in applied social psychology*. New York: Plenum Press.

Singer, E. (1984). Public reactions to some ethical issues of social research: Attitudes and behavior. *Journal of Consumer Research, 11*, 501–509.

Spielberger, C. D. (with G. Jacobs, R. Crane, S. Russell, L. Westberry, L. Barker, E. Johnson, J. Knight, & E. Marks). (1979). *Preliminary manual for the State–Trait Personality Inventory (STPI)*. Tampa: University of South Florida Press.

Spohn, H. E., & Fitzpatrick, T. (1980). Informed consent and bias in samples of schizophrenic subjects at risk for drug withdrawal. *Journal of Abnormal Psychology, 89*, 79–92.

Strohmetz, D. B., Alterman, A. I., & Walter, D. (1990). Subject selection bias in alcoholics volunteering for a treatment study. *Alcoholism: Clinical and Experimental Research, 14*, 736–738.

Suls, J. M., & Rosnow, R. L. (1981). The delicate balance between ethics and artifacts in behavioral research. In A. J. Kimmel (Ed.), *New directions for methodology of social and behavioral science: Ethics of human subject research* (No. 10, pp. 55–67). San Francisco, CA: Josey-Bass.

Veatch, R. M. (1982). Limits to the right of privacy: Reason, not rhetoric. *IRB: A Review of Human Subjects Research, 4*, 5–7.

Warner, S. L. (1965). Randomized response: A survey technique for eliminating evasive answer bias. *Journal of the American Statistical Association, 60*, 63–69.

Warner, S. L. (1971). The linear randomized response model. *Journal of the American Statistical Association, 66*, 884–888.

SPECIAL TOPICS
AND ISSUES

32

THE INSTITUTIONAL REVIEW BOARD AS A MIRROR OF SCIENTIFIC AND ETHICAL STANDARDS

RALPH L. ROSNOW, MARY JANE ROTHERAM-BORUS, STEPHEN J. CECI, PETER DAVID BLANCK, AND GERALD P. KOOCHER

Over the past two decades, psychologists doing research in a number of areas have witnessed a proliferation in the ethical standards to which they are held accountable, especially when the research involves human participants. Because of changes in ethical standards commensurate with changes in scientific practices, psychologists not only must be concerned with the protection of autonomy, privacy, and justice in the process of recruiting research participants but must ensure that the highest standards of ethical and scientific conduct will be followed throughout the research process (Christakis, 1988; Williams, 1984). Given the broad range of scientific and ethical challenges punctuating the social and scientific zeitgeist, the Board of Scientific Affairs (BSA) of the American Psychological Association (APA) revised the name and functions of the former Committee for the Protection of

Reprinted from the *American Psychologist*, 48, 821–826. Copyright 1993 by the American Psychological Association.

Human Participants in Research (CPHPR) to become the Committee on Standards in Research (CSR; see Grisso et al., 1991).

This change in title and purpose was intended to expand the area of concern in which the CPHPR had previously operated. It would now include (a) promoting freedom of research consistent with the highest ethical and scientific standards, (b) monitoring attitudes and concerns regarding the use of human and animal participants in research, (c) preparing written and oral statements relevant to research ethics and scientific conduct, and (d) updating the *Ethical Principles for the Conduct of Research with Human Participants* (APA, Committee for the Protection of Human Participants in Research, 1982). Recently, the CSR invited suggestions and experiences from psychological researchers and practitioners, editors of APA journals, and other interested parties to prepare for the task of revising the APA's document on ethical principles for research using humans (Mitchell-Meadows, 1992). The CSR has also sought to foster the view of research ethics as an opportunity for increased scientific and societal rewards rather than as an affront to the integrity of sound research (Blanck, Bellack, Rosnow, Rotheram-Borus, & Schooler, 1992).

In this article, the CSR continues its public discussion of problems that it believes are in need of study. The general issue addressed here concerns criticisms directed against institutional review boards (IRBs) as overly zealous in exercising their gatekeeping function at the expense of scientists, who also have the ethical imperative to do sound research (see Ceci, Peters, & Plotkin, 1985; Rosenthal & Rosnow, 1984). By opening this issue to discussion, we seek to accomplish three goals:

First, we hope to shed light on the difficulties faced by IRBs in assessing the rewards and potential conflicts of ethical choices in research with human participants. The title of this article encapsulates the idea that IRBs are presumed to mirror the incipient ethical dilemmas facing the scientific community and, in the process of evaluating risks and benefits, to mirror the current standards of scientific practice. As the number and sheer complexity of dilemmas increase, the role assigned to IRBs could become more multifaceted.

Second, we begin to explore how changes and emerging trends in the ways that IRBs choose to perform their role may affect freedom of inquiry in science. Just as standards of research practice have undergone evolution, so have the ethical criteria implemented by IRBs. To illustrate this point, we examine some of the difficulties faced in establishing consistent ethical procedures for research on the acquired immunodeficiency syndrome (AIDS) pandemic. Researchers in other areas of psychology have also experienced paradigmatic changes, but perhaps no area of human subjects research has been more affected by change than AIDS research.

Third, we aim to stimulate interest in the development of mechanisms to guide and monitor the IRB process. In so doing, we strive to ensure that there will be no cessation of studies that need to be done in order to answer important scientific and societal questions. We believe there are potential gains to be realized by both science and the general public as IRBs become more sensitive to the idea that the failure to conduct a study that has been proposed is as much an act to be evaluated on ethical grounds as is the conducting of a study (Rosenthal & Rosnow, 1984; Rosnow, 1990). We also hope to facilitate more consistent implementation of ethical standards across a field of research.

ASSESSING RISKS AND BENEFITS IN HUMAN RESEARCH

A central responsibility of IRBs is to ensure that the potential benefits to the individual research participants (and to society) will be greater than any risks that may be encountered by participation in the research (Stanley & Sieber, 1992). Before the 1950s, researchers were not held to a systematic evaluation of whether their studies met this requirement. There were no IRBs and few standard practices against which to assess whether the investigators were operating in an ethical manner. A radical shift occurred in 1954, when the United States Public Health Service decided to organize a large-scale experiment to test the efficacy of the Salk vaccine to protect children against polio.

Involving almost two million children, this was the first large-scale field trial ever mounted, and it raised a number of controversial issues (Meier, 1989). A basic concern was whether to use a randomized design that would place untreated (control) participants at greater risk than treated participants or to give all the children the poliomyelitis vaccine. It was decided that the only scientifically acceptable way to find out whether the Salk treatment really worked was to administer a placebo to a control group of children in such a way that none of the subjects would know whether they had received the therapeutic vaccine or the placebo. This and other features of this pioneering study would become technical standards to consider when the concept of the IRB was realized a decade later (Mitchell & Steingrub, 1988).

To be sure, the criteria originally invoked by IRBs continue to evolve, in part because of pressures by advocacy groups. For example, groups have lobbied for quicker release of relevant drugs for dying patients, drug companies have marshaled support for changes in access of research participants to experimental treatments, and researchers who see deficiencies in the medical community's and general public's understanding of the meaning of informed consent have pressed for education of these constituencies (Mitchell & Steingrub, 1988). Such pressures can produce a ripple effect leading to changes in national and regional criteria for the evaluation of research, ultimately affecting IRBs that are obliged to incorporate such standards.

The criteria used by medical school IRBs to address the issues with which they grapple in evaluating clinical trials have also come to be applied to behavioral and social science (Cann & Rothman, 1984). With the introduction of these criteria into a wider sphere have come concerns by psychologists as to the potential for misapplications (Ceci et al., 1985). One issue is whether evaluating the technical (not just the ethical) merit of a study is within the purview of IRBs. Historically, the role of review boards was to ensure that informed consent was obtained, the confidentiality of participants was safeguarded, and the recruitment process allowed equal access to all relevant potential participants. The objective was to preserve the autonomy of potential participants to the maximum extent possible. In recent years, the role of IRBs has often been expanded to include issues not specifically related to the autonomy of research participants.

A broad range of design issues is now included in many IRB discussions. The design of a drug trial is generally viewed as deficient unless there are adequate controls, random assignment, and a sufficient number of observations to ensure that the results due to the experimental intervention can be detected. It is not difficult to imagine how the strict application of standards developed in drug trials could pose problems for researchers in other areas. On the other hand, not including design issues as a prerequisite for approval could have negative ramifications (Meier, 1992). For example, if a large clinical trial were proposed to examine the efficacy of an experimental drug for halting progression of fatal illness and prolonging a high quality of life, the design must allow clear conclusions to be drawn. The failure to meet standards of control and sample size in such trials could result in a waste of governmental, institutional, public, and personal resources.

One question we raise is whether the composition of IRBs should be systematically expanded to include persons with expertise in areas not specifically directed to the autonomy issue. Should the membership include people who are sensitive to nuances in the interface of ethical and technical aspects of behavioral and social research (see, e.g., Suls & Rosnow, 1981)? Even if psychological researchers were to support this idea, considerable variability would exist among IRBs in deciding whether issues of design and methodology fall within their responsibility. Among the members of the CSR, there is also disagreement over whether technical aspects of the research are a proper concern of IRBs or whether such scientific issues should be resolved before submission to the IRB. Suppose an IRB insisted that a psychological study be radically redesigned to conform to criteria that the researcher, with a track record of successes in the area, viewed as an unrealistic demand. What recourse does the researcher have to press his or her claim or to resolve the disagreement expediently?

In practice, IRBs in medical schools are likely to be more intrusive in their critique of scientific merit than are review boards located in academic departments in liberal arts colleges. This greater intrusiveness is predicated on the belief that there is generally greater potential risk to participants in clinical trials and studies using invasive therapeutic procedures than in those using traditional behavioral procedures. Since the identification of AIDS in the early 1980s, the virus has presented a series of challenges to researchers attempting to maintain integrity in the application of ethical and scientific standards (Bayer, Levine, & Murray, 1984). The social stigma of AIDS, as much as the association of AIDS and death, intensifies the challenge (Bayer & Gostin, 1990). In the context of a life-threatening disease, it is critical that the principles of privacy, justice, and autonomy be consistently applied at every stage of the research. However, the definition of ethical practice and researchers' ability to ensure confidentiality and justice among human immunodeficiency virus (HIV) infected persons has changed over the last decade.

To illustrate, when an IRB makes decisions about maintaining confidentiality regarding a communicable disease that poses a substantial threat to the public's health, there is inherently a tension between an individual's desire to control personal information and society's desire to gain access to information (Bayer et al., 1984). The strain is increased because those at risk are often politically, socially, and economically stigmatized. In the midst of the AIDS pandemic, it is often not clear that researchers can ensure the confidentiality of their participants in research. Even researchers who have obtained "certificates of confidentiality" from the National Institutes of Health (NIH) ponder the consequences should the issue of confidentiality be challenged in the courts. Confidentiality is not the only source of tension, nor are issues of confidentiality confined to HIV research (Blanck et al., 1992), but the tension seems almost palpable in the case of HIV research.

To give another example, the availability of prophylactic treatments has led to increased advocacy for HIV testing, especially of persons considered at high risk (Bayer & Toomey, 1992; Kutchinsky, 1988). Behavioral researchers working in this area are increasingly interested in evaluating the consequences and reactions to testing. However, their ability to protect the confidentiality of those who are tested has decreased. Knowing one's serostatus is seen as the basic first step to adopting safer sexual practices and, therefore, a desirable goal of public health officials. There is conflicting evidence that at least raises the possibility that those who know they are HIV seropositive are not necessarily more likely to adopt safer sexual practices or to disclose to sexual partners (Fox, Odaka, Brookmeyer, & Polk, 1987; Goedert, 1987; Ostrow et al., 1989). Given that it is seen as good public health policy to know one's results and that some states have mandated the reporting of serostatus, can research studies of HIV testing be conducted without jeopardizing the person's right to privacy and confidentiality concerning serostatus? Analogous issues have been raised in other areas of research in psychology, such as the problems in protecting confidentiality in field studies of child abuse or venereal disease (Blanck et al., 1992).

Indeed, the question of HIV testing becomes even more complex when children considered at high risk (e.g., runaway, gay-identified) are the focus of the study (Rotheram-Borus & Koopman, 1992). In some states, parents can mandate that their children be tested or that they as parents be informed of the results of testing. If adolescents participated in the research as mature or emancipated minors, they nevertheless may return home at some point in the future and be under the supervision of their parents. Are parents then entitled access to information obtained by researchers when the adolescent held a different status? New York State Public Health Law (New York State Laws, 1988) mandates that serostatus be recorded in medical charts. This law also stipulates that physicians be allowed to disclose serostatus to parents when necessary for care or treatment unless the youth already has the legal authority to consent to health care (see Greater New York Hospital Association, 1988). Even if adolescents remain out of their homes, recording information about serostatus in a medical chart opens the opportunity for disclosure to parents. Studies evaluating the impact of HIV testing could create nightmares for investigators who strive to maintain consistent ethical practice.

A different type of ethical dilemma was created for IRBs when HIV serological testing emerged in the 1980s. Homosexual research participants were enrolled in ongoing protocols when the ELISA (enzyme-linked immunosorbent assay) and Western blot test for HIV became available (Holder, 1985). Researchers in several studies assessed the serostatus of their participants in the ongoing longitudinal studies with informed voluntary consent. The researchers offered participants the option of knowing their serostatus, but participants could choose not to be informed of the results of their tests. Some participants agreed to be tested but did not want to know their status. Within several years, the NIH adopted the policy that persons tested must be informed of their serostatus in the interests of the general public's health.

Consider the implication of such a ruling for participants who agreed to be tested under one set of guidelines if the guidelines later shifted. Given such a ruling, how was the researcher to handle this situation when participants had agreed to be tested, were tested, and did not return for the results of their serostatus? Was the researcher required to inform the participants? Should the researcher send a letter informing each participant of the results of his or her test? Can researchers be expected to conduct studies that evaluate the impact of HIV testing even though this testing is not linked to ongoing health care? Are there hypotheses in social psychology, clinical psychology, developmental psychology, and so forth that cannot be addressed because of the researcher's inability to protect confidentiality? Questions such as these reveal how difficult it can be to maintain a sure moral footing regarding issues of autonomy and confidentiality when there is a slippery ethical slope.

INCONSISTENCIES IN DECISION MAKING

There appears to be great variability in the standards invoked, and in turn the recommendations put forward, among IRBs (Ceci et al., 1985; Prentice & Antonson, 1987). It has been reported, for instance, that although IRBs are relatively successful in ensuring privacy and overseeing consent, they are less effective in weighing risks and benefits (Williams, 1984). Inconsistencies in evaluating risks and benefits may stem from biases in the assessment of protocols, the composition of review boards, and the nature of committee action and interaction. The point is that different standards are being applied to research at different institutions and in different parts of the country. Inconsistent standards create the appearance, if not the possibility, of injustice (Rosenthal & Blanck, 1993). In one case, it often happened that the identical proposal that was approved without amendments at one university was amended or even disapproved at a nearby university in the same city (Ceci et al., 1985).

Kimmel (1991) asked a sample of psychologists to give their opinions about the ethical costs and benefits of hypothetical studies. He reported that respondents who tended to put a greater emphasis on research costs were primarily female; had recently received the PhD degree in counseling, school, or community psychology; and were employed in service-oriented contexts. By contrast, respondents who tended to put a greater emphasis on research benefits were primarily male, had held their doctorates in a basic psychology area (such as social, experimental, or developmental psychology) for a longer time, and were employed in research-oriented contexts. These results raise the suspicion that individual biases toward costs and benefits due to the composition of an IRB could influence how it ultimately decides particular cases (see Ceci et al., 1985; Hamsher & Reznikoff, 1967; Kallgren & Kenrick, 1990; Schlenker & Forsyth, 1977).

State laws that limit the types of information and degree of acceptable risk to research participants are an indirect source of variability among IRBs (e.g., New York State 14 NYCRR 527.10). To the extent that a state insists on such limitations, IRBs will be obliged to impose stricter standards, and, in turn, there will be fewer opportunities to conduct research of a critical nature in that state. In the case of AIDS research, such regional variability is likely to influence the selection of sites for vaccine trials.

At present, there are several potential drugs that may be tested in AIDS vaccine trials (Taylor, 1992). To be useful, the trials must be conducted with populations that have a current conversion rate of seropositivity of about 3%

a year. This implies that the trial be conducted on only those individuals who are at highest risk, which includes those who share intravenous drug needles and young men who identify themselves as gay. Large numbers of participants will need to be recruited in each locale. In addition, it will be necessary to ensure that participants recognize that receiving an experimental vaccine does not imply that they are protected against HIV. Also, there are unlikely to be any biological markers to signal whether any individual is immune to the virus.

These are rigorous constraints under which to mount a vaccine trial. Although community advisory boards ensure that the IRBs mirror local standards and norms (Valdiserri, Tama, & Ho, 1988), wariness and mistrust of scientists—particularly among minority participants at high risk—could be substantial in view of the experience in previous circumstances (Ad Hoc Advisory Board, 1973; Thomas & Quinn, 1991). Confronted by these constraints, it is not surprising that researchers find it tempting to carry out such studies in regions where they need not worry about community advisory boards, such as in the developing world rather than in industrial countries. However, think of the untold new ethical dilemmas if developing countries should become a testing ground for the rest of the world.

Investigators distressed by the actions of local IRBs often voice the complaint that the committees act as a police force rather than as a protector of the rights of the participants (Christakis, 1988). Those researchers conducting low-risk interventions or epidemiological surveys have felt especially burdened by the demands of IRB processes (Cann & Rothman, 1984). Protocols of low risk are actually excluded from the necessity of undergoing a full IRB review if they do not violate one of three basic criteria: (a) anonymity of responses, (b) absence of civil or criminal liability, (c) sensitive aspects of behavior (Department of Health and Human Services, 1981). Most epidemiological surveys are exempt from review by IRBs, given these criteria. However, concerns regarding liability and shifting standards for the protection of human participants can mean that the same criteria are being applied to noninvasive interview surveys as to invasive medical procedures (Cann & Rothman, 1984). Thus a further challenge is to prevent the erosion of confidence among researchers, particularly those engaged in low-risk studies, who may perceive the review process as arbitrary or even irrational.

Some of the difficulty stems from local practices that are inconsistent across institutions, and some of it derives from conceptual confusion at the national or policy level. Regarding the latter, consider the case of educational research. Under some circumstances, research can be recast as curricular or educational and may thereby qualify for either expedited review or no review at all. School district employees frequently implement new curricula or learning technologies, sometimes replete with a formal evaluation plan, and are not bound by the same standards that apply to university researchers who propose similar curricula or technologies. Major large-scale educational interventions that might produce a negative impact on the lives of children are implemented with little difficulty. Witness the introduction of the "good touching–bad touching" curriculum, which, its proponents claimed, would increase the reporting of sexual abuse, although others have argued otherwise (see Reppucci & Havgaard, 1989). Another example was the new-math curriculum, which is now widely viewed as having set back an entire cohort of youngsters.

More recent illustrations include drug-related skills (e.g., Hawkins, Catalano, & Kent, 1991) and sexual-health curricula (e.g., Patierno & Britton, 1992) aimed at high-risk behaviors. Notwithstanding the absence of pilot data to justify the implementation of educational interventions such as these, proponents are rarely held to a level of cost–benefit analysis comparable to the most innocuous list-learning study proposed by an MA student in experimental psychology. Put baldly, there is a perception of hypocrisy, in that researchers are being asked to justify relatively innocent procedures while others are allowed to pursue potentially damaging practices with little or no justification. If protecting children from risk of harm is a concern for university researchers, then fairness would seem to dictate that it be a concern of school employees as well. Similar examples can be found in common medical practices, the behavior of attorneys toward clients, and so forth. Researchers feel singled out.

In addition to a discussion of community standards in its deliberations, IRBs should be acquainted with national disciplinary standards. At present, such standards are not clearly articulated, but they can be surmised from an analysis of published articles. APA journals are replete with studies that entail deception, psychological stress, and deliberate avoidance of debriefing (e.g., where researchers fear that debriefing could lead to unwanted social repercussions, such as a diminution of helping behavior among subjects in a bystander apathy experiment). There needs to be a balance between local standards of IRBs and national standards because investigators have a foot in each of these communities.

TOWARD COST–BENEFIT IDENTIFICATIONS

In view of the shifting standards governing research and the unevenness with which different IRBs function (Ceci et al., 1985), a process is needed to maximize consistency across IRBs and at the same time keep them abreast of emergent issues. For a variety of reasons—not the least being the need to couch deliberations in the context of local community standards of ethics—no top–down national regulatory body is desirable. Instead, it would be valuable for IRB members to be supplied with a casebook of actual research protocols that have received extensive review and analysis by social scientists, bioethicists, and research participants (both investigators and subjects). Such a casebook should aid IRB members in making explicit the costs of doing research as well as the costs of not doing it. It might also give them an opportunity to expose their own ethical biases to scrutiny so that they can function judiciously and equitably.

Although a casebook ought to help sensitize IRB members to relevant costs and benefits, there will always be cases that require extrapolation and novel analysis. This raises the possibility of conflicts among the opinions and values of IRB members, investigators, and institutions. Although this is unavoidable, it could be alleviated by the creation of an advisory board within the Office for the Protection of Subjects From Research Risk. Parties to disagreements could request an analysis and review of an IRB decision by such a board. Its analysis could serve merely an educative function or, in cases in which all parties gave previous stipulation of their willingness to accept the analysis as determinative, it could be binding. A description of the mechanics of such a board (i.e., its creation, authority, membership, and operating procedures) is beyond the scope of this article, but we raise the idea here for further discussion.

CONCLUSION

We have looked at how the role of IRBs has expanded over the past two decades and the ways in which inconsistencies seem to adhere to decision criteria that mirror changing standards of fields that are in constant flux. Clearly, it is critical to establish guidelines for the evaluation of research protocols (Prentice & Antonson, 1987). There must also be a way to limit the power of review boards (instead of adopting the strategy of an ever-increasing role), but current proposals include evaluation of the technical merit of the study as one component of evaluating the risk–benefit ratio for involvement of human participants. Finally, we raised the idea of providing IRBs with a book of case studies and accompanying ethical analyses to sensitize members to troublesome issues and nuances in the behavioral and social sciences. Central to such case studies would be an explicit enjoinder that IRBs take into consideration not only the costs of doing the proposed research but also the costs of not doing it. In general, we believe that a mirror must also be held up to the review process, so that its existence, fairness, and effectiveness can be examined and justified (see Cowan & Adams, 1979; Hershey, 1985).

REFERENCES

Ad Hoc Advisory Board. (1973). *Tuskegee syphilis study* (Public Health Service Report). Washington, DC: U.S. Government Printing Office.

American Psychological Association, Committee for the Protection of Human Participants in Research. (1982). *Ethical principles in the conduct of research with human participants*. Washington, DC: Author.

Bayer, R., & Gostin, L. (1990). Legal and ethical issues relating to AIDS. *Bulletin of the Pan American Health Organization, 24*, 454–468.

Bayer, R., Levine, C., & Murray, T. H. (1984). Guidelines for confidentiality in research on AIDS. *IRB: A Review of Human Subjects Research, 6*(6), 1–7.

Bayer, R., & Toomey, K. E. (1992). HIV prevention and the two faces of partner notification: Policy, politics, and ethics. *American Journal of Public Health, 89*, 1158–1164.

Blanck, P. D., Bellack, A. S., Rosnow, R. L., Rotheram-Borus, M. J., & Schooler, N. R. (1992). Scientific rewards and conflicts of ethical choices in human subjects research. *American Psychologist, 47*, 959–965.

Cann, C. I., & Rothman, K. J. (1984). IRBs and epidemiologic research: How inappropriate restrictions hamper studies. *IRB: A Review of Human Subjects Research, 6*(4), 5–7.

Ceci, S. J., Peters, D., & Plotkin, J. (1985). Human subjects review, personal values, and the regulation of social science research. *American Psychologist, 40*, 994–1002.

Christakis, N. A. (1988). Should IRBs monitor research more strictly? *IRB: A Review of Human Subjects Research, 10*(2), 8–10.

Cowan, D. H., & Adams, B. R. (1979). Ethical and legal considerations for IRBs: Research with medical records. *IRB: A Review of Human Subjects Research, 1*(8), 1–4.

Department of Health and Human Services. (1981). Final recommendation amending basic HHS policy for the protection of human research subjects (45 CFR, Pt. 46). *Federal Register, 46*, 8366–8392, 19195.

Fox, R., Odaka, N. J., Brookmeyer, R., & Polk, B. F. (1987). Effect of HIV antibody disclosure on subsequent sexual activity in homosexual men. *AIDS, 1*, 241–246.

Goedert, J. J. (1987). What is safe sex? Suggested standards linked to testing for human immunodeficiency virus. *New England Journal of Medicine, 316*, 1339–1442.

Greater New York Hospital Association. (1988). *AIDS confidentiality law*. New York: Author.

Grisso, T., Baldwin, E., Blanck, P. D., Rotheram-Borus, M. J., Schooler, N. R., & Thompson, T. (1991). Standards in research: APA's mechanism for monitoring the challenges. *American Psychologist, 46*, 758–766.

Hamsher, J. H., & Reznikoff, M. (1967). Ethical standards in psychological research and graduate training: A study of attitudes within the profession. *Proceedings of the 75th Annual Convention of the American Psychological Association, 2*, 203–204.

Hawkins, J. D., Catalano, R. F., & Kent, L. A. (1991). Combining broadcast media and parent education to prevent teenage drug abuse. In L. Donohew, H. E. Harper, & W. J. Bukosi (Eds.), *Persuasive communication and drug abuse prevention* (pp. 283–294). Hillsdale, NJ: Erlbaum.

Hershey, N. (1985). IRB jurisdiction and limits on IRB actions. *IRB: A Review of Human Subjects Research, 7*(2), 7–9.

Holder, A. R. (1985). Is this a job for the IRB?: The case of the ELISA assay. *IRB: A Review of Human Subjects Research, 7*(6), 7–8.

Kallgren, C. A., & Kenrick, D. T. (1990, March). *Ethical judgements and nonhuman research subjects: The effects of phylogenetic closeness and affective valence.* Paper presented at the Eastern Psychological Association meeting, Philadelphia.

Kimmel, A. J. (1991). Predictable biases in the ethical decision making of American psychologists. *American Psychologist, 46,* 786–788.

Kutchinsky, B. (1988). *The role of HIV testing in AIDS prevention.* Copenhagen: Institute of Criminal Science.

Meier, P. (1989). The biggest public health experiment ever: The 1954 field trial of the Salk poliomyelitis vaccine. In J. M. Tanur, F. Mosteller, W. H. Kruskal, E. L. Lehmann, R. F. Link, R. S. Pieters, & G. R. Rising (Eds.), *Statistics: A guide to the unknown* (3rd ed., pp. 3–14). Belmont, CA: Wadsworth.

Meier, P. (1992, May 12). *Ethical and scientific issues in drug trials with human participants.* Presentation to the APA Committee on Standards in Research, New York.

Mitchell-Meadows, M. (1992, December). Input is sought on guidelines for research using humans. *The APA Monitor,* p. 22.

Mitchell, S. C., & Steingrub, J. (1988). The changing clinical trials scene: The role of the IRB. *IRB: A Review of Human Subjects Research, 10*(4), 1–5.

New York State Laws. (1988). Ch. 584, Art. 27-F, §2782, ¶8. (Effective Feb. 1, 1989)

Ostrow, D. G., Joseph, J. G., Kessler, R., Soucy, J., Tal, M., Eller, M., Chmiel, J., & Phair, J. P. (1989). Disclosure of HIV antibody status: Behavioral and mental health correlates. *AIDS Education and Prevention, 1,* 1–11.

Patierno, C., & Britton, P. (1992). *Talk about sex.* New York: SIECUS.

Prentice, E. D., & Antonson, D. L. (1987). A protocol review guide to reduce IRB inconsistency. *IRB: A Review of Human Subjects Research, 9*(1), 9–11.

Reppucci, N. D., & Havgaard, J. J. (1989). The prevention of child sexual abuse: Myth or reality? *American Psychologist, 44,* 1266–1275.

Rosenthal, R., & Blanck, P. D. (1993). Science and ethics in conducting, analyzing, and reporting social science research: Implications for social scientists, judges, and lawyers. *Indiana Law Journal, 68.*

Rosenthal, R., & Rosnow, R. L. (1984). Applying Hamlet's question to the ethical conduct of research: A conceptual addendum. *American Psychologist, 39,* 561–563.

Rosnow, R. L. (1990). Teaching research ethics through role-play and discussion. *Teaching of Psychology, 17,* 179–181.

Rotheram-Borus, M. J., & Koopman, C. (1992). Protecting children's rights in AIDS research. In B. Stanley & J. Sieber (Eds.), *Social research on children and adolescents: Ethical issues* (pp. 143–161). Newbury Park, CA: Sage.

Schlenker, B. R., & Forsyth, D. R. (1977). On the ethics of psychological research. *Journal of Experimental Social Psychology, 13,* 369–396.

Stanley, B., & Sieber, J. (Eds.). (1992). *Social research on children and adolescents: Ethical issues.* Newbury Park, CA: Sage.

Suls, J. M., & Rosnow, R. L. (1981). The delicate balance between ethics and artifacts in behavioral research. In A. J. Kimmel (Ed.), *Ethics of human subject research* (pp. 55–67). San Francisco, CA: Jossey-Bass.

Taylor, R. (1992). Hesitation blues: AIDS researchers struggle to prepare candidate HIV-1 vaccines for large scale efficiency trials. *Journal of NIH Research, 4*(7), 89–93.

Thomas, S. B., & Quinn, S. C. (1991). The Tuskegee syphilis study, 1932 to 1972: Implications for HIV education and AIDS risk education programs in the Black community. *American Journal of Public Health, 81,* 1498–1505.

Valdiserri, R. O., Tama, G. M., & Ho, M. (1988). The role of community advisory committees in clinical trials of anti-HIV agents. *IRB: A Review of Human Subjects Research, 10*(4), 5–7.

Williams, P. C. (1984). Success in spite of failure: Why IRBs falter in reviewing risks and benefits. *IRB: A Review of Human Subjects Research, 6*(3), 1–4.

33

CURRENT NIH PERSPECTIVES
ON MISCONDUCT IN SCIENCE

MARY L. MIERS

Until recently it would have been highly unusual for a staff member of a federal agency to receive an invitation to prepare an article for a professional journal on the subject of misconduct in science. Although the scope and causes of such misconduct are not fully understood—and indeed, raise interesting questions for study—there is little doubt that the increased visibility of the aberrant scientist has colored both the public and professional view of the research enterprise (Brandt, 1983; Broad & Wade, 1982; Jackson & Prados, 1983; Kilbourne & Kilbourne, 1983; Relman, 1983; Schmaus, 1983; U.S. House of Representatives, 1983; Wigodsky, 1984). The impact of recent developments can be appreciated if one measures that form of significant social commentary, the editorial cartoon, a small collection of which now graces my bulletin board.

It is important to recall that fraud and misrepresentation of various kinds have always occurred in science. Although the popular concept of "pure" science emphasizes the quest for knowledge for its own sake, every scientist knows that the object of the quest is an exciting finding, and furthermore, the

Reprinted from the *American Psychologist*, 40, 1985, 831–835. In the public domain.

elucidation and publication of that finding in advance of one's colleagues. The temptation and opportunity to exploit the process have doubtless existed since the development of science as an organized activity, moderated by some combination of individual ethics, intellectual rigor, and the safeguards imposed by the processes of experimentation and publication. However, the sheer size of the research enterprise today and its dependence on public support present special dilemmas for both the patrons and practitioners of research when misconduct seems to have—or actually has—occurred.

Although fraud in science is not a new phenomenon, there is no question that the incidence of *reported* misconduct has increased dramatically. In the past three years, NIH has received an average of two reports per month of possible misconduct that appears to go beyond the traditional kinds of issues encountered in the fiscal and administrative management of grants, cooperative agreements, and contracts. About half of the reports have proven to be factual. Some of those reflected not fraudulent intent but some error in methodology or sloppy technique. Others appeared to be the result of the failure to develop and communicate appropriate policies and internal controls within academic and research institutions. The reports of misconduct cover a full range of behaviors. A few have involved possible egregious misuse of funds, but the majority are concerned with departures from accepted research practices, including fabrication, misrepresentation or selective reporting of results, inadequate attention to the rights of human subjects, and unacceptable treatment of laboratory animals.

Viewed against a denominator of more than 20,000 NIH awards active at any instant, these numbers are small, almost insignificant. They have, however, given rise to well-founded concerns about the efficacy of traditional practices often cited as safeguards against misconduct. Those practices include peer review of research proposed for funding or publication and replication of significant findings. Such safeguards are based on the assumption that individual investigators are honest and well intentioned, although they may make errors in methodology or theory. These procedures are not designed to detect clever, systematic cheating or research practices that are markedly at variance with what they are reported to be.

The realization that traditional safeguards of science cannot entirely prevent misconduct has been accompanied by increasing evidence that awardee institutions, funding agencies, and professional organizations are often ill prepared to deal with allegations or evidence of wrongdoing. Most funding agencies have access to some type of audit or investigative unit to pursue cases involving apparent misuse of funds or possible criminal activities. Recent trends such as the establishment of Offices of Inspector General throughout the federal government have underscored the importance of integrity in publicly funded programs of all kinds. Within the Department of Health and Human Services (DHHS), the Office for Protection from Research Risks (OPRR) has played an important role in detecting and dealing with failure to comply with requirements designed to protect the welfare of human subjects and animals, in addition to its role in developing and refining the needed policies and procedures.

The biomedical research community has been quick to recognize that the research institutions play a critical role in preventing, detecting, and dealing with misconduct in science. Professional organizations have traditionally assumed varying degrees of responsibility for the integrity of their members. Both the Association of American Medical Colleges (AAMC) and the Association of American Universities (AAU) have developed statements of principles and model procedures for the guidance of their member institutions (AAMC, 1982; AAU, 1982). Several institutions have developed their own guidelines or are in the process of doing so.

Until recently, NIH tended to treat reports of misconduct as isolated events, employing ad hoc procedures for each case on the assumption that the probability of encountering a similar incident was minimal. In the past few years, it has become clear that more explicit and predictable procedures are needed to enable the funding agencies to deal with some level of recurring activity involving allegations or evidence of misconduct. Of equal concern has been the lack of guidance to awardee institutions and investigators regarding their rights and responsibilities.

It is clear in retrospect that the lack of established policies and procedures led to false starts and inordinate delays in some cases. Nothing in previous NIH experience had prepared agency staff to deal with the conflicting demands of accountability and fiscal stewardship, on the one hand, and respect for civil liberties on the other. A more positive (and, one hopes, not too self-serving) assessment of recent NIH performance might conclude that the incremental approach taken in a series of investigations served to develop a body of knowledge and experience that could form the basis for development of more formalized procedures.

Although most of the recent attention has been centered on NIH, the problems posed by misconduct in science are not limited to that agency. In the fall of 1981, Secretary of Health and Human Services Richard S. Schweiker identified as a major management initiative the development of policies and procedures for dealing with misconduct in science. Early efforts undertaken by the research agencies included: (a) conducting regional seminars for investigators, academic officials, and institutional review board members regarding protection of human subjects and related regulations and policies; (b) discussing with members of NIH advisory councils and peer review groups their responsibilities related to misconduct in science and soliciting their views on approaches to be taken; (c) improving internal NIH procedures for identifying incoming grant applications and contract proposals from individuals or institutions under investigation or subject to postinvestigational sanctions; (d) modifying the coding and processing of competing grant applications to ensure that all requirements for protection of human subjects are met; and (e) developing a uniform procedure for documenting the results of agency staff review of annual progress reports.

NIH also undertook an intensive review of its policies and procedures to identify the need for improved guidance to agency staff and awardee investigators and institutions. This led to publication of a notice in the *NIH Guide for Grants and Contracts* in July 1982, inviting comments and suggestions. About two dozen responses were received. These were about evenly divided among those who believed firmer action was needed, those who suggested NIH was addressing a nonproblem and was proposing to repeal the Bill of Rights, and those who felt the situation was serious but under control. There was general agreement that the primary responsibility for preventing and dealing with misconduct rested with the academic institutions.

In August 1982, Assistant Secretary for Health Edward N. Brandt, Jr., directed NIH to take the lead in developing policies and procedures for all Public Health Service (PHS) research programs. This effort was not intended to override or replace the internal management controls of awardee institutions or the conditions imposed through routine grant and contract management practices. Rather, it was designed to deal with the special problems created by potentially serious breaches of the canons of science or conditions of the funding relationship. An interagency committee focused on the following broad types of misconduct: (a) serious deviations from accepted practices in the conduct or reporting of research, such as fabrication, falsification, or plagiarism; and (b) material failure to comply with federal requirements affecting specific aspects of the conduct of research, for example, protection of the welfare of human subjects and laboratory animals.

The committee has proposed a set of detailed policies and procedures for dealing with possible misconduct in research funded, regulated, or conducted by PHS. These documents were accepted by Brandt and his agency heads and were transmitted to appropriate offices in DHHS for review and approval. The latter process is nearly completed. It is expected that the documents will be made widely available for comment; and, where appropriate, some aspects will be incorporated into regulations. In brief, their coverage is as follows:

GENERAL POLICIES AND PRINCIPLES

This brief statement of policy is intended to underscore the commitment to integrity in all research funded, conducted, or regulated by the PHS.

POLICIES AND PROCEDURES FOR AWARDING AGENCIES

This step-by-step guide for agency staff will cover the "life cycle" of an incident. It will outline procedures for evaluating the significance of allegations, conducting an investigation, taking interim administrative actions when appropriate, and imposing postinvestigational sanctions when warranted. It will emphasize the need to protect the rights of accused individuals and "whistle blowers" and to provide an adequate public record of the agencies' actions without violating the civil liberties of individuals. An important section of this document is a statement of expectations for awardee institutions that underscores the institutions' responsibility to take prompt and appropriate action when misconduct is known or suspected and to inform the funding agency when the matter is judged to be serious enough to warrant an investigation.

POLICIES AND PROCEDURES FOR RESEARCH
CONDUCTED BY PHS

This document will provide guidance for agency research managers who may confront allegations or evidence of misconduct in an agency's intramural research program. It will embody many of the same principles enumerated above, adapted to take into account the employer–employee relationship, and will serve as the PHS internal counterpart of procedures now in place or being developed at many research institutions.

POLICIES AND PROCEDURES AFFECTING
RESEARCH REGULATED BY PHS

This document is a compendium of regulatory procedures, primarily those of the Food and Drug Administration (FDA), with special attention to the interface of regulatory requirements and research funded or conducted by PHS. It differs from the preceding two documents in that it is primarily a distillation and summary of existing, well-known procedures used by the agencies to ensure the integrity of regulated research.

PHS ALERT SYSTEM

As noted earlier, NIH has a mechanism in place for identifying incoming applications and proposals from individuals and institutions under investigation or subject to some sanction as the result of investigational findings. Because NIH has 14 different awarding components, some process was needed to ensure appropriate follow-up to completed investigations if an action were taken that would affect future funding. Similarly, although the fact that an investigation is ongoing does not preclude an award, there is a need for responsible NIH officials to consider all available information before a decision is made. This last document represents an effort to define the appropriate boundaries for sharing information among the various PHS agencies and to provide safeguards comparable to the strict confidentiality built into the NIH system when investigations are still underway. In addition to the public commentary planned for all these documents, a description of the proposed PHS ALERT will be published as a proposed major modification to the NIH ALERT, which is a system of records under the Privacy Act.

It may be of some interest to describe the approaches currently being used by NIH. In general, NIH staff share the concern, often expressed by representatives for the research community, that administrative solutions not create more problems than they solve. This agency has moved cautiously in an effort to develop sensible and equitable approaches based on precedent and the best advice available.

An early and critical step is distinguishing between frivolous or malicious allegations and those that may have some basis in fact. Although it is often difficult to make this distinction, it is generally possible to make a discreet, preliminary inquiry without compromising individual reputations or the integrity of research projects. NIH relies primarily on the awardee institutions to investigate, take actions when warranted, and provide agency staff with the information needed to make reasonable and equitable decisions regarding awards and pending applications. A typical incident would be handled in the following manner. When NIH staff become aware of allegations or other information suggesting misconduct may have occurred, the Office of Extramural Research and Training (OERT) is notified. Depending on what awards or pending applications are involved, one or more awarding units or investigative offices will participate in deciding what action should be taken. If there is general agreement that the allegation or report is plausible, the appropriate office will initiate an inquiry. Typically, this includes asking the institution and/or individual to respond. If the responses to the initial inquiry suggest that more fact-finding is necessary, an investigation will be undertaken. NIH does not conduct secret investigations, although in very rare instances a law enforcement agency may direct us to take no action because an investigation of possible criminal activity is underway.

It is not unusual to find that an active award or pending application is involved. This presents a very difficult problem. On the one hand, it is essential that agency staff not prejudge the outcome; at the same time, they are obligated to protect NIH interests based on the best information available at the time. When it appears that some interim action is necessary, every effort is made to minimize the effects of possibly premature decision. An awarding component may, for example, extend a current budget period for a few months—with or without funds—rather than make a new noncompeting award on the anniversary date. The process of investigation is a highly interactive one, designed to obtain the views of both the individuals suspected of misconduct and appropriate institutional officials. It is standard procedure to invite comments on a draft report and to change the report if warranted.

Even if NIH does not change its findings, the affected parties may have their comments appended to the report as part of the record.

In cases in which misconduct is not established, NIH attempts to minimize any harmful results of an unsubstantiated allegation or suspicion. Specific actions may include a letter to employers, removal of interim restrictions on awards, or briefing of agency staff and peer reviewers who may have incomplete or incorrect information. If misconduct has been established, a range of actions may be called for, depending on the circumstances. As a first step, the final report, including comments and rebuttals, is shared with a group of senior staff charged with making a recommendation to the NIH director. This "decision group" includes representatives from the OERT, affected awarding units, the DHHS Office of General Counsel, and at least one senior official with no direct involvement in the matter. Sanctions could include special prior approval requirements, consideration of relevant findings in future review and award processes, suspension or termination of an active award, or a recommendation that the Secretary of DHHS initiate proceedings to debar the individual or institution from eligibility for funding for some period of time.

As a general rule, pending investigations are not considered in the review of applications for scientific merit. Occasionally, when there has been media publicity or rumor about a particular case, reviewers are informed of the known facts in an effort to avoid compromising the review. Another option is to defer the review, although that may not work to the advantage of the applicant.

A similar process obtains when the alleged misconduct involves an intramural scientist. In such instances, inquiries and investigations are the responsibility of intramural officials, and actions are taken in accordance with regulations affecting civil service or PHS commissioned corps staff. The Office of Extramural Research and Training may be consulted at any time during the investigation and is required to assess the significance of established misconduct as it may affect an individual's eligibility for extramural funding.

The full impact of recent events on the research enterprise will probably not be understood for some period of time. In some instances, the reputations of individuals or institutions have suffered, and there have been instances of damage to research projects. More subtle and potentially more serious effects could include an erosion in public confidence in science, as well as inhibition of collaborative relationships among individual scientists and groups.

On balance, the response of the research community can be viewed as a reaffirmation of traditional scientific practices and values. And NIH, after the initial shock wave, is accommodating to the task of dealing with possible misconduct as an infrequent but significant feature of the agency's role as the largest supporter of biomedical research.

One of the most striking features of this process of adaptation is the extent to which it has been self-directed. For the casual observer, the topic of misconduct in science brings to mind the publicity generated by one or more recent cases. Both the general and scientific presses have published fairly detailed accounts of these—notably, plagiarism and falsification of results by Vijay Soman, irregularities in consent documents and protocols carried out under Marc Straus, Martin Cline's use of recombinant DNA in human subjects without required approvals, and most recently, John Darsee's fabrication of research findings. These examples and others have prompted considerable discussion about the adequacy of actions taken by research institutions and funding agencies. It is noteworthy, however, that NIH has experienced remarkably little outside pressure related to either the details of general procedures or actions to be taken in specific cases. We view this as encouraging evidence of public confidence in the integrity of the research enterprise, and we welcome the cooperation of the research community in maintaining that confidence.

REFERENCES

Association of American Medical Colleges. (1982). *The maintenance of high ethical standards in the conduct of research*. Washington, DC: Author.

Association of American Universities. (1982, April). *Report of the Association of American Universities Committee on Integrity of Research*. Washington, DC: Author.

Brandt, E. N., Jr. (1983). PHS perspectives on misconduct in science. *Public Health Reports, 98*, 136–139.

Broad, W. J., & Wade, N. (1982). *Betrayers of the truth: Fraud and deceit in the halls of science*. New York: Simon & Schuster.

Jackson, C. I., & Prados, J. W. (1983). Honor in science. *American Scientist, 71*, 462–465.

Kilbourne, B. K., & Kilbourne, M. T. (Eds.). (1983). *Proceedings of the 63rd Annual Meeting of the Pacific Division, American Association for the Advancement of Science: Vol. 1, Part 2. The dark side of science*. Washington, DC: Author.

National Institute of Health, Office of Extramural Research and Training. (1982). Misconduct in science. *NIH Guide for Grants and Contracts, 11*, 1–2.

Relman, A. S. (1983). Lessons from the Darsee affair. *New England Journal of Medicine, 308*, 1415–1417.

Schmaus, W. (1983). Fraud and the norms of science. *Science, Technology and Human Values, 8*, 12–22.

U.S. House of Representatives, Committee on Science and Technology, Subcommittee on Investigations and Oversight. (1981). *Fraud in biomedical research* [Hearings] (pp. 77–661). Washington, DC: U.S. Government Printing Office.

Wigodsky, H.S. (1984). Fraud and misrepresentations in research—Whose responsibility? *IRB, 6*(2), 1–5.

34

REFLECTIONS ON DETERMINING AUTHORSHIP CREDIT AND AUTHORSHIP ORDER ON FACULTY–STUDENT COLLABORATIONS

MARK A. FINE AND LAWRENCE A. KURDEK

Scholarly activity is an expected and rewarded enterprise for many professionals (Keith-Spiegel & Koocher, 1985). In academic settings, decisions regarding promotion, tenure, and salary are heavily influenced not only by the number of publications in peer-reviewed journals but also by the number of first-authored publications (Costa & Gatz, 1992). Similarly, in applied settings, professionals with strong publication records are often considered to have more competence and expertise than their less published counterparts.

Clearly, authorship credit and authorship order are not trivial matters. Because of the importance of authorship credit, dilemmas may arise when more than one person is involved in a scholarly project. In this article, we

Reprinted from the *American Psychologist*, 48, 1141–1147. Copyright 1993 by the American Psychological Association.

specifically address collaborative efforts between faculty and undergraduate or graduate students. The importance of authorship in the faculty–student research context was underscored by Goodyear, Crego, and Johnston (1992), who found that authorship issues were among the "critical incidents" identified by experienced researchers in faculty–student research collaborations.

The purpose of this article is to contribute to the discussions regarding the determination of authorship credit and order of authorship—in the faculty–student research context. There are six parts to the article. To provide a context for the discussions, the first part presents four hypothetical cases. Because the final authorship decisions in these cases are based on considerations reviewed later in the article, the cases end before the final decisions were determined. The second part reviews available guidelines for determining authorship credit and order. The third part describes ethical issues related to authorship credit and authorship order when faculty and students collaborate. The fourth part of the article highlights several ethical principles that may provide assistance in resolving authorship dilemmas. The fifth part provides tentative recommendations for faculty who collaborate with students on scholarly projects. The final part revisits the four hypothetical cases with our opinions regarding what authorship decisions would have been appropriate.

HYPOTHETICAL CASES

Case 1

A student in a clinical psychology doctoral program conducted dissertation research at a practicum site. The initial idea for the study was developed between the practicum supervisor (a psychologist) and the student. The dissertation committee was composed of the chair, who was a psychology faculty member in the student's graduate department; the practicum supervisor; and another psychology faculty member in the same department. After the dissertation was approved, the chair of the committee raised the possibility of writing a journal article based on the dissertation. The student agreed to write the first and subsequent drafts of the manuscript, the committee chair agreed to supervise the writing process, and the practicum supervisor agreed to review drafts of the paper. On initial drafts, the student, practicum supervisor, and committee chair were first, second, and third authors, respectively. However, after numerous drafts, the student acknowledged losing interest in the writing process. The committee chair finished the manuscript after extensively reanalyzing the data.

Case 2

An undergraduate student asked a psychology member to supervise an honors thesis. The student proposed a topic, the faculty member primarily developed the research methodology, the student collected and entered the data, the faculty member conducted the statistical analyses, and the student used part of the analyses for the thesis. The student wrote the thesis under very close supervision by the faculty member. After the honors thesis was completed, the faculty member decided that data from the entire project were sufficiently interesting to warrant publication as a unit. Because the student did not have the skills necessary to write the entire study for a scientific journal, the faculty member did so. The student's thesis contained approximately one third of the material presented in the article.

Case 3

A psychologist and psychiatrist collaborated on a study. A student who was seeking an empirical project for a master's thesis was brought into the investigation after the design was developed. The student was given several articles in the content area, found additional relevant literature, collected and analyzed some of the data, and wrote the thesis under the supervision of the psychologist. After the thesis was completed, certain portions of the study, which required additional data analyses, were written for publication by the psychologist and the psychiatrist. The student was not asked to contribute to writing the journal article.

Case 4

An undergraduate student completed an honors thesis under the supervision of a psychology faculty member. The student chose the thesis topic and took initiative in exploring extant measures. Because no suitable instruments were found, the student and the faculty member jointly developed a measure. The student collected and entered the data. The faculty member conducted the statistical analyses. The student wrote the thesis with the faculty member's guidance, and few revisions were required. Because the student lacked the skills to rewrite the thesis as a journal article, the faculty member wrote the article and the student was listed as first author. Based on reviewers' comments to the first draft of the manuscript, aspects of the study not included in the thesis needed to be integrated into a major revision of the manuscript.

AVAILABLE GUIDELINES FOR DETERMINING
AUTHORSHIP CREDIT AND ORDER

In each of the four hypothetical cases described above, decisions regarding the authorship credit and order were required. Until the last decade, there were few published guidelines that provided assistance in this decision-making process.

As an initial guideline, the American Psychological Association's (APA's) Ethics Committee (1983) issued a policy statement on authorship of articles based on dissertations. The statement indicated that dissertation supervisors should be included as authors on such articles only when they made "substantial contributions" to the study. In such instances, only second authorship was appropriate for the supervisor because first authorship was reserved for the student. The policy also suggested that agreements regarding authorship be made before the article was written.

This policy statement was important because it recognized that dissertations, by definition, represent original and independent work by the student. Given the creative nature of the student's dissertation, an article that he or she writes based on that dissertation should have the student identified as first author. The faculty supervisor, at most, deserves second authorship.

Although this policy statement was helpful, it did not clearly define the key term *substantial contributions*. Furthermore, because the policy statement applied only to dissertation research, it did not provide guidance for faculty who engaged in collaborative projects with students outside of dissertations.

Current guidelines for making decisions regarding authorship credit and order are presented in the APA *Ethical Principles of Psychologists and Code of Conduct* (1992), which supersedes the 1983 policy. The APA code has a section relevant to the determination of authorship on scholarly publications. Section 6.23, Publication Credit, states

> (a) Psychologists take responsibility and credit, including authorship credit, only for work they have actually performed or to which they have contributed.
> (b) Principal authorship and other publication credits accurately reflect the relative scientific or professional contributions of the individuals involved, regardless of their relative status. Mere possession of an institutional position, such as Department Chair, does not justify authorship credit. Minor contributions to the research or to the writing for publication are appropriately acknowledged, such as in footnotes or in an introductory statement.
> (c) A student is usually listed as principal author on any multiple-authored article that is based primarily on the student's dissertation or thesis.

Although this section is clearer and more detailed that the comparable section in previous versions of the *Ethical Principles of Psychologists*, it fails to provide comprehensive guidance to faculty who publish with students. In particular, terms such as *professional contribution* and *minor contribution* are unclear and, as a result, are open to different interpretations (Keith-Spiegel & Koocher, 1985). In the absence of clear guidelines regarding authorship credit and authorship order on faculty–student collaborative publications, disagreements may occur, and one or both parties may feel exploited.

ETHICAL ISSUES INVOLVED IN DETERMINING AUTHORSHIP CREDIT AND ORDER ON FACULTY–STUDENT COLLABORATIVE PROJECTS

The ethical dilemmas that arise when faculty collaborate with students on work worthy of publication stem from the unique nature of the faculty–student relationship. Although collaboration between two professionals can occur on an egalitarian basis, collaboration between faculty and their students is inherently unequal. By nature of their degrees, credentials, expertise, and experience, many faculty supervise students. Supervisors are responsible not only for facilitating the growth and development of supervisees but also for portraying supervisees' abilities accurately to others. For example, faculty may write letters of recommendation for their supervisees, evaluate their work, assign grades, or give critical feedback to representatives of their undergraduate or graduate programs. Thus, faculty who function as supervisors must balance the potentially competing duties of fostering the growth of their trainees and presenting them to others in a fair and accurate manner.

We believe that there are two potential ethical dilemmas in faculty–student collaborations. The first dilemma arises when faculty take authorship credit that was earned by the student. Many of the authorship-related critical incidents identified in the Goodyear et al. (1992) and Costa and Gatz (1992) studies concerned faculty taking a level of authorship credit that was not deserved and not giving students appropriate credit. As one might expect, Tabachnick, Keith-Spiegel, and Pope (1991) found that faculty respondents perceived "accepting undeserved authorship on a student's published paper" as unethical.

The second dilemma occurs when students are granted undeserved authorship credit. There are three reasons why this dilemma is an ethical one. First, a publication on one's record that is not legitimately earned may falsely represent the individual's scholarly expertise. Second, if, because he or she is now a published author, the student is perceived as being more skilled than a peer who is not published, the student is given an unfair advantage professionally. Finally, if the student is perceived to have a level of competence that he or she does not actually have, he or she will be expected to accomplish tasks that may be outside the student's range of expertise.

How often do faculty give students the benefit of the doubt with respect to authorship on collaborative publications? Although we are aware of many instances when supervisors engaged in this practice, systematic empirical evidence related to the prevalence of this practice is rare. Twenty years ago, Over and Smallman (1973) found that "distinguished psychologists" had reduced rates of first-authored papers in the years following receipt of APA Scientific Contribution Awards. Zuckerman (1968) had similar findings in a study of Nobel laureates. Recently, Costa and Gatz (1992), in a survey of faculty and students asked to assign publication credit in hypothetical dissertation scenarios, found that higher academic rank and more teaching experience were positively related to faculty giving students more authorship credit.

One explanation of this positive relation between faculty experience and granting students high levels of authorship credit is that senior faculty are more likely than junior faculty to be sought after for research consultation by students and new faculty. However, it is also possible that they may be more generous—perhaps overly so—in granting students authorship because publication pressures have lessened for them. Interestingly, Costa and Gatz found that faculty were more likely than students to give the student authorship credit in the hypothetical scenarios.

ETHICAL PRINCIPLES IN DETERMINING AUTHORSHIP CREDIT AND ORDER ON FACULTY–STUDENT COLLABORATIVE PROJECTS

Three ethical principles are relevant to ethical dilemmas that arise with regard to authorship on faculty–student collaborative projects: beneficence, justice, and parentalism. These principles, from which ethical codes (e.g., the *Ethical Principles of Psychologists and Code of Conduct*) are developed, may provide guidance when the codes themselves are inadequate (Kitchener, 1984).

To be beneficent is "to abstain from injuring others and to help others further their important and legitimate interests, largely by preventing or removing possible harms" (Beauchamp & Walters, 1982, p. 28). In the context of the authorship issue, *beneficence* implies that supervisors should help students further their careers by including them as authors when their contributions are professional in nature. In our opinion, to avoid harming students and others in the long run, beneficence implies that faculty should grant students authorship credit and first author status only when they are deserved.

Justice—the second ethical principle—refers to the ethical duty to treat others fairly and to give them what they deserve: "An individual has been treated justly when he has been given what he or she is due or owed, what he or she deserves or can legitimately claim" (Beauchamp & Walters, 1982, p. 30). The principle of justice is often interpreted to infer that one should treat another unequally only if there is a morally relevant difference between them (Beauchamp & Walters, 1982). In the authorship setting, if students are not considered to be meaningfully different from professional colleagues, then they should be awarded authorship credit and order on the same basis as those of nonstudent colleagues. However, if one makes the contrasting assumption that students have less power and competence than nonstudent collaborators, then justice would be served by giving students differential treatment.

Parentalism—the final ethical principal—refers to "treatment that restricts the liberty of individuals, without their consent, where the justification for such action is either the prevention of some harm they might do to themselves or the production of some benefit they might not otherwise secure" (Beauchamp & Walters, 1982, p. 38). Parentalistic actions are generally considered to be most appropriate when they are directed toward persons who are nonautonomous (i.e., lack the capacity for self-determination; Beauchamp & Walters, 1982). Thus, the appropriateness of parentalistic behavior in the authorship context depends on the student's level of autonomy.

A supervisor who is acting parentistically might alone decide the level of authorship credit a student receives. Even if students are consulted in the decision-making process, supervisors may use their power to influence the nature of the decision and discount student input. Parentalism is also relevant to the issue of when authorship credit is decided. When the supervisor makes the decision after the work is completed, the student makes his or her contributions without knowing the extent of authorship that he or she will receive. Thus, even when the supervisor does not consult the student in the decision-making process, later decisions are more parentalistic than those rendered before the work has been completed.

RECOMMENDATIONS FOR DETERMINING AUTHORSHIP CREDIT AND ORDER

How do the principles of beneficence, justice, and parentalism, in aggregate, provide guidance in determining authorship credit and order? To answer this question, we argue that two separate aspects of the authorship determination procedure need to be considered: (a) the process of how collaborators decide who will receive a given level of authorship credit for specified professional contributions and (b) the outcome resulting from the decision-making process. In this section, recommendations in each of these two areas are proposed.

Process Recommendations

As noted earlier, the principle of justice dictates that supervisors should treat students unequally only if there is a meaningful difference between them. With particular reference to the authorship decision-making process, we argue that faculty and students are not meaningfully different because faculty and students—particularly graduate students—have the autonomy, rationality, problem-solving ability, and fairness to mutually decide on authorship credit. Therefore, we propose that both faculty and students should have the opportunity to participate in the process of determining authorship credit. In addition, we argue that it is inappropriate for supervisors to assume a parentalistic stance in this process.

Our position should not be misinterpreted to indicate that faculty and students are equals in power, status, competence, and expertise. There are typically substantial differences between them in these areas. Rather, we believe that faculty and students are both sufficiently autonomous to mutually decide on what level of authorship credit will be awarded to each collaborator for specified professional contributions.

Several specific recommendations follow from the proposition that both faculty and students should meaningfully participate in the authorship decision-making process:

1. Early in the collaborative endeavor, the supervisor should provide the student with information related to how authorship decisions are made, the nature of professional and nonprofessional contributions to publications, the meaning of authorship credit and order, and the importance of both parties agreeing on what contributions will be expected of each collaborator for a given level of authorship credit. This information will provide the student with the knowledge necessary to exercise his or her autonomy and to choose whether to participate in the authorship determination process.

2. The supervisor and student should assess the specific abilities of each party, the tasks required to complete the scholarly publication, the extent of supervision required, and appropriate expectations for what each collaborator can reasonably contribute to the project.

3. On the basis of this assessment, the collaborators should discuss and agree on what tasks, contributions, and efforts are required of both parties to warrant authorship and to determine the order of authorship (Shawchuck, Fatis, & Breitenstein, 1986). Although they will not prevent disagreements from arising, such discussions may reduce their likelihood.

This recommendation is consistent with the notion of informed consent, which governs the development of agreements between psychologists and clients and between researchers and participants (Keith-Spiegel & Koocher, 1985). If authorship expectations are clearly established and agreed on early in the collaborative process, both the supervisor and the student have given their informed consent to participate in the project (Goodyear et al., 1992).

Although we are not necessarily advocating the use of signed informed consent forms, we see nothing in principle that would argue against their use. After all, written consent agreements are often developed by therapists and clients, researchers and subjects, and professors and students engaged in independent studies. In fact, in a similar vein, APA has considered requiring authors of submitted papers to include an "authorship paper," which would require authors to agree in writing to the use of their name on the paper and to the placement of their name in the listing of authors (Landers, 1988). If such forms are not used, we advocate making the agreement as clear as possible.

It should be recognized that some students may choose not to participate in the authorship decision-making process and may defer to the supervisor. As long as the student has been provided with sufficient information regarding authorship-related issues and has been encouraged to participate in this process, we believe that the student's choice should be respected. In such cases, the supervisor may appropriately make decisions regarding authorship credit and order without student input.

4. Agreements regarding authorship credit and order may need to be renegotiated for two reasons. First, scholarly projects often take unexpected turns that necessitate changes in initial agreements made in good faith. Second, many manuscripts need to be revised substantially before they are accepted for publication. These revisions may require additional professional contributions beyond those necessary for the completion of the initial draft of the manuscript. Thus, when such revisions are required, the supervisor and student should reexamine their original agreement and determine whether it needs to be modified.

Outcome Recommendations

We argue that the principles of beneficence and justice justify the use of a "relative standard" for determining authorship credit. According to this stance, there should be a varying standard for the level of professional contribution that is requried to attain a given level of authorship credit. Because collaborators differ in their scholarly expertise, their competence to contribute professionally to scholarly publications should be viewed as lying along a continuum. On one end of the continuum are collaborators who have limited competence in scholarly activities and who require intensive supervision. On the other end are collaborators who have considerable competence in scholarly endeavors and who function independently.

On the basis of the principle of justice, we advance the potentially controversial position that the level of contribution expected of a collaborator should depend on where he or she falls on this competence continuum. For the same level of authorship credit, one should expect greater professional contributions from collaborators who have more competence than from those who have less competence. When those who initially had less competence increase their levels of expertise, they should be expected to make more substantial professional contributions for the same level of authorship credit. This is consistent with the generative aspect of faculty–student collaboration—to provide students with experiences that will eventually allow them to conduct independent scholarship and to assist future students.

Where do students fall on the competence continuum? Of course students, as a group, are less competent in scholarly endeavors than faculty are. However, there are important individual differences in students' abilities. Some students function quite independently and have considerable talent in one or more areas related to scholarly activity. Others have less expertise and require intensive supervision. The key implication of this position is that, for the same level of authorship credit, justice is served by expecting relatively less of less competent collaborators than of more competent ones.

For example, a senior faculty member engaged in a collaborative project with an undergraduate psychology major should be expected to make more complex data analysis decisions than the student. However, if the student participated in the development of the research design, in the process of making data analysis decisions, and in the interpretation of the findings, within the limits of the student's limited expertise, his or her contributions should be considered professional and should be recognized with authorship credit. As the student's competence grows with increased coursework and experience, he or she should be expected to make greater contributions for the same level of authorship credit.

Therefore, we propose that faculty and students use a relative standard to determine authorship credit and order. However, we underscore the important point that in all cases when students are granted authorship, their contributions must be professional in nature. Our operational definition of *professional* is discussed below.

Several specific recommendations follow from the use of a relative standard for determining authorship credit and order:

1. To be included as an author on a scholarly publication, a student should, in a cumulative sense, make a professional contribution that is creative and intellectual in nature, that is integral to completion of the paper, and that requires an overarching perspective of the project. Examples of professional contributions include developing the research design, writing portions of the manuscript, integrating diverse theoretical perspectives, developing new conceptual models, designing assessments, contributing to data analysis decisions, and interpreting results (Bridgewater, Bornstein, & Walkenbach, 1981; Spiegel & Keith-Speigel, 1970). Such tasks as inputting data, carrying out data analyses specified by the supervisor, and typing are not considered professional contributions and may be acknowledged by footnotes to the manuscript (Shawchuck et al., 1986).

Fulfillment of one or two of the professional tasks essential to the completion of a collaborative publication does not necessarily justify authorship. Rather, the supervisor and student—in their discussions early in the collaborative process—must jointly decide what combination of professional activities warrants a given level of authorship credit for both parties. By necessity, there will be some variation in which tasks warrant authorship credit across differing research projects.

Particularly in complex cases, Winston's (1985) weighting schema procedure may be useful in determining which tasks are required for a given level of authorship credit. In this procedure, points are earned for various professional contributions to the scholarly publication. The number of points for each contribution varies depending on its scholarly importance, with research design and report writing assigned the most points. A contributor must earn a certain number of points to earn authorship credit, and the individual with the highest number of points is granted first authorship. This procedure has the advantage of helping all parties involved to carefully examine their respective responsibilities and contributions. However, in our opinion, it cannot be used in all cases because of collaborator differences in scholarly ability and because the importance of various professional tasks differs across projects. With modification (i.e., a weighting of points earned based on each collaborator's level of scholarly competence), it could be appropriate for the relative standard position that we advocate.

2. Authorship decisions should be based on the scholarly importance of the professional contribution and not just the time and effort made (Bridgewater et al., 1981). In our opinion, even if considerable time and effort are spent on a scholarly project, if the aggregate contribution is not judged to be professional by the criteria stated above, authorship should not be granted.

3. Although this may be another controversial position, we believe that authorship decisions should not be affected by whether students or supervisors were paid for their contributions or by their employment status (Bridgewater et al., 1981). In our opinion, it is the nature of the contribution that is made to the article that determines whether authorship credit is warranted and not whether participants received compensation for their efforts. We believe that financial remuneration is not a resource that can serve as a substitute for authorship credit.

4. As is often advocated when psychologists are confronted with ethical dilemmas (Keith-Spiegel & Koocher, 1985), we advise supervisors to consult with colleagues when authorship concerns arise. Furthermore, supervisors should encourage their students to do the same, whether with faculty or with student peers. With the informal input generated from such consultations, it is possible that new light will be shed on the issues involved and that reasonable and fair authorship agreements will result.

5. If the supervisor and student cannot agree, even after consultations with peers, on their authorship-related decisions, we recommend, as do Goodyear et al. (1992), the establishment of an ad hoc third party arbitration process. Whether this mechanism should be established at the local, state, or national level is unclear. Ethics committees, institutional review boards (IRBs), unbiased professionals (Shawchuck et al., 1986), or departmental

committees composed of faculty and students (Goodyear et al., 1992) are possible candidates for such an arbitration mechanism. The important point is that, given that both parties are considered to be equal contributors to this aspect of their work together, disputes need to be settled by outside parties. In such cases, arbitrators may find Winston's (1985) method helpful, because it requires as systematic review of all contributors' scholarly contributions (Shawchuck et al., 1986).

THE FOUR CASES REVISITED

In this final section, we return to the four hypothetical cases described at the outset of the article. First, we present our views on when authorship discussions should take place and then we offer our opinions regarding what authorship decisions are defensible in each case.

In Case 1, the discussion regarding authorship credit and order should ideally have taken place during the development of the thesis proposal but should certainly have occurred after the decision was made to attempt to publish the results. The clinical supervisor should also have been included in these deliberations. Similarly, in Cases 2 and 4, the discussion should have occurred during the initial stages of planning the honors project and no later than when the decision was made to submit a version of the thesis to a peer-reviewed journal. In Case 3, in addition to there being a need for the psychiatrist and supervisor to form an agreement regarding authorship credit, the student should have been a part of further authorship deliberations when brought into the project. Finally, in Case 4, the student should have been consulted when the revisions recommended by the reviewers were received by the faculty member.

Given the ethical considerations discussed in this article, what authorship decisions seem defensible in these cases? In Case 1, the student deserved authorship given the professional nature of his contribution: He participated in generating the idea, developing the research design, writing the proposal, collecting data, and producing several drafts of manuscript. The more difficult decision is whether the student deserved first authorship, given that he lost motivation toward the end of the writing process and the paper was finished by the faculty member who served as dissertation committee chair. In our opinion, the appropriateness of the student receiving first authorship depends on whether the collaborators believed that first authorship would be retained by the student if he did not fulfill the agreed-upon responsibilities. Similarly, the level of authorship credit received by the clinical supervisor depends on the extent to which he made professional contributions to the article as specified in the original agreement.

In Case 2, the student deserved authorship credit given that she generated the topic, participated somewhat in the design of the study, and wrote the paper for her honors project. Does she deserve first authorship? In our opinion, the ethical appropriateness of the student being first author revolves around whether she had the interest, motivation, and skill to expand her honors thesis so as to incorporate the complexity of the entire project. If she had the desire and commitment to do so, and therefore assumed responsibility for most components of the writing task, the supervisor had the ethical obligation to help her through this process and she would be listed as first author. If she had neither the interest nor the inclination to participate in this additional writing task, then it would be ethically appropriate for the supervisor to be identified as first author and the student as second author. In this latter instance, a footnote to the manuscript might be included that indicated that part of the article was based on the student's undergraduate honors thesis.

Case 3 presents a somewhat different dilemma. Did the student's contribution warrant authorship credit? The student did not participate in the generation of the research idea or design, he was given a great deal of assistance in conducting a literature review, and he did not participate in writing the manuscript for possible publication. Therefore, he was lacking in these areas of professional contribution. On the other hand, he gathered some additional literature, participated in some data analysis decisions, and wrote drafts of his thesis. These efforts were professional in nature.

Although further data analyses were conducted by the supervisor and the writing of the manuscript was completed by the supervisor and the psychiatrist, our position is that the student deserved third authorship. Although his participation was minimal, his contributions were, in a cumulative sense, professional. Furthermore, he functioned up to his relatively low level of scholarly competence.

Case 4 underscores the need for supervisors and students to recognize that their agreement may need to be reevaluated as the review process unfolds. The student clearly deserved authorship because she generated the research topic, participated in the design of the study and the development of assessments, and—given her relative inexperience—required surprisingly little supervision. We believe that the student should have been contacted when the reviews were available and should have been given an opportunity to participate in the revision process. If she did so, our position is that she would still deserve first authorship.

CONCLUSION

Collectively, these cases illustrate the potential complexities involved in determining authorship credit and order on faculty–student collaborative publications. In addition, they highlight our position that supervisors cannot expect as much from students as from experienced professional colleagues.

We hope that the issues raised, principles reviewed, and recommendations made in this article will help faculty engage in the process of making—in conjunction with their students—appropriate authorship decisions. We encourage faculty to give the appropriate amount of attention to the important issue of authorship through early, thorough, and systematic discussions leading to explicit agreements with their students.

REFERENCES

American Psychological Association Ethics Committee. (1983, February). *Authorship guidelines for dissertation supervision.* Washington, DC: Author.

Beauchamp, T., & Walters, L. (1982). *Contemporary issues in bioethics* (2nd ed.). Belmont, CA: Wadsworth.

Bridgewater, C. A., Bornstein, P. H., & Walkenbach, J. (1981). Ethical issues in the assignment of publication credit. *American Psychologist, 36,* 524–525.

Costa, M. M., & Gatz, M. (1992). Determination of authorship credit in published dissertations. *Psychological Science, 3,* 354–357.

Ethical principles of psychologists and code of conduct. (1992). *American Psychologist, 47,* 1597–1611.

Goodyear, R. K., Crego, C. A., & Johnston, M. W. (1992). Ethical issues in the supervision of student research: A study of critical incidents. *Professional Psychology: Research and Practice, 23,* 203–210.

Keith-Spiegel, P., & Koocher, G. P. (1985). *Ethics in psychology: Professional standards and cases.* New York: Random House.

Kitchener, K. S. (1984). Intuition, critical evaluation and ethical principles: The foundation for ethical decisions in counseling psychology. *The Counseling Psychologist, 12,* 43–55.

Landers, S. (1988, December). Should editors be detectives, too? *APA Monitor,* p. 15.

Over, R., & Smallman, S. (1973). Maintenance of individual visibility in publication of collaborative research by psychologists. *American Psychologist, 28,* 161–166.

Shawchuck, C. R., Fatis, M., & Breitenstein, J. L. (1986). A practical guide to the assignment of authorship credit. *The Behavior Therapist, 9,* 216–217.

Spiegel, D., & Keith-Spiegel, P. (1970). Assignment of publication credits: Ethics and practices of psychologists. *American Psychologist, 25,* 738–747.

Tabachnick, B. G., Keith-Spiegel, P., & Pope, K. S. (1991). Ethics of teaching: Beliefs and behaviors of psychologists as educators. *American Psychologist, 46,* 506–515.

Winston, R. B., Jr. (1985). A suggested procedure for determining order of authorship in research publications. *Journal of Counseling and Development, 63,* 515–518.

Zuckerman, H. A. (1968). Patterns of name ordering among authors of scientific papers: A study of social symbolism and its ambiguity. *American Journal of Sociology, 74,* 276–291.

VII

PUBLICATION AND COMMUNICATION OF RESEARCH

The publication and communication of research findings are essential to progress in science. The written report of research findings adds to the cumulative record of what has been learned. Although many avenues are available for communicating research findings (e.g., convention presentations, books and book chapters, technical or working reports), journal publication is the most common outlet. The tasks of preparing reports are similar across many different formats, even though journal publication has its own special challenges (e.g., the review process, squeezing massive amounts of details within a limited page range, intensive psychotherapy after reading the comments of reviewers). These tasks consist of addressing substantive issues that served as impetus for the investigation and conveying the rationale and decision-making process underlying the methodology and design.

It is important to underscore the central role of methodology and methodological issues in preparing the research report. Decisions pertaining to who served as participants, what constructs and measures were selected, and why various comparison, control, or other conditions were or were not included are central to the report. The study might have been designed and executed in any number of ways, each of which is likely to have strengths and weaknesses. The rationale for methods that were selected and the consequences that various decisions have on the results are important to elaborate within the report. Readers of the article will want to know what the findings are but also what limits might be placed on their interpretation. Sampling issues (e.g., special characteristics of the sample), measurement issues (e.g., poor reliability of observational measures, no evidence for validity of critical measures, only one measure to operationalize a particular construct), data evaluation issues (e.g., insufficient power, failure to control for a confounding factor), and others (e.g., no evidence for reliability of diagnoses if delineation of patients is important, absence of measures of treatment integrity), if present, require the researcher to qualify the claims that are made about the results.

The written report is evaluated by multiple criteria including the following: (a) Does this report make an important substantive contribution to the area of research? (b) Does the methodology (design and its execution) permit one to draw the conclusions the author wishes to make? and (c) Is the report well organized and complete in explaining what was done and why and how it was done? In addition to presentation of the research, the written report is an opportunity to influence the direction of the field. The author is in a special position to comment on the next steps in research, any lacunae in theory, and methodological obstacles that need to be resolved. The contribution of the study is not only in what questions were addressed but also in the questions, advances in theory, and changes in methods that the study provokes.

Articles in the present section are designed to facilitate preparation of research reports. The articles focus on the questions to be answered by the report, the integration of the study into a broader context of existing theory and research, and recommendations for presenting the material clearly. The articles are not about writing, although they include many good recommendations about writing; rather, the articles are about ways of thinking about one's own research and research in the field. Thus, publication and communication of results extend beyond describing the study and include all of the critical issues about methodology raised in prior sections.

The articles address preparation of reports of research in different ways, including articles that communicate the findings of a particular study or that review or evaluate a literature and proposals that are submitted for grant support. In the first article, I discuss preparation of research reports for journal publication. The article discusses the task of the author in broad terms, that is, what is expected by readers and reviewers for journal publication. Furthermore, each section of the manuscript (e.g., Introduction, Method, Results) is presented to convey the specific questions that are to be addressed. The article presents guidelines in the context of preparing reports of empirical studies related to assessment (e.g., measurement development and validation). Consequently, assessment issues also are discussed.

Authors often prepare and publish review articles. Indeed, in graduate training, completion of a review article may be a requirement or used as the basis for formulating an empirical study. Developing a study that contributes significantly to the literature obviously is enhanced by knowing the current status of that literature, including strengths and limitations of substantive findings and methodological approaches. In the second article, Daryl Bem provides guidelines for writing a review article, including recommendations for writing clearly, organizing the review, and obtaining the necessary feedback to make revisions. There are many helpful hints. In passing, Bem comments on what many researchers have experienced in writing, namely, the sense of elation we feel about a phrase that we consider to be clever, pithy, or otherwise brilliant. Such phrases are often the last to be deleted as we revise the article; indeed, through various revisions we might even build paragraphs around them. The sooner one can treat one's writing with less attachment to individual phrases and sections, the easier the writing and revision process becomes. The review, however well organized and written, is evaluated for its contribution. A summary of the relevant research is not enough; as Bem notes, a substantive contribution is needed as well. Consequently, the quality and contribution of review articles often is evaluated on the basis of what comes after the review portion, that is, what the author says about theory, new lines of research, and future directions. The review of existing studies is valuable insofar as this helps the author move to these other topics.

In the article by Scott Maxwell and David Cole, the focus is on preparing methodological articles. The article is a guide for writing and reading such methodological papers, but it includes a number of points that have broader generality. Among the guidelines are the importance of having the precise audience in mind, alerting the reader to a critical issue that warrants attention in the literature (i.e., the rationale for the article), and presenting technical material in a way that is palatable. Methodological articles are not necessarily difficult to read. In the present volume, for example, many articles convey how critical methodological issues are presented in the hands of extremely skilled and engaging writers. Most of us may not have this level of skill (given my own writing deficits, I have difficulty in getting people to read my graffiti). Consequently, the concrete guidelines for technical writing, provided at the end of the article by Maxwell and Cole, are particularly helpful.

Meta-analysis is now a commonly used technique to summarize a body of research and in this use is an alternative to the more traditional narrative or qualitative review. The article by Robert Rosenthal conveys how these reviews are completed and the type of information they ought to include. The article addresses how to search the literature, the criteria for including studies, how to use studies where critical information may be missing, how to characterize studies that are reviewed, and options for estimating effect size. Researchers have learned over the years that meta-analysis, as other methods for data evaluation, includes a number of assumptions and computational options and that variation in how the meta-analysis is conducted can alter the conclusions (Matt & Navarro, 1997). Rosenthal underscores the importance of describing precisely what was done along the dimensions that permit the reader to understand the conclusions. He also discusses ways of presenting and analyzing the data. The article is instructive also for those who read meta-analyses by conveying what to look for and how to interpret the results.

The final article shifts the focus slightly from journal publication to grant proposals. Many of the publication and communication issues are the same, namely, the rationale for decisions made by the author need to be presented in ways discussed in the prior articles. For a grant proposal, of course, one is providing the rationale for the study that is to be completed. In this article, E. R. Oetting discusses how to present the study, including clarification of the rationale and how the study will contribute to knowledge. The article is engaging because of its description of the grant process, including the many slings and arrows awaiting the person who applies for funding. There are special advantages to grant writing for those engaged in research, beyond the benefits of obtaining funding. The demands of grant writing require one to formalize a research plan with special care, to make the case for the study before it is to be done, and to present and justify all facets of the methodology. The demands sharpen the focus of the investigator because of the many questions that need to be addressed. Moreover, the feedback from the review of a grant is provided before the study has begun and hence the wisdom or concerns of reviewers, usually experts in the area, can be integrated into the design. This feedback can greatly improve the study and its yield. In any case, preparing grant proposals requires integration of all of the issues that have emerged in other sections of this book.

35

PREPARING AND EVALUATING RESEARCH REPORTS

ALAN E. KAZDIN

The research process consists of the design and execution of the study, analysis of the results, and preparation of the report (e.g., journal article). The final step seems straightforward and relatively easy, given the nature and scope of the other steps. In fact, one often refers to preparation of the article as merely "writing up the results." Yet the implied simplicity of the task belies the significance of the product in the research process. The article is not the final step in the process. Rather, it is an important beginning. The article is often a launching platform for the next study for the authors themselves or for others in the field who are interested in pursuing the findings. Thus, the report is central to the research process.

The article itself is not only a description of what was accomplished, but it also conveys the extent to which the design, execution, and analyses were well conceived and appropriate. Recognition of this facet of the report is the reason why faculty require students in training to write a proposal of

Reprinted from *Psychological Assessment*, 7, 228–237. Copyright 1995 by the American Psychological Association.
  Completion of this research was supported by Research Scientist Award MH00353 and Grant MH35408 from the National Institute of Mental Health.

the study in advance of its execution. At the proposal stage, faculty can examine the thought processes, design, planned execution, and data analyses and make the necessary changes in advance. Even so, writing the full article at the completion of the study raises special issues. At that point, the authors evaluate critical issues, see shortcomings of the design, and struggle with any clashes or ambiguities of the findings in light of the hypotheses.

The purpose of this article is to discuss the preparation and evaluation of research reports (articles) for publication.[1] Guidelines are presented to facilitate preparation of research articles. The guidelines cover the types of details that are to be included, but more important, the rationale, logic, and flow of the article to facilitate communication and to advance the next stage of the research process. Thus, preparation of a research report involves many of the same considerations that underlie the design and plan of the research.

Reports of empirical studies have many characteristics in common, whether or not they focus on assessment. Even so, the present focus will emphasize studies that are designed to evaluate assessment devices, constructs that the measures are intended to reflect, and studies of test validation. Issues that commonly emerge in articles of assessment and hence the design of assessment studies are highlighted as well.

GUIDELINES FOR PREPARING REPORTS FOR PUBLICATION

Preparation of the report for publication involves three interrelated tasks, which I shall refer to as description, explanation, and contextualization. Failure to appreciate or to accomplish these tasks serves as a main source of frustration for authors, as their articles traverse the process of manuscript review toward publication. *Description* is the most straightforward task and includes providing details of the study. Even though this is an obvious requirement of the report, basic details often are omitted in published articles (e.g., the gender and race of the participants, means, and standard deviation; see Shapiro & Shapiro, 1983; Weiss & Weisz, 1990). *Explanation* is slightly more complex insofar as this task refers to presenting the rationale of several facets of the study. The justification, decision-making process, and the connections between the decisions and the goals of the study move well beyond description. There are numerous decision points in any given study, most of which can be questioned. The author is obliged to make the case to

---

[1] Preparation of manuscripts for publication can be discussed from the perspective of authors and the perspective of reviewers (i.e., those persons who evaluate the manuscript for publication). This article emphasizes the perspective of authors and the task of preparing an article for publication. The review process raises its own issues, which this article does not address. Excellent readings are available to prepare the author for the journal review process (Kafka, *The Trial*, The Myth of Sisyphus, and Dante's *Inferno*).

explain why the specific options elected are well suited to the hypotheses or the goals of the study. Finally, *contextualization* moves one step further away from description of the details of the study and addresses how the study fits in the context of other studies and in the knowledge base more generally. This latter facet of article preparation reflects such lofty notions as scholarship and perspective, because the author places the descriptive and explanatory material into a broader context.

The extent to which description, explanation, and contextualization are accomplished increases the likelihood that the report will be viewed as a publishable article and facilitates integration of the report into the knowledge base. Guidelines follow that emphasize these tasks in the preparation and evaluation of research reports. The guidelines focus on the logic to the study; the interrelations of the different sections; the rationale for specific procedures and analyses; and the strengths, limitations, and place of the study in the knowledge base. It may be helpful to convey how these components can be addressed by focusing on the main sections of manuscripts that are prepared for journal publication.

Main Sections of the Article

Abstract

At first glance, the abstract certainly may not seem to be an important section or core feature of the article. Yet, two features of the abstract make this section quite critical. First, the abstract is likely to be read by many more people than is the article. The abstract probably will be entered into various databases that are available internationally. Consequently, this is the only information that most readers will have about the study. Second, for reviewers of the manuscript and readers of the journal article, the abstract sometimes is the first impression of what the author studied and found. Ambiguity, illogic, and fuzziness here is ominous. Thus, the abstract is sometimes the only impression or first impression one may have about the study. What is said is critically important.

Obviously, the purpose of the abstract is to provide a relatively brief statement of purpose, methods, findings, and conclusions of the study. Critical methodological descriptors pertain to the participants and their characteristics, experimental and control groups or conditions, design, and major findings. Often space is quite limited; indeed, a word limit (e.g., 100- or 120-word maximum) may be placed on the abstract by the journals. It is useful to make substantive statements about the characteristics of the study and the findings rather than to provide general and minimally informative comments. Similarly, vacuous statements (e.g., "Implications of the results are discussed" or "Future directions for research are suggested") should be replaced with comments about the findings or one or two specific implications and research directions (e.g., "The findings raise the prospect that there is a Big One rather than a Big Five set of personality characteristics").

Introduction

The introduction is designed to convey the overall rationale and objective of the research. The task of the author is to convey in a clear and concise fashion why this particular study is needed and the current questions, void, or deficiency the study is designed to address. The section should not review the literature in a study-by-study fashion, but rather convey issues and evaluative comments that set the stage for the study that is to follow. The task of contextualization is critically important in this section. Placing the study in the context of what is and is not known and conveying the essential next step in research in the field require mastery of the pertinent literatures and reasonable communication skills. Saying that the study is important (without systematically establishing the context) or noting that no one else has studied this phenomenon often are viewed as feeble attempts to circumvent the contextualization of the study

Limitations of previous work and how those limitations can be overcome may be important to consider. These statements build the critical transition from an existing literature to the present study and establish the rationale for design improvements or additions in relation to those studies. Alternatively or in addition, the study may build along new dimensions to advance the theory, hypotheses, and constructs to a broader range of domains of performance, samples, settings, and so on. The rationale for the specific study must be very clearly established. If a new measure is being presented, then the need for the measure and how it supplements or improves on existing measures, if any are available, are important to include. If a frequently used measure is presented, the rationale needs to be firmly established what precisely this study will add.

In general, the introduction will move from the very general to the specific. The very general refers to the opening of the introduction, which conveys the area of research, general topic, and significance of a problem. For example, if an article is on the assessment of alcohol abuse or marital bliss (or their interrelation), a brief opening statement noting the current state of the topic and its implications outside of the context of measurement is very helpful. Although reviewers are likely to be specialists in the assessment domain, many potential readers would profit from clarification of the broader context.

The introduction does not usually permit authors to convey all of the information they wish to present. In fact, the limit is usually two to four manuscript pages. A reasonable use of this space involves brief paragraphs or implicit sections that describe the nature of the problem, the current status of the literature, the extension that this study is designed to provide, and how the methods to be used are warranted. To the extent that the author conveys a grasp of the issues in the area and can identify the lacunae that the study is designed to fill greatly improves the quality of the report and the chances of acceptance for journal publication.

Method

This section of the article encompasses several points related to who was studied, why, how, and so on. The section not only describes critical procedures, but also provides the rationale for methodological decisions. Initially, the research participants (or subjects) are described, including several basic descriptors (e.g., age, genders, ethnicity, education, occupation, and income). From a method and design standpoint, information beyond basic descriptors can be helpful to encompass factors that plausibly could affect generality or replication of the results or that might influence comparison of the data with information obtained from normative or standardization samples.

The rationale for the sample should be provided. Why was this sample included and how is it appropriate to the substantive area and question of interest? In some cases, the sample is obviously relevant because participants have the characteristic or disorder of interest (e.g., parents accused of child abuse) or are in a setting of interest (e.g., nursing home residents). In other cases, samples are included merely because they are available (college students or a clinic population recruited for some other purpose than the study). Such samples of convenience often count against the investigator. If characteristics of the sample are potentially objectionable in relation to the goals of the study, the rationale may require full elaboration to convey why the sample was included and how features of the sample may or may not be relevant to the conclusions the author wishes to draw. A sample of convenience is not invariable a problem for drawing valid inferences. Yet, invariably, a thoughtful discussion will be required regarding its use. More generally, participant selection, recruitment, screening, and other features warrant comment. The issue for the author and reviewer is whether features of the participant selection process could restrict the conclusions in some unique fashion or, worse, in some way represent a poor test of the hypotheses.

Assessment studies may be experimental studies in which groups vary in whether they receive an intervention or experimental manipulation. More commonly, assessment studies focus on intact groups without a particular manipulation. The studies form groups based on subject selection criteria (e.g., one type of patient vs. another, men vs. women) for analyses. The rationale for selecting the sample is obviously important. If the sample is divided into subgroups, it is as critical to convey how the groups will provide a test of the hypotheses and to show that characteristics incidental to the hypotheses do not differ or do not obscure interpretation of the results (see Kazdin, 1992). Also, the selection procedure and any risks of misclassification based on the operational criteria used (e.g., false positives and negatives) warrant comment. Reliability of the assessment procedures used to select cases, especially when human judgment is required, is very important because of the direct implications for interpretation and replication of the findings. A common example for which this arises in clinical research is in invoking psychiatric diagnoses using interview techniques.

Several measures are usually included in the study. Why the constructs were selected for study should be clarified in the introduction. The specific measures and why they were selected to operationalize the constructs should be presented in the method section. Information about the psychometric characteristics of the measures is often summarized. This information relates directly to the credibility of the results. Apart from individual assessment devices, the rationale for including or omitting areas that might be regarded as crucial (e.g., multiple measures, informants, and settings) deserves comment. The principle here is similar to other sections, namely, the rationale for the author's decisions ought to be explicit.

Occasionally, ambiguous statements may enter into descriptions of measures. For example, measures may be referred to as "reliable" or "valid" in previous research, as part of the rationale for use in the present study. There are, of course, many different types of reliability and validity. It is important to identity those characteristics of the measure found in prior research that are relevant to the present study. For example, high internal consistency (reliability) in a prior study may not be a strong argument for use of the measure in a longitudinal design in which the author hopes for test–retest reliability. Even previous data on test–retest reliability (e.g., over 2 weeks) may not provide a sound basis for test–retest reliability over annual intervals. The information conveys the suitability of the measure for the study and the rationale of the author for selecting the measure in light of available strategies.

Results

It is important to convey why specific analyses were selected and how a particular test or comparison addresses the hypotheses or purposes presented earlier in the article. It is often the case that analyses are reported in a rote fashion in which, for example, the main effects are presented first, followed by the interactions for each measure. The author presents the analyses in very much the same way as the computer printout that provided multiple runs of the data. Similarly, if several dependent measures are available, a particular set for analyses is automatically run (e.g., omnibus tests of multivariate analyses of variance followed by univariate analyses of variance for individual measures). These are not the ways to present the data.

In the presentation of the results, it is important to convey why specific tests were selected and how these tests serve the specific goals of the study. Knowledge of statistics is critical for selecting the analysis to address the hypotheses of interest and conditions met by the data. The tests ought to relate to the hypotheses, predictions, or expectations outlined at the beginning of the article (Wampold, Davis, & Good, 1990). Presumably, the original hypotheses were presented in a special (nonrandom) order, based on importance or level of specificity. It is very useful to retain this order when the statistics are presented to test these hypotheses. As a general rule, it is important to emphasize the hypotheses or relations of interest in the results; the statistics are only tools in the service of these hypotheses.

It is often useful to begin the results by presenting basic descriptors of the data (e.g., means and standard deviation for each group or condition) so the readers have access to the numbers themselves. If there are patterns in the descriptors, it is useful to point them out. Almost-significant results might be noted here to err on the side of conservatism regarding group equivalence on some domain that might affect interpretation of the results, particularly if power (or sample size) was weak to detect such differences.

The main body of the results presents tests of the hypotheses or predictions. Organization of the results (subheadings) or brief statements of hypotheses before the specific analyses are often helpful to prompt the author to clarify how the statistical test relates to the substantive questions. As a step towards that goal, the rationale for the statistical tests chosen or the variations within a particular type of test ought to be noted. For example, within factor analyses or multiple regression, the options selected (e.g., method of extracting factors, rotation, and method of entering variables) should be described along with the rationale of why these particular options are appropriate. The rationales are important as a general rule, but may take on even greater urgency because of the easy use of software programs that can run the analyses. Default criteria on many software programs are not necessarily related to the author's conceptualization of the data, that is, the hypotheses. (Such information is referred to as "default criteria" because if the results do not come out with thoughtless analyses, it is partially "de fault of the criteria de investigator used.") Statistical decisions, whether or not explicit, often bear conceptual implications regarding the phenomena under investigation and the relations of variables to each other and to other variables.

Several additional or ancillary analyses may be presented to elaborate the primary hypotheses. For example, one might be able to reduce the plausibility that certain biases may have accounted for group differences based on supplementary or ancillary data analyses. Ancillary analyses may be more exploratory and diffuse than tests of the primary hypotheses. Manifold variables can be selected for these analyses (e.g., gender, race, and height differences) that are not necessarily conceptually interesting in relation to the goals of the study. The author may wish to present data and data analyses that were unexpected, were not of initial interest, and were not the focus of the study. The rationale for these excursions and the limitations of interpretation are worth noting. From the standpoint of the reviewer and reader, the results should make clear what the main hypotheses were, how the analyses provide appropriate and pointed tests, and what conclusions can be reached as a result. In addition, thoughtful excursions (i.e., with the rationale guiding the reader) in the analyses are usually an advantage.

Discussion

The discussion consists of the conclusions and interpretations of the study and hence is the final resting place of all issues and concerns. Typically, the discussion includes an overview of the major findings, integration or relation of these findings to theory and prior research, limitations and ambiguities and their implications for interpretation, and future directions. The extent that this can be accomplished in a brief space (e.g., two to five manuscript pages) is to the author's advantage.

Description and interpretation of the findings may raise a tension between what the author wishes to say about the findings and their meaning versus what can be said in light of how the study was designed and evaluated. Thus, the discussion shows the reader the interplay of the introduction, method, and results sections. For example, the author might draw conclusions that are not quite appropriate given the method and findings. The discussion conveys flaws, problems, or questionable methodological decisions within the design that were not previously evident. However, they are flaws only in relation to the introduction and discussion. That is, the reader of the article can now recognize that if these are the types of statements the author wishes to make, the present study (design, measures, and sample) is not well suited for making them. The slight mismatch of interpretive statements in the discussion and the methodology is a common, albeit tacit basis for not considering a study as well conceived and well executed. A slightly different study may be required to support the specific statements the author makes in the discussion; alternatively, the discussion might be more circumscribed in the statements that are made.

It is usually to the author's credit to examine potential sources of ambiguity given that he or she is in an excellent position because of familiarity with procedures and expertise to understand the area. A candid, nondefensive appraisal of the study is very helpful. Here, too, contextualization may be helpful because limitations of a study are also related to prior research, trade-offs inherent in the exigencies of design and execution, what other studies have and have not accomplished, and whether a finding is robust across different methods of investigation. Although it is to the author's credit to acknowledge limitations of the study, there are limits on the extent to which reviewers grant a pardon for true confessions. At some point, the flaw is sufficient to preclude publication, whether or not it is acknowledged by the author. At other points, acknowledging potential limitations conveys critical understanding of the issues and directs the field to future work. This latter use of acknowledgment augments the contribution of the study and the likelihood of favorable evaluation by readers.

Finally, it is useful in the discussion to contextualize the results by continuing the story line that began in the introduction. With the present findings, what puzzle piece has been added to the knowledge base, what new questions or ambiguities were raised, what other substantive areas might be relevant for this line of research, and what new studies are needed? From the standpoint of contextualization, the new studies referred to here are not merely those that overcome methodological limitations of the present study, but rather those that focus on the substantive foci of the next steps for research.

Guiding Questions

The section-by-section discussion of the content of an article is designed to convey the flow or logic of the study and the interplay of description, explanation, and contextualization. The study ought to have a thematic line throughout, and all sections ought to reflect that thematic line in a logical way. The thematic line consists of the substantive issues guiding the hypotheses and the decisions of the investigator (e.g., with regard to procedures and analyses) that are used to elaborate these hypotheses.

Another way to consider the tasks of preparing a report is to consider the many questions the article ought to answer. These are questions for the authors to ask themselves or, on the other hand, questions reviewers and consumers of the research are likely to want to ask. Table 1 presents questions that warrant consideration. They are presented according to the different sections of a manuscript. The questions emphasize the descriptive information, as well as the rationale for procedures, decisions, and practices in the design and execution. Needless to say, assessment studies can vary widely in their purpose, design, and methods of evaluation, so the questions are not necessarily appropriate to each study nor are they necessarily exhaustive. The set of questions is useful as a way of checking to see that many important facets of the study have not been overlooked.

General Comments

Preparation of an article is often viewed as a task of describing what was done. With this in mind, authors often are frustrated at the reactions of reviewers. In reading the reactions of reviewers, the authors usually recognize and acknowledge the value of providing more details that are required (e.g., further information about the participants or procedure). However, when the requests pertain to explanation and contextualization, authors are more likely to be baffled or defensive. This reaction may be reasonable because graduate training devotes much less attention to these facets of preparing

TABLE 1
Major Questions to Guide Journal Article Preparation

Abstract

What were the main purposes of the study?
Who was studied (sample, sample size, special characteristics)?
How were participants selected?
To what conditions, if any, were participants exposed?
What type of design was used?
What were the main findings and conclusions?

Introduction

What is the background and context for the study?
What in current theory, research, or clinical work makes this study useful, important, or of interest?
What is different or special about the study in focus, methods, or design to address a need in the area?
Is the rationale clear regarding the constructs to be assessed?
What specifically were the purposes, predictions, or hypotheses?

Method

Participants
  Who were the participants and how many of them were in this study?
  Why was this sample selected in light of the research goals?
  How was this sample obtained, recruited, and selected?
  What are the participant and demographic characteristics of the sample (e.g., gender, age, ethnicity, race, socioeconomic status)?
  What if any inclusion or exclusion criteria were invoked (i.e., selection rules to obtain participants)?
  How many of those participants eligible or recruited actually were selected and participated in the study?
  Was informed consent solicited? How and from whom, if special populations were used?

Design
  What is the design (i.e., longitudinal, cross-sectional) and how does the design related to the goals of the study?
  How were the participant assigned to groups or conditions?
  How many groups were included in the design?
  How were the groups similar and different in how they were treated in the study?
  Why were these groups critical to address the questions of interest?

Assessment
  What were the constructs of interest and how were they measured?
  What are the relevant reliability and validity data from previous research (and from the present study) that support the use of these measures for the present purposes?
  Were multiple measures and methods used to assess the constructs?
  Are response sets or styles relevant to the use and interpretation of the measures?
  How was the assessment conducted? By whom (as assessors/observers)? In what order were the measures administered?
  If judges (raters) were used in any facet of assessment, what is the reliability (inter- or intrajudge consistency) in rendering their judgments/ratings?

Procedures
  Where was the study conducted (setting)?
  What materials, equipment, or apparatuses were used in the study?
  What was the chronological sequence of events to which participants were exposed?

TABLE 1 (continued)

What intervals elapsed between different aspects of the study (e.g., assessment occasions)?

What procedural checks were completed to avert potential sources of bias in implementation of the manipulation and assessments?

What checks were made to ensure that the conditions were carried out as intended?

What other information does the reader need to know to understand how participants were treated and what conditions were provided?

Results

What were the primary measures and data on which the predictions depend?

What are the scores on the measures of interest for the different groups and sample as a whole (e.g., measures of central tendency and variability)?

How do the scores compare with those of other study, normative, or standardization samples?

Are groups of interest within the study similar on measures and variables that could interfere with interpretation of the hypotheses?

What analyses were used and how specifically did these address the original hypotheses and purposes?

Were the assumptions of the data analyses met?

If multiple tests were used, what means were provided to control error rates?

If more than one group was delineated, were they similar on variables that might otherwise explain the results (e.g., diagnosis, age)?

Were data missing due to incomplete measures (not filled out completely by the participants) or due to loss of participants? If so, how were these handled in the data analyses?

Are there ancillary analyses that might further inform the primary analyses or exploratory analyses that might stimulate further work?

Discussion

What were the major findings of the study?

How do these findings add to research and how do they support, refute, or inform current theory?

What alternative interpretations can be placed on the data?

What limitations or qualifiers must be placed on the study given methodology and design issues?

What research follows from the study to move the field forward?

Note. Further discussion of questions that guide the preparation of journal articles can be obtained in additional sources (Kazdin, 1992; Maher, 1978). Concrete guidelines on the format for preparing articles are provided by the American Psychological Association (1994).

research reports than to description. Also, reviewers' comments and editorial decision letters may not be explicit about the need for explanation and contextualization. For example, some of the more general reactions of reviewers are often reflected in comments such as "Nothing in the manuscript is new," "I fail to see the importance of the study," or "This study has already been done in a much better way by others."[2] In fact, such characterizations may be true.

---

[2] I am grateful to my dissertation committee for permitting me to quote their comments at my oral exam. In keeping with the spirit embodied in their use of pseudonyms in signing the dissertation, they wish not to be acknowledged by name here.

Alternatively, the comments could also reflect the extent to which the author has failed to contextualize the study to obviate these kinds of reactions.

The lesson for preparing and evaluation research reports is clear. Describing a study does not eo ipso establish its contribution to the field, no matter how strongly the author feels that the study is a first. Also, the methodological options for studying a particular question are enormous in terms of possible samples, constructs and measures, and data-analytic methods. The reasons for electing the particular set for options the author has chosen deserve elaboration.

In some cases, the author selects options because they were used in prior research. This criterion alone may be weak, because objections levied at the present study may also be appropriate to some of the prior work as well. The author will feel unjustly criticized for a more general flaw in the literature. Yet, arguing for a key methodological decision solely because "others have done this in the past" provides a very weak rationale, unless the purpose of the study is to address the value of the option as a goal of the study. Also, it may be that new evidence has emerged that makes the past practice more questionable in the present. For example, investigators may rely on retrospective assessment to obtain lifetime data regarding symptoms or early characteristics of family life, a seemingly reasonable assessment approach. Evidence suggests, however, that such retrospective information is very weak, inaccurate, and barely above chance when compared with the same information obtained prospectively (e.g., Henry, Moffitt, Caspi, Langley, & Silva, 1994; Robins et al., 1985). As evidence accumulates over time to make this point clear and as the domain of false memories becomes more well studied, the use of retrospective assessment methods is likely to be less acceptable among reviewers. In short, over time, the standards and permissible methods may change.

In general, it is beneficial to the author and to the field to convey the thought processes underlying methodological and design decision. This information will greatly influence the extent to which the research effort is appreciated and viewed as enhancing knowledge. Yet, it is useful to convey that decisions were thoughtful and that they represent reasonable choices among the alternatives for answering the questions that guide the study. The contextual issues are no less important. As authors, we often expect the latent Nobel Prize caliber of the study to be self-evident. It is better to be very clear about how and where the study fits in the literature, what it adds, and what questions and research the study prompts.

COMMON INTERPRETIVE ISSUES IN EVALUATING ASSESSMENT STUDIES

In conducting studies and preparing reports of assessment studies, a number of issues can be identified to which authors and readers are often sensitive. These issues have to do with the goals, interpretation, and generality of the results of studies. I highlight three issues here: test validation, the relations of constructs to measures, and sampling. Each of these is a weighty topic in its own right and will be considered in other articles in this issue. In this article, they are addressed in relation to interpretation and reporting of research findings.

Interpreting Correlations Among Test Scores

Test validation is a complex and ongoing process involving many stages and types of demonstrations. As part of that process, evidence often focuses on the extent to which a measure of interest (e.g., a newly developed measure) is correlated with other measures. Interpreting seemingly simple correlations between measures requires attention to multiple considerations.

Convergent Validation

Convergent validity refers to the extent to which a measure is correlated with other measures that are designed to assess the same or related constructs (Campell & Fiske, 1959). There are different ways in which convergent validity can be shown, such as demonstrating that a given measure correlates with related measures at a given point in time (e.g., concurrent validity) and that groups selected on some related criterion (e.g., history of being abused vs. no such history) differ on the measure, as expected (e.g., criterion or known-groups validity).[3] In convergent validity, the investigator may be interested in showing that a new measure of a construct correlates with other measures of that same construct or that the new measure correlates with measures of related constructs. With convergent validity, some level of agreement between measures is sought.

In one scenario, the investigator may wish to correlate a measure (e.g., depression) with measures of related constructs (e.g., negative cognitions and anxiety). In this case, the investigator may search for correlations that are in the moderate range (e.g., $r = .40-.60$) to be able to say that measure of interest was correlated in the positive direction, as predicted, with the other (criterion) measures. Very high correlations raise the prospect that the measure is assessing the "same" construct or adds no new information. In cases in which the investigator has developed a new measure, the correlations of that measure will be with other measures of the same construct. In this case, high correlations may be sought to show that the new measure in fact does assess the construct of interest.

Interpretation of convergent validation data requires caution. To begin

---

[3] There are of course many different types of validity, and often individual types are referred to inconsistently. For a discussion of different types of validity and their different uses, the reader is referred to other sources (Kline, 1986; Wainer & Braun, 1988).

with, the positive, moderate-to-high correlations between two measures could well be due to shared trait variance in the construct domains, as predicted between the two measures. For example, two characteristics (e.g., emotionality and anxiety) might overlap because of their common psychological, biological, or developmental underpinnings. This is usually what the investigator has in mind by searching for convergent validity. However, other interpretations are often as parsimonious or even more so. For example, shared method variance may be a viable alternative interpretation for the positive correlation. *Shared method variance* refers to similarity or identity in the procedure or format of assessment (e.g., both measures are self-report or both are paper-and-pencil measures). For example, if two measures are completed by the same informant, their common method variance might contribute to the magnitude of the correlation. The correlations reflect the shared method variance, rather than, or in addition to, the shared construct variance.

The correlation between two measures that is taken to be evidence for validity also could be due to shared items in the measures. For example, studies occasionally evaluate the interrelations (correlations) among measures of depression, self-esteem, hopelessness, and negative cognitive processes. Measures of these constructs often overlap slightly, so that items in one particular scale have items that very closely resemble items in another scale (e.g., how one views or feels about oneself). Item overlap is not an inherent problem because conceptualizations of the two domains may entail common features (i.e., share trait variance). However, in an effort of scale validation, it may provide little comfort to note that the two domains (e.g., hopelessness and negative cognitive processes) are moderately to highly correlated "as predicted." When there is item overlap, the correlation combines reliability (alternative form or test–retest) with validity (concurrent and predictive).

Low correlations between two measures that are predicted to correlate moderately to highly warrant comment. In this case, the magnitude of the correlation is much lower than the investigator expected and is considered not to support the validity of the measure that is being evaluated. Three considerations warrant mention here and perhaps analysis in the investigation. First, the absolute magnitude of the correlation between two measures is limited by the reliability of the individual measures. The low correlation may then underestimate the extent to which the reliable portion of variance within each measure is correlated. Second, it is possible that the sample and its scores on one or both of the measures represent a restricted range. The correlation between two measures, even if high in the population across the full range of scores, may be low in light of the restricted range. Third, it is quite possible that key moderators within the sample account for the low correlation. For example, it is possible that the correlation is high (and positive) for one subsample (men) and low (and negative) for another subsample. When these samples are treated as a single group, the correlation may be low or zero, and nonsignificant. A difficulty is scavenging for these moderators in a post hoc fashion. However, in an attempt to understand the relations between measures, it is useful to compute within-subsample correlations on key moderators such as gender, ethnicity, and patient status (patient vs. community) where relations between the measures are very likely to differ. Of course, the study is vastly superior when an influence moderating the relations between measures is theoretically derived and predicted.

Discriminant Validity

Discriminant validity refers to the extent to which measures not expected to correlate or not to correlate very highly in fact show this expected pattern.[4] By itself, discriminant validity may resemble support for the null hypothesis; namely, no relation exists between two measures. Yet, the meaning of discriminant validity derives from the context in which it is demonstrated. That context is a set of measures, some of which are predicted to relate to the measure of interest (convergent validity) and others predicted to relate less well or not at all (discriminant validity). Convergent and discriminant validity operate together insofar as they contribute to construct validity (i.e., identifying what the construct is and is not like). A difficulty in many validational studies is attention only to convergent validity.

With discriminant validity, one looks for little or no relation between two or more measures. As with convergent validity, discriminant validity also raises interpretive issues. Two measures may have no conceptual connection or relation but still show significant and moderate-to-high correlations because of common method variance. If method variance plays a significant role, as is often the case when different informants are used, then all the measures completed by the same informant may show a similar level of correlation. In such a case, discriminant validity may be difficult to demonstrate.

Discriminant validity raises another issue for test validation. There is an amazing array of measures and constructs in the field of psychology, with new measures being developed regularly. The question in relation to discriminant validity is whether the measures are all different and whether they reflect different or sufficiently different constructs. The problem has been recognized for some time. For example, in validating a new test, Campbell (1960) recommended that the measure be correlated with measures of social desirability, intelligence, and acquiescence and other response sets. A minimal criterion for discriminant validation, Campbell proposed, is to show that the new measure cannot be accounted for by these other constructs. These other constructs, and no doubt additional ones, have been shown to have a

---

[4] Discriminant validity is used here in the sense originally proposed by Campbell and Fiske (1959). Occasionally, discriminant validity is used to refer to cases in which a measure can differentiate groups (e.g., Trull, 1991). The different meanings of the term and the derivation of related terms such as *discriminate, discriminative,* and *divergent validity* reflect a well-known paradox of the field, namely, that there is little reliability in discussing validity.

pervasive influence across several domains, and their own construct validity is relatively well developed. It is likely that they contribute to and occasionally account for other new measures.

Few studies have adhered to Campbell's (1960) advice, albeit the recommendations remain quite sound. For example, a recent study validating the Sense of Coherence Scale showed that performance on the scale has a low and nonsignificant correlation with intelligence ($r = .11$) but a small-to-moderate correlation ($r = .39$) with social desirability (Frenz, Carey, & Jorgensen, 1993). Of course, convergent and discriminant validity depend on multiple sources of influence rather than two correlations. Even so, as the authors noted, the correlation with social desirability requires explanation and conceptual elaboration.

General Comments

Convergent and discriminant validity raise fundamental issues about validation efforts because they require specification of the nature of the construct and then tests to identify the connections and boundary conditions of the measure. Also, the two types of validity draw attention to patterns of correlations among measures in a given study and the basis of correlation. The importance of separating or examining the influence of shared method factors that contribute to this correlation pattern motivated the recommendation to use multitrait and multimethod matrices in test validation (Campbell & Fiske, 1959). In general, demonstration of convergent and discriminant validity and evaluation of the impact of common method variance are critical to test validation. In the design and reporting of assessment studies, interpretation of the results very much depends on what can and cannot be said about the measure. The interpretation is greatly facilitated by providing evidence for both convergent and discriminant validity.

Constructs and Measures

Assessment studies often vary in the extent to which they reflect interests in constructs or underlying characteristics of the measures and in specific assessment devices themselves. These emphases are a matter of degree, but worth distinguishing to convey the point and its implications for preparing and interpreting research reports. Usually researchers develop measures because they are interested in constructs (e.g., temperament, depression, or neuroticism). Even in cases in which measures are guided by immediately practical goals (e.g., screening and selection), there is an interest in the bases for the scale (i.e., the underlying constructs).

The focus on constructs is important to underscore. The emphasis on constructs draws attention to the need for multiple measures. Obviously, a self-report measure is important, but it is an incomplete sample of the construct. Perhaps less obvious is the fact that direct samples of behavior also are limited, because they are only a sample of the conditions as specified at a given time under the circumstances of the observations. Sometimes investigators do not wish to go beyond the measure or at least too much beyond the measure in relation to the inferences they draw. Self-report data on surveys (e.g., what people say about a social issue or political candidate or what therapists say they do in therapy with their clients) and direct observations of behavior (e.g., how parents interact with their children at home) may be the assessment focus. Even in these instances, the measure is used to represent broader domains (e.g., what people feel, think, or do) beyond the confines of the operational measure. In other words, the measure may still be a way of talking about a broader set for referents that is of interest besides test performance. Anytime an investigator wishes to say more than the specific items or contents of the measure, constructs are of interest.

Any one measure, however well established, samples only a part or facet of the construct of interest. This is the inherent nature of operational definitions. In preparing reports of assessment studies, the investigator ought to convey what constructs are underlying the study and present different assessment devices in relation to the sampling from the construct domain. A weakness of many studies is using a single measure to assess a central construct of interest. A single measure can sample a construct, but a demonstration is much better when multiple measures represent that construct.

The focus on constructs draws attention to the interrelation among different constructs. Although a researcher may wish to validate a given measure and evaluate his or her operational definition, her or she also wants to progress up the ladder of abstraction to understand how the construct behaves and how the construct relates to other constructs. These are not separate lines of work, because an excellent strategy for validating a measure is to examine the measure in the context of other measures of that construct and measures of other constructs. For example, a recent study examined the construct psychological stress by administering 27 self-report measures and identifying a model to account for the measures using latent-variable analyses (Scheier & Newcomb, 1993). Nine latent factors were identified through confirmatory factor analyses (e.g., emotional distress, self-derogation, purpose in life, hostility, anxiety, and others). Of special interest is that the study permitted evaluation of several scales to each other as well as to the latent variable and the relation of latent variables (as second-order factors) to each other. This level of analysis provides important information about individual measures and contributes to the understanding of different but related domains of functioning and their interrelations to each other. At this higher level of abstraction, one can move from assessment to understanding the underpinnings of the constructs or domains of functioning (e.g., in development), their course, and the many ways in which they may be manifested.

Although all assessment studies might be said to reflect interest in constructs, clearly many focus more concretely at a lower level of abstraction. This is evident in studies that focus on the development of a particular scale, as reflected in evaluation of psychometric properties on which the scale depends. Efforts to elaborate basic features of the scale are critically important. Later in the development of the scale, one looks to a measure to serve new purposes or to sort individuals in ways that elaborate one's understanding of the construct. It is still risky to rely on a single measure of a construct no matter how well that validational research has been. Thus, studies using an IQ test or an objective personality inventory still raise issues if only one test is used, as highlighted later. For a given purpose (e.g., prediction), a particular measure may do very well. Ultimately, the goal is understanding in addition to prediction, and that requires greater concern with the construct and multiple measures that capture different facets of the construct.

In designing studies that emphasize particular measures, it is important to draw on theory and analyses of the underlying constructs as much as possible. From the standpoint of psychology, interest usually extends to the theory, construct, and clinical phenomena that the measure was designed to elaborate. Also, research that is based on a single assessment device occasionally is met with ambivalence. The ambivalence often results from the view that a study of one measure is technical in nature, crassly empirical, and theoretically bereft. The focus on a single measure without addressing the broader construct in different ways is a basis for these concerns. And, at the level of interpretation of the results, the reliance on one measure, however well standardized, may be viewed as a limitation.

At the same time, there is a widespread recognition that the field needs valid, standardized, and well-understood measures. Programs of research that do the necessary groundwork are often relied on when selecting a measure or when justifying its use in a study or grant proposal. When preparing articles on assessment devices, it is important to be sensitive to the implications that the study has for understanding human functioning in general, in addition to understanding how this particular measure operates. Relating the results of assessment studies to conceptual issues, rather than merely characterizing a single measure, can greatly enhance a manuscript and the reactions of consumers regarding the contribution.

Sample Characteristics and Assessment Results

Sampling can refer to many issues related to the participants, conditions of the investigation, and other domains to which one wishes to generalize (Brunswik, 1955). In assessment studies, a special feature of sampling warrants comment because of its relevance for evaluating research reports. The issue pertains to the structure and meaning of a measure with respect to different population characteristics. Occasionally, the ways in which studies are framed suggest that the characteristics of a scale inhere in the measure in some fixed way, free from the sample to which the scale was applied.

It is quite possible that the measure and indeed the constructs that the measure assesses behave differently across samples, as a function of gender, age, race, and ethnicity (e.g., McDermott, 1995). Such differences have important implications for test standardization and interpretation beyond the scope of the present discussion. Sensitivity to such potential differences and evaluation of such differences in the design of research can be very helpful. Ideally, an assessment study will permit analyses of the influence of one or more sample characteristics that plausibly could influence conclusions about the measure. For example, in a recent evaluation of scales to study motives for drinking alcohol, analyses showed that the factor model that fit the measure was invariant across male and female. Black and White, and older and younger adolescents (Cooper, 1994). The inclusion of multiple samples and a sufficient sample size to permit these subsample analyses ($N > 2,000$) enabled the research to make a significant contribution to assessment and scale structure. From the study, it was learned that the structure of the measure is robust across samples. Apart from scale characteristics, the generality of the model may have important implications for adolescent functioning in general.

A more common research approach is to sift through separate studies, each representing an attempt to replicate the factor structure with a slightly different population (e.g., Derogatis & Cleary, 1977; Schwarzwald, Weisenberg, & Solomon, 1991; Takeuchi, Kuo, Kim, & Leaf, 1989). Such research often shows that the central features of the measure differ with different samples. One difficulty lies in bringing order to these sample difference, in large part because they are not tied to theoretical hypotheses about characteristics of the samples that might explain the differences (Betancourt & Lopez, 1993). Also, from the standpoint of subsequent research, guidelines for using the measure are difficult to cull from the available studies.

Evaluating assessment devices among samples with different characteristics is important. However, one critically important step before evaluating these assessment devices is the replication of the scale results with separate samples from the same population. Some studies include large standardization samples and hence provide within-sample replication opportunities. More common among assessment studies is the evaluation of the measure with smaller samples. It is important to replicate findings on the structure of the scale or the model used to account for the factors within the scale. Even when separate samples are drawn from the same population, the findings regarding scale characteristics may not be replicated (e.g., Parker, Endler, & Bagby, 1993). Evaluation of multiple samples is very important in guiding use of the measure in subsequent research.

Sampling extends beyond issues related to participants. Sampling refers to drawing from the range of characteristics or domains to which one wishes to generalize (Brunswik, 1955). In relation to assessment studies, the use of multiple measures to assess a construct is based in part on sampling considerations. Conclusions should not be limited to a single operation (measure or type of measure). There may be irrelevancies associated with any single measure that influences the obtained relation between the constructs of interest. A study is strengthened to the extent that is samples across different assessment methods and different sources of information.

The familiar finding of using multiple measures of a given construct is that the measures often reflect different conclusions. For example, two measures of family functioning may show that they are not very highly related to each other. One measure may show great differences between families selected because of a criterion variable, whereas the other measure may not. These results are often viewed as mixed or as partial support for an original hypothesis. The investigator usually has to prepare a good reason why different measures of seemingly similar constructs show different results. However, the study is stronger for the demonstration when compared with a study that did not operationalize family functioning in these different ways. An issue for the field is to make much further conceptual progress in handling different findings that follow from different methods of assessment.

CONCLUSION

Preparing reports for publication involves describing, explaining, and contextualizing the study. The descriptive feature of the study is essential for the usual goals such as facilitating interpretation and permitting replication of the procedures, at least in principle. However, the tasks of explaining the study by providing a well thought-out statement of the decisions and contextualizing the study by placing the demonstration into the field more generally are the challenges. The value of a study is derived from the author's ability to make the case that the study contributes to the literature, addresses an important issue, and generates important answers and questions.

In this article, I discussed some of the ways in which authors can make such a case when preparing a research article.[5] Generally, the task is to convey the theme or story line, bringing all of the sections of the study in line with that, and keeping irrelevancies to a minimum. In the context of assess-

---

[5] In closing, it is important to convey that recommendations in this article regarding manuscript preparation and journal publication derive from my experiences as an editor rather than as an author. As an author, the picture has not always been as pretty. For example, over the course of my career, such as it is, two journals went out of business within a few months after a manuscript of mine was accepted for publication and fowarded to production. Although this could be coincidence in the career of one author, in this case the result was significant ($p < .05$), using a chi round test and correcting for continuity, sphericity, and leptokurtosis.

ment studies, three issues were highlighted because they affect many studies and their interpretation. These include interpretation of correlations between measures, the relation of constructs and measures, and sampling. Each issue was discussed from the standpoint of ways of strengthening research. Test validation, development of assessment methods from constructs, and sampling raise multiple substantive and methodological issues that affect both the planning and reporting of research. Many of the articles that follow elaborate on the issues.

REFERENCES

American Psychological Association. (1994). *Publication manual of the American Psychological Association* (4th ed.). Washington, DC: Author.

Betancourt, H., & Lopez, S. R. (1993). The study of culture, ethnicity, and race in American psychology. *American Psychologist, 48*, 629–637.

Brunswik, E. (1955). Representative design and probabilistic theory in a functional psychology. *Psychological Review, 62*, 193–217.

Campbell, D. T. (1960). Recommendations for APA test standards regarding construct, trait, and discriminant validity. *American Psychologist, 15*, 546–553.

Campbell, D. T., & Fiske, D. (1959). Convergent and discriminant validation by the multitrait–multimethod matrix. *Psychological Bulletin, 56*, 81–105.

Cooper, M. L. (1994). Motivations for alcohol use among adolescents: Development and validation of a four-factor model. *Psychological Assessment, 6*, 117–128.

Derogatis, L. R., & Cleary, P. A. (1977). Factorial invariance across gender for the primary symptom dimensions of the SCL-90. *British Journal of Social and Clinical Psychology, 16*, 347–356.

Frenz, A. W., Carey, M. P., & Jorgensen, R. S. (1993). Psychometric evaluation of Antonovsky's Sense of Coherence Scale. *Psychological Assessment, 5*, 145–153.

Henry, B., Moffitt, T. E., Caspi, A., Langley, J., & Silva, P. A. (1994). On the "remembrance of things past": A longitudinal evaluation of the retrospective method. *Psychological Assessment, 6*, 92–101.

Kazdin, A. E. (1992). *Research design in clinical psychology* (2nd ed). Needham Heights, MA: Allyn & Bacon.

Kline, P. (1986). *A handbook of test construction: Introduction to psychometric design*. London: Methuen.

Maher, B. A. (1978). A reader's, writer's, and reviewer's guide to assessing research reports in clinical psychology. *Journal of Consulting and Clinical Psychology, 46*, 835–838.

McDermott, P. A. (1995). Sex, race, class, and other demographics as explanations for children's ability and adjustment: A national appraisal. *Journal of School Psychology, 33*, 75–91.

Parker, J. D. A., Endler, N. S., & Bagby, R. M. (1993). If it changes, it might be unstable: Examining the factor structure of the Ways of Coping Questionnaire. *Psychological Assessment, 5,* 361–368.

Robins, L. N., Schoenberg, S. P., Homes, S. J., Ratcliff, K. S., Benham, A., & Works, J. (1985). Early home environment and retrospective recall. *American Journal of Orthopsychiatry, 55,* 27–41.

Scheier, L. M., & Newcomb, M. D. (1993). Multiple dimensions of affective and cognitive disturbance: Latent-variable models in a community sample. *Psychological Assessment, 5,* 230–234.

Schwarzwald, J., Weisenberg, M., & Solomon, Z. (1991). Factor invariance of SCL-90-R: The case of combat stress reaction. *Psychological Assessment, 3,* 385–390.

Shapiro, D. A., & Shapiro, D. (1983). Comparative therapy outcome research: Methodological implications of meta-analysis. *Journal of Consulting and Clinical Psychology, 51,* 42–53.

Takeuchi, D. T., Kuo, H., Kim, K., & Leaf, P. J. (1989). Psychiatric symptom dimensions among Asian Americans and native Hawaiians: An analysis of the symptom checklist. *Journal of Community Psychology, 17,* 319–329.

Trull, T. J. (1991). Discriminant validity of the MMPI–Borderline Personality Disorder scale. *Psychological Assessment, 3,* 232–238.

Wainer, H., & Braun, H. I. (Eds.). (1988). *Test validity.* Hilldale, NJ: Erlbaum.

Wampold, B. E., Davis, B., & Good, R. H., III. (1990). Hypothesis validity of clinical research. *Journal of Consulting and Clinical Psychology, 58,* 360–367.

Weiss, B., & Weisz, J. R. (1990). The impact of methodological factors on child psychotherapy outcome research: A meta-analysis for researchers. *Journal of Abnormal Child Psychology, 18,* 639–670.

36

WRITING A REVIEW ARTICLE FOR *PSYCHOLOGICAL BULLETIN*

DARYL J. BEM

You have surveyed an experimental literature and arrived at conclusions you believe are worth sharing with the wider psychological community. Now it is time to write. To publish. To tell the world what you have learned. The purpose of this article is to enhance the chances that the editors of *Psychological Bulletin* will let you do so.

According to the recent revision of the *Publication Manual of the American Psychological Association*,

> **review articles,** including meta-analyses, are critical evaluations of material that has already been published. By organizing, integrating, and evaluating previously published material, the author of a review article considers the progress of current research toward clarifying a problem. In a sense, a review article is tutorial in that the author
>
> - defines and clarifies the problem;
> - summarizes previous investigations in order to inform the reader of the state of current research;

Reprinted from the *Psychological Bulletin*, *118*, 172–177. Copyright 1995 by the American Psychological Association.

- identifies relations, contradictions, gaps, and inconsistencies in the literature; and
- suggests the next step or steps in solving the problem. (American Psychological Association [APA], 1994, p. 5)

The inside front cover of *Bulletin* further notes that reviews "may set forth major developments within a particular research area or provide a bridge between related specialized fields within psychology or between psychology and related fields."

As these statements imply, *Bulletin* review articles are directed to a much wider audience than articles appearing in more specialized journals. Indeed, the current editor asserted in his first editorial that "*every* psychologist should read *Psychological Bulletin* . . . [b]ecause there is no better way to stay up-to-date with the field of psychology as a whole. . . . The *Bulletin* [provides] the best single vehicle for a continuing education in psychology" (Sternberg, 1991, p. 3). Moreover, the journal is frequently consulted by journalists, attorneys, congressional aids, and other nonpsychologists.

This means that your review should be accessible to students in Psychology 101, your colleagues in the Art History department, and your grandmother. No matter how technical or abstruse a review is in its particulars, intelligent nonpsychologists with no expertise in statistics, meta-analysis, or experimental design should be able to comprehend the broad outlines of your topic, to understand what you think the accumulated evidence demonstrates, and, above all, to appreciate why someone—anyone—should give a damn.

Thus, many of the writing techniques described in this article are designed to make your review article comprehensible to the widest possible audience. They are also designed to remain invisible or transparent to readers, thereby infusing your prose with a "subliminal pedagogy." Good writing is good teaching.

BEFORE WRITING

Let me begin on a pessimistic note: The chances that your review will be accepted for publication in *Psychological Bulletin* are only about 1 in 5. According to the current editor, "the #1 source of immediate-rejection letters is narrowly conceived topics" (R. J. Sternberg, personal communication, August 2, 1994). Translation: Nobody will give a damn. So the first question to ask about your intended review is whether it is likely to be interesting to a general audience of psychologists. If not, can it at least be made interesting—perhaps by extending its reach or setting it in a broader context? If your answer is that you think so, then you have already improved your chances. Read on.

The second obstacle to publication arises from the nature of the genre itself: Authors of literature reviews are at risk for producing mind-numbing lists of citations and findings that resemble a phone book—impressive cast, lots of numbers, but not much plot. So the second question to ask about your intended review is whether it has a clear take-home message. Again, editor Sternberg (1991):

> Literature reviews are often frustrating because they offer neither a point of view nor a take-home message. One is left with a somewhat undigested scattering of facts but little with which to put them together. I encourage authors to take a point of view based on theory and to offer readers a take-home message that integrates the review. . . . [T]o be lively and maintain reader interest, they need to make a point, not simply to summarize all the points everyone else has made. (p. 3)

As an additional antidote to dullness, Sternberg (1991) also encouraged authors to "*take risks in choosing topics, writing articles, and making submissions*" and not to be deterred because "they represent too much of a departure from current conventions, whether in conceptualization or methodology." In return, he pledged to "make every effort to ensure that top-quality work is rewarded rather than punished" (p. 3). So if an off-beat topic genuinely excites you, try submitting a review of it. (As a consumer service to readers, I have pretested the editor's sincerity by submitting an article on extrasensory perception [ESP]. He published it [Bem & Honorton, 1994].)

WRITING

The primary criteria for good scientific writing are accuracy and clarity. If your manuscript is written with style and flair, great. But this is a subsidiary virtue. First strive for accuracy and clarity.

Achieving Clarity

The first step toward clarity is to write simply and directly. A review tells a straightforward tale of a circumscribed question in want of an answer. It is not a novel with subplots and flashbacks but a short story with a single, linear narrative line. Let this line stand out in bold relief. Clear any underbrush that entangles your prose by obeying Strunk and White's (1979) famous dictum, "omit needless words," and by extending the dictum to needless concepts, topics, anecdotes, asides, and footnotes. If a point seems tangential to your basic argument, remove it. If you can't bring yourself to do this, put it in a footnote. Then, when you revise your manuscript, remove the footnote. In short, don't make your voice struggle to be heard above the ambient noise of cluttered writing. Let your 90th percentile verbal aptitude nourish your prose, not glut it. Write simply and directly.

A corollary of this directive is not to confuse *Bulletin* reviews with the literature reviews found in doctoral dissertations (even though some *Bulletin* reviews derive therefrom). Typically, these *are* novels with subplots and flashbacks, designed to assure dissertation committees that the candidate has covered any and all literatures conceivably related to the topic. If a dissertation proposes that love relationships in human adults recapitulate infant attachment styles, the biopsychologist on the committee will want to see a review of imprinting and its mating consequences in zebra finches. *Bulletin* readers will not. Omit needless literatures.

Organization

The second step toward clarity is to organize the manuscript so that it tells a coherent story. A review is more difficult to organize than an empirical report (for which there is a standardized APA format). Unfortunately, the guidance given by the *Publication Manual* (APA, 1994) is not very helpful: "The components of review articles, unlike the sections of reports of empirical studies, are arranged by relationship rather than by chronology" (p. 5). The vague generality of this guidance reflects that a coherent review emerges only from a coherent conceptual structuring of the topic itself. For most reviews, this requires a guiding theory, a set of competing models, or a point of view about the phenomenon under discussion.

An example of a review organized around competing models is provided by a *Bulletin* article on the emergence of sex differences in depression during adolescence (Nolen-Hoeksema & Girgus, 1994). The relevant literature consists primarily of studies examining specific variables correlated with depression, a hodgepodge of findings that less creative authors might have been tempted to organize chronologically or alphabetically. These authors, however, organized the studies in terms of whether they supported one of three developmental models: (a) The causes of depression are the same for the two sexes, but these causes become more prevalent in girls than in boys in early adolescence; (b) the causes of depression are different for the two sexes, and the causes of girls' depression become more prevalent in early adolescence; or (c) girls are more likely than boys to carry risk factors for depression before early adolescence, but these lead to depression only in the face of challenges that increase in prevalence in early adolescence. With this guiding structure, the findings fell into a recognizable pattern supporting the last model.

An example of a review organized around a point of view is provided by any of several *Bulletin* articles designed to convince readers to accept— or at least to seriously entertain—a novel or controversial conclusion. In these, tactics of persuasive communication structure the review. First, the commonly accepted conclusion is stated along with the putative reasons for its current acceptance. Next, the supporting and nonsupporting data for the author's view are presented in order of descending probative weight, and counterarguments to that view are acknowledged and rebutted at the point where they would be likely to occur spontaneously to neutral or skeptical readers. Finally, the reasons for favoring the author's conclusion are summarized.

This organizational strategy was the basis for the *Bulletin* article in which Charles Honorton and I sought to persuade readers to take seriously new experimental evidence for ESP (Bem & Honorton, 1994). Similar organization characterizes a *Bulletin* article whose authors argued that left-handers die at earlier ages than do right-handers (Coren & Halpern, 1991), a subsequent rebuttal to that conclusion (Harris, 1993), and an article whose author argued that the cross-cultural evidence does not support the commonly held view that there is universal recognition of emotion from facial expression (Russell, 1994).

There are many other organizing strategies, and Sternberg's (1991) editorial emphasizes that there is no one right way to write a review. As noted earlier, a coherent review emerges from a coherent conceptual structuring of the domain being reviewed. And if you remember to organize your review "by relationship rather than by chronology," then, by Jove, I think you've got it.

Metacomments

It is often helpful to give readers of a review article an early overview of its structure and content. But beyond that, you should avoid making "meta-comments" about the writing. Expository prose fails its mission if it diverts the reader's attention to itself and away from the topic; the process of writing should be invisible to the reader. In particular, the prose itself should direct the flow of the narrative without requiring you to play tour guide. Don't say, "now that the three theories of emotion have been discussed, we can turn to the empirical work on each of them. We begin with the psychoanalytic account of affect . . . ." Instead, move directly from your discussion of the theories into the review of the evidence with a simple transition sentence such as, "each of these three theories has been tested empirically. Thus, the psychoanalytic account of affect has received support in studies that . . . ." Any other guideposts needed can be supplied by using informative headings and by following the advice on repetition and parallel construction given in the next section.

If you feel the need to make metacomments to keep the reader on the narrative path, then your plot line is probably already too cluttered or pretzel shaped, the writing insufficiently linear. Metacomments only oppress the prose further. Instead, copy edit. Omit needless words—don't add them.

Repetition and Parallel Construction

Inexperienced writers often substitute synonyms for recurring words and vary their sentence structure in the mistaken belief that this is more creative and interesting. Instead of using repetition and parallel construction, as in "women may be more expressive than men in the domain of positive emotion, but they are not more expressive in the domain of negative emotion," they attempt to be more creative: "Women may be more expressive than men in the domain of positive emotion, but it is not the case that they are more prone than the opposite sex to display the less cheerful affects."

Such creativity is hardly more interesting, but it is certainly more confusing. In scientific communication, it can be deadly. When an author uses different words to refer to the same concept in a technical article—where accuracy is paramount—readers justifiably wonder if different meanings are implied. The example in the preceding paragraph is not disastrous, and most readers will be unaware that their understanding flickered momentarily when the prose hit a bump. But consider the cognitive burden carried by readers who must hack through this "creative" jungle:

> The low-dissonance participants were paid a large sum of money while not being given a free choice of whether or not to participate, whereas the individuals we randomly assigned to the small-incentive treatment (the high-dissonance condition) were offered the opportunity to refuse.

This (fictitious) writer should have written.

> Low-dissonance individuals were paid a large sum of money and were required to participate; high-dissonance individuals were paid a small sum of money and were not required to participate.

The wording and grammatical structure of the two clauses are held rigidly parallel; only the variables vary. Repetition and parallel construction are among the most effective servants of clarity. Don't be creative; be clear.

Repetition and parallel construction also serve clarity at a larger level of organization. By providing the reader with distinctive guideposts to the structure of the prose, they can diminish or eliminate the need for meta-comments on the writing. For example, here are some guidepost sentences from earlier in this section:

> The first step toward clarity is to write simply and directly. . . .
> The second step toward clarity is to organize the manuscript so that . . . .
> An example of a review organized around competing models is provided
>   by . . . .
> An example of a review organized around a point of view is provided
>   by . . . .

If I had substituted synonyms for the recurring words or varied the grammatical structure of these sentences, their guiding function would have been lost, the reader's sense of the section's organization blurred. (I try so hard to be helpful, and I bet you didn't even notice. That, of course, is the point.)

Terminology

The specialized terminology of a discipline is called jargon, and it serves a number of legitimate functions in scientific communication. A specialized term may be more general, more precise, or freer of surplus meaning that any natural language equivalent (e.g., the term *disposition* encompasses, and hence is more general than, beliefs, attitudes, moods, and personality attributes; *reinforcement* is more precise and freer of surplus meaning than *reward*). Also, the technical vocabulary often makes an important conceptual distinction not apprehended in the layperson's lexicon (e.g., genotype vs. phenotype).

But if a jargon term does not satisfy any of these criteria, opt for English. Much of our jargon has become second nature and serves only to muddy our prose. (As an editor, I once had to interrogate an author at length to learn that a prison program for "strengthening the executive functions of the ego" actually taught prisoners how to fill out job applications.) And unless the jargon term is extremely well known (e.g., reinforcement), it should be defined—explicitly, implicitly, or by context and example—the first time it is introduced.

For example, in our article on ESP, Honorton and I decided that we could not proceed beyond the opening paragraph until we had first explicitly defined and clarified the unfamiliar but central theoretical term:

> The term *psi* denotes anomalous processes of information or energy transfer, processes such as telepathy or other forms of extrasensory perception that are currently unexplained in terms of known physical or biological mechanisms. The term is purely descriptive: It neither implies that such anomalous phenomena are paranormal nor connotes anything about their underlying mechanisms. (Bem & Honorton, 1994, p. 4)

Here is how one might define a technical term (ego control) and identify its conceptual status (a personality variable) more implicitly:

> The need to delay gratification, control impulses, and modulate emotional expression is the earliest and most ubiquitous demand that society places on the developing child. Because success at so many of life's tasks depends critically on the individual's mastery of such ego control, evidence for life-course continuities in this central personality domain should be readily obtained.

And finally, here is a (made-up) example in which the technical terms are defined only by the context. Note, however, that the technical abbreviation, MAO, is still identified explicitly when it is first introduced.

> In the continuing search for the biological correlates of psychiatric disorder, blood platelets are now a prime target of investigation. In particular, reduced monoamine oxidase (MAO) activity in the platelets is sometimes correlated with paranoid symptomatology, auditory hallucinations

or delusions in chronic schizophrenia, and a tendency toward psycho-pathology in normal men. Unfortunately, these observations have not always replicated, casting doubt on the hypothesis that MAO activity is, in fact, a biological marker in psychiatric disorder. Even the general utility of the platelet model as a key to central nervous system abnormalities in schizophrenia remains controversial. The present review attempts to clarify the relation of MAO activity to symptomatology in chronic schizophrenia.

This kind of writing would not appear in *Newsweek*, and yet it is still accessible to a nonspecialist who may know nothing about blood platelets, MAO activity, or biological markers. The structure of the writing itself adequately defines the relationships among these things and provides enough context to make the basic rationale behind the review comprehensible. At the same time, this introduction is neither condescending nor boring to the technically sophisticated reader. The pedagogy that makes it accessible to the nonspecialist is not only invisible to the specialist but also enhances the clarity of the review for both readers.

Ending

Most *Bulletin* reviews end with a consideration of questions that remain unanswered along with suggestions for the kinds of research that would help to answer them. In fact, suggesting further research is probably the most common way of ending a review.

Common, but dull. Why not strive to end your review with broad general conclusions—or a final grand restatement of your take-home message—rather than precious details of interest only to specialists? Thus, the statement, "further research is needed before it is clear whether the androgyny scale should be scored as a single, continuous dimension or partitioned into a four-way typology," might be appropriate earlier in the review but please, not your final farewell. Only the French essayist, Michel de Montaigne (1580/1943), was clever enough to end a review with a refreshing statement about further research: "Because [the study of motivation] is a high and hazardous undertaking, I wish fewer people would meddle with it" (p. 126).

You may wish to settle for less imperious pronouncements. But in any case, end with a bang, not a whimper.

Discussing Previous Work

Summarizing Studies

One of the tasks most frequently encountered in writing a *Bulletin* review is summarizing the methods and results of previous studies. The *Publication Manual* (APA, 1994) warns writers not to let the goal of brevity mislead them into writing a statement intelligible only to the specialist. One technique for describing an entire study succinctly without sacrificing clarity is to describe one variation of the procedure in chronological sequence, letting it convey an overview of the study at the same time. For example, here is one way of describing a complicated but classic experiment on cognitive dissonance theory (Festinger & Carlsmith, 1959):

> Sixty male undergraduates were randomly assigned to one of three conditions. In the $1 condition, the participant was first required to perform long repetitive laboratory tasks in an individual experimental session. He was then hired by the experimenter as an "assistant" and paid $1 to tell a waiting fellow student (a confederate) that the tasks were fun and interesting. In the $20 condition, each participant was hired for $20 to do the same thing. In the control condition, participants simply engaged in the tasks. After the experiment, each participant indicated on a questionnaire how much he had enjoyed the tasks. The results showed that $1 participants rated the tasks as significantly more enjoyable than did the $20 participants, who, in turn, did not differ from the control participants.

This kind of condensed writing looks easy. It is not, and you will have to rewrite such summaries repeatedly before they are both clear and succinct. The preceding paragraph was my eighth draft.

Citations

Reviews typically contain many more citations than other kinds of articles. The standard journal format permits you to cite authors in the text either by enclosing their last names and the year of publication in parentheses, as in (a) below, or by using their names in the sentence itself, as in (b).

> (a) "MAO activity in some patients with schizophrenia is actually higher than normal" (Tse & Tung, 1949).
> (b) "Tse and Tung (1949) reported that MAO activity in some patients with schizophrenia is actually higher than normal."

In general, you should use the form of (a), consigning your colleagues to parentheses. Your narrative should be about MAO activity in patients with schizophrenia, not about Tse and Tung. Occasionally, however, you might want to focus specifically on the authors or researchers: "Theophrastus (280 B.C.) implies that persons are consistent across situations, but Montaigne (1580) insists that they are not. Only Mischel (1968), Peterson (1968), and Vernon (1964), however, have actually surveyed the evidence in detail." The point is that you have a deliberate choice to make. Don't just intermix the two formats randomly, paying no attention to your narrative structure.

Ad Verbum Not Ad Hominem

If you take a dim view of previous research or earlier articles in the domain you reviewed, feel free to criticize and complain as strongly as you feel is commensurate with the incompetence you have uncovered. But criticize the work, not the investigators or authors. Ad hominem attacks offend editors and reviewers; moreover, the person you attack is likely to be asked to serve as one of the reviewers. Consequently, your opportunity to address— let alone, offend—readers will be nipped in the bud. I could launch into a sermonette on communitarian values in science, but I shall assume that this pragmatic warning is sufficient.

Formatting and Further Guidance

Your manuscript should conform to the prescribed format for articles published in APA journals. If it diverges markedly from that format, it may be returned for rewriting before being sent out for review. If you are unfamiliar with this format, you should consult recent issues of *Bulletin* and the new edition of the *Publication Manual* (APA, 1994). Even experienced writers should probably check this revision for recent changes in formatting style, new information on formatting with word processors, and instructions for submitting final versions of manuscripts on computer disk for electronic typesetting.

In addition to describing the mechanics of preparing a manuscript for APA journals, the *Publication Manual* (APA, 1994) also has a chapter on the expression of ideas, including writing style, grammar, and avoiding language bias. Sternberg (1993) has also written an article on how to write for psychological journals. Finally, this article has borrowed heavily from my earlier chapter on how to write an empirical journal article (Bem, 1987).

REWRITING

For many writers revising a manuscript is unmitigated agony. Even proofreading is painful. And so they don't. So relieved to get a draft done, they run it through the spell checker—some don't even do that—and then send it off to the journal, thinking that they can clean up the writing after the article has been accepted. Alas, that day rarely comes. Some may find solace in the belief that the manuscript probably would have been rejected even if it had been extensively revised and polished; after all, most APA journals, including *Bulletin*, accept only 15–20% of all manuscripts submitted. But from my own experience as an editor of an APA journal, I believe that the difference between the articles accepted and the top 15–20% of those rejected is frequently the difference between good and less good writing. Moral: Don't expect journal reviewers to discern your brilliance through the smog of polluted writing. Revise your manuscript. Polish it. Proofread it. Then submit it.

Rewriting is difficult for several reasons. First, it is difficult to edit your own writing. You will not notice ambiguities and explanatory gaps because *you* know what you meant to say; *you* understand the omitted steps. One strategy for overcoming this difficulty is to lay your manuscript aside for awhile and then return to it later when it has become less familiar. Sometimes it helps to read it aloud. But there is no substitute for practicing the art of taking the role of the nonspecialist reader, for learning to role-play grandma. As you read, ask yourself, "Have I been told yet what this concept means? Has the logic of this step been demonstrated? Would I know at this point what the dependent variables of this study were?" This is precisely the skill of the good lecturer in Psychology 101, the ability to anticipate the audience's level of understanding at each point in the presentation. Good writing is good teaching.

But because this is not easy, you should probably give a copy of a fairly polished manuscript to a friend or colleague for a critical reading. If you get critiques from several colleagues, you will have simulated the journal's review process. The best readers are those who have themselves had articles published in psychological journals but who are unfamiliar with the subject of your manuscript.

If your colleagues find something unclear, do not argue with them. They are right: By definition, the writing is unclear. Their suggestions for correcting the unclarities may be wrongheaded; but as unclarity detectors, readers are never wrong. Also resist the temptation simply to clarify their confusion verbally. Your colleagues don't want to offend you or appear stupid, so they simply mumble "oh yes, of course, of course" and apologize for not having read carefully enough. As a consequence, you are pacified, and your next readers, *Bulletin*'s reviewers, will stumble over the same problem. They will not apologize; they will reject.

Rewriting is difficult for a second reason: It requires a high degree of compulsiveness and attention to detail. The probability of writing a sentence perfectly the first time is vanishingly small, and good writers rewrite nearly every sentence of a manuscript in the course of polishing successive drafts. But even good writers differ from one another in their approach to the first draft. Some spend a long time carefully choosing each word and reshaping each sentence and paragraph as they go. Others pound out a rough draft quickly and then go back to extensive revision. Although I personally prefer the former method, I think it wastes time. Most writers should probably get the first draft done as quickly as possible without agonizing over stylistic niceties. Once it is done, however, compulsiveness and attention to detail become the required virtues.

Finally, rewriting is difficult because it usually means restructuring. Sometimes it is necessary to discard whole sections of a manuscript, add new ones, and then totally reorganize the manuscript just to iron out a bump in the logic of the argument. Don't get so attached to your first draft that you are unwilling to tear it apart and rebuild it. (This is why the strategy of crafting each sentence of a first draft wastes time. A beautiful turn of phrase that took me 20 minutes to shape gets trashed when I have to restructure the manuscript. Worse, I get so attached to the phrase that I resist restructuring until I can find a new home for it.) A badly constructed building cannot be salvaged by brightening up the wallpaper. A badly constructed manuscript cannot be salvaged by changing words, inverting sentences, and shuffling paragraphs.

Which brings me to the word processor. Its very virtuosity at making these cosmetic changes will tempt you to tinker endlessly, encouraging you in the illusion that you are restructuring right there in front of the monitor. Do not be fooled. You are not. A word processor—even one with a fancy outline mode—is not an adequate restructuring tool for most writers. Moreover, it can produce flawless, physically beautiful drafts of wretched writing, encouraging you in the illusion that they are finished manuscripts ready to be submitted. Do not be fooled. They are not. If you are blessed with an excellent memory (or a very large monitor) and are confident that you can get away with a purely electronic process of restructuring, do it. But don't be ashamed to print out a complete draft of your manuscript; spread it out on table or floor; take pencil, scissors, and scotch tape in hand; and then, all by your low-tech self, have at it.

If, after all this, your manuscript still seems interesting and you still believe your conclusions, submit it.

REWRITING AGAIN

Long ago and far away, a journal editor allegedly accepted a manuscript that required no revision. I believe the author was William James. In other words, if your review is provisionally accepted for publication "pending revisions in accord with the reviewers' comments," you should be deliriously happy. Publication is now virtually under your control. If your review is rejected, but you are invited to resubmit a revised version, you should still be happy—if not deliriously so—because you still have a reasonable shot at getting it published.

But this is the point at which many writers give up. As an anonymous reviewer of this article noted,

> in my experience as an associate editor, I thought a good deal of variance in predicting eventual publication came from this phase of the process. Authors are often discouraged by negative feedback and miss the essential positive fact that they have been asked to revise! They may never resubmit at all or may let an inordinate amount of time pass before they do (during which editors and reviewers become unavailable, lose the thread of the project, and so forth). An opposite problem is that some authors become defensive and combative, and refuse to make needed changes for no reason.

So don't give up yet. Feel free to complain to your colleagues or rail at your poodle because the stupid reviewers failed to read your manuscript correctly. But then turn to the task of revising your manuscript with a dispassionate, problem-solving approach. First, pay special attention to criticisms or suggestions made by more than one reviewer or highlighted by the editor in the cover letter. These *must* be addressed in your revision—even if not in exactly the way the editor or reviewers suggest.

Next, look carefully at each of the reviewers' misreadings. I argued earlier that whenever readers of a manuscript find something unclear, they are right; by definition, the writing is unclear. The problem is that readers themselves do not always recognize or identify the unclarities explicitly. Instead, they misunderstand what you have written and then make a criticism or offer a suggestion that makes no sense. In other words, you should also interpret reviewers' misreadings as signals that your writing is unclear.

Think of your manuscript as a pilot experiment in which the participants (reviewers) didn't understand the instructions you gave them. Analyze the reasons for their misunderstanding and then rewrite the problematic sections so that subsequent readers will not be similarly misled. Reviewers are almost always more knowledgeable about your topic, more experienced in writing manuscripts themselves, and more conscientious about reading your review than the average journal reader. If they didn't understand, neither will that average reader.

When you send in your revised manuscript, tell the editor in a cover letter how you have responded to each of the criticisms or suggestions made by the reviewers. If you have decided not to adopt a particular suggestion, state your reasons, perhaps pointing out how you remedied the problem in some alternative way.

Here are three fictitious examples of cover-letter responses that also illustrate ways of responding to certain kinds of criticisms and suggestions within the revision itself.

1. *Wrong:* "I have left the section on the animal studies unchanged. If Reviewers A and C can't even agree on whether the animal studies are relevant, I must be doing something right."

Right: "You will recall that Reviewer A thought that the animal studies should be described more fully, whereas Reviewer C thought they should be omitted. A biopsychologist in my department agreed with Reviewer C that the animal studies are not really valid analogs of the human studies. So I have dropped them from the text but cited Snarkle's review of them in an explanatory footnote on page 26."

2. *Wrong:* "Reviewer A is obviously Melanie Grimes, who has never liked me or my work. If she really thinks that behaviorist principles solve all the problems of obsessive–compulsive disorders, then let her write her own review. Mine is about the cognitive processes involved."

Right: "As the critical remarks by Reviewer A indicate, this is a contentious area, with different theorists staking out strong positions. Apparently I did not make it clear that my review was intended only to cover the cognitive processes involved in obsessive–compulsive disorders and not to engage the debate between cognitive and behavioral approaches. To clarify this, I have now included the word 'cognitive' in both the title and abstract, taken note of the debate in my introduction, and stated explicitly that the review does not undertake a comparative review of the two approaches. I hope this satisfactory."

3.   *Right:* "You will recall that two of the reviewers questioned the validity of the analysis of variance, with Reviewer B suggesting that I use multiple regression instead. I agree with their reservations regarding the ANOVA but believe that a multiple regression analysis is equally problematic because it makes the same assumptions about the underlying distributions. So I have retained the ANOVA, but summarized the results of a non-parametric analysis, which yields the same conclusions. If you think it preferable, I could simply substitute this nonparametric analysis for the original ANOVA, although it will be less familiar to *Bulletin* readers."

Above all, remember that the editor is your ally in trying to shape a manuscript that will be a credit to both you and the journal. So cooperate in the effort to turn your sow's ear into a vinyl purse. Be civil and make nice. You may not live longer, but you will publish more.

REFERENCES

American Psychological Association. (1994). *Publication manual of the American Psychological Association* (4th ed.). Washington, DC: Author.

Bem, D. J. (1987). Writing the empirical journal article. In M. P. Zanna & J. M. Darley (Eds.), *The compleat academic: A practical guide for the beginning social scientist* (pp. 171–120). New York: Random House.

Bem, D. J., & Honorton, C. (1994). Does psi exist? Replicable evidence for an anomalous process of information transfer. *Psychological Bulletin, 115,* 4–18.

Coren, S., & Halpern, D. F. (1991). Left-handedness: A marker for decreased survival fitness. *Psychological Bulletin, 109,* 90–106.

de Montaigne, M. (1943). Of the inconsistency of our actions. In D. M. Frame (Trans.), *Selected essays: Translated and with introduction and notes by Donald M. Frame* (pp. 119–126). Roslyn, NY: Walter J. Black. (Original work published 1580)

Festinger, L., & Carlsmith, J. M. (1959). Cognitive consequences of forced compliance. *Journal of Abnormal and Social Psychology, 58,* 203–210.

Harris, L. J. (1993). Do left-handers die sooner than right-handers? Commentary on Coren and Halpern's (1991) "Left-handedness: A marker for decreased survival fitness." *Psychological Bulletin, 114,* 203–234.

Nolen-Hoeksema, S., & Girgus, J. S. (1994). The emergence of gender differences in depression during adolescence. *Psychological Bulletin, 115*, 424–443.

Russell, J. A. (1994). Is there universal recognition of emotion from facial expression? A review of the cross-cultural studies. *Psychological Bulletin, 115*, 102–141.

Sternberg, R. J. (1991). Editorial. *Psychological Bulletin, 109*, 3–4.

Sternberg, R. J. (1993). How to win acceptance by psychology journals: Twenty-one tips for better writing. In R. J. Sternberg (Ed.), *The psychologist's companion* (3rd ed., pp. 174–180). New York: Cambridge University Press.

Strunk, W., & White, E. B. (1979). *The elements of style* (3rd ed.). New York: Macmillan.

37

TIPS FOR WRITING (AND READING) METHODOLOGICAL ARTICLES

SCOTT E. MAXWELL AND DAVID A. COLE

For some psychologists, writing a methodological article is a fine art of obfuscating needlessly tedious and complex trivia. For others, reading a methodological article ranks right up there with a visit to the dentist's office. Many methodological articles, however, are not accessible to their intended readers, not necessarily because the material is so sophisticated but because the presentation of the materials is so obtuse. Our goal in this article is to provide a few suggestions for writing methodological articles. Excellent articles are available on the writing of general psychology articles (e.g., Bem, 1987; Sternberg, 1988, 1992). Hence, we try to avoid repeating these points, except to say that all the rules for good nontechnical writing are at least as important for good technical writing if only because the material is often more complex. Our specific focus is on writing methodological articles for nonspecialists, although some of our comments may also pertain to authors who target specialists.

Reprinted from the *Psychological Bulletin*, *118*, 193–198. Copyright 1995 by the American Psychological Association.

753

Quantitative methods articles in psychology take many different forms. Some articles are similar to substantive *Psychological Bulletin* articles insofar as they are literature reviews. The authors of these articles typically synthesize relevant methodological literature or present new statistical methods in a format that is appropriate to a nonstatistical audience. Other authors present the results of original research. The topics range from evaluations and comparisons of current statistical technologies to developments and introductions of qualitatively new research methodologies. Such articles may include highly technical mathematics or extensive computer simulation. Because of the diversity of these articles, we attempt to make points that are useful to as wide a range as possible of current and future methodological article authors.

PREPARATION

Defining Your Audience

"Perhaps the most important principle of good writing is to keep the reader uppermost in mind" (Knuth, Larrabee, & Roberts, 1989, p. 3). This principle is especially important in technical writing, where your audience may be remarkably diverse, ranging from methodologists who specialize precisely in the topic under investigation to researchers in very different fields who hope to apply a specific new technique in their next study.

Authors often overlook the fact that they wield considerable control over their readership by carefully choosing the journals to which they submit their work. At least three questions should be considered when selecting a journal in which to publish a methodological article. First, how technical is your presentation? The perfect article for a highly technical outlet such as *Psychometrika* may be almost unintelligible to the majority of *Psychological Bulletin* readers. Many journals (*Psychological Bulletin* included) explicitly proscribe the use of complex mathematics, such as calculus or matrix algebra. If not, the editor either requests the author to find a more accessible way to make the points or suggests to the author to submit the work to a more technical journal. Second, how specific is your methodological point? Among methodological journals, some (e.g., *Psychological Bulletin*) target a readership that uses a wide variety of methodologies. In general, articles in which highly specific points about a particular statistical technique are made belong in more specialized methodological journals (e.g., *Structural Equation Modeling*). If the point is more general or pertains to a wider variety of research paradigms, then broader methodological outlets may be more appropriate. Third, how specific are the implications of your article for a particular subdiscipline of psychology? Articles submitted to journals with broad readerships should have implications for researchers almost irrespective of their content area. Even when the technical level of the presentation is low, authors must still face the question of whether the practical implications of the article are broad enough to warrant publication in a journal such as *Psychological Bulletin* or whether a more specialized substantive journal might be more appropriate. Many area journals publish occasional methodological articles (e.g., *Journal of Applied Psychology*), have special sections on methodological advances (e.g., *Journal of Consulting and Clinical Psychology*), or even publish special issues on methodology (e.g., *Journal of Counseling Psychology* and *Journal of Family Psychology*). Consequently, an article on a specific topic, such as reaction times in cognitive tasks, would probably fit well in a cognitive journal, whereas an article on reaction time research in general might cut across disciplines and thus be more appropriate for a journal with a broader readership.

After selecting a journal, continue to strive to write for as broad an audience as possible. Failure to relate specific methodological points to the variety of situations to which they might pertain unnecessarily limits the impact of the article. Use examples from diverse research areas; refer the reader to wide-ranging applications of your procedure; and elaborate on the implications of your methodology for diverse research paradigms. Pitching your article to too narrow an audience may not get it the attention it deserves.

Most articles have multiple audiences. A hierarchical structure permits an article to be read for its general ideas by some readers and for its specific details by others. Presenting a general overview of the problem and the solution early in the article enables all readers to walk away with the overall gist of the message. Then, increasing the amount of detail as the article progresses allows readers to go as far as they want (or need) into the intricacies of the methodology. At the same time, authors and readers alike need to be sensitive to the dangers of stopping too soon. Authors might motivate readers to persevere by issuing periodic cautionary notes that describe potential hazards of implementing this new technique (among other things) before reading the next section.

Obtain feedback on the article from a variety of sources. For example, sharing a draft of the article with other authors who have written articles in the same general area may provide valuable expert feedback. It may be especially useful to seek the opinions of individuals whose expertise and perspective differ from your own. For example, some authors may benefit from involving a methodological expert who can ensure the technical accuracy of the article. All authors may benefit from the input of a knowledgeable nonspecialist, who can endow the work with a healthy respect for some of the readers' primary concerns, paraphrase statistical jargon, enrich the article with substantive examples from nonquantitative journals, and maintain a focus on the article's practical implications.

Motivating the Reader

Most psychologists are content to continue plying the traditional statistics and methodologies learned in graduate school. A pretty serious wake-up call is needed to alert psychology authors to new alternatives. Before proving anything with numbers and formulas, prove to the reader that what you propose can make a real difference. A specialist who encounters your article may immediately appreciate the relevance and potential importance of your article simply by reading the title and the abstract. The nonspecialist, however, is likely to need more guidance. Consequently, be as explicit as possible about the purpose of the article. Furthermore, make the point as early as possible in the article; otherwise, many readers may not struggle beyond the first paragraph or even the abstract.

To some extent, the point is the same as Sternberg's (1992) advice that all psychology authors should "tell readers why they should be interested" (p. 12). This point is even more important when writing a methodological article, however, if only because there is likely to be a larger gap between the author's background and the reader's. The author may be drawn to the topic because of its theoretical elegance or mathematical challenge, whereas readers are more likely to be interested in knowing whether this article means that they should design their studies differently or analyze their data with a new technique.

As Knuth et al. (1989) stated, "present the reader with something straightforward to start off with" (p. 76). Hand the readers a statement that explains what the article is about and why they should read it. Most *Psychological Bulletin* articles have one of the following points at their center:

1. Methodological advances allow interesting questions to be answered that previously were not amenable to a solution.
2. Here is a way to increase your statistical power.
3. You may not be testing the hypothesis you thought you were.
4. If you have data that depart from standard assumptions, there may be better ways to analyze your data.
5. A new statistic is better than the standard statistic.

Remember, presenting a new solution is of little value if the reader does not understand the problem yet. A voluminous review of every nuance of a methodological conundrum is unlikely to hold anyone's interest unless one is working on the particular problem. If the problem is truly important, an author should be able to state in a few sentences at the beginning of the article what the problem is, why it is important for psychologists, and why it has been difficult to solve.

Reviewing the Literature

Stipulating that prospective authors conduct a thorough literature search prior to formulating a methodological article is hardly an earth-shattering notion. Less obvious, however, is that searching the relevant literature for methodological articles is often quite different from reviewing the literature for substantive articles. The multidisciplinary nature of the methodology requires that the researcher be familiar with previous work in a variety of other disciplines. What appears to be a new statistical technique in psychology may have already been proposed in the statistics literature. The *Current Index to Statistics* (American Statistical Association, 1994), an annual keyword index, is extremely useful for identifying relevant statistical literature on a particular topic.

Quantitative psychologists must also be aware of the methodological literatures in other social sciences. For example, authors on structural equation modeling often must be familiar with recent advances that have appeared in sociology literature (such as *Sociological Methods and Research* and *Sociological Methodology*). Finally, methodologists must be cognizant of the ideas transmitted to the next wave of researchers through recent methodology textbooks. Articles that critique methodologies from texts published a decade ago are not of much value if those presentations no longer appear in more recent books. Similarly, articles that constitute pedagogical reviews of already published methodologies must differ substantively from modern textbook presentations of the same material. Synthesizing literature that has heretofore appeared exclusively in specialized methodology journals may be quite valuable. Once new methodologies appear in textbooks, however, they are likely to be inappropriate journal topics even if previous literature reviews have not appeared in journal format.

Occasionally, relevant literature lurks in unexpected places. In statistics, problems can sometimes be transformed in such a way that they take on an entirely different appearance (even though they are technically unchanged). Under the alternative guise, new literature, if not new insights, may be hiding.

COMMUNICATING TECHNICAL MATERIAL

Many psychologists' worst adult memories are from their first graduate statistics class. With a few well-chosen mathematical proofs and equations, you have the power to dredge up nightmares of endless take-home exams and to rekindle feelings of deep-seated insecurity—not exactly the recipe for tempting the reader past the first few opening paragraphs of your article. You might rationalize that these simply are not the people who will read your article anyway, but that is precisely the (unfortunate) point.

Some authors appear to operate from the assumption that clarity and rigor represent opposite ends of the same dimension: These authors argue that if everyone can understand their arguments, then their points must not have much insight. Certainly some arguments require a great deal of prior knowledge without which even the clearest prose fails to be comprehensible. Nevertheless, it does not follow that clarity and rigor are enemies of one another. The author must adopt a different attitude, such as by wondering how he or she can make this inherently difficult (and potentially tedious) material as accessible as possible.

Clarity is especially critical in technical writing where the presentation of ideas is usually cumulative. If the author does not communicate the first points clearly, readers will probably be lost and therefore be unable to appreciate the remainder of the article. Be aware of what the reader knows because either the material has already been presented in the article or some background knowledge can be safely assumed (Knuth et al., 1989). If your article is closely related to an earlier article, it is usually necessary to summarize the major points of the previous article in considerable detail. Do not expect readers to be familiar with recent articles, and do not require them to read the articles before they can comprehend yours. Good advice is generally to start at a lower technical level than you would think. Even more difficult, however, is to anticipate what the reader expects next. Prepare the reader for the relations between different sections of the article so that individual pieces become a coherent whole.

Presume that many readers will skim (or altogether skip) anything that even slightly resembles an equation. Why fight it? Too much mathematical material in an article written for nonspecialists may effectively reduce actual readership to zero. The most obvious solution is to relegate technical details to an appendix. This is frequently a useful strategy; however, authors must take care that the main message of the article is clear even to those who do not read the appendix.

At times, equations are necessary for the main message of the article, in which case they should not be placed in an appendix. Indeed, a statistics article in a specialized journal may (and perhaps should) contain as many equations as words. When it comes time for the unavoidable mathematical argument, consider a few simple steps:

1. Tell the reader what you are going to show and why it is important.
2. Define your terms clearly when you first introduce them (and do not be afraid to remind the reader of key terms along the way).
3. Within the mathematics section, do not forget that you can use words too. Phrases such as "substituting Equation 3 into

Equation 4 produces the following" are far superior to phrases such as "it follows that" or insults such as "obviously." Remember, too, that symbolic expressions are parts of sentences and should be punctuated as such as well.

4. Pause periodically to explain particular equations and comment on how they fit into the big picture.
5. At the end of the mathematics section, provide a verbal summary of the main points and why they are important.

Formulas can often be made more comprehensible by the presentation of "special cases." For example, some formulas may become simpler when sample size becomes extremely large. Simplifications may also arise when certain terms are assumed to be equal to one another or to zero. Yet another simplification sometimes emerges when a formula is written for the special case of two groups or in its univariate form instead of the more general multivariate form. Even if the rest of the article uses the more complex form of the formula, readers will usually find this presentation to be more meaningful if they have been able to grasp the essential meaning of the formula through special cases.

Of course, authors must also exercise good judgment about how much verbal explanation surrounding the mathematical presentation will be useful to readers. Unnecessary verbiage simply slows readers down and can make concentrating on the major points more difficult. On a related point, although word variety can reduce repetition and subsequent boredom, technical terms should generally not be interchanged even when they have the same precise meaning because many readers may not know whether the change in wording reflects a change in meaning.

Notation

The wise use of symbols in a quantitative article provides a clear and parsimonious form of communication. It is much simpler for both the reader and the author to write σ_j instead of "population standard deviation within group j." Whereas the advantage is most obvious in equations, the careful use of symbols in text can also prevent awkward and excessive verbiage. Careless or thoughtless notation, however, may frustrate the most dedicated reader even when the expository text of the article is exemplary. A few straightforward rules go a long way to ensure that symbols help rather than hinder the reader. For example, providing an explicit definition of each symbol when it is first introduced is essential. Even something as seemingly straightforward as n may need to be defined. Although the American Psychological Association's *Publication Manual* (1994) stipulates that n be used to denote sample size within a group and N be used to denote total sample size, some readers may not be aware of this notation. Even when the initial meaning is explicit and clear, readers may benefit from an occasional reminder of what a symbol represents, especially if it has not been used for several pages. Also helpful is to take advantage of mnemonic coding wherever possible. Standard notation should be used if it has been established. The *Publication Manual* (1994) provides an extensive list of common statistical abbreviations and symbols. Even when standard notation does not exist, it is still important to follow general conventions, such as using Greek letters to represent population parameters and Latin letters for sample statistics. Needless to say, the same symbol should never be used to represent two different concepts, nor should two different symbols be used to represent the same concept. Finally, authors must be aware of the need to balance the parsimony obtained from symbols with the added burden placed on readers to remember what each symbol represents. In general, the best advice is to use as few symbols as possible.

Examples and Figures

A mathematician's natural tendency is to derive the most general form of an expression first and only then consider special cases. This strategy can be effective in articles written for nonspecialists if the author explains the general problem thoroughly and builds a compelling case for needing the general form in the first place. Nonspecialists, however, often crave a few special cases as appetizers, which then whet their appetite for the most general case. Although this sequence is typically less elegant mathematically, beginning with concrete examples may allow nonspecialists to follow the underlying logic more easily. This approach is similar to the *particular–general–particular* teaching technique recommended by Rourke (as cited in Mosteller, 1980). To explain an abstract idea, begin with a specific example that motivates the need to develop a solution to the problem. A general approach to the problem can then be considered along with a general solution. A sense of closure and full understanding may be absent, however, unless the general principles are followed by their application to a specific problem.

Using the particular–general–particular strategy is often consistent with using appropriate examples. Numerical examples are especially helpful in methodological articles. Authors can fulfill the first step of Rourke's (cited in Mosteller, 1980) strategy by providing an initial discussion of a problem in need of a solution. Once the author has presented the general solution, the initial problem can be revisited through a numerical example. A dilemma facing the author is to make the example complicated enough to be realistic and yet simple enough to illustrate the general methodological principle clearly. At times, the best resolution of this dilemma may involve a succession of increasingly complicated examples (see Cole, 1987). Ideally, examples also provide sufficient information to allow readers to work through computations or programming themselves, so they can check the accuracy of their understanding as well as their ability to apply procedures to actual data. Sometimes providing a numerical example on the basis of a small number of cases is either so unrealistic as to be misleading or it is simply infeasible. However, authors should be aware that useful alternatives may exist in these cases. For example, Willett and Sayer (1994) provided complete longitudinal data on a subsample of cases and effectively integrated their presentation of the subsample with their discussion of the actual total sample. For some types of problems, presenting the sample covariance matrix (or other summary statistics) may be sufficient to allow readers to duplicate the authors' results (see MacCallum & Browne, 1993, for an example). Willett and Sayer's inclusion of the LISREL program code in an appendix also illustrates an additional approach for helping readers to check their understanding of the proposed method and to use it appropriately for their own data. Although examples are often essential for clear communication, both authors and readers must understand that examples in and of themselves do not establish desirable properties of a proposed method.

The juxtaposition of specific and general issues may be ideally suited for methodological articles that demonstrate how advances in computer software can offer new methodological opportunities. The impact of such a presentation can usually be greatly increased by couching the presentation in terms of more general methodological issues. Try to use software examples to illustrate fundamental methodological principles. Good examples are O'Brien and Kaiser's (1985) demonstration of how syntax choices in SPSS multivariate analysis of variance yield different analyses in repeated measures designs and Bryk and Raudenbush's (1987) discussion of how hierarchical linear modeling addresses basic questions in the analysis of change. The combination of computer software, a broad consideration of more general quantitative issues, and specific numerical examples enables readers to not just use the statistical program but also better understand the advantages and disadvantages of various data analytic strategies.

Another useful tool for communicating technical material is the use of figures. Figures may be useful for showing results from numerical examples or for displaying the results of simulation studies. An often overlooked advantage of figures, however, is their use for depicting mathematical relationships. Plotting mathematical functions often illuminates the meaning underlying an abstract mathematical expression. For example, some of our own work (Maxwell, 1994; Maxwell, Cole, Arvey, & Salas, 1991) illustrated how contour plots can show the meaning and practical implications of mathematical derivations. Recent advances in graphics software open the door to a multitude of possibilities for visual representations of multivariate data and relationships. Methodologists should be at the forefront of advances in graphics (see Cleveland, 1985, 1993; Tufte, 1983, 1990).

Simulation Studies

Much of the methodological work submitted to psychology journals involves simulation studies. Simulations can be extraordinarily valuable because they allow the author to describe properties of statistics under suboptimal conditions where underlying assumptions have not been met. As a consequence, mathematical derivations of properties may be cumbersome if not impossible. Effective communication of simulation studies involves special considerations beyond those of other methodological articles; simulation studies are experiments and must be described and interpreted in this light.

For example, careful thought must be given to the selection of specific parameter values to manipulate. An infinite number of ways exist for distributions to depart from homoscedasticity. How does the author select a realistic sample of distributions to examine? Although there is no simple answer, some sources can supply useful evidence of the types of distributions obtained in actual empirical work in the behavioral sciences (e.g., Micceri, 1989). Sawilowsky and Blair (1992) provided an example of how this type of information can be incorporated into the design of simulation studies. Of course, previous simulation studies in related areas can also provide a useful framework for selecting conditions to simulate.

As in all experiments, the author should be prepared to interpret the results obtained from the specific parameter values in the context of a broader theoretical framework. For example, the specific results obtained with exactly 20 or 50 participants per group in the simulation are valuable only to the extent that the author can establish a case for generalizing the findings to other sample sizes (even if these specific values were not included in the simulation). The author must also plan an appropriate number of simulation replications so that obtained results are sufficiently precise. Obtaining 8 significant results out of 100 simulated replications at an alpha level of .05 does not necessarily indicate that the test under consideration is liberal. The excessive error rate might simply reflect sampling error. Many replications are quite appropriate when a high degree of precision is required.

Simulation studies typically produce an enormous amount of data. After doing all of the work to generate the data, the author may be tempted to show the reader all the results of this massive effort. Authors, however, must distill this mass of information down to its essence, especially for a nonspecialist readership. Most important, the author must decide what conclusions emerge from systematic patterns in the data and organize the presentation of results accordingly. In addition to typical reports of proportions, means, and standard errors, Maxwell (1980) illustrated how correlates of the primary statistics can provide an even broader context for interpreting results obtained for the selected parameter values. Other approaches for establishing a broad framework include making an approximate argument (see the appendix of

Hedges & Olkin, 1984, for an example) and using exact theory for simplified cases and developing large sample theory (see Hedges, Cooper, & Bushman, 1992, for both of these approaches). In addition, Harwell (1992) discussed methods for integrating results from simulation studies, which are valuable ideas for the prospective simulation researcher.

A final (or "first") concern for simulation studies is that they are sometimes completely unnecessary. Authors occasionally fail to appreciate the value of the analytic proof. If properties of a statistic can be derived mathematically under specified conditions, then there is no need to study the statistic through simulations under these same conditions. Such simulations add no information whatsoever to what is already known mathematically. Such simulations only serve to validate the algorithms used in the simulation itself. Thus, including such conditions in a simulation may be useful to verify that the simulation is correct under baseline conditions. Authors should not, however, make the mistake of inferring that these results are informative in and of themselves.

Once Burned, Twice Shy

Identify the limits of your findings early in the article. Imagine a reader's frustration at having plowed through a statistical treatise on distribution-free alternatives to maximum likelihood structural equation modeling only to discover at the end of the article that the sample size requirements are 10 times what the reader usually has available. Trudging through a second methodological masterpiece may not end up very high on this reader's list of things to do.

One frequent way in which limitations manifest themselves is through assumptions. Unfortunately, authors sometimes fail to state assumptions explicitly. Without a clear statement of assumptions, the reader has no starting point for statistical claims made in the article. Although a detailed statement of assumptions might best appear in an appendix, most articles would benefit from a general overview of the assumptions near the initial statement of the problem and proposed solution.

In a related vein, authors should avoid the temptation to present a new methodology as a panacea. In all likelihood, any new method carries with it some disadvantages as well as advantages. Authors do readers a disservice when their presentation is one sided. Although a certain degree of enthusiasm is understandable and even desirable, balance is also important.

TIPS FOR READING METHODOLOGICAL ARTICLES

Not surprisingly, many of the tips for writing methodological articles apply equally well to reading quantitative articles. Ideally, the goals of the author and the reader are virtually identical. In many cases, the advice for authors can be generalized to readers simply by substituting *reader* for *author*.

Just as authors should often strive for a hierarchical structure, readers may also benefit from approaching a methodological article hierarchically. For many readers, attempting to read a technical article word for word from beginning to end is a guaranteed prescription for frustration. Instead, it is often far better to skim the article initially to develop a broad understanding of the article. A second reading might involve close reading of the introduction and the conclusion, again simply skimming the details of the justifications for the conclusions. Only on the third reading might there be any serious attempt to begin to understand the details of the actual argument. In any case, readers should frequently expect that they will need to reread methodological articles before they feel comfortable with their understanding of the material. Throughout this process, it is often helpful to take notes on the key points of the introduction and conclusions as well as on the basis for the conclusions. Similarly, readers can benefit from making a list of symbols and brief descriptions of what they represent.

Just as authors can improve the clarity of technical points by presenting special cases, readers can also check their understanding of such points by considering special cases even if the author does not provide them for the reader's convenience. Along these lines, readers can also attempt to reproduce the results from a numerical example. Finally, when all else fails, readers can ask for help. Just as authors usually benefit from the advice of someone with a different perspective, readers may also discover that sharing an article with a colleague allows both individuals to reach a higher level of understanding.

SUMMARY

Attention to fundamental rules for good writing is especially important when writing articles on methodology or statistics. Such basic rules are insufficient, however. Additional concerns arise as the content of psychological articles becomes increasingly technical or mathematical. With an eye toward improving the written presentation of methodological material, we outline a number of tips for technical writing:

1. Keep the reader uppermost in mind.
2. Select the journal for your article carefully.
3. Write for as broad an audience as possible.
4. Obtain feedback from someone whose expertise and perspective is different from your own.
5. Be especially clear at the onset because methodological presentations are often cumulative.

6. Convince your reader that it is important to read this article.
7. Be aware of the unusually diverse literature that is relevant to methodological articles.
8. Be sensitive to what your readers do and do not know.
9. Strategically define your symbols.
10. Encapsulate and clearly summarize technical material.
11. Consider using the particular–general–particular approach to technical presentations.
12. A figure is worth a thousand equations.
13. Keep the work relevant to read-world situations.
14. Be mindful of the value of mathematical proofs.
15. Confess the limitations and shortcomings of even the best new methodologies.

Needless to say, following these guidelines and 100 others will not guarantee publication. The packaging will make the product pretty, it will get the article read, and it will help the material to be understood, but the bottom line will always be the quality of the authors' ideas and their ultimate relevance to psychological research.

REFERENCES

American Psychological Association. (1994). *Publication manual* (4th ed.). Washington, DC: Author.

American Statistical Association. (1994). *Current index to statistics*. Alexandria, VA: Author.

Bem, D. J. (1987). Writing the empirical journal article. In M. P. Zanna & J. M. Darley (Eds.), *The complete academic* (pp. 171–201). New York: Random House.

Bryk, A. S., & Raudenbush, S. W. (1987). Application of hierarchical linear models to assessing change. *Psychological Bulletin, 101*, 147–158.

Cleveland, W. S. (1985). *The elements of graphing data*. Monterey, CA: Wadsworth.

Cleveland, W. S. (1993). *Visualizing data*. Summit, NJ: Hobart Press.

Cole, D. A. (1987). The utility of confirmatory factor analysis in test validation research. *Journal of Consulting and Clinical Psychology, 55*, 584–594.

Harwell, M. R. (1992). Summarizing Monte Carlo results in methodological research. *Journal of Educational Statistics, 17*, 297–313.

Hedges, L. V., Cooper, H., & Bushman, B. J. (1992). Testing the null hypothesis in meta-analysis: A comparison of combined probability and confidence interval procedures. *Psychological Bulletin, 111*, 188–194.

Hedges, L. V., & Olkin, I. (1984). Nonparametric estimators of effect size in meta-analysis. *Psychological Bulletin, 96*, 573–580.

Knuth, D. E., Larrabee, T., & Roberts, P. M. (1989). *Mathematical writing*. Washington, DC: Mathematical Association of America.

MacCallum, R. C., & Browne, M. W. (1993). The use of causal indicators in covariance structure models: Some practical issues. *Psychological Bulletin, 114,* 533–541.

Maxwell, S. E. (1980). Pairwise multiple comparisons in repeated measures designs. *Journal of Educational Statistics, 5,* 269–287.

Maxwell, S. E. (1994). Optimal allocation of assessment time in randomized pretest–posttest designs. *Psychological Bulletin, 115,* 142–152.

Maxwell, S. E., Cole, D. A., Arvey, R. D., & Salas, E. (1991). A comparison of methods for increasing power in randomized between-subject designs. *Psychological Bulletin, 110,* 328–337.

Micceri, T. (1989). The unicorn, the normal curve, and other improbable creatures. *Psychological Bulletin, 105,* 156–166.

Mosteller, F. (1980). Classroom and platform performance. *The American Statistician, 34,* 11–17.

O'Brien, R. G., & Kaiser, M. K. (1985). MANOVA method for analyzing repeated measures designs: An extensive primer. *Psychological Bulletin, 97,* 316–333.

Sawilowsky, S. S., & Blair, R. C. (1992). A more realistic look at the robustness and Type II error properties of the *t* test to departures from population normality. *Psychological Bulletin, 111,* 352–360.

Sternberg, R. J. (1988). *The psychologist's companion* (2nd ed.). New York: Cambridge University Press.

Sternberg, R. J. (1992). How to win acceptances by psychology journals: 21 tips for better writing. *APS Observer, 5,* 12–13, 18.

Tufte, E. R. (1983). *The visual display of quantitative information*. Cheshire, CT: Graphics Press.

Tufte, E. R. (1990). *Envisioning information*. Cheshire, CT: Graphics Press.

Willett, J. B., & Sayer, A. G. (1994). Using covariance structure analysis to detect correlates and predictors of individual change over time. *Psychological Bulletin, 116,* 363–381.

38

WRITING META-ANALYTIC REVIEWS

ROBERT ROSENTHAL

The purpose of this article is to provide some guidelines for the preparation of meta-analytic reviews of literature. *Meta-analytic reviews* are quantitative summaries of research domains that describe the typical strength of the effect or phenomenon, its variability, its statistical significance, and the nature of the moderator variables from which one can predict the relative strength of the effect or phenomenon (Cooper, 1989; Glass, McGaw, & Smith, 1981; Hedges & Olkin, 1985; Hunter & Schmidt, 1990; Light & Pillemer, 1984; R. Rosenthal, 1991).

The goal is not to explain the various quantitative procedures used in meta-analytic practice, for these are described in detail in the textbooks by the authors just cited, in less detail in R. Rosenthal (1993), and in far greater detail in a new handbook edited by Cooper and Hedges (1994). Another goal the writer does not have is to convince readers of the value of meta-analytic research summaries because this too has been addressed in all the previously referenced texts and in many other sources. The heart of this

Reprinted from the *Psychological Bulletin*, 118, 183–192. Copyright 1995 by the American Psychological Association.

Preparation of this article was supported in part by the Spencer Foundation and by a sabbatical award from the James McKeen Cattell Fund and the Faculty of Arts and Sciences of Harvard University.

article is a discussion of what should be considered for inclusion in a meta-analytic report. Not all of the suggestions apply equally well to all meta-analytic undertakings, but on average important omissions are likely to be minimized if these suggestions are at least seriously considered.

Who should be thinking of writing meta-analytic reviews? Anyone considering a review of literature, or a specifiable subset of the literature, may as well do it quantitatively as nonquantitatively because all of the virtues of narrative reviews can be preserved in a meta-analysis that merely adds the quantitative features as a bonus. The level of quantitative skill and training required to use basic meta-analytic procedures is so modest that researchers capable of analyzing the results of their own research will be capable of readily learning the small number of calculations required to answer standard meta-analytic questions (e.g., What is the mean and standard deviation of this list of correlation coefficients or other effect size estimates?).

As is the case of data analysis of any study, the analysis of a set of studies can vary greatly in complexity. For example, the texts of the six authors previously listed can be roughly divided into two levels of complexity and completeness. The books by Glass et al. (1981), Hedges and Olkin (1985), and Hunter and Schmidt (1990) are more detailed and more quantitatively demanding than those by Cooper (1989), Light and Pillemer (1984), and R. Rosenthal (1991). There are theoretical differences among these six texts as well, and this article is intended to be useful to meta-analysts working within any of these frameworks. Thus, although some of the more complex procedures described by Hedges and Olkin and by Hunter and Schmidt are not specifically mentioned, researchers working within their frameworks can easily add those analyses to the basics covered in this article. Regardless of how complex the meta-analytic procedures may become in a given review of the literature, reporting the basics makes a meta-analysis easier for the reader to follow and to understand at a deeper level. Reporting the basics also makes it easier for a reader to check the tenability of conclusions drawn by the meta-analyst.

Thus, keeping at least the basic meta-analytic procedures used descriptive, simple, and clear is a positive virtue. In 20 years of reviewing meta-analytic literature syntheses, I have never seen a meta-analysis that was "too simple," but I have often seen meta-analyses that were very fancy and very much in error.

The most important part of a meta-analysis is the descriptive part in which the effect sizes (e.g., correlation coefficients) are displayed and their distribution and central tendency are summarized. Good meta-analytic practice, similar to good data-analytic practice in general, adopts an exploratory orientation toward these displays and summaries (Tukey, 1977); for this valuable enterprise, little "high-tech statistication" is required. Indeed, the computations required for the most basic meta-analytic work are so trivial that in my own meta-analytic work of the last 30 years or so, I have never felt the need to use a software package that "does meta-analysis."

Good software for meta-analytic procedures can, of course, be a great time saver. However, a drawback to the development of sophisticated software for the computation of meta-analytic (or any other data-analytic) computations is that some researchers who feel less expert than they might like believe the software will "do the analysis." Alas, that is not the case. The software does a variety of computations and it does them fast, but for any given application the computations may be wise or they may be foolish. Staying simple, staying close to the data, and emphasizing description help to avoid most serious errors. It is better to consult with a more experienced colleague who knows exactly what is being computed by the software than to trust the software to do the analysis. That advice applies to all data-analytic undertakings, of course, not merely to meta-analytic procedures.

Without any implication that all good meta-analyses look alike and incorporate all the suggestions to follow, for the remainder of this article I discuss what might be reported in most meta-analyses and what should probably be at least considered for almost all meta-analyses.

INTRODUCTION TO A META-ANALYTIC REVIEW

The introduction to a meta-analysis is not very different strategically from the introduction to any scientific article. It tells readers why they should read the article, what makes it important, and how it achieves what has not been achieved before.

If the literature is made up of several types of study, it is helpful to describe a typical study from each of the types. If the results of the research differ widely—for example, some results strongly favor the treatment condition and some results strongly favor the control condition—it is useful to give examples of studies showing this wide variation in results.

METHOD SECTION OF A META-ANALYTIC REVIEW

Literature Searches

In this section, the meta-analyst should tell readers how the studies summarized were located, what databases were searched, what journals were painstakingly gone through, what research registers were consulted, and what steps were taken to retrieve the "fugitive literature." For those meta-analysts not trained as information scientists, the new *Handbook of Research Synthesis* edited by Harris Cooper and Larry Hedges (1994) may offer considerable help and enlightenment. Most of what any meta-analyst needs to know (and even more) about retrieving the data for a meta-analysis is contained in about 50 pages of the four chapters prepared by White (1994), Reed and Baxter (1994), Dickersin (1994), and M. C. Rosenthal (1994).

The reason for trying to locate all the research on the topic of a meta-analysis is primarily to avoid the biased retrieval of searching only the major journals, which may selectively publish only the results characterized by lower p values and larger effect sizes. If the domain searched has a great many studies, more than the meta-analyst has the resources to analyze, it is better to sample the exhaustive listing of results than to select only the more readily retrievable results.

Criteria for Inclusion

Information Available

Not all the reports retrieved are appropriate for inclusion in a meta-analysis. Some turn out to have no data of any kind, some have collected data but report on the data so poorly that they are unusable. Some are borderline cases where the meta-analyst is given enough data that good detective work allows him or her to obtain at least an approximate effect size estimate and significance level. Many studies, for example, simply say "there was no effect of X on Y" or "the effect was not significant." Meta-analysis involves the summarization of data, not of an author's conclusions, so the previous statements are of little help to the meta-analyst. However, if the meta-analyst has the relevant means and standard deviations, he or she can compute the effect sizes. If, in addition, sample sizes are given, the meta-analyst can also compute accurate p values.

For studies claiming "no effects" or "no significant effect," the meta-analyst may want to assign an effect size estimate of 0.00 and a one-tailed p of .50 ($Z = 0.00$). Experience suggests that this procedure is conservative and leads to effect size estimates that are too small. The alternative of not using those studies, however, is likely to lead to effect size estimates that are too large and almost surely to p values that are too small, that is, too significant. Confronted with this choice of procedures, it is usually best to "do it both ways" to learn just how much difference it really makes to the overall view of the data. Considerations of alternative approaches to the data are part of the process of "sensitivity analysis" described by Greenhouse and Iyengar (1994).

Study Quality

Of the studies retrieved, some may be methodologically exemplary and others may be stunningly bad. Should the meta-analyst include them all or only the good ones? The question of quality criteria for inclusion is really a question of weighting by quality (R. Rosenthal, 1991). Including good studies and excluding bad ones is simply a 1,0 weighting system which is often suspect on grounds of weighter bias. The meta-analyst is too likely to think of his or her own studies, those of his or her students, those of friends, and those of others who successfully replicate his or her work as good studies. In addition, the meta-analyst is too likely to think of the studies of his or her enemies and of those who fail to replicate his or her work as bad studies. As protection against biases, a meta-analyst would do better to evaluate the retrieved studies for quality by some procedure that allows disinterested coders or raters to make the required judgments. Indeed, some workers feel that coders or raters should be blind to the results of the study.

Coding of studies for their quality usually requires only simple judgments of the presence or absence of desirable design features, such as randomized experiment, experimenter blind to hypothesis, or controlled demand characteristics. Quality points can then be assigned on the basis of the number of desirable features present. Rating of studies usually requires a more global, overall assessment of the methodological quality of a study using, for example, a 7-point rating scale. Reliability of coding or rating should be reported. The quality weightings obtained for each study can then be used as (a) an adjustment mechanism in computing average effect size and (b) as a moderator variable to determine whether quality is, in fact, related to obtained effect size. Further details on quality assessment, weighting, and reliability are available in Hall, Tickle-Degnen, Rosenthal, and Mosteller (1994); R. Rosenthal (1991); and Wortman (1994).

Independence

For a database of any size, the meta-analyst soon discovers that many studies are not independent of one another; that is, the same participants have been used in two or more studies. Perhaps slightly different dependent variables were reported in the multiple reports on the same participants. For example, if responses had been recorded in video, audio, or transcript form, new ideas for dependent variables can be evaluated years later. Although such multiple usage of data archives can be scientifically valuable, they present a problem for the unwary meta-analyst. Most computational procedures dealing with significance testing require that the studies summarized be independent. Treating nonindependent studies as independent leads to significance test errors. These errors can be avoided by treating the several nonindependent studies as a single study with multiple dependent variables (R. Rosenthal, 1991; R. Rosenthal & Rubin, 1986; for a more technical treatment of problems of nonindependence, see Gleser & Olkin, 1994).

Minimum Number of Studies

What if meta-analytic efforts result in only a few studies retrieved? How few studies are too few for a meta-analysis? Meta-analytic procedures can be applied to as few as two studies; but when there are very few studies, the meta-analytic results are relatively unstable. When there are very few studies available on a given research question, it would be more economical of journal space and editors' and reviewers' time to incorporate the meta-analysis as an extension of the results section of the last study in the series of a few studies. Thus, if my study finds a correlation r between the two variables of interest, I might end my results section by combining and comparing my correlation and my p values with those few obtained earlier by other investigators.

Recorded Variables

Study Characteristics

Describe what information was recorded for each study. For example, the number, age, sex, education, and volunteer status of the participants (R. Rosenthal & Rosnow, 1991) might be recorded for each study regardless of whether participants themselves were the sampling unit or whether classrooms, therapists, groups, wards, clinics, or other organizations served as the unit of analysis (e.g., the basis for computing degrees of freedom for the analysis). Was the study conducted in a laboratory or in the field? Was it an observational study or a randomized experiment? What was the year of publication and the form of publication (book, article, chapter, convention report, bachelor's or master's thesis, doctoral dissertation, technical report, or unpublished manuscript)? The particular study characteristics mentioned are just some of what are often included. However, each meta-analysis should also include all the variables that the meta-analyst's knowledge of the literature and intuition suggest may be important correlates of the magnitudes of the obtained effect sizes. More detailed discussions of the selection, coding, and evaluation of study characteristics have recently become available (Lipsey, 1994; Orwin, 1994; Stock, 1994). All of the foregoing study characteristics are used in two ways: as descriptions of the study set retrieved and as potential moderator variables.

Summarizing the Characteristics

An overview of the various study characteristics is often valuable. The range and median of ages used in the assembled studies, of dates of published and unpublished studies, and of the proportions of sample participants who were female or male and the proportions found in various types of publication formats, of laboratory or field studies, and of studies that were randomized experiments rather than observational studies are readily summarized statistics that will be useful to readers.

Other Moderator Variables

All of the study characteristics recorded for each study and summarized for the set of studies can be used as moderator variables, that is, variables correlated with the magnitude of obtained effect size for the different studies. In addition to these fairly standard potential moderators, however, there are specific moderator variables with particular meaning for the specific area of research summarized.

For example, in a recent meta-analysis of "thin slices" of expressive behavior, short periods (under 5 min) of observation of expressive behavior were surprisingly predictive of various objective outcomes (Ambady & Rosenthal, 1992). One of the moderator variables examined was the presence or absence of verbal content accompanying the nonverbal behavior. It was found that studies including verbal content did not yield a higher average effect size of predictive accuracy. Another example of a moderator variable analysis grew out of a meta-analysis of the effects of teachers' expectations on pupils' IQ gains (Raudenbush, 1994). Using the moderator variable of how long teachers had known their pupils before the teachers were given randomly assigned, favorable expectations for pupils' IQ, Raudenbush (1994) found that the longer teachers had known their pupils before the experiment began, the smaller were the effects of experimentally induced teacher expectations.

Effect Size Estimates

Effect size estimates are the meta-analytic coin of the realm. Whatever else may also be recorded for each study, the estimated effect size should be recorded for each study in the meta-analysis.

The two main families of effect sizes are the r family and the d family. The two most important members of the former are Pearson's product–moment correlations (r) and Z_r, Fisher's r-to-z transformation. The three most important members of the d family are Cohen's d, Hedges's g, and Glass's Δ, all of which are differences between means divided by a standard deviation. Detailed explanations of these and other effect size estimates are given elsewhere (R. Rosenthal, 1991, 1994; for categorical data, see also Fleiss, 1994).

Significance Levels

Though far less important than effect size estimates, significance levels should be recorded for each study unless the meta-analyst is certain that questions of statistical significance for the overall results of the meta-analysis will not arise. All such levels should be computed as accurately as possible and recorded as the one-tailed standard normal deviates associated with the

p value. Thus, ps of .10, .01, .001, and .000001 are reported as Zs of 1.28, 2.33, 3.09, and 4.75, respectively. Results that are significant in the unpredicted or uncharacteristic direction are reported as negative Zs (e.g., if $p = .01$ one-tailed, but in the wrong direction, it is recorded as -2.33).

RESULTS SECTION OF A META-ANALYTIC REVIEW

Descriptive Data

The heart of a meta-analytic review is a description of the obtained effect sizes. Unless the number of studies is very small, it is often very valuable to provide a visual display of the obtained effect sizes as well as various indices of central tendency and variability.

Visual Display

A great many different visual displays may be useful under different conditions, and many of these are described by Cooper (1989); Glass et al. (1981); Greenhouse and Iyengar (1994); Hedges and Olkin (1985); Light and Pillemer (1984); Light, Singer, and Willett (1994); R. Rosenthal and Rosnow (1991); and Tukey (1977). Sometimes a specially prepared graphic can be most useful, one not found in any of these references. It would be instructive in that case to consult some of the general texts on visual displays, for example, those by Cleveland (1985), Kosslyn (1994), and Tufte (1983). However, there is not space here to illustrate even a few of the visual displays that may be instructive (e.g., box plots, funnel plots, and stem-and-leaf displays). As a single example of an often useful visual display, Tukey's stem-and-leaf display is a versatile picture of data that perfectly describes the distribution of results and retains each of the recorded effect sizes. Table 1 is a stem-and-leaf display from a recent meta-analysis of 38 studies on the predictive value of thin slices of nonverbal and verbal behavior. Each of the 38 effect sizes (r) is recorded with the first digit in the "stem" column and the second digit in the "leaf" column. The top three entries of Table 1, therefore, are read as three rs of .87, .73, and .74, respectively.

Central Tendency

Several indices of central tendency should be reported, and differences among these indices should be discussed and reconciled. The unweighted mean effect size, the weighted mean effect size, and the median—and optionally, the proportion of studies showing effect sizes in the predicted direction—should be given. The number of independent effect sizes on which these indices are based should be reported and, optionally, the total number of participants on which the weighted mean is based and the median num-

TABLE 1
Stem and Leaf Display
of 38 Effect Size *rs*

Stem	Leaf
.9	
.8	7
.7	3, 4
.6	3, 8
.5	0, 2, 2, 3, 4, 4
.4	0, 0, 0, 1, 7
.3	1, 3, 5
.2	1, 1, 1, 2, 3, 3, 4, 5, 6, 6, 7, 8, 9
.1	0, 0, 4, 5, 6, 6
.0	

Note. Effect size *rs* are based on Ambady and Rosenthal (1992); *rs* include relationships between two continuous variables (*r*), two dichotomous variables (phi), and one dichotomous and one continuous variable (point biserial *r*).

ber per obtained effect size. The weighted mean effect size refers to weighting by size of study (e.g., *df*), but other weightings can also be used. For example, weighting may also be done by the quality of the study or by any other study characteristic likely to be of substantive or methodological interest. In larger meta-analyses, subsets of studies that can be meaningfully grouped together on the basis of study characteristics can be examined separately, subset by subset, with respect to central tendency or other descriptive features.

Variability

The most important index of variability of effect sizes is simply their standard deviation. It is also helpful to give the maximum and minimum effect size and the effect sizes found at the 75th percentile (Q_3) and the 25th percentile (Q_1). For normally distributed effect sizes, the standard deviation is estimated at .75 ($Q_3 - Q_1$). Appendix A provides a checklist of descriptive data that should often, if not always, be reported.

Examining the distance (e.g., in units of S) of the maximum and minimum effect sizes from the mean, median, Q_1, and Q_3 of the full distribution of effect sizes is a useful start in data analysis for outliers. Valuable discussions of the problem of outliers are found in Barnett and Lewis (1978), Hedges and Olkin (1985), Hunter and Schmidt (1990), and Light and Pillemer (1984).

Several meta-analysts discuss the separation of the overall variability among effect sizes into components associated with "ordinary sampling error" and variability associated with other sources (Hedges & Olkin, 1985; Hunter & Schmidt, 1990; Light & Pillemer, 1984). This can be especially valuable in alerting meta-analysts to "nonsampling error" variability that must then be investigated. However it should be noted, a conclusion that all the effect size variability is due to "ordinary sampling error" does not mean that meta-analysts cannot or should not investigate the variability by means of moderator variables. Indeed, scientific progress can be defined in terms of scientists' continually reducing the magnitude of sampling error by increasing their understanding of moderator variables.

Inferential Data

Significance Testing

A good many procedures are available for testing the significance of an estimate of the typical effect size found in a particular meta-analysis (e.g., Mosteller & Bush, 1954, described 3; R. Rosenthal, 1991, described 9; and Becker, 1994, listed 18). One of the most generally useful of these methods is the Stouffer method in which one needs only to compute the standard normal deviate (Z) associated with each p value in the meta-analysis. Then, one simply adds all Zs (one per study) and divides the sum by $\sqrt{k}$, where k is the number of independent studies, to find the new Z that tests the overall result of the meta-analysis.

A related procedure for significance testing has been described in detail by Hedges, Cooper, and Bushman (1992). This procedure, the lower confidence limit (LCL) method, also yields a standard normal deviate, Z. The LCL Z and the Stouffer Z agree most of the time (nearly 99%); where they disagree, the LCL method may be more powerful unless the smaller studies summarized in the meta-analysis are associated with the larger effect sizes, a likely state of affairs. The LCL method tends to reject the null hypothesis when it is true (a Type I error) more often than does the Stouffer method; but because it may well be that the null hypothesis is essentially never true, that is not a serious problem (Cohen, 1994).

In both the Stouffer and LCL methods to get its magnitude, Z depends on the obtained effect sizes and the size of the studies, and it is interpreted as a fixed effect. That is, generalization of the results is to other participants of the type found in the specific k studies of the meta-analysis; generalization is not, ordinarily, to other studies.

Because of this limitation of the generalizability of fixed effect analyses, it is desirable also to use a random effects test of significance that permits generalization to other studies from the same population from which the retrieved studies were sampled. A simple once-sample t test on the mean effect size serves this purpose (Mosteller & Bush, 1954). For example, if one is working with Fisher Z-transformed rs, t is the mean Z_r, divided by the square foot of the quantity SD^2/k, where SD is the standard deviation of Z_rs and k is the number of independent Z_rs. This t ($df = k - 1$) tends to be more conservative than Stouffer's Z but should nevertheless also be used because of its greater value in generalizing to other studies.

Another random effects approach to significance testing likely to be even more conservative than the one-sample t test is the one-sample $\chi^2(1)$ test of the null hypothesis in which there is no difference in the proportion of studies showing positive effect sizes rather than negative effect sizes. When there are fewer than 10 effect sizes, the binomial test tends to give more accurate p values than $\chi^2(1)$ (Siegel, 1956).

Note the difference between the fixed effect and the random effect view of the obtained results in the meta-analysis. When a meta-analyst adopts a fixed effect view of the results, the significance testing is based on the total number of sampling units (e.g., research participants, patients, or organisms), but the generalization is restricted to other sampling units that might have been assigned only to the same studies of the meta-analysis. The fixed effect good news, therefore, is greater statistical power; the bad news is more limited generalizability. When a meta-analyst adopts a random effect view of the results, the significance testing is based not on the total number of sampling units but only on the total number of studies included; the generalization is beyond the specific studies retrieved to others that can be seen to belong to the same population from which one obtained the studies. The random effect good news, therefore, is somewhat increased generalizability; the bad news is decreased statistical power. One should try not to be overly precise in an application of "random effects" because there is precious little random sampling of studies in meta-analytic work. Indeed, even in the fixed effect model, when one generalizes to other sampling units within the studies, one assumes that the new sampling units will be randomly sampled within the study from the same population from which one sampled the original sampling units. However, it is very seldom that in behavioral or biomedical research one samples participants or patients randomly. Hence, "random" should be thought of as quasi-random at best.

To give an intuitive feel for the fixed versus random effect issue, Tables 2 and 3 have been prepared. Table 2 shows a simple meta-analytic model in which 10 studies have been retrieved, each with a treatment and a control condition of 20 participants in each of the $2 \times 10 = 20$ cells. Table 3 shows the expected mean squares and F tests when studies are regarded as fixed versus random (Snedecor & Cochran, 1989). With treatment always regarded as a fixed effect, the F tests for studies and for the Treatment $\times$ Studies interaction are the same whether studies are regarded as fixed or random. However, the treatment effect is tested against different error terms when studies are fixed versus random, and the degrees of freedom for the F test are also different. In Tables 2 and 3, when studies are viewed as fixed, the error term is the one expected to be the smallest (variation within cells), and $df = 380$. When studies are viewed as random, the error term will often be larger than when viewed as fixed, to the extent that there are nonzero Treatment $\times$ Study interaction effects, and the df will be smaller (9 instead of 380 in this

TABLE 2
Meta-Analytic Model Illustrating
Fixed Versus Random View
of Summarized Studies

Study	Condition	
	Treatment	Control
1		
2		
3		
4		
5		
6		
7		
8		
9		
10		

Note. Assume $n = 20$ for each of the $2 \times 10 = 20$ cells.

example). The most recent (and more detailed) discussions of the fixed versus random effect issue can be found in Hedges (1994), Raudenbush (1994), and Shadish and Haddock (1994).

Confidence Intervals

Confidence intervals should be computed around the mean effect size, preferably using a simple random effects approach. That is, the standard error of the mean effect size estimate (e.g., Z_r) should be computed as $S/\sqrt{k}$, with k being the number of independent effect sizes. The 95% confidence interval should be recorded at least; sometimes it is also useful to give the 90%, the 99%, and other intervals as well.

For example, suppose $k = 25$ independent studies available with an unweighted mean $d = .50$ and a standard deviation of these 25 $ds = 1.00$. Then the standard error for the 25 ds is $SD/\sqrt{k} = 1.00/\sqrt{25} = .20$. The 95% confidence interval is then given by the rough and ready mean $d \pm 2\ (SE)$ or $.50 \pm 2(.20) = .10-.90$. A more accurate interval is obtained by replacing the 2 by the critical .025 one-tailed value of t for the appropriate df, that is, $k - 1$. That critical value of t for $k = 25$ $(df = 24)$ is 2.06. Therefore, in this example, the confidence interval is $.50 \pm (2.06)\ (.20) = .09-.91$ (R. Rosenthal & Rubin, 1978). The interpretation of this confidence interval is that if the claim of the effect size for the population (from which the 25 studies must be viewable as a random sample) falls within the 95% confidence interval, the claim will be correct 95% of the time.

This example is based on the conservative random-effects procedure in which studies, not individuals within studies, are used as the sampling unit. It is often useful also to compute confidence intervals in which individuals

TABLE 3
EMSs and F Tests When Studies Are Viewed as Fixed Versus Random

Source	df	Studies fixed[a]		Studies random[b]	
		EMS	F	EMS	F
T	1	$\sigma^2 + 200K_T^2$	T/U	$\sigma^2 + 20\sigma_{TS}^2 + 200K_T^2$	T/TS
S	9	$\sigma^2 + 40K_S^2$	S/U	$\sigma^2 + 40\sigma_S^2$	S/U
TS	9	$\sigma^2 + 20K_{TS}^2$	TS/U	$\sigma^2 + 20\sigma_{TS}^2$	TS/U
U	380	σ^2		σ^2	

Note. EMS = expected mean square; T = treatment (fixed effect); S = studies; TS = Treatment × Studies interaction; U = units in cells; K = population variance of the effect in question.
[a] These 10 studies are recognized as the entire population of studies that are of interest.
[b] These 10 studies are regarded as a "random" sample from a larger population of studies to which the meta-analyst would like to generalize.

rather than studies are used as the sampling unit. However, the confidence intervals obtained by such procedures can appear dramatically more optimistic (i.e., narrower) than those based on the previously illustrated random effects procedures. Computational procedures for confidence intervals on the basis of individuals as sampling units are described in varying degrees of detail by Hedges (1994). Hedges and Olkin (1985), Hunter and Schmidt (1990), and Shadish and Haddock (1994).

Heterogeneity Tests

Statistical tests of the heterogeneity of significance levels (R. Rosenthal & Rubin, 1979) and of effect size estimates (Hedges, 1982; R. Rosenthal & Rubin, 1982b) are readily available. Usually one is more interested in the heterogeneity of effect sizes than of significance levels, and it is often useful to present the results of such an analysis. However, two common problems in the use of these tests must be pointed out.

First, there is a widespread belief that a test of heterogeneity must be found to be significant before contrasts can be computed among the obtained effect sizes; this is not the case. Contrasts, particularly planned contrasts, can and should be computed among the obtained effect sizes whether the overall test of heterogeneity is significant or not. The situation is identical to that in a one-way analysis of variance where many investigators believe it is improper to compute contrasts unless the overall F is significant. Actually, planned contrasts should be computed without reference to the overall F, and even unplanned contrasts can be computed with appropriate adjustments of their levels of significance (R. Rosenthal & Rosnow, 1985, 1991). If overall tests of heterogeneity are not to serve as licenses to pursue contrast analyses, why compute them at all? They do provide some useful information. If very significant, they alert the meta-analyst to the likelihood that all the effect sizes are not cut from the same cloth and that he or she should try to find the moderator variables accounting for the significant heterogeneity of the effect sizes. Thus, a very significant χ^2 for heterogeneity "morally" obligates one to search for moderators, but a nonsignificant χ^2 does not preclude the search.

The second common problem in the use of heterogeneity tests is to treat them as though they were estimates of the magnitude of heterogeneity; they are not. They are tests of significance and as with all tests of significance they are a function of the magnitude of the effect and the sample sizes. Thus, the widely varying ($SD = .40$) effect sizes (r) .80, .40, and .00 may not differ significantly if they are based on small sample sizes (e.g., $n = 10$), whereas the homogeneous ($SD = .05$) rs of .45, .40, and .35 may differ significantly if they are based on large sample sizes (e.g., $n = 800$). The magnitude of the effect size heterogeneity is given by the indices of variability previously described—in particular by the standard deviation of the effect sizes.

Some meta-analysts like to present separately one or both of the ingredients of the standard deviation of the effect size. These two ingredients can be illustrated by examining in Table 3 the expected mean squares for the Treatment $\times$ Studies interaction when studies are viewed as random. The two components of variance are σ^2 and σ^2_{TS}. The estimate of σ^2 is obtained directly from the mean square for units nested in conditions, and the estimate of σ^2_{TS} is obtained in two steps:

$$(a)\ MS_{TS} - MS_U = (\sigma^2 + 20\sigma^2_{TS}) - (\sigma^2) = 20\sigma^2_{TS})$$

and

$$(b)\ \sigma^2_{TS} = 20\sigma^2_{TS}/20,$$

where 20 is the number of units in each cell. The estimate of σ^2 gives the basic "noise level" of the dependent variable, whereas the estimate of σ^2_{TS} gives the interaction variation of the study outcomes above that basic noise level.

Contrasts

The statistical significance of the relationship between a moderator variable and the obtained effect sizes is given by the computation of a contrast test (R. Rosenthal, 1991; R. Rosenthal & Rubin, 1982b; or more complex procedures of fitting models to effect size data in the spirit of multiple regression, Hedges & Olkin, 1985). As with the case for tests of heterogeneity, the tests of significance of contrasts do not give a direct indication of the magnitude of the moderator variable's relationship to the obtained effect sizes. Such an indication is readily available, however, simply by correlating the obtained effect sizes with their corresponding "score" on the moderating variable. Such a correlation, in which the sample size is the number of independent studies, reflects a random effects view of the data with generalizability to other potential results drawn from the same population that yielded the obtained results. When the number of studies retrieved is quite small, such correlations of effect sizes with their moderators are not very stable, and a meta-analyst may be forced to take a less generalizable, fixed effect view of the data (Raudenbush, 1994). In such cases, a meta-analyst can get a serviceable indicator of the moderator effect's magnitude by dividing the obtained test of the significance of the contrast, Z, by the square root of the sum of the sample sizes contributing to the computation of Z. This fixed effect type r tends to be smaller than the random effects r but tends to be associated with a more significant test statistic. Appendix B provides a checklist of inferential data that should often, if not always, be reported.

Interpretive Data

In this section, a number of procedures and statistics are summarized that are often useful in helping to understand and interpret the descriptive and inferential data of the meta-analysis. They are described here more as a reminder of their availability and usefulness than as a standard requirement of all meta-analyses.

Binomial Effect Size Display

The binomial effect size display (BESD) is a procedure that shows the practical importance of an effect size (R. Rosenthal & Rubin, 1982a). The input to the BESD is a specific effect size estimate, the Pearson r; but because any other effect size estimate can be converted to r, the BESD can be used to display the mean or median effect size estimate of any meta-analysis.

In a BESD, the Pearson r is shown to be the simple difference in outcome rates (e.g., proportion successful or proportion performing above the overall median) between the experimental and control groups in a standard table, column, and row, totals of which always add up to 100. The BESD is computed from any obtained effect size r by computing the treatment condition success rate as $.50 + r/2$ and the control condition success rate as $.50 - r/2$. Thus, an r of .20 yields a treatment success rate of $.50 + .20/2 = .60$ and a control success rate of $.50 - .20/2 = .40$, or a BESD of

Condition	Success	Failure	Σ
Treatment	60	40	100
Control	40	60	100
Σ	100	100	200.

Had a meta-analyst been given the BESD to examine before knowing r, he or she could easily have calculated it mentally; r is simply the difference between the success rates of the experimental versus control group $(.60 - .40 = .20)$.

Coefficient of Robustness

Although the standard error of the mean effect size along with confidence intervals placed around the mean effect size are of great value (R. Rosenthal & Rubin, 1978), it is sometimes helpful to use a statistic that does not increase simply as a function of the increasing number of replications. Thus, if a meta-analyst wants to compare two research areas for their robustness, adjusting for the difference in number of replications in each research area, he or she may prefer the robustness coefficient, which is simply the mean effect size divided by the S of the effect sizes. The metric is the reciprocal of the coefficient of variation (R. Rosenthal, 1990, 1993). The coefficient of robustness (CR) can also be viewed in terms of the one-sample t test on the mean of the set of k effect sizes. Thus, CR is given by $t/\sqrt{k}$, or t adjusted for the number of studies.

The usefulness of this coefficient is based on two ideas—first, that replication success, clarity, or robustness depends on the homogeneity of the obtained effect sizes, and second, that it also depends on the unambiguity or clarity of the directionality of the result. Thus, a set of replications grows in robustness as the variability (S) of the effect sizes (the denominator of the coefficient) decreases and as the mean effect size (the numerator of the coefficient) increases. Incidentally, the mean may be weighted, unweighted, or trimmed (Tukey, 1977). Indeed, it need not be the mean at all but any measure of location or central tendency (e.g., the median).

The CR can be seen as a kind of second-order effect size. As an illustration, imagine that three meta-analyses of three treatments have been conducted with mean effect size ds of .8, .6, and .4, respectively. If the variability (S) of the three meta-analyses were quite similar to one another, the analysis showing the .8 mean d would, of course, be declared the most robust. However, suppose Ss for the three analyses were 1.00, 0.60, and 0.20, respectively. Then the three CRs would be .8/1.00 = .8, .6/.60 = 1.0, and .4/.20 = 2.0. Assuming reasonable and comparable sample sizes and numbers of studies collected for the three analyses, the treatment with the smallest effect size (i.e., .4) would be declared most robust, with the implication that its effect is the most consistently positive.

Counternull

A new statistic was recently introduced to aid the understanding and presentation of research results: the counternull value of the obtained effect size (R. Rosenthal & Rubin, 1994). The counternull statistic is useful in virtually eliminating two common errors: (a) equating failure to reject the null with the estimation of the effect size as equal to zero and (b) equating rejection of a null hypothesis on the basis of a significance test with having demonstrated a scientifically important effect. In most meta-analytic applications, the value of the counternull is simply twice the magnitude of the obtained effect size (e.g., d, g, Δ, Z_r). Thus, with mean $r = .10$ found to be nonsignificant, the counternull value of $r = .20$ is exactly as likely as the null value of $r = .00$. For any effect size with a symmetric reference distribution such as the normal or any t distribution, the counternull value of an effect size can always be found by doubling the obtained effect size and subtracting the effect size expected under the null hypothesis (usually zero). Thus, if meta-analysts found that the overall test of significance of the mean effect size (e.g., $\bar{d}$ or $\bar{z}_r$) did not reach the chosen level (e.g., .05), the use of the counternull would keep them from concluding that the mean effect size was, therefore, probably zero. The counternull value of $2\bar{d}$ or $2\bar{z}_r$ would be just as tenable a conclusion as conducting $\bar{d} = 0$ or $z_r = 0$.

File Drawer Analysis

The *file drawer problem* refers to the well-supported suspicion that the studies retrievable in a meta-analysis are not likely to be a random sample of all studies actually conducted (R. Rosenthal, 1991). The suspicion has been that studies actually published are more likely to have achieved statistical significance than the studies remaining squirreled away in the file drawers (Sterling, 1959). No definitive solution to this problem is available, but reasonable boundaries can be established on the problem, and the degree of damage to any research conclusion that could be done by the file drawer problem can be estimated. The fundamental idea in coping with the file drawer problem is simply to calculate the number of studies averaging null results that must be in the file drawers before the overall probability of a Type I error can be brought to any desired level of significance, say $p = .05$. This number of filed studies, or the *tolerance for future null results*, is then evaluated for whether such a tolerance level is small enough to threaten the overall conclusion drawn by the meta-analyst. If the overall level of significance of the research review is brought down to the *just significant* level by the addition of just a few more null results, the finding is not resistant to the file drawer threat.

Details of the calculations and rationale are given elsewhere (R. Rosenthal, 1991); briefly, a meta-analyst finds the number (X) of new, filed, or unretrieved studies averaging null results required to bring the new overall p to .05 with the following equation: $X = [(\Sigma Z)^2/2.706] - k$, where ΣZ is the sum of the standard normal deviates associated with the one-tailed ps of all the k studies retrieved.

Meta-analysts should note that the file drawer analysis addresses only the effects of publication bias on the results of significance testing. Very sophisticated graphic (Light & Pillemer, 1984) and other valuable procedures are available for the estimation and correction of publication bias (e.g., Begg, 1994; Hedges & Olkin, 1985; Hunter & Schmidt, 1990).

Power Analysis

In large meta-analyses, it is usually the case that the null hypothesis is found to be unlikely at a very low p value. In smaller meta-analyses, however, it can happen that the overall results are not found to be significant. Before concluding that the population value of the effect size is zero, it is helpful to perform a power analysis along with computing the counternull value of the overall obtained effect size. In this application, meta-analysts should assume a population effect size equivalent to the actually obtained overall effect size and simply use Cohen's (1977, 1988) tables to find the power at which the null hypothesis is tested. If that power level is low, the evidence for the null hypothesis is weak and should be reported as such. Appendix C provides a checklist of interpretive data that should often be considered and reported when appropriate.

DISCUSSION SECTION OF A META-ANALYTIC REVIEW

The discussion section could begin with a summary of the meta-analytic results, followed by tentative explanations of these results. These explanations may be in terms of the theories of the area in which the meta-analysis was done, or they may require new theory (Hall et al., 1994). The implications for theory—old or new—for practice, if relevant, and for further primary level research could be discussed.

The overall goal of the discussion may be seen as the answer to the question, "Where are we now that this meta-analysis has been conducted?" The meta-analysis is placed into the context of the field, and the field, very often, is placed into the context of the meta-analysis.

REFERENCES AND APPENDIX TO A META-ANALYTIC REVIEW

The reference list should include full references for each of the studies included in the meta-analysis, with the following text directly under the heading: "Studies preceded by an asterisk were included in the meta-analysis"; and an asterisk should be inserted before each reference entry.

An appendix in the form of a table should give for each of the included studies the overall effect size, the sample size, the Z corresponding to an accurate p value, and the coded or rated "score" for each study of the primary study characteristics and moderator variables used in the meta-analysis. The journal editor and reviewers will then have important information to guide them in their evaluation of the meta-analysis. If this appendix table makes the article too long, the author note should include where to get a copy of it.

CONCLUSION

Most reviews of the literature should be quantitative, just as most primary research studies should be quantitative. The statistical procedures used in meta-analyses range from the basic to the very complex, as do the statistical procedures of primary research studies. There is no one way to do a meta-analysis or to report a meta-analysis, any more than there is just one way to do or to report the data analysis of a primary research study. Therefore, the goal of this article was not prescriptive in the sense that every meta-analysis should include everything suggested in this article. The goal instead was to provide some general guidelines that may be considered by meta-analysts following the standard procedures of the various authors of meta-analytic textbooks. My own bias has been to keep it simple, basic, and intuitive. Even when complex analyses are undertaken, their reporting should be kept simple, basic, and intuitive. When one writes a meta-analytic review, after all, it is intended for a far larger audience than the other authors of texts and articles on meta-analytic methodology.

REFERENCES

Ambady, N., & Rosenthal, R. (1992). Thin slices of expressive behavior as predictors of interpersonal consequences: A meta-analysis. *Psychological Bulletin, 111*, 256–274.

Barnett, V., & Lewis, T. (1978). *Outliers in statistical data*. New York: Wiley.

Becker, B. J. (1994). Combining significance levels. In H. Cooper & L. V. Hedges (Eds.), *Handbook of research synthesis* (pp. 215–230). New York: Russell Sage Foundation.

Begg, C. B. (1994). Publication bias. In H. Cooper & L. V. Hedges (Eds.), *Handbook of research synthesis* (pp. 399–409). New York: Russell Sage Foundation.

Cleveland, W. S. (1985). *The elements of graphing data*. Monterey, CA: Wadsworth.

Cohen, J. (1977). *Statistical power analysis for the behavioral sciences* (Rev. ed.). New York: Academic Press.

Cohen, J. (1988). *Statistical power analysis for the behavioral sciences* (2nd ed.). Hillsdale, NJ: Erlbaum.

Cohen, J. (1994). The earth is round ($p < .05$). *American Psychologist, 49*, 997–1003.

Cooper, H. M. (1989). *Integrating research: A guide for literature reviews* (2nd ed.). Newbury Park, CA: Sage.

Cooper, H., & Hedges, L. V. (Eds.). (1994). *Handbook of research synthesis*. New York: Russell Sage Foundation.

Dickersin, K. (1994). Research registers. In H. Cooper & L. V. Hedges (Eds.), *Handbook of research synthesis* (pp. 71–83). New York: Russell Sage Foundation.

Fleiss, J. L. (1994). Measures of effect size for categorical data. In H. Cooper & L. V. Hedges (Eds.), *Handbook of research synthesis* (pp. 245–260). New York: Russell Sage Foundation.

Glass, G. V., McGaw, B., & Smith, M. L. (1981). *Meta-analysis in social research*. Beverly Hills, CA: Sage.

Gleser, L. J., & Olkin, I. (1994). Stochastically dependent effect sizes. In H. Cooper & L. V. Hedges (Eds.), *Handbook of research synthesis* (pp. 339–355). New York: Russell Sage Foundation.

Greenhouse, J. B., & Iyengar, S. (1994). Sensitivity analysis and diagnostics. In H. Cooper & L. V. Hedges (Eds.), *Handbook of research synthesis* (pp. 383–398). New York: Russell Sage Foundation.

Hall, J. A., Tickle-Degnen, L., Rosenthal, R., & Mosteller, F. (1994). Hypotheses and problems in research synthesis. In H. Cooper & L. V. Hedges (Eds.), *Handbook of research synthesis* (pp. 17–28). New York: Russell Sage Foundation.

Hedges, L. V. (1982). Estimation of effect size from a series of independent experiments. *Psychological Bulletin, 92,* 490–499.

Hedges, L. V. (1994). Fixed effects models. In H. Cooper & L. V. Hedges (Eds.), *Handbook of research synthesis* (pp. 285–299). New York: Russell Sage Foundation.

Hedges, L. V., Cooper, H., & Bushman, B. J. (1992). Testing the null hypothesis in meta-analysis: A comparison of combined probability and confidence interval procedures. *Psychological Bulletin, 111,* 188–194.

Hedges, L. V., & Olkin, I. (1985). *Statistical methods for meta-analysis*. New York: Academic Press.

Hunter, J. E., & Schmidt, F. L. (1990). *Methods of meta-analysis: Correcting error and bias in research findings*. Newbury Park, CA: Sage.

Kosslyn, S. M. (1994). *Elements of graph design*. New York: Freeman.

Light, R. J., & Pillemer, D. B. (1984). *Summing up: The science of reviewing research*. Cambridge, MA: Harvard University Press.

Light, R. J., Singer, J. D., & Willett, J. B. (1994). The visual presentation and interpretation of meta-analyses. In H. Cooper & L. V. Hedges (Eds.), *Handbook of research synthesis* (pp. 439–453). New York: Russell Sage Foundation.

Lipsey, M. W. (1994). Identifying potentially interesting variables and analysis opportunities. In H. Cooper & L. V. Hedges (Eds.), *Handbook of research synthesis* (pp. 111–123). New York: Russell Sage Foundation.

Mosteller, F. M., & Bush, R. R. (1954). Selected quantitative techniques. In G. Lindzey (Ed.), *Handbook of social psychology: Vol. 1. Theory and method* (pp. 289–334). Cambridge, MA: Addison-Wesley.

Orwin, R. G. (1994). Evaluating coding decisions. In H. Cooper & L. V. Hedges (Eds.), *Handbook of research synthesis* (pp. 139–162). New York: Russell Sage Foundation.

Raudenbush, S.W. (1994). Random effects models. In H. Cooper & L. V. Hedges (Eds.), *Handbook of research synthesis* (pp. 301–321). New York: Russell Sage Foundation.

Reed, J. G., & Baxter, P. M. (1994). Using reference databases. In H. Cooper & L. V. Hedges (Eds.), *Handbook of research synthesis* (pp. 57–70). New York: Russell Sage Foundation.

Rosenthal, M. C. (1994). The fugitive literature. In H. Cooper & L. V. Hedges (Eds.), *Handbook of research synthesis* (pp. 85–94). New York: Russell Sage Foundation.

Rosenthal, R. (1990). Replication in behavioral research. *Journal of Social Behavior and Personality, 5,* 1–30.

Rosenthal, R. (1991). *Meta-analytic procedures for social research.* Newbury Park, CA: Sage.

Rosenthal, R. (1993). Cumulating evidence. In G. Keren & C. Lewis (Eds.), *A handbook for data analysis in the behavioral sciences: Methodological issues.* Hillsdale, NJ: Erlbaum.

Rosenthal, R. (1994). Parametric measures of effect size. In H. Cooper & L. V. Hedges (Eds.), *Handbook of research synthesis* (pp. 231–244). New York: Russell Sage Foundation.

Rosenthal, R., & Rosnow, R. L. (1985). *Contrast analysis: Focused comparisons in the analysis of variance.* Cambridge, England: Cambridge University Press.

Rosenthal, R., & Rosnow, R. L. (1991). *Essentials of behavioral research: Methods and data analysis* (2nd ed.). New York: McGraw-Hill.

Rosenthal, R., & Rubin, D. B. (1978). Interpersonal expectancy effects: The first 345 studies. *Behavioral and Brain Sciences, 3,* 377–386.

Rosenthal, R., & Rubin, D. B. (1979). Comparing significance levels of independent studies. *Psychological Bulletin, 86,* 1165–1168.

Rosenthal, R., & Rubin, D. B. (1982a). A simple, general purpose display of magnitude of experimental effect. *Journal of Educational Psychology, 74,* 166–169.

Rosenthal, R., & Rubin, D. B. (1982b). Comparing effect sizes of independent studies. *Psychological Bulletin, 92,* 500–504.

Rosenthal, R., & Rubin, D. B. (1986). Meta-analytic procedures for combining studies with multiple effect sizes. *Psychological Bulletin, 99,* 400–406.

Rosenthal, R., & Rubin, D. B. (1994). The counternull value of an effect size: A new statistic. *Psychological Science, 5,* 329–334.

Shadish, W. R., & Haddock, C. K. (1994). Combining estimates of effect size. In H. Cooper & L. V. Hedges (Eds.), *Handbook of research synthesis* (pp. 261–281). New York: Russell Sage Foundation.

Siegel, S. (1956). *Nonparametric statistics.* New York: McGraw-Hill.

Snedecor, G. W., & Cochran, W. G. (1989). *Statistical methods* (8th ed.). Ames: Iowa State University Press.

Sterling, T. D. (1959). Publication decisions and their possible effects on inferences drawn from tests of significance—or vice versa. *Journal of the American Statistical Association, 54,* 30–34.

Stock, W. A. (1994). Systematic coding for research synthesis. In H. Cooper & L. V.

Hedges (Eds.), *Handbook of research synthesis* (pp. 125–138). New York: Russell Sage Foundation.

Tufte, E. R. (1983). *The visual display of quantitative information*. Cheshire, CT: Graphics Press.

Tukey, J. W. (1977). *Exploratory data analysis*. Reading, MA: Addison-Wesley.

White, H. D. (1994). Scientific communication and literature retrieval. In H. Cooper & L. V. Hedges (Eds.), *Handbook of research synthesis* (pp. 41–55). New York: Russell Sage Foundation.

Wortman, P. M. (1994). Judging research quality. In H. Cooper & L. V. Hedges (Eds.), *Handbook of research synthesis* (pp. 97–109). New York: Russell Sage Foundation.

APPENDIX A
Checklist of Descriptive Data for the Results Section

Visual Displays of Effect Sizes (Often Useful)

stem-and-leaf plots (as in Table 1)
box plots (if many are to be compared)
funnel plots (e.g., to investigate publication bias)
other plots (as needed)

Central Tendency

unweighted mean
weighted mean[A1]
median (repeated for convenience as Q_2 below)
proportion of positive effects
k (the number of independent studies)
N (the number of independent participants)
n (median number of participants per study)

Variability

SD (the standard deviation) [A2]
maximum effect size[A3]
Q_3 (75th percentile effect size)

[A1] Weighting is usually by degrees of freedom; means weighted by study quality or by other weightings should also be reported, if computed.

[A2] It is also often valuable to report separately the variability "corrected" for sampling variation.

[A3] This is useful in a preliminary check for outliers.

Q_2 (50th percentile effect size)
Q_1 (25th percentile effect size)
minimum effect size[A3]
normal-based $SD = .75 \, (Q_3 - Q_1)$

APPENDIX B
Checklist of Inferential Data for the Results Section

Significance Testing

combined (Stouffer) Z (and other such tests as needed)
t test (one-sample)
test of proportion positive (Z)

Confidence Intervals

	From	To
90% (optional)		
95% (almost always desirable)		
99% (optional)		
99.9% (optional)		
standard error $(S/\sqrt{k})$		

Heterogeneity Tests

$\chi^2(k - 1)$
p of χ^2
S (magnitude of heterogeneity or other indices of magnitude not dependent on sample size)

Contrasts

For each contrast or predictor variable give
test of significance
effect size of contrast.

[A3] This is useful in a preliminary check for outliers.

APPENDIX C
Checklist of Interpretive Data for the Results Section

Binomial Effect Size Display Procedure

Independent variable	Dependent variable		Total
	High	Low	
High			100
Low			100
Total	100	100	200

Coefficient of robustness: M/SD[a]
Counternull (especially if overall results not significant)
File Drawer analysis (tolerance for future null results)
Power analysis (if overall results not significant)

[a] Several coefficients may be reported using weighted or unweighted mean or median effect size for the numerator and weighted or unweighted standard deviation for the denominator.

39

TEN FATAL MISTAKES
IN GRANT WRITING

E. R. OETTING

I have just stepped down as the Chair of the National Institute on Drug Abuse (NIDA) Initial Review Group for Epidemiology, Prevention, and Services Research. The massive title means only that I chaired the meetings of the group of scientists who reviewed the grant proposals that many psychologists and other scientists submitted: grants to study epidemiological, social, psychological, or treatment aspects of drug abuse. Our primary task was to decide whether the research had scientific merit. If, in our judgment, the proposed study was good science, we then assigned a priority score to the grant: a score showing how much we thought the research would contribute to scientific knowledge about drug abuse.

Those ratings were extremely important; they almost always determined whether a proposal could eventually be funded. While I was on the committee, not one single grant that the committee rejected was funded.

Reprinted from the *Professional Psychology: Research and Practice*, 17, 570–573. Copyright 1986 by the American Psychological Association.

Furthermore, more than 90% of the time, the proposals that were funded were selected from those that had the best priority numbers.

I do not want to discuss how to prepare a good grant proposal or even list all of the little things that can go wrong. There are excellent materials available elsewhere on how to write a grant (Gordon, 1978; Holtz, 1979; Lindholm, Marin, & Lopez, 1982). After participating in this review process for several years, however, I decided that there were a few very basic mistakes that people made, mistakes that almost always led to rejection of their proposals. I saw these same fatal flaws time and again at NIDA, and also when serving as a special reviewer for other agencies. Avoiding these errors might keep one from wasting a lot of time and effort in preparing a proposal that would have almost no chance of being funded.

MISTAKE 1: "LET'S GET A GRANT TO PAY FOR TREATMENT"

Careful reading of the goals of the grant and the budget reveals that the primary aim is to get more treatment staff or to fund treatment staff that have been cut by budget reductions. The research plan is weak, and the emphasis is on how much good will be done by providing service.

It is, of course, possible to provide service on a research grant, if it is an integral part of the research. A project, for example, could be conducted to test treatment effectiveness, if the research plan would actually allow determination of what kind of treatment worked, for whom it worked, and how well it worked. Many proposals, however, are dominated by service delivery and include only a sparse and patched-together research plan. They are often, but not always, submitted by a service agency, with a research plan added by an academic from a nearby institution. The goal is clearly to provide service, not to answer important questions about how and why treatment works. Even if the committee agrees that providing the service is laudable, they still must rate the project in terms of its contribution to science, and just providing service does not usually add much to knowledge.

MISTAKE 2: SIGNING UP FOR THE WRONG RACE

If you were a sprinter, fast but without much endurance, it would be a blatant error to sign up for a marathon. Despite this obvious principle, NIDA receives grant proposals from scientists that do not enable them to use their greatest strengths, and instead focus on areas in which they are relatively weak. I have deep sympathy for some of the personal and professional goals that lead to this error. One researcher, for example, applies for a grant to study an idea that is totally novel and does not fit into his or her past research. Another scientist is trying to use grant funds to retrain, to move into a different area of research. Still another scientist, highly skilled and experienced in psychological assessment, tries to be thorough and includes extensive physiological measures in the proposal despite minimal experience with physiological measurement.

In an ideal world, all of these behaviors should be encouraged. Unfortunately, given current conditions of funding, any of these proposals is likely to end up being rejected. A decade ago, when more grant funds were available, a proposal that was only reasonably good, or one that entailed considerable risk of failure, might have been funded. Today, a proposal has to be very strong to be funded, and that usually means that the risk of failure has to be low.

It is hard enough to design a tight and carefully controlled experiment when you already have considerable research experience in an area. When the idea is really new, creating innovative measurement techniques and experimental methods can be very difficult, and a proposal is likely to leave doubts in the minds of at least some members of the committee. Sadly, funding for research is tight enough so that even one or two committee members with doubts can be enough to put a priority score out of the funding range. The scientist who is trying to retrain or move into a new area, or the one who includes areas outside of his or her expertise, is at a real disadvantage: The proposal will be read by people who are already skilled and knowledgeable in that other area, and the proposal is likely to look unsophisticated and weak to those experts.

A strong consultant or a co-principal investigator (Co-PI) who is an expert in the new area could solve some of these problems. All too often, however, the consultant is an afterthought and was not deeply involved in writing the proposal or in designing the study, and the proposal remains weak. Investigators might be better off if they thought seriously about their strengths and considered how they might contribute to knowledge by using their existing talents, skills, and experience, while retraining or polishing new skills or innovative ideas until they can be winners.

MISTAKE 3: "TRUST ME—I'M AN EXPERT!"

The principal investigator does not provide details of how important tasks will be done, pointing only to a past record of solving similar problems. This may appear to be arrogance, but there is a good chance that it is not. Part of the problem that experienced researchers have is that they are excruciatingly familiar with a particular aspect of the problem or with a particular method. It is hard to remember that others may not have the same familiarity.

Being famous is definitely not enough to automatically get you a grant. No matter how "important" the scientist is, or how experienced, providing complete details in the grant proposal is essential. Proposals are not reviewed "blindly." In fact, part of the committee's task is to evaluate the credentials of the investigator and to judge whether the investigator is competent to complete the project and likely to succeed. Having a strong publication record can be an asset; the past record is important because it demonstrates that the principal investigator (PI) does have the capability to complete research and bring it to fruition. But in some ways, the committee expects more of an established scientist. An experienced researcher is expected to have a firm grasp of the literature and should have the ability to write a proposal in which he or she perfectly describes procedures, methods, and instrumentation. If the proposal is not excellent, the committee is likely to wonder why. Although committee members try to maintain complete objectivity, they are human and are likely to be more critical of the expert's proposal than if it came from a relative novice.

Sometimes young investigators feel that they are at a disadvantage, but this may not be entirely true. The new investigator, proposing a reasonably well-designed study, is often viewed with considerable sympathy. The risk with a new investigator may be somewhat higher, but in assigning a priority score, the committee may weigh the value of recruiting and encouraging a new scientist fairly heavily, particularly if the cost of the study is reasonable. When this weight is added to the perceived value of producing the study, a proposal may receive a very favorable priority number.

It is not only senior scientists who fail to provide enough detail. The single most frequent reason for rejecting a reasonably good proposal or approving it with a low priority number may be that it did not include enough detailed information.

MISTAKE 4: IGNORING THE "PINK SHEETS"

When your grant proposal is evaluated by the committee, you get feedback. The results of the review are printed on baby pink paper. If you really want to have your research funded, these "pink sheets" are more precious than rubies. They tell you, in detail, just what the committee saw as the strengths and the weaknesses of the proposal.

When you resubmit the proposal, the information on the pink sheets can be used to emphasize the strengths and to deal specifically and clearly with every weakness in the proposal. This may seem obvious, but many investigators do not resubmit, and others send the proposal back with only cosmetic changes and do not deal with the weaknesses that were clearly specified on the pink sheets. Dealing directly and effectively with every weakness does not guarantee that you will be funded, but ignoring a weakness or glossing over it does ensure that you will be rejected again.

Incidentally, a criticism of your proposal does not necessarily mean that you are "wrong." Your approach could be perfectly appropriate, but you need to communicate better, showing exactly why what you plan to do is the best way to do it. You do not have to refute the pink sheets; you can clarify, present the material from a different angle, or provide what is missing to make your point clear. Why are you doing it in this way? Why are you doing this project at all? A criticism on the pink sheets means that you have not convinced the committee.

The pink sheets may also show that you were approved, but with a poor priority. This means that the committee thought that your proposal had scientific merit and did not have any fatal flaws, but that you have not convinced the committee that the result, as you planned the study, would be highly valuable. The criticisms provide a good set of ideas about how you might modify your proposal, but you cannot just answer the questions. You need to rethink the proposal, clean it up, make it really relevant and important. In short, make it better science.

MISTAKE 5: "I'M GOING TO DEVELOP A SCALE"

When I see this statement on a proposal, I always hear Andy Hardy shouting, "Let's do a show!" Andy thought that doing a show was going to solve everyone's problems. In all too many grant proposals, "I will build a scale" is presented in the same way: as the solution to all of the project's problems.

Building a scale is usually listed as a supposedly minor part of the project. The author finds that there is no already tested method for assessing one or more of the variables that have to be measured. The answer is to build a scale. That would be fine, but the proposals that are likely to be rejected usually present "building a scale" as a simple solution to the problem. There may be a few short sentences mentioning that the scale will be tested for reliability, but the author provides no details to show that he or she is aware of the technical steps needed to construct a reliable and valid measure, or of how difficult the task really is.

Unless, for example, the author includes samples of items that may appear on the scale, the committee may find it difficult to even begin evaluating whether a scale will be able to take its place as an important part of the research. Experienced researchers and the members of the committee have a great deal of experience, know how hard it is to write good items, and are likely to want to see what kinds of items the author is capable of creating. Are they clear? Will the research subjects be able to read and understand them? Could they have more than one meaning? Do they relate to the construct being assessed?

The PI sometimes mentions testing the new scale for reliability but does not mention what will happen if the scale is not reliable. There is no pilot test, no opportunity for revision, and no alternative plans, simply an assumption that the scale will be reliable. The reviewer has no choice but to mark a proposal like this unfavorably because if the scale does not work, the research is usually of little or no value.

Constructing a reliable and valid scale is a very difficult, technically complex, and challenging task. If a new measure must be constructed for a study, the PI has to show in-depth awareness of the theoretical and practical problems involved, show knowledge about where and when things might go wrong, and show how adjustments and alterations can be made so that eventually an adequate measure will be produced. If the value of the research depends totally on the adequacy of a new scale that is yet to be constructed, it is essential to present at least pilot data showing that there is very good reason for believing that with a minimum of further work, a reliable and valid scale will be produced.

MISTAKE 6: "IF I 'TACK ON' DRUG ABUSE, NIDA WILL FUND MY RESEARCH"

This kind of proposal usually results when the principal investigator has a consistent and ongoing research program in an area other than drug abuse. Sometimes funding has been cut off by another agency; sometimes the scientist wants to expand research into new areas. The result is a proposal that can be very strong in those parts that deal with the investigator's true love and very superficial in the parts that link that research with drug abuse.

The committee has little choice but to reject the resulting proposal because it would usually contribute little to scientific knowledge about drug abuse. Rejection is often accompanied by real regret because drug use, like other human behaviors, is cross-linked to a very wide range of human problems and personal and social characteristics, because the investigator is often a very good researcher, and because the proposal sometimes presents interesting possibilities and ideas.

The solution is obvious: the scientist sending a proposal to NIDA has to recognize that drug use is as important to the proposed research as the rest of the study and warrants the same in-depth review of the literature and the same careful and sophisticated consideration as the other variables in the study. One approach might be to include a Co-PI or consultant who is experienced in research on drug abuse and who has a major involvement in preparing the proposal. Another is simply to do your homework: to truly study the literature in drug use as you would the literature related to your own initial field of interest.

MISTAKE 7: THE "NO-PROBLEM" PROBLEM

Suppose one proposed a study to examine drug use by high school superintendents, or another to provide expensive drug avoidance training for institutionalized handicapped youth. In neither of these situations is there any evidence that a real drug use problem exists, and in both of them there is fairly good reason to believe that there will be relatively minimal drug involvement. Neither study seems to attack a real problem.

Another kind of "no-problem" involves the hypothesis that is hardly worth testing: for example, "I am going to find out how the make of car that a person owns relates to drug use."

You could, of course, make a case that no one really knows whether high school superintendents have drug problems. They do have high-stress jobs and might be tempted to use drugs to relieve that stress. If no hard choices about research funding had to be made, an argument that high school superintendents are an important group and that people should know about their drug use might be cogent.

You might also draw up some inferences about what automobiles symbolize to people and how particular drugs match those symbols. You might also argue that people could learn something about Freudian theory from the relationship between cars and drugs. But research funds are severely limited. When there are obvious and serious drug problems, cogent and important theoretical hypotheses that need to be tested, and not enough funds to do the research that really needs to be done, a proposal to study a "non-problem" is likely to get short shrift.

The argument "little is known about . . ." is not a very good one. Little is known about making love in a canoe while standing up, but then again, why bother? If you really believe that what you want to study represents a serious problem, then you will probably have to do the pilot research to demonstrate that fact, and write a very persuasive section on significance of the research, before you will get funding.

MISTAKE 8: EXCUSES—EXPLAINING WHY THE STUDY CANNOT BE DONE RIGHT

"The administrators of the clinic would not agree to a control group." "Subjects in School D cannot be given saliva tests because the administration will not allow those tests." If you are writing a proposal, you have to remember that the purpose of the research grant program is to fund good research, not to fund your research. An excuse counts for nothing; it is only the quality of the research that will actually be done that counts. If a control group or a saliva test would be important to producing a good study, and if either one is not possible, then the study is not worth funding as it stands.

This is not to say that control groups or saliva tests or any other specific conditions are essential for good research. If, however, particular experimental conditions or methods would ordinarily be needed for a good research plan and cannot, for some reason, be provided, you have to present a strong case showing why they are not essential parts of your proposed study.

Failure to provide control conditions in treatment or prevention studies can be particularly serious. Although the reviewers know that they are difficult to construct and that it is hard to obtain approval for them, not having adequate comparisons or controls may not only damage the ability of the study to reach conclusions, but also suggests that the PI may not have real control over other essential conditions of the study. If administrators or staff feel the need to dictate conditions and do not understand or are not in sympathy with research goals and needs, it may be symptomatic of other potential problems. What other changes might be dictated by treatment staff or administration either before or during the course of the study that may negate the value of the research?

MISTAKE 9: USING INAPPROPRIATE TESTS OR MEASURES

I can list only a few of the many different ways that this mistake has been made:

1. Giving a test or scale developed on college students to 7th grade students, and not presenting any data showing that it is reliable or valid for that group;
2. Giving a test validated on one cultural group to another, with no recognition of the need to determine whether it is reliable or valid in that group;
3. Giving a test such as the Minnesota Multiphasic Personality Inventory to determine "adjustment difficulties" with no discussion on how it will be interpreted;
4. Stating that a particular test or measure will be used but providing no data on its reliability or validity, thus forcing the reviewer either to look it up or to guess at its suitability;
5. Listing tests or scales to be used with no mention of why they are being used;
6. Presenting a test or scale and claiming prior use in one's own research, but presenting no data from that prior use;
7. Presenting pilot data on a test, but data with internal inconsistencies that show that the data are inaccurate;
8. Picking a measure of a particular characteristic on the basis of

the name of the test or trait, when examination of the test items would show that it would not enable one to assess what the investigator really wants to measure;

9. Giving so many tests or repeating tests so often that they are almost bound to be reactive and lead to inaccurate results;
10. Changing the method of test administration from written to oral without considering possible effects.

MISTAKE 10: THE CRITICAL MISTAKE THAT ONE NEVER SEES

A minister prayed again and again, asking to win the lottery in order to use the money for good works. Time and again the lottery went by and the minister did not win. Finally, one night after a hard session of prayer, the minister asked, "Why don't you answer my prayers? I am a good man and I have promised to use the money for good works. Why won't you let me win the lottery?"

Suddenly a voice spoke from the heavens, "Buy a ticket!"

The biggest mistake of all is not to write a proposal. It is absolutely fatal. You cannot get funded without trying.

Writing a proposal and having it rejected is painful. You will invest a lot of work, and will almost undoubtedly invest considerable ego. Being rejected is no fun. But it is not necessarily a waste of time even then. There are secondary benefits that can be important. Writing a proposal makes you consider seriously the significance of what you are doing, forces you to review the recent literature, and encourages detailed planning of your next research efforts. The pink sheets provide feedback on your effort. The exercise sharpens your thinking and creativity, and will improve your work regardless of whether you are funded.

And there is always the chance that you can convince the committee that your ideas will really advance science. Then you will have money and time to invest in your research that you could not hope to get in any other way. Go ahead and "Buy a ticket!"

REFERENCES

Gordon, J. (1978). Research work book: A guide for initial planning of clinical, social, and behavioral research projects. *Journal of Family Practice*, 7(1), 145–160.

Holtz, H. (1979). *Government contracts, proposalmanship and winning strategies*. New York: Plenum.

Lindholm, K. J., Marin, G., & Lopez, R. E. (1982). *Proposal writing strategies* (Monograph No. 9). Los Angeles: University of California, Spanish Speaking Mental Health Research Center.

REFERENCES

Abelson, R. (1985). A variance explanation paradox: When a little is a lot. *Psychological Bulletin, 97,* 129–133.

Addis, M. E. (1997). Evaluating the treatment manual as a means of disseminating empirically validated treatments. *Clinical Psychology: Science and Practice, 4,* 1–11.

Aiken, L. S., West, S. G., Sechrest, L., & Reno, R. R. (1990). Graduate training in statistics, methodology, and measurement in psychology: A survey of Ph.D. programs in North America. *American Psychologist, 45,* 721–734.

Alter, C., & Evens, W. (1990). *Evaluating your practice: A guide to self-assessment.* New York: Springer.

American Psychological Association. (1992). Ethical principles of psychologists and code of conduct. *American Psychologist, 47,* 1597–1611.

Barlow, D. H., Hayes, S. C., & Nelson, R. O. (1984). *The scientist practitioner: Research and accountability in clinical and educational settings.* New York: Pergamon.

Baron, R. M., & Kenny, D. A. (1986). The moderator-mediator variable distinction in social psychological research: Conceptual, strategic, and statistical considerations. *Journal of Personality and Social Psychology, 51,* 1173–1182.

Berkson, J. (1938). Some difficulties of interpretation encountered in the application of the chi-square test. *Journal of the American Statistical Association, 33,* 526–542.

Borkovec, T., & Rachman, S. (1979). The utility of analogue research. *Behaviour Research and Therapy, 17,* 253–261.

Clement, P. (1996). Evaluation in private practice. *Clinical Psychology: Science and Practice, 3,* 146–159.

Cohen, J. (1962). The statistical power of abnormal-social psychological research: A review. *Journal of Abnormal and Social Psychology, 65,* 145–153.

Dawes, R. M. (1994). *House of cards: Psychology and psychotherapy built on myth.* New York: Free Press.

Fisher, R. A. (1925). *Statistical methods for research workers.* London: Oliver & Boyd.

Haynes, S. N. (1992). *Models of causality in psychopathology: Toward dynamic, synthetic, and nonlinear models of behavior disorders.* Needham Heights, MA: Allyn & Bacon.

Hoagwood, K., & Hibbs, E. (Eds.). (1995). Special section: Efficacy and effectiveness in studies of child and adolescent psychotherapy. *Journal of Consulting and Clinical Psychology, 63,* 683–725.

Kazdin, A. E. (1978). Evaluating the generality of findings in analogue therapy research. *Journal of Consulting and Clinical Psychology, 46,* 673–686.

Kazdin, A. E. (1993). Evaluation in clinical practice: Clinically sensitive and systematic methods of treatment delivery. *Behavior Therapy, 24,* 11–45.

Kazdin, A. E. (1998). *Research design in clinical psychology* (3rd. ed.). Needham Heights, MA: Allyn & Bacon.

Kraemer, H. C., Kazdin, A. E., Offord, D. R., Kessler, R. C., Jensen, P. S., & Kupfer, D. J. (1997). Coming to terms with the terms of risk. *Archives of General Psychiatry, 54*, 337–343.

Lipton, D., Martinson, R., & Wilks, J. (1975). *The effectiveness of correctional treatment: A survey of treatment evaluation studies.* New York: Praeger.

Matt, G. E., & Navarro, A. M. (1997). What meta-analyses have and have not taught us about psychotherapy effects: A review and future directions. *Clinical Psychology Review, 17*, 1–32.

Meehl, P. (1978). Theoretical risks and tabular asterisks: Sir Karl, Sir Ronald, and the slow progress of soft psychology. *Journal of Consulting and Clinical Psychology, 46*, 806–834.

Miller, D. J., & Hersen, M. (Eds.). (1992). *Research fraud in the behavioral and biomedical sciences.* New York: Wiley.

National Academy of Sciences, Committee on the Conduct of Science. (1989). *On being a scientist.* Washington, DC: National Academy Press.

Neyman, J., & Pearson, E. S. (1928). On the use and interpretation of certain test criteria for purposes of statistical inference. *Biometrika, 294*, 175–240 (Part 1), 263–294 (Part 2).

Rosenthal, R., & Gaito, J. (1963). The interpretation of levels of significance by psychological researchers. *Journal of Psychology, 55*, 33–38.

Rosenthal, R., & Rosnow, R. L. (1991). *Essentials of behavioral research: Methods and data analysis* (2nd ed.). New York: McGraw-Hill.

Rosnow, R. L., & Rosenthal, R. (1989). Statistical procedures and the justification of knowledge in psychological science. *American Psychologist, 44*, 1276–1284.

Roth, A., & Fonagy, P. (1996). *What works for whom: A critical review of psychotherapy research.* New York: Guilford Press.

Sechrest, L., White, S. O., & Brown, E. D. (Eds.). (1979). *The rehabilitation of criminal offenders: Problems and prospects.* Washington, DC: National Academy of Sciences.

Sedlmeier, P., & Gigerenzer, G. (1989). Do studies of statistical power have an effect on the power of studies. *Psychological Bulletin, 105*, 309–316.

Shadish, W. R., Matt, G. E., Navarro, A. M., Siegle, G., Crits-Christoph, P., Hazelrigg, M. D., Jorm, A. F., Lyons, L. C., Nietzel, M. T., Prout, H. T., Robinson, L., Smith, M. L., Svartberg, M., & Weiss, B. (1997). Evidence that therapy works in clinically representative conditions. *Journal of Consulting and Clinical Psychology, 65*, 355–365.

Shrout, P. E. (Ed.). (1997). Should significance tests be banned? Introduction to a special series exploring the pros and cons. *Psychological Science, 8*, 1–20.

Weisz, J. R., & Weiss, B. (1993). *Effects of psychotherapy with children and adolescents.* Newbury Park, CA: Sage.

Weisz, J. R., Weiss, B., & Donenberg, G. R. (1992). The lab versus the clinic: Effects of child and adolescent psychotherapy. *American Psychologist, 47,* 1578–1585.

Wilson, G. T. (in press). Manual-based treatment and clinical practice. *Clinical Psychology: Science and Practice.*

INDEX

significance of methodology, 8–9
theory linkage, 301–302, 315–316,
    508–509
tools for, 420
use of null hypothesis testing, 380
Cognitive processes
    recurrence of ideas, 39–40
    subjective probability, 298–299
Cognitive psychology, 19–20, 508–509
Cohen, J., 286
Cole, D., 713
Collaborative research, 507–508
    allocation of credit, 599, 633
    for increasing clinical relevance,
        572–573
    See also Authorship credit
Comorbidity, 547–549
Comparison
    anchor scales, 228
    ethnic groups, 267–268
    metaphorical thinking, 41–42
    of psychotherapies, 513–514
Compensation to research subjects, 631,
    650
Competence, therapist
    boundary issues, 612
    ethical issues, 609–610
    evaluating, 472, 473–491, 516–517
Computer technology
    analytical limitations, 322–323
    default criteria in statistical software,
        721
    meta-analysis software, 768–769
    written descriptions of software
        analysis, 761
Concept mapping, 53–54
Conceptualization of research project
    evaluation of, 52–55
    importance of, 55
    mediator–moderator terminological
        problems, 95–96
    scale development, 218–219
    significance of, 9–10
    statement of, 54
    strategies, 40–41
Confidence intervals
    alternative to significance testing,
        358, 359–360
    application, 333, 380–381
    error rates, 359

as indicators of effect size, 358
meta-analysis, 778–779
Confidentiality
    AIDS/HIV research, 659–660, 677–
        679
    certificate of, 657–658
    in community-based research, 657
    ethical issues, 625–628, 646–648, 652
    rationale, 657
    subject self-disclosure and, 658–659
    subpoenas for information and, 657–
        658
Conformity, 168
Construct-irrelevant variance, 244–247
Construct representation/underrepresen-
    tation, 207, 244, 251
Construct validity, 189
    analysis for, 243–244
    argument-based analysis, 253–254
    assessment generalizability, 249, 251–
        252
    attenuation paradox, 232–233
    consequential basis of test interpreta-
        tion, 255, 256–257
    construct-irrelevant variance, 244–
        246
    construct representation/underrepre-
        sentation, 207, 244, 251
    content relevance, 249–250
    content representativeness, 250, 251
    discriminant validity and, 729–730
    establishing, 217
    evidential basis of test interpretation,
        255–256
    external correlations, 249, 252
    functional aspects, 248–249, 253
    hypothesis validity and, 315
    priorities of evidence, 253–254
    scoring models, 251
    significance for testing, 216–217
    sources of evidence, 246–248, 249,
        252–253
    sources of invalidity, 244–246
    structural issues, 249, 251
    theoretical rationales, 249, 250–251
    Type III errors and, 506
Consultations and referrals
    confidentiality and, 626–627
    ethical guidelines, 616, 626–627
Contrast testing, 780–781

Control conditions
  generalizability to clinical settings,
    549–551
  minimal treatment, 550
  usual-care, 550–551
Control of experimental conditions, 7, 8
Convergent validity, 727–729, 730
Coping research, 98–101
Correlation analysis
  cross-validated, 323–324
  measure of effect size, 330
Correlation bias, 209
Correlation coefficient, 164
Cost–benefit analysis, 400, 583–585
  client perspective, 585–593
  impediments to analysis, 587–590
  outcomes analysis in, 586
  rationale, 587
  recommendations for, 573–574
  reporting trends, 564, 569
  treatment effectiveness, 563
Cost-effectiveness
  analytical methodology, 585
  causal relationship, 579–581, 583–
    585
  comparison between treatments, 586
  impediments to analysis, 587–590
  rationale for analysis, 587
  See also Cost–benefit analysis
Cost of research
  funding for outcomes research, 451–
    452, 464
Costs of treatment
  effectiveness of treatment and. See
    Cost-effectiveness
  ethical issues in financial arrange-
    ments, 617–618
  significance for research, 577–579
  treatment resources used and, 581
Counseling psychology scales, 193, 197,
  198, 200, 210
Cowles, M., 285
Creativity
  in developing research ideas, 14
  in theory formation, 32
Criteria keying, 225–226
Cross-cultural research, research with;
    Ethnicity–race, 272–275. See also
    Ethnic minorities
Cross-validated correlation, 323–324

d measure, 773
Data analysis
  current research practice, 368–370
  design considerations, 283–284,
    285–286
  disadvantages of computer programs,
    322–323
  goals, 283
  in meta-analytic reviews, 768–769
  methods, 283
  outlier data, 322
  significance of, 6–7
  statistical techniques, 284
  See also Analysis–interpretation of
    findings
Data collection
  anchor scales, 228
  in case studies, 406–407, 414
  discovery-oriented research, 67–69,
    73–74
  ethical issues in documentation, 617,
    626–628, 651–652
  scale development, 228
  for treatment integrity evaluation,
    474–478
  See also Assessment; Scales
Davis, B., 286
Davis, C., 285
Dawis, R., 188
Debriefing, 660–661
Deception research, 650–651
Dependent variables
  choice of, to demonstrate important
    effects, 167–169
  number of, 320
  psychological models of behavior, 31
Depression, 452
  anxiety and, 465–466
  design of single-case experiment,
    455–459
  outcomes of single-case experiment,
    459–464
Design of research, 114–116
  APA code of conduct, 640–641, 643,
    645
  between-subject vs. within-subject,
    175–176
  collaborative studies, 507–508
  conceptualization, 9–10, 40
  control conditions, 549–551

proving, 329
quantitative evaluation, 374
significance testing and, 286–287
test applications, 376, 381, 389
testing practical applications, 380
testing predictive models, 376–377
theory testing, 379–380
Type I error, 320, 341, 351
Type II error, 351–352
Nuremberg trials, 657

Oetting, E. R., 714
Omnibus tests, 311–314
Ordinal claims
definition, 375
experimental support, 377–378
null hypothesis testing for, 375–376
in psychology laws and theories, 378–379
Outcomes
Aptitude × Treatment Interactions hypothesis, 495–496
client variables, 503
clinically significant, 397–398
component analysis, 547
concept of effect size, 115
consequences of nonequivalence, 126–129
cost–benefit analysis, 400, 586
cost-effectiveness analysis, 586
cost-related, 579–581, 583–585
delivery-related vs. technique-related, 582–585
discovery-oriented research questions, 72–73
efficiency of treatment, 498–499
equivalence of groups, 124–126
evaluation methodologies, 395–398
experimental comparison of therapies, 513–514
external validity, 147
generality of, 114
generalizability of findings, 152–155, 563
hard-criterion measures, 563, 568
influence of method on, 4
measures of therapist adherence/competence, 474–478, 480, 483–486
mediator effects, 85

obstacles to research, 451–452, 495, 542
policy-making role of research, 561–562
recommendations for reporting, 570–571
reporting trends, 564–570
single-case experimental design, 452–453, 459–464
small sample size, 121
therapeutic relationship as factor in, 510
therapist adherence/competence factors, 472, 516–517, 545–546
treatment withdrawal, 431–434
Type III errors, 505–506
written description of findings, 720–722
Outlier data, 322

p level, 285
arbitrariness of .05 level, 292, 325–326
confidence intervals as alternative for, 380–381
development of .05 convention, 291–292
effect size and, 330
historical development, 293–298
null hypothesis testing, 373, 382–383
power analysis, 328–329
researcher confidence correlated with, 367
role of, 326
significance reporting, 326–327, 333–334
subjective probability rationale, 298–299
Panic control treatment, 457–458, 459
Path analysis, 90–92
interpretation of effect size, 171
Pathology, misuse of terminology, 27
Pearson, K., 327–328, 360
Pediatric psychology
adjustment research, 84, 93–101
exemplary uses of mediator–moderator effects, 101
mediation–moderation testing, inconsistencies in, 92–101

Perception
    current conceptualization, 23
    testing, 378–379
Performance assessment, 242, 245
    generalizability, 251–252
Personal experience, scientific legitimacy
        of, 21
Persuasion research, 183
Physical attractiveness, 167
Pilot studies, 197, 228
Placebo-attention control condition, 549–
        550
Placebos, 509–510
    in efficacy–effectiveness research,
        549–550
Plagiarism, 633
Policy-making
    clinical research issues, 399–400
    cost-of-treatment research and, 589–
        590
    environment for psychotherapy, 561–
        562
    presentation of findings for, 563, 570
Polio vaccine, 675
Popper, K., 325–326
Power analysis
    advantages, 329
    effect size, 329–330, 342–344
    goals, 339–340
    historical development, 328–329, 334
    in meta-analysis, 784
    method, 320, 328–329, 341–344
    neglect of, 340–341
    sample size, 342
    significance criterion, 341–342
    for specific test situations, 344–347
    treatment interactions research, 503
    trends, 334–335, 340
Practice effects, 178–180
Predictors
    methodological rigor in treatment
        delivery, 546
    quantitative, null hypothesis testing,
        376–377
    weighting, 323–324
Prentice, D., 115
Presentation of research, 563
    advantages of graphic representation,
        322
    ethical issues, 633, 651–652
    graphics schemes, 42–43

number of decimal places in numeri-
        cal results, 321
    See also Publication of findings
Privacy, 646–648, 652. See also Confiden-
        tiality
Probability theory
    function, 298
    historical development, 293–294,
        295–297
    subjective probability, 298–299
Probable error, 294–295, 297
    adjusting alpha to reduce, 387
Proposals, research, 715–716
Psycholinguistics, 22
Psychological Bulletin, 737–750
Psychology, generally
    body of knowledge, 63–65
    conceptual basis, 19–22
    conceptualization of behavior,
        27–29, 31
    conceptualization of individual
        differences, 29
    conceptualization of individual
        potential, 24
    current research practices, 368–370
    imperviousness of theories, 60–63
    level of analysis, 22–23
    mentalistic concepts, 24–27
    nature–nurture conceptualization, 23
    operational definitions of concepts,
        29–31
    requirements for theory development,
        31–33
    underlying values, 33–34
Psychometric evaluation, 206–210, 229–
        236
Psychometric research goals, 31
Psychophysics, 378–379
Public Health Service, 690–694
Publication of findings, 11
    abstract, 717–718
    for career advancement, 695
    clinical experiments, 445
    criteria for evaluation, 712
    critical reviews, 723–726
    editorial process, 748–750
    ethical issues, 633–634, 651–652
    goals for content, 711–712, 715
    meta-analysis, 713–714
    outcomes data base, 562
    policy-making issues, 562

in *Psychological Bulletin*, 737, 738–739
significance of, 711, 715
trends, 564–570
trends in meta-analysis, 368–369
writing, 713
See also Authorship credit; Presentation of research; Report writing; Review writing

Q sorts, 197, 198–199, 294
Quantitative evaluation, 283
null hypothesis testing, 374
psychology teaching, 349–350, 369–370

r measure, 330, 773
Race. *See* Ethnic minorities, research with; Ethnicity–race
Random sampling, 123–124
minimum sample size, 131
Randomization
advantages of, 120
disadvantages of, 120
efficacy research, 121–123
minimum sample size, 131
role of, 119
with small samples, 120, 121, 129–130
Randomized response technique, 659 n.
Rank-order scales, 199–200
Recruitment
ethical issues, 664–665
for sample representativeness, 552–554
use of volunteers, 662–665
See also Sampling
Reference population, 209
Referrals and consultations, 616, 626–627
Regression analysis
difficult applications, 88–89
ethnic considerations in test analysis, 274–275
external criterion scales, 205
interpretation of effect size, 171
plotting, 88
for testing mediated effects, 90–92
for testing moderated effects, 86, 87–89
too many variables, 321
Relations between variables
in case studies, 403–404

contrast testing in meta-analysis, 780–781
goals of research, 5–6
interpreting correlations, 727–730
intervening variable theorizing, 25–27
mediator effects, 85–86, 90
moderator effects, 84–86
nonlinear, 7
research design issues, 14–15
See also Mediators; Moderators
Reliability
scale evaluation, 206–207
scale homogeneity and, 230–231
standards, 230
structural analysis for, 233–235
Replication studies, 762
recommendations for, 571–572
trends, 564, 567
Report writing
abstract, 717–718
assessment studies, 726–727, 734–735
central tasks, 716–717, 734
description of measures, 720
description of methodology, 719–720, 726
interpreting correlations, 727–730
introduction section, 718–719
proposal stage, 715–716
questions for review, 723
results section, 720–722
underlying constructs of assessment studies, 730–731
See also Methodological articles; Publication of findings; Review writing
Representative design, 114, 140–142
in laboratory setting, 157–159
Research populations
animals, 632–633, 649
compensation for, 631, 650
confidentiality issues, 657–660
debriefing, 660–661
equivalence groups, 114
ethical issues, 644–645, 657
ethnic minority, 266–275
generality of results, 114
guidelines for ethical practice, 655–656
lack of autonomy in, 645–646

Treatment (*continued*)
  experimental comparison of thera-
    pies, 513–514
  generalizability across settings, 114–
    115, 547–549
  integrated intervention regime, 547,
    548–549
  integrity. *See* Treatment integrity
  interaction of variables in, 396–
    397
  manipulation check, 472, 473
  projections for recovery, 408–409
  single-case research, 394–395, 429–
    431
  strength of, 510–512
  withdrawal, 430–434
  See also Therapeutic change
Treatment integrity, 395
  contextual variables, 479–480, 486–
    487
  evaluating, 472, 473
  measures of, 474–478
  problems in assessment of, 478–481
  recommendations for assessing, 481–
    491
Treatment manuals, 396
  assessing therapist adherence, 481–
    491, 545–546
  development of, 473
  implications for research, 471–472,
    543–544
  outcome factors, 512
  for replicating research, 572
  role of, 471
  therapist adherence, 472, 543–545
Treatment matching, 396
  for therapeutic relationship, 499–
    500
  See also Aptitude × Treatment
    Interactions
Two-tailed testing, 353
Type I error, 320, 341, 352, 505
  adjusting alpha to reduce, 388
  definition, 351
  trends, 356, 357
Type II error, 352, 505
  adjusting alpha to reduce, 388
  in ANOVA, 353
  definition, 351
  trends, 356, 357
Type III errors, 504–507

Unidimensionality of scales, 230–232
Unit weights, 323–324

Validity, 189
  assessment issues, 242–243
  convergent, 727–729, 730
  definition, 243
  establishing, 384
  scale evaluation, 206, 207
  selection–maturation interaction
    and, 120
  significance of, 241–242
  statistical conclusion, 505
  theoretical, 505, 506–507
  unified concept, 253–255
  values implications, 242–243, 247,
    249, 255–258
  See also specific type
Values, 33–34
  assessment validity and, 242–243,
    247, 249, 255–258
  implications in testing, 189
Variables
  ethnicity as, 265
  number of, 320–321
  range of, 512–513
  scale design, 194–195
  selection of, 32
Videotapes
  for discovery-oriented research, 73–
    74
  as laboratory stimulus, 139
Videotaping, 67
Visual analog scales, 223
Volition research, 20
Volunteers, research, 662–665

Waltz, J., 396
Wampold, B., 286
Watson, D., 188
Wen, F., 399
Wicker, A., 14
Within-subject designs, 115–116
  carry-over effects, 181–182
  context effects, 176, 178–182, 184
  external validity, 182–184
  indications for, 175–176
  practice effects, 178–180
  sensitization effects, 180–181
  statistical power, 177–178
  violation of assumptions, 178

Writing
    concept paper, 54
    grant applications, 791–799
    rewriting, 746–750
    See also Meta-analysis; Methodologi-
       cal articles; Report writing;
       Review writing

Yates, B., 400

Z scores, 199, 200, 298, 776

ABOUT THE EDITOR

Alan E. Kazdin is professor and chairman of the Department of Psychology at Yale University, professor in the Child Study Center (Child Psychiatry), and director of the Yale Child Conduct Clinic, an outpatient treatment service for children and their families. He received his PhD in clinical psychology from Northwestern University in 1970. Prior to going to Yale, he was on the faculty of The Pennsylvania State University and the University of Pittsburgh School of Medicine. His research focuses primarily on the evaluation of factors that contribute to the development, treatment, and clinical course of antisocial behavior in children and adolescents and the factors that influence child, parent, and family participation in psychotherapy. He has been a fellow of the Center for Advanced Study in the Behavioral Sciences, president of the Association for Advancement of Behavior Therapy, and recipient of the Distinguished Scientific Contribution and Distinguished Professional Contribution Awards in Clinical Psychology. He has been editor of various journals (*Journal of Consulting and Clinical Psychology*, *Behavior Therapy*, *Psychological Assessment*, and *Clinical Psychology: Science and Practice*). Currently, he is editor of the *Encyclopedia of Psychology* (American Psychological Association and Oxford University Press) and the book series on Developmental Clinical Psychology and Psychiatry (Sage). Some of his other books include *Research Design in Clinical Psychology* (3rd. ed., Allyn & Bacon); *Single-Case Research Designs: Methods for Clinical and Applied Settings* (Oxford University Press), *The Clinical Psychology Handbook* (with Alan S. Bellack and Michel Hersen, Pergamon Press); *Behavior Modification in Applied Settings* (5th ed., Brooks/Cole), *Conduct Disorder in Childhood and Adolescents* (2nd ed., Sage), and *Child Psychotherapy: Developing and Identifying Effective Treatments* (Allyn & Bacon).